ENVIRONMENTAL
DESIGN
RESEARCH
volume two
symposia and workshops

Community Development Series

The papers gathered in this volume support the notion that *information* may be as important a generator of design in the years ahead as building technology, symbolism, and aesthetic impulse were in the past. The concepts of form and function are not new to those who are designing our environment, but insights based on research can now give new meanings to those words. For practitioner, client, and general reader, these volumes illuminate and detail a new dimension in the environmental arts.

Series Editor: Richard P. Dober, AIP

ENCLOSING BEHAVIOR / Robert Bechtel
URBAN ENVIRONMENTS AND HUMAN BEHAVIOR: An Annotated Bibliography / edited by Gwen Bell, Edwina Randall, and Judith Roeder
EDUCATIVE ENVIRONMENTS FOR CHILDREN: Implications for Design and Research / edited by Gary Coates
COMPUTER GRAPHICS FOR COMMUNITY DEVELOPMENT / William Fetter
DESIGNING FOR HUMAN BEHAVIOR / edited by Jon T. Lang, Charles H. Burnette, and David A. Vachon
APPLYING THE SYSTEMS APPROACH TO URBAN DEVELOPMENT / Jack LaPatra
ENVIRONMENTAL DESIGN: The Role of Preference, Perception and Satisfaction / George L. Peterson
ENVIRONMENTAL DESIGN RESEARCH, VOL. I: Selected Papers / edited by Wolfgang F. E. Preiser
ENVIRONMENTAL DESIGN RESEARCH, VOL. II: Symposia and Workshops / edited by Wolfgang F. E. Preiser
TERRAIN ANALYSIS: A Guide to Site Selection Using Aerial Photographic Interpretation / Douglas Way

Community Development Series

ENVIRONMENTAL DESIGN RESEARCH
volume two
symposia and workshops

editor   Wolfgang F E Preiser

fourth international edra conference

Dowden, Hutchinson & Ross, Inc.
Stroudsburg, Pennsylvania

PREFACE

This is the second volume of ENVIRONMENTAL DESIGN RESEARCH, the proceedings of the
Fourth International Environmental Design Research Conference, was held on April
15-18, 1973 at the College of Architecture of Virginia Polytechnic Institute and
State University. Volume One of the proceedings contains a collection of research
papers which were selected from the responses to the "Call for Papers". The contents
of this book represent the invited contributions to the conference and are broken
down into three parts: Special addresses, symposia and workshops.

Special addresses at this conference were conceptualized to view environmental design research in a holistic way, incorporating changing societal and political conditions. The need for shifts in basic value orientations in man-environment and
man-man relationships is expressed. Further, the acceptance of cultural heterogeneity
as a necessary and enriching force in civilizatory development is proposed. And
lastly, the recognition of man's biological functioning and limitations as information processing system is emphasized.

The purpose of the symposia was to provide a broad overview of the theoretical and
methodological issues addressed at the conference and they are intended to fill in
the gaps left by the selected papers reporting current research findings. The symposia focus on six themes considered to be representative of ongoing work in the
field of environmental design research.

The symposium "Environmental Design Research In The Social and Political Context"
focuses on the consideration of need fulfillment on the individual, social and
ecological levels of functioning. Realization of research potential requires institutional innovations to (a) enable coordination of effort among mission-restricted
institutions and agencies whose combined effort is essential to resolve environmental
problems. Public awareness of issues needs to be increased and the communication
gap between design researchers and policy makers needs to be bridged. Furthermore,
only holistic theory can form the basis for actions that will contribute to system
stability with options for adaptive evolution.

The symposium "Theory of Man-Environment Relations" attempts to bring together
the theoretical positions of some of the leading researchers in the field. Topics
range from current philosophical models and attempts toward theoretical concepts in
man-environment relations to characteristics of behavioral ecology and behavioral
ecosystems technology for the design of artificial environmental systems.

Ways of analyzing man-environment relations are critically assessed in the symposium
on "Selected Instruments and Measures in Environmental Analysis". Included are
obtrusive and unobtrusive measures of user response analysis, such as interview and
semantic differential techniques, survey research methods, photographic analysis,
and time-budgeting. The application of several complementary measurement techniques to a given topic of investigation is advocated.

The perceptions and knowledge of attributes of the spatial social, political and
cultural environment are the concern of the symposium on "Environmental Cognition".
It comprises papers by researchers, mainly doctoral candidates, in the fields of
geography, psychology and environmental design.

The "Design Languages and Methods" symposium seeks to explore the means by which information is expressed, organized and brought to bear on problems of environmental design. Both the manner in which information is represented and the process by which it is structured and synthesized are covered. The intention is to provide an overview of the various systems of description and methods of synthesis now under development, and to examine these languages and methods in order to better comprehend the problems and potentials which they manifest. The symposium topics range from problems of symbolic notation and meaning to issues in decision theory. The characteristic differences between English and American work are examined, and an agenda for the future in terms of needed research, priorities, proposals and communication between participant interests concludes the symposium.

A critical look at the future of computer-aided design is taken in the symposium entitled "For the Environment: Major Thrusts in Computer Activity". According to some of the authors, the days of ad-hoc computer programs to aid environmental designers are, or at least should be, coming to an end. Some questions are asked: How do we integrate the knowledge and expertise we have gained? What are the advantages and dangers of developing larger computer systems? Where do we put our energies and resources in the future to assure both that computers will be used as design tools and that their use will result in a truly better environment?

The purpose of the 17 workshops is to provide an interactive forum between the audience and the workshop participants. Contained in this volume are the outlines as well as some of the abbreviated presentations at the workshops. The workshops cover a wide range of topics from the differences in designers' and researchers' intelligence to the discussion of the concept of the architectural school as an institution rendering services to communities and other clients.

The 4th International Environmental Design Research Conference was attended by over 600 participants from the U.S. and foreign countries, mainly Canada, Great Britain, Sweden, Germany and Switzerland. Included in this number is an encouragingly large contingent of student registrants, representing disciplines ranging from psychology to geography and environmental design.

Blacksburg, Virginia
May, 1973
Wolfgang F. E. Preiser

ACKNOWLEDGEMENTS

The preparation of this conference would not have been possible without the generous assistance of a great number of individuals at Virginia Polytechnic Institute & State University and throughout the United States. The listing of the conference organization in Volume One contains most of the contributors' names. The help of the following additional persons is gratefully acknowledged:

Graphic Design Coordination, Peter Prendergast, Steven House, Lee Quill/Photography, David Schultz, Mark Major/Exhibitions, John Payne, Patrick Rand/Multi-Media Shows, Fred Kirchner/Television Recording, Robert Steffen/Conference Coordinators, Nancy Smith, Salahuddin Choudhury, Charles Hildebrand, Lynn Crafts, Dixon Hanna.

Special thanks are owed to C. Craig Frazier, Omer Akin and Mark Lapping for their contributions and editorial assistance in the preparation of the conference proceedings. The royalties resulting from the conference proceedings will go into the Educational Foundation of the College of Architecture at Virginia Polytechnic Institute & State University in order to establish a design research scholarship.

The hospitality and assistance of the Alpha Rho Chi National Architectural Fraternity in hosting over 150 visiting students is acknowledged. A book exhibit was made possible through the generosity of the following publishers who donated the exhibit copies to the library system of Virginia Polytechnic Institute & State University:

Addison-Wesley/Crane, Russak, & Company, Inc./Dowden, Hutchinson & Ross, Inc./Free Press/Harvard University Press/University of Illinois Press/ Oxford University Press/Pelican Publishing Co./Penguin Books Inc./ Pergamon Press/Plenum Press/Pyne Press/University of Toronto Press/Van Notstrand-Reinhold Company/John Wiley & Sons/Wittenborn and Company/ Yale University Press.

Thanks are owed to Dowden, Hutchinson & Ross, Inc., the Virginia Foundation for Architecture Education and Virginia Polytechnic Institute & State University for making honorary funds available.

Special mention is made of the host institution, the College of Architecture, for providing facilities and the donation of faculty time as well as the necessary support facilities for the organization of the conference.

CONTENTS

WORKSHOPS

INVITED ADDRESSES

CHANGING CONTEXTS OF ENVIRONMENTAL POLITICS

Lynton K. Caldwell
Arthur F. Bentley Professor of Political Science and
Professor of Public and Environmental Affairs
Indiana University
Bloomington, Indiana 47401

Abstract

Modern society is in transition from attitudes and social arrangements based on open system assumptions to new priorities and controls based on closed system necessities. Political leadership in this transitional period is caught in a struggle over priorities that it is not equipped to resolve. The dominant political ideologies of the Modern world reflect past conditions and do not afford adequate rationale for public actions required to cope with the environmental problems that society is now encountering. Environmental experts in the science and design arts are handicapped in the extent of their assistance to public officials on environmental issues because of this incongruity between traditional assumptions and unprecedented problems. A new political ideology is needed to provide a basis for a reordering of public priorities.

Introduction

In his book, THE LIFE OF REASON (1), George Santayana observed that "Those who cannot remember the past are condemned to repeat it." It may as truly be said that "Only those able to perceive the future have any chance to shape it."

But out of personal knowledge no one can recall the past nor forsee the future in other than fragments so small as to be historically insignificant. The complex and changing matrix of the present continues patterns from the past and contains the elements of an evolving future. The events that we experience are, in relation to history, like Werner Heisenberg's atomic particles. The behavior of an individual particle may not be predictable even when the tendency of the phenomenon as a whole is known. For the individual life, the principle of indeterminacy governs; but for societies over time, aggregated events, like the actuarial tables of insurance companies, permit at least a prognosis of possible futures.

Concern for the future is not new with men, nor is there novelty in the mere fact of transition in society. But there are many reasons for believing that Modern society is approaching a critical stage unlike any yet encountered in human history. This conclusion has been reached by a number of our most thoughtful contemporary observers--largely it seems as the basis of their own independent analyses. (2) There is a substantial concurrence among these analyses. Cumulatively they present a thesis about the meaning and direction of change in Modern society that no person concerned with his own future or that of humanity can afford to ignore. And no persons are more directly involved in this critical future than those engaged in environmental design.

For the transition of our times is not less than a reshaping of societies everywhere. A major part of this task is a reordering of man-environment relationships and a redesigning of the physical expression of these relationships in settlements, landscapes, dwellings and work-places. This assertion is not mere philosophic rhetoric; the concept of better environmental relationships in the future is being written into our public law and political expectations. For example, under Section 102 of the National Environmental Policy Act the Congress has directed that to the fullest extent possible: " . . . all agencies of the Federal Government shall . . . utilize a systematic, interdisciplinary approach which will insure the integrated use of the natural and social sciences and the environmental design arts in planning and in decision making which may have an impact on man's environment."

That the Federal Government has not willingly or adequately obeyed this directive should not be surprising. Its implications are inconsistent with the long established assumptions and practices of most governmental agencies, and its purpose does not appear to be among the higher priorities of the present administration. Legislative instructions have limited effectiveness; the Congress cannot control the President and the Executive Branch in the exercise of their constitutional prerogatives and cannot mandate their values or priorities. Nevertheless the law stands as an authorization and directive for a new approach to the shaping of man's environment available to a political leadership committed to its use and purpose.

Although the conditions of the Modern world are very complex, the circumstance which now confronts us can be simply stated. Modern society (largely synonymous with the industrialized world) has through its major efforts and successes brought itself to a threshold of critical instability. The future development of society cannot proceed on the basis of the assumptions, goals, and methods that have been dominant for the past 500 years. But the concepts and the institutions now available for surmounting this impending crisis are instruments of the very social forces that created it. And the means which modern societies have largely used to overcome their self-made difficulties are largely those that have created their present dangers.

The Thesis

The thesis of the transition now underway may be most simply but abstractly stated as a change from societies based on open-system assumptions to new social arrangements based on closed-system necessities. For historical biological man, the Earth was and is a closed system, but its finite character did not preclude open-system assumptions of infinite space and material abundance. The illusion of infinity was plausible so long as human demands upon the Earth did not approach its inherent limits. Only in the latter half of the 20th Century have these limits come into view. These are not the temporary and localized limits that men have encountered in time of drought and famine. They are not limits which can be evaded by the discovery of new continents or of new technologies. They are inherent in the nature of the Earth and the nature of man; and for the first time in human experience they are confronted by man as a species.

Various metaphors or analogies have been used to symbolize the circumstance that the Club of Rome calls the "predicament of mankind." They are obvious over-simplifications, but they are not intended as models in detail. Their purpose is to exemplify a global circumstance that individuals from their limited viewpoints do not readily see and who, by their cultures, have been conditioned to dis-believe. These analogies have been attacked as misleading models of reality, with the most frequent complaint being that they fail to take into account human ingenuity. Criticism of the Club of Rome "Limits to Growth" model has more often been directed toward the technical validity of the model rather than toward the probability of the developments that it was intended to exemplify. But never-theless there is reason to suspect that it is the closed-system predicament rather than the imperfect model that is the real source of objection among the critics.

If the analogical models of spaceships, islands, or life boats are true, then some basic assumptions of modern liberal, democratic, and economic thought are false. And socialist doctrine is no more valid than is free-enterprise dogma-- both are wrong in the premises which they share regarding man's relationship to the planet Earth. Their differences are primarily instrumental; their view of the world is the same, but they would organize and apportion the exploitation of the Earth according to different concepts of equity. All modern political ideologies profess the same abstract goals in principle--peace, economic welfare, health, education and justice. All assume an Earth infinitely responsive to human demands. The only limit to man's achievement that they perceive is man himself; and for both Marxists and liberal democrats the perfectibility of mankind (although by different means) is an article of faith. Thus the "Limits to Growth" thesis is an affront to the hopes and beliefs of socialists and capitalists alike.

With the dominant forces of social, economic and political power going against it, what can the thesis of limited environment have going for it? The answer is: reality.

Persuasiveness is not a quality residing solely in the persuaders; there must also be an audience willing to be persuaded. People are seldom willingly per-suaded in the absence of compelling evidence to abandon hopes and expectations for less optimistic views of the future. And unfortunately for their credi-bility, the future-oriented critics of limitless growth and ever-expanding economies are unable to prove their thesis. For the five centures of modern times the expansive thesis has prevailed, and experience has not proved it to be false. The logic of Spaceship Earth is unconvincing to people whose personal experience and political beliefs tell them that, if human institutions and relationships are properly ordered, the Earth can be made to answer all of man's demands.

Like old man Noah among his neighbors, the seers of a coming confrontation with the limits of the real world are vulnerable to ridicule as "false prophets of doom." Some among them doubt the feasibility of persuading peoples and govern-ments through information and logic alone. Experience is a harsh though not always persuasive teacher. Should socio-ecological disaster be the consequence of continuing the presently dominant behavior patterns, would societies be moved to alter course and to adopt goals and behavior patterns more consistent with the realities of Spaceship Earth which human ingenuity can neither change nor transcend?

Many variables must be taken into account in finding a valid answer to this question. There are wide differences in the socio-ecological state of the world; in Sweden the course of events may be very dissimilar to that in El Salvador. There are variations in the readiness of nations, classes and cultures to accept and to implement a philosophy of Spaceship Earth. And there are many forms and degrees of socio-ecological disaster--some localized, some universal, some salvageable--others irreversible.

There are many uncertainties. What percentage of the leadership of a society must be persuaded of the need for a new orientation to alter the direction of social policy, and in what positions in society must they be placed? Answers to this question may differ widely as between, for example, the United States and the Soviet Union; or between Australia and Brazil. The answer involves not only the intentions of the leaders but their ability to implement policy. Insofar as history is a reliable indicator, one might surmise that in Australia a relatively high percentage of the leadership and of the population might be persuaded to adopt a "spaceship" orientation; and, once accepted, the policy could be effectively implemented. In Brazil a relatively small number of strategically placed individuals might restate the nation's policies, but would find great difficulty in implementation; whereas in China an even smaller number of persons might obtain swift and far-reaching compliance with the new order.

These variations in the condition and capabilities of peoples and governments make difficult any aggregation of trends and responses for the globe as a whole. The Club of Rome study was criticized for aggregating statistical trends for the entire Earth when, if the aggregated phenomena were broken down by geographical and cultural components, the course of events in different areas might proceed at significantly differing rates and in differing directions. This objection may, however, be based on assumptions regarding political ideas and organizational behaviors heavily influenced by the recent historical past. Modern industrial society has woven a globe-circling network of dependencies that grows ever more comprehensive and complex. The multi-national corporation and the international intergovernmental agency exemplify this matrix of association which could now be broken only at enormous social, economic and political cost.

Historical man has at times paid high prices for realization of his convictions. There is little reason to believe that he may not do so again. The major question for humanity in the remaining years of the 20th Century is: What price will be paid for what outcome? For there must be payment. The evidences of resource depletion, of environmental pollution, of food shortage, of interpersonal stress, are too clear to be denied. To continue to force historically obsolete doctrines upon a world no longer able to respond is to exact a heavy price in human welfare and happiness in the short run--and with disaster at the end of the road. To re-direct social efforts toward a new ordering of priorities will exact heavy costs in psychic commitment; in political expectations, in economic advantages and in ideological allegiances. But the road may possibly lead to a world that, avoiding disaster, might endure.

The Task

The thesis of modern man's transitional crisis from an "open system" world of expansion to a "closed system" world of control has been disseminated widely among literate people. Its reception ranges along a continuum from total acceptance to total rejection. But, mostly, the nature of man's life-support system is not debated in such abstract terms. The "nature of the system" issue more often arises in connection with problems of man's environmental relationships, particularly with problems of energy and of pollution. "Environment" is a key opening a door upon the most fundamental questions of man's relationships with the physical world.

The environmental "key" does not, however, always work well; "environmental quality" is rarely a clearcut issue and its implications are seldom fully developed in political debate and are not fully understood by most people. Public opinion polls in the United States and Scandinavia indicate an unmistakable popular desire for public action on behalf of environmental quality. (3) Where environment has been an issue, environmental quality candidates have generally fared well in election to public office. But in most political contests "environment" has not been an issue, and the exact distribution of popular attitudes, their variations, intensities, and stability is nowhere known. This uncertainty is troublesome for political decision-makers, caught between commitment to the aims and values that have heretofore prevailed, and demands for a new approach to environmental relationships for which the nature and extent of public support, while known to be significant, is uncertain.

In such efforts as they may make to reduce this uncertainty, the makers and administrators of the public laws have received little aid or guidance from professional experts on environmental policy issues. Why this assistance has not been forthcoming is basic to the political problem of reordering public priorities and will presently be analyzed. But first, it would be useful to distinguish two separate sources of expert information on environmental problems.

The first source of information is environmental science. Its expert practitioners cover a broad range in the spectrum of the natural sciences and engineering. They are the primary sources of basic and technical knowledge of relationships and processes in the environment. As concerned citizens, many of these scientific and technical professionals have been in the forefront of efforts to develop social awareness of environmental jeopardy. They have contributed to the analysis of environmental problems and, within the limits of present knowledge, have often proposed solutions. But the solutions are characteristically substantive rather than operational. The advice is directed toward the substance of what should be done, but rarely toward how to attain the objective through political action. "The Blueprint for Survival" signed by 36 British scientists, (4) illustrates the difficulty. Public officials are unable to act upon advice that departs radically from popular norms or that provides no practical means for implementation. Only where technical solutions have been feasible, as in certain pollution control measures, has the environmental scientist been able to package his information in a form that administrators may directly receive and apply.

The second source of information is more heterogeneous and may be described as environmental planning and design. Its spectrum includes behavioral scientists, economists, architects and urban and regional planners. In theory, these professionals might be expected to translate information generated by natural scientists and engineers into operational plans and programs. In fact, they have seldom been able to do so. This is partly because an interdisciplinary approach to environmental problem solving, specified, for example, in the National Environmental Policy Act of the United States, has nowhere been institutionalized in practice. It is also because the public official has no way of acting upon the advice of technical and professional experts without assistance at the operational level which environmental expertise is seldom able to provide.

The literature of environmental policy and administration has provided the decision-maker with little more than historical background and descriptions of comparative organization and procedure. Some of it contains philosophic insights that could assist a public official in analysis of policy alternatives. But it has offered little practical counsel, and for a reason which becomes apparent when the full implications of environmental policies are seen in their political contexts.

On balance, the politics of the environment is a politics of values rather than of interests. It resembles more the politics of morals and religion than the politics of who gets what, when, where, and how. It is easier to bargain over wages, hours, working conditions, and over price supports and insurance rates, than over immaculate conception, birth control, or preservation of a wilderness area. Moreover, the problems of environmental values and choice are seldom amenable to technical solutions. Technology may influence a policy choice, notably on questions of feasibility, but it rarely can determine a social choice.

In non-ideological democratic societies the public official acts within the context of competing interests, nowhere better described than by James Madison in THE FEDERALIST. If there is a democratic ideology, it includes the proposition that one man's ideas may be as good as another's--popular preferences in some sense providing guidance for the law-maker and the administrator. Scientific inquiry is not immune to value judgments and to the influence of popular preference. But the tests of truth in science are not the tests of feasibility in politics. For example, the degree of human tolerance for carbon monoxide is not a suitable subject for bargaining; but the feasibility of choices among air quality standards (within limits) might be.

Environmental science provides no built-in guidance for policy implementation; behavioral science has seldom offered such guidance, and the instances of effective application have been relatively infrequent--with an important exception.

This exception pertains to those few cases wherein the public goals or purposes are relatively clear and unequivocal--unembarrassed by incompatible commitments. But this exception contrasts sharply with the actual state of environmental politics everywhere at the present time.

The context of politics in the latter third of the 20th Century is a transition in the state of the world that may be as profound as any that has yet occurred. Within this context, the priorities that have dominated Western and industrial societies for 500 years are being stressed by socio-ecological circumstances generated by imprudent implementation of these same priorities. These priorities are also being challenged by a quality-of-life ideology that, although rooted in the past, was subordinated by the expansive and aggressive tendencies of modern societies. The movement for environmental quality is a new aspect of this politics of values; it has been reinforced simultaneously by the difficulties of resource depletion and pollution, along with the growth of scientific knowledge that not only reveals hitherto unperceived environmental relationships and dangers, but that also provides an informational basis for remedial technologies.

The public leadership in this period of transition is caught in a struggle over priorities that it cannot itself resolve. The new manifestation of a politics of values does not fit easily into a structure of concepts and institutions evolved out of a politics of interests. The particular values and assumptions that dominate the interest-based politics of the United States (and most Western industrial democracies) are not easily modified by considerations of environmental quality. The new values of "quality of life" are not yet dominant in the "practical" world and have only begun to modify traditional behavior patterns. Efforts to integrate environmental protection measures with traditional politics have been awkward and only partially successful. For example, efforts to cope with the environmental aspects of land use would, in many countries, threaten the whole structure of politics, especially at local levels.

The formal commitment of many governments and of the United Nations to policies of environmental quality and protection is established fact. But this commitment will rapidly encounter frustration unless a way is found to state environmental policies in specific operational terms that are consistent with the full range of human needs. A principal theme of the United Nations Conference on the Human Environment was the integration of environmental and developmental concepts, especially in the less developed nations. How this task is to be accomplished has not yet been clarified. The task may be assisted by technical methods, but only when the desired outcomes of the effort have been specified in operational language. Intended outcomes are achieved by translating values into actions leading to specified desired results. An ideology of values is insufficient to achieve results; to be effective it must be joined to an ideology of means or action toward desired results. Until outcomes can be described in language of time, place and condition, the means to action cannot be specified, nor their costs and benefits estimated.

If they are to respond to the most urgent needs of society in transition, environmental professionals--scientists, designers, engineers--must now directly confront the issue of conflicting priorities, must identify options, and propose operational strategies for the attainment of specified objectives. A possible outcome of such effort could well be a new political ideology--and no less an outcome may be required to move modern society to a higher level of social and ecological sophistication.

Changing the Context of Priorities

In certain of its more superficial aspects, the man-environment issue can be regarded as "just another set of interests." But those persons who regard the environmental issue fundamentally as one of survival and of the quality of life do not regard their "cause" as just another issue. Its advocates do not see their mission as on parity with the interests of land developers, oil companies, highway lobbyists or the forest products industries. But in the conventional perspective of Federal hearing officers, judges, administrators, many Congressmen and even some social scientists, the "environmentalist" is seen as another interest-group lobbyist.

Advocates of environmental quality are therefore seldom able to help the public decision-makers within the context of the laws, traditions, pressures, values and priorities under which they presently operate. They are widely regarded by public officials as "special pleaders," with biased views. Environmental scientists and planners are today constrained in their advisory roles by the practical need of the public official to accommodate his action to a wide range of conflicting priorities. Their influence is effective chiefly in tipping the balance in controversial issues toward environmentally preferable outcomes. But if sanity and survival are really at stake, incremental compromises and modest ad hoc victories will not reform national commitments and will not actualize the values of the environmental quality movement.

The outcome of the struggle for priorities depends upon the context in which the contending values are interpreted, weighted, and applied. The present political context is only partially favorable to quality of life and environmental priorities. The context is changing, but its complexities and contradictions make the future political climate uncertain. For example, it is not clear how efforts to deal with an impending crisis of energy will affect environmental quality in the United States. Will high voltage electric lines increasingly criss-cross the country like huge spider webs, and will areas the size of New England be bulldozed into wastelands of spent oil shale throughout the Rocky Mountain states? For the government of the United States there is a declaration of national environmental policy, but that declaration has not yet been built into the political beliefs, values and folkways of the American people. Its purpose and precepts have only begun to penetrate the awareness and the imperfectly articulated assumptions of the average man. The politics of environmental quality will be a politics of defense until a new ideology takes possession of men's minds and habits, and shapes their expectations toward a more stable, diverse, and enduring world.

Political ideology has acquired a bad reputation in liberal and democratic thought, principally perhaps because most modern ideologies have provided rationalization for dogmatic and intolerant tyrannies. But dogmatism and intolerance are hazards in any system of thought--liberal and democratic belief systems not excepted. The malevolence in ideologies may perhaps be explained by the relative ease with which men can be mobilized through fear or hatred of other men, as contrasted with the difficulty of obtaining their cooperation on constructive, non-controversial issues. Ideas powerful in substance and powerfully expressed have nevertheless seized the imaginations and energies of men. If ideas are to be acted upon, however, they must be stated so as to be applicable to practical affairs. Exhortations are seldom self-executory.

The great need for the reordering of social priorities for quality of life and environment is a persuasive theory of man's best possible future, coupled to a practical prescription for the action needed to attain it. This linkage of a persuasive idea to the means of attainment has been the formula employed by all successful reshapers of societies from Mohammed to Marx. But more than in most ideologies or theologies, an operational philosophy for man's relationships with the planet Earth will be subject to tests of rational effectiveness. Its results will be measurable in the real world, and it cannot be credible if it does not work. That ideologies have survived the falsity of their premises implies no assurance of their continuing to do so in the future.

In relation to issues in which scientific confirmation is increasingly needed for credibility, the tenets of an operational ideology must at least be consistent with the state of verified knowledge. In the long run, propositions that are untrue cannot provide a reliable foundation for human relationships with a natural world whose systems conform to natural "laws" over which man has only limited control. Political fiat cannot modify the nitrogen cycle or repeal the laws of thermodynamics.

Public opinion appears to be growing more critical, and the percentage of literate, informed and educated individuals in society is everywhere becoming more numerous. And although erudition confers no immunity to self-delusion, the increasing popular exposure to ideas, and the increasing popular acceptance of scientific methods as tests of truth, suggest that the politics of the future can be more rational than those prevailing in the past.

A corollary of this need for confirmable propositions is the need to put man in realistic perspective. The business of politics is to manage the public affairs of man; but those affairs now involve all of nature. Political ideologies inherently have been focused on man and his activities; but historically few other aspects of life and the world have been considered. Today governments legislate for all life, for all ecosystems, and for the atmosphere, the oceans, and the land. But only in the United Nations Declaration on the Human Environment adopted in Stockholm on June 16, 1972 has a major political declaration attempted to put man into the perspective of the living world. (5) Nature has no votes in the assemblies of men, but its response to abuse is recorded in the resulting effects upon the human environment. Men must now legislate with regard to the capabilities, requirements, and limitations of nature--including human nature-- if self-destruction is not to be the destiny of a post-Modern world.

Another corollary of the need for realism and for an honest effort to achieve valid perspective is a comprehensiveness of doctrine sufficient to include major related aspects of public policy. This need is exemplified by the efforts of the United Nations Conference on the Human Environment to bring environmental protection and economic development into a consistent and mutually supportive relationship. To achieve this objective it will be necessary to jettison much of the dogma of conventional economics that has infused the public policies of nearly all nations with abstract concepts of living standards, of economic growth, and of national well-being and productivity. And advocates of environmental quality will serve their cause by assisting a more valid formulation of criteria for economic welfare. They must also adopt strategies more effective than mere prohibitions to divert and redirect social and economic behaviors that would otherwise impair environmental quality.

However old some of its ingredients may be, an effective political ideology for the future must be free from the unverifiable dogmas of past ideologies. Its formulation must be in concepts and in metaphors that all people everywhere should be able to accept. It would of course be possible to have national interpretations of a global ideology; by analogy socialism and democracy have assumed distinctive national expressions. The need for universality, however, is inherent in the involvement of all nations in the task of protecting the planetary biosphere--the life-support system of all mankind. Until most nations (and especially the greater powers) share at least the rudiments of a basic political ideology there can be little prospect for effective international governance of man's common assets and necessities in the air, sea, and ecosystems that link together all forms of life in a common biosphere. A universal ideology, moreover, should not impair the dignity or the identity of any nationality or ethnic group. It should clearly express the sense, perhaps the only true sense, in which all men are alike and equal: as temporary passengers on Spaceship Earth, commonly exposed to the vulnerabilities of the only place known to man where life, as man has known it, can exist.

There is no way a priori that the feasibility of such an action-oriented political philosophy can be proved or disproved. That elements of such an international ideology already exist could be inferred from the recommendations of the UNESCO sponsored Biosphere Conference of 1968; from some (but not all) of the declarations of United Nations conferences; and from the records of international non-governmental associations such as the International Council of Scientific Unions and the International Union for Conservation of Nature and Natural Resources. In view of the rise and spread of religious and political belief-systems in the past, it does not appear that world-wide adoption of an ideology of man-environment relationships would be less plausible than the universalizing of Christianity, Marxism, or Islam. A more plausible case could be made for the near certainty that at least elements of a new political ideology of universal applicability will coalesce before the end of the 20th Century, and that a major part of it will concern man's environmental relationships.

In a world governed by nations, it is at the national level that changing values and beliefs reorder political priorities and change the direction of public affairs. The new political orientation may find expression through existing political parties or may be advanced through new parties that challenge established political systems. The principal political parties in the world today are almost without exception rooted in 19th Century causes and concepts. In many countries parties have been preoccupied with issues that growing sectors of the public, and particularly the youth, find of diminishing relevance. In New Zealand the newly established Values Party received 2 percent of the votes cast in the first election in which it offered candidates. (6) This appears to be the first political party to be organized around quality of life considerations, and its future may be instructive.

We may not yet be at a point at which substantial consensus could be achieved on any particular set of principles comprising an ideology for man-environment relationships. Among nations differing circumstances indicate the need for different rankings even within a common set of priorities. There are, however, certain propositions so fundamental to man's continuing relationship to the Earth that they must somehow be incorporated in any effective environmental ideology. This is not the place to argue the case for these propositions, but it is necessary to identify them so as to illustrate the fundamental change in human attitudes that will be necessary if humanity is to move from its traditional role of exploitation to an indefinitely sustainable role of managed renewal and conservation. Each of the problem areas represented by these propositions was recognized in the statement of principles adopted by the United Nations Conference at Stockholm; but great concessions to ethnic, political, and religious biases were required in order to obtain even minimal agreement on the principal areas of concern.

Four broad areas of concern may be identified as essential components of an eco-logical ideology. The following propositions may suggest the magnitude of changes that the ideology would require:

1.

The reproduction of human beings must be socially controlled.

Unless human population growth stabilizes by involuntary mechanisms, social control must eventually be imposed if the natural life-support system of man is to be maintained. Permits are required to hunt wildlife, to drive automobiles, or to operate barber shops; but modern liberal society leaves the most portentous human activity, with its immense implication for the human environment, almost totally uncontrolled. It seems a strange logic for governments to require licenses for men and women to live together in wedlock, but to permit them to reproduce with no assessment of the social costs and implications involved. Only a thoroughly conventional mind could fail to puzzle at the political logic that limits the number of spouses to one at a time, but allows offspring unlimited. Is it more logical for society to tell a woman how man husbands she may legally have at any given time than to tell her, in accordance with socially approved criteria, how many children she may produce?

This far-reaching proposition is presently widely unacceptable, but is neither utopian nor impractical. Socially sanctioned controls over population growth and over who reproduces, and when, are as old as human society. If life is as precious as some moralists contend, its transmission should be one of the most carefully guarded functions of society. To leave it to accident is among the more gross of social irresponsibilities.

There are undeniable risks in a deliberate policy of population control, but the risks of no policy may be greater. The problem of numbers may soon be dwarfed by possibilities in genetic technology for which human society has no precedent. The conjectured possibility of duplicating individuals through "cloning" should be sufficient to persuade even the most reluctant to place population control on the agenda of public policy.

2.

Land, like labor, is more than a commodity; only under carefully limited conditions should its use and disposition be decided by the economics of the market.

The "right" of persons to use land and other natural resources must be more strongly qualified than at present. For the United States, criteria for the permissible uses of land and the limitations on its use as a commodity are perhaps the most urgently needed elements of an effective policy for environmental quality. The mechanisms for control are at hand, but the will to employ them has been missing. For example, profits in land speculation could be totally recovered through taxation. But the establishment and enforcement of effective socio-ecological criteria for land use could bring day-long nightmares to large numbers of public officials. Their environmental responsibilities would have to be reinforced by a new set of political norms that treated all land as a public trust and thereby broke the near monopoly of land use decisions in countries like the United States, by the triumvirate of developers, lenders, and lawyers.

A major responsibility of man in relation to land (and sea) is the effect of his actions upon all other living things. All wildlife above the microbial stage now lives by human sufferance. If human society "develops" the world to its full potential perhaps the greater part of the plant and animal species now living will eventually die out--crowded off the planet by "the ethical animal" who accords no rights to other species.

3.

The advancement of technology, wisely employed, is a concomitant of the advancement of civilization; but wisdom requires that technology serve life rather than be permitted, in effect, to become an abstract master over man and nature.

A third unavoidable aspect of any effective policy for man-environment relationships is the management of technology. The development of criteria for the development and application of technology is a long-delayed need. Some needs for criteria are readily apparent. Among these are guidelines for the selective use of technology in relation to demands upon energy and natural resources, in relation to the nature and fate of its residual products including its ultimate disposition, and in relation to its effects upon human welfare and happiness.

There is need for new technologies that are conserving of ecological and environmental values and provide alternative methods for meeting human needs.

4.

A major responsibility of society through government is to reshape and maintain the habitate of man in accordance with the best available knowledge of human needs and values and man's relationship to the natural world.

This fourth element of an environmental ideology relates to the design and construction of the man-made environment. It is a major aspect of coping with the communal aspects of life. Human settlements have only in small part reflected our best knowledge of human needs. The world's great cities may be technological and logistical triumphs, but many of them are threatened with disaster as civic institutions. If cities are to be saved as centers of civilized and "urbane" values, perhaps they must be regarded, as they once were by great city builders in the past, as "civil works"--the epitomy of political and civic arts in the days of their builders.

The environmental movement has often been misunderstood as relating solely to wild nature and the aesthetics of natural beauty. These are important elements, not only for their intrinsic value, but also for the perspective they provide on human vanity and ambition. And yet, as self-appointed custodian of the world, man must be mindful of his own care and custody. The quality of life for all people is intimately connected to the places in which they live, work and gather for purpose of public affairs and recreation. It is profoundly true that "In Wilderness is the Preservation of the World," and its corollary is that "In Cities is the Preservation of the Wilderness." For unless the ideology of ecology and of man's responsibilities for his terrestrial future gains dominion in the cities, it can hardly govern the larger society. Unless this political-philosophy of man-environment relationships can be exemplified in the cities, it can never capture the imagination and the allegiance of a critical mass of humanity.

It is ironic that hostility toward the environmental quality movement has often been expressed by defenders of poor and displaced people. Ecology is somehow perceived as irrelevant to low cost housing, to public health, transportation, and employment at satisfying work. But the ecology of man is of greatest relevance to all of these concerns, and this point has been forcefully presented by Barbara Ward, René Dubos, and Ian McHarg among many others. Nonetheless, the misconception persists and challenges the conceptual and communications skills of the advocates of a politics of ecology.

The example of these four broad areas of public responsibility--control over human reproduction and population; control over use of land and natural resources; control over technology; and control over civil works and the civic arts should be sufficient to illustrate a point that all persons concerned with the future of humanity need to understand: the action that must be taken to maintain or to advance man's well being on earth is not consistent with the conventional assumptions of contemporary politics anywhere. This new politics of ecology cannot meaningfully be categorized by the expressions "right," "left" or "center." An ideology for man-environment relationships that deals realistically with funda- mental issues will be radical in the precise sense of that term; it will also be conservative. Whether this political ideology will prove to be compatible with liberal democracy as presently understood is at least questionable. Yet it need not follow that some form of ecological totalitarianism is necessary. The orienta- tion which has been suggested will diminish some freedoms for some people, but may simultaneously enlarge more freedoms for more people.

It would be a mistake to assume that people embrace an ideology because they like it. They may accept it reluctantly because no alternative seems as likely to serve their perceived needs. And the last persons to discover that a new ideology is about to displace the old are "the establishment" presiding over the old. De Toqueville's comment on the coming of the French Revolution epitomizes the curious blindness that characterizes the governors of old regimes: " . . . for never were there events more important, longer in ripening, more fully prepared, or less forseen." (7)

Of the world's peoples the Americans may find greatest difficulty in adapting to an ideology of control, for of all peoples they--or most of them--have enjoyed the widest general freedoms. But Americans may have misled themselves in their reliance upon the "natural rights" folklore of political tradition, expressed in the Declaration of Independence. They have not studied the "ecology of freedom" and have failed to understand that all "rights" are "conditional" and conditions are changing in ways that threaten all "freedoms."

The loss of freedoms that will follow if a change of direction does not occur will almost certainly be greater than the restrictions that will be required for safe- guarding the fundamental freedoms that are realizable within the limits of Space- ship Earth. The transition to a rational world of foresight and prudence, of restraint and controls, will not come easily--possibly not without the bitterness and violence that has usually characterized mankind's major social transitions. The tactics of transition to a new form of society cannot be foreseen clearly at this time. The fact of the transition is becoming ever more apparent, and the major outlines of strategy include those that have been described in the foregoing pages. The events themselves belong to the history of the future.

Notes and References

(1) THE LIFE OF REASON, OR THE PHASES OF HUMAN PROGRESS. Second Edition. New York: Charles Scribner's, 1924, p. 284.

(2) See for example: John Platt, "What We Must Do," SCIENCE, Vol. 166 (28 November 1969), 1115-1121; Geoffrey Vickers, FREEDOM IN A ROCKING BOAT. London: Allen Lane The Penguin Press, 1970; Donella H. Meadows, et al. THE LIMITS TO GROWTH. New York: Universe Books, 1972.

(3) See "The U.S. Public Considers Its Environment," A NATIONAL OPINION TRENDS
     REPORT. Princeton, New Jersey: The Gallup Organization, Inc. February 1969;
     "Pollution Resistance Grows - The Harris Survey," CHICAGO TRIBUNE, July 26,
     1971, Sec. A-1; and Lennart Lundquist, "Sweden's Environmental Policy,"
     AMBIO, Vol. 1 (June, 1972), 90-101.

(4) THE ECOLOGIST. Vol. 2 (January, 1971).

(5) REPORT OF THE UNITED NATIONS CONFERENCE ON THE HUMAN ENVIRONMENT HELD AT
     STOCKHOLM, 5-16 JUNE 1972. New York: United Nations General Assembly,
     3 July, 1972, pp. 124 plus annexes.

(6) NEW YORK TIMES, November 26, 1972, p. 1.

(7) ON THE STATE OF SOCIETY IN FRANCE BEFORE THE REVOLUTION OF 1789. London:
     John Murray, 1856, p. 1.

PRINCIPLE OF HETEROGENIZATION AND SYMBIOTIZATION: IMPLICATIONS FOR PLANNING
AND ENVIRONMENTAL DESIGN

Magoroh Maruyama
3403 May Road
Richmond, California

Abstract

There are, among many other paradigma, three basically different paradigms in
planning and environmental design as well as in various fields of science: (1)
unidirectional causal paradigm: This stems from the Greek logic, is hierarchical,
uniformistic and universalistic, and achieves design "unity" by similarities and
repetitions. (2) random process paradigm: This is the basis of thermodynamics and
Shannon's information theory. Its premise is that basically the universe tends to
random and independent events. In planning and design, this manifests in atomistic,
isolationistic, "individualistic", non-contextual principles. (3) mutual causal
paradigm: This is the newest of the three paradigms, and has developed in three
phases. (3a) First phase (1940's and 1950's): deviation-counteracting, equilibrating mutual causal processes, which are commonly called "negative feedback
systems" or "self-regulating systems". (3b) Second phase (1960's and early 1970's):
differentiation-amplifying mutual causal processes which generate and increase
heterogeneity, structuredness, patterns and complexity, and which are commonly called "positive feedback systems" or "self-evolving systems". (3c) Third phase (from
mid-1970's on): symbiotization of heterogeneity thus generated. The mutual
causal paradigm corresponds to heterogenistic design, cultural and individual
diversities in the community, planning from grass-roots up, and finding symbiotic
combinations among the heterogeneous elements.

Introduction

Our world consists of heterogeneous human cultures, individuals, and species of
animals and plants. Therefore the principle of our planning and environmental
design needs to be heterogenistic. People in different cultures respond to the
same situation in quite different ways. There is an old joke about what two men
and a woman, shipwrecked on an island, will do:

* If they are Spanish, one of the men will kill the other.
* If they are Italian, the woman will kill one of the men.
* If they are Korean, the woman will kill both men.
* If they are Japanese, one of the men will feel the awkwardness of the
  situation, and in order to make the situation easier for the others he will
  commit suicide. Then the second man will blame himself for the death of
  the first man and will commit suicide. Then the woman, feeling responsible
  for the death of the two men, will commit suicide.
* If they are English, nothing will happen because they haven't been introduced.
* If they are French, no problems.
* If they are regular Americans, they will discuss how to manufacture
  contraceptives.

* If they are <u>hippies</u>, they will form a commune.
* If they are <u>radical Americans</u>, they will organize a Women's Liberation Movement.
* If they are <u>hustlers</u>, one man will pimp the woman to the other man.
* If they are <u>religious</u>, they will establish a monastery and a nunnery for the salvation of mankind.

And we can go on and on enumerating the heterogeneous "solutions" to the same problem proposed or practiced by different people. This was only a joke to illustrate the point, but there are many real examples.

For example, Americans try to "solve" the population "problem" by the <u>mechanical</u> means of contraceptives. But there is a culture which has been practicing the system of "staggered marriage" which resulted in low fertility rates: Young men married old women. When they themselves got older and their partners died off, they married young girls. In this culture everybody, both men and women, married at least twice, and it was reported that everybody had fun. Of course, the life expectancy was not high, and most people died before they were too old.

Another example involves a much more profound, philosophical difference between two cultures. It deals with the concept of "waste disposal". In the Greek-European-American logic, the universe consists of "things" which have permanence and "identity". When the "thing" changes, it loses its identity and it is no longer the "thing" it used to be, and therefore it is <u>no-good</u> any more as the original thing. The Greek-European-American logic handles this situation in one of the two ways: either the changed thing must be thrown away, or it has to be restored into its original shape. Thus, the thing becomes either "waste" or gets "recycled".

On the other hand, in the Chinese philosophy nothing is permanent and everything changes. Since it is normal for everything to change, "identity" in the sense of permanence is irrelevant. When things change, they do not become no-good. They are always good for some use. All you have to do is to find a new use for the changed things. Therefore things do not become "waste", and they do not have to be "recycled".

It is this kind of philosophical differences between cultures and between disciplines that I would like to discuss in this paper.

There are different terminologies which have been used to describe philosophical differences in different cultures and in different disciplines. Systems engineers, operational researchers and some experimental psychologists have used the term "models." Some philosophers and logicians have used the term "logics." Anthropologists and psycholinguists have used the term "cognitive structure," and more recently "epistemology" or "epistemologies." Sociologists have also used the term "epistemology," but more in the sense of "sociology of knowledge" than in the sense of experimental study of cognitive structure. More recently sociologists began using the term "paradigms" mainly because of their effort to gain their inspiration from physics, and because Thomas Kuhn's work (1) on paradigms in physics has become respectable among sociologists. In this paper I will use the term "paradigms" to indicate different philosophical structures of reasoning.

Examples of Paradigms

There exist many different paradigms, and there will undoubtedly be many more paradigms in the future which do not exist yet. Let us take three paradigms as examples. These are: 1) unidirectional causal paradigm; 2) random process paradigm; 3) mutual causal paradigm. These examples are not meant to be exhaustive. Nor are they mutually exclusive.

Any attempt at separating paradigms into non-overlapping categories is itself a victim of a paradigm which assumes that the universe consists of non-overlapping categories. Such an attempt excludes non-classificational paradigms, and therefore negates itself in the sense of Russell's paradoxes.(2)

In actuality, there are mixtures and overlappings between these three paradigms as well as between these and many other paradigms. For example, there are: (1-2) probabilistic unidirectional causal paradigm which is a mixture between the first and the third paradigms; (1-2-3) probabilistic mutual and unidirectional paradigm which is a mixture between the three paradigms. Let us discuss them one by one.

First, let me make a simplified table of the three "pure" paradigms:

	(1) Unidirectional Causal Paradigm	(2) Random Process Paradigm	(3) Mutual Causal Paradigm
Science:	traditional "cause" and "effect" model	thermodynamics; Shannon's information theory	post-Shannon information theory
Information	past and future inferrable from present	Information decays and gets lost. Blueprint must contain more information than finished product.	Information can be generated. Nonredundant complexity can be generated without pre-established blueprint.
Cosmology:	predetermined universe.	decaying universe.	self-generating and self-organizing universe.
Social organization:	hierarchical	individualistic	non-hierarchical interactionist
Social policy:	homogenistic	decentralization	heterogenistic coordination
Ideology:	authoritarian	anarchistic	cooperative

	(1) Unidirectional Causal Paradigm	(2) Random Process Paradigm	(3) Mutual Causal Paradigm
Philosophy:	universalism	nominalism	network
Ethics:	competitive	isolationist	symbiotic
Esthetics:	unity by similarity and repetition	Haphazard	harmony of diversity
Religion:	monotheism	freedom of religion	polytheistic harmonism
Decision process:	dictatorship, majority rule or consensus	do your own thing	elimination of hardship on any single individual
Logic:	deductive, axiomatic	inductive, empirical	complementary
Perception:	categorical	atomistic	contextual
Knowledge:	believe in one truth. If people are informed, they will agree.	why bother to learn beyond one's own interest.	Polyocular: must learn different views and take them into consideration.
Methodology:	classificational, taxonomic	statistical	relational, contextual analysis, network analysis
Research hypothesis and research strategy:	Dissimilar results must have been caused by dissimilar conditions. Differences must be traced to conditions producing them.	There is probability distribution. Find out probability distribution.	Dissimilar results may come from similar conditions due to mutually amplifying network. Network analysis instead of tracing of the difference back to initial conditions in such cases.
Assessment:	"impact" analysis.	What does it do to me?	Look for feedback loops for self-cencellation or self-reinforcement.

	(1) Unidirectional Causal Paradigm	(2) Random Process Paradigm	(3) Mutual Causal Paradigm
Analysis:	pre-set categories used for all situations.	limited categories for his own use.	changeable categories depending on situation.
Community people viewed as:	ignorant, poorly informed, lacking expertise, limited in scope.	egocentric	most direct source of information, articulate in their own view, essential in determining relevance.
Planning:	by "experts." Either keep community people uninformed, or inform them in such a way that they will agree.	laisser-faire.	generated by community people.

(1) Unidirectional causal paradigm. There is the paradigm which, until recently, has been commonly regarded as "the" scientific way of thinking. In this paradigm, there is a one-way flow of influence from the "cause" to the "effect." There is nothing in the "effect" which cannot be traced back to its "cause." Therefore there cannot be less information in the cause than in its effect. If you know the conditions of the "cause," you can deduce the conditions of the "effect." On the other hand, if you know the conditions of the "effect," you can infer the conditions of the "cause." The past and the future can be inferred from the present if we have a complete knowledge of the present. For the same reason, the present can be inferred from the past or from the future if we have complete information. The "scientific method" consists in identifying the "cause" when the "effect" is known, and predicting the "effect" when the "cause" is known. If there are differences in the "effect," there must be corresponding differences in the "cause". The strategy of scientific research is aimed at discovering these differences in the "cause."

(1-2) Probabilistic unidirectional causal paradigm. This is a paradigm which became fashionable since the discovery of indeterminism and informational indeterminablism in quantum mechanics. This paradigm continues to be fashionable in the philosophy of science and in sociology, even though physical and biological sciences have already moved out from this paradigm. According to this paradigm, there is a one-way flow of influence from the "cause" to the "effect." But the influence occurs with some probability rather than with certainty. "Effect" can be predicted from the "cause" with some probability, and the "cause" can be inferred from the "effect" with some probability. Complete information can never be obtained even

on the present condition because of the fact that the information-collecting
instrument interfers with the observed phenomena and the act of information-collecting disturbs the phenomena. The "scientific method" consists in discovering the
probability distribution in the "effect" when the cause is hypothetically specified
(neither cause nor effect can be completely accurately measured), and in establishing the limits of accuracy of observation. Multivariate statistical analysis such
as factor analysis, correlation analysis, regression analysis, etc. can be attempted
in the study of phenomena which are not completely amenable to laboratory experiments,
such as weather tropospheric scattering of electromagnetic waves and social revolution. If statistical relations between two variables are found, this may be
due to one of the following unidirectional causal relations: a) one causes the other
with some probability either directly or through other intermediate variables; or
b) both are influenced by some common cause with some probability. The causal direction cannot be known from statistics alone, and must be determined by logical considerations.

(2) Random process paradigm. This paradigm is due to the development of thermodynamics in the nineteenth century. It is based on logic similar to that of tossing
coins. The coin-tossing situation, each toss is considered to be independent from
other tosses. The outcome of the first toss should not influence the outcome of
the second toss. The third toss should not have influence from the outcome of the
two previous tosses, etc. This assumption is considered true even if the coin itself may be "unfair," i.e. heavy on one side. For example, if the coin is unfair
and is heavy on one side, and has the probability of 30-70 for the head on each toss,
the second toss should have the same probability of 30-70 regardless of whether it
was a head or a tail at the first toss.

Suppose you have 1,000 coins, each of which is similarly unfair, having the head-
tail probability of 30-70. Suppose you paint the head side of all coins blue, and
the tail side of all coins yellow. Suppose you put them in a box, shake the box
well, and pour the coins onto a tray. You will see coins spread over the tray,
mostly yellow but some blue. If you put the tray on the table in your garden, go
to the airport, rent a helicopter and hover over your garden, you will see the
tray without being able to distinguish individual coins. The tray will look yellow-
ish-green.

If the probability of each coin is 30-70, the chances of getting two heads out of
two coins are $0.3 \times 0.3 = 0.09$ or nine percent. The chances of getting two tails
out of two coins is $0.7 \times 0.7 = 0.49$, or forty-nine percent.

The chances of getting 1,000 heads out of 1,000 coins are very small, even though
such a possibility exists. Therefore the chances of getting a completely blue-
looking tray is very small. So are the chances of getting a completely yellow-
looking tray. Most of the time you get a green-looking tray, more to the yellow
side than to the blue side.

How about the chances of one-half of the tray looking completely blue and the other
half looking completely yellow? Again, such a possibility exists, but very small.
Most of the time both sides of the tray have about the same hue.

Similar reasoning can be applied to the distribution of temperature in thermo-dynamics. Heat is caused by movements of molecules. If left alone for a long time without interference to or from outside, the most probable distribution of temperature in a non-living isolated object is even distribution.

If an isolated "system" is found in a state in which the temperature distribution is not even, it is thermodynamically in an improbable state. The more uneven the distribution of the temperature, the more improbable its state. The heat tends to move from warmer zones to colder zones either by direct transmission through solid body, by being carried by the flow of liquid or gas, or by radiation. The system tends to change from a low-probability state to a higher-probability state, even though there is a small probability that the change might occur in the other direc-tion, just as once in a while the coin-tossing might produce a very improbable distribution of hues.

This tendency is called the "law of increase of entropy." "Entropy" is defined in such a way that the higher the degree of homogeneity of the distribution of temp-erature, the higher the entropy.

The change from a low-entropy state to a higher-entropy state occurs gradually, because it takes time for the heat to move. The change does not occur by a sudden jump. There is some degree of continuity in the sense that the state of the system at a given time is related to the state of the system at a previous time. Therefore this change is not "independent" in the sense of coin-tossing. In fact, the state at a later time is related to the state at an earlier time with a certain probability distribution, and this type of change is called "stochastic process."

So this second paradigm may be called a "stochastic paradigm" instead of "random process paradigm." But I prefer to call it "random process paradigm" because entropy is defined on the basis of the system's closeness to the state of random distribution.

Shannon's theory of information (3) is based on the same paradigm. Working in the Bell Telephone Laboratories, Shannon had to deal with the problem of loss of trans-mitted information in telephone circuits due to overloading or due to noise. He also had to develop ways to pack information in compact coded forms in order to make maximum use of transmission circuits.

In telephone circuits the human voice is converted into patterns of electric os-cillation. At the listener's end, these electric oscillations are reconverted into vibration of air which corresponds to the original voice of the talker. In the transmission lines there are random movements of electrons caused either by am-plifiers themselves or by external electro-magnetic phenomena such as lightning. These random movements of electrons interfere with the transmitted patterns of electronic oscillations, and decrease the amount of information. It was therefore natural for Shannon to define the amount of information as the degree of non-random-ness of the patterns. It is not surprising that the mathematical formula for the amount of information thus conceptualized by Shannon turned out to be exactly the same as the mathematical formula for thermodynamic entropy.(4)The only difference is that while thermodynamic entropy was defined in such a way that it is greater when the degree of randomness is higher, the amount of information was defined in such a way that it is greater when the degree of randomness is lower. Thus, mathematically, the formula for the amount of information has a negative sign as compared to the formula for thermodynamic entropy.

This can be restated in many ways. One way to restate is that the amount of information corresponds to the degree of improbability of the given pattern on the basis of the assumption of random independent events. For example, a series of footprints on a sand beach is improbable on the basis of the assumption of the sand being blown randomly by the wind, and conveys the "message" that something other than wind was present. When the footprints are left to the winds or waves, they decay. The more details of the footprints remain, the more "information" they have as to what kind of an animal was there.

Just as in thermodynamic process in which the distribution of temperature in an isolated system became more and more homogeneous, in the information theory as formulated by Shannon the amount of information gradually decays if left to random influences. Shannon's information theory was partly aimed at combatting this decay and restoring the lost information. It was not intended to, and cannot, generate new information. The other part of Shannon's information theory was aimed at coding and packing information in a compact form in order to maximize the total amount of information transmitted in a given channel. For example, suppose you want to transmit a black-and-white image on a television screen. An uneconomical way is to transmit the brightness of all the points on the image. A more economical way is to indicate only the places where the brightness changes in the scan. In this way you can pack the information more efficiently. There are still other ways of packing the same information more efficiently.

If you notice, the procedure of indicating only the places where the brightness changes is a procedure which ignores the homogeneous parts and pays attention only to heterogeneous parts. In this sense, homogeneous parts have less "information" than heterogeneous parts. For the same reason, repetition of identical elements has less "information" than combinations of different elements. If the same element is repeated several times, it suffices to transmit information on one element and indicate how many times it is repeated, instead of transmitting the same information several times. It is worth remembering that the amount of Shannonian information is greater when the degree of heterogeneity is greater, as we will reconsider this point in the discussion of the mutual causal paradigm.

The purpose of science based on the paradigm of Shannonian information theory is to identify the amount of information, the type of coding and decoding, and the mode of transmission in living organisms and in man-made control and communication devices. Since noise and overloading of channels result in loss of information, and since information can never be increased, the primary concern of this type of science was the economy and the efficiency in the coding and decoding as well as the maximum use of channel capacity without creating overloading.

Examples of fields of specialization which flourished under this paradigm are: the study of so-called "genetic codes"; neurophysiology; coded data transmission in space technology; data bank and information retrieval.

(3) <u>Mutual causal paradigm</u>. This paradigm attained a sophisticated mathematical formulation in the Western science during the Second World War, although it existed in the philosophies of many non-Western cultures for a few thousand years. The development of this paradigm in the Western science occurred in two phases: a) The phase of the deviation-counteracting and equilibrating mutual causal paradigm. This phase occurred in the period extending from 1940's to 1950's; b) the phase of the differentiation-amplifying and heterogeneity-increasing mutual causal paradigm extending from the early 1960's to present. There may yet be the third phase to develop, characterized by mathematical elaboration of the diversity-symbiotizing mutual causal paradigm.

Even though intuitive formulations of mutual causality in the Western science can be traced back to Darwin, Adam Smith and several others in different fields of specialization((5),(6)); the notion of mutual causality had not become a "respectable" scientific paradigm until it was formulated with some mathematical sophistication in mid-20th Century.

The mathematical formulation which marked the beginning of the first phase of the mutual causal paradigm occurred during the Second World War, when anti-aircraft artillery became equipped with a corrective feedback loop consisting of a radar and a computer (7). The initial mathematical formulation for the second phase occurred in 1960 when mathematician Stanislaw Ulam developed a theory that complex patterns can be generated by means of simple rules of interaction (8),(9). The mathematical formulation for the third phase is yet to be made.

The history of the development of the conceptualization of the mutual causal paradigm both before and after the Second World War is discussed elsewhere (10), (11) (12).

Deviation-counteracting equilibrating mutual causal loops can be found in many self-regulating processes in biology, ecology and man-made devices; for example, the self-regulation of body temperature, the prey/predator ratio and the auto-pilot mechanism.

In such a causal loop the effect of any change in one element comes back to itself through other elements in the loop in such a way that the change is counteracted and cancelled out. For example, if for some reason the number of preys decreases, the predators starve and their number decreases. If the predators decrease in number, less preys are eaten, and as a result the number of preys increases. Similarly, if the number of preys increase, the predators get well-nourished and a greater number of their off-springs survive. Therefore the number of predators increases. This, in turn, decreases the number of preys. Thus any change in the number of preys has the effect of cancelling itself out through the change in the number of predators. Similarly, any change in the number of predators has the effect of cancelling itself out through the change in the number of preys. There is a mutual deviation-counteracting equilibrating mutual causal relationship between the number of preys and the number of predators.

Differentiation-amplifying heterogenizing mutual causal loops can be found in many biological and social processes which increase complexity, diversity and structure.

For example, in the interaction between a species of moth and a species of bird which feeds on it, camouflaged mutants of the moth will survive better and the mutants of the bird who are clever at discovering the camouflaged moths will survive better. As a result, the moth gets more and more camouflaged generation after generation, and the bird gets more and more skillful in discovering the camouflaged moths will survive better. As a result, the moth gets more and more camouflaged generation after generation, and the bird gets more and more skillful in discovering the camouflaged moth. Another example is the growth of a city on a homogeneous plain. Suppose that there is a plain which is homogeneous before the arrival of human pioneers. One day someone arrives and settles down on a certain spot. The choice of the spot may be accidental, due to such reasons as the man's being too tired to go any further, the horse becoming ill, etc. But once he is settled, someone else may come and join him, and gradually a village may grow. This increases the attractiveness of the spot to other pioneers, and more people will come. Gradually industries develop, and a city grows. The plain is no longer homogeneous. Within the city many types of differentiation and heterogenization take place; business sections and residential sections become differentiated; several different kinds of vocational schools are built, etc.

Ulam's formulation has profound implications in these processes. He discovered that when a complex pattern is generated by interaction, it often takes more "amount of Shannonian information" to describe the finished pattern than to describe the interaction rules which generated the pattern. In other words, the "amount of Shannonian information" grows in such processes. We remember that in Shannon's formulation based on the random process paradigm, the amount of information can never increase. In the random process paradigm, structures decay and information decreases. On the other hand, the deviation-counteracting equilibrating mutual causal processes can maintain structures and information against decay, and the differentiation-amplifying heterogenizing mutual causal processes can generate and increase structures and information.

This solves one of the puzzles of science. Thermodynamics based on the random process paradigm could not explain how living organisms decreased the entropy (increased temperature differentiation). It simply begged the question by saying that living organisms are not isolated systems. But this question-begging was as unsatisfactory as the attempt at explaining how a computer works by saying that it works because it is plugged into a power source. A more satisfactory explanation lies in the recognition that the biological processes are mutual causal processes, not random processes.

Because the mutual causal processes can maintain and increase heterogeneity, they are sometimes called "anti-entropic processes." Furthermore, deviation-counteracting equilibrating mutual causal processes are sometimes called "morphostatic processes," and differentiation-amplifying heterogenizing mutual causal processes are called "morphogenetic processes."

Let us recall for a moment the example of the footprints on a sand beach. As late as in 1953 Hans Reichenbach, one of the leading philosophers of science of that period, denied the possibility of mutual causal processes (13) and advanced the following argument.

There are several types of time-asymmetrical processes. If you take a movie film of a time-asymmetrical process and run the film backward, you can tell it is run backward because the process does not obey the laws of physics.

As an example of one of the types of time-asymmetrical processes, Reichenbach discussed the process of a footprint on a sand beach being blown by winds. He said that the actual event runs in the direction of gradual decay of the footprint. If you take a movie film of this event and run it backwards, you can recognize that the film is being run backward. His argument was that it is highly improbable, though not completely impossible, that random influences consistently accumulate in such a way as to gradually produce a structure. Faced with the question of how structures came about in the first place, Reichenbach tended to think that structures can be created by sudden events such as an explosion, but not by a gradual, slow process.

His unidirectional causal paradigm could not explain gradual growth of structure such as we have seen in the case of the growth of a city on a homogeneous plain. He had to introduce the notion of "finality," i.e. the future determining the present, in order to account for the processes which he could not explain with his unidirectional causal paradigm.

Some of the readers may have noticed the affinity of Reichenbach's explosion theory to LeMaitre's "Big Bang Theory" in astronomy. There are currently two theories in astronomy regarding how the universe got started. One is the "Big Bang Theory" which says that the universe began with a big explosion. The other is the "Condensation Theory" which says the universe initially consisted of homogeneously distributed gas matters which gradually condensed into astronomic bodies due to mutual gravity.

The condensation theory is in the mutual causal paradigm. An interesting question the Condensation Theory poses is the following: If we regard the entire universe as an isolated system, then the entropy decreases in this isolated system provided the condensation theory is correct. This is a very interesting paradigmatic possibility.

At the end of the 19th Century, Boltzmann (14) proposed another paradigm. He proposed that there may be other universes in which the direction of time runs opposite to ours. We cannot receive any information from such a universe, because any information leaving it according to its time direction would be seen by us as going to that universe. But if it were possible to observe such a universe, the decays in it would look as growth, and growth in it would look like a decay. It would not be easy to talk about decay and growth in such a case.

Let us return to the discussion of the mutual causal paradigm and discuss its third phase. The third phase, which is not yet mathematically formulated, is going to have to deal with the question of symbiotization of diversities at a more sophisticated level than is now practiced. There is already a great deal of data from ecology and biology regarding symbiosis and heterogeneity. But in ecology and biology we have been studying so far the symbiotic relations which are already established between diverse species. We do not concern ourselves with the possibility of creating new symbiotic relations between the species which are not yet interacting. Yet this is the kind of concern we need to develop in dealing with the social and cultural change taking place in our world, not only in order to avoid possible catastrophes but also in order to explore positive alternatives.

In most cases the ecological and biological thinking proceeds with two assumptions: a) That the animal species and plant species have no "alternatives." They live the way they live. b) That the ecological relationship established among them should be maintained as much as possible. A change in any of its parts may affect the whole eco-system, and may have disasterous and irreversible consequences.

On the other hand, our social thinking proceeds with two different assumptions: a) that each culture, each social group or each individual has its own goal, and there are several alternative ways to attain this goal; b) They are homogenistic, and cannot even deal with the heterogeneity in our own culture; c) Consequently they do not even conceive the problem of finding possible symbiotic combinations among heterogeneous elements; d) Not many of them include the consideration of existence of alternatives.

The formulation of the third phase of the mutual causal paradigm can begin with considerations such as the following. Suppose there are three individuals, A, B and C. A has his goal which we call Ga. B has his goal which we call Gb. C has his goal which we call Gc. Suppose A has five different ways to accomplish his goal Ga; B has two different ways to accomplish his goal Gb; and C has three different ways to accomplish his goal Gc. Then there are 5 times 2 times 3 = 30 different combinations of these alternative ways in which all three individuals can attain their different goals. Some of these 30 combinations may produce symbiosis among the three individuals, while other combinations may not. Our problem is to find these combinations of alternatives which produce symbiosis. We need not only a mathematically sophisticated but also practically implementable formulation to deal with symbiotization of a wide range of heterogeneous elements.

In the unidirectional, quantitative and competitive paradigm, "the survival of the fittest" was misinterpreted as the survival of the strongest, the most aggressive, etc. But in the mutualistic causal paradigm, the survival of the fittest is interpreted as the survival of the most symbiotic, not the strongest. The random process paradigm can be called the "decay principle"; the deviation-counter-acting equilibrating mutual causal paradigm and the differentiation-amplifying heterogenizing mutual causal paradigm can be called the "life principle." The diversity-symbiotizing mutual causal paradigm, when developed more fully, might as well be called the "love principle" (the name given by Elise Boulding).

One of the characteristics of deviation-counteracting equilibrating mutual causal processes is that dissimilar conditions are counteracted and the result converges to similar conditions. On the other hand, the differentiation-amplifying heterogenizing mutual causal processes have a characteristic that similar initial conditions may produce very dissimilar results. These properties have very profound theoretical consequences: a) Neither the past nor the future can be inferred from the present, nor the present can be inferred from the past or from the future. This is not because of the "indeterminism" and "probabilism," but because of the deviation-counteracting and differentiation-amplifying mutual causal loops. b) In the research method, the existence of a "difference in the initial condition" cannot be assumed on the basis of a difference in the result. One would be looking for a non-existing straw man if one looked for a difference in the initial condition. One must look for the amplification network. For example, the difference in the national character between Denmark and Holland may not come from the difference in climate, geography, racial origin, and such "conditions." Instead, it may be more worthwhile to look into how within each culture the various aspects reinforce one another.

The research method regarding "information" also changes considerably in the mutual causal paradigm. In the random process paradigm of Shannon's information theory, the amount of information can never grow. Therefore, all existing information must have come from somewhere. For example, the genes must contain the amount of information necessary to describe the adult body. For each part of the adult body, there must be a corresponding unit of information locatable in the genes. The research therefore aims at locating these units.

On the other hand, in the mutual causal paradigm the amount of information as defined by Shannon may grow by interaction. Therefore it may be more profitable to discover the rules of cellular interaction than try to locate in the genes the information units corresponding to each part of the adult body. Therefore experiments in embryonic grafting or embryonic interference may be performed instead of the analysis of genes per se.

(2-3) _Probabilistic mutual causal paradigm_. As we have seen, even _without_ the introduction of probabilistic indeterminism the mutual causal paradigm does not conform to the notion that "similar conditions produce similar results." In the _deterministic_ mutual causal paradigm, dissimilar conditions may end up with similar results due to deviation-counteracting, or similar conditions may produce dissimilar results due to differentiation-amplifying.

But when we combine the indeterminism with the mutual causal paradigm, we obtain the following: a) The _same_ conditions may produce different results. b) Different conditions may produce the _same_ results.

(a) This is because a very small initial difference, which is within the range of high probability, may be amplified to the degree which would be very improbable in the probabilistic unidirectional causal paradigm.

(b) In the deterministic deviation-counteracting process, the equilibrium is usually reached asymptotically, but not necessarily completely. The process approaches the ideal equilibrium but does not completely attain it. On the other hand, if small probabilistic fluctuations are allowed, it is possible that the process jumps into the ideal equilibrium state once in a while, even though it may jump out of it as well.

(1-3) _Deterministic mutual and unidirectional causal paradigm_. In this paradigm, not all causal relations are mutual. There are some unidirectional causal relations mixed with mutual causal relations.

(1-2-3) <u>Probabilistic mutual and unidirectional causal paradigm</u>. This is the most flexible combination of the three paradigms discussed. This contains the characteristics of all three "pure" paradigms.

There are many other paradigms. The above have been given as examples, and were not intended to be exhaustive.

<u>Implications for planning and environmental design.</u>

Paradigmatic differences affect <u>the planning procedure</u> as well as <u>the design principles</u>.

a) <u>Planning procedure</u>: As we have seen in the table at the beginning of this paper, in the unidirectional causal paradigm the planning is made from the top down by socalled "experts". In the random process paradigm, there is hardly any planning. In the mutual causal paradigm, the planning is made from the grass-roots up, with constant interaction, input and feedback between different groups in the community as well as between the community and the administration.

b) <u>Design principles</u>: Esthetic principles vary from culture to culture. Some of the Islamic designs are characterized by intricate repetitions of minute details. The European Vitruvius principle which stems from the unidirectional causal paradigm achieves its design unity by repetitions of similar elements. On the other hand, the Japanese gardens and flower arrangements avoid repetitions and redundancies, and create harmony of <u>dissimilar</u> elements. In Japan repetitiousness, whether in design, in poetry or in human behavior, is considered "kudoi" (heavy, overdone, obnoxious) and is avoided. The contrary of "kudoi" is "sappari" (fresh, clear), and is a very important consideration in the Japanese esthetics.

In China, however, we find both the principle of repetition and the principle of sappari. The Chinese architecture and decorations can be highly elaborate, repetitious and strong in color, and some of the ancient Chinese poems are quite profuse in extravagant adjectives, while the traditional Chinese paintings as a whole have non-repetitious compositions.

Nor is the one or the other principle characteristic of exclusively Western or exclusively Eastern cultures. The Hopi design is elaborate, while much of the Swedish design is sappari.

There are also different basic numbers in different cultures. In Navajo, the basic number seems to be 4, particularly in songs. In Sioux, the basic numbers seem to be 4 and 6, corresponding to the four directions, with sky and earth sometimes included as two additional directions. The Japanese Ikebana (flower arrangement) is usually based on various principles of making a composition out of 3, 5, 7 or 9 <u>different</u> elements. Many Japanese designs use a triangle or <u>un</u>equal sides as the basic layout, often with secondary triangles added, which should be <u>dissimilar</u> from the main triangle, unlike the European architectural design in which the "subdominant" forms are supposed to repeat the main form.

There are also cultural differences in the concept of a design object in relation to other objects. For example in the Japanese architecture there has been, and there still is, a great concern in harmonizing the building with its surrounding environment. On the other hand, many of the American architects, particularly the urban architects, tend to regard the building mainly as an expression of its individuality.

The existence of these cultural differences in esthetic principles indicate that even in esthetics there are heterogenistic as well as homogenistic principles, and that harmony and beauty can be created by heterogeneity.

These considerations make us further ask to ourselves questions like: (1) whether we can apply esthetic principles of heterogeneity to social hardware such as urban and regional planning; (2) whether we can devise over-all esthetic meta-principles capable of combining several designs, some of which are based on homogenistic principles while some others are based on heterogenistic principles.

The answer to the first question cannot yet be given, because examples of such hardware have hardly been produced yet. There are numerous urban designs which include various buildings with different functions. But usually the philosophy of such designs is to bring these buildings to unity by means of some shared features, similar details, similar proportionality, etc. An urban area with an overall design with components based on different principles, or a building consisting of suites or rooms with contrasting philosophies, is yet to be created. A shopping center built with such an over-all consideration, or even a student dormitory consisting of rooms in different styles, would be very attractive and interesting.

The answer to the second question seems positive. There already exist some examples of such meta-principles. Kenzo Tange's Olympic Sports Building Complex can be regarded as an example of such a meta-principle. The overall design is heterogeneous based on the principle of dynamic balance of flow of lines (which, in this case, coincide with the direction of movements of pedestrians), and is asymmetrical and non-redundant. If you take the components separately, some of them are homogeneous and redundant inside themselves, while other components are heterogeneous.

Such meta-principles have not yet been applied to urban planning. But in some cities there is an emergence of different cultural principles in architecture, which later can be used as components of an overall meta-design. For example in San Francisco the residents of the Chinatown have designed and proposed some housing projects which have a high ratio of the number of occupants per square footage, and which will enable old-age persons to stay near younger generations. This is all in accordance with the Chinese culture. In another part of San Francisco, some Black architects designed houses which have a shower and bath facility directly attached to the large living room. This is congruent with the Black tradition in this country. The Black families in cities often receive migrants from rural areas. These new arrivals stay and sleep in the living room until they find a job and a place to live. The receiving family is able to express its hospitality by having a bathroom attached to the living room.

At present, each community is acting independently in such an endeavor. But as our society moves toward increased heterogenism, overall urban designs to anticipate,

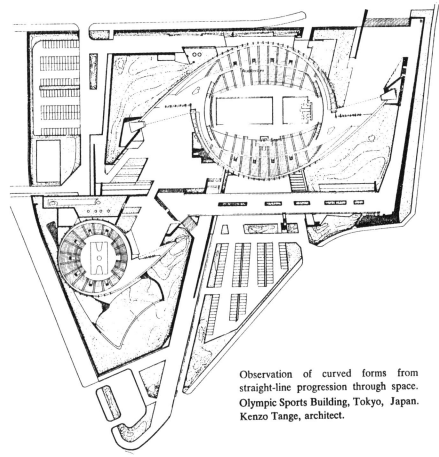

Observation of curved forms from straight-line progression through space. Olympic Sports Building, Tokyo, Japan. Kenzo Tange, architect.

Illustration taken from Edmund Bacon's "Design of Cities", Viking Press.

accomodate and symbiotize the heterogeneity become necessary and useful.

There are two ways the heterogenization may proceed: <u>localization</u> and <u>interweaving</u>. In localization, heterogeneity between localities increases, while each locality may remain or become homogeneous. In interweaving, heterogeneity in each locality increases, while the differences between localities decrease. At the present, localization is more conspicuous than interweaving. At the stage of localization, the meta-principles apply to inter-locality designs. In the next stage of our social heterogenization, interweaving may increase. At that stage the meta-principles will be needed for intra-locality designs and designs for individual buildings. We need to develop esthetic meta-principles of heterogenization and symbiotization of heterogeneity both for localization and interweaving.

Notes and References

(1) Kuhn, T., THE STRUCTURE OF SCIENTIFIC REVOLUTIONS, Chicago: University Chicago Press, 1962.

(2) Bertrand Russell gave several examples of logical paradoxes. One of them is the statement written on a sheet of paper: "Any statement written on this sheet is false." If this statement is true, then it must be false. But if this statement is false, then in a bi-value logic its negation is true, i.e. the statement must be true. Hence a paradox. Gregory Bateson gave another paradox (1956). It is a command: "Be self-assertive." If someone becomes self-assertive, he is obeying this command and is therefore not self-assertive. If he becomes un-self-assertive, he is disobeying the command and is therefore self-assertive. As pointed out be Bateson, the solution to these paradoxes, including ours, lies in distinguishing the statements from the comments on statements. But if we do this in our own example, we will still be falling into a classificational paradigm.

(3) Shannon, C., et al., MATHEMATICAL THEORY OF COMMUNICATION, Urbana: University of Illinois Press, 1949.

(4) The conditions for the determination of the formula are given by Shannon (1949).

(5) Maruyama, M., The Second Cybernetics: Deviation-Amplifying Mutual Causal Processes, AMERICAN SCIENTIST, Vol. 51: pg. 164-179; 250-256, 1963.

(6) Milsum, J., POSITIVE FEEDBACK, Pergamon, 1968.

(7) Maruyama, M., EXTRAPOLATION, INTERPOLATION AND SMOOTHING OF STATIONARY TIME SERIES WITH ENGINEERING APPLICATIONS, 1949.

(8) Ulam, S., On Some Mathematical Problems Connected With Patterns of Growth Figures, PROCEEDINGS OF SYMPOSIUM ON APPLIED MATHEMATICS, Vol. 14: pg. 215-224, 1962.

(9) Maruyama, M., Generating Complex Patterns By Means Of Simple Rules of Interaction, METHODOS, Vol. 14: pg. 17-26, 1963.

(10) Maruyama, M., The Second Cybernetics: Deviation-Amplifying Mutual Causal Processes, AMERICAN SCIENTIST, Vol. 51: pg. 164-179; 250-256, 1963.

(11) Milsum, J., POSITIVE FEEDBACK, Pergamon, 1968.

(12) Buckley, W., MODERN SYSTEMS RESEARCH FOR THE BEHAVIORAL SCIENTIST, Chicago: Aldine, 1968.

(13) Reichenbach, H., DIRECTION OF TIME, Los Angeles: University of California Press, 1956.

(14) Boltzmann, L., VORLESUNGEN ÜBER GASTHEORIE, Barth, 1898.

ON CONSTRUCTING A REALITY

Heinz Von Foerster
Professor of Biophysics and Electrical Engineering
Biological Computer Laboratory, 216 EERL
University of Illinois
Urbana, Illinois 61801

Abstract

"Draw a distinction!" (1)

The Postulate

I am sure you remember the plain citizen Jourdain in Moliere's "Bourgeois Gentil-homme" who, nouveau rich, travels in the sophisticated circles of the French aristocracy, and who is eager to learn. On one occasion with his new friends they speak about poetry and prose, and Jourdain discovers to his amazement and great delight that whenever he speaks, he speaks prose. He is overwhelmed by this dis-covery: "I am speaking Prose! I have always spoken Prose! I have spoken Prose throughout my whole life!"

A similar discovery has been made not so long ago, but it was neither of poetry nor prose--it was the environment that was discovered. I remember when, perhaps ten or fifteen years ago, some of my American friends came running to me with the delight and amazement of having just made a great discovery: "I am living in an Environment! I have always lived in an Environment! I have lived in an Environ-ment throughout my whole life!"

However, neither M. Jourdain nor my friends have as yet made another discovery, and that is when M. Jourdain speaks, may it be prose or poetry, it is he who invents it, and likewise when we perceive our environment, it is we who invent it.

Every discovery has a painful and a joyful side: painful, while struggling with a new insight; joyful, when this insight is gained. I see the sole purpose of my presentation to minimize the pain and maximize the joy for those who have not yet made this discovery; and for those who have made it, to let them know they are not alone. Again, the discovery we all have to make for ourselves is the following postulate:

The Environment As We Perceive It Is Our Invention.

The burden is now upon me to support this outrageous claim. I shall proceed by first inviting you to participate in an experiment; than I shall report a clinical case and the results of two other experiments. After this I will give an inter-pretation, and thereafter a highly compressed version of the neurophysiological basis of these experiments and my postulate of before. Finally, I shall attempt to suggest the significance of all that to aesthetical and ethical considerations.

Experiments   Figure <u>1</u>

((i) Blindspot) Hold book with right hand, close left eye and fixate asterisk of
Fig. 1 with right eye. Move book slowly back and forth along line of vision until
at an appropriate distance (from about 12 to 14 inches) round black spot dis-
appears. Keeping asterisk well focused, spot should remain invisible even if book
is slowly moved parallel to itself in any direction. ● This localized blindness
is a direct consequence of the absence of photo receptors (rods or cones) at that
point of the retina, the "disc", where all fibers, leading from the eye's light
sensitive surface, converge to form the optic nerve. Clearly, when the black spot
is projected onto the disc, it cannot be seen. Note that this localized blindness is not perceived as a dark blotch in our visual field (seeing a dark blotch
would imply "seeing"), but this blindness is not perceived at all, that is,
neither as something present, nor as something absent: whatever is perceived is
perceived "blotch-less".

((ii) Scotoma) Well localized occipital lesions in the brain (e.g., injuries from
high velocity projectiles) heal relatively fast without the patient's awareness
of any perceptible loss in his vision. However, after several weeks motor dysfunction in the patient becomes apparent, e.g., loss of control of arm or leg movements of one side or the other, etc. Clinical tests, however, show that there is
nothing wrong with the motor system, but that in some cases there is substantial
loss (Fig. 2) of a large portion of the visual field (<u>scotoma</u>) (2). A successful
therapy consists of blindfolding the patient over a period of one to two months
until he regains control over his motor system by shifting his "attention" from
(non-existent) visual clues regarding his posture to (fully operative) channels
that give direct postural clues from (proprioceptive) sensors embedded in muscles
and joints. Note again absence of perception of "absence of perception", and

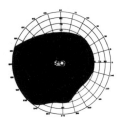 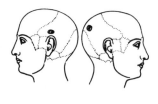 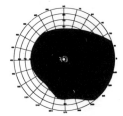

Figure <u>2</u>

also the emergence of perception through sensory-motor interaction. This prompts two metaphors: "Perceiving is Doing"; and "If I don't see I am blind, I am blind; but if I see I am blind, I see."

((iii) Alternates) A single word is spoken once into a tape recorder and the tape smoothly spliced (without click) into a loop. The word is repetitively played back with high rather than low volume. After one or two minutes of listening (from 50 to 150 repetitions) the word clearly perceived so far abruptly changes into another meaningful and clearly perceived word: an "alternate". After 10 to 30 repetitions of this first alternate, a sudden switch to a second alternate is perceived, and so on (3). The following is a small selection of the 758 alternates reported from a population of about 200 subjects who were exposed to a repetitive playback of the single word COGITATE: AGITATE; ANNOTATE; ARBITRATE; ARTISTRY; BACK AND FORTH; BREVITY; CA D'ETAIT; CANDIDATE; CAN'T YOU SEE; CAN'T YOU STAY; CAPE COD YOU SAY; CARD ESTATE; CARDIO TAPE; CAR DISTRICT; CATCH A TAPE; CAVITATE; CHA CHA CHE; COGITATE; COMPUTATE; CONJUGATE; CONSCIOUS STATE; COUNTER TAPE; COUNT TO TEN; COUNT TO THREE; COUNT YER TAPE; CUT THE STEAK; ENTITY; FANTASY; GOD TO TAKE; GOD YOU SAY; GOT A DATE; GOT YOUR PAY; GOT YOUR TAPE; GRATITUDE; GRAVITY; GUARD THE TIT; GURGITATE; HAD TO TAKE; KINDS OF TAPE; MAJESTY; MARMALADE....

((iv) Comprehension (Literally: con = together; prehendere = to seize, grasp.)) Into the various stations of the auditory pathways in a cat's brain microelectrodes are implanted which allow a recording ("Electroencephalogram") from the nerve cells first to receive auditory stimuli (Cochlea Nucleus, CN) up to the Auditory Cortex (4). The so prepared cat is admitted into a cage that contains a food box whose lid can be opened by pressing a lever. However, the lever-lid connection is operative only when a short single tone (here C_6, that is about 1000 Hz) is repetitively presented. The cat has to learn that C_6 "means" food. Figures 3 to 6 show the pattern of nervous activity at 8 ascending auditory stations, and at four consecutive stages of this learning process (4). The cat's behavior associated with the recorded neural activity is for Fig. 3: "Random search"; Fig. 4: "Inspection of lever"; Fig. 5: "Lever pressed at once"; and for Fig. 6: "Walking straight toward lever (full comprehension)". Note that no tone is perceived as long as this tone is uninterpretable (Figs. 3,4; pure noise), but the whole system swings into action with the appearance of the first "beep" (Figs. 5,6; noise becomes signal) when sensation becomes comprehensible, when our perception of "beep", "beep", "beep", is in the cat's perception "food", "food", "food".

Figures

3: Sess.3, Tr.1;   4: Sess.3, Tr.13;   5: Sess.4, Tr.20;   6: Sess.6, Tr.9

Interpretation

In these experiments I have cited instances in which we see or hear what is not "there", or in which we do not see or hear what is "there", unless coordination of sensation and movement allows us to "grasp" what appears to be there. Let me strengthen this observation by citing now the "Principle of Undifferentiated Encoding":

> "The response of a nerve cell does not encode the physical nature of the agents that caused its response. Encoded is only "how much" at this point on my body, but not "what".

Take, for instance, a light sensitive receptor cell in the retina, a "rod", which absorbs the electro-magnetic radiation originating from a distant source. This absorption causes a change in the electro-chemical potential in the rod which will ultimately give rise to a periodic electric discharge of some cells higher up in the post-retinal networks (see later, page 7) with a period that is commensurate with the intensity of the radiation absorbed, but without a clue that it was electro-magnetic radiation that caused the rod to discharge. The same is true for any other sensory receptor, may it be the taste buds, the touch receptors, and all the other receptors that are associated with the sensations of smell, heat and cold, sound, etc.: they are all "blind" as to the quality of their stimulation, responsive only as to their quantity. Although surprising, this should not come as a surprise, for indeed "out there" there is no light and no color, there are only electro-magnetic waves; "out there" there is no sound and no music, there are only periodic variations of the air pressure; "out there" there is no heat and no cold, there are only moving molecules with more or less mean kinetic energy, and so on. Finally, for sure, "out there" there is no pain. Since the physical nature of the stimulus--its quality--is not encoded into nervous activity, the fundamental question arises as to how does our brain conjure up the tremendous variety of this colorful world as we experience it any moment while awake, and sometimes in dreams while asleep. This is the "Problem of Cognition", the search for an understanding of the cognitive processes. The way in which a question is asked determines the way in which an answer may be found. Thus, it is upon me to paraphrase the "Problem of Cognition" in such a way that the conceptual tools that are today at our disposal may become fully effective. To this end let me paraphrase (→) "cognition" in the following way:

COGNITION → computing a reality

With this I anticipate a storm of objections. First, I appear to replace one unknown term, "cognition", with three other terms, two of which, "computing" and "reality", are even more opaque than the definiendum, and with the only definite word used here being the indefinite article "a". Moreover, the use of the indefinite article implies the ridiculous notion of other realities besides "the" only and one reality, our cherished Environment; and finally I seem to suggest by "computing" that everything, from my wristwatch to the Galaxies, is merely computed, and is not "there". Outrageous!

Let me take up these objections one by one. First, let me remove the semantic sting that the term "computing" may cause in a group of women and men who are more inclined toward the humanities than to the sciences. Harmlessly enough,

computing (from com-putare) literally means to reflect, to contemplate (putare)
things in concert (com-), without any explicit reference to numerical quantities.
Indeed, I shall use this term in this most general sense to indicate any operation
(not necessarily numerical) that transforms, modifies, re-arranges, orders, etc.,
observed physical entities ("objects") or their representations ("symbols"). For
instance, the simple permutation of the three letters A,B,C, in which the last
letter now goes first: C,A,B, I shall call a computation. Similarly, the operation that obliterates the commas between the letters: CAB; and likewise the
semantic transformation that changes CAB into TAXI, and so on.   I shall now turn
to the defense of my use of the indefinite article in the noun-phrase "a reality".
I could, of course, shield myself behind the logical argument that solving for
the general case, implied by the "a", I would also have solved any specific case
denoted by the use of "the". However, my motivation lies much deeper. In fact,
there is a deep hiatus that separates the "The"-school-of-thought from the "A"-
school-of-thought in which respectively the distinct concepts of "confirmation"
and "correlation" are taken as explanatory paradigms for perceptions. The "The-
School": My sensation of touch is confirmation for my visual sensation that here
is a table. The "A-School": My sensation of touch in correlation with my visual
sensation generate an experience which I may describe by "here is a table".
I am rejecting the THE-position on epistemological grounds, for in this way the
whole Problem of Cognition is safely put away in ones own cognitive blind spot:
even its absence can no longer be seen.

Finally one may rightly argue that cognitive processes do not compute wristwatches
or galaxies, but compute at best descriptions of such entities. Thus I am yield-
ing to this objection and replace my former paraphrase by:

COGNITION → computing descriptions of a reality.

Neurophysiologists, however, will tell us (5) that a description computed on one
level of neural activity, say a projected image on the retina, will be operated
on again on higher levels, and so on, whereby some motor activity may be taken
by an observer as a "terminal description", for instance the utterance: "here is
a table". Consequently, I have to modify this paraphrase again to read:

COGNITION → computing descriptions of ⸺⸺⸺
                              ⬆_____⏋

where the arrow turning back suggests this infinite recursion of descriptions of
descriptions...etc. This formulation has the advantage that one unknown, namely,
"reality" is successfully eliminated. Reality appears only implicit as the operation of recursive descriptions. Moreover, we may take advantage of the notion
that computing descriptions is nothing else but computations. Hence:

COGNITION → computations of ⸺⏋
                        ⬆_____⏋

In summary: I propose to interpret cognitive processes as never ending recursive
processes of computation, and I hope that in the following tour de force of
neurophysiology I can make this interpretation transparent.

Neurophysiology

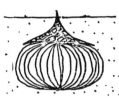

Fig. 7

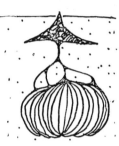

Fig. 8

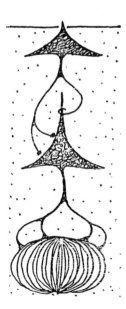

Fig. 9

((i) Evolution) In order that the principle of recursive computation is fully appreciated as being the underlying principle
of all cognitive processes--even of life itself, as one of the
most advanced thinkers in biology assures me (6)--it may be
instructive to go back for a moment to the most elementary--
or as evolutionists would say, to very "early"--manifestations
of this principle. These are the "independent effectors", or
independent sensory-motor units, found in protozoa and metazoa
distributed over the surface of these animals (Fig. 6). The
triangular portion of this unit, protruding with its tip from
the surface, is the sensory part, the onion-shaped portion
the contractile motor part. A change in the chemical concentration of an agent in the immediate vicinity of the sensing
tip, and "perceptible" by it, causes an instantaneous contraction of this unit. The resulting displacement of this or any
other unit by change of shape of the animal or its location
may, in turn, produce perceptible changes in the agent's concentration in the vicinity of these units which, in turn, will
cause their instantaneous contraction,...etc. Thus, we have
the recursion:

$$\rightarrow \text{change of sensation} \rightarrow \text{change of shape} \rightarrow$$

Separation of the sites of sensation and action appears to have
been the next evolutionary step (Fig. 8). The sensory and
motor organs are now connected by thin filaments, the "axons"
(in essence degenerated muscle fibers having lost their con-
tractility), which transmit the sensor's perturbations to its
effector, thus giving rise to the concept of a "signal": see
something here, act accordingly there. The crucial step,
however, in the evolution of the complex organization of the
mammalian central nervous system (CNS) appears to be the
appearance of an "internuncial neuron", a cell sandwiched
between the sensory and the motor unit (Fig. 9). It is, in
essence, a sensory cell, but specialized so as to respond only
to a universal "agent", namely, the electrical activity of the
afferent axons terminating in its vicinity. Since its present
activity may affect its subsequent responsivity, it introduces the element of computation in the animal kingdom, and
gives these organisms the astounding latitude of non-trivial
behaviors. Having once developed the genetic code for assembling an internuncial neuron, to add the genetic command
"repeat" is a small burden indeed. Hence, I believe, it is
now easy to comprehend the rapid proliferation of these neurons
along additional vertical layers with growing horizontal connections to form those complex interconnected structures we
call "brains".

((ii) Neuron) The neuron, of which we have more than ten
billion in our brain, is a highly specialized single cell
with three anatomically distinct features (Fig. 10): (a)
the branch-like ramifications stretching up and to the side,
the "dendrites"; (b) the bulb in the center housing the
cell's nucleus, the "cell body"; and (c), the "axon", the
smooth fiber stretching downward. Its various bifurcations
terminate on dendrites of another (but sometimes (recursively) on the same) neuron. The same membrane which en-
velopes the cell body forms also the tubular sheath for
dendrites and axon, and causes the inside of the cell to be
electrically charged against the outside with about one
tenth of a volt. If in the dendritic region this charge is
sufficiently perturbed, the neuron "fires" and sends this
perturbation along its axons to their terminations, the
synapses.

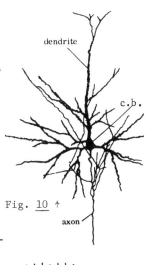

Fig. 10 ↑

((iii) Transmission) Since these perturbations are electrical, they can be picked up by "micro-probes", amplified and
recorded. Fig. 11 shows three examples of periodic dis-
charges from a touch receptor under continuous stimulation,
the low frequency corresponsing to a weak, the high frequency to a strong stimulus. The magnitude of the discharge
is clearly everywhere the same, the pulse frequency
representing the stimulus intensity, but the intensity only.

((iv) Synapse) Fig. 12 sketches a synaptic junction. The
afferent axon (Ax), along which the pulses travel, terminates in an end bulb (EB) which is separated from the
spine (sp) of a dendrite (D) of the target neuron by a
minute gap (sy), the "synaptic gap" (Note the many spines
that cause the rugged appearance of the dendrites in Fig.
10). The chemical composition of the "transmitter sub-
stances" filling the synaptic gap is crucial in determining
the effect an arriving pulse may have on the ultimate
response of the neuron: under certain circumstances it may
produce an "inhibitory effect" (cancellation of another
simultaneously arriving pulse); in others a "facility
effect" (augmenting another pulse to fire the neuron). Consequently, the synaptic gap can be seen as the "micro-
environment" of a sensitive tip, the spine, and with this
interpretation in mind we may compare the sensitivity of the
CNS to changes of the internal environment (the sum-total
of all micro-environments) to those of the external environment (all sensory receptors). Since there are only a
hundred million sensory receptors, and about ten-thousand
billion synapses in our nervous system, we are 100,000
times more receptive to changes in our internal than in our
external environment.

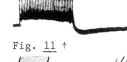

Fig. 11 ↑

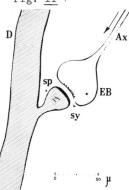

Fig. 12 →

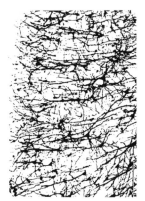

Fig. 13

Fig. 14

1 2   3   4 5 67

Fig. 15

((v) Cortex) In order that one may get at least some per-spective on the organization of the entire machinery that computes all perceptual, intellectual and emotional exper-iences, I have attached Fig. 13 (7) which shows magnified a section of about 2 square millimeters of a cat's cortex by a staining method which stains only cell body and dendrites, and of those only 1% of all neurons present. Although you have to imagine the many connections among these neurons provided by the (invisible) axons, and a density of packing that is a hundred times that shown, the computational power of even this very small part of a brain may be sensed.

((vi) Descartes) This perspective is a far cry from that being held, say three hundred years ago (8): "If the fire A is near the foot B (Fig. 14), the particles of this fire, which as you know move with great rapidity, have the power to move the area of the skin of this foot that they touch; and in this way drawing the little thread, c, that you see to be attached at base of toes and on the nerve, at the same instant they open the entrance of the pore, d,e, at which this little thread terminates, just as by pulling one end of a cord, at the same time one causes the bell to sound that hangs at the other end. Now the entrance of the pore or little conduit, d,e, being thus opened, the animal spirits of the cavity F, enter within and are carried by it, partly into the muscles that serve to withdraw this foot from the fire, partly into those that serve to turn the eyes and the head to look at it, and partly into those that serve to ad-vance the hands and to bend the whole body to protect it." Note, however, that some behaviorists of today still cling to the same view (9) with one difference only, namely, that in the meantime Descartes' "animal spirit" has gone into oblivion.

((vii) Computation) The retina of vertebrates with its associated nervous tissue is a typical case of neural com-putation. Fig. 15 is a schematic representation of a mam-malian retina and its post-retinal network. The layer labeled #1 represents the array of rods and cones, and layer #2 the bodies and nuclei of these cells. Layer #3 identifies the general region where the axons of the receptors synapse with the dendritic ramifications of the "bipolar cells" (#4) which, in turn, synapse in layer #5 with the dendrites of the ganglion cells" (#6) whose activity is transmitted to deeper regions of the brain via their axons which are bundled together to form the optic nerve (#7). Computation takes place within the two layers labeled #3 and #5, that is, where the synapses are located.

Figure 16   Figure 17

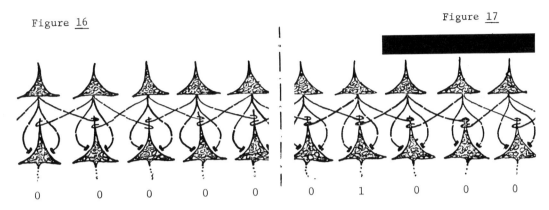

As Maturana has shown (10) it is there where the sensation of color and some clues as to form are computed.   Form computation: take the two-layered periodic network of Fig. 16, the upper layer representing receptor cells sensitive to, say, "light". Each of these receptors is connected to three neurons in the lower (computing) layer, with two excitatory synapses on the neuron directly below (symbolized by buttons attached to the body), and with one inhibitory synapse (symbolized by a loop around the tip) attached to each of the two neurons, one to the left and one to the right. It is clear that the computing layer will not respond to uniform light projected on the receptive layer, for the two excitatory stimuli on a computer neuron will be exactly compensated by the inhibitory signals coming from the two lateral receptors. This zero-response will prevail under strongest and weakest stimulation as well as to slow or rapid changes of the illumination. The legitimate question may now arise--"Why this complex apparatus that doesn't do a thing?"   Consider now Fig. 17 in which an obstruction is placed in the light path illuminating the layer of receptors. Again all neurons of the lower layer will remain silent, except the one at the edge of the obstruction, for it receives two excitatory signals from the receptor above, but only one inhibitory signal from the sensor to the left. We now understand the important function of this net, for it computes any spatial variation in the visual field of this "eye", independent of intensity of the ambient light and its temporal variations, and independent of place and extension of the obstruction.   Although all operations involved in this computation are elementary, the organization of these operations allows us to appreciate a principle of considerable depth, namely, that of the computation of abstracts, here the notion of "edge".   I hope that this simple example is sufficient to suggest to you the possibility of generalizing this principle in the sense that "computation" can be seen on at least two levels, namely, (a) the operations actually performed, and (b) the organization of these operations represented here by the structure of the nerve net. In computer language (a) would again be associated with "operations", but (b) with the "program". As we shall see later, in "biological computers" the programs themselves may be computed on. This leads to the concepts of "meta-programs", "meta-meta-programs",...etc. This, of course, is the consequence of the inherent recursive organization of those systems.

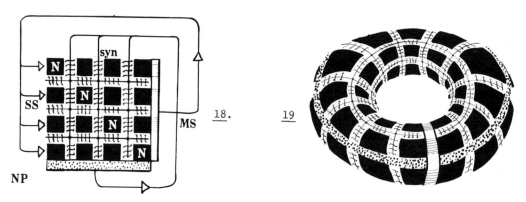

18.   19

((viii) Closure) By attending to all the neurophysiological pieces, we may have
lost the perspective that sees an organism as a functioning whole. In Fig. 18
I have put these pieces together in their functional context. The black squares
labeled N represent bundles of neurons that synapse with neurons of other bundles
over the (synaptic) gaps indicated by the spaces between squares. The sensory
surface (SS) of the organism is to the left, its motor surface (MS) to the right,
and the neuropituitary (NP) the strongly enervated mastergland that regulated
the entire endocrinal system, is the stippled lower boundary of the array of
squares. Nerve impulses traveling horizontally (from left to right) ultimately
act on the motor surface (MS) whose changes (movements) are immediately sensed
by the sensory surface (SS), as suggested by the "external" pathway following
the arrows. Impulses traveling vertically (from top to bottom) stimulate the
neuropituitary (NP) whose activity releases steroids into the synaptic gaps, as
suggested by the wiggly terminations of the lines following the arrow, and thus
modify the modus operandi of all synaptic junctures, hence the modus operandi
of the system as a whole. Note the double closure of the system which now recursively operates not only on what it "sees" but on its operators as well.
In order to make this twofold closure even more apparent I propose to wrap the
diagram of Fig. 18 around its two axes of circular symmetry until the artificial
boundaries disappear and the torus (doughnut) as in Fig. 18 is obtained. Here
the "synaptic gap" between the motor and sensory surfaces is the striated meridian in the front center, the neuropituitary the stippled equator. This, I
submit, is the functional organization of a living organism in a (dough)nut
shell. ● The computations within this torus are subject to a non-trivial constraint, and this is expressed in the Postulate of Cognitive Homeostasis:

> "The nervous system is organized (or organizes itself) so that it
> computes a stable reality."

This postulate stipulates "autonomy", i.e., "self-regulation", for every living
organism. Since the semantic structure of nouns with prefix "self-" becomes
more transparent when this prefix is replaced by the noun, "autonomy" becomes
synonymous with "regulation of regulation". This is precisely what the doubly
closed, recursively computing torus does: it regulates its own regulation.

Significance

It may be strange in times like these to stipulate
autonomy, for autonomy implies responsibility: If
I am the only one who decides how I act then I am
responsible for my action. Since the rule of the
most popular game played today is to make someone
else responsible for my acts--the name of the game
is "heteronomy"--my arguments make, I understand, a
most unpopular claim. One way of sweeping it under
the rug is to dismiss it as just another attempt to
rescue "solipsism", the view that this world is only
in my imagination and the only reality is the imag-
ining "I". Indeed, that was precisely what I was
saying before, but I was talking only about a single
organism. The situation is quite different when
there are two, as I shall demonstrate with the aid
of the gentleman with the bowler hat (Fig. 20).
He insists that he is the sole reality, while everything else appears only in his imagination. However,
he cannot deny that his imaginary universe is populated with apparitions that are not unlike himself.
Hence, he has to concede that they themselves may
insist that they are the sole reality and everything
else is only a concoction of their imagination. In
that case their imaginary universe will be populated
with apparitions, one of which may be he, the gentleman with the bowler hat. According to the Principle of Relativity which rejects a hypothesis when it
does not hold for two instances together, although
it holds for each instance separately (Earthlings
and Venusians may be consistent in claiming to be
in the center of the universe, but their claims fall

Figure 20

to pieces if they should ever get together), the solipsistic claim falls to pieces
when besides me I invent another autonomous organism. However, it should be noted
that since the Principle of Relativity is not a logical necessity, nor is it a
proposition that can be proven to be either true or false, the crucial point to
be recognized here is that I am free to choose either to adopt this principle or
to reject it. If I reject it, I am the center of the universe, my reality are my
dreams and my nightmares, my language is monologue, and my logic mono-logic. If
I adopt it, neither me nor the other can be the center of the universe. As in the
heliocentric system, there must be a third that is the central reference. It is
the relation between Thou and I, and this relation is IDENTITY:

Reality = Community.

What are the consequences of all this in ethics and aesthetics?

The Ethical Imperative: Act always so as to increase the number of choices.

The Aesthetical Imperative: If you desire to see, learn how to act.

Acknowledgement

I wish to express my gratitude to my students Valarie Lamont and Stuart Umpleby who encouraged me to develop some of these ideas under the auspices of their Grant GY10766 with the National Science Foundation, and to the Department of Electrical Engineering which graciously permitted me to use its facilities. To Lebbeus Woods, Rodney Clough and Gordon Pask I am indebted for offering their artistic talents to embellish this paper with Figs. (7,8,9,16,17), (18,19), and (20) respectively, and last but not least to Kathy Roberts whose aesthetic sense, competence and patience allowed this article to become what it is.

References

(1) Brown, G. S., LAWS OF FORM, New York, Julian Press, page 3, 1972.

(2) Teuber, H. L., "Neuere Betrachtungen über Sehstrahlung und Sehrinde" in Jung, R., Kornhuber, H. (Eds.) DAS VISUELLE SYSTEM, Berlin, Springer, pages 256-274, 1961.

(3) Naeser, M. A., and Lilly, J. C., "The Repeating Word Effect: Phonetic Analysis of Reported Alternates", JOURNAL OF SPEECH AND HEARING RESEARCH, 1971.

(4) Worden, F. G., "EEG Studies and Conditional Reflexes in Man", in Brazier, Mary A. B., THE CENTRAL NERVOUS SYSTEM AND BEHAVIOR, New York, Josiah Macy Jr. Foundation, pages 270-291, 1959.

(5) Maturana, H. R., "Neurophysiology of Cognition" in Garvin, P., COGNITION: A MULTIPLE VIEW, New York, Spartan Press, pages 3-23, 1970.

(6) Maturana, H. R., BIOLOGY OF COGNITION, University of Illinois, 1970.

(7) Sholl, D. A., THE ORGANIZATION OF THE CEREBRAL CORTEX, London, Methuen, 1956.

(8) Descartes, R., L'HOMME, Paris, Angot, 1664. Reprinted in OUERVRES DE DESCARTES, XI, Paris, Adam and Tannery, pages 119-209, 1957.

(9) Skinner, B. F., BEYOND FREEDOM AND DIGNITY, New York, Knopf, 1971.

(10) Maturana, H. R., "A Biological Theory of Relativistic Colour Coding in the Primate Retina", ARCH. BIOLOGIA Y MEDICINA EXPER., SUPPL. No. 1, Soc. Biologia de Chile, Santiago, Universidad de Chile, 1968.

SYMPOSIA

ONE   ENVIRONMENTAL DESIGN RESEARCH IN THE SOCIAL AND POLITICAL CONTEXT

Chairman: John B. Calhoun, National Institute of Mental
Health, Bethesda, Maryland

Authors: John B. Calhoun, "Introductory Remarks To The
Symposium"
Charles H. Kahn, "Dilemmas Of Research In Open-
Ended Problems"
Robert G. Shibley, "Design For Research: The
U.S. Army Corps of Engineers Architectural
Research Plan"
Penelope C. Starr, "Getting Environmental
Design Research Into The Social and Politi-
cal Context"
Alan W. Steiss, "Environmental Design Research:
A Pentagonal Model"
Martin S. Baker, "Implication Of The National
Environmental Policy Act"

John B. Calhoun
Section on Behavioral Systems
Laboratory of Brain Evolution and Behavior
National Institute of Mental Health
Building 112, NIHAC, 9000 Rockville Pike
Bethesda, Maryland 20014

Abstract

A perspective to the symposium is presented. Environmental design research entails
consideration of need fulfillment at the individual, social and ecological levels
of function. Realization of research potential requires institutional innovations
to (a) enable coordination of effort among mission-restricted institutions and
agencies whose combined effort is essential to resolve environmental problems, (b)
increase public awareness of issues, and (c) bridge the communication gap between
design researchers and policy makers. Furthermore, only holistic theory can form
the basis for actions that will contribute to system stability with options for
adaptive evolution.

Introduction

The title of this symposium includes two key concepts, "research" and "context,"
with further qualifiers to clarify the scope of a domain of concern. In analyzing
literature relating to comparable conceptual domains I have found that the many
included concepts can be condensed to a set of thirteen generic ones, with a central major concept and with the remaining twelve further falling naturally into
four groups of three. Not having specifically examined literature from the point
of view of the conceptual domain that is being considered in this symposium, I
cannot know with any precision what the twelve major generic concepts may be that
relate to "environment" as the major one. However, it may prove useful to make an
approximation as a tool in influencing the direction of reports prepared by the
participants and to assist the audience and readers of the symposium in relating
and evaluating the separate contributions. To this end, the accompanying conceptual circumplex was prepared. The following overview follows clockwise around the
circumplex from recognition of needs to action bringing application through implementation of design.

Conceptual Quartile 1: NEEDS

Environmental designing implies introducing changes that rearrange the spatial and
functional relationships among individuals, or aggregates of them extending to the
entire biosphere, and not just man. Designing further implies that the anticipated changes will fulfill needs appropriate to the levels of biological and social organization on which the implemented design will have an impact. Thus, for
environmental designing to proceed effectively these needs must be stated explicitly. In fact, the check off list of needs should be much more extensive than
that encompassing those toward which the specific design effort is directed. This

50

Circumplex of the Conceptual Domain:

ENVIRONMENTAL RESEARCH DESIGN in the SOCIAL AND POLITICAL CONTEXT

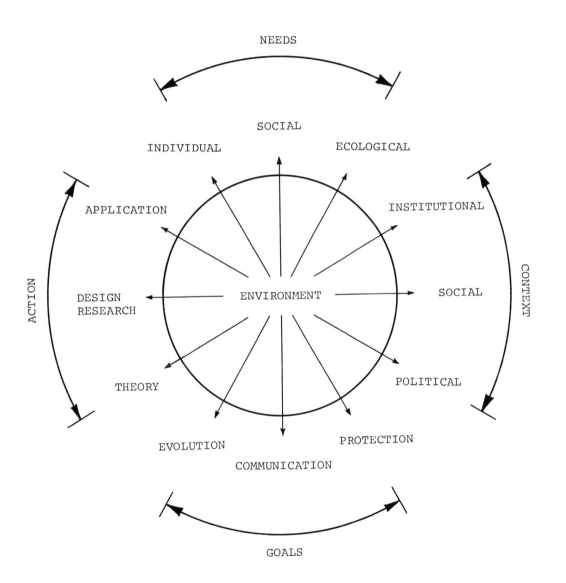

is a precautionary procedure to increase recognition of possible undesirable consequences.

Conceptual Quartile 2: CONTEXT

Efforts to modify the environment, whether at initial design phases or more terminal implementation phases, require information transmission, decision making and policy formation within and between institutions or formal organizations. Broad topics such as implied by the term "environment" are too encompassing to be effectively dealt with under the rubric of the mission of any single institution. In fact, many institutions now finding it necessary to cope with various aspects of environmental issues are straddled with a compartmentalized, categorically focused hierarchical organization unsuited to coping with problems whose resolution requires simultaneous attention by several of the organizational units. Both intra- and inter-institutional networking capacities are called for with the concurrent establishment of coordinative units having the responsibility and authority to maintain networking relationships.

The more diffused social context that affects environmental designing research presents an even greater degree of intransigency. This arises not from a lack of willingness of the general public to become involved, but from the sheer lack of effective means of bringing awareness rapidly to people about future options while at the same time providing opportunity for them to express preferences soon enough to alter the course of design before its implementation becomes an incontrovertible fact altering continued living.

The political context involves influencing opinion in both legislative and administrative spheres -- wherever decisions are made that become institutionally codified. Research, design or otherwise, has historically been subjected to a series of buffers shielding it from the decision making political sphere as reflected by the appellation "ivory tower." During times when human generations or centuries measured the pulse of social and technological change, such buffers served a useful function of protecting deviant change designers from the rigidity inherent to traditional society. Now the shoe is on the other foot. Administrators and legislators are shielded from the sources of idea generation capable of producing designs meeting the needs of society more attuned to change and with an ever increasing expectation of future options. Like Sleeping Beauty administrators and legislators sit somnolent in their towers awaiting the kiss from the prince that will bring them back into the light of external reality. I am not advocating politicizing researchers, or converting professional societies into lobbies, but merely pointing out the necessity for the development of some means for more effectively bridging the communication gap between the design research field and the political sphere.

Conceptual Quartile 3: GOALS

Given the accomplishment of that bridging, goals may more rationally be clarified to enhance the matching of actions being designed to recognized needs. The first major goal is to insure protection from insults or threats while reachieving functional stability after introduction of change. Designed environments, both physical and social, serve as vehicles for the transfer of information, as well as its codification into more meaningful language (1). Therefore, the second major goal is to structure environment so as to enhance these functions. Promoting evolution may be taken as the ultimate goal via the subsidiary goals of increasing environmental diversity and complexity with accompanying codification of network dependencies that bring adaptive resiliency through choice and redundancy, the ultimate consequence of which is to increase the awareness and responsiveness of the total living system.

Conceptual Quartile 4:   ACTION

Under the pressures of responding to recognized needs it is all too easy to ignore that action, that behavior, which most distinctively sets Homo sapiens apart from other animals. This is his capacity to develop new paradigms, new ways of looking at the world, that can guide the simpler and more stereotyped individual and institutional behavior having an applied connotation. Developed theory couples mind and action; it harmonizes the mind-body dichotomy. Without theory, design remains art only. This is not to denigrate art, but merely to recognize that theory makes rationally explicit with predictive value those artistic syntheses intuitively grasped. Without a basis of theory, design research, as a profession, can neither justify increased public support nor anticipate that the results of their research when applied will have the desired impact.

But theorizing appropriate to environmental design research must extend beyond that characterizing most current fields of normal science research. The very notion of design implies synthesis, synergy, holism and an evolutionary and systems perspective in contrast to the reductionist approach that most of normal science follows in its theory building. This means that an effort must be made to identify the disciplines, kinds of individuals and settings which must be brought into interface relationships to promote development of a truly scientific discipline of environmental design research. Unlike a great deal of current scientific effort, design research cannot proceed effectively without a clear enough delineation of purpose to guide establishing priorities.

The following excerpts from articles I have previously published help to clarify the role and purpose of design research, all of which is ultimately environmental. In these the word design is here underlined for emphasis.

Set 1, from: Promotion of Man pp. 38-58 in Global Systems Dynamics, E.O. Attinger, Ed. (S. Karger, Basel/New York, 1970):

(a) Direction of evolution implies establishment of goals attainable only through a reworking of existing values, creation of new values, and choice among alternatives. In essence we need a strategy for developing a design for the future. The processes of making such design possible may be represented by the word dialogue. At a planning conference on transportation, (L.J.) BAKANOWSKY remarked: "The goal of design is to provide a richer human experience. The designer's role is to define what is meaningful." And he went on to say that design should provide meaningful variety. These comments lead directly to a concise definition of design: design is the creation of meaning.

(b) Regarding growth (K.W.) DEUTSCH says: "Growth also should mean an application of learning capacity toward an increase in openness, that is, an increase in the range, diversity, and effectiveness of an organization's channels of intake of information from the outside world...And, finally growth should mean an increase in the range and diversity of goals the organization is able to follow, including the power to change goals and to add new ones." And, in elaborating on what he calls the decider subsystem of any system, (J.G.) MILLER adds: "Discovering purposes or goals -- in this stage is determined the internal steady state, or external target or relationship which the system should attempt to attain; this becomes the comparison signal for the system's feedback adjustment processes, like the temperature for which a thermostat is set." As consciousness arises and a decider begins to function through the existence of channels connecting nodes, we have the origin of mind. Of mind (K.W.) DEUTSCH remarks: "Mind...is the pattern of information flow within...communication channels and storage devices;...Mind is not a machine, but a run. It is a single run pattern of information flow." We have here, then, the essential ingredients of the really not so mystic concept of the noosphere elaborated by TEILHARD de CHARDIN arising from the interconnectedness of people forming a network around the earth.

Dialogue is the process whereby individuals and institutions become units in a mind greater than themselves, and through this involvement gain the identities and the purpose they have so largely lost in our complex mass society. But (J.A.) WHEELER in discussing the views of MICHAEL POLANYI cautions us about expectations without effort: "He makes the case that by itself the universe is meaningless. Nowhere in that reach of space can one read any sure direction. Physical forces act, molecules collide, galaxies separate. Radiation flows outward. Evolution proceeds. In all this blind activity there is no purpose, he argues. Whatever purpose there is, man himself has to supply -- this is his leading theme." POLANYI here uses purpose in its most advanced sense of the conceptualization of an intentional design for the creation of meaning. WHEELER concludes his remarks on purpose by saying: "We ourselves can make the purpose of life what we collectively choose. If we do not set the goals, no one will do it for us. We can let this planet hurtle through space to a dreadful fate. We can let rich planetary landscapes elsewhere lie forever untrodden by human beings. We can let evolution take its blind course. We can let humanity degenerate into a single crowded planet of large-scale ants, collectivized and regimented, with all diversity of thought extinguished. Or we can recognize that the fate of man lies in our own hands...We, the human species, can and must take control of our own fate. How else can we survive over the long pull?"

(c) Dialogue is thus the process by which we seek and accept new information and reassemble it through the design process into a new form which is the establishment of the new goal, while at the same time providing the conceptual framework for its implementation through altering the prior work processes of the system. If the concept of dialogue is to become functional, it must assure that each individual and each institution must have greater opportunity for enlarging its store of knowledge, expanding its awareness, and exerting influence. A system with such capacities when faced with continuing demands for change, cannot be rigid.

Set 2, from: Man of the Environment. Journal of Environmental Health, 35, No. 3, pp. 236-247 (1972):

(d) The need for challenge and exploration arises mostly out of the blockage of fulfillment of lower level needs, giving rise to a pervading restlessness. Out of this restlessness there arises much pathology as searchers collide with established structuring and functioning of the environment. Out of this restlessness there also arises a small cadre of creative deviants whose insights and inventions have provided the leverage which has enabled man to increase his standard of living and his compassionate concern for his fellows. Our success in being human has so far derived from our honoring deviance more than tradition. Template changing has always gained a slight, though often tenuous, lead over template obeying. Now we must search diligently for those creative deviants from whom alone will come the conceptualizations of an evolutionary <u>designing</u> process which can assure us an openended future -- toward whose realization we can all participate.

Assuming that my circumplex conceptual matrix does provide a condensation of the scope of the domain, "Environmental design research in the social and political context," one must then ask: "How may it be utilized to formulate some approach to this domain?" One might assume that each major generic concept could be related to each other one. With an N=13 of major concepts, the total paired concept relationships is $N(N-1)/2=78$. This is a burdensome complexity. However, if the logic of the circumplex has been sufficiently rigorous a smaller number of paired relationships among concepts will be more fruitful to examine. Each concept has a companion polar opposite one which should have complementarity to it. For example, the "Goal of Communication" stands opposite to "Social Needs." There are 12 such complementarity sets. Furthermore, each generic concept on the circumplex has two others orthogonal to it, one sinistral and one dextral. For "Social Needs," "Social Context" stands sinistral to it, and "Design Research" dextral. There are 12 such orthogonal pairs. This reduces the conceptual relationships to 18 sets, less than 25% of the total. The 18 total conceptual relationships are summarized in the accompanying table.

Each person utilizing this strategy, even if followed similarly from relationship 1 through 18, would produce a unique contribution because of personal idiosyncracies of conceptual bias and focus on emphasis. However, in concentrating on the present conceptual domain, every interrelationship explored should at least tangentially relate to both "environmental design research" and to "the political and social context." This introduction to this symposium was made available to all participants during the preparation of their contributions. It was not meant to be coercive in dictating their separate formulations. However, it was made available in the spirit of possibly contributing to more coherence and comprehensiveness among the collected contributions. Lastly, and perhaps principally, it will assist me as chairman, and perhaps you as listner or reader in structuring an evaluation of this symposium.

References

(1) DeLong, Alton J. "The Communication Process: A Generic Model for Man-environment Relations," MAN-ENVIRONMENT SYSTEMS, Vol. 2, No. 5, pp. 263-313, 1972/

Accounting procedure providing comprehensive coverage of question asking and explication with respect to the conceptual domain "environmental design research in the social and political context."

Starting Concept	Related Concept		
	Polarity	Orthongonality	
	Complementary	Sinistral	Dextral
Individual Needs	1 Protective Goals	2 Institutional Context	3 Theory necessary for action
Social Needs	4 Communication Goals	5 Social Context	6 Design Research
Ecological Needs	7 Evolutionary Goals	8 Political Context	9 Application of Design
Institutional Context	10 Theory necessary for action	11 Protective Goals	2 (Same as 2 above)
Social Context	12 Design Research	13 Communication Goals	5 (Same as 5 above)
Political Context	14 Application of Design	15 Evolutionary Goals	8 _____
Protective Goals	1 _____	16 Theory necessary for action	11 _____
Communication Goals	4 _____	17 Design Research	13 _____
Evolutionary Goals	7 _____	18 Application of Design	15 _____
Theory necessary for action	10 _____	3 _____	16 _____
Design Research	12 _____	6 _____	17 _____
Application of Design	14 _____	9 _____	18 _____

Charles Howard Kahn
Professor of Architecture
School of Architecture and Urban Design
University of Kansas
Lawrence, Kansas 66044

Abstract

This paper discusses the difficulty in the attempted application of traditional
research theories and techniques to the types of issues inherent in the social and
political spheres. It is not merely a question of the added level of difficulty
in problem-definition and goal definition. It involves the possibility of structuring a reasonable process for handling the numerous complex interdependent variants
present in such issues. The paper poses the thesis that the theory of incrementalism applicable in other research activities, may not be applicable to this type of
research. It also raises the issue that, when a reasonable level of implementation
resources is not available, research into the social and political context may be
dysfunctional. Therefore different issues must be resolved before investigators
need to develop and implement theories and programs for research which have as their
goal the rectification of perceived environmental problems. The paper suggests
that the development of methods both for modifying societal priorities and for
handling the type of "mean" problems, as defined in the referenced article by
Rittel and Webber, peculiar to social and political issues should be the priority
activity before investigators initiate programs which disturb even the undesirable
status quo.

Over the past ten to fifteen years, those involved in environmental design, particularly those deeply committed to education, have been caught up in a successive
series of movements intended to modify, if not completely change, the either seemingly or real lack of a scientific basis for the activity of design. These movements
have run the gamut from the preoccupation with building structure of the fifties,
to the methodology bias of the early sixties, to the present pre-occupation of some
with the efficacy of research as a basic tool for the activity of design. Certainly
the arguments which point out the almost unique status of environmental design as
an activity without a solid and legitimate existing research base are very persuasive. Because of this it is only logical that large numbers of very able and creative people have turned their considerable energies to relevant work in this area.

However, in the process of developing a research legitimacy we have convinced ourselves that any problem in any area of the environment, even if it does not yield
to direct solution by the application of research techniques, cannot be further
damaged by such activity, and that the long-term benefits cannot help but be positive. Perhaps it is time to re-evaluate this bias that all problems may be studied
through research methods and techniques with a high probability of success that
widely and generally applicable and acceptable problem solutions will result and
to consider the thesis that either in some areas, or in all areas when the con-

ditions are not totally propitious, certain kinds of research activity and results can be counter-productive both to the reasonable goals of well-intentioned investigators and to the expectations of the group for whom the benefits of the research was intended.

What I propose to discuss in this paper is the weakness inherent in attempting to approach open-ended problems such as those which exist in the social and political spheres through the theories, the methods and the rationals of research procedures in the more traditional areas. It will bring into question the whole concept of the applicability of the theory of incrementalism to the solution of problems in the context under discussion. Indeed, the crux of the argument may be in the recognition that, in the social and political context of environmental design, it is impossible to state explicitly either the goal to be desired or the problem to be investigated.

To consider the tenability of such a thesis, some basic agreements must be reached concerning at least the classical, scientific definition of research, its process and its conclusions. It would seem that research may be broken down into basically two types: experimental investigation through which conclusions are based on the interpretation of the data generated; and library research in which conclusions are based on a study of precedent examples. It is obvious that most actual research consists of a combination of the two, but usually one is the dominant form through which the conclusions are generated. I will concentrate my comments on the former as more relevant to our subject since precedent-based conclusions tend to preserve the status quo and have traditionally formed the basis for the legitimization of many of the socially-based environmental problems which we face today. Within the context of this typology, it would seem reasonable to accept that experimentally-based research can be defined as the systematic testing of a stated thesis by a process which can be replicated by another investigator with essentially the same results within previously established and agreed-upon limits of error. Certainly this has been the basic mode of scientific investigation. Interpretive conclusions resulting from the data may differ, but the data remain consistent from the various experiments. This assumes that the reputability of the research data is largely dependent upon their ability to be duplicated under similar circumstances and procedures, and that those circumstances and procedures are not so unique as to defy exact repetition. The acceptance of these basic premises inevitably brings up several issues, possibly unique to the social and political context of a system such as ours, which, when combined with the economic constraints of the same system, cast serious doubt on the possibility of the same type of research in this area as a generator of measurable change in the environment as is possible in the sciences.

One of the major problems which arises with investigation into issues in the social and political spheres is that the number of the variants is so large and their character so complex and inter-related that either the requirement of experimental duplication of resultant data may not be within the realm of reasonable expectation or that it may be possible to expect results which are minimal and of only academic significance. This does not automatically assume that the data which result from such investigations are automatically judged incorrect but merely that verification in the same manner that data resulting from research in the hard sciences is verified may not be possible. Data resulting from such sources is unlikely to gain widespread credence, especially within the political arena where change must be legislated and funded. It may also be argued, with reasonable justification, that the experimental and analytical tools now available to us to handle the number and complexity of the variants present in issues involving human behavior in the social and political context are not sufficiently sophisticated to allow their simultaneous consideration. Ordinarily, a researcher faced with this problem will circumvent the issue by excluding enough variants and conditions to allow a defensible measurement of the effect of his research into those variants which are chosen to be manipulated. Unfortunately, each variant arbitrarily held constant in an area such as the social and political context of the environment diminishes the validity of the results. While it is difficult to state with any precision the point at which the elimination of any particular one of the relevant variants of an experiment produces results which are meaningless or useless, the question of data legitimacy resulting from such constraint manipulation remains.

A second problem exists with respect to the results of research. All research must obviously allow for the possibility that the thesis proposed may not be able to be substantiated. Indeed, in most research, the proof of the non-viability of a thesis is equally valuable to its verification. However, in the social context, for instance, can we afford to initiate an investigation the objective of which is the betterment of the environment and then develop data which leads to the conclusion that the proposed action is not tenable? Moreover, and even more critical to research in the area with which we are concerned in this workshop, must be the realization that the very conduct of such research when it involves contact with actual people as subjects modifies the conditions under which the research was conducted and the social and political behavior and expectations of those who have been involved as sources or target populations. Few investigations with which I am familiar either by social scientists or by environmental designers active in the area of the social sciences, have provided in their process of data gathering for a sophisticated method of taking into account the effect which the mere asking of a question has on the respondent's conception or awareness of the problem or his behavior, initially or over time. This is not the same as the so-called Hawthorne effect but merely the recognition that questions the investigator considers relevant may trigger problem identification and solution expectation not present in the respondent before the question was asked. This is probably a continuing characteristic of open-ended problems such as those in the political and social spheres. It has critical importance on the validity of the interpretations made from the initial data and is not an inconsequential issue when considering the continually changing character of question/perception/response. The relatively low repute in which investigators in the social sciences and environmental design are held in inner city communities is ample evidence of the lack of attention paid to this issue by people who, for one reason or another, involve themselves in social research.

If one accepts the thesis that the asking of a question changes, in time, the conditions which generated the answer, it would still be difficult to predict which of the two possible results of the research thesis would be the most counter-productive to the stated goals: results which showed that the proposed thesis was incorrect; or results which showed that the proposed thesis was correct but for which implementation resources were not available. This is the equivalent of an interruption of the circumplex proposed by Doctor Calhoun and the basic validity of such a circumplex rests with its continuity and cyclic possibilities. A basic requirement for researchers in the social and political context is that they have control over the entire range of the elements in the circumplex, at least to the extent that implementation, the "action" phase as listed in the circumplex, can be triggered at the direction of the researcher on the verification of his data. It would only be gratuitous at this time to point out why this is neither the present situation nor the likely situation in the near future.

There is another issue raised by Dr. Calhoun's circumplex which may even more succintly point out the dilemma in which research, and therefore, researchers, in the social and political context finds itself. This involves the inclusion of "Design Research" itself in the "action" realm of the circumplex. To do so represents, in my estimation, a basic misinterpretation of the character of "action" necessary to legitimize the entire process. The process of research is action only to the researcher and, as such, presents us with the obvious pitfall that the investigator may identify what satisfies his own needs, either of legitimizing his own position and activities or furthering his academic credibility, with the actual social and political needs of those outside the confines of research academia. Such activity may bear no relation at all to those needs of the social organism with which we are dealing and for which we are ostensibly seeking effective action mechanisms.

In many ways, the questions I have raised concerning the dilemmas of research in the social and political realms bear a striking similarity to questions raised by Philip Arctander about the relationships between planning and research in a recent edition of CITY. In addition to recognizing the debilitating effect of the "immensely complex interdependency of all the intersecting factors" and the danger that, in simplifying the variables to manageable limits, "researchers in their isolation will select and define distorted problems for research, and gradually develop their own standards, their own ends, their own fairyland", two observations which are equally applicable to our own situation, he also points out clearly the dichotomy between the desires and needs of those funding (for the most part) the research and those for whom the research is carried out. It is the rare funding agency, either of initial research or the implementation of that research, which will allow a type of research which will result in the kinds of even moderately radical action necessary to meet the expectations of the people for whom the research was initiated. Governmental units, the federal government in particular, are not likely to fund both the research necessary to generate a real systems break and the implementation of that radical step. Reading neither evil nor stupidity into this reluctance, it is merely a reasonable statement of the political and economic facts of life. Because of the types of problems investigated, such research is basically geared toward modest revolutionary change while government and vested interests are prepared to accept, at best, evolutionary change. The only other result can be planned maintenance of the status quo. This basic conflict cannot be resolved when the distribution of power between the two participants, researcher and funder, in their uncomfortable symbiotic relation has such an enormous disparity.

Nor can research in this realm operate on the assumption that the continual amassing of small bits of applicable data will, in the long run, eventually result in the critical mass necessary to guarantee meaningful action. The incrementalism of other types of research may not be applicable here. Expectations will consistently outrun the abilities of the delivery system even if the political and economic power structure is altruistic enough to allow research into critical problems rather than peripheral, insignificant ones. It is essentially the reluctance on the part of those who have a heavy investment in the status quo, for all its deficiencies, that works against any reasonable hope for successful action in the context of any proposed circumplex. It is certainly not a question of the lack of reasoned thought or the logic of Dr. Calhoun's proposal. It is merely the acceptance of the fact that the necessary ingredient of continuity throughout any circumplex of which implementation is a critical element is precluded in the existing political and economic reality.

While Dr. Calhoun does indicate a recognition of these issues in his position paper, I must take exception to the overall tenor of the recognition. The very uniqueness of the action which sets homo sapiens apart from the other (so called) lower forms of animals presents simultaneously the greatest potential and the greatest danger. It can be demonstrated relatively easily that history is on the side of danger winning out. Theories are not necessarily liberating elements, and most theories have tended to end up as rationalizations for oppressive social, economic, or political action. Certainly a highly intellectualized theory which is generated by a third party to the intended social structure has not proven to be the most effective method to generate the type of change necessary to intervene effectively in the environment. This is not anti-intellectualism, but merely a statement of the belief that intellectualizations are not what are needed to sway public opinion. Does one really believe that the existence of a refensible and rational intellectualized theory would change the present majority feeling in this country or the interpretation of it by the President?

Although I am not very sanguine about the possibility at this time of reasonable goal-formulation and problem definition in a pluralistic society, let us accept the thesis that no research can proceed effectively "without a clear delineation of purpose to guide establishing priorities." The question remains who will establish that purpose and through what mechanisms?

I am convinced that the standard doubt which exists concerning the empathetic understanding of the desires and needs of the society which form the intended beneficiaries of the research and the researchers themselves is not an insurmountable problem. It is merely that the better we understand the basic constraints under which we operate the more useful will be the results and the more likely that implementation will be at all possible or allowed.

None of the foregoing argument is intended to indicate that research in the social and political context is for all time an activity of dubious legitimacy and minimum effectiveness. It does suggest, perhaps, that there are several issues which must be settled first before time and energy are wasted, both by researcher and the population for whom the researcher is, at least partially, the advocate. There is no more debilitating fact than to realize that the energy and creativeness one has invested in a thesis is so counterproductive as to result in backward movement at the time when one is convinced one is advancing the cause of a better environment for people.

The issues which must be solved, while lying in the social and political context, lie completely outside the realm of research. It is not research which will identify the basic needs or set the parameters for the desired goals. Given the right climate, those needs will become apparent. What is necessary is the basic redirection of priorities within the society which will accept modest revolutionary change in some sectors as part of a non-zero-sum game rather than the traditional zero-sum game; the establishment of implementation mechanisms concurrently with research mechanisms even though implementation may change some basic power structure alignments; an acceptance of the principle that people, deciding for themselves their own destinies, may make some basic mistakes which result in economic inefficiencies in both the research and implementation.

This latter point is extremely critical to the entire process of the legitimization of research in the social and political realm. Neither in private industry nor in government-sponsored research in the "hard" sciences or technology is there an assumption that each research thesis be automatically assured of success before substantial resources are committed. One need not even point out the extremes of the research by the Navy into the potential applicability of the Frisbee principle to military hardware or the Mohole project to make the point. Social and political problems are much more complex and less amenable to finite definition and solutions are much more difficult to evaluate than are those in science and technology. It is illogical to assume that research in the former can be profitable under tighter constraints than is the case in the latter. What is critical is that the same priority be given to issues in the realm under discussion in our workshop as has been given to science and technology in the past and that the same acknowledgement be made of the susceptibility of problems to solutions when massive implementation resources are committed. For it would seem that research results aimed at changing social structure or political context should either be filed away in vaults or generate meaningful change. It is my feeling that, at the present time, if the latter is not possible the former will be dysfunctional. If that is the case, such investigations should not be conducted until the social and political climate will accept such change.

References

(1) Andreski, Stanislav SOCIAL SCIENCES AS SORCERY, Andre Deutsch Ltd. 1972.

(2) Arctander, Philip. DUBIOUS DOGMAS OF URBAN PLANNING AND RESEARCH, CITY, Winter, 1972.

(3) Braybrooke, David and Lindblom, Charles. A STRATEGY FOR DECISION, The Free Press, New York, 1963.

(4) Evans, K.M. PLANNING SMALL-SCALE RESEARCH, National Foundation for Educational Research, England, 1968.

(5) Lindblom, Charles E. THE INTELLIGENCE OF DEMOCRACY, The Free Press, 1965.

(6) RIBA Board of Education. STRATEGIES FOR ARCHITECTURAL RESEARCH, 1969.

(7) Rittel, Horst W.J. and Webber, Melvin. DILEMMAS IN A GENERAL THEORY OF PLANNING, Institute of Urban and Regional Development, University of California, Berkeley, 1972.

DESIGN FOR RESEARCH: THE U.S. ARMY CORPS OF ENGINEERS ARCHITECTURAL RESEARCH PLAN

Robert G. Shibley
Office of the Chief of Engineers
Military Construction, Engineering Division
ATTN: DAEN-MCE-A
Forrestal Building, Washington, D.C. 20314

Abstract

The Volunteer Army concept has been the impetus for many serious examinations of the quality of military life. The U.S. Army Corps of Engineers architectural research is one such examination aimed at improving the current process of facility planning, design, construction, and maintenance for military installations. The research, in part, is a response to apparent inadequacies in the state-of-the-art in architectural design. Currently, the profession of architecture is not accountable for the social and, to a large extent, the behavioral consequences of its decisions. The profession does not have the comprehensive, well defined operating principles or evaluation guidelines necessary to be made accountable. It is the position of the Military Construction Directorate of the Office of the Chief of Engineers that increased architectural accountability through more comprehensive, clearly defined criteria prescription methods, operating procedures for design, and design evaluation techniques is necessary for good quality control in design administration.

Three unique characteristics of the Corps Research Program discussed in the paper are: 1. The program exists in direct support of a complex management system that is responsible for approximately one billion design and construction dollars per year in support of military installations all over the world; 2. The program is a mix of criteria development and communication research and studies in design methods, simulation, and assessment; and 3. The program embodies theory-based research and development and context related problem solving that are immediately applicable.

The discussion of the characteristics is clarified in the paper with an explanation of the military context and statements of research bias particularly related to the development of research problem statements. Given these qualifications, the paper describes the research organization and provides a technical objectives summary of selected individual work units.

The Military Context

The Military Construction Directorate of the Army Corps of Engineers (not to be confused with Civil Works, Postal, Real Estate, or other Corps Directorates) is responsible for planning, design, construction and maintenance support for military installations all over the world. Military installations are, in effect, small cities. Some installations have populations over 60,000 people, and all contain a wide variety of housing, work, recreational and support facilities.

There are three major personnel elements that assist the Military Construction Directorate in meeting its architectural and planning responsibilities. First, there is an in-house professional staff of architects and engineers responsible for facility functional and engineering requirements and contract monitorship. Second, there are professional architects and engineers on contract to the Corps, and third, there are research laboratories that answer to problems directly related to Corps-wide design, construction, and administration responsibilities. Two such laboratories that are directly involved in research of specific interest to this symposium are the Construction Engineering Research Laboratory (CERL) in Champaign, Illinois, and the Cold Regions Research and Engineering Laboratory (CRREL) in Hanover, New Hampshire.

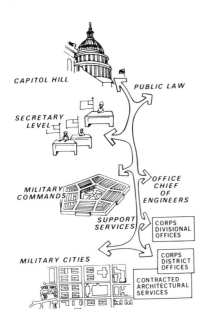

Given this simplified description of elements working for the Director of Military Construction in the Office of the Chief of Engineers, it is important to see how the elements relate to the rest of the military management system. The diagram demonstrates agency involvement from Congress to the client (military cities). Each echelon diagrammed has the capability to influence the final facility quality. Each has a say in what the determinates of quality are.

A management system of this size with its administrative control on large amounts of design and construction money can potentially influence the profession of architecture and governmental perceptions of quality design. Problem statements forwarded to the research laboratories by the Office of the Chief of Engineers relate to what the precise nature of these influences should be.

Figure 1

Research Bias

The problem statements were not formulated without a certain bias, however, and it is important that the bias be documented in order to allow for an accurate assessment of the program. The bias has been formulated into five specific assumptions which will be tested during the conduct of the research.

Assumption one: There are significant correlations between the quality of the environment and military personnel recruitment, retention, professional performance, and social/personal growth.

This assumption, relative to troop retention, has been documented by several questionnaire surveys, many related to the cost effectiveness of Volunteer Army experimental sites. One such survey done by the Research Analysis Corporation in December 1971 indicated that such things as barrack improvement, improved common rooms, new recreational facilities and special services all tended to significantly enhance re-enlistment potential.(1) The impact of such improvements on recruitment, professional performance, and concepts of personal and social growth is much more difficult to assess, but no less significant. Much of the Corps research is structured to test this assumption and make clear the precise nature of the significant correlations.

Assumption two: Quality in architectural design is partially dependent on design responsiveness to a well defined hierarchy of interrelated physical, social, and psychological needs, values, and behaviors.(2)(3)

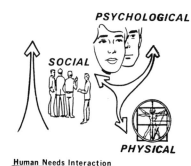

PSYCHOLOGICAL

SOCIAL

PHYSICAL

Human Needs Interaction

Figure 2

Current governmental efforts to establish a minimum standard for housing, for example, do not appear to successfully address anything more than minimum physical standards. Testimony in the Congressional hearings on the Military Construction Authorizations is full of phrases like "minimum physical standard" or "adequate physical facilities." This assumption implies that design research should collect the objective evidence and develop the objective methodologies necessary to re-establish minimum standards based on social and psychological behaviors as well as minimum physical considerations.

Assumption three: It is valid to seek out general or generic principles of architecture and planning that relate this hierarchy of needs to the statement of design criteria and to design methodology.

Many of these principles have already begun to appear in the current literature. Concepts of "personal space," "territoriality," "proximics," "field dependence/ independence," and many others provide some insight into the complex relationships between social, psychological, and physical behaviors and the configuration of space. It may be argued that these only have significance in a specific context or as related to a specific set of functions, but this assumption states that in an organization such as the Corps of Engineers, with its responsibility for the management of a very large design and construction program, the quality control provided by general principles is necessary. It is also reasonable to assume that architectural education would benefit from such a base line of principles from which to operate.

Assumption four: That these general principles, applied in specific situations, can be stated objectively as testable design criteria (in architectural contract documents, for example). These principles can be revealed through the interaction between criteria research on specific facilities, design demonstration, and theoretical research into the physical implications of the hierarchy of needs and values.

This is the assumption that led to the basic research design illustrated in figure 3. It is an assumption similar to those utilized by Christopher Alexander in the evolution of a generic pattern language(4); and by Robert Sommer in the generalization of research results in his books PERSONAL SPACE and DESIGN AWARENESS.(5)(6)

Assumption five: Many of the qualitative attributes of environmental design can be objectively evaluated. The research program should develop evaluation procedures that improve on the current mix of stylism, aesthetic theory, and traditional functionalism.

The Organization Plan

The research that is responding to problem statements derived from the above assumptions is centered at CERL in a Special Projects Division headed by Robert Dinnat, and in an Architectural Branch within that Division led by Architect Richard Cramer. One work unit in Cold Regions Habitability is centered in the CRREL and selected demonstration work is sponsored by the Office of the Chief of Engineers (OCE). OCE is also responsible for the preparation of problem statements for research, for detailed research review and the application of research results to the Military Construction Program.

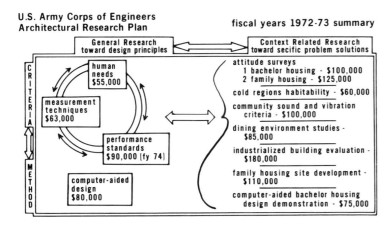

Figure 3

The basic organization or research plan is based on studies in criteria concerns and design methodology. The research areas are further defined as general research toward design principles and context related research toward specific problem solutions. The diagram (figure 3) indicates by work unit title abstracts and dollar amounts, the general nature and scope of each work unit. These are further detailed in the selected research objective summaries that follow. The interaction between the basic elements is critical to the success of the program. While the research in specific situations yields short-range benefits, it is only when these research results are processed through the general work units that one arrives at principles for guidance in the overall design/construct program administration. At the same time, general principles are difficult to understand without the clear examples of application given in specific situations. The principles are, in fact, difficult to generate without the use of design as a learning tool.

Selected Research Objective Summaries

The Identification and Classification of Human Needs in Military Facilities (Human Needs)
Principal Investigator - Roger Brauer, PhD

Technical Objective: The collection of information about the physical, social, and psychological needs, values and behaviors of military personnel and the objective definition of relationships between those needs, management concerns, and the design and planning of military facilities.

The research plan for this work unit involves several small scale trial and error information systems that relate human needs and values criteria to physical design implications and management concerns. Some of the techniques to be investigated include: Matrix systems that interrelate needs, physical implications, and activities; analyzing portions of the environment in terms of desired or required behavior settings(7); behavioral circuit systems of design prescription(8); and derivations of the pattern language work of Christopher Alexander. All of these techniques and others have demonstrated various degrees of usefulness in a variety of design processes. Ideally, this work unit will develop a composite system that organizes research information for design criteria prescription and for the evaluation of design products in simulated or constructed form.

Measuring Techniques to Determine User Satisfaction in Facility Environments (Measurement Techniques)
Principal Investigator - Charles Lozar, PhD

Technical Objective: The development, evaluation, and selection of measurement techniques that objectively determine the relative strengths of identified human and management needs and relate these strengths to priorities in the military facilities planning and design process.

After an initial study of the state of the art in environmental assessment, specific methods are being tested on a trial and error basis with results to be utilized in the establishment of construction priorities and in the understanding of human needs and values under study in the Human Needs work unit. Some of the methods currently being investigated involve time lapse photography, semantic differential attitude sampling(9), human factors checklists, behavior setting surveys(10), questionnaires, interviews, activity logs, paired comparison of 35 mm slides, and others. Many of these techniques have been or will be applied in the specific context related research.

The Development of Performance Standards for Use as Architect-Engineer Design
Guidance (Performance Standards)
Principal Investigator - not selected

Technical Objective: This work unit will provide the organizational model in
performance language for the specific criteria and principles generated from the
other work units. It will develop this model in terms of specific information
requirements for funding justification for facility construction, facility programing, criteria requirements for designers and master planners, evaluation parameters for design reviewers, and built facility evaluation parameters for renovation
programing and feedback to criteria requirements.

Attitude Survey of Enlisted Bachelor Housing Users (SAMVA Survey)
Principal Investigator - Roger Brauer, PhD

Technical Objective: The assessment of troop attitudes about barracks housing
and related support facilities through the use of questionnaires, activity logs,
personality investories, and 35 mm slide comparisons. The data from the survey,
administered to 2,000 soldiers at six installations, compares current behaviors
with preferred choices of behavior related to existing and desired facility characteristics.

Habitability Criteria for Military Installations in Cold Regions (Cold Regions
Habitability)
Principal Investigator - C. Burgess Ledbetter

Technical Objective: The development of specific performance criteria for the
habitability and architectural design of remote cold regions military facilities.
The criteria will cover all aspects of the facilities encountered by the users during their work, rest, and recreational activities. They will be derived from the
application of a comprehensive behavior setting survey at several cold regions
sites.

Dining Environment Studies
Principal Investigator - Richard Cramer, AIA

Technical Objective: The testing of user responses to dining environments both
before and after the renovation of existing dining facilities in order to evaluate
the validity of stated design assumptions and specific design criteria in actual
settings. The work unit is directed specifically at the development of interior
design data related to interior building materials and furnishings in dining areas
used by military customers, rather than food service processes, layouts, operations,
and equipment. Many of the assessment tools mentioned in the measuring techniques
work unit are utilized in these studies.

Industrialized Building Evaluation
Principal Investigator - G. Gordon Bagby, PhD

Technical Objective: To assess the current state of the art in industrialized
building. The research to date has involved a detailed survey of the industry

experience and capabilities in industrialized building. The follow-on work is a demonstration project testing those survey results. The evaluation parameters for the demonstration related to this paper deal with the assessment of user attitudes toward the industrialized housing utilized prior to occupancy and six months after occupancy of demonstration units.

Computer Aided Architectural Design Research
Principal Investigator - Richard Cramer, Karl Kelly

Technical Objective: The investigation of the state of the art and the development of advanced computer-aided architectural design systems that will enhance the overall speed and quality of Military Construction Programs. Primary areas of research focus relate to the organization and utilization of complex design criteria in architectural design administration. This study will include an investigation of the transfer of program and criteria information throughout the various agencies involved in military construction and will involve the implementation of objective design evaluation techniques.

An additional objective of this work unit has been to test and evaluate an operating computer-aided design system in a practical situation. This portion of the research, administered by the author in the Office of the Chief of Engineers, has involved a demonstration project with the Boston architectural firm of Perry, Dean and Stewart. This firm now owns and operates an in-house computer system which is essentially an on-line interactive graphics system with process routines related to space allocation, plan optimization, and material and system trade-offs.

A Difficult Solution of Inclusiveness

Robert Venturi, in his COMPLEXITY AND CONTRADICTION IN ARCHITECTURE, speaks out against those who would make architects into social scientists. He takes a position similar to Sir John Summerson when he quotes from HEAVENLY MANSIONS, "I have not tried to 'improve the connections between science and technology on the one hand and the humanities and the social sciences on the other...and try and make of architecture a more human and social art.'"(11), He goes on to indicate that he accepts "...what seem to...(him)...architecture's inherent limitations, and attempts to concentrate on the difficult particulars within it rather than the easier abstractions about it." He believes this "...because the arts (in architecture) belong to the practical and not the speculative intelligence" and because "...there is no surrogate for being on the job."(12) (brackets by author)

The philosophy of the Corps research program is in general accord with these attitudes. The utilization of "on the job" demonstrations of research results and the use of design itself as a method of inquiry are essential to the establishment. of generalized principles for application in the on-going construction program. Our research that attempts to "improve connection...and make of architecture a more human social art" does so in compliance with the Venturi quest for a "richness of meaning rather than clarity of meaning; for implicit function as well as explicit function."(13)

The research teams are making a concerted effort to develop a design model that addresses the "complexity and contradiction" inherent in the nature of man. Extensive efforts at coordinating research work units are largely based on the belief that we need better, more objective tools to help insure this responsiveness to the human condition, and that these tools will only be valuable if they are the resultant products of a difficult union of wide-ranging issues rather than the cleaner, easier, but questionable tools generated from singular issue engagement and resolution.

References

(1) Rae, William R., et al, COST EFFECTIVENESS EVALUATION OF THE 1971 MODERN VOLUNTEER ARMY FIELD EXPERIMENT (VOLAR-E), Research Analysis Corporation, 1971.

(2) Barker, Roger, ECOLOGICAL PSYCHOLOGY, CONCEPTS AND METHODS FOR STUDYING THE ENVIRONMENT OF HUMAN BEHAVIOR, Stanford University Press, 1968.

(3) Maslow, Abraham, TOWARD A PSYCHOLOGY OF BEING, Van Nostrand Reinhold Co., New York, 1968.

(4) Alexander, Christopher, PATTERN LANGUAGE WHICH GENERATES MULTI-SERVICE CENTERS, Center for Environmental Structure, University of California, Berkely, 1968.

(5) Sommer, Robert, PERSONAL SPACE, THE BEHAVIORAL BASIS OF DESIGN, Prentice Hall Inc., 1969.

(6) _____; _____, DESIGN AWARENESS, Rinehart Press, 1972.

(7) Barker, Roger, ECOLOGICAL PSYCHOLOGY, CONCEPTS AND METHODS FOR STUDYING THE ENVIRONMENT OF HUMAN BEHAVIOR, Stanford University Press, 1968.

(8) Perin, Constance, WITH MAN IN MIND, The MIT Press, 1972.

(9) Osgood, Charles, THE MEASURE OF MEANING, University of Illinois, Urbana, 1957.

(10) Bechtel, Robert, ARROWHEAD REPORT, Environmental Research Development Foundation, 1971.

(11) Summerson, Sir John, HEAVENLY MANSIONS, W. W. Norton and Co. Inc., 1963, pg 197.

(12) Venturi, Robert, COMPLEXITY AND CONTRADICTION IN ARCHITECTURE, Museum of Modern Art Papers in Architecture, 1966, pp 20-21.

(13) Ibid, pg 23.

Penelope C. Starr
Staff Associate
Arthur D. Little, Inc.
Washington, D. C. 20006

Abstract

This paper uses as an example of the importance of the social and political context in environmental design, the findings of work done by Arthur D. Little, Inc. (ADL) for a state housing agency that was concerned with the future of its low income housing program. This work is discussed in terms of the views low income people have of their housing and the social environment in which it is placed. The paper then describes some of the ways in which environmental design research now enters and becomes a part of the social and political context and identifies several areas in which environmental design research might increase our capabilities of dealing with today's urgent developmental issues. It closes with some remarks aimed specifically at those carrying on environmental design research, suggesting ways in which they can make themselves more aware of the social and political realities relating to their work.

Introduction

The evolution of the public housing program from a fond wish for what Reinhold Niebuhr has called "salvation by bricks" to its present complex web of social, political and economic variables can serve as a good illustration of the similar evolution of environmental design research. Getting environmental design research into the social and political context is not easy. It is far simpler to design an effective and livable environment for astronauts than it is to design one for public housing tenants. A space capsule has voluntary inhabitants who make their voyages singularly unaffected by social and economic conditions in the earth they have left. In contrast, public housing tenants are usually involuntary inhabitants who have been placed there because of their social and economic condition.

Environmental design research then has, of necessity, moved out of the solely physical realm into the social and political context: research into the needs and desires of individuals, groups and institutions and into the institutional barriers and reviews through which projected changes must pass before they can become implemented.

Environmental Design and Public Housing

Our present public housing program was born of New Deal idealism. It was assumed that many of the terrible physical and social conditions of slums would be eradicated by putting people into decent housing. It appeared then, and still does, that good neighborhoods promote better family life and more healthful and contented living. There was, however, very little research into what constituted a good neighborhood and how, if at all, the leap was to be made from provision of good housing to creation of successful neighborhoods.

Jane Jacobs, a keen observer of and writer about living in cities, has cogently
described a successful neighborhood not by the facilities it has but by what it is
able to accomplish:

> "A successful city neighborhood is a place that keeps sufficiently
> abreast of its problems so it is not destroyed by them. An un-
> successful neighborhood is a place that is overwhelmed by its defects
> and problems and is progressively more helpless before them." (1)

The ultimate in unsuccessful neighborhoods seems to have arrived just as she was
writing these words: the huge high-rise public housing projects of our big cities,
Pruitt-Igoe in St. Louis, South side Chicago, Columbia Point in Boston. These
towers of neglect hold their tenants as fearful prisoners while youths, alcoholics,
junkies claim the corridors and elevators as their own turf. This filing cabinet
approach to housing the poor appears to have been designed to actually prevent any
hope of a successful neighborhood.

Because public housing tenants today make up the most socially difficult and
potentially hostile housing market, the rewards of responsive environmental design
are potentially greater here than in many other sectors of society, although local
housing authorities would usually be content just to reduce the crime and vandalism
rate. In fact, many of the measures taken appear to reflect the siege mentality:
grills or plastic windows, strong lighting in outside areas, guards at reception
areas. Some measures are merely cosmetic: new uses of materials, varied facades,
more landscaping. Some go further: scattered site public housing, rehabilitation
of individual houses for public housing tenants, rent subsidies in conventional or
moderate income housing, "sweat" equity and other forms of home ownership.

Consumer Views of Public Housing

Recognizing the problems public housing faced, a state agency in 1969 asked ADL's
help in planning for its future program of low-income housing. (2) Part of ADL's
task was to identify consumer needs and wants that could be translated into housing
design requirements. ADL therefore convened "consumer panels" made up of mothers
receiving Aid to Dependent Children, young couples living in housing projects,
elderly couples living in projects, and low and moderate income people renting or
owning homes outside housing projects. Needs and preferences in housing design
were identified partly through discussion and partly through a "Design Your Own
Home" kit developed by ADL. The latter allowed panelists to specify their housing
needs and wants and then to modify these specifications to meet realistic rent
levels. An analysis of the original designs, items removed, and items substituted
provided not only design priorities for housing meeting the needs of various low-
income groups, but also provided information on people's perceptions and aspirations
in regard to housing, the extent to which these are realistic, and the manner in
which they influence housing decisions.

The following were among the most significant findings:

1. Social services and institutional operations surrounding housing are more important to low-income households than is housing itself. The problems of garbage collection, snow removal, maintenance and repair, adequate schools, secure play spaces for parents with small children, and physical security on the streets of the neighborhood were more important than the problems of housing per se. Similarly, the project management's attitude toward tenants, its efforts to keep the premises usable, its expenses, and its honesty were most important to both public housing and private rental tenants. Many tenants of public housing projects complained of "inmate" attitudes on the part of housing managers, such as locking up the clothes drying room and utility meter room, charging for lockouts, charging for children playing in the hall, checking on one's income, encouraging "squealing" on one's neighbors' moonlighting activities to earn additional money, etc.

2. When the housing preferences of the panelists had to be modified to meet rents that they could afford, they generally tried to preserve dining space and work space, even at the expense of extra bedroom space. The general belief has been that the top priority space need of low-income families is for more bedroom space.

3. The process of construction is not important. There are no inherent drawbacks to the concepts of "prefabricated," "modular," or "factory built" housing. The key criteria for construction are durability, useful design for household needs, and general appearance.

4. The mixing of persons having different socioeconomic, household, and racial characteristics is crucial in multiple-family dwellings. Panelists felt that the clustering of a single category of low-income persons (mothers on ADC, young black couples with children, and so forth) reinforces the poverty cycle by depriving people of varied examples of ways to cope with and overcome poverty (for instance, by saving money to buy a house, or by undertaking one's own routine maintenance). Furthermore, such homogeneous units become derogatorily stereotyped, thus adding to the problems of self-respect and responsible behavior. The exception to this feeling concerned housing for the elderly poor, where homogeneous groupings were not as resented.

5. Opportunities for home ownership and for the sharing of responsibilities for maintaining the environment, appeal to a large proportion of low-income households, but:

   • They need education in home care. An understanding of how to repair and maintain property is crucial to home ownership and was a key distinguishing factor between homeowners and renters in the black community.

- The housing must be small in scope and cooperatively owned rather than large in scope (hundreds of units) or condominium. Low-income persons, like middle- and high-income persons, want some degree of control over the type of neighbors they have and how his property is maintained.

- An insurance pool mechanism needs to be developed to minimize perceived and actual risk. When employment is uncertain or seasonal and savings are limited, to use savings for a down payment on real property involves a serious risk. If the family should find itself temporarily unable to make mortgage payments because of seasonality or temporary lay-off, the mortgage can be foreclosed. A simple insurance pool for full or partial payment of interest and accrued taxes during a limited period of unemployment could alleviate much of the perceived risk in such situations and encourage home ownership.

6. The households with the greatest needs are receiving least attention or satisfaction.

I have chosen to discuss the public housing program because it seems to illustrate so succinctly the relationship between critical environmental design issues and the social and political problems of today's society. There are, however, many other places where these issues are important: design of mass transportation, college housing, hospitals, schools, highways, airports, shopping centers, new communities, to name some of the most obvious.

Getting Environmental Design Into the Social and Political Context

Why is the "social and political context" so important? First, it is the most volatile aspect of project planning. In the late '60's and early '70's, not just in the United States but all over the world, a wide variety of projects has been delayed, stopped, or significantly changed when people felt, for one reason or another, that the project represented an outrage against society. Secondly, of all aspects of environmental responsiveness, the social and political aspects are hardest to quantify or adequately describe.

Our problem may be seen as fourfold. First, it is to identify the points at which environmental design meets the social and political context. Secondly, it is to develop data on environmental design research needs. Thirdly, it is to analyze these data and formulate alternative strategies whereby environmental design can assist in meeting the social and physical needs of our population. Fourthly, it is to see that the environmental design strategies formulated actually get incorporated into project design.

The very fact that this conference is considering the social and political context of environmental design research is an indication that the first of these problems is being addressed. Further, it has been our experience at ADL that academic and institutional communities are constantly developing very useful data concerning

environmental design. It is, therefore, to the third and particularly the fourth
of the above problems that I would address the attention of the Fourth International
EDRA Conference: the formulation of strategies to make environmental design relevant
to the social and physical needs of people and the introduction of these environmental strategies into the actual project design. Here is where the vast amounts
of environmental design research already done, some of which has been described in
other parts of this conference, can be brought into the social and political context.

At present, wherever environmental design is consciously brought into the social
and political context, it is usually done on an ad hoc basis. Literally thousands
of projects having a significant impact on the human environment are started each
year and most of them are designed, approved and executed as off-the-shelf items.
Maybe one hundred such projects are sufficiently large or controversial to cause
the sponsor some concerns for "environmental design." Sometimes the only measure
of a plan's environmental responsiveness is the degree to which people accept it.
If there is no serious opposition, it must be all right. However, most discouraging
of all is that even extensive environmental research and multidisciplinary cooperation by a group, such as the one assembled to select a second site for the new
Miami Jetport, may not be politically responsive. Recently the Dade County
Commissioners rejected by a vote of 4 to 3 the site recommended by a $1.2 million
task force which investigated 42 proposed locations, after the original Everglades
site was rejected on environmental grounds. It is possible that such a project
cannot be located on "rational" grounds at all. In some cases the decision will
be political.

Further Research Needed

What appears to be needed are better indicators of the social and political values
placed on such things as growth, economic development, ecological balance, the
preservation of life styles, the need for quiet, etc. We know that most people
resist change and resent noise, but what are they willing to give up to attain
their ideal? We need a widely applicable tool along the lines of our "Design Your
Own Home" kit described earlier--a Design Your Own Environment kit whereby the
financial, social and political costs of alternative actions are made more readily
apparent. When I say widely-applicable, I mean that this tool should be available
to, and used by, not just the consumer, or the sponsor, but the political officials
affected and staffs of the relevant reviewing agencies.

The National Environmental Policy Act of 1969 (NEPA), seems to have given us,
albeit unwittingly, a framework on which to build. The environmental impact statement required by Section 102(2)(C) of NEPA has become an imperfect and variable
but nevertheless very useful working model. The required consideration of alternatives combined with the widespread distribution and reviews that such statements
get is already forcing discussion of the land use, social, economic and design
implications of a project as well as its more strictly "environmental" issues.
Further, these issues are also discussed at public hearings, quite vigorously on
the more controversial projects. In these discussions, the question of environmental design takes on its broadest meaning. For instance, is bigger always

better? Is growth necessary or even desirable? Who is going to absorb the burden
of the secondary impacts? Until very recently these questions were rarely asked.
Now the impact statement and its related hearings gives a widespread public the
chance not only to ask questions but to expect answers. Further, readers of impact
statements have begun to expect the statement to prove not just that a generic project is needed but that this project, in this place and at this time is needed.

However, even this process has its problems. The volume of impact statements is
high and the level of training and skills in evaluating the statements is low. At
present there just do not seem to be many ways for the environmental impact statement readers to evaluate with any real degree of effectiveness the information
they are reading. There are few units of measurement, particularly in the area of
human values and lack of consistent data often prohibits comparison. Additionally,
there doesn't seem to be much experience with actual working models of the interrelationship between environmental design and the social and political realities.
Models in books are at best only a generator of ideas from which to build. But
new ideas are constantly being tried and from these should come some valuable
lessons. For instance, further research might show us what constants there are
between the workings (and results) of a weekend design charrette for a new junior
high school in Washington and a months long citizen effort to help locate and design
a new airport in Kentucky.

Role of the Researcher

This paper appears to raise more questions than it answers. Possibly this is
because my personal experience has been with the difficult task of taking the
environmental research available and plugging it in to projects on the self same
ad-hoc basis mentioned above. But there are some constants, and the same questions
do come up over and over again: the ones about growth and life styles and
pollution (be it air, water or noise) and privacy.

However, there are some suggestions I would like to leave with research-oriented
readers, assuming they are interested in seeing their basic research applied to
real problems. One is quite direct. Don't be afraid to talk in English. A
harried public agency staff member will give up in despair if a potentially useful
theory is couched in such obscure language that he can't understand it. He also
may never even find the theory if it is published in a journal speaking only to
other researchers. A second suggestion is to get in touch with those who
implement projects. Go to some local zoning commission meetings and find out what
the locally important issues are. Attend a few public hearings on controversial
projects. Go to conferences at which your discipline is not in the majority. If
there is a design feature you would like to see more widely incorporated in
certain projects, find out what national or local groups have an interest in that
type of project and get in touch with them. A third suggestion is more directly
political. Find out what the state and Federal agencies in your field are doing.
You may be very helpful to them and may even be able to affect their policies.
Find out which Congressional committees are interested in your field of research
and see what they are doing. You may be able to exchange information or more

importantly, affect legislation.

It is not news but it's still true; the day has passed when researchers and implementors can afford to disregard each other. Environmental design research <u>must</u> take into account the social and political context and the best way to see that it is done is for the two groups to keep in touch.

References

(1) Jacobs, J. DEATH AND LIFE OF GREAT AMERICAN CITIES, New York, Random House, 1961, page 112.

(2) Arthur D. Little, Inc., TECHNOLOGY IN CONNECTICUT'S HOUSING DELIVERY SYSTEM, A Report to the Department of Community Affairs. July 1969.

Alan Walter Steiss
Assistant Dean & Chairman
Division of Environmental & Urban Systems
College of Architecture
Virginia Polytechnic Institute & State University
Blacksburg, Virginia   24061

Abstract

It is far easier to advocate a "systems approach" to the analysis of complex environmental design problems than it is to apply such an approach. A great deal
of groundwork must be laid before wholesale transfer of systems techniques can
be made to the field of environmental design. In fact, outright transfers may
be neither possible nor desirable. This paper discusses the basis for a "hybrid"
systemic approach, formulated to retain the scientific applications of systems
oriented disciplines and the human value orientations of more traditional environmental design professions.

The Search for a Systems Approach

The task confronting the environmental design professions in contemporary society
is a most difficult one. In addition to building a professional body of knowledge capable of examination by other related disciplines, the designer must learn
from a vast accumulation of research and technology that now is before him. Failing to address these challenges, the "traditional" designer may soon find his
professional responsibilities assumed by other disciplines better equipped and
more capable than his. The designer's technique of "muddling through," supported
by some nebulous "professional ideology of creativity," will increasingly prove
inadequate to the task.

Upon examination, the challenge before the design professions, in their attempt
to grasp the ever increasing and changing complexities of the environmental system,
might be reduced to a choice between two widely differing models: (1) intuitive
approaches, suggesting an emphasis on subjectivity, experience, and faith; or (2)
systemic approaches with a focus on deduction, empiricism, and the scientific
method. Admittedly, these two broadly generalized models should exist side-by-
side, one complementing the other. For the most part, however, past design efforts
have been characterized by intuitive approaches. As Forrester has observed,
intuitive solutions to the problems of complex systems will be wrong most of the
time. (1)

A model based on General Systems Theory--built on the assumption that all real
phenomena can be described and studied in systemic terms--provides a useful tool
to give further substance to these points. While many social scientists have
accepted the notion that comtemporary society can be analyzed as a system composed

of various social groups, institutions, activities, and processes, consensus has yet to be reached as to the proper vehicle for such analysis.

The concept system may be applied in two different but closely related senses. First, it may be used to refer to observable, empirical phenomena, i.e., the things that environmental analysts seek to explain and understand. These phenomenal realities might be labelled empirical or functional subsystems with respect to some explanatory theory concerning the broader system, i.e., society. They are functional subsystems because they are designed to carry out certain basic functions necessary to the continued operation (and survival) of the total society. Thus, for example, the functional subsystem of "education" prepares new members of a society for full-scale participation through the socialization process. While this process is carried out by different components (e.g., the family, peer groups, formal schooling, etc.), the functional subsystem of education is a necessary ingredient of every society.

The concept system also may be used to refer to a set of abstractions (symbols) through which the behavior of the empirical subsystems is identified, delimited, and described. System here applies to sets of ideas or theories; hence, they may be thought of as theoretical or conceptual subsystems. The value of conceptual subsystems lie in the adequacy with which they correspond to the functional subsystems that they are designed to explain.

By definition, conceptual and functional subsystems may be assumed to possess systemic characteristics. Among these are: (1) an established order or arrangement of component parts (a structural configuration), reflecting a set of relationships among elements and subsystems; (2) a set of processes, often difficult to perceive or understand from outside the subsystem; (3) a series of inputs which pass through the subsystem or are operated upon by it to produce outputs; and (4) a relationship to the basic functions for which the subsystem was established to serve (i.e., goal-directedness or teleos, involving a monitoring of performance through some sort of feedback mechanism). Each conceptual and functional subsystem also operates within a larger environment, i.e., the society.

Society as a Polystable System

A fundamental concept in General Systems Theory is that of difference, either that two things are recognizably different or that one thing has changed with time. In the first instance, difference refers to those characteristics or parameters which set apart one system from another. In the second case, the differences are internal to the system, occurring over time. When such changes take place, it is said that the system has moved from one state to another, a state of a system being any well-defined condition or property that can be recognized if it occurs again. Any system, of course, can have many possible states.

While any society may exist in a variety of states, for purposes of analysis, a society may be conceived as operating in three main sets of states: (1) states which merely sustain the society; (2) states which result in growth and adaptation; and (3) states of crisis of one kind or another. As shown in Figure 1, there is more than one state of equilibrium or stability in each of these sets, and some cycling will occur. Therefore, any society can be viewed as a polystable system.

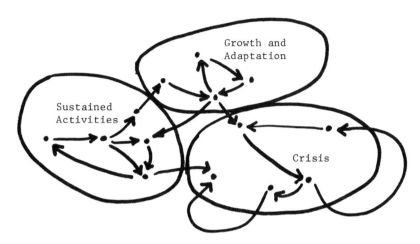

Figure 2. Society as a Polystable System

As long as the cycling which occurs is kept within reasonable bounds, no harm is done. Further, some alteration between the growth mode and sustaining activities may be beneficial, as when the society attempts to "consolidate the gains" achieved through "progress." Some states of the system, however, are near the boundaries of crisis. If proper care is not exercised in responding to pressures at these boundaries, the society can end up in the trapped state of crisis--where every attempt to get out leads straight back in. (2) If the system is to survive, some kind of regulatory mechanism eventually must be introduced to realign the states of the system; it no longer is possible to simply yield to pressures in the trapped state. Thus a society, to remain viable, must offer avenues for social reform-- for planned change.

As Dr. Calhoun has observed, environmental design implies the introduction of planned change, resulting in the rearrangement of spatial (structural) and functional relationships among individuals and aggregates of individuals. Design further implies that these planned changes will fulfill certain biological and social needs of the society. In short, environmental design involves the development of regulatory mechanisms which contribute to social reformation.

Social reform efforts have met with a degree of success when they have dealt with the inputs to a system or have attempted to introduce new states into the structure of the system. Conversely, such reform efforts have been frustrated when they have attempted to deal exclusively with the existing structure of the system or with the ongoing processes. One of the most important contributions derived from General Systems Theory is that any system is rapidly dominated by its error-actuated feedback rather than by its inputs. The inputs to a system may be varied over a wide range; the parameters of the system may change; the functions which characterize the behavior of elements within the system may be transferred over a broad spectrum. As long as the systemic structure remains unchanged, the critical outputs of the system will remain invariant.

This conclusion assumes that the structure of a system is hierarchical, exceedingly complex, full of interaction, and rich in negative feedback to permit self-correcting action. If these assumptions are valid, then it is primarily the structure--the basis on which a system is organized--which conditions the characteristic behavior of a system. This structure, in turn, is the consequence of the interaction of a set of functional imperatives and prerequisites, i.e., a given structural configuration emerges in response to certain societal needs. Therefore, the most critical component of any system is its structure, and social reforms--planned changes--must be directed primarily toward the introduction of new states within the structure of the system.

To date, the planning and design processes required to bring about these objectives have not been sufficiently developed or understood. Instead, planning and design have been relegated to the level of the functional subsystems--land use, housing, transportation, health, law and criminal justice, and so forth. As a consequence, "planning" and "design" have become pejorative words in many circles. Planning and design processes are not seen to be rising to the needs of the total society. Moreover, the coordination of the various planning and design processes operating at the level of functional subsystems has become so complicated that it has ground to a screeching halt. The desire to preserve initiative at every functional level has resulted in an incapacity to show initiative anywhere.

Functional Imperatives and Functional Prerequisites

It is my contention that environmental design research in a social and political context must begin with an understanding of the functional exigencies of society. (3) These functional limitations are of two classes: (1) functional imperatives-- conditions which must be met if society is to retain its stable and durable character; and (2) imperatives of compatibility--those conditions which limit the range of coexistence of structure elements in a given society. As an example of this latter class of functional exigencies if a society has a given occupational role structure, the type of kinship system which supports this structure must fall within certain specifiable limits.

FIGURE 2. FUNCTIONS OF THE URBAN SYSTEM

SURVIVAL-STABILITY	DEVELOPMENT	CONTROL	GOAL ACHIEVEMENT	UTILITY-WELFARE
Functions of the Social Subsystem				
survival stability continuity	dynamic change adaptiveness effectiveness	formation of norms order socialization	goal identification satisfaction gratification status allocation	cohesion & solidarity fusion cultural development mobility
Functions of the Economic Subsystem				
provision of goods & services (supply) production consumption (demand)	growth & expansion domination	coordination regulation efficiency	allocation distribution rewards	utility welfare resources
Functions of the Political Subsystem				
protection survival security	guidance to development conflict resolution	power regulation codification	goal identification social welfare redistribution of power & wealth	justice equality indoctrination acculturation integration
Functions of the Physical-Environmental Subsystems				
habitat provision of raw materials & basic resources	space-time relationships	physiographic constraints	spatial distribution of people & activities	territoriality
Functions of the Behavioral Subsystem				
physiological needs physical safety & security nutrition reproduction	personality development & stability plasticity of human behavior	sensitivity to attitudes of others control of poten- tially disrup- tive behavior	self-actualization esteem identity prestige	positive motivation rewards sense of justice belongingness

In Figure 2, an attempt has been made to summarize the basic functions of society according to five conceptual subsystems--social, economic, political, physical-environmental and behavioral. The five broadly defined dimensions--survival-stability, development, control, goal achievement, and utility-welfare--may be equated with the concept of functional imperatives, i.e., any society must meet these functions (goals) if it is to survive. The particular manifestations of these imperatives, assuming each to be a continuum, reflect the imperatives of compatibility. The various terms listed under each of the functional imperatives represent functional prerequisites which either are a "consequence of" or a "pre-determinant of" these functional exigencies. These functional prerequisites must exist for the emergence of or significant changes in any societal system. This is not to suggest a direct cause and effect relationship among these functional categories, but rather, that as a society emerges and develops, a series of iterations or functional cycles are evident. With each cycle, the cumulative "effects" of the functional imperatives and functional prerequisites interact to reinforce one another until the full network of relationships is complete and operative. To illustrate this point, Figure 2 might be converted to a "flow diagram," as shown in Figure 3.

Reading the "flow diagram" from left to right, it is apparent that the functional imperative of SURVIVAL-STABILITY is of primacy in the initial stages of an emerging system. From this functional imperative "flows" the need for continuity, security and physical safety, provision of basic physiological needs (including nutrition and reproduction), and dynamic change. (4) In addition, certain physiographic constraints must be overcome or controlled at an acceptable level of tolerance if the society is to achieve stability. The prerequisite of continuity leads to the development of a system of production to provide for the basic consumptive needs of the society. Such a production system necessitates that the society have access to raw materials. The system of production also relates in subsequent cycles to the emergence of mechanisms for social motivation (which, in turn, are linked to the functional imperative of CONTROL and the functional prerequisite relating to the development and stability of individual personalities). The functional prerequisite of security and physical safety leads to the development of a system of protection and the emergence of mechanisms for social control (i.e., the formulation of regulations governing the activities of individuals and groups, and in subsequent cycles, the codification of mores and norms into formal laws). One of the basic elements in the system of protection is the need for a "habitat" --a region or place where individuals or groups have achieved a certain degree of control over their environment. As these habitats become more formalized, there is an interactive process with the physiographic constraints relating to time and space. This interaction, in turn, yields patterns of spatial distribution of people and activities which are of crucial significance to the environmental designer. The emergence of an organized system of protection also results in a differentiation in the distribution of power (the protected and the protectors, the governed and the governors, the conquered and the conquerors). In more complex societies, the functional prerequisite of coordination and efficiency in

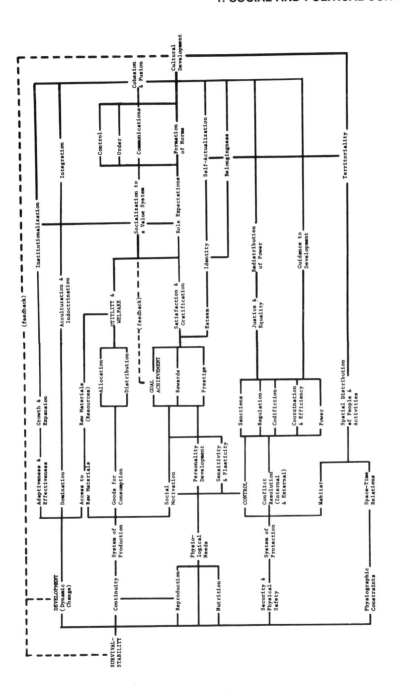

social and economic activities become integral parts of the system of protection. The prerequisite of <u>dynamic change</u> requires access to raw materials and presumes a minimum level of adaptiveness to change. A society which cannot adapt to change while retaining its basic stability is not likely to survive. In subsequent cycles, adaptation and change frequently are tied to the search for greater effectiveness in the operations of the system. Achieving these prerequisites ultimately leads to further growth and expansion of the society both in absolute numbers and in territorial aspects. At some point, however, expanding systems encounter one another, resulting in external conflict. Ultimately, one system emerges as the dominant force and other systems are "acculturated" to the dominant system. In order to maintain its dominance, however, the system must establish formal and informal mechanisms for the indoctrination and integration of subsequent participants.

The functional imperative of GOAL ACHIEVEMENT represents a complex interaction among the mechanisms of social motivation, the factors of plasticity and sensitivity in personality development, the functional prerequisites of rewards, sanctions, and prestige, and the individual's needs for satisfaction, gratification, and esteem. This interaction also underlines the importance of examining the structure of society in terms of a continuum which includes the needs of: (1) individuals, (2) social groups, (3) social networks, i.e., specialized groups which exist in response to deep-seated needs of the society, (4) social institutions, as well as (5) the society as a whole. Two fundamental properties of "human nature" must be recognized in connection with social motivation and control: (a) the "plasticity" of the human organism, i.e., man's capacity to learn any one of a large number of alternative patterns of behavior; and (b) the "sensitivity" of individuals to the influence of attitudes of others in the social interaction process. Man's plasticity" frees him from the very limited range of alternative behavior patterns established by his genetic constitution. Man's "sensitivity" produces a dependence on receiving particular and specific reactions as a consequence of interaction with others. The significance of cultural and social factors as independent determinants must be sought within the limits of the "plasticity" of man. Man's "sensitivity," on the other hand, provides the motivational basis for the accessibility of influence in the learning (socialization) process. Thus, the notion of "plasticity" forms the outer parameters of personality development in the context of the social system, while the concept of "sensitivity" to the expectations of others provides the exertive force which pushes outward, often to the limits of these parameters. As indicated in the flow diagram, there is a primary feedback link between GOAL ACHIEVEMENT and the processes whereby individuals and groups are socialized to a value system. This socialization process yields a number of role expectations which also are linked with the psychological needs of satisfaction and gratification and the critical functional prerequisites of self-identity and self-actualization.

One further link in this rather complex set of relationships involves the functional imperative of UTILITY AND WELFARE. The stability and continuity of a society is dependent upon the emergence of some mechanisms of social welfare as related to the allocation and distribution of goods. Individual choices can be made, within certain limits, on the basis of some "utility function," i.e., the satisfaction or gratification that an individual receives from his choices. However, since not all individuals have the same range of choices or the same freedom to make their selections, other mechanisms must be developed (social and economic welfare mechanisms) to provide the basis for a more equitable distribution of goods. The mechanisms which emerge and the level of "equality" deemed appropriate in a given society, in turn, will depend upon the value system.

Again it must be emphasized that the elements illustrated in the "flow diagram" represents a composit of numerous iterations. A value system for a given society emerges gradually over many cycles and, in turn, requires the institutionalization of certain acceptable modes of behavior (collective and individual) which must be communicated to subsequent generations of participants in order to achieve the functional prerequisites of cohesion and fusion. These latter prerequisites also are dependent upon a formal system of justice to insure greater equality under law (which, in turn, may result in a redistribution of power), certain policies or guidelines regarding the development of the system, and an individual sense of belongingness (which, in turn, relates to the concept of territoriality--the willingness to give allegiance to a particular locality).

Conceptual Models of Threes and Fives

The title of this symposium has led Dr. Calhoun to postulate a most thought-provoking "circumplex of the conceptual domain," based primarily on the number three, i.e., each of the basic quartiles of the circumplex has been subdivided into three secondary sectors. I tend to think in terms of the number five, and therefore, my first reaction is to expand Dr. Calhoun's conceptual model to include five sectors under each quartile. First, I would add to the key contextual terms--social and political--in the title of this symposium what I perceive to be the other major subsystems of society--economic, behavioral, and physical-environmental (or ecological). Secondly, I would view the goals quartile in terms of five functional imperatives and the related functional prerequisites--conditions which must be met if society is to retain its stable and durable character. Thirdly, I envision the conceptual quartile of "needs" as a continuum, ranging from individual needs, through the needs of social groups, social networks, and social institutions, to the needs of society as a whole. Finally, I would expand the action quartile to include issues of: (1) objectives--what is to be accomplished; (2) means--how is it to be accomplished; (3) locus--where is it to be accomplished; (4) priorities--given limited resources, what is to be accomplished first; and (5) standards for evaluation and control.(5) Thus, I would propose that the research task of the environmental designer must encompass the five basic subsystems of society, must reflect the five components in the broad continuum of needs, must recognize the five functional imperatives of society and the related functional prerequisites, and must be translated into the five categories of action.

Notes

(1) Jay W. Forrester, "Should We Improve Our Cities? Can We?" paper presented
     at the NATO International Conference on Cities, Indianapolis, Indiana,
     May 25-28, 1971.

(2) In a polystable system, the interaction of error-actuated feedback at every
     level determines the dominant behavioral characteristics of the system.
     This phenomenon is somewhat analogous to the "pendulum effects" which can be
     observed in contemporary society--a swing too far to the left is countered
     by a swing to the far right. In a closed system, a pendulum will oscillate
     in decreasing arcs until a point of equilibrium is achieved. In an open
     system, however, forces may act on the motion of the pendulum such that
     equilibrium is never achieved; in fact, these forces may result in an ampli-
     fication of the pendulum's arc. In such cases, it is difficult to predict
     outcomes or to intervene in the system to predictable ends. Thus, society
     today may become entrapped in a potential state of crisis.

(3) Without these functional limitations, it would be impossible to account for
     the fact that the known range of actual structural configurations of any
     society is only a fraction of those which conceivably could result from
     random arrangements of the permutations and combinations of possible struc-
     tural components.

(4) This latter prerequisite becomes analogous to the functional imperative of
     DEVELOPMENT in subsequent iterations. In its initial emergence, however,
     it tends to be in conflict with the functional imperative of SURVIVAL-
     STABILITY, i.e., change can be disruptive (dysfunctional) to efforts to
     achieve stability in the early stages of a system's development.

(5) For a further discussion of the five components of the action quartile, see:
     Alan Walter Steiss, PUBLIC BUDGETING AND MANAGEMENT (Lexington, Mass.:
     D. C. Heath and Company, 1972), Chapter 9.

Martin Stuart Baker

Demov, Morris, Levin &Shein
New York, New York 10019

There is sufficient statutory authority in the National Environmental Policy Act of 1969 and in other environmental legislation for the broad acceptance of socio-physical and design insights into federal and private programs. These environmental laws have been used to date to direct private and public attention to a wide range of hard pollution issues - air, noise, water, solid waste, etc. Attention is now being directed for the first time to "ecological" issues - those issues which study the physical relationship of various systems upon each other - and the effect intrusions on one system have upon another.

However, the range of environmental design issues which have been discussed at this and prior EDRA conferences have been largely ignored by governmental and private decision makers - those with direct responsibility for building environments. It is my thesis that there is an obligation upon those of us here to deliver to these decision makers the insights and tools necessary to sensitize their decisions to issues of environmental design.

Environmental design and socio-physical insights are not generally shared by the businessmen, politicians and government officials whose decisions direct our built environment. The lack of enlightenment is evidenced in the forms, shape and products we produce, the lack of sensitivity of which you are accutely aware. The professions and professionals with various ranges of socio-physical insights - the psychologists, architects, behaviorists, sociologists and other socio-physical professionals - have, even to this time, neglected the processes by which their sensitivities can be brought to bear on the institutions and processes which determine the sensitivity of our built environment.

There is a significant opportunity provided to you by the environmental law, including the National Environmental

Policy Act. It is clear however that there is little recognition of this opportunity by socio-physical professionals. If the sensitivities and insights of your research are to be brought to bear in the public and private sector, your recognition of the opportunities presented, and your activity in those forums is essential.

The landmark general statute for the built environment can be the National Environmental Policy Act of 1969. In this Act the Congress broadly declared the "continuing responsibility of the Federal Government" to be the use of

"all practicable means, consistent with other essential considerations of national policy, to improve and coordinate Federal plans, functions, programs, and resources to the end that the Nation may -

(1) fulfill the responsibilities of each generation as trustee of the environment for succeeding generations;

(2) assure for all Americans safe, healthful, productive, and esthetically and culturally pleasing surroundings;

(3) attain the widest range of beneficial uses of the environment without degradation, risk to health or safety, or other undesirable and unintended consequences;

(4) preserve important historic, cultural, and natural aspects of our national heritage, and maintain, wherever possible, an environment which supports diversity and variety of individual choice;

(5) achieve a balance between population and resource use which will permit high standards of living and a wide sharing of life's amenities; and

(6) enhance the quality of renewable resources and approach the maximum attainable recycling of depletable resources."

The Congress recognized that this declaration of

policy would not, alone, redirect the process by which
decisions are made. To this end the Congress provided certain
"action forcing" requirements which are to be met in all Federal
decision making. Among these "action forcing" requirements the
Congress stated that

> "(1) The policies, regulations, and
> public laws of the United States shall
> be interpreted and administered in
> accordance with the policies set forth."

It was further provided that

> "all agencies of the Federal Government
> shall -
>
> (A) utilize a systematic, interdis-
> ciplinary approach which will insure the
> integrated use of the natural and social
> sciences and the environmental design arts
> in planning and in decisionmaking which
> may have an impact on man's environment;
>
> (B) identify and develop methods and
> procedures...which will insure that presently
> unquantified environmental amenities and
> values may be given appropriate consideration
> in decisionmaking along with economic and
> technical considerations;"

The Congress also required that for every major Federal
action "significantly affecting the quality of the human
environment" an environmental impact statement is to be
prepared. This environmental impact statement is to
specify the environmental impact of the proposed action,
any adverse environmental effects of such action, and
alternatives to the proposed action. The environmental
impact statement is conceived as being the vehicle by
which environmental implications of proposed actions are
to be considered. This statement is to be an integral
part of the documentation of each proposed action, is to
follow the proposed action throughout the decision making
process, and is to be made available to the public for
comment at a timely stage during decision making.

In addition, each agency of the Federal Government was directed to conduct studies into the environmental
impacts of its programs so as to advance the state of art
of environmental analysis.

Of these "action forcing" requirements, the environmental impact statement has received the most attention from the Federal bureaucracies. Little or no attention has been given to "systematic, interdisciplinary approaches", to "the environmental design arts", to insuring "that presently unqualified environmental amenities and values be given appropriate consideration", and to the study of the range of environmental implications of project decisions. With reference to the design and socio-physical technologies, this inaction represents, up to this time, an unrequited opportunity.

Similar policy language is found in basic housing, transportation, education, anti-pollution and open spaces legislation. Similar inattention, finding its basis in lack of sensitivity and lack of knowledge, is found in each of these specific program areas.

It is the responsibility of those of you with professional understanding of the opportunity and implications of these legislative phrases to actively investigate and explain them and to encourage their implementation.

Each Federal agency should have, by now, appropriate guides and revised administrative regulations covering environmental issues. Most do. But they do not incorporate environmental design sensitivity into their regulations. For example, the basic standards for decent, safe and sanitary housing utilized by the U.S. Department of Housing and Urban Development should - but don't - evidence this sensitivity. So should the standard for jails - they don't, either.

The guidelines by which environmental analysis is directed - those guides for the preparation of environmental impact statements - do not mention or open consideration of the issues we have been discussing this week.

I believe that the greatest leverage for environmental design or socio-physical technologies exists in the administrative arena. I urge that serious attention be given to that arena by those researchers who are serious about wanting to improve the sensitivity of public and private sector decisions - the decisions which determine the quality of the built environment. I will leave to the other members of this panel the more detailed description of the processes by which you can be instrumental in effecting these administrative regulations and processes.

Selected Judicial Decisions

There are several recent court cases which offer
examples of how the National Environmental Policy Act is being
interpreted by the courts. These decisions are important
because they are consistently requiring Federal programs
and projects to be responsive to a wide range of environmental
issues. Now that the courts are requiring programs to be responsive, properly at issue, and of interest to those of us, is what
environmental factors they must be responsive to.

The HUD Section 236 Multi-Family Housing Program was at
issue in Silva v. Romney, decided by the First U.S. Circuit Court
of Appeals on February 22, 1973. This case held that an apartment
house development in Stoughton, Massachusetts, could not be built,
and the ground could not even be cleared for it, until a full
environmental impact statement had been prepared. This case is
important because it requires the preservation of the "status quo"
until all environmental factors have been considered. The Chief
Judge of the Circuit Court stated in this decision "We are also
impelled to go beyond the strict necessities of this case, in
view of the increasing frequency of this kind of litigation, and
urge the adoption by HUD of suitable 'status quo' regulations."
That is an unusual admonition by the court.

The urban renewal programs of HUD were brought into the
scope of the National Environmental Policy Act in the case of
San Francisco Tomorrow v. Romney, decided by the Ninth U.S. Circuit Court of Appeals on January 18, 1973. This Court held that
the change of purpose of an urban renewal area from an industrial
park to a neighborhood development is a "major Federal action"
requiring the preparation of an environmental impact statement. In
this case the range of issues related to the change in character
of a neighborhood were at issue. General Services Administration's
Public Building Program came into scrutiny in the case of Save
Our Ten Acres v. Kreger, decided by the Fifth Circuit on January 16,
1973. In this case the Court allowed potential employees of a
Federal office building proposed for construction in Mobile,
Alabama to question GSA's decision not to prepare an environmental
impact statement. The environmental factors at issue in this case
included traffic congestion, air pollution and ground water. The
Court required an impact statement be prepared.

The Law Enforcement Assistant Administration was required to prepare an environmental impact statement in connection
with approving Federal funds for the construction of a prison
reception and medical center in Green Springs, Virginia. The
Court's opinion in the case of Ely v. Velde, describes the area
as follows:

"Green Springs is an area of land consisting of
approximately 10,000 acres located in the western
part of Louisa County. It is a uniquely historical
and architecturally significant rural community...
The proposed [prison] Center will consist of at least
four concrete faced buildings, a 30 foot guard tower
and a surrounding fence."

The facts and the law were interpreted to require the preparation
of an impact statement.

General prison conditions were at issue in the case of
Campbell v. Rodgers, in the U.S. District Court for the District
of Columbia. Members of this panel and of this conference participated in forming the issues in this case. They gave expert testimony and, when this case is decided, may well have advanced the
state of acceptance of environmental design issues. This case was
brought to improve the conditions in the D.C. jail. The D.C. jail
is hopelessly overcrowded. The effects of overcrowding on the inmates was put at issue. The plaintiffs alleged that their constitutional rights were violated because, in part, "the jail is overcrowded; the heating, ventilation and other aspects of the physical conditions all constitute a health threat". The memorandum in
support of the plaintiffs' position discusses the physiological
and psychological implications of the jail conditions citing,
among others, the work of Wohlwil and Carson, Esser, Altman and
Haythorn, Audrey, Lorenz, Calhoun, and Myers.

This is the kind of professional support that parties
who bring actions and their attorneys need in this environmental
field. Attorneys badly need new precedents if your positions
are to be accepted into the case law.

The case of Calvert Cliff's Coordinating Committee v.
AEC makes clear that major agency programs can be redirected by
court action. This case required the preparation of a detailed
environmental impact statement as part of all AEC licensing procedures. Most importantly, I believe, it required the AEC to balance
the benefits and costs of each particular project. The court
stated "in each individual case the particular economic and technical benefits of planned action must be assessed and then weighed
against the environmental costs; alternatives must be considered
which would affect the balance of values".

There is a particular danger to cost-benefit analysis.
This is a danger for which the design and socio-physical professional must be alert. Subjective environmental values cannot, and
probably should not, be quantified. Because of this, the tendency to ignore them in quantification analysis, cost-benefit
analysis, is great.

The case of Goose Hollow Foothills League v. Romney was decided by the United States District Court in Oregon on September 9, 1971. In this case, the Court required the preparation of an environmental impact statement relating to the effect of the construction of a 16 story apartment building on the character of the neighborhood.

Numerous highway, airport and other projects or programs have been delayed or cancelled due to procedural deficiencies in their development.

It is just becoming clear that the courts are willing to evaluate the substantive adequacies of the consideration of "unquantifiable" environmental implications of projects. The environmental impact statement provides the vehicle for such consideration. Other members of this panel have written such statements and can comment on your role in their preparation.

In this area the design and socio-physical professional has great leverage. Working closely with attorneys familiar with the environmental law, issues can be drawn and evidence developed which clearly place specific issues of the built environment before the courts. The D.C. jail case is a good example. As more courts are willing to hear and decide environmental cases, precedents will develop which can serve to expand the range of environmental consideration by Government bodies.

The courts will soon be hearing cases which challenge not only a specific project, but Government processes and whole programs. The need for substantive, professional imput from the design and socio-physical professionals is great. Your imput can be to evaluate and provide evidence for such litigation.

I would caution, however, against litigation where there is any other remedy available - and there usually are such remedies.

Several Federal Departments have actively sought policy and technical guidance relating to the impact of the National Environmental Policy Act on their programs. I have advised several federal agencies regarding the impact of environmental law on their programs and procedures. I have advised clients on the legal requirements of preparing environmental impact statements. I have found them to be receptive to thoughtful, professional policy and technical critiquing and advice.

There are people at the Department of Housing and Urban Development who are trying to understand the implications of the new environmental laws on the policies, programs and projects of that Department. Similar efforts are taking place at the Department of Interior, the Department of Health, Education and Welfare and at the National Science Foundation. They have been trying for several years now - and they need help.

It will take concerted effort to direct these discussions at certain departments. There is a need to move from discussion and research to implementation stages, particularly in the design and socio-physical arenas. I state again that this opportunity is the challenge to you as the researchers and professionals in these fields. There is a lack of coherent presentation from recognized professionals in the socio-physical technologies in the language of these departments' programs. This lack of support does not encourage those people in these departments who are willing or would be sensitive to these issues.

Several observations are of relevance to our discussion today:

1. Opportunities are present to encourage sensitivity to environmental design issues. These opportunities are not being fully utilized. As these opportunities are not met it may become more difficult to sensitize processes and institutionalize these issues in both private and public sector decision making.

2. General legislation in this field is sufficient. Specific legislation should be developed as clearer professional understanding of design and socio-physical issues emerges.

3. Attention to institutional procedures is important for encouraging the consideration of the full range of environ- mental implications of Government decisions. However, attention to process alone will not produce the kind of sensitivity with which we are concerned. Such attention alone can be counter- productive.

4. Quantifiable environmental issues, such as pollution issues, are conceptually different from unquantifiable environmental issues. This conceptual distinction requires a dif- ference in sensitivity and approach to these different types of environmental effects.

5. Attention must be given to broadening the range of substantive analysis of potential environmental impacts. In do- ing so, we must not be reserved about recognizing the subjective nature of the range of "unquantifiable" environmental issues.

6. Administrative approaches, such as guidelines and standards can be developed for quantifiable environmental effects. Some kind of guidance is necessary for the institutionalization and consideration of unquantifiable environmental effects, though such guidance should not embody guidelines and standards.

7. A conceptual scheme must be developed to refine the understanding of the range of environmental impacts.

For example, in work with Arthur D. Little, Inc., we developed the following scheme: An environmental impact can be described in terms of its "amount", "effect" and "value". The "amount" is a quantity related to the physical or social processes that occur, such as noise generation or displacement of people. The "effect" relates to the response engendered by the "amount", as experienced by people, wildlife, or fauna and flora subject to an environmental disturbance. The "value" is an indicator of the cost of the impact. Conceptually, the three terms are determinable and related to each other. At the present time, however, only the "amount" can ordinarily be measured or forecast quantitatively, and even this is generally only possible for physical impacts.

TWO THEORY OF MAN–ENVIRONMENT RELATIONS

Chairman: Irwin Altman, Department of Psychology,
University of Utah

Authors: Irwin Altman, "Some Perspectives On The Study
of Man-Environment Phenomena"
Aristide H. Esser, "Structures of Man-Environ-
ment Relations"
Amos Rapoport, "An Approach To The Construction
of Man-Environment Theory"
Raymond G. Studer, "Man-Environment Relations:
Discovery Or Design"
Edwin P. Willems, "Behavioral Ecology As A
Perspective For Man-Environment Research
Joachim F. Wohlwill, "The Environment Is Not
In The Head!"

Adapted from: *Representative Research in Social Psychology*, Vol. IV, No. 1, published by Department of Psychology,
University of North Carolina at Chapel Hill

Irwin Altman
Professor and Chairman
Department of Psychology
University of Utah
Salt Lake City, Utah 84112

Abstract

This paper examines differences in value systems and approaches of behavioral scientists and practitioners, reviews briefly the history of relations between practitioners and scientists, and examines alternative philosophical models implicit in present day research in the field. These models include mechanistic, perceptual-cognitive-motivational, behavioral, and ecological-social systems approaches.

Introduction

From the perspective of one who has been both a witness and participant, the field of man-environment studies has been growing continuously and is presently characterized by theoretical, methodological and substantive diversity, confusion and controversy. Considerable energy is being directed toward man-environment phenomena by practitioners and academic researchers, conferences are frequent and well-attended (even poor papers are received with attentiveness and rapture), organizations and newsletters are endlessly spawned, and the various disciplines try frantically to communicate with one another. In many instances, the alienated from several disciplines have come together, disenchanted by the provincialism of their parent professions. These include practitioners who want to build environments in terms of man's capabilities and needs and who criticize their own disciplinary "establishments" on the grounds that they are largely interested in creating personal monuments to designers. And, there are behavioral scientists who feel that their disciplines have neglected man's unity with his physical environment. Some talk of a coming unity of the scientist and the practitioner. Others foresee a Tower of Babel which will ultimately lead all back to their provincial disciplinary languages, values and approaches.

This paper examines the historical and sociological status of the man-environment field, with an eye toward providing some perspective about its roots, progress to date, philosophical underpinnings and potential future. The first section contrasts styles of problem-solving by practitioners and behavioral scientists (primarily psychologists). The second section discusses the history of relations between behavioral scientists and practitioners. The last part of the paper outlines some philosophical "models of man" implicit in present-day work in the man-environment field, which may be considered as alternative strategies. The discussion is designed to provide an historical and philosophical perspective, to facilitate decisions by researchers and practitioners about how to expend their energies, and to assist them in consciously moving the field in directions which they consider worthwhile.

The Differing "Psyche" of Practitioners and Behavioral Scientists

A major barrier to progress in man-environment research is lack of productive communication between practitioners and behavioral scientists. It is our thesis that
there are, in fact, basic differences in strategies among practitioners and
behavioral scientists. But, their different approaches should not necessarily be
compromised. Rather, each side should learn the other's strategy, gain skill in
translating from one approach to the other, and should begin to develop some "role-
playing" skills so as to be able, temporarily, to get into the "psyche" of one
another. Thus, understanding and solution of man-environment problems may well come
from preservation of the divergent approaches of practitioners and scientists, not
from a search for consensus or the elimination of differences.

But, how do their strategies differ? Figure 1 differentiates practitioner and
researcher approaches in terms of units of study, environmental phenomena and stages
of the environmental design process.

The first dimension, unit of study, refers to places, from molecular units such as
individual family homes to complex units such as cities and urban areas. The second
dimension refers to environmental phenomena or social processes, e.g., privacy,
territoriality. The typical practitioner, whether he be an architect or urban planner, usually focuses on a particular unit or place--a home, neighborhood, or city.
His interest is in specifiable environmental units having spatial boundaries. In
designing a place he necessarily deals with a variety of processes, whether they
be the ones listed on the second dimension (privacy, territoriality) or other issues
such as economic, political, and technological matters. In short, he fixes at a
particular level on the place dimension and scans across phenomena or processes.

On the other hand, the behavioral scientist is usually process oriented. He studies
such issues as privacy, territoriality or crowding, often in any setting which
facilitates answers to his questions. For example, Galle, Gove and McPherson (2)
examined the impact of various types of crowding in terms of people per room in
apartments (home unit), number of apartment units per house (apartment house unit),
number of apartment houses per residential neighborhood (neighborhood unit) and
number of residents per census tract (community unit). Thus, they scanned across
places in studying the phenomenon of crowding. As another example, studies of
proximity and friendship are often not concerned with family, neighborhoods and
communities per se, but compare such places to the extent that they provide information about the phenomenon of friendship. In short, the behavioral scientist focuses
his microscope on processes and scans across places, whereas the practitioner examines places and scans across phenomena. Obviously, not all behavioral scientists
rigidly adopt this strategy; a number emphasize a particular cell in the two-dimensional space, e.g., privacy in the home. And, others emphasize more than single
processes, e.g., the sociology of the family may involve study of privacy in the
home and the role of the family in the community. Thus, some deal with a block of
space, not just a vertical or horizontal slice. In general, however, the typical
practitioner and the typical behavioral scientist seem to have different approaches
in their respective emphasis on units and places vs. processes and phenomena.

The third dimension refers to the design process or the steps necessary to create a

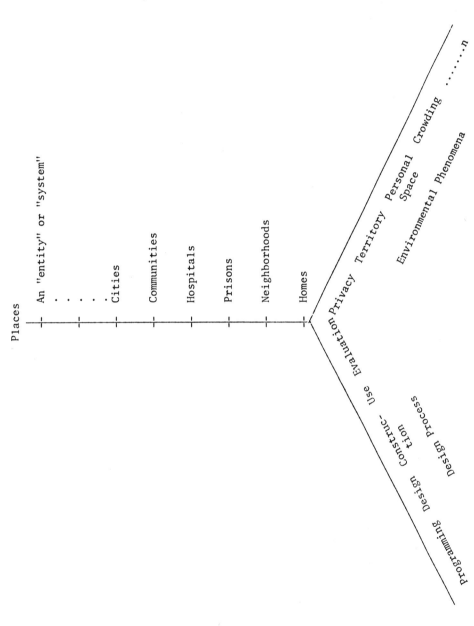

Figure 1. Behavioral Scientist and Design Practitioner Orientations to Man-Environment Issues.

building, home, or city [Zeisel (3)]. Briefly, programming involves identification of design criteria or the goals of the unit; design is a specific plan to achieve programming goals. Construction includes building the place; use refers to user activities and adaptations to completed units. Evaluation includes assessment of whether the completed unit satisfied original programming goals. Historically, researchers have not been involved in the design process. And, when they have participated, it has largely been in the evaluation stage, i.e., Is the place doing what it was supposed to do; does it have "validity"? For example, Bechtel (4) identified problems associated with a low-cost housing development. Unique to his approach was the feeding of evaluative limitations into a rehabilitative design process.

While practitioners have occasionally recruited behavioral scientists to participate in the design process, their success has been limited. Researchers are not prone to deal easily with such questions as: "How can the cultural background of group X be translated into the design of a home?" or "What design features should be built into this specific community for poor people?" Researchers do not typically pose questions in such specific place/locale form. The average scientist often replies that he can research the problem, but that his answers will be tentative and restricted in generality, and that the problem will require many studies, long-term funding and development of a body of theory. The practitioner, caught in the bind of a place to be built immediately, and operating with limited dollars, often throws up his hands in dismay, pleading that the design process must go on, and that decisions must be made in spite of incomplete knowledge. He goes on to say that he will accept educated guesses, but that the behavioral scientist must assume some responsibility, in spite of his uncertainty. The behavioral scientist often then steps aside, unwilling to assume such responsibility, to be driven by schedules and dollar limitations, and to act in the absence of thorough and scholarly documentation. Furthermore, he is often not interested in an applied product focused on a particular place or entity.

Implicit in this three-dimensional framework and in the paraphrased dialogue of miscommunication are several other differences in approach.

1. Criterion-oriented vs. process-oriented approaches

So-called "applied" researchers who work on weapon, transportation, education, and health care "systems" share much in common with environmental designers and are divergent from "basic" researchers. The practitioner and applied researcher are typically criterion- or problem-oriented in that they begin with a statement of goals or end-points to be achieved. They have a known criterion with known properties, e.g., a building or community to house X people and to provide X services, a transportation system which is to achieve a given flow of traffic in a specified period of time, etc. The job is to solve a specific problem and to produce a workable product. The practitioner or applied researcher then proceeds backwards from the criterion, gathering information and conducting research directed specifically towards problem solutions. While there may be by-products which go beyond immediate concerns, their perspective is directed primarily toward solving a particular problem. Thus, the practitioner and applied researcher are dependent variable oriented and work backwards only to those independent variables which may affect goal achievement. The basic researcher generally proceeds in the opposite direction. While interested in behavioral outcomes, his style is to pose first the question "What are the major classes of factors which affect behavior X?" His specification of behavior X is initially in fairly global terms. The next step, particularly if the researcher is experimentally oriented, is to design a multifactor study, with considerable attention devoted to properties of the laboratory setting and to careful specification and manipulation of independent or antecedent variables. In a sense, detailed description of behavioral or dependent variables comes last and is often contingent on what can be measured in the situation. And, the researcher is usually not concerned with a particular level of behavioral proficiency, but wishes to demonstrate how independent variables produce reliable differences in behavioral outcomes. In summary, he tends to be independent variable oriented, at least in terms of starting point.

Is it any wonder that practitioners and researchers encounter communication difficulties, when the practitioner poses a criterion or dependent variable question, e.g., "How can we satisfy people's needs for privacy in the design of this home?" and the researcher translates this into an independent variable framework, "What factors can I study as independent variables which will yield demonstrable effects of privacy?" The practitioner will not obtain the answer to his specific problem from the researcher's strategy, and the researcher is not accustomed to posing his research in the form requested by the practitioner. The result is an impasse.

2. Analysis vs. synthesis

Embedded in the preceding discussion is an issue which has been of philosophical and scientific interest for centuries. The practitioner often describes his job as "putting everything together" to solve problems. Not only must he worry about an array of technological questions—architectural design, plumbing, electricity, materials, transportation, building codes—but he must also deal with sociological and psychological matters. His job is to synthesize these different areas in order to create a viable entity.

Implicit in many behavioral science approaches is an analytic strategy, i.e., the unraveling of the contribution of individual and clusters of variables to behavioral outcomes. Thus, scientists usually focus on specific behaviors, specific settings, and specific independent variables. While the ultimate goal is broad generalization, immediate goals usually involve dimensionalizing phenomena, partialing out of variance, and detailed analysis of the impact of specific variables on specific behaviors. Or, to put it somewhat facetiously, the behavioral scientist is primarily interested in behavior, and only secondarily in putting information together to describe whole people or whole groups. So, when the practitioner poses the question "What does this particular cultural group need by way of privacy, availability to transportation, cultural centers, etc.?" the behavioral scientist not only translates this into the independent variable strategy described above, but he also may reply, "I am a specialist in religious institutions of rural members of that group and, therefore, can only speculate about the many other parts of your question." The result is another mutual frustration.

3. Doing and implementation vs. knowing and understanding

The environmental practitioner is action-oriented; he is a "doer" whose energies are directed toward a specific end product. The typical behavioral scientist is less compelled to achieve an immediate "real world" product. His goal is usually a published study or a theory, with unknown or limited immediate application. Again, these differences in orientation can lead to an impasse. The practitioner, geared toward rebuilding a city or designing a low-cost housing project, must take immediate action. The behavioral scientist devotes his energies to understanding rather than to direct action, and in controlled settings where he can tease out relevant sources of variance. He is generally less driven to directly and immediately apply his knowledge.

While these distinctions are not categorical, they collectively point to differences in approach of behavioral scientists and practitioners. And, as noted earlier, the ideal relationship is not necessarily one of consensus or homogeneity of style. Divergencies in approach are probably healthy, for they will bring to bear a variety of knowledge and strategies to the same problems. Furthermore, it will be particularly unhealthy if divergencies are seen by either party as inadequacies on the part of the other, or if there is a refusal to undertake translation between approaches. Such translation can take any of several forms. Practitioners and researchers can shift roles, i.e., the scientist can attempt occasionally to translate his work into the practitioner's framework, and vice versa. Or, we can try to develop a new breed of scientist-practitioner, who has a commitment to both types of professions, who works at the boundary of disciplines, and who becomes skilled at the translation process on an everyday basis. In any case, the theme proposed here is that differences in style exist, and need to be understood and bridged, not obliterated.

Evolutionary Stages of Researcher-Practitioner Contacts

The momentum for researchers and practitioners to join forces began in the late 1950's, when long smoldering discontents began to surface in the design professions and in behavioral science fields. Many practitioners rebelled against what they termed an egocentric approach to the design process, where the main product was accused of being for the benefit of the designer's aesthetic and personal aspirations, and not for the benefit of the human user. The needs of the environmental consumer became primary in the eyes of the malcontents, even at the expense of beauty in design. This led to a reaching out toward disciplines who presumably knew something about man's limitations, motivations and needs--sociology, psychology, political science, anthropology.

In the social and behavioral sciences (speaking primarily of psychology), a complementary discontent mounted about the same time. Some began to question the use of laboratory experimentation as the sole approach to understanding behavior and called for the study of behavior in "real world" settings. The hold of the laboratory was quite firm at the time, and it was not popular to conduct field research. However, there had been several notable field studies [Barker & Wright (5); Barker (6), (7); Sommer (8)] which demonstrated that meaningful information could be obtained using field experimental or observational techniques. Neverthe-less, those who advocated field studies were often alienated from the mainstream of research. Second, a realization grew that psychology traditionally had been examin-ing behavior almost independent of the physical environment. When it was consider-ed, the environment had been treated primarily as an independent variable and physi-cal determinant of responses, e.g., lighting, noise, color. It was not really con-ceived of as a social milieu or as a modifier of social structures and interaction patterns. Furthermore, the environment had rarely been studied in a dependent vari-able sense, as a manifestation and extension of behavior, e.g., privacy mechanisms, personal space, territorial behaviors.

Sommer (9) and Barker [Barker (10), (11); Barker & Wright (12)] demonstrated how environments serve as a social milieu, calling forth complex patterns of social behavior. And, the work of Hall (13), (14), undertaken from an anthropological perspective, and that of Kuethe (15), (16), done in a laboratory context, were early illustrations of the role of personal space mechanisms in different social situa-tions. These early efforts sensitized researchers to the role of the environment as an essential feature of social behavior. The result was a reaching out to disci-plines who dealt with the environment-architecture, interior design, geography, urban planning. Thus, in the early 1960's a critical mass of professionals develop-ed, who wanted to break away from the constrictions of their own disciplines.

During this initial period, spontaneous and organized interdisciplinary discussions took place, some under the sponsorship of formal organizations, and others as ad hoc meetings. From these meetings new channels of communication and more organized activities emerged, such as formal conferences and symposia, newsletters and infor-mal journals, interdisciplinary organizations, and academic programs to train man-environment researchers and practitioners.

In the mid- to late 1960's it appeared as if the early honeymoon was over, as basic value systems and styles of behavioral scientists and practitioners began to clash. The criterion-oriented, problem-directed, unit/place strategy of the practitioner was not being satisfied by the researcher, and vice versa. That state continues to exist to some extent, but one also has the impression that, having gone through a period of unreal expectations and subsequent disillusionment, a new stage of rela-tionship now exists. Both sides seem ready to make a more realistic assessment of each others' points of view and mutual advantages and disadvantages. It is essen-tial that continued efforts be made in this direction, else the study of man-envi-ronment relations will fragment, and once again be approached from the myopic view of individual disciplines.

A Models-of-Man View of the Field

The conduct of environmental research by practitioners and scientists has increased dramatically in the past few years--as evidenced in conference proceedings, techni-cal reports, newsletters and journal articles. And, there is apt to be an even greater outpouring in the coming years. Aside from the question of which research topics are popular or desirable to pursue [see Craik (17); Proshansky, Ittelson & Rivlin (18); Sommer (19), (20)], there is the less tangible issue of which philosophical models underlie present-day research. What general conceptions or models of man seem to be implicit and are in vogue in existing studies? Do these represent historical, evolutionary stages of the man-environment field? Are there philosophical viewpoints which may be fruitful to pursue but which are not yet evident in current research? Even brief consideration of these questions may make salient guiding assumptions underlying current research. And, other perspectives about which researchers and practitioners are not yet wholly aware may evolve from such an analysis. (See the paper by Rapaport in this volume for a more extensive list of various models of man.)

1. The mechanistic model of man

This model was one of the first applied to the study of man-environment relations. Its origin was in the human engineering, hardware-oriented systems work of the 1950's and 1960's, when it was a maxim that the design of complex systems had to include considerations of human users. The "man-machine systems" approach called for the design of equipment built around physical, sensory, motor and intellectual capabilities and limitations of man, with one motto being, "Fit the machine to man." The roots of this approach were in the early industrial psychology studies of time and motion, energy expenditure, etc. In modern times this approach has been translated into layout analyses, traffic flow systems, lighting, color, heating analyses of environments.

Several assumptions are implicit in this model. Man is viewed primarily as a _performing_, task-oriented organism. As a consequence, emphasis has been placed on his capabilities for sensing, processing, and interpreting inputs, and on his skills in evaluating and selecting action alternatives. Motivational and emotional states and interpersonal processes are either of secondary interest or are treated as factors which enhance or degrade man's system-like functioning. Such processes are not usually considered in and of themselves, but are cast in the context of efficient performance output.

Another feature of this approach is its extensive concern with environmental design, or the shaping of physical environments. The goal has been to insure that man's performance-related skills are maximized and that his limitations are not exceeded or unduly stressed. While training for maximum performance is often undertaken, emphasis has been placed on the design of physical environments, with man as one major constraint on that environment. Thus, environments are designed _for man_, often in a static sense and with relatively few options for him to alter environments or to function in them in a flexible fashion. In this sense, man is merely another system component with limited degrees of operating freedom.

While this approach achieved popularity in the 1950's and early 1960's, and still has relevance today, current man-environment research does not appear to rely heavily on this model.

2. The perceptual-cognitive-motivational model of man

The major present-day approach in environmental research conceptualizes man in terms of a variety of internal processes. These include _perceptual reactions_ to the environment (how he senses, perceives, and organizes environmental stimuli), moti-vational and emotional states associated with environmental stimuli (stress, nega-tive and positive affect), cognitive responses to the environment (subjective esti-mates of the richness, complexity, meaning and evaluation of the environment). This model conceives of man as an internal processing organism, and is more concerned with subjective psychological processes in relation to the environment than with overt behavioral responses.

Historically, psychology has relied heavily on an "internal state" model of man. This has been especially true in clinical psychology which, stemming from the earlier Freudian tradition, emphasized man's emotional and motivational states. This model has also been prevalent in social psychology, with its emphasis on: (1) attitudes and belief systems, (2) personality-oriented social states such as need achievement, affiliation, and dominance, and (3) interpersonal psychological states involving cooperation and competition, interpersonal attraction, conformity and influence, etc.

Research-oriented practitioners have been quick to adopt this model, perhaps because there is a large body of available theory and measurement techniques. The goal has been to uncover how man sees, perceives, feels and reacts to aspects of his environ-ment. Use has been made of questionnaire and rating procedures such as the semantic differential, where environments are rated on scales tapping evaluative (good-bad), activity (dynamic quality of environments), and potency (impact characteristics of environment) dimensions. Other approaches include "cognitive maps," where people are literally asked to draw their neighborhoods, streets, and cities, or are inter-viewed as they move through environments. The goal is to determine subjective per-ceptions of an environment, independent of its "objective" characteristics. One of the earliest examples of this approach involved taking people on a walk and asking them to give subjective impressions as they moved about [Lynch & Rivkin (21)]. Recently, Ladd (22) asked black children to draw their neighborhoods and streets, and then content analyzed their responses. Various aspects of cognitive map re-search and techniques have been summarized by Stea and Downs (23).

A massive body of data is building in this area and it seems that this model of man dominates research at the present time. It is also interesting to consider this approach from an extended historical perspective. Early in the history of modern psychology, during the last third of the nineteenth century, a substantial aspect of research involved "introspection," or the systematic analysis and self-reporting of internal cognitive and psychological events. In fact, there was an attempt by Wilhelm Wundt and his associates to establish a "mental chemistry." In many re-spects the cognitive map movement in man-environment research is analogous to the introspectionist movement of the 19th Century, as it also seeks to unravel how man cognizes, perceives and feels about the environment. It will be interesting to see how long this "inside the head" model of man remains prominent in man-environment research. A comprehensive analysis and criticism of this approach is presented by Wohlwill in this volume.

3. The behavioral model of man

This approach emphasizes study of overt behavior rather than internal, subjective states. What man does is stressed rather than how he feels, perceives or cognizes.

The work of Roger Barker and his associates [Barker (24), (25); Barker & Gump (26); Barker & Wright (27)] is representative of this approach, with detailed observations made of people's movements and activities as they function in various environments.

Behavioral analyses are not restricted to naturalistic observation. Much of the work of Sommer and others [Sommer (28)] involves field experimentation coupled with behavioral measurement, e.g., how people overtly interact, protect spaces, occupy chair locations, and approach others at varying distances as a function of manipulated variables such as nature and degree of intrusion, status, etc. There is also an increasing volume of research in laboratory settings on such factors as personal space, crowding and territorial behavior, all of which deals with overt behavioral events. [See Altman (29); Lett, Clark & Altman (30); Proshansky, Ittelson & Rivlin (31); Sommer (32) for reviews of some of this literature.] While this approach generally emphasizes overt behavior, many studies also simultaneously examine internal motivational states. (The chapters by Willems and Studer in this volume describe several facets of behavioral approaches.)

The behavioral approach is beginning to have an impact on practitioners. Many early conferences were dominated by the cognitive map approach, as practitioners sought to gain better understanding of man's internal needs and perceptions. And it appeared as if everyone scampered about, armed with questionnaires, rating instruments and interview schedules designed to tap all manner of internal states. More recently the behavioral approach has begun to gain momentum. For example, Barker-type work occupies more and more time at conferences, sessions are increasingly crowded, students and practitioners now talk about committing themselves to behavioral observation. It is likely that the coming years will show a surge of energy in this direction.

4. A social systems, ecological model of man

This approach has not been well established in the behavioral and social sciences, although the present author and others (see Willems' chapter in this volume) have formulated some ideas in this direction [Altman (33); Altman, Nelson & Lett (34); Altman & Taylor (35)]. A central theme underlying this model is that human interpersonal behavior is part of a complex ecosystem which has several features:

1. Environment and behavior are closely intertwined. This involves more than the accepted dictum that "environment affects behavior." It also states that behavior cannot be wholly understood independent of its intrinsic relationship to the physical environment, and that the very definition of behavior must be within an environmental context [Barker (36)]. To a great extent the social and behavioral sciences, especially psychology, have historically studied man almost as if he were separate from physical environments. What is now called for is recognition that man is at one with his environment and that the appropriate unit of study is a behavior-environment or organism-environment unit.

2. There is a mutual and dual impact between man and his environment. Not only does the environment act upon men, but man acts on environments, in a true ecological sense. Historically, researchers and practitioners have emphasized the environment as an independent variable--as something which acts on, determines, or causes

behavior. Thus, one often encounters the view that environments must be designed for people to be placed in, to meet their needs and to satisfy their purposes. Implicit in this traditional notion is the idea that man's control over his environment is to be limited, that environments are tailored to him in somewhat of a static, nonmodifiable form. More recently, however, increased emphasis has been given to the design of flexible, changing environments which men can manipulate, shape and alter. Here, man becomes an environmental change agent, not merely a recipient of environmental influences. And, according to this approach, the environment becomes an extension of man's being and personality. Concepts such as territory (the use and possession of places), privacy (control of input from others) and personal space (spatial distances from others) all refer to an active, coping use of the environment by people, not merely reactive responses to environmental stimuli.

3. A third feature of this ecological approach concerns the dynamic, changing quality of man-environment relations. These are not static, immutably fixed or intransigent relationships. Territories shift, functions alter, group composition changes. While a seemingly obvious truism, practitioners and researchers often act as if their products and knowledge were fixed and unchanging through time. Social systems adapt, cope and struggle, and both research and practice need to incorporate this idea.

4. A final theme of this approach is that man-environment relations occur at several levels of behavioral functioning, and as a coherent system. The man-machine, perceptual-motivational-cognitive and behavioral models emphasize different facets of human functioning, and almost presume that each is sufficient unto itself to understand man-environment relationships. It is proposed here that many such levels of behavior occur simultaneously and must be considered as a coherent set. Thus, perceptions, cognitions, feelings and emotional states serve as internal forces which eventually become translated into several levels of overt behavior, such as: (a) verbal content and paraverbal behaviors, including tone, pitch, interruptions and other stylistic features of speech; (b) nonverbal behaviors, including body postures and positions, and dynamic body behaviors such as eye contact, smiling, hand and feet movements and gestures, (c) environmentally oriented behaviors, or active use of objects and areas in the environment, such as personal space or physical distance, arrangements of furniture and other objects, selection and use of environmental objects.

Explicit in this last theme is the idea that different levels of behavior fit together as a "system," with the various levels capable of substituting, complementing or amplifying one another. Thus, a verbal statement can substitute for a smile or a head nod, or vice versa, or can be combined with a particular body position or use of the physical environment. This results in a wide repertoire of behaviors which are coordinated in various patterns. While sole emphasis on one level of behavior may be necessary in a particular research study, continued particularistic analysis without integration of behavioral levels can lose sight of the system quality of man-environment relations.

From the perspective of this paper, the social systems approach is the most potentially fruitful "model" of man for several reasons. For example, it may be useful in establishing connections between the other models. Furthermore, it seems to fit

more appropriately the complex nature of man-environment relationships. It also may
help bridge the gap between the place-oriented approach of the practitioner and the
process-oriented approach of the behavioral scientist. That is, a model based on
several levels of behavior which function as a coherent system may permit a synthesis of a total organism--a person, group or person-environment unit--as separate
levels of behavior are interrelated. If carried to its logical possibilities, this
approach can be analogous to understanding and managing a symphony orchestra, in
terms of simultaneous knowledge of separate instrument sections as well as the whole
orchestral unit. If this can be achieved, then place-unit and process-oriented
approaches can be bridged, as can analysis and synthesis strategies.

Summary and Conclusions

Progress in the man-environment area depends on the joining of forces by scientists
and practitioners. However, barriers to mutual understanding exist, because of
differences in styles of practitioners and researchers. Researchers are primarily
analytic and independent variable-oriented, and less concerned with solving "real
world" problems. Their efforts are directed toward behavioral processes, and less
emphasis is placed on whole organismic units, i.e., places or people. The typical
practitioner operates according to a goal-directed, criterion-oriented, place-
focused strategy. He seeks to synthesize information, and deals with processes only
if specific information is necessary to design a viable place or unit. Because of
these different strategies, practitioners and scientists have often miscommunicated.
To understand and solve man-environment problems, it is important that these differences be understood and bridged. For example, scientists and practitioners may find
it useful to translate their knowledge into one another's frameworks--the scientist
viewing his data in terms of its potential application, and the practitioners becoming more analytic, even at the expense of ignoring immediate applications of knowledge. It is not advocated that each should become the other, nor that they necessarily achieve total mutual consensus. Rather the goal should be to occasionally
view a problem from the perspective of the other. In this way the strengths of
each approach might generate new modes of attack.

Researchers and practitioners have implicitly adopted one of several theoretical
"models of man." While none of the following models are "correct" in an absolute
sense, they have served to guide research and practice:

1. A mechanistic model, with man viewed primarily as part of a complex man-machine
system, and emphasis placed on performance-related behaviors; 2. a perceptual-
cognitive-motivational model, with man conceived of as an internal, subjective,
inside-the-head processor. This model is presently popular in man-environment
research, in the form of studies of cognitive maps and subjective reactions to
environmental stimuli; 3. a behavioral model, which places emphasis on overt behavior rather than internal psychological processes. According to this position,
man-environment relations are best understood through study of overt transactions
between man and his physical environment; 4. an ecological, social systems model,
which conceives of man-environment events as involving: (a) several behavioral
levels, e.g., subjective internal processes, overt verbal, nonverbal and environmental behaviors, which (b) function as a coherent system of interrelated, substitu-
tible and complementary behaviors and (3) where there is a mutual relationship

between environment and behavior, each influencing and shaping the other, (d) in a dynamic time-linked sense.

The position was taken that no single model is complete, but that the ecological social systems approach held considerable promise for understanding man-environment relations for several reasons: 1. it treats man and environments as the central units, not men alone or environments alone; 2. it holds the potential for bridging between the approaches of practitioners and researchers. That is, it calls for scientists to synthesize separate behavioral events into total organismic units and calls for practitioners to examine social processes in an analytic fashion; 3. its emphasis on multi-level behaviors brings together several areas of the behavioral and social sciences; and 4. it views man-environment relations in a way which stresses flexibility of environments and active organisms shaping environments.

The understanding and solution of man-environment problems cannot be approached from a dogmatic and doctrinaire perspective. What is most important, and the primary goal of this paper, is to point out alternative strategies and implicit assumptions underlying differences in styles of problem solving. In this way those interested in the field can pursue a line of attack consciously, with some perspective on its history and sociology.

Notes and References

(1)   A lengthier version of this paper appeared in REPRESENTATIVE RESEARCH IN SOCIAL PSYCHOLOGY, 4, 1973, revised with permission of the editor, D. Stokols.

(2)   Galle, O. R., Gove, W. R., McPherson, J. M., "Population Density and Pathology", SCIENCE, 176, pages 23-30, 1972.

(3)   Zeisel, J., FRONTIER PAPER ON SOCIOLOGY OF ARCHITECTURE (unpublished manuscript), Harvard University, 1972.

(4)   Bechtel, R. B., THE PUBLIC HOUSING ENVIRONMENT: A FEW SURPRISES, paper presented at Environmental Design Research Association, Los Angeles, California, 1972.

(5)   Barker, R. G., and Wright, H. F., MIDWEST AND ITS CHILDREN, New York, Harper and Row, 1955.

(6)   Barker, R. G. (Ed.), THE STREAM OF BEHAVIOR, New York, Appleton-Century-Crofts, 1963.

(7)   Barker, R. G., ECOLOGICAL PSYCHOLOGY, Stanford, California, Stanford University Press, 1968.

(8)   Sommer, R., PERSONAL SPACE: THE BEHAVIORAL BASIS OF DESIGN, Englewood Cliffs, New Jersey, Prentice Hall, 1969.

(9)   Sommer, R., PERSONAL SPACE: THE BEHAVIORAL BASIS OF DESIGN, Englewood Cliffs, New Jersey, Prentice Hall, 1969.

(10) Barker, R. G. (Ed.), THE STREAM OF BEHAVIOR, New York, Appleton-Century-Crofts, 1963.

(11) Barker, R. G., ECOLOGICAL PSYCHOLOGY, Stanford, California, Stanford University Press, 1968.

(12) Barker, R. G., and Wright, H. F., MIDWEST AND ITS CHILDREN, New York, Harper and Row, 1955.

(13) Hall, E. T., THE SILENT LANGUAGE, New York, Doubleday, 1959.

(14) Hall, E. T., THE HIDDEN DIMENSION, New York, Doubleday, 1966.

(15) Kuethe, J. L., "Social Schemas", JOURNAL OF ABNORMAL AND SOCIAL PSYCHOLOGY, 64, pages 31-38, 1962.

(16) Kuethe, J. L., "Social Schemas and the Reconstruction of Social Object Displays from Memory", JOURNAL OF ABNORMAL AND SOCIAL PSYCHOLOGY, 65, pages 71-74, 1962.

(17) Craik, K., NEW DIRECTIONS IN PSYCHOLOGY, New York, Holt, Rinehart & Winston, 1970.

(18) Proshansky, H., Ittelson, W., and Rivlin, L., ENVIRONMENTAL PSYCHOLOGY, New York, Holt, Rinehart & Winston, 1970.

(19) Sommer, R., "Small Group Ecology", PSYCHOLOGICAL BULLETIN, 67, pages 145-152, 1967.

(20) Sommer, R., PERSONAL SPACE: THE BEHAVIORAL BASIS OF DESIGN, Englewood Cliffs, New Jersey, Prentice Hall, 1969.

(21) Lynch, K., and Rivkin, M., "A Walk around the Block", LANDSCAPE, 8, pages 24-34, 1959.

(22) Ladd, F., "Black Youths View their Environment: Neighborhood Maps", ENVIRONMENT AND BEHAVIOR, 2, pages 74-99, 1970.

(23) Stea, D., and Downs, R. (Eds.), COGNITIVE MAPPING: IMAGES OF SPATIAL ENVIRONMENTS, Chicago, Aldine Press, 1972.

(24) Barker, R. G. (Ed.), THE STREAM OF BEHAVIOR, New York, Appleton-Century-Crofts, 1963.

(25) Barker, R. G., ECOLOGICAL PSYCHOLOGY, Stanford, California, Stanford University Press, 1968.

(26) Barker, R. G., and Gump, P., BIG SCHOOL, SMALL SCHOOL, Stanford, California, Stanford University Press, 1964.

(27) Barker, R. G., and Wright, H. F., MIDWEST AND ITS CHILDREN, New York, Harper and Row, 1955.

(28) Sommer, R., PERSONAL SPACE: THE BEHAVIORAL BASIS OF DESIGN, Englewood Cliffs, New Jersey, Prentice Hall, 1969.

(29) Altman, I., "The Communication of Interpersonal Attitudes: An Ecological Approach" in Huston, T. L., PERSPECTIVES ON INTERPERSONAL ATTRACTION, New York, Academic Press, 1973.

(30) Lett, Evelyn E., Clark, W., and Altman, I., A PROPOSITIONAL INVENTORY OF RESEARCH ON INTERPERSONAL DISTANCE (Technical Report No. 1), Naval Medical Research Institute, Bethesda, Maryland, 1969.

(31) Proshansky, H., Ittelson, W., and Rivlin, L., ENVIRONMENTAL PSYCHOLOGY, New York, Holt, Rinehart & Winston, 1970.

(32) Sommer, R., PERSONAL SPACE: THE BEHAVIORAL BASIS OF DESIGN, Englewood Cliffs, New Jersey, Prentice Hall, 1969.

(33) Altman, I., "The Communication of Interpersonal Attitudes: An Ecological Approach" in Huston, T. L., PERSPECTIVES ON INTERPERSONAL ATTRACTION, New York, Academic Press, 1973.

(34) Altman, I., Nelson, Patricia, and Lett, Evelyn E., THE ECOLOGY OF HOME ENVI-RONMENTS (Final Report, Project No. 0-0502, Grant No. OEG-8-70-0202 (508), Office of Education, Department of Health, Education and Welfare), University of Utah, 1972.

(35) Altman, I., and Taylor, D. A., THE DEVELOPMENT OF INTERPERSONAL RELATIONSHIPS: SOCIAL PENETRATION, New York, Holt, Rinehart & Winston, 1973.

(36) Barker, R. G., ECOLOGICAL PSYCHOLOGY, Stanford, California, Stanford University Press, 1968.

Aristide H. Esser
Director, Central Bergen Community Mental Health Center
Saddle Brook, New Jersey 07662
President, ASMER, Inc., P. O. Box 57
Orangeburg, New York 10962

Abstract

A model for the structural components in the field of Man-Environment Relations
based on the organization of the Central Nervous System is described. The importance of linkages between the components is stressed: individual development and
continued evolution depend on functional compatibility between cognitive and environmental structures. Pollution is explained as inherent conflicts between those
structures which are typically human and those which man shares with the animals.
Design implications of this concept are discussed. The process of synergy may lead
to a possible systematic integration.

Introduction

The neurosciences have illustrated the possibility that built-in CNS functions represent aspects of the environment: the logic of our environment relates to the
logic of our brain. (1) The Central Nervous System, as the seat of experiencing,
constructs man's transactions with his environment. I therefore propose a structural model of Man-Environment Relations based on the anatomical and functional organization of the CNS.

We know that the human CNS is complex, shows differences in operation depending on
its levels and its hemispheres, and may partake in diverse states of consciousness.
(2) A systematic understanding of the increasing complexity encountered on different levels of human CNS functioning is facilitated by MacLean's concept of the Tri-
une Brain. (3) In the course of evolution, man acquired three interpenetrating CNS
subsystems, representing what MacLean calls the reptilian, old mammalian and new
mammalian stages of behavior, responsible for different environmental transactions.
Associated with the reptilian brain in the brainstem (reticular system) is biological behavior, including stereotyped actions for self-preservation, orientation,
establishment and maintenance of territory, etc. The old mammalian brain in the
limbic system is associated with emotional behavior, grouping for the preservation
of the species, establishment of social order, etc. Associated with the new mammalian brain in the (neo)cortex is intellectual behavior which has enabled mankind to
change the environment deliberately. (4)

For the purpose of this presentation, I will combine the biosocial functions of the
first two CNS levels and contrast these with the sociocultural functions of the neo-
cortex. The fact that biosocial behavior in part contrasts with sociocultural behavior makes for the great number of dichotomies in human life. For instance, on
the biosocial level the environment largely determines behavior; to this extent we
therefore may agree with the suggestion that there is an environmental solution to
human behavior. (5) On the other hand, on the sociocultural level man conceptua-

lizes via language and artifact. The environment then clearly is part of a negotiating system in which man takes an active role in influencing and shaping the environment. (6,7)

Even if we do not know the details of the exact linkages between CNS and environment, it is possible to hypothesize on their systems characteristics by following the structuralist tradition. This approach looks for organized totalities by focusing on domains which appear to be coherent and to be central to human experience. The assumptions are that the study of animal and human groups can give insight into the whole of human experience, and that the brain as a biological structure reflects this whole; we refer to it as Mind, the collective of experience. (8,9)

Structures of CNS Functioning

In the Western tradition we discern two major groups of structures provided by the CNS: Mental (or Cognitive) and Environmental. These can be represented in a model for Man-Environment Relations as shown in Figure 1, with a further subdivision into Biosocial Cognition and Nonverbal Behavior shared by man with other animals, and Sociocultural Cognition and Language and Artifacts which are typically human. I propose to discuss briefly the contents of each subdivision, or box, and to examine their linkages in order for us to understand the role of design in the evolution of man-environment relations.

The assumption that structures in cognition are produced by CNS functioning is readily understandable when we realize that cognition is the abstraction of private experiencing, made possible by one's individual brain. However, it may be difficult initially to realize that structures in environment are reflections of CNS functioning, since these are public. But once we understand that the environment, which includes our behavior therein, only obtains structure through consensual validation of multiple private experiences, we are able to accept that our Weltbild rests on the restraints shared by all of our individual brains. (10)

Non-Verbal Behavior

I will begin the discussion of the model in Figure 1 with nonverbal behavior (NVB), since its study has led to the conceptualization of cognitive structures.

The first cognitive structures related to the natural environment. Studies of animals have revealed that NVB structures their environment. In this sense birds do not see trees, they see the others. Man has kept this way of structuring the natural part of the environment in the NVB of his reptilian and paleo-mammalian brain. (11) This is the basis for his emotional experiences, his bio-social cognition. Man's relations to his fellowmen rest on pre-verbal mechanisms such as orientation toward the parent or the familiar, withdrawal from the stranger, grooming and sex, gestures and emotional expressions, play, etc. Most of NVB is out-of-awareness, and NVB is possibly 65% of all environmental communication. (12) NVB is well adapted to the dictates of the environment, since, for the animal, knowing is doing.

As is the case with all structures in environment, NVB is public, shared and observable. These characteristics make an objective study of NVB a possibility, but

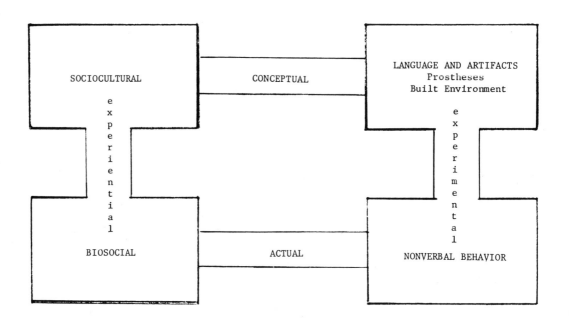

Figure 1
STRUCTURAL ASPECTS OF CNS FUNCTIONING

should not encourage behavioral scientists, notably Skinner, (13) to pretend that it is all that is needed to account for man-environment relations. More astute observers have seen that when an animal is perfectly adapted to its natural environment, it appears that its behavior is based upon a plan, a model of its interactions (e.g., Tolman's cognitive map). (14) The linkage between NVB and its cognitive counterpart, Biosocial Cognition, can only be attained by the actual interactions of the animal in nature. (15) For all practical purposes, there is an equilibrium maintained by feedback processes between these boxes.

Biosocial Cognition

Ethologists, studying animals in their natural habitats, have contributed most to the understanding of biosocial structures. They demonstrated the complex structures of instincts and their logic, which antedates the logic of the behavior, (16) such as territory serving biological life and peck-order serving social life. In a purely behavioristic study, the "plans", which may be hypothesized as underlying the structure of territorial and dominance behavior, (17) could not have been discovered.

Biosocial structures have to be inferred from observable NVB. Piaget has shown convincingly that sensory motor schemes can be found in the private acts of children, and the theoretical Test-Operate-Test-Exit (TOTE) unit has been useful in bridging the gap between image and behavior. (18,19) The genetic work by Waddington describes best the fit between biosocial structures (the organism) and its environment: their relations can be considered a cybernetic loop whereby the organism selects its environment while being conditioned by it. (20) This viewpoint is implicit in the reconciliation of the behaviorist model based on conditioning and learning (dependent on environmental structures) with the ethologist model of imprinting and fixed motor patterns (dependent on cognitive structures) as proposed by Lorenz. (21)

The transformations biosocial structures undergo before they become part of the sociocultural structures are complex. (22,23) In children, the transit time from sensory motor to truly operational schemes encompasses the period from age 1 1/2 - 6, according to Piaget. (24) During these years the child becomes uniquely human. This fact underlines the importance of early childhood experiences as the linkage between general biosocial structures (leading to relatively inflexible behavior) and specific sociocultural structures, on which rest the apparently limitless adaptability of man.

Sociocultural Cognition

This component of CNS functioning includes the most evolved cognitive processes. These, as defined by Von Foerster, form "the hierarchy of mechanisms, transformational operations and processes that lead from sensation over perception of particulars to the manipulation of generalized internal representations of the perceived, as well as the inverse transformations that lead from general commands to specific actions, or from general concepts to specific utterances." (25, p.24) Only with CNS cortical functioning do we find generalized internal representations of the environment, the "true" representational schemes of Piaget, and symbolic structures. Construction of these representations is possible through the tremendous development of memory, the sequential functioning of intellect and reason, and, most of all, the language capability of the dominant hemisphere.

Language is especially important in structuring, since it is an objectifying tool of man. Beyond that function, language also provides the only viable possibility of linkage between the components in this model. It is language that enables man to know and refer to his own biosocial structures as "self", and to the environment as "other". In the same breath, man becomes able to link direct experience and conceptual activities. We know that structuring strategies developed by children strongly depend on the technology, including language, needed for culturation and participation.

It is important to note that of all the linkages in Figure 1, only the one between the typically human structures systematically provides a feed-forward mechanism. That is, the conceptual linkage implies those strategies whereby one attempts to predict the consequences of the implementation of a structure. Sociocultural cognition and man-made structures augment each other and this feed-forward process guarantees that equilibrium will never be reached.

Man-made Structures

The man-made environment is a CNS function as different from NVB as sociocultural cognition is from biosocial cognition. It is not that animals do not make permanent changes, "ipsefacts", in the environment. Bee hives, termite heaps, etc. have a recognized influence on the behavior of each species: "ipsefacts have ecological significance." (26)

But, not only do man-made environments have ecological significance, they are being used consciously more and more to change our nonverbal behavior (an adaptational function) and enlarge consciousness itself (a creative function). Thus, man-made structures have come to be used as <u>prostheses</u>, artificial substitutes and extensions: "(Man) is distinguished from other animals by virtue of the fact that he has elaborated what I have termed extensions of his organism. By developing his extensions, man has been able to improve or specialize various functions. The computer is an extension of part of the brain, the telephone extends the voice, the wheel extends the legs and feet. Language extends experience in time and space while writing extends language." (27, p.3) Man-made changes in the environment appear to parallel the neocortical functions, freeing man from the bondage of biosocial cognition. For instance, linear reasoning appears in the symbolic notations on bone, stone, etc. made in the Upper Paleolithic, whose purpose Marshack describes as the <u>sequential</u> accumulation of sets, subsets and super-ordinate sums. (28) Man-made environmental structures also may replace NVB as environmental adaptation mechanisms, since they do not suffer from the biosocial restraints of the human organism. The linkage between biosocial cognition and behavior is subject to organic constraints, circadian rhythms (necessitating periodic inactivity, sleep), fatigue, etc. Man-made structures and their conceptual linkage to CNS functions are only subject to physical restraints, cf., the computers processing the data while the astronauts are safely asleep in their space capsule.

The linkage between man-made structures and NVB rests on experiment. Until we have actually constructed we will not know the consequences: "First we shape our buildings and they then shape us." No matter how much we conceptualize and predict, there is always the possibility of an unexpected result. Concerning environmental design it is therefore a truism to say that the experiment is the solution. (29)

Application of the Model

This structural conceptualization of CNS function can be used to clarify social and environmental pollution, and to see the implications of environmental design.

Pollution is a typical human problem, it is impurity in what was once pure, a disturbance of equilibrium. The biosocial and NVB structures man shares with animals are at equilibrium: they are polluted by man-made environmental structures and sociocultural cognition. In terms of the model, pollution most clearly occurs when structures in non-adjacent boxes interact. (Figure 2) The absence of linkage makes non-compatible development likely. We need sex-clinics because modern sociocultural imagery impaired non-verbal pairing behavior (social pollution). We fouled up the earth because our territorial images prevented us from seeing that we cannot get rid of something without it coming back to plague us.

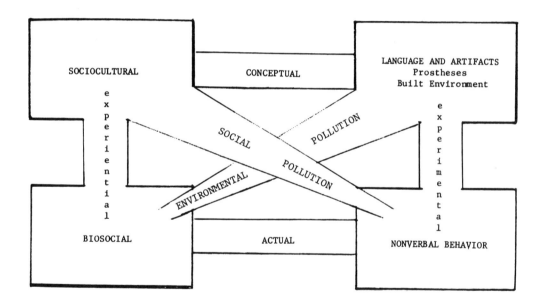

Figure 2
CONCEPT OF POLLUTION

Environmental pollution is the accumulation of unwanted side-effects of man-made structures: its greatest threat is to biosocial cognition. The CNS has no direct ways of perceiving the threats of man-made structures to human survival and procreation. This explains why DDT, CO, radioactive fallout, etc. caught us unaware, and even when we finally registered these threats to our vital functions we still need changes in sociocultural structures before the side-effects of insecticides, the automobile and atomic weapons can be effectively combated. We have come to realize that the conservatism of established sociocultural cognitive structures reflects the stereotyped ways of the reptilian and paleomammalian brain systems. And "successful" environmental structures (industrial revolution) have made for seemingly immutable cultural structures.

Social pollution has been described as the inevitable disturbance of biological and emotional imagery by rational thinking, (30) in terms of the model: the endangering of nonverbal behavior structures by sociocultural cognitive structuring. The accent in sociocultural cognition is on the formal learning experience, intellectual sequential reasoning. But, as mammals, our earliest learning experience was social, based on the emotional ties within our primary group. Thus, shared individual experiences of intimate nonverbal behavior in small group life are replaced in intellectual learning by collectively accumulated verbal structures showing logical association and coherence. Here cultural man may clash with himself, since the nonverbal structures of personal-social experience cannot always be transformed comprehensively into language. (31)

As to the potentials and limitations of environmental design: we may distinguish adaptational design for NVB, and creative design for prosthetic functions.

Adaptational design can direct itself to influencing the four important factors in the survival of animals: weather, predators and disease, food and other resources, and other individuals. (32) In modern society only the last factor is relevant, and then only to preserve rather than to improve. Better adaptation of man to increase his survival chances is not needed and may be counterproductive. Ecologically speaking, man has surpassed the animal density-dependent mechanisms for population regulation. Thereby man has made it impossible to stop his population growth by NVB, except when using large-scale antisocial behaviors: alienation, violence and war. As Calhoun remarked: there is no reason why man should not go to standing room only. (33) Adaptational design therefore has a limited but essential task: to preserve the essence of man by providing opportunity for proper emotional growth. Keeping in mind the components of NVB, this would mean design for privacy needed for emotional bonding and design for community life especially for the pre-school child, etc. This preserving function of adaptational design must be directed against social pollution and toward full emotional development. It must not succumb to "successful" sociocultural concepts which cannot enhance NVB in the child, e.g., "enrichment" of young children through academic learning.

Creative design is directed toward our evolution, it cannot serve what is "average" in man. Incidentally, we do not know what the "average man" is, it is therefore folly to look for perfect adaptation in utopias. Creative design must take into account its feedback linkage with NVB. Determining the success of design experiments with user-evaluation is one way. More importantly, creative design should enhance

the variety of sociocultural cognition. The research task here is to prevent harmful side-effects, the pollution of those structures to which there is no direct linkage and thus no direct feedback. Nobody would have predicted that sociocultural concepts of apartment-living new to the user-subculture would destroy social behavior
patterns in Pruitt-Igoe. Thus, creative design has to look for a principle which
will prevent a run-away effect of its structures; it must guard against making sor-
cerer's apprentices.

Going Beyond the Model: Synergy

As professionals, a possible way out of the boxes in which we are caught is the attempt at integration of CNS functions through synergy: the increase of organization
resulting from a combined action of all parts of the system. (34) The mechanisms to
bring this about all derive from an attitude of tolerance. We have to learn to em-
pathize with all aspects of our brain as well as other people's lives, and try to
dissolve our most harmful dichotomies: I-it; conscious-unconscious; man-animal;
male-female; familiar-stranger....

I propose a scientific and professional adherence to theoretical pluralism and methodological tolerance, (35) without preconceptions about the "nature" of things. I
believe this to be a subjective choice, since it rests on the individual and commitment.

Notes and References

(1)   Von Foerster, H., "Logical Structure   of Environment and its Internal
       Representation" in Eckerstrom, R.E., INTERNATIONAL DESIGN CONFERENCE: ASPEN
       1962, Zeeland, Michigan, H. Miller, Inc., 1963.

(2)   For a summary of brain-mind research, see Calder, N., THE MIND OF MAN, New
       York, Viking, 1970.

(3)   MacLean, P.D., "Man and his Animal Brains", MODERN MEDICINE, 32, pages 95-106,
       1964.

(4)   Esser, A.H., "Social Pollution", SOCIAL EDUCATION, 35, pages 11-18, 1971.

(5)   Skinner, B.F., CONTINGENCIES OF REINFORCEMENT, New York, Appleton-Century-
       Crofts, 1969.

(6)   See especially chapter 3 in Klausner, S.Z., ON MAN IN HIS ENVIRONMENT, San
       Francisco, Jossey-Bass, Inc., 1971.

(7)   Tibbetts, P., "The Transactional Theory of Human Knowledge and Action", MAN-
       ENVIRONMENT SYSTEMS, 2, pages 37-59, 1972.

(8)   e.g., Gardner, H., THE QUEST FOR MIND, New York, A.H. Knopf, 1973.

(9)   Esser, A.H., "Social Pollution in the Evolution of Mankind's Communal Imagery",
       in White, J., FRONTIERS OF CONSCIOUSNESS, New York, Julian Press, in press.

(10) See Reference (1).

(11) The fact that this behavior is so stereotyped that it resembles reflex action has made some believe that environment can be sufficiently restructured through behavior modification.

(12) De Long, A.J., "The Communication Process: A Generic Model for Man-Environment Relations", MAN-ENVIRONMENT SYSTEMS, 2, pages 263-313, 1972.

(13) See Reference (5).

(14) Miller, G.A., Gallanter, E., Pribram, K.H., PLANS AND THE STRUCTURE OF BEHAVIOR, New York, Holt, Rinehart, and Winston, 1960.

(15) Yet we know that at times the two can be dissociated, as in the Rapid Eye Movement (REM) sleep, whereby intense mental activities (vivid dreams) occur without clear environmental counterparts. This spontaneous CNS state which structures only cognitively and not behaviorally, remains mysterious.

(16) Piaget, J., STRUCTURALISM, New York, Basic Books, 1970.

(17) See Reference (14).

(18) Esser, A.H., "Evolving Neurologic Substrates of Essentic Forms", GENERAL SYSTEMS, 17, pages 33-41, 1972.

(19) See Reference (14).

(20) See Reference (16).

(21) Lorenz, K., EVOLUTION AND MODIFICATION OF BEHAVIOR, University of Chicago Press, 1965.

(22) See Reference (16).

(23) Esser, A.H., "War as Part of Social Pollution", to appear in Givens, A., Nettleship, A. and Nettleship, M., WAR, ITS CAUSES AND CORRELATES, The Hague, Mouton.

(24) Furth, H., PIAGET AND KNOWLEDGE, New Jersey, Prentice-Hall, Inc., 1969.

(25) Von Foerster, H., "What is Memory that it May Have Hindsight and Foresight as Well?" in Bogosh, S., PROCEEDINGS OF THE THIRD INTERNATIONAL CONFERENCE: THE FUTURE OF THE BRAIN SCIENCES, New York, Plenum, 1969.

(26) Audy, J.R., "The Ipsefact" in Esser, A.H., BEHAVIOR AND ENVIRONMENT: THE USE OF SPACE BY ANIMALS AND MEN, New York, Plenum, 1971.

(27) Hall, E.T., THE HIDDEN DIMENSION, Garden City, N.Y., Doubleday, 1966.

(28) Marshack, A., "Upper Paleolithic Engraving", CURRENT ANTHROPOLOGY, 13, pages 445-447, 1972.

(29) Studer, R.G., "The Dynamics of Behavior-Contingent Physical Systems" in Broadbent, G., DESIGN METHODS IN ARCHITECTURE, London, Humphries, 1969.

(30) See References (4) and (9).

(31) See Reference (23).

(32) Andrewartha, H.G., "Population Growth and Control: Animal Populations" in Allison, A., POPULATION CONTROL, New York, Penguin Books, 1970.

(33) Calhoun, J.B., "Population" in Allison, A., POPULATION CONTROL, New York, Penguin Books, 1970.

(34) The synergy concept is differently conceived in different disciplines. For a further discussion, see, e.g., Benson, D., "Synergetics: The Study and Practice of Synergy", MAN-ENVIRONMENT SYSTEMS, 2, pages 195-199, 1972; Esser, A.H., "Strategies for Research in Man-Environment Systems" in Smith, W.M., BEHAVIOR, DESIGN, AND POLICY ASPECTS OF HUMAN HABITATS, Green Bay, Wis., Regents of the University of Wisconsin System, 1972, and Reference (9).

(35) e.g., see Lakatos, I., "Methodology of Scientific Programmes" in Lakatos, I. and Musgrave, A., CRITICISM AND GROWTH OF KNOWLEDGE, Cambridge University Press, 1970.

Amos Rapoport
Associate Professor of Architecture and Anthropology
University of Wisconsin-Milwaukee
Milwaukee, Wisconsin 53201

Abstract/Introduction

It is not my intention to become overly involved in epistemological problems. It
is, however important to consider why man-environment studies should require
theory at this point - as I among others have been arguing for some time. This
inevitably involves considering theory in general, but the major thrust will be to
the _specific_ rationale regarding man-environment studies.

After having, as it were, specified some general characteristics of theory as we
need it in our field, the specific characteristics will be examined. In the light
of these two sets of criteria current models will be examined. It will be suggested that no one model meets all needs and several models must be used - and preferably combined.

Then another way of approaching the problem will be mentioned briefly. Here specific questions and issues are tackled and are considered from various points of
view and perspectives, using different models. (Clearly the choice of these two
approaches is partly arbitrary and the task could be approached in terms of scale,
of contrast of descriptive and comparative studies or according to methodologies
used.) (1)

1. Why Theory?

The need for a theory can be argued on _general_ grounds. Thus it has been suggested that in any fully developed field we find a continuum from practitioners tack-
ling real problems through methodologists, to theoreticians and philosophers developing models. The first lot are involved in front-line problems and the latter
are more detached and contemplative. (2) If any one of these groups dominates
unduly the field is not adequately developed. The design disciplines have been
weak in theory and methodology which explains the recent development of man-environment studies and design methodology. But within the man-environment studies
field itself we have had more "practitioners" than theoreticians. Thus to balance
the field more theory is needed.

Since we are dealing with design related theory we must be concerned not only with
the conventions for formulating theory (3) but also with specifying performance
criteria and then evaluating the success of design decisions based on them. In
order to do this we need to know how the various components of man-environment
relations interact. In the most general terms this leads to three general basic
questions to which I have often referred:
  1. What characteristics of people as individuals and groups are important in
      shaping the environment?

2. How and to what extent does the environment affect people?

3. What are the mechanisms that link people and environment?

In order to deal with these questions it is essential to use a broad sample and be flexible with regard to methodology. To cope with the great variety of elements ordering schemas are essential. In general terms (and using Henry Margenau's model) events which are numerous must be structured and classified using various ordering systems which lead from events to constructs and concepts – and these differ according to the system used. (4) (Hence part 2 of this paper). This also inevitably means that empirical work alone is not enough and theory is needed. (5)

Any theory developed at this stage, even if initially inadequate, will help to develop and extend ideas and make them more precise. Once formulated operationally, such a theory can be tested, revised, and ultimately verified. It can also become additive and cumulative which is essential. Design disciplines have not been either cumulative nor additive – each building, each piece of design was isolated. Yet design basically is hypothesis and feedback is essential to verify the hypothesis, such verification being used to generate further hypotheses. While this problem is partly institutional (there is no provision made for an evaluation stage), it is also due to the difficulty of stating objectives. The failure to state operational goals which design can achieve and which can be evaluated is then partly a function of lack of theory. It is much easier to state objectives and to go on to evaluation if one begins with some theory linking people and environments.

Several more specific reasons for the need for a theory can be listed.
1. One major reason is the need to make sense of thousands of papers and items of empirical data and hence order the confusion resulting from too many disparate pieces of work. We need to see pattern in an apparent mass of detail and to see anomalies in an apparent pattern. I have argued previously that this mass of material can be in fact counter-productive since it inhibits the use of such work. The need is for constructs, concepts and so on, i.e. theory, which will group items so as to reduce and order the confusion. (6) For example, I have collected nearly 700 references on the effect of the environment on behavior pro and con. Many of these have extensive bibliographies so that the total number of references is even greater. Yet it is not possible to give a firm opinion about these effects and their extent, or about how they occur and under what specified conditions – yet this seems to be a crucial point for design theory.

2. A framework to reduce such confusion must provide for a wide variety of work on many aspects of man-environment interaction. Since many of these pieces of work are contradictory, or are not comparable, this is bad for both theory and practice. Thus another reason for theory building is to reveal gaps, inconsistencies as well as agreement, to suggest problem areas needing replication or clarification and generally raise questions, thus helping in research. While this can be achieved partly through general articles, bibliographies, information systems, etc. the most rewarding way is to create a framework, i.e. a theory. By creating a theoretical framework much of the material should fall into place, patterns can

be discerned, gaps located, inconsistencies exposed and studies then replicated. This seems to be the most urgent order of business - and a number of people in the field (including myself) are, in fact, trying to do just this.

3. An important role of theory is to lead from description to explanation and ultimately to prediction, although the latter is a distant goal. One problem at this point is that we are remarkably weak even in description, which itself involves both a process of selection of what is important and at least an implicit classification and hence a notion of theory. We do not really know even how adequately to describe. It may thus be suggested that the very attempt to build theory will help improve description, as well as leading beyond it to explanation. The process is one of describing significant elements and deriving concepts which have design utility. Thus begins a theoretical orientation. (7)

4. Theory is also urgently needed to help in teaching. (This is linked to 1 above). It is very difficult to teach man-environment studies because it appears to consist of masses of pieces of empirical work and case studies. For example, there are many specific indications of concepts of environmental quality but no attempt to link them in any theoretical way which would relate them or show where any particular case belongs. It is undoubtedly true that every teacher tries to link work through theoretical formulations which are his alone. But we need more, and effective theories generally are the result of many people's efforts constantly reworked into a more general and more systematic form - so that what is esoteric information at one point can become part of the undergraduate curriculum a few years later.

5. Related to this (i.e. related to 1 and 4) is the final need - and this is an essential one - which is to help in applying man-environment data to design and planning practice. Although practitioners often complain about the lack of data on man-environment relations which they might use, there is much more than they suspect - or even most researchers suspect. It is unknown, and remains unused because it is concealed by mountains of single pieces of information. The only way such data can be used in design is if it is linked into theoretical systems which are easy to know, remember and transmit and which are flexible enough to encompass a wide variety of human and environmental characteristics and viewpoints. The arguments among researchers essential to the progress of research are counter-productive for practitioners. In this connection the distinction between nomothetic and idiographic approaches becomes important. Designers stress the idiographic since each problem is in a sense unique; scientists tend to the nomothetic, generalizing for classes of phenomena. One can suggest that the traditional design stress on uniqueness is not good enough (it is one reason for man-environment studies), but on the other hand science tends to over-generalize and reduces differences due to culture, context and so on, yet the specifics of needs, ways of doing things etc. are terribly important as are the perceptible characteristics of things. Thus both generalization and specificity are needed and a major question is - what degree of each?

These general requirements for a theory, then have one theme in common - the need to systematize, condense, combine, reveal pattern and regularity. This then suggests the need to specify the type of theory we need. This is the subject of the next section.

2. <u>What theory</u>?

In this section I will try to specify in somewhat more detail (while remaining general) some of the characteristics which a theory for man–environment relations will need to possess.

The first and possibly the most important point is that any theory must have design implications or consequences. Since I believe that the most important characteristics of design relate to space organization this means primarily that such a theory must have spatial implications. However, since the mechanisms linking people and environments are multiple, there may also be consequences relating to the nature of materials, control of the thermal, acoustic, lighting, etc. environments, color or whatever, as well as those physical elements which relate to social environments of various sorts. This basic and fundamental requirement may mean rethinking the implications of much existing work which we now use, since much of it does <u>not</u> have such design implications. (8) Parenthetically this will mean that we need to know what work there is and make it accessible and available and such stocktaking is, therefore, an essential first step in any systematic theory building. Some design implications may emerge as a result of theory itself, but some pieces of work will inevitably need to be replicated with new questions in mind – questions related to the physical environment. This may, in some cases, require retesting laboratory studies in real life settings and vice-versa, applying a wide range of methods and approaches to the material, evaluating existing and historical environments and so on.

Regarding laboratory studies consider one example related to psychology. It soon becomes apparent when one tries to apply perception studies to environmental perception that much of it is not directly useful – both because of the unnatural conditions in the laboratory compared to people freely active in the environment and also because most experiments are on <u>one</u> sense modality (with many modalities not studied at all) and very little work available on how the different senses work together – whether they are additive, multiplicative, whether they cancel out or whatever. This also applies to other variables, generally, and how they work in combination rather than singly. For example, regarding the fundamental question of the importance of the designed environment on human behavior, mood, satisfaction and so on we need to know whether the direct and indirect, the physical and social environment, spatial and aspatial components all work together or against each other, complement, cancel out or whatever. And also how the <u>context</u> affects the effects.

There are of course, very difficult questions. How then can we get to them as efficiently and quickly as possible? One way, and I have argued for this before, is to use a very broad sample. A single sample, or even set of examples, a single cross-section is not enough. We need a representative sampling of environments, ideally, a sample of all possible environments, behaviors, value systems, definitions of environmental quality, ways of doing things – and in real life situations. This is necessary so that we can understand how and why people behave the way they do, how they shape environments – and how environments affect them. We need to trace regularities, patterns, differences, constancy and change to do this. We need to get the range of environments, of people, of their characteristic behaviors, and also a range of theories of behavior. A theory must, then be broadly valid cross-culturally in time and in space. It must assume a wide variety of environmental and specific expressions, behaviors, etc. This has very important philosophical and methodological implications. (9) Theory also needs to be applied and be applicable in so far as is at all possible at all scales - or as many as possible so that continuities and commonalities from region to room can be traced and one could then concentrate on the differences.

There are some problems inherent in enlarging our sample in the way described above and, as it were, working semi-inductively from existing work and starting with both existing and past environments.

One of these problems concerns the difficulty of identifying the goals and objectives embodied in various environmental solutions. Yet in order to derive criteria and hypotheses which can be tested (through experiment, observation or those natural experiments called designs) the successes and failures of projects must be in terms of the objectives set.

Another problem (which also affects interdisciplinary work) lies in the difficulty of identifying the methodologies used as well as the specific theoretical orientation, i.e. the variability of results of various pieces of work may be due to epistemological differences rather than to "real" variability. This of course, means examining the underlying theoretical and paradigmatic assumptions - and hence the next section of the paper which examines the models used in man-environment studies.

A Models

Each conceptual framework, based, as it is, on underlying concepts and philosophical premises, orders the world differently. It leads to a model of reality which, in a way, is a self-fulfilling prophecy. If one takes a specific view of the world it tends to "behave" accordingly. This has been called the "epistemological snare" and makes it necessary to identify and look at a number of models. This very identification in itself involves implicit definitions of the environment, implicit views of man, but the very process of listing and briefly examining a variety of models should be useful.

Ideally, the advantages and disadvantages of each model should be tested against the specifications for a theory described so far, and what these various models have in common, wherein they differ and so on should be identified.

In principle, this should lead to the development of new larger models ("meta-models"). This is, in fact, the main need - it is important to reduce the number of models in the same way as the number of separate pieces of data need to be "reduced" but this needs to be done so as not to destroy or lose any models - all of which should be subsumed in the metamodels.

I do not pretend this will happen here in this paper, but a first step, and an important one, in getting at theory is a <u>survey</u> of models and alternative approaches. In terms of the three general man-environment interaction questions it seems to be possible to identify at least the following models, which will be discussed generally and briefly. Examples, when given, are merely to show that these models have been used at least once. There is no intention of an exhaustive literature review in this connection.

1. Perception Based

These begin with the notion that perception is the essential mechanism linking people and environments. Since one must perceive problems and opportunities before they can be evaluated and decisions made, I have taken this view in several articles Most work on complexity in the environment, landscape, and environmental preference, much geographical work on perception of hazard, of opportunity, of perceived landscape etc. is based on this model. The notion of "filters" which I have stressed (i.e. cultural effects in environmental perception) also belong to this group. One problem is the lack of immediate application to design. Another, and more serious, is too general a use of the term "perception". It seems important to distinguish betweenperceptual and associational/symbolic aspects and also perceptual, cognitive and evaluative aspects.

2. Cognitive And Image-Based

While implicitly admitting the importance of perception, these models stress the cognitive processes which follow - or precede. They concentrate on the mental maps and images formed, how they distort "reality", how they relate to cues and features in the environment and how images in turn, affect behavior and decision. To be classified as part of this approach are all learning-based models. These stress how people learn to use the environment and thus how they build up knowledge of the environment, mental maps and images (e.g. Golledge; EDRA 3 Cognitive Seminar) and consequently how environments can be designed as fields for learning (Studer, Fatouros). Another interpretation of cognitive models is one which I have stressed - how do various spatial forms and environmental domains correspond to the cognitive categories used by people.

3. Behavior Setting Models

These have, since EDRA 2, become important and influential. They start with the problem of the effect of the environment on behavior, having moved from environmental determinism through the unimportance of the physical environment to the environment as inhibiting, facilitating, or neutral (10) and the environment as catalyst (Wells). This approach led to the notion of a setting for behavior (Barker, Gump, et.al.), and can be seen together with Goffman's dramatic analogy. It has been used to study hospitals, (Willems, et.al.) offices, (Duffy) and other environments. Implicit is the notion that people behave differently in different settings (and in different roles).

4. Environment As Communication, Non-Verbal Communication, Symbolism

Given that people behave differently in different settings, we can interpret the environment as providing cues for behavior - i.e. communicating. There is, in fact, a body of work on the communicative function of the environment - space as communication (Hall), the notion of coding and decoding and problems when codes are misunderstood (DeLong in fact argues that "environment as communication" generally can be seen as the generic model for man-environment relations); non-verbal communication generally; symbolism etc. These notions all link up. For example, Hall's fixed feature, semi-fixed feature and informal (nonfixed feature) aspects relate to Rosenthal's studies on the effects of laboratories on experimental results, i.e. the environment affects behavior both directly and indirectly. Gestures, body postures etc., are then part of the non-fixed feature environment (Hall, Efron, Birdwhistell, etc.). Clothing, furniture, etc. can then be seen as semi-fixed feature while walls, space organization, etc. can be seen as fixed feature - all interacting and forming a system, thus linking social and physical environments through symbols and communication.

5. Competence And Adaptation

Given the underlying systemic notion of a two-way interaction of people and environment as well as the evidence on the importance of the involvement of organisms (both animals and people) with their environment the notion of competence inevitably comes up. Based on White's concept this has been developed theoretically by Perin. This relates to personal and socio-cultural variables, previous experience and the notion of open-ended or indeterminate design (which has been proposed by Weeks, myself, Habraken, and others) as well as personalization etc. (Sommer and many others).

6. Information Flow Models

These conceive of the environment as facilitating or inhibiting information flows between people. They have mainly been developed in rather abstract terms in planning (Meier, Webber, Deutsch, etc.) and have been used in geography (Goodey), but can be seen as implicitly influential and used on smaller scales in studies of offices (office landscapes), schools (open schools), medical facilities etc., and, more generally as important in dealing with density and privacy in terms of controlling unwanted communication (as I have recently done).

7. Ecological Models

This can be seen in terms of an approach - not man and environment but man in environment, and systemic, affecting many other models indirectly. This has been important in proposed definitions of the environment (for example by Lawton and Ittelson), and has been central to much research, for example in behavior settings, (see model 3 above). Related is the notion of habitat selection which I have stressed and the stress on real life studies, rather than laboratory situations which has affected methodology (for example Lipman; Willems and Rausch; anthropological methods generally).

8. Ethological Models

These can be seen in several ways. Firstly, they have affected methodology through

the use of ethological techniques (related to 7 above) (Esser, Ittelson, et.al.
etc.) and the notion of studying the same species (man) in different environments,
both natural and experimental. Secondly, they have been important in introducing
concepts such as behavioral sinks, personal space, crowding, etc. (Calhoun, Sommer,
Esser, etc.). Thirdly, these models have been influential by introducing spatial
concepts, primarily those generally termed territoriality and relating these to
dominance etc. (e.g. Sundstrom and Altman, Esser, Carson and Pastalan, etc.) I
have used an ethological spatial approach in elaborating a five-element model of
the human use of space. (11) (12)

9. Evolutionary Models

These begin with the notion of constancy — that people are as they always have been
and that there may be problems and dangers with certain environmental arrangements
and some forms of human adaptation (e.g. Dubos). In this view, important insights
about human characteristics, predispositions and limits can be obtained from the
physical and social environment in which man evolved (Boyden, Tiger and Fox). Related is the developmental model — of ontogeny reflecting phylogeny, which relates
to 2 above (e.g. cognitive Seminar at EDRA 3, applications of Piaget, etc.). Also
it can be seen tackled in terms of future evolution. (Esser, Calhoun).

10. Socio-Cultural Models

These accept the premise that the important thing for design (within certain
limits) is the specific way in which given groups of people define and solve problems. Culture is the important mediating variable in determining how things are
done and consequently the form of the environment (Hall, myself, King, Esber, etc.)
This relates to values, images, choices, preferences etc. (13)

11. Preference In Environmental Quality

This model begins with the notion implicit in several models already described,
that by studying people's preference structures we can understand their decisions
and choices they make. Within the constraints of economics, knowledge etc. it
is assumed that environmental quality as defined and perceived will be the criterion by which people make choices. I have used this approach in several studies
and it is implicit in many others.

12. Performance-based Models

These tend to be more "hard" — and try to study performance under various sets of
conditions — noise, crowding, overload, etc. They tend to be empirically oriented
but implicit is a theoretical model based on physical sciences rather than on
ethological or anthropological approaches.

There are surely a number of models which have been omitted, and some of those
listed are implicit ones, based on my interpretation of the work, but two things
should be clear:
  a. There is quite a range of models used.
  b. They are not mutually exclusive — in fact in writing this section it was

almost impossible to avoid cross-referencing (although this was avoided as much as possible).

This suggests that most approaches already use more than one model. In fact, this is the major point to be made - we need all, or most of these models. Thus, in addition to asking what are their advantages and disadvantages, we need to consider what they have in common and wherein they differ and in what ways they can be combined into "meta-models", (or a "meta-model"). Such a meta-model would be the start of a theory, if it could begin to answer the three basic questions - for individuals and groups, in different cultures and periods, at different scales.

That many models are involved in any useful interpretation can most easily be shown through examples. While this is all that I will do in this report, it would be useful, in fact, essential, in the long run to consider several additional questions. These are:

a. What are the relative advantages and disadvantages of these models in terms of the discussion earlier in this paper?
b. What do these models have in common and conversely, wherein do they differ; what are the inconsistencies?
c. How are they used together now and from that, how can they most usefully be combined to form meta-models?

Question (a) will require a detailed analysis of the numbers of studies, identifying the underlying models and comparing their effectiveness. In a sense questions (b) and (c) are basically one question, since it is through an analysis of how they work together now and where they overlap that the outlines of a meta-model will begin to emerge. Both these things I hope to report at a later stage.

Let us, as a preliminary, merely consider one example and show how all, or most models, have a contribution to make and must be used together.

1. If we consider a part of a city as an urban setting, we then find that habitat selection (where people live) is an ecological-ethological concept. This is linked to environmental quality and preference. This latter concept is multidimensional, but involves a perceptual aspect (e.g. complexity) as well as symbolic (status, preference for nature, proximity of services etc.). These differential preferences involve cultural variables while the migration and decision-making involve cognitive aspects which also enter into the learning of the new area (as well as the areas among which one chooses - mental maps). This then links once again with ethological concepts in terms of home range, core area, etc. There are also socio-cultural variables related to clustering of people with like characteristics and preferences, i.e. of people homogeneous along certain dimensions. This then relates to notions of stress and sensory/social over-load relating to definitions of privacy, density, etc.; such stress being reduced by agreement on rules, manners, and behavior. These agreements are also embodied in space organization, buildings and other artefacts, and thus linked to nonverbal communication and the behavior-setting concept. Environmental preference in terms of proximity or separation of facilities also relates to traffic and transportation, and hence time-budgets and activity systems. The speed and mode of travel is then linked to perceptual model (complexity) and also to learning models and so on. This example could both be

elaborated and expanded to include all models in much more detail, but the principal point has been made.

Thus we can dimly see a theory (or metamodel) emerging. The perception of the world is essential before evaluation, but is affected by images, values and expectations. These affect evaluation even more, and evaluation is essential for decisions regarding habitat selection or design. These are thus closely related to images, ideas, and also involve activity and feelings of competence.

These are related to experience, and thus, learning and they are also affected by culture and embedded in culture (and its values and images) thus also affecting behavior and rules. The behavior settings which constitute the given environment provide cues for behavior (non-verbal communication) and the environment is thus a catalyst rather than merely facilitating or inhibiting (in geographical terms, it is probabilistic rather than merely possibilitic) and so on.

B. Issues

The example above and the discussion of it in effect begin to overlap the domain of what might be called issues. By this I mean the consideration of questions or problem areas from various points of view and perspectives, using not only a variety of disciplines and data but also a variety of models and theoretical approaches.

Once again this is most easily done through examples. A number suggest themselves, although none will be developed in detail.
  (i)   The nature and meaning of space and how people use it. (14)
  (ii)   Crowding, density, privacy etc.
  (iii) Complexity
         (ii) and (iii) are linked and combine and can best be tackled by
         applying a variety of ethological, social-psychological, anthropological,
         historical, perceptual, information, theory and other approaches and
         models.
  (iv)   Preference and evaluation of environments
         (iii) and (iv) are also related, and by being considered in this multi-
         faceted and multi-model way this link could be greatly clarified.
  (v)   Environment as communication
  (vi)   Effect of environment on people generally (direct and indirect).
  (vii) A specific environment – whether school, housing, urban area analyzed
         from the different points of view.

This is basically a "problem-oriented" approach. Any given issue is exposed to all the available evidence and different ways of looking at it, and is, in effect, "triangulated"(as in radio-location).

In this respect, the two approaches, through models and through issues, have some common characteristics. In light of this, and in light of the fact that they are mutually enlightening, a case can be made for using both.

In each case, one should start with the historical and cross-cultural data, using existing environments and case studies as the point of entry, as already discussed. By thus starting with evaluation, two objectives will be achieved. Firstly, the broad base will be provided which is essential for a consideration of the constancy-change argument. Secondly, it will help designers who traditionally use case study approaches in their "research", and would also introduce the notion of feedback, which is the weakest link in any practice-oriented research. Only through feedback studies of design seen as hypotheses and natural experiments can we get a cumulative body of knowledge.

Using this approach then, and by using it broadly, we will simultaneously be evaluating the evidence as well as the models and approaches. Since we would be considering empirical and theoretical aspects together, working at both models and themes, a theory would emerge which would achieve the objectives described - linking separate pieces of work, linking approaches and disciplines, linking theory and design. It would also begin to reveal underlying regularities, patterns, agreement and disagreement. (This approach has problems similar to those described on p. 10 - in fact, problems common to any approach relying on a large body of existing work).

It is clear that in the same way that I had previously argued for an eclectic approach to methodology, I am now arguing for an electic and open approach to the construction of theory.

Regarding research, the emergence of theory might be enough initially, but regarding practice (and partly teaching) some additional problems would still have to be faced. These are partly off the subject of this paper, but need briefly to be raised. The research-practice gap will persist even when the information is simplified and clarified through rules and theory. It will be caused by problems of the form in which this information is provided and the easy retrieval of information (requiring new information systems). In addition there are more basic problems. Research is more abstract by its very nature. Researchers have more time available and are not working against the kinds of deadlines that practitioners are working against. At the same time the members of the two groups have very different world views; they use different language and terminology, which affects both the communication in teams and the understanding of the literature. They have different orientations. They often represent different personality types. In effect, these latter problems are typical of those between different groups, different cultures and sub-cultures generally. These require both institutional changes in the design professions and some value changes on the part of both designers and researchers. But the type of theory which I have been outlining should at least begin the process of making man-environment studies more useable - by beginning to provide information in a more useable and more easily transmitted form.

References

(1) Altman,I.,et.al.,THE ECOLOGY OF HOME ENVIRONMENTS,Washington,D.C. HEW Office of Education, Bureau of Research, January, 1972.

(2) Abler, R.,et.al.,SPATIAL ORGANIZATION, Englewood Cliffs, New Jersey, Prentice-Hall, 1971, p.4.

(3) Chapin, F.S.,"Selected Theories of Urban Growth and Structure," in Bourne, L.S. (ed.), INTERNAL STRUCTURE OF THE CITY, New York, Oxford, 1971, p. 141 ff.

(4) Abler,R.,et.al.,SPATIAL ORGANIZATION,Englewood Cliffs, N.J.,Prentice-Hall, 1971 pp.12-15; see also Oliver,R.& Hornsby,J.,"On Equivalence" in Adams,P.(ed.) LANGUAGE IN THINKING, Harmondsworth, Penguin Books, 1972, p. 306-320.

(5) Rapoport, A.,"A Plea for Interdisciplinary Design for the Environment", A.A. QUARTERLY, Vol. 3, No. 4, October, 1971.

(6) Rapoport, A.,"A Plea for Interdisciplinary Design for the Environment", A.A. QUARTERLY, Vol. 3, No. 4, October, 1971.

(7) Timms,D.,THE URBAN MOSAIC,Cambridge,Cambridge University Press,1971, p.44-46.

(8) One such difference between design and science-oriented theory (idiographic/ nomothetic) is apparent from Wohlwill's paper in this symposium. From the designer's viewpoint the differences in perceiving, reacting to and evaluating physical variables are precisely what leads to specific designs. These subjective factors become more rather than less significant. It is still important to relate the subjective (perceived) environment to the objective one and to generalize at certain levels.

(9) Rapoport,A.,"An Approach to the Study of Environmental Quality",EDRA 1;"The Design Professions and The Behavioral Sciences",A.A. QUARTERLY, Vol.1,No.1, 1969;"Some Thoughts on the Methodology of Man-Environment Studies" INTERNATIONAL JOURNAL OF ENVIRONMENTAL STUDIES, (in press).

(10) Rapoport,A.,"Environment and People" in Rapoport,A.(ed.) AUSTRALIA AS HUMAN SETTING, Sydney, Angus and Robertson, 1972, p.12-13; Barker,R.,"The Nature of the Environment", JOURNAL OF SOCIAL ISSUES, Vol. 22, 1963.

(11) Rapoport,A.,"Some Perspectives on the Human Organization and Use of Space", paper given to the Annual Meeting of The Australian and N.Z. Association of Social Anthropologists, Melbourne, May, 1972 (mimeo.).

(12) Rapoport,A.,"Australian Aborigines and the Definition of Place", EDRA 3.

(13) This links with fn. 7 and Wohwill's paper in this symposium.

(14) Rapoport,A.,"The Study of Spatial Quality",JOURNAL OF AESTHETIC EDUCATION,Vol. 4,No.4,Oct.1970;Rapoport,A.,"Some Perspectives of the Human Organization and Use of Space".

Raymond G. Studer
Professor and Director
Division of Man-Environment Relations
College of Human Development
The Pennsylvania State University
University Park, Pennsylvania 16802

Abstract

The relationship between environmental-behavioral research and environmental design
has not been adequately documented. Some of the problems, prospects and technical
resources linking these two domains are explicated. Two inimical world views, i.e.
interventionist and non-interventionist, are identified as problematic for this
applied task. Behavioral technology and behavioral ecology are explicated as
offering complementary resources in the design of artificial systems. An environmental design and management strategy is explicated as an instrument to synthesize
relevant aspects of behavioral research. These and other issues addressed lead to
the arguments for and the outlines of a behavioral ecosystems technology.

Introduction

The systematic study of human behavior and social structure as these relate to the
day-to-day physical environment is a domain of research activity with a limited
history. Although lacking on established research tradition, this area of inquiry
has produced a body of "findings" (as they are guardedly called) which document
empirically derived relationships between man and his physical surroundings. The
expectation has been that the physical designer, armed with this empirically based
information would surely act upon it to effect a higher order of environmental organization; but this has not been the case. Why are these research findings so
difficult to apply to environmental design? The behavioral scientist is not typically concerned with such issues, and research in environmental psychology and
sociology per se implies neither the commitment nor the means (methods) to facilitate the application of empirical findings to environmental design processes. The
subject of this paper is behavioral euthenics--the prospects for a technology of
man-environment systems design and management.

The proposition that designed environments should respond to--be dependently related to--human rather than other classes of requirements, is one readily embraced
by all concerned (which is about everybody); thus our interest in environmental-
behavioral research. Attempts to technically implement this commitment--to apply
behavioral findings to the design of human settings--expose a discouraging array of
discontinuities in the behavioral sciences. These discontinuities and conflicts
may or may not impede the development of normal science per se (1), but they do
produce horrendous conceptual problems for the environmental designer. The behavioral scientist's problems now become the environmental designer's problems. Some
of the intrinsic difficulties encountered in collaborative efforts between behavioral scientist and environmental designer have been developed elsewhere (2).
There is perhaps a more fundamental problem which requires resolution before the

136

relevance of particular behavioral "findings" to the design task can be documented
and before the appropriate linkages between the domains of research and design can
be consummated.

The issue requiring attention can perhaps best be identified by depicting two world
views: that of the Non-Interventionist (e.g. certain ecologists, ethologists,
ethnologists), and that of the Interventionist (e.g. certain behavioral and other
technologists). The Non-Interventionist sees man as an integral part of all natural
living systems although unique in certain dimensions. Since man is a product of
natural evolutionary processes, his behavior and social structure are more or less
"natural", and by implication ultimately ecologically sound, if only allowed to
flourish. The research task is to discover and systematically describe the immutable man-environment relations--or states and systems of them--in the finest tradition of descriptive science. The designer holding this view attempts to accommodate and hopefully nurture these discovered relations. This perspective is
implicitly optimistic regarding man's nature as an extension of other living systems
and his evolutionary course. The principal threat is seen as technology and intervention generally (the difficulty here being that technology is also a "natural"
product of man). The more primitive a culture the more viable it is likely to be
seen, and exercises in futuristics are anathema to this world view. Man's short-
term adaptive capacities are viewed as highly limited and the interdependencies
among humans and between these and the impinging environment operate within small
tolerances. In short, this view is quite conservative regarding intervention and
change in human systems, i.e., "nature knows best".

The Interventionist perspective, while sharing certain tenets with the first (both,
for example, place high value on rigorous empirical research), contrasts with it in
several important ways. This view is basically pessimistic regarding man's capacity
to self-correct dysfunctional tendencies through "natural" processes. It sees man
as a partially evolved organism, not completely rational yet certainly able to bias
his evolutionary course. He is also seen as highly adaptable in his behavior.
Technology is seen not as a threat but as the means to survival, and human problems
are dealt with as they arise, optimistically employing the appropriate technological
means. Somewhat ahistorical in its outlook, this view tends to embrace utopian or
futuristic speculations as a necessary exercise in charting a course toward an appropriate future. Systematic intervention and change are thus seen as both necessary and possible. Experimental rather than naturalistic research paradigms
guide the search for functional rather than discursive models of man-environment
systems.

Although grossly overgeneralized, the above depicts two extant views of human reality which would seem to depict inimical approaches to the analysis, design and
management of man-environment systems. This is indeed the case, for they clearly
generate disparate strategies for dealing with problems, or even classifying a
human situation as a problem. Each of the strategies generated will in turn suggest which paradigms, methods or findings in behavioral science are seen as relevant to the design task. We thus find researchers and designers alike committed to
particular, often divergent, modes of dealing with man-environment problems. In
their most stereotyped form these two seemingly antithetical perspectives can be
compared somewhat as follows:

Non-Interventionist	Interventionist
- conservative view of intervention and change	- radical view of intervention and change
- pessimistic regarding technology	- optimistic regarding technology
- embraces historical perspective	- deemphasizes historical perspective
- rejects futuristic and utopian analyses	- embraces futuristic and utopian analyses
- optimistic regarding human survival via "natural" processes	- pessimistic regarding human survival via "natural" processes
- naturalistic research methods	- experimental research methods
- seeks discursive models	- seeks functional models
- predictions based on forecasts from present data	- predictions are self-realizing and based on "if . . . then" relations
- human organism capable of fairly limited behavioral adaptations	- human organism capable of highly adaptive behaviors (malleable)
- discovery of man-environment relations	- design of man-environment relations
- sees both animal and human behavior as lawful	- sees both animal and human behavior as lawful

Each of these views of the problems of applied environmental research and design embodies principles essential to our survival and well-being. On the other hand, comprehensive implementation of either would surely lead to disaster. That is, both non-intervention and incompetent intervention involve comparable risks. The mood of the culture in this historical situation is to put down the technologist in favor of the ecologist, i.e., "stop everything" until we understand all the implications. This sort of ecological rhetoric, as opposed to technical solutions, has pretty much run its course. In the interest of getting on with it, let us review some of the positive and negative implications of the above, ostensibly divergent perspectives.

The evidence is in regarding the dangers of technological intervention in a number of living and non-living systems (3). The second- and third-order effects of physical technology on human biological systems are becoming dramatically felt. Similarly the unintended effects of technology on human social and behavior systems is, while perhaps less well documented, quite apparent (4). Beyond its negative side effects, remedial technological intervention is often simply ineffective in dealing with a particular problem under analysis; in which case we get the costs without any benefits. The demand for more physical technology to solve problems created by physical technology provides the most telling example of this technological impotence, e.g., the energy conversion and consumption of natural resources outweigh the ecological benefits. Indeed, we may be reaching a plateau, if not the limits, of physical technology. Social/behavioral intervention as now practiced often embodies the same problems, i.e., the strategies either don't work or they affect contingent systems in unexpected ways.

In summary, then, we do not appear to have sufficient technical understanding of the interdependencies amongst most man-environment systems to understand and isolate dysfunctional aspects (problem boundaries), or to predict the direct and indirect effects on contingent systems. The question is whether this leads us to an atechnological posture or toward the development of new technologies capable of dealing with problems of interest.

While the risks of embracing a technological (interventionist) perspective have been generally acknowledged, those related to the ecological (non-interventionist) perspective have not been. If the non-interventionist perspective sees human systems as extensions of--as interdependent with--all natural systems, then man's place and the subtleties of these interdependencies in the ecosystem has not been adequately documented. Human biological and behavioral processes are clearly extensions of lower animal forms and similar in many important dimensions. Man's advanced evolutionary state, however, requires a different kind of analysis (hardly a profound observation even from a behaviorist). One evidence for man's uniqueness is the unfortunate incompatibility of his behavior with other natural systems which raises the question: what is a natural behavioral state and which social structure is more natural than another? Is it man's "nature" to foul his environment, kill his own and other species, squander scarce life-supporting resources, poison himself? Many ethologically oriented researchers insist that certain behaviors, e.g. aggression, are residual manifestations of more primitive evolutionary states--which may be true. On the other hand if we assume that whatever man does is natural, and therefore valuable to survival of the ecosystem, then we indeed have no solvable problems. We can merely set about to study human processes (employing naturalistic methods of course) ostensibly self-correcting toward ecological stability via the biological, psychological and social demise of masses of humans and other life forms. If, on the other hand, we see man's behavior as incompatible with survival, a vigorous intervention strategy seems mandatory. While the negative side effects of technological intervention are well understood in some domains, in others these are no better understood by the ecologist than the technologist. Empirical knowledge is thus replaced by a <u>belief</u> that intervention can only make things worse!

What all of this comes down to is that we are faced with two equally unacceptable alternatives. We will, of course, adopt neither approach <u>per se</u>. We will either muddle through, randomly applying and resisting technological intervention, or we will move toward a technical understanding of ecologically based human system design and chart a course for a viable future.

Ecological Technology and Human Systems

What the ecologist is saying is that what appear to be somewhat independent random events in both living and non-living systems are in fact highly systematic, and maintained via a subtle and tenuous network of interdependencies. A system has been defined as " a whole which is a whole by virtue of the interdependence of its parts" (5). Disruption at critical levels has been dramatically documented in both biological and physical systems. Ecologically-oriented psychologists argue that behavior systems are subject to similar disruptions which also threaten human viability. In the sense that survival is directly dependent upon effective behavior patterns, this is probably the case. Ecological psychology and behavioral technology thus find themselves on an apparent collision course. However, the opportunity and necessity for an important synthesis of these seems apparent (6).

In order to understand the issues involved we must recognize the existence of two classes of phenomena, i.e., natural and artificial (7,8); human existence is simultaneously dependent upon both. Herbert Simon has attempted to deal with distinctions between artificial and natural phenomena. He points out that the realization of artificial systems involves synthesis or design; the concern is with "how things ought to be in order to attain goals and to function" (7). The design of artificial systems, then, involves normative as well as descriptive issues. We cannot maintain the traditional exclusion of normative considerations (as opposed to description of how things are) when we move from natural to artificial phenomena--from analysis to synthesis.

Artificial systems are organized and maintained by man in response to human goals; natural systems are not so organized. We are and have for some time been committed to the organization of artificial, i.e., goal-directed, human systems. The complexities of these--the intensity and distribution of dysfunctions within several classes of them, e.g. economic, political, physical--produces a design problem of immense proportions. To reverse critical environmental-organismic tendencies requires recognition of both the artificial nature of contemporary human settings and the technical dimensions of their design. The only issue is how we can bring our technical knowledge to bear on this design task. Few, if any, human problems emerge as discretely biological, psychological or social. For example, we now understand that high incidence of a particular disease (a biological dysfunction) can only be understood and affected through an analysis of the social, economic, physical and other environments (9). That is, environmental alteration in response to human dysfunction generally involves more than one system and necessarily involves analysis of several; such is the ecological reality. The decision to intervene--to design and implement a new system state--must be conditioned by mandatory ecological principles: e.g. realization of appropriate: 1) interrelationships amongst the various artificial man-environment systems, 2) intrarelationships within these and 3) interfaces between artificial and natural systems to maintain states of both within tolerable levels of dissonance.

So much for man, the ecosystem and biological survival. The remaining comments will deal with but a modest subset of such issues. They will focus on an approach to environment-behavior systems design and maintenance intended to accommodate both ecological and technological principles essential to a viable state of human well-being in the future.

Human problems are ultimately behavioral problems requiring behavioral solutions. Attempts to implement findings, principles and methods from the behavioral sciences have been notably unsuccessful, and the difficulty might lie in either or both of two areas: 1) environmental problems are not formulated so as to admit realistic (empirically verifiable) behavioral solutions, or 2) behavioral data, principles and methods are not in a form relevant to the environmental design task. Historically we did not presume to directly apply the laws of mechanics to the design of physical structure. Before these resources from physical science could be found useful in the practical problems of shelter, technologies had to be developed, and it was these that eventually facilitated general applicability. In addressing problems of environmental-behavioral design we are clearly not drawing upon a mature science such as physics, but there are certain developmental analogies.

We are in need of two kinds of enterprises: 1) environmental-behavioral <u>research</u> and 2) environmental-behavioral <u>technology</u>, and we should not confuse these two do- mains of development. Basic research in environmental psychology and sociology seeks to expand our general knowledge base. As such these may contribute to but certainly will not <u>per se</u> directly produce an applied science useful to environ- mental designers. Descriptive studies of the kind most prevalent in current research efforts attempt to document, e.g. the attitudes, preferences, propensities, values, of a particular population vis-a-vis a particular environment. Even when executed with consummate skill such studies have limited generalizability to other settings. Before such findings become valuable to design decisions they must be demonstrated as generalizable across many populations <u>and</u> many environments. Moreover, since the designer must necessarily make "if . . . then" kinds of predictions (i.e., if environment <u>e</u> is implemented, behavior <u>b</u> will emerge), he is understandably inter- ested in <u>functional</u> rather than discursive models of man-environment phenomena. Little of the current research in man-environment relations purports to incorporate appropriate levels of rigor to assert functional, predictive models on the grounds that we as yet know too little of real, complex human settings. This may be true but is of little consolation to the designer who must make predictions (or guess) daily regarding the effects of his decisions on human outcomes. In any event, it is fairly clear that it is the <u>methods</u> of behavioral research and <u>not</u> specific findings which must be incorporated into the environmental design process.

There is a research paradigm and a related technology the elaboration of which can be demonstrated as having direct relevance to environmental design and management. The plan for the remainder of this paper is to explicate elements of: 1) behavioral technology, 2) behavioral ecology and 3) a resultant systems oriented environmental design and management strategy which utilizes these and other relevant areas in the behavioral sciences.

Behavioral Technology and Environmental Design

Many researchers concur that environmental design and management should be directed toward the realization of an appropriate state of <u>congruence</u> between environmental and behavioral structures (10,11). The lack of such congruence in a particular setting constitutes a problem to be solved. Such an objective implies that neither system must conform to nor form the other. Rather the objective is to realize an environment-behavior <u>ensemble</u> which fulfills the goals of the human setting under analysis within the constraints of the external environment affected.

Any decision to intervene in a human setting is occasioned by a behavioral dysfunc- tion, i.e., certain behaviors <u>are</u> occurring which are incompatible with the goals of the setting, and/or certain behaviors are <u>not</u> occurring which are required by the goals of the setting. Clearly any design problem (as contrasted with a research problem) implies the need to change and maintain a behavioral system in a new state, otherwise the setting would not require intervention. The principles and tech- niques of a technology of behavior are thus central to environmental design and man- agement processes. The empirical and theoretical basis for a behavioral technology grew out of the laboratory using various organisms emitting small samples of behav- ior. The experimental analysis of behavior sometimes called operant psychology has produced profound and incontrovertible evidence for systematically relating aspects of environmental structure to observed behaviors (12)   We are now witnessing an ever widening application of these principles in applied human settings (13).

The methods for bringing operant behavior under control of elements of the environment involve an analysis of the spatial/temporal relations between behavior and its (positive or negative) consequences. These consequences, i.e., reinforcers, affect the probabilities of the behaviors recurrence. Behavior change and maintenance is effected through the spatial/temporal organization and management of the contingencies of reinforcement operating in a particular environment. Another important area of behavior analysis of particular relevance to environmental design is that of stimulus control (14). When particular behaviors are iteratively reinforced in the presence of particular stimuli, these stimuli come to elicit those behaviors in the future. The process is discrimination learning and successful behavior in the designed environment depends heavily upon the participants' development of a complex system of discriminations. Environmental elements acquire "meaning" when discrimination of them leads to positively reinforcing events or the absence of aversive events. Aspects of new environments thus come to support new behaviors through this dynamic. Behavior change and maintenance via acquisition of stimulus control offers a direction for overcoming one of the intrinsic problems of environmental design, i.e., varying environmental propensities in aggregate populations. Evidence from the laboratory suggests that the environmental designer's task is not to discover (or guess at) what kind of human response to an environmental element is likely to occur. The task is rather to arrange environmental contingencies such that particular stimuli and behavior become functionally linked through discriminative learning. The environmental-behavioral relationship is thus designed and implemented, not discovered to exist prior to implementation of an environmental system. Attention to linguistic principles (15)   together with the techniques of discrimination learning identifies an approach to stimulus organization in which interpersonal response probabilities can be effectively developed in spite of widely varying ontogenies.

A central problem in behavioral accommodation is identifying a class of elements in the environment which are likely to have reinforcing potential. Any organism will attempt to stay in contact with, move toward, a positively reinforcing state; conversely, it will avoid or attempt to escape from an aversive state. In general the more effective behavior change strategy involves the identification and organization of positive reinforcers. Identifying the reinforcing potential of a population requiring alternative behavioral topographies becomes an important technical task for which we fortunately have effective strategies.

More cognitively-oriented behavioral scientists (16)   of course argue that humans do not respond moment-to-moment to environmental events as they are presented but anticipate--make certain predictions--regarding future environmental states and responses to them. People are said to have an internal dynamically organized "environmental model" or "template" which directs probable responses to environmental stimuli. This internalized environmental model represents a particular ontogeny (and phylogeny), a person's environmental representations and expectations; implicit therein is an individual's reinforcement potential, both positive and negative.

A great deal of current research in man-environment relations is involved in externalizing and assessing people's environmental propensities. The place of this research--the function of the methods involved vis-a-vis a behavior change strategy--is to reveal and define (and hopefully generalize) the probable reinforcing aspects of the participants' milieu. Strategies to reveal social and physical attitudes, preferences, expectations, beliefs, perceptions and cognitions (17,18) of a population must be seen as integral components of a behavioral change strategy (and thus environmental design) since they reveal both a population's behavioral goals and their reinforcement potential.

Behavioral technology is the application of operant principles developed in the experimental laboratory, two components of which require consideration: 1) contingency management and 2) stimulus control. These are the principal techniques effecting behavior change and maintenance. Contingency management simply involves arranging the environment such that the probabilities of reinforcing consequences are made contingent upon, increase as a function of, appropriate behaviors. As noted above, acquisition of stimulus control occurs when certain behaviors are iteratively reinforced in the presence of certain stimuli.

Behavior modification utilizing both contingency management and/or stimulus control involves the following sequential components (see Figure 1): 1) baseline analysis of environmental-behavioral structures, 2) development of new behavioral objectives, 3) manipulation of appropriate environmental structures (contingencies), 4) assessment of the new behavioral baseline, 5) iteration of 3 and 4. This well-documented behavior modification strategy clearly has application to a problem situation where environmental alteration is indicated. Systematic behavior modification is not accomplished in an "all or none" fashion. Research in human learning confirms that transformation from one complex state to another involves a series of intermediate states, i.e., behavioral shaping or successive approximation. Modifying behavior toward a viable or specified state, (e.g. stimulus control of certain features of the spatial environment via the acquisition of appropriate stimulus discriminations) involves multiple and varying presentations. Appropriate responses to complex, high-performance environments generally come about as an organism acquires increasingly complex repertories. An environment which reinforces such acquisitions is one which is constantly modified.

A program of extensive behavior change for most human settings appears an extremely complex enterprise. If entirely new repertories were required of all participants, the task would, of course, be impossible. Relative to the total behaviors emitted in a setting, the elements requiring modification represent but a small subset. Three functional elements are involved: 1) strengthening of extant requisite behaviors; 2) extinction of undesirable behaviors; and 3) shaping of new requisite behaviors. That is, some of the behaviors in extant repertories are assumed to remain, some are intensified and some are eliminated.

The above contains only the barest elements of a highly complex explication of the principles of behavior change and maintenance but they will suffice to document their relevance to environmental design. Environmental designers control either directly (e.g. physical stimuli) or indirectly (e.g. social stimuli) a number of variables which profoundly structure the kinds of contingencies which maintain present forms and could be organized to effect new forms of behavior. Because the above principles are not generally implemented in extant design processes, new environments--the organization of these contingencies--either exert a random and unexpected influence incommensurate with people's goals, or they exert little influence on the desired state of affairs. That is, every man-environment setting embodies a high potential for behavioral development which is realized only when the operating contingencies are understood and organized into an appropriate texture.

Behavioral Ecology and Environmental Design

Operant principles growing out of the experimental analysis of behavior have been extensively and successfully applied to human problems in a number of settings. A behavioral technology is not a remote, future eventuality but an established fact of life in the present, i.e., it is a technology in current use. The prospect of more comprehensive, larger-scale applications of this technology, however, raises serious questions which go beyond the obvious and popular ones, i.e., the who controls the controller syndrome. Behavioral technology as well as the laboratory science upon which it is based have typically focused upon limited repertoires of single organisms. The issue is whether this approach to behavior analysis and change is adequate to deal with larger populations emitting more complex behaviors. What is suggested is that this technology requires elaboration to include an ecological perspective.

One thing is quite certain; if Homo sapiens is to have a future, much less a viable one, it will be because he becomes an effective designer of artificial systems. His place in the ecosystem has been maintained at great expense to and through the tenacity of natural systems to survive. As we move toward the status of a planning culture and the systematic design of life sustaining artificial systems, we would do well to look to natural systems to provide the necessary analogues. Successful natural systems embody recurring powerful and pervasive principles which have been revealed through extensive, empirical and theoretical research (19).   Natural ecosystems, both living and non-living, exhibit such characteristics as heirarchical levels of complexity and subtle interdependencies among both elements and subsystems. These systems are open and the transfer of energy at the boundaries producing a dynamic adaptation to changing inputs; that is, they exhibit self-regulating behavior via intra- and inter-system feedback linkages.

Ecological behavioral analyses of human settings have documented similar characteristics (20,21,11).   Longitudinal studies of interpersonal behavior systems in "naturally occurring" environments have revealed a complexity of "system-like" interdependencies amongst individual behavioral repertories and between these and the environmental setting. The behavior setting is one in which sustained and recurring topographies are exhibited across a number of individuals in a number of situational contexts, e.g., the classroom, a baseball game, an opera. These behavior settings invariably operate within supporting environments which also exhibit consistent patterns. Operating out of slightly different research paradigms, other researchers have also identified system-like interdependencies which maintain stable interpersonal behavior networks and the mediation of these by supporting environmental elements and constraints (22).   In short, behavior settings have been documented as influencing, e.g., roles of participants; relationships amongst participants;

relationships amongst behaviors; numbers of participants; quantity and quality of behaviors emitted.

The importance of behavioral ecology to environmental design cannot be overstated, however, before it can become effective in this enterprise certain difficulties must be overcome, i.e., this area of research to date offers: 1) an inadequate functional explanation of behavior setting phenomena (as contrasted with a description of them), 2) observational techniques which are complex and extremely time-consuming, and 3) inadequate tools of analysis to make these phenomena tractable for design purposes. A functional explanation of behavior settings would describe the means by which the patterns of behavior are maintained within them. What "drives" the system and what constitutes the "glue" amongst constituent behavioral elements within it?

Anything like a complete explanation is considerably beyond the scope of this paper; however, an operant analysis is predicted to provide useful insights. Behavior settings can be viewed as the building blocks of social/physical environments of a culture or subculture. A behavior setting by definition assumes that a system of behaviors is organized around implicitly or explicitly (probably implicitly) defined goals. These goals generate a system of interdependencies amongst the behaviors emitted. By inference these goals also define the number of functioning actors (human units) which can be or must be accommodated by the setting (see overmanned and undermanned aspects of behavior settings). The linkage, or "glue" could be appropriately described as the contingencies amongst the behaviors (social stimuli) and/or other elements of the behavior setting environment (e.g. physical stimuli). That is, the functional networks can no doubt be analyzed as systems of contingencies. While the behavioral ecologists argue for an ecological perspective, they have not really integrated their arguments into a general systems format. But more importantly they have inexplicably not implemented the tools of systems analysis to deal with behavioral ecosystems phenomena. The question which this raises is whether such settings merely exhibit "system-like" (6) behavior or can they truly be described as systems! If the latter is being asserted then the tools of systems modeling would seem to follow as an integral aspect of behavioral ecology.

The argument being made here is that the principles and methods of behavioral ecology should be incorporated into or synthesized with those of behavioral technology to form the underpinnings of an environmental design and management strategy. However, if behavioral ecosystems are to be effectively analyzed, the change agents, whether they be environmental designers or behavioral technologists, will require more powerful monitoring techniques and tools of analysis which will render behavior setting structures, constraints, functional relations and interdependencies tractable (in a reasonable amount of time). But analysis of behavior setting phenomena is clearly not the only issue. To approach human problems through environmental design requires that behavior settings be (partially or wholly) designed as well. Some behavior settings may indeed exist but operate at ineffective levels in terms of a population's goals. Others may exist but be antithetical to these goals, e.g. the behavior setting: "lynching". A behavioral technology provides the appropriate means of implementing new or phasing out undesirable behavior settings. In short, the principles of behavioral ecology are compatible with, indeed essential to, an appropriate behavioral technology. A systems oriented, behavior based environmental design and management strategy provides a synthesizing format and the impetus for applying the principles in each of these as well as other research domains mentioned above.

Environmental Design and Management

Environmental reorganization is required when there is an incongruence between behavioral objectives and the supporting environment. An alternative environment-behavior ensemble implies a change in behavior and thus the supporting (designed) environment. Environmental design, then, is an activity necessarily committed to and organized around the objective of behavior change and maintenance. Arguments for an appropriate strategy have been developed elsewhere (2,23); these can be briefly summarized and elaborated in the light of the above comments.

The arguments for a behavior-contingent approach to physical design grow out of the realization that designed environments should, but often do not, reduce the disparity between human intentions and their accomplishments. Since accomplishments depend upon what people do, i.e., upon their behavior, requirements for physical systems must be developed in the same dimensions. The objective of environmental design, then, is to realize an alternative state of human affairs, to interpose a system of energy and matter between human behavioral objectives and antithetical elements in the general milieu. In directing our attention to the behavioral requirements of populations, we are in a position to identify a research and problem-solving paradigm within which disparate areas of information and expertise can be more incisively focused. Figure 1 depicts the behavior-modification strategy discussed in some detail earlier. A systems oriented problem-solving paradigm is depicted in Figure 2. The integration of these two produces the environmental design and management strategy depicted in Figure 3. In summary environmental-behavioral design and management involves the following sequential functions:
1. EMPIRICAL OBSERVATION of the human setting of problematic concern is required to develop an understanding of the environmental-behavioral baseline states.
2. MODELING functions in the problem-solving process are required to describe three classes of phenomena:
    a. An empirical model structures the observations of the baseline conditions; that is, it describes the properties of the environment-behavior ensemble as it exists, i.e., a functional description of the behavioral ecosystem.
    b. A normative behavioral model describes the system of behaviors required to meet the goals of the population; it operationalizes the goals of the setting in dimensions of empirically accessible units of behavior (i.e., the way things ought to be). When these requisite behaviors are compared with the existing ones the discrepancy (between ought and is) defines a behavior-modification problem.
    c. An environment-behavior ensemble model describes an alternative environment required to realize a new state of behavioral affairs, i.e., to move the behaviors from where they are to where they ought to be to meet the defined goals. This is a predictive model which carries the assertion: if a particular environmental structure is implemented then certain behaviors will emerge.
3. SIMULATION functions are required to validate and refine the environment-behavior ensemble model prior to implementation. No algorithms exist for solving this class of problems: simulation, therefore, is necessary to reduce the economic, social and other risks involved in implementing untested models. Iterative

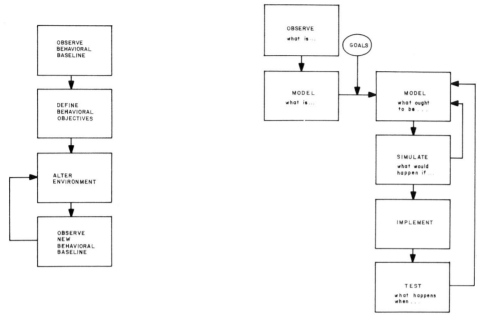

FIGURE 1
BEHAVIOR MODIFICATION STRATEGY

FIGURE 2
GENERAL PROBLEM-SOLVING STRUCTURE

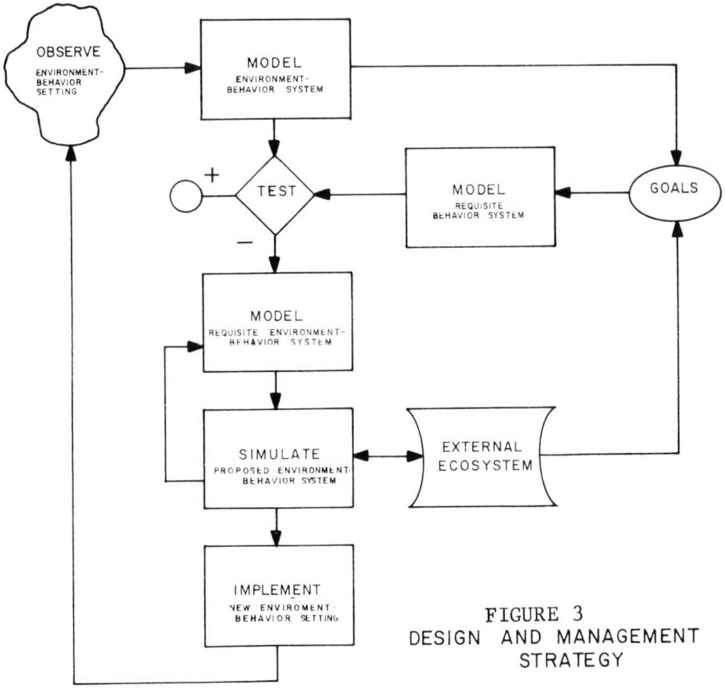

FIGURE 3
DESIGN AND MANAGEMENT
STRATEGY

simulation-(re)modeling functions (in various modes) minimize this risk via experimentation in the "laboratory".   The simulation tests the ensemble in its functioning state subject to the constraints operating in the exogenous environment.
4.   IMPLEMENTATION is simply the act of placing the proposed environment-behavior
ensemble in the actual setting. It is in fact the realization of an experiment to
test an hypothesis regarding a particular man-environment interface, one predicted
to produce a new state of behavioral affairs.
5.   TESTING this new environment-behavior ensemble involves the assessment of the
new behavioral baseline states. Does the ensemble behave as predicted via the
model and simulation experiments? Very often it will not, in which case iterative:
(1) reprogramming of certain aspects, (2) testing via simulation, (3) implementation
and (4) empirical validation, are necessary.

Implementation of appropriate environment-behavior ensembles via the above operations is indeed a complex undertaking considering available tools and knowledge.
The task is made even more difficult, however, when one realizes that such systems
are not finite-state, but, like all living (open) systems, subject to constant
change. Areas of variability include: (1) changes in the settings goal structure,
(2) changes in exogenous constraints, (3) changes in various (endogenous) environments, e.g. political, economic, social, and (4) changes in the human participants,
e.g. states of deprivation, adaptation, learning. A change in any one of these
will bring about dissonance in the environment-behavior ensemble and the need for
its reprogramming. Considering the variable nature of human systems, together with
the uncertainties involved in behavioral predictions generally, it is clear that a
solution is not really a solution but an hypothesis. Implemented environment-
behavior systems should be viewed quite literally as on-going experiments. The
above decision-making process then is appropriately seen as iterative--a dynamic
experiment designed to move an ensemble toward consonance in response to changing
goals and controlling conditions.

Although clearly based on the principles and techniques of behavioral technology,
the above environmental design and management strategy contains operational elements
not ordinarily included. The emphasis on system modeling and simulation experiments
lies outside the literature and current programs in behavior modification. There
are several reasons for this. Such programs generally operate in contexts where
appropriate terminal behaviors are easily defined (e.g. educational) or where behavioral dysfunctions are critical (e.g. mental hospitals). Thus the risks of implementing behavior-change programs relative to extant conditions are not considered
great. Also such programs deal with quite modest samples of behavior and ostensibly
present no significant or complicated ecological consequences. Finally, most behavior modifiers are simply ignorant of the tools of systems modeling and simulation,
or they are routinely skeptical regarding their effectiveness as predictive instruments. Indeed model building and simulation merely increase the probability of,
but do not insure perfect predictions. However, as behavior change and maintenance
programs are implemented which involve and accommodate larger behavioral ecosystems
a more elaborate strategy such as the above will most certainly be required.

Conclusion: Toward a Behavioral Ecosystems Technology

This discussion began with the observation that establishment of a research tradition in environmental psychology and sociology will not <u>per se</u> facilitate the implementation of their findings. In addressing the problems of realizing an applied discipline for this task, two notable,somewhat antithetical world views appear endemic among applied researchers and designers. The first sees man—environment relations in natural settings as somewhat immutable, subject to and maintained via fairly delicate system-like interdependencies. The research objective is essentially to discover these man—environment relationships and support obesrved human behavioral tendencies via organization of appropriate environmental structures. The second world view focuses on the human capacity for extensive behavioral change (in response to altered features of the environment) and the need to reorganize man-environment settings in response to changing goals. This second world view thus speaks to the design and not the discovery of particular man—environment ensembles. It was argued that strict adherence to either of these dichotomous approaches is equally untenable, leading as they do to a future in which human survival becomes somewhat equivocal.

The characteristics of artificial versus natural phenomena were explicated in order to more closely depict the conditions of the design act, i.e., goal-directed synthesis toward a defined state as contrasted with analysis to explicate how things are. The self-conscious design of artificial human systems raises serious questions regarding man's place in the ecosystem generally, as well as the essential characteristics of successful man-made settings. The design act necessarily focuses attention on the relationship between existing human settings, and intervention to create new settings. It was argued that successful natural or artificial systems have similar characteristics of maintenance, be these infrahuman, human, living or non-living.

The design objective, it was noted, is to realize a state of congruence between environmental and behavioral structures organized around defined goals. Both systems are seen to require modification in order to realize the appropriate states. Whatever else the environmental design effort requires, its central concern is a change in and the maintenance of new behavioral states. Thus, the underlying scientific principles as well as the applied format for a behavioral technology were explicated as these apply to an environmental design and management strategy. Behavior modification via contingency management or acquisition of stimulus control both require an understanding of a population's reinforcement potential. This aspect of behavior analysis and change is linked to other current environmental research methods which focus on analysis of human propensities for certain environmental configurations.

It was noted that behavioral technology as presently implemented (i.e., limited organisms emitting limited repertories) is probably inadequate for dealing with reorganization of larger behavioral ecosystems. Such networks are subject to system-wide influences and complexities which require not only more sophisticated environmental design strategies but the adoption of an ecological perspective generally. Although criticized as lacking certain essential technical tools, e.g., systems modeling, ecological psychology, or more generically behavioral ecology, was identified as an important resource requiring integration into environmental design processes.

It is generally agreed that the socioenvironmental problems facing ours and other cultures are critical. The implicit challenge to the resourcefulness of the scientific and technological community could not be greater. The purpose of these comments has been to challenge the widespread belief that human environmental problems can be solved through more knowledge of man-environment relations alone. I have attempted to outline one approach to an applied format for implementing some of the relevant methods of behavioral science. Even in their generality, examination of the issues moves one toward the conclusion that we need a <u>behavioral</u> <u>ecosystems technology</u> in order to deal with the complexities of human environmental problems. Some of the resources upon which such a technology can be built have been identified, but its full realization will be a tedious enterprise involving numerous attempts to deal directly with the reality of human behavioral problems.

References

(1) Kuhn, T., THE STRUCTURE OF SCIENTIFIC REVOLUTIONS, Chicago, University of Chicago Press, 1962.

(2) Studer, R.G., "The Organization of Spatial Stimuli", in J.F. Wohlwill and D.H. Carson (Eds.), BEHAVIORAL SCIENCE AND PROBLEMS OF THE ENVIRONMENT, Washington, American Psychological Association, (in press).

(3) Commoner, B., THE CLOSING CIRCLE, New York, Alfred A. Knopf, Inc., 1968.

(4) Bauer, R.A. (Ed.), SECOND-ORDER CONSEQUENCES, Cambridge, Massachusetts, The Massachusetts Institute of Technology Press, 1969.

(5) Rapoport, A., Foreward, MODERN SYSTEMS RESEARCH FOR THE BEHAVIORAL SCIENTIST, W. Buckley (Ed.), Chicago, Aldine, 1968.

(6) Willems, E., "Behavioral Ecology and Experimental Analysis: Courtship is not Enough", in J. Nesselroade (Ed.), LIFE-SPAN DEVELOPMENTAL PSYCHOLOGY, New York, Academic Press, (in press).

(7) Simon, H.A., SCIENCES OF THE ARTIFICIAL, Cambridge, MIT Press, 1969.

(8) Studer, R.G., "Human Systems Design and the Management of Change", GENERAL SYSTEMS, XVI, pages 131-143, 1971.

(9) Cassel, J., "Social Science Theory as a Source of Hypotheses in Epidemiological Research", AMERICAN JOURNAL OF PUBLIC HEALTH, 54, No. 9, pages 1482-1488, 1964.

(10) Michelson, W., MAN AND HIS URBAN ENVIRONMENT, Reading, Addison-Wesley, 1970.

(11) Wicker, A.W., "Processes which Mediate Behavior-Environment Congruence", BEHAVIORAL SCIENCE, 17, No. 3, 1972.

(12) Honig, W. (Ed.), OPERANT BEHAVIOR: AREAS OF RESEARCH AND APPLICATION, New York, Appleton-Century-Crofts, 1966.

(13) Ulrich, R., T. Stachnik, and J. Mabry, CONTROL OF HUMAN BEHAVIOR, (2 vols.) Glenview, Scott Foresman, 1966; 1970.

(14) Terrace, H.S., "Stimulus Control", in W.K. Honig (Ed.), OPERANT BEHAVIOR: AREAS OF RESEARCH AND APPLICATION, New York, Appleton-Century-Crofts, pages 271-344, 1966.

(15) Pike, K., LANGUAGE IN RELATION TO A UNIFIED THEORY OF A STRUCTURE OF BEHAVIOR, The Hague, Mouton and Co., 1967.

(16) Miller, G., Galanter, E., and Pribram, K., PLANS AND THE STRUCTURE OF BEHAVIOR, New York, Holt, Rinehart and Winston, 1960.

(17) Craik, K.H., "The Comprehension of the Everyday Physical Environment", JOURNAL OF THE AMERICAN INSTITUTE OF PLANNERS, 34, pages 29-37, 1968.

(18) Stea, D. and R. Downs (Eds.), "Cognitive Representations of Man's Spatial Environment", ENVIRONMENT AND BEHAVIOR, 2, No. 1, June, 1970.

(19) Watt, K.E.F., PRINCIPLES OF ENVIRONMENTAL SCIENCE, New York, McGraw-Hill, Inc., 1973.

(20) Barker, R., ECOLOGICAL PSYCHOLOGY, Stanford, Stanford University Press, 1968.

(21) Willems, E.P. and H. Raush (Eds.), NATURALISTIC VIEWPOINTS IN PSYCHOLOGICAL RESEARCH, New York, Holt, Rinehart and Winston, 1969.

(22) Altman, I., "An Ecological Approach to the Functioning of Social Groups", in J.E. Rasmussen (Ed.), INDIVIDUAL AND GROUP BEHAVIOR IN ISOLATION AND CONFINEMENT, Chicago, Aldine Press, 1973.

(23) Studer, R.G., "The Dynamics of Behavior-Contingent Physical Systems", in H. Proshansky et al (Eds.), ENVIRONMENTAL PSYCHOLOGY: MAN AND HIS PHYSICAL SETTING, New York, Holt, Rinehart and Winston, pages 56-76, 1970.

Edwin P. Willems
Associate Professor of Psychology
University of Houston
Houston, Texas 77004

Abstract

Neither those professions whose primary mandate is to design for human living and
intervene to correct its problems nor the behavioral sciences to which the design
professions look for insight and technology have fully apprehended the extent to
which human behavior is implicated in organism-environment-behavior systems. A true
behavioral ecology, which would provide the grounds not only for the basic understanding of the complexities of everyday behavior but for appropriate and effective
design and intervention, is still in its infancy. Some of the major values, assumptions, and programmatic guidelines of an emerging behavioral ecology are spelled out
and illustrated.

Introduction

Members of the planning-design professions and their compatriots in the behavioral
sciences stand in a painful and difficult position. They experience tremendous
pressures from many sources to solve environmental problems, to alleviate human suffering, and to revolutionize the designing of human environments. Their professional
and humane sense then inclines them to do something. What connects the pressures and
the doing--what is applied--is a set of skills, insight, and information that is constrained by the traditional ways in which they do their work. One purpose of this
paper is to argue that this is not enough and that we must create something new to
place between the pressures and the doing. Why? Because we do not know what happens
when we act. Most of our concerted actions are intended to affect human behavior in
some way. The problem is twofold. (a) We seldom really know to what extent we achieve
our intended results. (b) Our actions have unanticipated and unintended effects. Can
we build a society in which each person not only has the resources to meet his ele-
mental needs, but is also an integral and optimally healthful part of the societal
whole? The answer is no because we have so limited a conception of the nature of the
person-environment-behavior systems that make up societal wholes. Being an integral
part of ecological systems involves behavior and behavioral well-being just as much
as it involves biological and physical well-being. If this is so, then we must mobi-
lize a whole new cluster of resources and commitments in the pursuit and refinement
of a true behavioral ecology, a systematics of behavior, a formal rendering of the
ways in which human behavior is caught up in the interdependencies of ecological
systems. Thus, the second purpose of this paper is to present and illustrate a
perspective on behavior called behavioral ecology that should help both the behavioral
scientist and the designer to deal more effectively with the realities of human
behavior.(1)

The Problem of Behavior-Environment Systems

In ways that often become clear only in retrospect and for reasons that are often
mysterious, the application of known techniques to produce change can lead to very
troubling results. The case of hybrid corn is illustrative. Corn leaf blight destroyed
15 per cent of the domestic corn crop in 1970. The blight struck only one kind of
corn, but it was the kind of corn grown by almost all farmers. The ecological problem
here was only recognized after the fact. On the one hand, technology was available
to produce high-yield seeds, which were highly uniform. Also, uniform crops are
easier for the farmer to manage. Thus, the technology of upgrading crops and pressures toward ease of production both encouraged greater genetic uniformity. On the
other hand, when a parasite (blight) with a preference for the characters controlled
by the reduced set of genes came along, a major epidemic resulted. In other words,
the uniformity (created for very positive, humane reasons) was responsible for the
size of the epidemic. The possibilities for disaster are immense when we consider
that many of the world's major grains and vegetables are now being bred to uniformity
at a rapid rate. We also know by now that the use of insecticides and the building
of large dams, both of which are often carried out to enhance human living conditions,
lead to unanticipated results that are pernicious and highly disruptive of human living conditions. It is clear that our humane efforts to apply proven technology and
to alleviate human suffering on a large scale can go awry in the most vexing ways.
More importantly, there is something pervasively wrong with our available understanding of environment-inhabitant systems and the impact of singular intrusions into
those systems. In the cases of crops, insecticides, dams, as well as others, we are
now quite sure that they are ecological phenomena whose complexity was not anticipated because we know now what happened--someone has discovered the principles that
govern such events.

Micro-Ecology of Behavior. A similar problem shows up in our understanding of behavior and behavior change. Proshansky, Ittelson, and Rivlin report an attempt to
increase the therapeutic effectiveness of psychiatric facilities through appropriate
design in one ward of a mental hospital. (2) The ward was laid out on a long corridor,
with a nurses' station at one end and a solarium at the other end, with bedrooms, a
bathroom, and a day-room in between. When the psychologists came, the solarium,
which was meant to be a place of relaxation and recreation, was overheated, poorly
furnished, and generally unappealing, with intense sunlight pouring in through a
bank of uncovered windows. It was used very little, even though there was a TV set
there. What patients did most consistently in the solarium was to stand alone for
long periods of time in a state of preoccupation, detachment, and withdrawal--that
singular behavior pattern in which severely disturbed persons engage so much. This
isolated standing was one of the behavior patterns that the hospital staff wished to
change. The psychologists changed the solarium by adding furniture, drapes, and other
accessories. Soon, larger numbers of patients began spending longer periods of time
there, and the solarium took on the air of a pleasant recreational and social area.
More importantly, the rate of isolated standing behavior went down so that very
little of it was now occurring in the solarium. The psychologists had achieved their
purpose--for the solarium. However, all they had succeeded in doing was to change
the location of the isolated standing behavior--a great deal of it now took place at
the other end of the corridor, by the nurses' station. Luckily, these environmental
designers did not restrict their behavior observations to the solarium, but studied

a whole environment-behavior system, of which the solarium was only one component. Creating the environmental conditions for damping down the level of troubling behavior in one part of the system had only shifted the troubling behavior to another part.

A second issue in the micro-ecology of behavior raises questions about the use of successful technologies of behavior change. Applied behavior analysis, or the operant approach to the modification of behavior, is a behavioral technology of proven effectiveness which changes the course of behavior through the control of its pleasant and unpleasant consequences. The problem here is twofold. First, despite some significant exceptions, this technology is applied to narrowly-specified conditions--one person at a time, one or few behaviors at a time, one reinforcer at a time, and one setting at a time. Second, although desired and intended outcomes can be specified with great precision, it is possible for many forms of unintended effects to occur and unintended effects are much more difficult to measure. In one case (3), investigators arranged for a preschool teacher to try to change a child's initiated speech to her (nagging) by ignoring the initiations. This tactic was successful in reducing the nagging, but it produced systematic changes in other behavior by the child in the same setting and in another setting as well. Some of the ''side-effects'' were desirable (increasing speech initiated to children, increasing cooperative play) while some were undesirable (decreasing task-appropriate behavior, increasing disruptive behavior) and some were neutral (use of girls' toys). Sajwaj et al. consider it distinctly possible that modifying one behavior modifies the larger setting. We know almost nothing as yet about governing principles in such systems or about the ways in which behaviors and behaviors and environments form clusters or co-varying units in the everyday world. Such system-like phenomena at the level of behavioral micro-ecology must be elucidated if we are ever to use rational anticipation and planning in the application of behavioral technologies.

We can see why the behavioral ecologist worries about the simplistic tinkering of the behavioral technologist. We need to find out which kinds of unintended effects occur most frequently and why they occur. Such information will tell us a great deal about behavior-organism-environment systems, but it will also enable us to predict the effects of interventions and develop the means to avoid instigating long-term harm while creating short-term good. Evidence is accumulating in drug research to suggest that the safety and effectiveness of specific chemicals, taken for specific purposes, can often be affected in profound ways, not only by intra-organismic interactions with other chemicals, but also by interactions with pharmaceutical agents and chemicals in the environment. Analogously, it may be that the safety and effectiveness of behavior modification by means of simple behavioral technology may be affected by interactions within persons and between persons and environments that await discovery.

In another case, an ornithologist with a European zoo wished to add a small bird called the bearded tit to the zoo's collection. Armed with all the relevant information he could find about the tit, the ornithologist went to great pains to build the right setting. Bringing in a male and female, he noted that, by all behavioral criteria, the birds functioned very well. Unfortunately, soon after the birds hatched babies, they shoved the babies out of the nest, onto the ground, where they died. This cycle, beginning with mating and ending with the babies dead on the ground, repeated itself many times. The ornithologist tried many modifications of the setting, but none forestalled the systematic infanticide. After many hours of renewed, direct observation of tits in the wild, the ornithologist noted three patterns of behavior that had missed everyone's attention. First, throughout most of the daylight hours in the wild, the parent tits were very active at finding and bringing food for the infants. Second, the infants, with whose food demands the parents could hardly keep pace, spent the same hours with their mouths open, apparently crying for food. The third pattern was that any inanimate object, whether eggshell, leaf, or bettle-shell, was quickly shoved out of the nest by the parents. With these observations in mind, the ornithologist went back to observe his captive tits and he found that, during the short time a new brood of infants lived, the parents spent only brief periods feeding them by racing between the nest and the food supply, which the ornithologist had supplied in abundance. After a short period of such feeding, the infants, apparently satiated, fell asleep. The first time they slept for any length of time during the daylight hours, the parents shoved them (two inanimate objects, after all) out of the nest. When he made the food supply _less_ abundant and _less_ accessible and thereby made the parents work much longer and harder to find and bring food, the ornithologist found that the infants spent more daylight time awake, demanding food, and that the tits then produced many families and cared for them to maturity.

Infanticide is a behavior problem and there are several important implications of this story. The first is that neither the designer's good will nor the technologist's respect or love for his clients will themselves ensure his creating the right environment. Good intentions by environmental agents and social engineers do _not_ necessarily ensure habitability. The second implication is more complex and has to do with the criteria we use in making evaluative inferences about our efforts. All the indicators in the behavior of the parent tits suggested that their captive environment was congenial and hospitable and that it fulfilled their needs. Yet, the long-range criterion of survival of the captive representatives of the species (a surprise, a shock to the ornithologist) pointed to a very different conclusion about the environment. The implication is that day-to-day and moment-by-moment behavioral criteria, as well as indicators or expressions of enjoyment, comfort, and satisfaction, can be very misleading indicators of how functional an environment is. The parents had to work much harder in the second environment than in the first, but their babies _survived_ in the second and _not_ in the first. We must pick and choose our criteria with the greatest care, perhaps flying in the face of what common sense, accepted social wisdom, and even past success with our technologies tell us is humane, important, and worthwhile. The third implication involves even more speculation. It is the reminder, the caution, that the complicated systems comprising everyday environments, their human inhabitants, and the links among them probably involve lawful interdependencies whose subtlety has eluded us completely. In the case of the bearded tits and environmentally-induced infanticide, the interdependencies involved (a) some aspects of a total physical environment, (b) the ongoing, short-range individual and social behavior of the birds, e.g., child-rearing practices and characteristic ways of dealing with the environment, and (c) a long-range outcome. Who knows, for example, what aspects of personal, familial, neighborhood, and general social behavior and their environmental surroundings combine to account for troublesome symptoms such as irritability, alcoholism among housewives, drug abuse, vandalism, child abuse, truancy, motiveless murder, interpersonal and intergroup tension, and the deterioration of human amenities? The point is that we do not know. Unless we find out, we may make changes and interventions that only create new and unanticipated problems, no matter how humane and decent the reasons for making the changes.

Macro-Ecology of Behavior. Extremely unpleasant effects also follow from intervention in larger environment-behavior systems. Turnbull (4) describes the social and behavioral disintegration of the Iks, a group of hunter-gatherers who inhabit part of the Kidepo Valley in Northern Uganda. Turnbull, who lived among the Iks and observed them for 18 months, reports that the traditional way of life among the Iks had involved highly cooperative forms of hunting across the reaches of the valley and living in small, widely-dispersed bands. Terrain, rituals, traditional beliefs, and day-to-day behavior all combined to form an interrelated whole over time. Then, partly in the interests of wildlife conservation, the Ugandan government defined the Kidepo Valley as a national park, herded the Iks to the edges of the park, set up police outposts to keep the Iks out of the valley, and encouraged the Iks to take up farming on the mountain slopes. The social and behavioral fabric of the Ik society fell apart completely. Malicious competition replaced cooperation. Hostility and treachery replaced kindness. Laughter became a raucous response to the misfortunes of people, rather than an expression of good will and humor. Members of the group were left to die and sometimes goaded to die instead of being nursed and helped. Strong isolation in booby-trapped enclaves replaced openness and companionship between people.

The case of the Iks is dramatic and disturbing because it reflects society turned inside out to display malevolence and behavioral disturbance and because it displays the effects of the fundamental disruption of the ecological links between habitat and social and behavioral adaptation. Even more disturbing are the parallels between the ways the Iks now live and the ways that many 20th century members of industrialized society live. Many of the data, complaints, and fears of present-day city dwellers and inhabitants about the degradation and disorientation of daily life sound very much like the developments for the Iks. All around us, we see and hear about new forms of behavioral pathology that bewilder us because our traditional assumptions offer no means to understand them or attribute motives to them. Perhaps the fire storm of behavioral difficulty that threatens to overwhelm many persons is fueled by fundamental disruptions of the relationships between habitat and living style which we do not recognize only because they occur more gradually than the upheaval of the Iks. Much work must be done on large-scale issues of behavioral ecology because appropriate intervention and change presupposes much more far-reaching understanding than we now have.

General Implications

Paradoxically, the ecological perspective on human behavior and behavioral difficulty as target phenomena is still in its infancy; ''paradoxically'' because Americans are worried about behavioral problems. Human behavior and its emergence into troubling forms represent serious threats to persons, societies, and the species. The sense of fear over crime and social disintegration and the forbidding and growing sense of vulnerability to the acts of persons are, perhaps, more dramatic and widespread than apprehension over lung cancer, auto accidents, or heart trouble. The sciences and technologies of human behavior must overcome their sense of futility over understanding this pell-mell course.

At many levels, behavior is implicated in very complex organism-environment-behavior systems. If we think of the implications of such phenomena and what they suggest about human behavior in general and if we think about the growing pressure to apply known behavioral technologies and known capabilities for environmental design, the following observation emerges: We have become fairly conservative and sophisticated about introducing new biotic elements and new chemicals into our ecological systems, but we display almost childish irresponsibility in our attitudes toward behavioral and behavioral-environment systems. Agents of change including economic planners, housing authorities, architects, psychotherapists, social workers, industrial consultants, educational planners, psychopharmacologists, and operant behavior modifiers have at their disposal various means to affect behavior-environment systems. The questions of larger and unintended effects within interpersonal and environmental contexts and over long periods of time beg for evaluation and research, because lessons learned in other areas suggest that we should always be sensitive to ''other'' effects of both small and large intrusions.

Every intervention, every human artifice, has its price, no matter how well-intentioned the agent of intervention may be. The counter-argument often is, ''Don't try to immobilize us with all that alarmist talk. We'll deal with side-effects when they come up. After all, we're not stupid!'' However, when we think in terms of environment-behavior systems, we can see that there is a fundamental misconception embedded in that popular term, ''side-effects.'' This phrase means, roughly, ''effects which I hadn't intended, hadn't foreseen, or don't want to think about.'' What we so glibly call ''side-effects'' no more deserve the adjective, ''side,'' than does the ''principle'' effect—they are all aspects of the interdependencies which we need so badly to understand. It is hard to think in terms of systems and we warp our language to protect ourselves and our favorite approaches from the necessity of thinking in terms of interdependent systems of behavior and environment.

For the student of behavior, there is much to be learned from this emerging ecological orientation and there is immediate and pervasive need for an expansion of perspective. Until a few years ago, technologists believed that most, if not all, of their developments would be useful in a rather direct and simple sense. We know now that this is not necessarily true--feasibility and even intrinsic success are not sufficient grounds for immediate application.

> With each decade, scientific findings translated into technology radically reshape the way we live. Technical capacity has been the ruling imperative, with no reckoning of cost, either ecological or personal. If it could be done, it has been done. Foresight has lagged far behind craftsmanship. At long last we are beginning to ask, not can it be done, but should it be done? The challenge is to our ability to anticipate second- and third-order consequences of interventions in the ecosystem before the event, not merely to rue them afterward. (5, p. 123)

This widening awareness--the ecological perspective--suggests that many things that can be done either should not be done or should be done most judiciously and that more technology will not provide solutions to many technologically-induced problems. Before we can be truly effective at designing human environments and alleviating human suffering, we must know much more about the principles that characterize and govern the systems into which such designs and alleviating efforts must, of necessity, intrude.

One implication of this line of argument may well be a conservatism with regard to intervention in behavior-environment systems and the clear hint that the most adaptive form of action may sometimes be <u>inaction</u>. Such conservatism has developed in other areas, but not in the behavioral sciences and their applied areas. The problem is that we know little as yet about the circumstances under which the price for a particular action outweighs the price of inaction and vice versa. So, if we give the above examples and arguments a slight interpretive twist, we arrive at another implication that is even more important. This is the clear suggestion that we need a great deal more basic research and theoretical understanding that takes account of the ecological, system-like principles that permeate the phenomena of behavior and environment. There is immediate need for a systematic scientific basis to plan environmental designs, behavioral interventions, and technologies in such a way that they will not produce unanticipated negative costs in behavior-environment systems.

Some Components of the Ecological Perspective

The behavioral ecologist sees a world in which behavior is intertwined with phenomena at many levels so as to form ecosystems that function according to laws of balance, reciprocity, conservation, and succession over time. He would argue that a new form of ecological understanding must be placed between pressures to influence human behavior and programs of action. The purpose of this section is to list some of the major earmarks of behavioral ecology, a list which can be seen as specifying some of the work that must be placed between pressure and action.

<u>Behavior-and-Environment</u>. Behavioral ecology places a great deal of emphasis upon the mutual and interdependent relations among organism, behavior, and environment.

> ...both organism and environment will have to be seen as systems, each with properties of its own, yet both hewn from basically the same block. Each has surface and depth, or overt and covert regions ... the interrelationship between the two systems has the essential characteristics of a ''coming-to-terms.'' ... It follows that, much as psychology must be concerned with the texture of the organism or of its nervous processes and must investigate them in depth, it also must be concerned with the texture of the environment as it extends in depth away from the common boundary. (6, p. 5)

Thus, one of the central conceptual issues of behavioral ecology is the transactional character of organism-environment systems wherein behavior represents the primary mediating process, the ''coming-to-terms'' across the boundaries. On this view, bits of behavior or bits of environment taken independently (as in a simple S-R model), as well as the ''independent'' and ''dependent'' variables of most experiments, are abstractions from functioning, interactional systems.

<u>Systems Concepts</u>. Sometimes because of the extensiveness and complexity of the phenomena under study, sometimes because systems theory brings to bear an appropriate and powerful set of formal principles, and sometimes simply because ecologists slip into the use of the jargon of systems analysis, it is common to find that the work of the ecologist is couched in terms of systems. It is only reasonable that ecologists would turn to this formal discipline for tools of conceptual representation and analysis because systems theory and its various derivatives offer the tools for representing interdependence and time-related complexity. General ecology has become quite sophisticated in its use of formal quantitative representation and systems theory, but

behavioral ecology's use of such concepts is still in its infancy. The use of systems concepts in behavioral ecology is often common-sensical, crude, and analogical in form--e.g., my frequent use of the phrase, ''environment-behavior system,'' in contexts where I cannot specify precisely what that means. Some writers speak of interdependent components and interrelationships in environment and behavior without using systems terminology. Others use systems terminology in more explicit fashion, e.g., Barker's application of servomechanistic thinking to represent self-regulation and control in behavior settings.(7) However, behavioral ecology has a long way to go. These developments will be important because, like the development of general taxonomies (see below), they promise to enhance communication among professional specialists. In behavioral ecology, it is critically important that each professional and consumer know a great deal about the work of others, because the phenomena that are implicated do not restrict themselves to any one of our dearly-held specialties. Systems theory may provide the necessary terminology for communication.

Transdisciplinary Emphasis. The behavioral ecologist assumes that the phenomena of behavior participate in a much larger network of phenomena, descriptions, and disciplines. Thus, ecology tends to be highly eclectic and the ecologist tends to borrow and lend concepts, methods, and hypotheses freely, with little sense of preciousness about boundaries between disciplines. The need for eclecticism and professional symbiosis arises because of the nature of the phenomena and because of the nature of professional specialization. Behavior, the principle means by which organisms carry on commerce with the environment, is embedded in and relates to phenomena at many levels, which themselves form hierarchies of embedded systems, e. g., molecules, cells, tissues, organs, organ systems, organisms, settings, facilities, institutions, political systems, economic systems. Behavior is a mid-range phenomenon and its full contextual understanding requires models and approaches developed by persons who study the various levels of embeddedness.

Molar Phenomena and Nonreductionism. The ecological perspective tends, generally, to place more emphasis upon molar phenomena than upon molecular ones. Closely related is a relative emphasis upon environmental, behavioral, and organismic holism and simultaneous, complex relationships. This is so in part because, all the way from survival of a species, through adaptive functioning, down to day-to-day and moment-by-moment adaptive processes, the emphasis is upon the organism's and the population's behavioral commerce with the environmental packages they inhabit. Adaptation to and long-range functional performance in everyday settings places relative focus on various forms of coming to terms with the environment. Furthermore, the ecologist is much more willing than many of his peers to work from the complex to the simple as his strategy of choice and to accept complicated, intact phenomena as his arena. Space does not permit the delights of arguing this point extensively, but the ecologist, with some support from other scientists, operates on the assumption that the functioning of his relatively large units of phenomena cannot always be reduced to or understood in terms of more molecular events; that the exhaustive understanding of system-level phenomena often requires the formulation of models and principles at the level of the system. Since many of the crucial problems of behavior lie at the level of behavior-environment systems, a true behavioral ecology must address its investigative efforts to phenomena at that level and create concepts that are commensurate with that level.

Site Specificity: The Importance of Place. One of the clearest generalizations from descriptive research on behavior is a high degree of predictability from place or situation to behavior; i.e., behavior tends to concentrate in characteristic ways with site or situation. In the conduct of everyday affairs, we depend upon behavior-environment congruence for predictability and social order. Two colleagues and I are involved in a program of research at a comprehensive rehabilitation facility in Houston, Texas. Adults with injuries to the spinal cord, resulting in severe functional impairments, are our target population. We are searching (a) for quantitative behavioral indicators of progress in rehabilitation, (b) for the ways in which the hospital's system of health care meets the patients, and (c) for the ways in which these relationships change over time. From direct observations of patient behavior, we can extract measures of behavioral independence, i.e., the proportion of behavioral events which patients initiate and engage in alone, and behavioral complexity, i.e., the proportion of time that patients do more than one thing at once. In this exercise in the micro-ecology of behavior, we have confronted some fascinating issues. First, even though many personological models of human behavior assume that independence is largely a matter of individual motivation and thus should reflect a high degree of personal constancy, we find, on the contrary, that behavioral independence varies dramatically when patients change from one hospital setting to another. Second, differences between settings account for far more variance in patient independence than do differences between patients. Finally, and most interestingly, differences between early and advanced patients in independence and complexity are much larger in some settings than in others. That is, there are powerful setting dependencies in the rate of growth in patient behavior.

Where the organism is located is never seen as accidental or unimportant by ecologists and clarifying the phenomena of congruence between setting and behavior is very important to the design professions. From the evolutionary standpoint, the human being's responsiveness that leads to behavior-environment congruence makes sense because adaptability and responsiveness are selected for and because behavior (doing things within environmental settings) accounts for a large share of the process of adaptation. One of the important issues of behavioral ecology is to understand the ways in which behaviors and their niches become patterned. The implications of site specificity are widespread, but three that are accepted by the behavioral ecologist are, first, that behavior is largely controlled by the environmental setting in which it occurs and second, that changing environmental variables results in the modification of behavior. Third, as has already been argued in various ways, there is the investigative problem, the description and classification of the types and patterns of such congruence in human behavior and the formulating of hypotheses to account for them. This effort is a key aspect of behavioral ecology and it promises to contribute much to programs of design and intervention in human environments.

Habitability. The ecological perspective devotes a great deal of effort to the question of habitability; that is, to the issue of what kinds of environments are fit for human beings to inhabit. The behavioral ecologist not only does this because it sets the stage for applied environmental design and social engineering, but because he believes that when he leaves his preoccupation with measures of time, latency, errors, number of trials, thresholds, and molecular physiology and concerns himself with such messy and molar problems as safety, convenience, comfort, satisfaction, adjustment, long-term functional achievement, adaptation, and cost, he may well be on the most direct path to basic theoretical understanding as well.

Ecological Diagnosis. The case of the bearded tit mentioned above raises some fundamental questions about the symptomatic value of behavior, the diagnostic process, and
targets of intervention. After he had confirmed his suspicion that the parent tits
were killing their infants, the ornithologist could have followed the example provided by diagnosticians of human affairs. That is, he could have assumed that the
mainsprings of the behavior resided inside the skins of the parents and he could have
diagnosed them as crazy or sick and in need of some form of help, perhaps psychother-
apy. Instead, he used a series of careful observations to converge on a contextual,
ecological diagnosis of the problem and he engaged in an ecological course of remedial action that makes great sense in retrospect; i.e., intervening with the
accessibility of the food supply. We have little difficulty accepting this kind of
ecological, contextual approach to infra-human animals, but we manage to blind ourselves to its implications for human behavior. Part of the problem lies in our models,
theories, and research, which are preoccupied with the unity and integrity of persons
taken one at a time and with what goes on inside them. After all, it is the person
who behaves, whose behavior we must understand, who misbehaves, and it is the person
who comes or is referred for help because of some serious internal disturbance, isn't
it? This is the way it has been in sciences of behavior, at least in psychology, but
these sciences need much more if they are to deal effectively with human problems.
The fact that the disturbance process has varying concentrations and is not necessarily
distributed equally throughout the ecological system should not divert us from the
principle that we ''... cannot speak only of the disturbance of the individual, but
... must speak of the disturbance of the system.'' (8, p. 559) ... ''We are, so to
speak, fishing in the stream of life, and bring up only that for which we have appropriate bait.'' (p. 563) This is true for both scientists and practitioners. When our
pet models lead us to attach our disturbance detectors to the individual, we will
detect disturbance in the individual and we will make him our target of intervention
and change. In the process, we disregard the fact that the problem, the disturbance,
the imbalance may lie at the level of an ecological system of which the individual is
only one component and that our scientific understanding of behavior, our principles
of diagnosis, and our interventions must be adjusted to that level of complexity.

Naturalistic Emphasis. The ecological perspective is largely naturalistic in its
methodological orientation. I say ''largely'' because it is not defined by any particular technique and because I am pointing to an emphasis rather than a necessary
condition. The ecologist's methodological statement of faith has two parts. First,
the ecologist says that you cannot understand the behavior of the organism in the
laboratory unless you understand his behavior in everyday life. Second, contrary to
widely-held canons, the ecologist believes that the investigator should manipulate
and control only as much as is absolutely necessary to answer his questions clearly.
The ecologist works with the continual reminder that holding constant experimental
conditions while varying a limited phenomenon is a figment of the experimental
laboratory which may result in the untimely attenuation of both findings and theories.

Distribution of Phenomena in Nature. Behavioral ecology concerns itself with the distribution of phenomena in nature; upon the range, intensity, and frequency of behavior
in the everyday, investigator-free environment. Space does not permit the full elaboration of this misleadingly simple but controversial issue. In areas outside the
behavioral sciences, great numbers of scientists have considered it scientifically
worthwhile to go out and simply observe, describe, count, measure, and classify the

distributions of elements and compounds in large environments and in animal tissues. We have nothing comparable in behavioral science. If we are to continue our attempts to influence, change, and accommodate human behavior, and especially, if such attempts are going to intensify and spread, then we must grow far beyond the hit-or-miss grounds we now use for deciding where and when to intervene and tinker. We must begin taking account of the much larger organism-behavior-environment systems within which our activities take place, of distributions of behavior within those systems, and of optimal proportions and combinations of behaviors across populations and subpopulations. Otherwise, at best, our work may confront behavioral bottlenecks or, at worst, we may tragically hasten our client-subjects toward behavioral bottlenecks and new forms of difficulty. The startling thing is that, at the present state of the art, we do not even recognize when we are guilty of either.

Taxonomy. Behavioral ecology is focally concerned with taxonomy. Together with naturalistic description of the distribution of behavioral phenomena, basic taxonomic research has been grossly neglected by American behavioral scientists. What are the units of environment, of behavior, and of environment-behavior linkages? Into what types of classifications do situations, behaviors, and environments fall? It is sometimes argued that behavior and its situations are too ephemeral, too spontaneous, and too malleable to be fitted into taxonomies. However, that is an evasion, because the fleeting and malleable quality of many chemical and biological phenomena have not prevented the creation of useful taxonomies. It is tempting to view the great advances now occurring in biology and physiology and assert (correctly) that those scientists are not going through the drudgery of basic taxonomic research. The error here lies in forgetting that all the current work presupposes and rests upon the work of taxonomists going far back into the history of science.

Taxonomies are important for several reasons.(9) First, there is the esthetic pleasure that accompanies scientific orderliness. Second, systems of classification represent the only comprehensive way to avoid being smothered by a great host of splintered, separate facts. The development of comprehensive theory depends, in part, upon a coherent classification of the empirical domain. Third, a good taxonomy can provide a common language and notational system (e.g., periodic table) for a field. Such translation into a common system permits comparison of various findings and concepts with each other. Fourth, an effective taxonomy can help scientists to pinpoint well-established results, confused or contradictory results, and areas of research that have been neglected (i.e., missing data). Fifth, a taxonomy can lead to predictions of new relationships that have not become obvious from separate studies. Finally, it is not difficult to see from all this that good taxonomies become particularly important to persons engaged in the applied, mission-oriented efforts of environmental design. It is when environmental agents set out to apply the substance of man-environment research to arrangements for living that the lack of orderly classification of knowledge becomes most painful. Seeking orderly, cross-classified information and principles and not finding them, it is easy to conclude that the areas of behavioral science and man-environment relations do not know much. We do know much, but, without classification systems, it is almost impossible to ascertain what we do and do not know.

Long Time Periods. In keeping with the characteristics of behavior-environment systems and the kinds of behavioral dimensions with which he often works (e.g., adaptation, accommodation, functional achievement, long-range behavior, and sometimes even survival), the ecologist not only allows, but sometimes demands, unusually long time periods and time dependencies in his research. Such long-range research often takes the form of monitoring interdependencies continuously, or nearly continuously, for extended periods of time. We know by now from other areas (e.g., crop diseases, pollution, insecticides) that empirical monitoring of very long sequences can be both scientifically illuminating and pragmatically critical, because the time-dependent phenomena can be very subtle and complex and because the true properties of ecological systems sometimes become clear only over time. The fact that the behavioral sciences cannot match the sophistication of ecological biochemistry or agronomy is no excuse to avoid this kind of research.

Small Rates. The behavioral ecologist is more willing than many of his peers to depend upon rate measures across whole populations in drawing conclusions. American behavioral scientists and their counterparts in the design professions are used to viewing things as effective or ineffective, important or unimportant, good or bad only if they lead to big changes in rate. Another way of saying this is that we do not view things from an ecological perspective. The ecologist lets himself view certain matters in terms of whole populations and in terms of small changes in rates in those populations. Minute changes in the concentrations of certain chemicals can mean the difference between rates that support life and rates that destroy life. Small changes in per cents or even fractions of per cents in such phenomena as tuberculosis, metallic poisoning, bubonic plague, cholera, or schistosomiasis can bear unambiguous information that something is wrong in the environment and in the relations between persons and the environment. If this is so, then why should it be different with social and behavioral phenomena? Does nearly everyone in a population have to be involved in rape, murder, suicide, drug addiction, alcoholism, assault, irritability, depression, malaise, uncooperativeness, or lack of social amenity before we conclude that there is something fundamentally wrong in the environment or in the interaction of that population with it? Probably not. However, we are not prepared to take rate measures seriously enough, partly because we do not yet have the kinds of models and theories that lead us to depend upon such rate measures. These are ecological problems and they are ecological problems for man-environment relations.

Evaluation of Natural Experiments. The final aspect of behavioral ecology is one which, to date, has probably done most to bring general ecology to the attention of the public. Many events--e.g., introduction of insecticides, building of dams, introduction of contraceptive techniques, increase in pollutants, uses of new seed crops, lumbering, introduction of organisms into new areas--are out of the direct control of ecologists and, therefore, represent natural experiments whose various effects they are able to study. Such natural experiments, when evaluated by ecologists, have provided data and generalizations that have made ecology a sophisticated and controversial enterprise. Behavioral ecology has begun to recognize the potential scientific value of natural experiments and should realize that the possibilities for advancing understanding are almost infinite, e.g., institutional reforms, refurbishing programs, social change programs, changes in trafficways and transportation systems, disruption of neighborhoods, increases in population and crowding, shifts from single-family to multi-family dwellings, programs of behavior modification.

Conclusion

I have argued (a) that behavioral scientists and their compatriots in the fields of environmental design are only beginning to apprehend the complexities and interdependencies that permeate the problems with which they work; (b) that the values, assumptions, theoretical characteristics, and methodological guidelines of an ecological perspective on behavior provide a highly appropriate framework within which to work; and (c) that there are some distinctive kinds of work that need to be done in order to build an appropriate capability for responding to pressures to act. The arguments of ecologists often crop up in the form of criticisms and disconcerting questions only after technologists, engineers, and designers have been hard at work and, therefore, tend to sound like second-guessing, carping from the sidelines, and Monday-morning quarterbacking. The ecologist is often seen to pounce on the efforts of others and to say, ''Hold on just a cotton-picking minute!'' If the ecological perspective on behavior is tenable and fruitful, then we must all become involved in conducting the research necessary to make it an anticipatory point of view and to make it an integral part of the planning of human environments as well as the thrust of the behavioral sciences that support the planning efforts.

Almost every day, we hear of a project or technology being turned down or halted on ecological grounds--because of the known complexity and delicacy of ecosystems. Those of us who think that the behavioral sciences and the behavioral design professions know enough and that arguments for a new effort in behavioral ecology are just so much window dressing should ask ourselves one question: How often have I heard of a program whose target is human behavior being turned down or halted on behavioral-ecological grounds--because of the known complexity and delicacy of eco-behavioral systems?

Notes and References

(1) The main arguments of this paper and supporting bibliographies are presented in more extensive detail in two papers by the author: (a) ''Behavior-Environment Systems: An Ecological Approach,'' MAN-ENVIRONMENT SYSTEMS, in press; and (b) ''Behavioral Ecology as a Perspective for Research in Psychology,'' in Deckner, C. W., METHODOLOGICAL PERSPECTIVES IN BEHAVIORAL RESEARCH, Springfield, Ill.: Charles C. Thomas, in press. Space permits only highlighting the issues here, with little elaboration.

(2) Chapters 3 and 43 in Proshansky, H. M., Ittelson, W. H., and Rivlin, L. G. ENVIRONMENTAL PSYCHOLOGY, New York, Holt, Rinehart and Winston, 1970.

(3) Sajwaj, T., Twardosz, S., and Burke, M. ''Side Effects of Extinction Procedures in a Remedial Preschool,'' JOURNAL OF APPLIED BEHAVIOR ANALYSIS, 5, pages 163-175, 1972.

(4) Turnbull, C. M. THE MOUNTAIN PEOPLE, New York, Simon and Schuster, 1972.

(5) Eisenberg, L. ''The Human Nature of Human Nature,'' SCIENCE, 176, pages 123-128, 1972.

(6) Brunswik, E. ''Scope and Aspects of the Cognitive Problem,'' in Gruber, H., Jessor, R., and Hammond, K., COGNITION: THE COLORADO SYMPOSIUM, Cambridge, Harvard University Press, 1957.

(7) Barker, R. G. ECOLOGICAL PSYCHOLOGY, Stanford, Standford University Press, 1968.

(8) Rhodes, W. C. ''An Overview: Toward Synthesis of Models of Disturbance,'' in Rhodes, W. C., and Tracy, M. L., A STUDY OF CHILD VARIANCE, Ann Arbor, University of Michigan Press, 1972.

(9) Highly pertinent discussions of the problem of taxonomy are presented in Altman, I. ''Choice-points in the Classification of Scientific Knowledge,'' in Indik, B. P., and Berrien, F. K., PEOPLE, GROUPS, AND ORGANIZATIONS, New York, Teachers College Press, 1968; and Altman, I., and Lett, E. E. ''The Ecology of Interpersonal Relationships: A Classification System and Conceptual Model,'' in McGrath, J. E., SOCIAL AND PSYCHOLOGICAL FACTORS IN STRESS, New York, Holt, Rinehart and Winston, 1970.

Joachim F. Wohlwill
Professor of Man-Environment Relations
The Pennsylvania State University (1)
University Park, Pennsylvania 16802

Abstract

This paper focuses on the subjectivist bias considered to permeate much of
the thinking and research on problems of environmental perception, cognition and
attitude, i.e., the dual tendency to define environmental variables in phenomenological or personalistic terms, rather than in terms of objective physical dimensions, and to emphasize the contribution of factors based in the individual
in the study of environment-behavior relations, at the expense of environmental
determinants per se. It is argued that this tendency has worked to the detriment
of progress in environmental psychology, both on the theoretical and the practical fronts. A contrary approach is outlined, emphasizing the specification of
objectively defined environmental determinants, and the study of their relationship to behavioral variables, alongside factors centered in the individual. This
approach is illustrated with reference to three problem areas: the differential
response to the natural as opposed to the man-made world, the role of adaptation
levels in the individual's assessment of environmental dimensions, and the interaction of the individual with his environment in a natural recreation area.

Introduction

In this paper I should like to voice a growing concern that I feel over a
tendency that I detect in much of the thinking, the writing and the research in
the environment-behavior field, and that I believe will be disastrous in its
consequences both for the advancement of theoretical aims and for an effective
attack on problems of an applied nature. This concern can best be stated by
paraphrasing Pogo's famous comment on the environmental crisis. It seems that
we, as psychologists, geographers, architects, have at last confronted the environment. And the environment -- that's us!

What I am referring to here is the widespread tendency to define the environment in subjective and personal terms, rather than objective, physical ones,
and as a correlary, the popularity of certain problems for study that supposedly
reveal the highly individual, personal nature of the perceived or experienced
environment, as well as the ready resort to methodological approaches that are
predicated on a similar subjectivist view of the environment.

There are good reasons for this state of affairs. Quite apart from the
fact that physicalism and operationism are going out of fashion as an epistemological base from which to study behavior, there is, for those coming from
outside of psychology, a special fascination with the notion of a personal,
subjectively experienced environment bearing little relationship to the real

world. This fascination has diverse roots. For geographers it appears to stem from the excitement of the discovery that there was a subject matter laying dormant beyond the realm of cartography, aerial photography, and other modes of describing and representing the features of terrestrial sphere -- a discovery that opened up an entirely new world to a profession in which dissatisfaction with the limitations of a purely physicalist account of the topographical as well as ecological aspects of human life on earth was becoming widespread. On the part of designers and architects, on the other hand, the concepts of personal space, of territorial behavior, of individual and idiosyncratic modes of experiencing and using the environments created by them has proved a welcome reinforcer for those in the profession who hoped to bring about not only a more functional, but more socially responsive form of design.

I have several reasons for wishing to oppose myself to this trend. Let me note two major ones. First, by starting inside the person, rather than at the level of the environment, we frequently wind up begging some of the most interesting questions that we might want to attack in our research. Thus, mental maps or urban imagery may well contain distortions of reality -- but we will never be able to investigate this admittedly intriguing phenomenon, if we do not start with the Gospel according to Rand-McNally, so that we have an objective standard against which to compare our internalized schemata of our world.

Indeed, to the extent that we fail to give proper attention to the definition and specification of the environmental variables to which we wish to relate behavior, to that extent we will be in danger of building an environmental psychology on a foundation of quicksand. Mentalistic or phenomenological approaches may have their place in certain areas of psychology, as in the study of dreams, creative activity and the like, just as the visions of Stanley Kubrick's Outer Space at the conclusion of the Film "2001--A Space Odyssey" properly belong in the study of the psychology of human imagination. As environmental psychologists, I submit, it is time we got back down to earth.

This brings me to my second point. I think it is particularly important for us to hasten our reentry into the sphere of mundane terrestrial problems, because that's where the problems are -- our problems. The problems that we are all concerned about, I take it, have to do with our environment and the mess we have made of it. I'm not thinking by any means exclusively of pollution and contamination of our earth, our rivers, our air. I'm also thinking of our man-made environment -- our suburban developments, our ribbons of concrete, our high-rise housing projects. But the problems with these aspects of our environment relate to the real world -- not the world of mental maps, personal space, or semantic-differential n-space, but the world of bricks and concrete, of pesticides and pollutants. They are of concern for us, furthermore, not only because they affect our behavior and our well-being, but because our behavior and our attitudes affect them. We are dealing, in other words, with behavior and environment in a mutually interacting system. It is impossible to analyze or understand such a system, without at the outset defining and conceptualizing the entities of that system in objective, independent terms. Thus, suppose that we find that a group of suburban residents systematically omit from their mental maps an area of a city that has turned into a conclave for an ethnic minority, or misplace its location, or reduce it in size. First of all, that becomes a phenomenon of interest as a manifestation of mental mapping only by relating the mental map to one constructed as a faithful representation of the environment. More important, the phenomenon in itself is of little interest to those involved in planning for the amelioration or more effective use of that environment. Such planning presupposes, not only that we study how the actual environment and changes proposed for it (e.g., a freeway splitting it in half) affect its residents, but how the behavior of those residents, as well as any others who may use it or traverse it affect that environment -- e.g., the environmental consequences to an area of a shift in shopping habits from Center City to suburban shopping centers.

A Simple Schema for Conceptualizing Environment-Behavior Relations

It is time to turn from this polemical tack to a more positive attempt to indicate how to place the study of behavior-environment relations on a sounder footing. To this end I wish to propose the following elementary schema to represent the Environment-Behavior Interaction Cycle:

In this schema, the meaning of E and B should be clear enough -- they refer to Environmental and Behavioral variables, respectively, defined in molar terms. On the "E" side they may refer to geographically or topographically defined settings, characteristics of interior or exterior space, or generic attributes of the environment such as noise levels, amount or intensity of stimulation, etc. On the "B" side they may refer to a variety of overt behaviors directed at specified features of the environment (e.g., environmental exploration, movements of approach or avoidance, modes or patterns of space use) or otherwise placed into relationship with the environment (e.g., task-performance, sexual activity, communicative behavior, etc.), as well as more dispositional variables such as attitudes, preferences, percepts, cognitive maps, etc. As for the "O" element, it is intended to include such variables as expectations, adaptation levels, motivational states, social and cultural attitudes or values, etc., which may modulate the individual's response to his environment.

This schema comprises three kinds of relations: First, direct, determinate relationships between features or attributes of the physical environment and aspects of behavior (e.g., the incidence of crime occurring in and around a housing project is related to the height of its buildings). Second, indirect relationships between environment and behavior, modulated by particular characteristics of the individuals involved (e.g., the incidence of crime around a housing project is related to the presence or absence of areas of empty space around that project that the particular residents of the project perceive as "defensible" or "communal" space). Third, effects of behavior on the environment (e.g., public space in a housing project perceived as non-defensible or non-communal will engender behavior leading to rapid deterioration of such public-space areas). (2)

It should be clear that, according to this formulation, the directness or indirectness of the E→B relationship is purely a question of whether the B variables can be satisfactorily predicted by specifying the E variables alone, or whether it is essential to invoke the role of personality or individual-difference factors modulating the effects of the E variables. Obviously, all E→B relations are necessarily mediated by processes going on in the individual, and for a full explanation of these we will need to concern ourselves with the mechanisms, perceptual, cognitive, motivational or whatever, that can account for them. But unless we can show that there are major differences in the way different individuals respond to the same environmental variables, it does not seem profitable to focus on perceptions, hypotheses or other internally based constructs as the determining variables.

The argument that is being made can now be stated simply as a two-fold plea: that the investigation of environmental questions demands due attention to the role of the variables on the E side, whether these be related to the B variables directly, or indirectly, as modulated by O-based processes, and that the E term be defined in objective, physical terms, and analyzed into its component variables, as much as possible, via operations that are independent of the subject whose behavior is under study.

Note that these two aspects of the argument, while clearly related, are separable. It is quite possible to subscribe to the resort to definition of environmental variables in objective, physical terms, while neglecting their role in the Environment-Behavior relation, and emphasizing instead the contribution of organismic determinants based in the individual. The perceptual work of Wapner and his associates (3) represents a good illustration of such an approach; in the environmental area it is similarly exemplified by work such as that of Sonnenfeld (4) who has studied differential responses by groups of individuals originating in different environments to aspects of the physical environment defined and represented in strictly geographic terms. The converse case, i.e., that of an environmental determinism in which environmental variables are yet defined in subjective terms is more difficult to find, though it may correspond to an extent to the approach to environmental perception on the part of cultural anthropologists (5).

The issue is by no means a purely theoretical one; on the contrary, it has direct implications for the formulation of strategies for effecting changes in a given environmental situation. Thus, to return to the housing-project example, we might be interested in rehabilitating either the environment or the behavior (or both). In either case, the schema suggests a choice of two alternative avenues of approach. Suppose we wish to reduce crime rate. We might alter the environment directly, as done most recently at Pruitt-Igoe, by cutting the height of the buildings in half, or, less drastically, by making the galleries around each floor more accessible to direct view from the apartments on that floor, thereby discouraging their use for muggings, rape, etc. Or we might operate on the "O" aspect, e.g., by trying to inculcate our residents with strong middle-class values to alter their behavior, or, alternatively, by simply replacing our lower-class residents by a middle-class group. Note that any of these actions would not only result in a change in the behavior, but a consequent change in the environment itself, which might have been the starting point for our concern -- i.e., a drop in incidence of broken windows and similar destruction of the environment; an enhancement in the appearance of the environment through communal responsibility (6). But any or all of these effects can only be achieved by coming to grips with the environment, literally -- rather than allowing ourselves, to quote Brunswik's (7) criticism of Lewin's "Field-theory of behavior," to remain "centrally encapsulated."

Let me turn from these general remarks to an attempt to apply the schema just presented, as well as the more general argument for anchoring our environmental variables on the stimulus side, to particular types of research problems. I will illustrate these points by reference to three problems on which I have carried out research recently. They are chosen, not because they provide pat, clean-cut answers to the questions I am raising, but rather because they are problems in which I have been most recently involved. In fact, none of them is ideal for the purposes of my argument; rather each raises some important questions that will need resolving.

The Natural vs. the Man-Made World

The distinction between the world of nature and that of the artifacts of man is, if not as old as the hills, at least as old as man. It is a recurrent theme in literature and the arts, and has been discussed by professionals in such diverse fields as biology, geography, forestry and landscape architecture. The dichotomy enters into issues of conservation, recreation and wild-life management, and is implied in such research as that of Hendee and McKechnie on individual differences in environmental attitudes (8).

Yet we know as yet very little concerning the stimulus-correlates of this distinction, assuming that there are any. It is of course conceivable that the distinction reflects a purely symbolic differentiation between what man has wrought, and that which he finds existing in his environment for which he cannot take credit -- perhaps in spite of himself. Yet this strikes me as an implausible, and eventually unsatisfactory basis on which to establish such a far-reaching dichotomy, with all the values and positive and negative affect associated with it.

The question is, incidentally, of more than purely theoretical interest, for if we knew just what it is that we prize in the natural environment we would be in a better position to argue for the desirability, if not necessity for its preservation. Conceivably we might also find out how to increase the attractiveness or livability of our man-made world, or how best to integrate the two in our approach to landscaping. (I am assuming, of course, that there is something more than avoidance of our fellow human being in our valuing of nature.)

But how may we study this problem? "Semantic Differential!" There's the open sesame to all our methodological problems -- or so it would seem from the widespread application of this technique to all sorts of situations in environmental perception and attitude. In my view, this frequently unthinking use of the semantic differential has, in the aggregate, exerted a negative impact on progress in the field of environmental perception. Let us remember, first of all, what the semantic differential was originally intended for, namely, to study the meaning of words in psychological terms, as an alternative to the formal approaches of the linguists, semanticists and dictionary compilers, as well as to the approaches via paired-associate and similar methods formerly current in the study of verbal behavior, which seemed to lack a clear structural base. Assuredly, the semantic differential can tell us something about the connotative meanings established to particular stimuli or concepts. But it not only remains a purely descriptive approach, with little power for the study of functional or causal processes, but when applied to the differentiation of environmental stimuli, it puts the cart before the horse, in a sense, since it provides us with differentiations at the behavioral level (i.e., that of psychological meaning) while detracting attention from the specification of the environmental variables to which behavioral differences might meaningfully and functionally be related. Thus, in the case of differentiating the natural from the man-made, we might quite likely find that as a category the two differ along such dimensions as fast-slow, noisy-quiet, clean-dirty, and possibly beautiful-ugly, warm-cold, etc. We would probably find resultant differences on Osgood's three dimensions (or at least the evaluative and potency ones), or on particular factors that might emerge from a factor-analysis carried out on such data. But we will have skipped the vital step of specifying the stimulus dimensions that are implicated in these differential evaluations. The results, in other words, would have told us something about the connotative meanings attached to the natural vs. the man-made world, but nothing about the environmental attributes that relate to that difference.

The specification of these attributes is, admittedly, no easy matter, though it is possible to speculate on the role of certain basically rather simple variables, such as shape and sharpness of contours, abruptness of change in color, texture and form, that may well turn out to differentiate the two worlds with some degree of consistency. This, it might be noted, would be the approach of a perception psychologist such as James Gibson, who has for some time advocated a "global psychophysics" aimed at specifying the stimulus-correlates of our perceptions in complex stimulus environments, and who has advocated the development of an "ecological optics" to carry out this task in systematic fashion (9).

Gibson's suggestion deserves to be put to the test in this problem area; indeed, Gibson himself considers that his ecological optics may hold the answer to the perceptual difference between the man-made and the natural world that is the object of our concern (10). It has the limitation, however, of being a purely perceptual approach, which has no reference to the behavioral domain from which the differentiation between these two worlds derives its greatest importance. I am referring to the domain of affective reactions, of responses of interest and boredom, of exploration and curiosity, of approach and avoidance -- in short, that of the aesthetics of the environment. A series of studies carried out in part by Rachel and Steven Kaplan at Michigan, and in part at Penn. State by myself with the collaboration of a number of graduate students (11), represents a beginning attempt to deal with this side of the problem.

The details of the somewhat checkered history of these parallel sets of studies need not concern us; accounts of earlier research are available in print (12), while more recent work is being reported by R. Kaplan elsewhere at these meetings, and will form the subject of an A.P.A. Symposium to be held in Montreal in August. Suffice it to note that this research brings out, first of all, the role of higher order stimulus variables in environmental exploration and preference, such as stimulus complexity, coherence (or "legibility") and identifiability -- all variables which are clearly one step beyond physically defined stimulus variables, relating rather to information content. They are thus compatible with the theoretical and empirical work of Berlyne on the stimulus determinants of behavior and arousal (13). At the same time they are independently definable stimulus attributes, and even if their objective measurement in ready-made environmental stimuli may pose problems, it is possible to treat human subjects as sensors of variations in such attributes with quite adequate reliability and consistency (14).

Let us turn now to another facet of this research, of more direct relevance to the differentiation between the natural and the man-made world that is under discussion. Both the findings of Kaplan, Kaplan and Wendt (1972) and those from our laboratories (Wohlwill, 1973) have shown a very consistent preference for natural scenes as opposed to those of man-made environments. Our own research extends this difference to the variable of amount of voluntary exploratory activity. At the same time the work of the Kaplans appears to indicate that as far as the complexity variable is concerned at least, it operates independently of the nature vs. man-made differentiation. Our own data seemingly corroborate this finding, since the functions obtained relating both preference and exploratory activity to our diversity scale were approximately parallel for both domains (15). As for the other variables emphasized by the Kaplans, such as coherence and identifiability, as well as "mystery," which seems to refer to the surprise potential of an environmental scene (16), there is no indication from their reports that they serve to account for the difference between the two domains; instead, Kaplan and Wendt emphasize the role of a set of supplementary variables that they designate as "primary landscape factors."

Before turning to the question what these factors may be, or more generally what residual differences between the stimulus characteristics of the two domains may be implicated in the differences observed in the responses to them, we must add an important qualifier, as well as methodological caveat, to the conclusion stated above concerning the independence of the effects of the complexity and the man-made vs. nature dimensions. In order to demonstrate such independence, it is necessary to select stimuli that are equated for the variable of complexity for each of the two values of the latter, according to a classical orthogonal-analysis of variance design. But in the process of constructing such sets, we confirmed a finding that we had ample reason to suspect all along: that there is in fact an intrinsic association between the two dimensions in the real worlds -- i.e., man-made stimuli are, on the average, more complex than those of the natural world. At the least we found it impossible to locate samples of the natural world of a level of complexity comparable to the most complex of our man-made stimuli. Thus an attempt to keep these variables orthogonal not only would have entailed a strongly biased selection of stimuli, but would have led to a highly misleading picture of the relationship between preference and com-plexity, since it is only by including the high-complexity stimuli (i.e., within the man-made set) that the true inverted -U shape of this relationship emerges.

This observation may serve as a warning against the blithe disregard of ques-tions of sampling of stimuli that may result from attempts to isolate the role of stimulus variables that are intrinsically related in the real world. Perhaps the solution lies in the application of the principles of ecologically representa-tive sampling of stimuli which Brunswik (17) has championed for students of per-ception, though this prescription is more easily enunciated than carried into practice; indeed, the very concept of representative sampling as applied to envi-ronmental stimuli has been questioned on conceptual grounds. (18)

Where does this leave us, then, in our attempts to resolve the question of the real basis for the differentiation between the natural and the man-made environment? Certainly stimulus complexity must be admitted as one of the factors contributing to this differentiation, but just as surely it cannot be said to account for all or even most of the behavioral differences associated with it.

Research currently under way at our laboratories at Penn. State may help to provide some partial answers to this conundrum. First of all, by investigating the problem in terms of preferential direction of looking from a focal point (with the subject being able to rotate around a full 360° circle in his explora-tion of a given setting), the difficult problem of stimulus selection alluded to above will be alleviated to a degree. That is, the nature vs. man-made dif-ferentiation will be studied within each setting, in terms of differential looking times and preference judgments associated with particular directions, which will be related to the balance between natural and man-made elements visible in those directions. An attempt will then be made to determine the stimulus-correlates of this balance, by specifying a number of a-priori defined variables, such as expansiveness or depth of field, sharpness of contrast, etc., that should permit us to predict both preference judgments and exploration times in terms of a

multiple regression equation. Finally, a comparison between results obtained
under field conditions and those obtained from photographic slides in the laboratory (with sets of eight slides being presented in a 360° panorama duplicating the
array of views present in the original scene), will not only indicate how validly
photographic slides can be taken as surrogates of the real world, but more particularly how judgments of preference and exploratory activity are affected by
the elimination of movement and sound. Indeed, one plausible hypothesis is that
the overall preference for natural stimuli may be in part an artifactual consequence of the reliance on still photos, since the deprivation of sound and motion
may act disproportionately to impoverish the man-made stimuli relative to the
natural ones. (25)

This lengthy foray into the thicket of environmental perception is clearly
not intended to resolve the diverse, formidable obstacles that have to be overcome in approaching this area of study on the basis of a thorough specification
of determining stimulus variables. It should serve, however, to indicate the
possibilities of such an approach, and the potential harvest of information it
promises regarding functional relationships between environmental variables and
behavioral variables. It is these relationships that will remain obscured in
short-cuts such as the semantic differential and other approaches that start from
the side of the individual, or from response-defined measures.

Adaptation Level and Environmental Evaluation

Those who would oppose themselves to the view being promulgated here, that
the physical environment must be defined in objective terms, independent of the
individual experiencing it, could make a seemingly potent case for the contrary
position by pointing to adaptation-level phenomena. They can argue cogently that
the manner in which a given environment is experienced by the individual is dependent on the frame of reference with which the individual comes to that environment, or more particularly the adaptation level he has established through his
past experience, which will modulate the effects of a given level of physical
stimulation on him.

At the risk of thus demolishing my own position, let me describe briefly a
pilot study carried out in collaboration with Imre Kohn (19) that dealt with this
very problem. I believe that is is possible to demonstrate that even on this
apparently unfavorable ground the general argument I am proposing remains tenable.

Kohn and I studied a group of families who had migrated to the Harrisburg,
Pa., area. We were interested in obtaining their assessment of their present
environment on a number of dimensions relating to the physical as well as the
social environment, such as how noisy, crowded, polluted they considered it to
be, how much of a problem they perceived vandalism and crime to be, etc. The
purpose was to relate their assessment of these variables to the adaptation level
that they might have been expected to have built up through living in the environment of their previous residence. Accordingly we compared a group of families
who had moved from large metropolitan areas with one that had moved from small-
town or rural areas. While our N was pitifully small (Harrisburg is not an ideal

community for the purposes of studying migration, but it was the only one accessible to us that fitted the criterion of an intermediate-sized urban area), the results still supported our hypotheses, although not for all of the variables that we dealt with. Thus, migrants from rural areas rated the Harriburg environment as significantly noisier, more polluted and more vandalism- and crime-ridden than did those from metropolitan areas.

In other words, the results appear to indicate that a person's perception of his environment is a function, not so much of the objective, physical conditions, but of his frame of reference, or adaptation level. Let us note, parenthetically, that the principle demonstrated here is hardly a new one; the work of Helson and his followers (20) is replete with illustrations of such frame-of-reference effects modulating judgments of sensory magnitudes, aesthetic stimuli, social-attitude statements, etc. It is equally familiar to sociologists, in the context of work on problems of "relative deprivation" and similar contextual effects in the area of personal satisfaction. (21)

Is the environment, then, really in the head, after all? Two points are to be noted, in gauging the significance of effects of this type for the study of environmental perception. The first is that the responses asked of the subjects are based on the use of a subjective, seven-point rating scale, which is not anchored at any point to an objective referent. The use of such scales renders the results altogether equivocal as indices of _perceived_ stimulus magnitudes. Thus, in the case of the dimension of noise, the fact that rural migrants gave a mean rating to Harrisburg of 4.1, as compared to 2.1 for the metropolitan group, _may_ mean that the latter group had been rendered less sensitive to noise as a result of their prolonged exposure to a large urban environment; alternatively, it may mean that their frame of reference for judging an environment as "noisy," i.e., for assigning a given number on this essentially arbitrary scale to a particular environment, was different. The point is that in order to make conclusive statements concerning perception, we need to have confidence in the status of our response measure as an index of perception. Subjective rating scales are clearly deficient in this respect, and their widespread use in the field of environmental perception, particularly through the growing popularity of the semantic differential, renders the significance of much of the work carried out in this field open to doubt.

The second point is that in spite of the susceptibility of our responses to frame-of-reference effects and the like, the environmental stimuli remain as objective standards against which the actual results can be judged. The study is in fact anchored in the objective stimulus environment in two essential respects: in the definition of the independent variable (size of community of origin) and in the postulation of a further stimulus dimension (e.g., noise) assumed to be correlated with the first. It is this correlation that allows for the assumption of a contrast effect, in accordance with adaptation-level principles.

It should be noted further that the apparent lack of determinancy of the objective environmental variables in our study is actually an artifact of the design, which calls for responses to but a single environment, that of the Harrisburg area. Thus community size, and the several variables assumed to be correlated with it, represent a constant in our study. Once we allow this factor to vary, we can generate a set of functions describing the relationship between perceived and objective stimulus magnitudes, as modulated by differential adaptation levels.

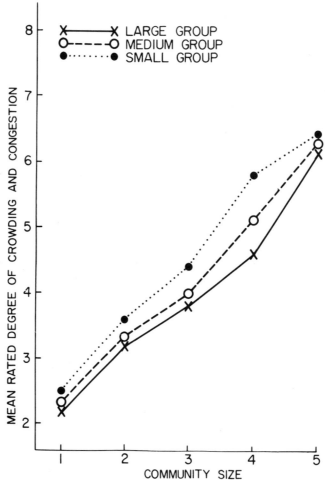

Fig. 1: Ratings of Crowdedness attributed to photographically portrayed communities varying in size, by three groups of migrants to New York City. (Preliminary data from dissertation in progress by I. Kohn.)

A good illustration comes from some recent dissertation research by Mr. Kohn in which he has extended our earlier study of migration by comparing migrants to New York City originating in small-town, intermediate-sized and large communities, not just with respect to their evaluation of New York City, but with respect to their evaluation of unspecified communities varying along the size dimension, presented through sets of photographs. Fig. 1 shows the results obtained with respect to one of the dimensions that Kohn used, that of crowding. The functions portrayed here indicate that perception is quite dependably related to the stimulus, but that the exact form of the relationship varies with the individual's adaptation level, which thus becomes a parameter of the function -- a prime illustration of the meaning of the B = f(E,O) paradigm.

The Environment as Independent and Dependent Variable

Probably the strongest argument for insisting that in any attempts to relate environment to behavior the former be defined and specified in objective, physical terms, is the fact that a complete account of the interrelationship between the two requires us to envisage them as acting reciprocally on each other. Thus, behavior is not only to some degree affected by the environment, but can itself effect changes in the environment -- a situation represented in our original schema, which simply amounts to recognizing that human (and for that matter animal) behavior enters as an element of the system of forces that we may designate as an ecosystem.

Consider, for instance, the relationship between the attractiveness of a natural recreation area and the degree of use to which it has been subjected. Let us start out with the assumption that there exists a specifiable degree of use conducive to maximal enjoyment of the area on the part of the recreationist. As use increases (as a function of publicity, population increase in the area, etc.), enjoyment should decrease, in turn causing a decline in use. We thus arrive at a negative feedback relationship between amount of use and its effects on the area, and consequently on further use.

It is obvious that this equilibrium model is so oversimplified as to be rarely if ever applicable in this realm, though there may be some problems, such as the use of grazing lands perhaps, that may come closer to fitting it. There are two factors, in particular, that need to be taken into account in the recreation-area case. One is that use is traditionally accompanied by development of facilities, which are typically irreversible in their environmental effects. The second is that as a function of this very development, as well as the usually correlated facilitation of access to the area, changes occur in the type of user attracted to the area. The result is frequently a positive rather than a negative feedback cycle, operating at least over an extended period of time, with development stimulating more use (even if the type of user and the reasons for their frequenting the area may undergo change), until a saturation point is reached, so as to result in the restoration of equilibrium at a different level. The case of Yosemite Valley may be taken as an instance in point. Here it was the National Park Service which was instrumental, first in promoting the development of the

Park for mass recreation and tourism (under the impetus of the "Mission 66" Program instituted in the Eisenhower Administration), and most recently, in trying to reverse the process of environmental deterioration from increasing use, by instituting corrective administrative measures -- notably the banning of the automobile from the Valley.

How might one go about studying this problem? Ideally it would require a long-term study of a particular area, monitoring the changes occurring over an extended period in the number of visitors, their reasons for coming to the area and their expectations of it, the amount of and kinds of development introduced into the area, and the concomitant changes in the ecosystem and the overall quality of the environment. We have not attempted anything that ambitious thus far, however. Instead, Harry Heft (a graduate student) and I have undertaken a pilot study, designed as a simple comparative study of the users of State Parks in an underdeveloped as opposed to a highly developed recreation area in Pennsylvania, specifically, the area of the Grand Canyon of Pennsylvania (in the North-Central portion of the State), compared to the Poconos area.

A comparison of the two groups with respect to several questionnaire-based measures, notably preferences for development, and general attitudes towards the social and man-made world as opposed to the world of nature show some interesting differences in the expected directions: The Poconos group had a significantly higher index of preference for development than the Grand Canyon group (based on a composite of responses to a set of eight Likert-type items dealing with the provision of specific facilities and services), and likewise showed attitudes oriented more towards civilization and less towards wilderness. This finding, indicating that those in the relatively undeveloped area of the Grand Canyon were content with much less in the way of facilities and services than those in the Poconos, fits in with the positive-feedback relationship between use and development suggested above as applying to natural-recreation areas.

This pilot study has been cited here mainly to point the way towards conceptualizing individual human behavior as an integral part of the ecosystem, and consequently to reemphasize the importance of studying functional relationships between behavioral variables and features or attributes of the physical environment, defined in objective terms. From the point of view of this analysis, it matters little that the beauty and environmental quality of the environment of Yosemite Valley, for instance, may be perceived as fairly constant over time, as a result of changing expectations or adaptation levels of successive populations of users. What does matter is the relationship between the objective characteristics of the environment and the behavior of the visitors at the site, and their density and ecological distribution over the area, as well as the changes in that environment resulting directly from the behavior and use to which it is subjected, and more indirectly from administrative responses to such use.

Conclusion

While the foregoing argument concerning the primacy of environmental variables in the study of environment-behavior relations may not find universal acceptance, it is reassuring to see others working in this area arriving at similar viewpoints. Consider the following quote, taken from the conclusion of Carr and Schissler's study of environmental perception: (22)

> "Perhaps the most significant and surprising finding of this study is the degree to which both perception and memory of the city as seen from a highway seem to be determined by the form of the environment itself. Whether analyzed in terms of eye fixations, head orientation, or the number of mentions in memory reports, it is clear that it is the structure of what is out there to be seen which largely determines what is seen by a diversity of subjects.... Much recent work in psychology has emphasized the importance of cognitive, affective, and individualistic factors in perception, sometimes seeming to suggest that the selective and constructive powers of the mind are all-important, with the environment merely providing the raw material. These results indicate otherwise, although cognitive and affective factors must be accounted for in any full explanation of the process. Even the subtitle of this paper, 'Perceptual Selection...' is misleading and should perhaps have been 'perceptual programming'." (pp. 31/32)

We might also call attention, in the same context, to work being undertaken in two very different fields, i.e., architecture and natural recreation, to devise ways of describing the physical environment in terms that are both precise and functional for the investigators' purposes. The first is that of Thiel, who has given us a highly detailed schema for specifying the variables in the spatial environment that are of relevance to the architect and the designer, (23) in terms that bring to mind the "ecological optics" advocated by Gibson. Similarly, Shafer and Thompson have followed an interesting mode of attack in trying to specify the environmental variables determining choice of campsites, by cataloguing a large number of physical and geographic dimensions along which such campsites vary and subjecting these to factor analysis so as to arrive at the main independent dimensions in terms of which the stimulus environment of campsites can be described. (24)

Note, finally, that acceptance of the present argument does not in any way commit one to the empty-organism approach. I have no quarrel with the utilization of intervening constructs, such as adaptation level, mental map, sensation-seeking needs, environmental attitudes, or whatever. They are in fact essential to account for the mode of interrelationship between stimulus variables and overt behaviors. What I do decry is the tendency in some quarters to emulate the sad history of the "new look in perception" movement which attempted to accomplish the prodigious feat of building a theory of perception while deliberately ignoring the stimulus input -- to the point of drawing weighty inferences about perceptual processes from findings obtained from tachistoscopically presented blank slides! Such a tack, in my view, can only serve to undermine our efforts to understand the individual's response to the physical environment, and to negate our pretense of contributing substantively towards an effective attack on environmental problems.

As psychologists, we cannot fail to deal with the mind. As environmental psychologists, however, I suggest that we at least provide our model of the mind with a window to the outside world.

Notes and References

(1) The author is indebted to a number of persons, notably Irwin Altman, John Archea, Eugene Bazan, Dan Carson and Arthur Patterson, for invaluable comments in response to an earlier draft of this paper.

(2) For evidence of this type, cf. Newman, O., DEFENSIBLE SPACE, Macmillan, New York, 1972; Yancey, W. L., "Architecture, interaction and social control", in Wohlwill, J. F. and Carson, D. C., ENVIRONMENT AND SOCIAL SCIENCE, A.P.A., Washington, D. C., 1972.

(3) cf. Wapner, S., & Werner, H., PERCEPTUAL DEVELOPMENT, Worcester, Mass., Clark University Press, 1957.

(4) Sonnenfeld, J., "Environmental perception and adaptation-level in the Arctic", in Lowenthal, D., ENVIRONMENTAL PERCEPTION AND BEHAVIOR, University of Chicago, 1967.

(5) Kluckhohn, F. R., & Strodtbeck, F. L., VARIATIONS IN VALUE ORIENTATIONS, Evanston, Illinois, Row, Peterson, 1961.

(6) Newman, O., DEFENSIBLE SPACE, Macmillan, New York, 1972.

(7) Brunswik, E., "The conceptual framework of psychology", in Neurath, O., et al., INTERNATIONAL ENCYCLOPEDIA OF UNIFIED SCIENCE, Vol. I, Pt. 2, University of Chicago, 1952.

(8) Hendee, J. C., RECREATION CLIENTELE (unpublished dissertation), University of Washington, 1970; McKechnie, G. E., "Measuring environmental dispositions with the environmental response inventory", in Eastman, C., & Archea, J., EDRA 2, Pittsburgh, 1970.

(9) Gibson, J. J., "Ecological optics", VISION RESEARCH, 19, pages 253-262, 1961.

(10) Gibson, J. J., Personal communication.

(11) The following individuals participated in this research: John Adams, Fred Hurand, Robert LeDoux, Brian Nealy, Joel Ostro, Romedi Passini, Elliot Reiff, Richard Titus, and Harry Watters.

(12) Wohlwill, J. F., "Amount of stimulus exploration and preference as differential functions of stimulus complexity", PERCEPTION AND PSYCHOPHYSICS, 4, pages 307-312, 1968; Kaplan, S., Kaplan, R., & Wendt, J. S., "Rated preference and complexity for natural and urban visual material", PERCEPTION AND PSYCHOPHYSICS, 12, pages 354-356, 1972.

(13) Berlyne, D. E., CONFLICT, AROUSAL AND CURIOSITY, McGraw-Hill, New York, 1960.

(14) For evidence on this point with respect to stimulus complexity, cf. Wohlwill, J. F., "Amount of stimulus exploration and preference", PERCEPTION AND PSYCHOPHYSICS, 4, pages 307-312, 1972.

(15) Wohlwill, J. F., "Factors in the differential response to the natural and the man-made environment" (to be presented at A.P.A. meetings, Montreal, 1973).

(16) Kaplan, S., & Wendt, J. S., "Preference and the visual environment: complexity and some alternatives", in Mitchell, W. J., EDRA 3, Los Angeles, 1972; Kaplan, R., "Predictors of environmental preference", in Preiser, W. F., EDRA 4, Blacksburg, Virginia, 1973.

(17) Brunswik. E., PERCEPTION AND THE REPRESENTATIVE DESIGN OF PSYCHOLOGICAL EXPERIMENTS, University of California, 1956.

(18) Hochberg, J., "Representative sampling and the purposes of perceptual research", in Hammond, K. R., THE PSYCHOLOGY OF EGON BRUNSWIK, Holt, Rinehart & Winston, New York, 1966.

(19) Wohlwill, J. F., & Kohn, I., "The environment as experienced by the migrant: An adaptation-level view", REPRESENTATIVE RESEARCH IN SOCIAL PSYCHOLOGY, 4 (1), 1973. (in press)

(20) Helson, H., ADAPTATION-LEVEL THEORY, New York, Harper & Row, 1964; Appley, M. (ed.), ADAPTATION-LEVEL THEORY: A SYMPOSIUM, New York, Academic Press, 1971.

(21) Kelley, H. H., "The two functions of reference groups," in Swanson, G. E., et al., READINGS IN SOCIAL PSYCHOLOGY (2nd ed.), New York, Holt, 1952.

(22) Carr, S., & Schissler, D., "The city as a trip", ENVIRONMENT AND BEHAVIOR, 1, pages 7-35, 1969.

(23) Thiel, P., "Notes on the description, scaling, notation, and scoring of some perceptual and cognitive attributes of the physical environment", in Proshansky, H. M., et al., ENVIRONMENTAL PSYCHOLOGY, New York, Holt, Rinehart & Winston, 1970.

(24) Shafer, E. L. Jr., & Thompson, R. C., "Models that describe use of Adirondack campgrounds", FOREST SCIENCE, 14, pages 383-391, 1968.

(25) The writer is pleased to acknowledge the role of Romedi Passini and Harry Watters in suggesting this 360° -panorama approach to the problem, as well as their skillful assistance, along with Brian Nealy, in translating this idea into experimental reality for both field and laboratory settings.

THREE   ENVIRONMENTAL COGNITION

Chairman: Reginald G. Golledge, Ohio State University,
    Columbus, Ohio

Authors: Reginald G. Golledge and Gary T. Moore,
    "Introductory Comments"
Ronald Briggs, "On The Relationship Between
    Cognitive and Objective Distance"
Martin T. Cadwallader, "A Methodological Ex-
    amination Of Cognitive Distance"
Ann S. Devlin, "Some Factors In Enhancing
    Knowledge Of A Natural Area"
David L. George, "Frame Dependence In
    Directional Orientation"
Georgia Zannaras, "The Cognitive Structures
    of Urban Areas"
Alcira Kreimer, "Building The Imagery of San
    Francisco: An Analysis of Controversy
    Over High-Rise Development, 1970-71"
Gary T. Moore, "Developmental Differences In
    Environmental Cognition"
Alfred J. Nigl and Harold D. Fishbein,
    "Children's Ability To Coordinate Perspec-
    tives: Cognitive Factors"
Roger Peters, "Cognitive Maps In Wolves and Men"
Susan Saegert, "Crowding: Cognitive Overload
    and Behavioral Constraint"

SYMPOSIUM ON ENVIRONMENTAL COGNITION: INTRODUCTORY COMMENTS   3.0

Reginald G. Golledge
Professor of Geography
Ohio State University
Columbus, Ohio 43210

Gary T. Moore
Canada Council Fellow
Department of Psychology
Clark University
Worcester, Massachusetts 01613

The Content of Papers

This symposium has been organized as a means of presenting a variety of current
approaches to the problem of environmental cognition. By environmental cognition
is meant individual and group knowledge of large scale environments, including
spatial, social, political and cultural environments. Participants include
graduate students and new Ph.D.'s from disciplines such as geography, psychology,
and environmental design. While some differences are obvious in terms of the
nature of the problems studied and the relative importance of theoretical and
empirical content, studies are unified by common aims and methods. This can best
be illustrated by summarizing the themes of contributed papers.

Environmental cognition is still a relatively new area of knowledge. It is of
considerable importance therefore, that some attention be paid to organizing
existing theoretical studies, and modifying or developing such theory as a
guide for future work. Moore continues his contribution to this aspect of the
field by examining developmental differences in the cognition of macro-environments based on Piagetan and Wernerian theory. Continued research into the philosophical and theoretical bases of the cognition of macro-environments, or the
spatial characteristics of such environments, is of the utmost importance if
further work is to be prevented from degenerating to a series of independent
empirical studies.

Relations between the cognitive and spatial structure of Columbus, Newark and
Marion (Ohio), and the images of a city (San Francisco) generated by the mass
media, are examined by Zannaras and Kreimer respectively. Both are concerned
with entire cities as cognitive units, and develop and discuss appropriate methods
for determining city images and the effect of these images on selected forms
of behavior in an urban environment. Working also at a macro-scale, Sloan-
Devlin and Peters concentrate on rural areas rather than cities. The first of
these two papers focuses on the interaction between humans and relatively unknown
"natural areas", while the second uses cognitive processes to interpret the
behavior of wolves in their natural habitat.

The relationship between cognitive and objective distance is investigated at
different scales by Cadwallader and Briggs. Cadwallader describes the relationship between the two distances in terms of intercity distance estimates in the
vicinity of Los Angeles. Briggs focuses more on distances within a city
(Columbus, Ohio), showing the nature of the distortion of cognised distance as
direction changes and as complex rather than straight line routes are examined.

Distance is but one characteristic of the spatial structure of environmental
cognitions. Saegert, for example, concentrates on the perception of density as
a factor likely to influence behavior; George argues that directional accuracy is
a function of an underlying frame dependence which is imposed on all cognitive
structures; Fishbein and Nigl examine the understanding of spatial relations
such as left-right, up and down, back and front, as a means for explaining how
children co-ordinate perspectives. All these papers clearly imply that cognitive
structures must be influences by these activities.

The Theoretical and Methodological Bases of the Papers

A variety of cognitive and spatial theories have been used as frameworks for the
symposium papers. Piaget and Wernerian type developmental ideas occur in several
papers and are made explicit in the papers by Moore and Fishbein and Nigl. Tolman's
cognitive place learning theory and Neisser's interpretations of cognitive
psychology provide conceptual backgrounds, terminology, and explanatory rationale
for papers by Zannaras, Briggs, Cadwallader, and to some extent, Peters and
Sloan-Devlin. The ideas of the latter two are also strongly influenced by Kaplan's
evolutionary perspective, and by Gibson's perceptual learning theories. Saegert's
work is tied less closely to any one specific theory, and instead relies heavily
on personal space concepts including those related to humans (e.g. Sommer), and
those related to animals (e.g. Calhoun). Human spatial orientation, as interpreted by George, has a long history of interest in psychology, and the theoretical
basis of his paper traces from Trowbridge to Asch to Angyal. Departing somewhat
from a primary emphasis of the above pages on psychological theory, Kreimer draws
on an exciting melange of social, communication, and architectural theory (e.g.
Barthes, Gerbner). The mixing of interdisciplinary theory is also evident in
papers by Zannaras, Briggs, and Cadwallader, who combine the geographer's theories
of spatial structure and density decay concepts with theories of cognitive
processes to discuss their selected problems.

The methodologies used in the symposium papers are as diverse as the theories
relied on. Moore uses a panel of judges to sort map-like representations of
macro-environments derived from a random sample of school children; Fishbein and
Nigl also use children but examine positional relations in arrangements of objects
and photos from different observer viewpoints to obtain their data. Saegert
observes the overt activities of people in a variety of crowded situations;
Sloan-Devlin uses verbal recall and graphic skills to provide here empirical
evidence. Peter's observes the activities of wolves for evidence of cognitive
processes at work; Kreimer examines newspapers and attitudinal questionnaires
to identify imageable characteristics procedures, such as interval and ratio
scaling methods, to obtain data and test their hypotheses. Zannaras adopts a
mixed mode methodology, using wayfinding tasks in experimental and real world
conditions, and scale modelsand slide presentations of actual environments to
elicit subjects' responses.

Directions for Future Research

For the most part theories related to cognitive processes have been developed for micro-scale environments. Interest in the cognition of macro-spatial environments is of a relatively recent origin. It is no surprise therefore, to see that the bulk of studies in this area are empirical ones, examining specific localized problems and using theories developed for somewhat different purposes from a variety of disciplines to help organize and define the slowly accumulating knowledge of the field. It is also obvious that continued work on the theoretical bases of environmental cognition should continue, and that this may be facilitated best by working in an interdisciplinary mode. Not only do we require a thorough understanding of cognitive processes, but we also require an understanding of the locational arrangements of environmental elements, and the individual and social meanings attached to those elements.

The variety of experimental designs and analytical methods used by participants in the symposium point to another area of necessary concentration of future effort. The question arises, can cognitive information be recovered in an objective form? If so, how can it be recovered? How can it best be presented? What analytical methods are most appropriate for obtaining relevant information? And what procedures are most appropriate for testing data? Finally, how much confidence do we have in the objective representation of internal images? There is at present no consensus of answers for these questions, for in many cases comparatively little attention has been paid to them. Papers in this symposium illustrate a wealth of measurement, testing, and representational methods which can be used to investigate problems of environmental cognition, and some objective assessment of the relativevalues of these procedures should be a focus of future work in the area.

The characteristics of the physical and human environment which appear to significantly influence the structure of images is another obvious avenue of future research. There has been a considerable (and increasing) volume of research into what elements of the general environment appear most likely to be noticed and used by persons in their commerce with the environment. Less attention has been paid to the actual and cognized nature of fundamental spatial properties of macro-environments such as location, proximity, distance, direction, density and position.

The papers of this symposium evidence a concern with problems of theory, method, and empirical data collection, and indicate a number of approaches which should be valuable for continued research in the field.

Ronald Briggs
Assistant Professor of Geography,
Research Associate, Population Research Center
University of Texas at Austin
Austin, Texas   78712.

Abstract

The importance of a relatively close correspondence between objective and cognized distance for efficient navigation in the urban environment is suggested. Some contradictions in the existing literature concerning this correspondence are noted. Possible mechanisms for the cognition of distance are suggested and discussed and one of these models is drawn upon for the design of an experiment to examine distortions in the cognition of distance between points within an urban environment. Results suggest the existence of distortions associated with the structure of the underlying physical environment and give some validity to one of the proposed mechanism for the cognition of distance.

Introduction

In his classic work Lynch (1) stressed the importance of the legibility of the physical structure of cities and suggested that this vitally effected the clarity of an individual's image of cities. For a geographer interested in the spatial behavior of individuals, it is the influence of the image upon individual movement patterns within the city which is of primary interest. Movement patterns primarily result from decisions made by individuals to utilize or interact with a specific facility or location within the urban fabric. The image provides the information input necessary both to make the decision and execute the consequent behavior. However, efficient decision making can only be accomplished if the image and the objective environment are in reasonably close correspondence. Particularly critical for spatial behavior is the correspondence between objective and cognitive distance since distance, or its close derivative, travel time, is one of the major dimensions upon which decisions are based. If distortions exist in the cognition of distance then the possibility is open for "inefficiencies" in travel behavior as well as inaccurate predictions of such behaviors obtained from any model of individual behavior based upon objective distance measures.

It appears that the most basic question to ask is whether or not distortions exist in the cognition of distance to places within the urban environment. If this is the case then attention should be directed to the sources of these distortions. If they are a consequence of the physical structure of the city they may be amenable to correction by appropriate environmental design strategies. On the other hand, if they follow from the nature of the cognitive processes, alternative strategies may be required.

The conclusions of existing studies on cognitive distance within an urban environment are contradictory. Lowrey (2) concludes that "judgements were closely related to geographic distances." On the other hand, Lee (3) and Golledge, Briggs and Demko (4) have shown the existence of systematic distortions related to the type of routes linking locations, the familiarity of the subjects with the locations, and orientation relative to downtown. However, the studies differ on several grounds. The scaling method utilized by Lowrey is that of ratio estimation whereas the other researchers obtained direct magnitude estimates of distances. Lowrey defines the function relating cognized and objective distance, whereas other authors do not. The present paper addresses itself to these contradictions and attempts to ascertain the correspondence between cognized and objective distance, with particular emphasis on the question as to whether or not the physical structure of the environment influences cognized distance.

Mechanisms For the Cognition of Distance

Despite the growing literature on the cognition of distance no author has suggested an appropriate mechanism. This is a serious shortcoming since there are several facets to the cognition of large environmental forms such as the city which differ from situations more commonly studied under the rubric of perception or cognition, thus traditional models in these fields are not immediately applicable. Perhaps the most significant difference is that when the relative spatial location of two or more places within the city is being examined the scale is such that the subject cannot receive stimulus information from both objects simultaneously. Thus, some process must be postulated by which stimulus inputs can be related together even though they are received by the subject when he is at different points in time and space. This necessitates the existence of a relatively complex process since, even in the simple situation of perceived distance between points within the subject's field of vision, complex processes involving the use of distance "clues" or cues are involved.

At least five possible mechanisms for distance cognition can be postulated. The first, motory response, may provide distance cognition from the amount of physical energy expended in moving. A second mechanism involves obtaining distance estimates from knowledge of the time and velocity involved in moving between two points by utilizing the simple mathematical relationships between these three variables. A third possibility utilizes the perception of distance (5). The space between two points which cannot be viewed simultaneously is assumed to have within it a series of "link-nodes," adjacent pairs of which can be viewed simultaneously. The processes producing perceived distances can then operate upon these adjacent pairs, and the cognized distance between the end points can be obtained by an additive process which sums the distances between the linknode pairs. Utilization of regular, or supposedly regular, patterns within the structure of the external environment is a fourth possible mechanism. Counting blocks, telephone poles or stop lights are possible examples. Finally, symbolic representations provide important sources of distance information. These would include maps, roadsigns giving distance, automobile odometers, etc.

Although all five of these mechanisms may operate, it is suggested that the third, namely distance perception, is the most general and critical. Motor response depends upon walking, a rather uncommon practice in the United States! Regarding time and velocity, as Fraisse (6) points out the experience of time is not a simple phenomena since it can pass without being "experienced." Given that access to speedometers is not universal it is difficult to conceive of velocity perception existing without a priori information concerning both time and distance. Thus the second mechanism may only assume importance in societies where time is important and thus noticed and velocity indicators are readily available. Regularly occuring features are relatively uncommon. Blocks, for instance, are not used as a concept in the European environment. Finally, concerning the last mechanism Appleyard (7) has found the existence of distance information in towns for which no public maps exist.

A mechanism for the cognition of distance based upon visual perception seems particularly appealing. Unlike other mechanisms it is not dependent upon the cultural artifacts of the society concerned. Furthermore, the postulated additive process accords well with recent theories which see cognition as a construction or reconstruction process (8), a view well in keeping with the concepts of Piaget and Inhelder (9). If images are reconstructed from memory traces of earlier perceptual constructions or image reconstructions, then we can easily envisage the image of the space between two end nodes being reconstructed from successive, separately perceived segments, and the total distance being cognized as the sum of the distances involved in each segment.

Viewing cognized distance as the sum of perceived distances has the important implication that factors which influence perceived distance must also influence cognized distance. Examination of the literature on these factors suggests that, in outdoor situations where distance cues are readily available, a relatively close correspondence is generally found between objective and perceived distance, with the important exception that perceived distance tends to be progressively underestimated as objective distance increases (10). For the model of cognized distance this has the important implication that the greater the number of segments into which the space between two end nodes is divided, the greater the cognized distance (Figure 1). Such a situation would be indicated by higher b values if a function

FIGURE 1.   The Influences of Segmentation Upon Cognized Distance

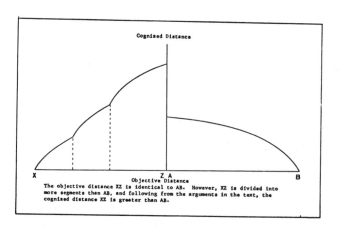

The objective distance XZ is identical to AB. However, XZ is divided into more segments than AB, and following from the arguments in the text, the cognised distance XZ is greater than AB.

of the form $Y=aX^b$ is used to relate objective to cognized distance. We may further suggest that the number of segments into which the space is divided is a function of the number of distinct and differentiable features, or "link-nodes", in the physical structure of the environment. Thus, it can be postulated that the underlying structure of the physical environment will influence cognized distance.

The Experiment

An experiment was designed and conducted the primary purpose of which was to ascertain whether distinct differences exist between cognized and objective distance (11). The hypothesized model of distance cognition suggests that situations which contrast distances from a common origin point to locations away from as against toward downtown, and locations involving straight routes as against those involving turns, are the most likely to show such discrepancies. Toward, as against away from, downtown there are marked contrasts in the underlying environmental structure. The density of buildings and population increases, thus the environment contains more potential link nodes. Furthermore, the slower speed of travel allows for more elements to be observed, and the greater frequency of use of the route allows more link-nodes to be identified. If a turn acts as a link node, routes involving turns will have potentially more link-nodes than straight routes. Thus it can be hypothesized that, for equivalent objective distances, cognized distance will be greater to location toward as against away from downtown (Hypothesis 1), and for routes involving bends as against straight routes (Hypothesis 2).

Twenty locations within Columbus, Ohio, were chosen such that each could be assigned to one of four groups determined on the basis of two binary variables: "away from downtown" versus "toward downtown" and "along a major north-south artery (straight routes)" versus "off this artery (routes with bends)." Distance estimates via the road net to each of these points from a twenty-first point, the main entrance to the University, which lies on the north-south artery about 2½ miles from downtown, were obtained by two methods from a sample of 248 students resident at the University. The first, a ratio estimation technique, followed Lowrey (12) and allowed a "scale value" estimate of cognized distance to be obtained for seven of the locations from any one subject. The other method, a direct magnitude technique, followed Lee (13) and resulted in a "mile estimate" measure of cognized distance for all twenty locations for each subject. It is critical to note the difference between these two techniques. The first is dimensionless and measures the cognition of relative distance itself. The second is a measure of an individual's cognition of the mile measurement scale and is dependent upon him possessing some conception of the amount of spatial separation corresponding to a mile unit.

A power function of the form $Y=aX^b$, where Y is cognized and X objective distance, was used to relate objective to cognized distance. The parameters, a and b, were estimated by regression, separate fits being obtained for each of the four groups to which the locations could be assigned: (1) locations away from downtown involving straight routes; (2) locations away from downtown involving routes with bends; (3) locations toward downtown involving straight routes; (4) locations toward downtown involving routes with bends. The relative positions of the regression lines and the values of the parameters for each group were compared in order to

	a Value	b Value	Test on b Values Hypoth. 1	Hypoth. 2
Individual Mile Estimates				
Straight Away (Group 1)	1.57	.54	} } $p < .025$	} $p < .005$
Bends Away (Group 2)	1.10	.74		
Straight Towards (Group 3)	1.49	.67	} } $p < .05$	} $p < .01$
Bends Towards (Group 4)	1.06	.90		
Individual Scale Values				
Straight Away (Group 1)	1.08	.76	} } $p < .005$	} opposes hypoth.
Bends Away (Group 2)	.85	.63		
Straight Towards (Group 3)	1.11	1.08	} } $p < .001$	} $p < .025$
Bends Towards (Group 4)	.98	1.48		

TABLE 1. Parameters of Power Functions for Location Groups

ascertain whether the underlying environment or route structure influences cognized distance (Table 1). Hypothesis 1 implies that the b values should be greater and the regression lines lie above in Group 3 against Group 1, and Group 4 against Group 2. Hypothesis 2 implies a similar situation for Group 2 against Group 1, and Group 4 against Group 3.

Results and Conclusions

The relative positions of the regression lines and the size of the b parameters indicated that, as hypothesized, distances to locations toward downtown are over-estimated relative to those away from downtown (Figure 2). Tests on both the b parameters (Table 1) and the overall coincidence of the regression lines established statistically significant differences in most cases. The comparison of straight routes against those involving turns showed higher b values for the latter as hypothesized, but markedly smaller a values and, as a consequence, regression lines for the former lie above the latter in apparent contradiction to the hypothesis (Figure 3). Since the a value is a scale factor this suggests that a different scale is being used by the subjects for routes with bends as against straight routes. It is suggested that this scale is the airline rather than road net distance. Thus, there appears to be an influence of airline distance in addition to that of turns themselves upon the cognition of distance for routes involving bends.

The differences in the functions relating cognized to objective distance for the mile estimate as against the scale value data should be noted, the parameter values for the latter being considerably closer to unity (and thus a one to one correspondence with objective distance) than for the former. This suggests that the cognition of relative distance itself, measured by the scale values, is considerably more accurate than cognition of the mile measurement scale.

In conclusion, the results do seem to suggest the existence of discrepancies between cognized and objective distance. Furthermore, an influence of environ-

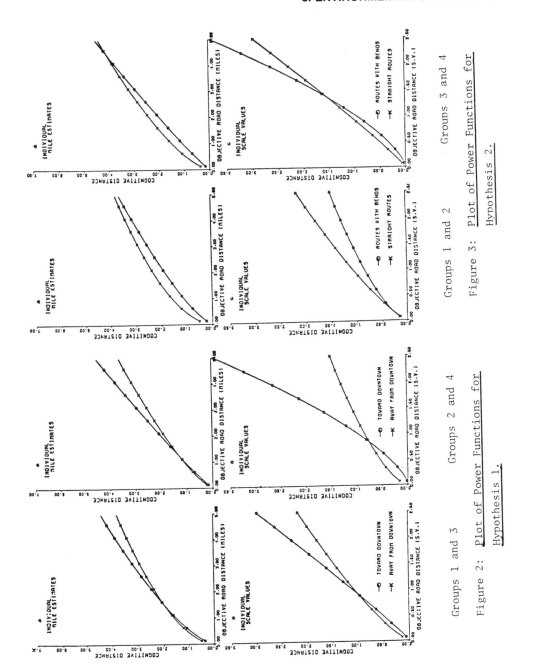

Groups 1 and 3   Groups 2 and 4

Figure 2:   Plot of Power Functions for
             Hypothesis 1.

Groups 1 and 2   Groups 3 and 4

Figure 3:   Plot of Power Functions for
             Hypothesis 2.

mental structure upon cognized distance may be indicated, although alternative hypotheses could be advanced to account for results observed here. Although they cannot be accepted as proof, the results of the experiment are also in keeping with the suggested mechanism for the cognition distance. Finally, the differences between the scale value and mile estimate measures of cognized distance suggest a need for the careful choice of appropriate scaling techniques in future studies.

Notes and References

(1) Lynch, K. THE IMAGE OF THE CITY, Cambridge, Mass., MIT Press, 1960.

(2) Lowrey, R. A., "Distance Concepts of Urban Residents", ENVIRONMENT AND BEHAVIOR, 2, pages 52-73, 1970.

(3) Lee, T., "Perceived Distance as a Function of Direction in the City", ENVIRONMENT AND BEHAVIOR, 2, pages 40-51, 1970.

(4) Golledge, R. G., Briggs, R., and Demko, D., "The Configuration of Distances in Intra-Urban Space", PROCEEDINGS OF THE ASSOCIATION OF AMERICAN GEOGRAPHERS, 1, pages 60-65, 1969.

(5) Perception is used here to refer to the situation where stimulus inputs are immediately available from the external environment.

(6) Fraisse, P., THE PSYCHOLOGY OF TIME, New York, Harper and Row, 1963, pages 199-200.

(7) Appleyard, D., "Styles and Methods of Stucturing a City", ENVIRONMENT AND BEHAVIOR, 2, pages 100-118, 1970.

(8) Neisser, U., COGNITIVE PSYCHOLOGY, New York, Appleton-Century-Crofts, 1967.

(9) Piaget, J., and Inhelder, B., THE CHILD'S CONCEPTION OF SPACE, New York, Norton, 1967.

(10) Teghtsoonian, M., and Teghtsoonian, R., "Scaling Apparent Distance in Natural Indoor Settings", PSYCHONOMIC SCIENCE, 16, pages 281-283, 1969.

(11) Briggs, R., COGNITIVE DISTANCE IN URBAN SPACE, unpublished Ph.D. dissertation, Department of Geography, The Ohio State University, 1972.

(12) Lowrey, R. A., "Distance Concepts of Urban Residents", ENVIRONMENT AND BEHAVIOR, 2, pages 52-73, 1970.

(13) Lee, T., "Perceived Distance as a Function of Direction in the City", ENVIRONMENT AND BEHAVIOR, 2, pages 40-51, 1970.

Martin T. Cadwallader
Department of Geography
University of California
Los Angeles
California 90024

Abstract

This paper examines the relationship between cognitive distance and real distance. Evidence is presented to suggest that, when trying to specify the form of the relationship between these two variables, results obtained at the aggregate level are not directly compatible with those obtained at the individual level. It is also shown that a methodological difference in data collection can influence the rate at which cognitive and real distances covary. Finally, estimation variation and the deviations between cognitive and real distances are analysed in terms of familiarity, attractiveness, and length of residence.

Introduction

In order to truly understand the nature of the perceived environment we must be able to specify the relationship between real and cognitive distance. Research into this relationship is not new, but it has generally suffered from a lack of consistency in the methodological procedures employed. This has made the comparison of results somewhat difficult. For example, the way in which subjects are required to provide distance estimates varies from study to study. Bratfisch (1) utilized the complete method of ratio estimation, which entails asking subjects to compare two distances and then estimate one distance as a per cent of the other. This general methodology was also followed by Lowrey (2). Lee (3), on the other hand, required direct mileage estimates, although this was accomplished via a scale on a piece of paper.

The above studies also vary with regard to whether subjects were asked to conceptualize straight-line distances or not. Lee used shortest walking distance, whereas Bratfisch used straight-line distance. This difference appears to be mainly a function of the spatial scale of the studies. Lee was concerned with intra-urban distances, while Bratfisch was using inter-city distances. Lowrey's study was different again in that, although he was working at the intra-urban scale, each subject estimated the distance to a different set of self-chosen points in the city. In the case of the other studies a common set of points was chosen by the experimenter. Finally, most studies which have used a common set of points have aggregated the individual results, consequently masking the possibility that a number of different relationships might exist between real and cognitive distance at the individual level.

Although it is not yet possible to conclusively specify the functional relationship between real and cognitive distance, this paper points to two methodological questions that must be taken into account. First, it shows that the relationship between these two variables appears to vary according to the estimation technique used, and second, that the relationship is not stable at the individual level. The second part of the paper is more substantive in nature. It tries to account for the varying degree of uncertainty exhibited in distance estimation, and for the deviations between real and cognitive distance.

Methodology

Data for the study was collected, via questionnaires, from fifty households in West Los Angeles. Subjects were asked to estimate the distance from their home to each of thirty cities in the Los Angeles Basin. This task involved estimating distances up to sixty-five miles. The subjects lived within three blocks of each other, so they were all estimating the same real distances. Because of the spatial scale of the study it was deemed most appropriate for the subjects to estimate the straight-line distances, although it is not yet known whether individuals always think in these terms.

Subjects were asked to estimate the same set of distances in two different ways. First, the subjects were asked to give absolute mileage estimates. Second, the method of direct magnitude estimation was used. In this procedure a particular stimulus along the given physical continuum is selected as a standard, and assigned a number (4). The subjects are then required to compare the complete set of variable stimuli with the standard, and assign each one a number which seems proportional to its subjective magnitude as compared to the standard. In the case of the experiments reported here the standard distance was given the value one hundred, and the other distances were estimated accordingly. Following Stevens (5), stimuli both longer and shorter than the standard were presented, and the order of presentation was randomized.

The Relationship Between Real And Cognitive Distance

The data was first analysed at the aggregate level. That is, the median estimates to each of the thirty cities were obtained, and then plotted against real distance. This was done for both the scaled estimates, from the method of direct magnitude estimation, and the mileage estimates. Medians were used because for every city the distribution of estimates, although displaying marked peakedness, was positively skewed.

The relationship, in both cases, appears to be linear, with Pearson correlation coefficients of 0.94 and 0.96 (Figs. 1 & 2). However, the slopes of the regression lines are different. When using the method of direct magnitude estimation, cognitive distance increases with real distance, but at a less than proportional rate. Alternatively, in the case of the mileage estimates, cognitive distance increases at a rate that is slightly more than proportional to real distance. These results illustrate the point that a methodological difference in data collection can influence the rate at which cognitive and real distances covary. It is also noteworthy that previous research, utilizing different methodologies, has suggested that the relationship between these two variables is non-linear (6, 7).

Figure One: <u>Relationship between real distance and mileage estimates.</u>   Figure Two: <u>Relationship between real distance and scaled estimates.</u>

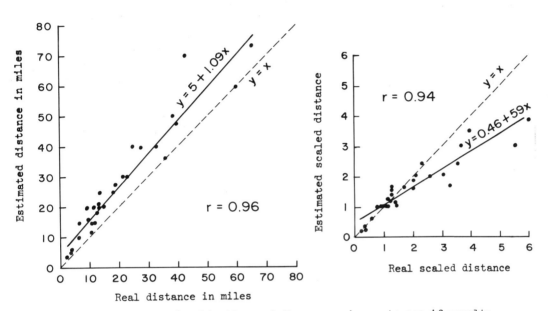

However, as one of the main objectives of the research was to see if results obtained at the aggregate level are compatible with those obtained at the individual level, the relationship between cognitive and real distance was examined further. Correlation coefficients and regression equations were calculated separately for each individual (Fig. 3). As can be seen from this analysis, the correlation coefficients obtained at the aggregate level exaggerated the strength of the relationship, although a large number of the coefficients are still in the vicinity of 0.8 or above. The same is true as regards the b values in the regression equations, where the distinction between the two cognitive distance measures is less clear than that suggested by the aggregate analysis. Noting that some of the correlation coefficients at the individual level were 0.75 or less, and bearing in mind the conflicting results of Bratfisch and Golledge et al., a sample of these were investigated more closely, in order to uncover any non-linearity. Scatter diagrams were plotted for each of the sample individuals, but there was no evidence of a curvilinear relationship that would fit the data more closely than the linear model originally chosen.

Estimation Variation

As previously stated, the second part of the research was concerned with trying to explain the estimation variation and the deviations between real and cognitive distance. In the case of the former it was hypothesized that the variance of the

Figure Three: <u>Histograms for the correlation and regression analysis performed on each individual subject.</u>

Pearson correlation coefficients for estimated scaled distance and real scaled distance.

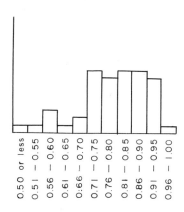

Pearson correlation coefficients for estimated distance in miles and real distance in miles.

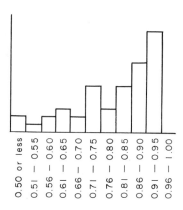

b values for estimated scaled distance and real scaled distance.

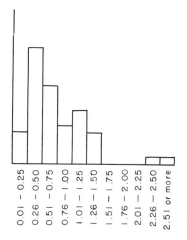

b values for estimated distance in miles and real distance in miles.

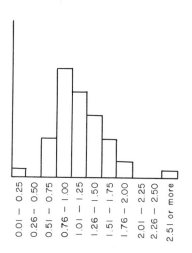

distribution of distance estimates to each city would decrease as familiarity increased, measured across cities. As these distributions were all positively skewed the inter-quartile range was chosen as the most appropriate measure of dispersion. The subjects' levels of familiarity with each of the cities was obtained using the method of direct magnitude estimation.

As one might expect, a correlation analysis indicated that there is a very strong positive relationship between estimation variation and real distance to the city. In the case of both the direct mileage estimates and the scaled estimates the Pearson correlation coefficient was over 0.9. There does not, however, appear to be any significant relationship between estimation variation and the average level of familiarity with each city. Although the correlation coefficient between familiarity and estimation variation was in both cases about -0.6, this can be explained by the fact that familiarity also decreased with distance at a fairly constant rate.

The Deviations Between Real And Cognitive Distance

It is important, in addition to specifying the nature of the relationship between real and cognitive distance, to examine why individuals make incorrect estimates. Length of residence, attractiveness, and familiarity variables were used to investigate the deviations between real and cognitive distance. Length of residence was measured in two ways; first, by how long the subject had been living in the Los Angeles Metropolitan Area, and second, by how long he had been living at his present address. An average level of attractiveness for each city, as a place to live in, was obtained by again using the method of direct magnitude estimation.

The deviations between real and cognitive distance, for each individual, were first divided by the real distance, as prior analysis showed that the deviations increased with increasing distance. It was expected that an increase in familiarity and length of residence would result in a decrease in the difference between real and cognitive distance. Also, following the suggestion of Lee (8), it was expected that the distance estimates would be influenced by the attractiveness of the city. These hypotheses were tested by using all the individual data, and performing a non-parametric correlation analysis to obtain both Spearman and Kendall correlation coefficients. Although the assumptions of these two procedures are not completely met by the data, because the observations are not all independent, it was felt that the analysis was sufficiently rigorous for exploratory purposes. The results failed to substantiate the hypothesized relationships. There were no correlation coefficients greater than 0.2.

There appear to be three main reasons for the present inability to account for the deviations between real and cognitive distance. First, the explanatory variables may have been inadequately measured. Second, previous research suggests that such factors as intervening barriers, direction, and driver/non-driver differences might have been profitably incorporated into the research design (9, 10, 11). Analysis of the influence of these factors is currently underway. Third, it is possible that subjects usually think in terms of time distance. This would then account for some of their inaccuracy when required to give mileage estimates.

In view of this the author is at present completing a study of the estimation of time distances.

Conclusion

This paper has pointed to two factors which must be taken into account when investigating the relationship between real and cognitive distance. First, the results reported here suggest that subjects react differently when presented with alternative ways in which to give their distance estimates. Second, this research has pointed out the need to work with individual data, as analysis at the aggregate level could well conceal some of the more important relationships. There are also two further questions that must be considered, although they have not been discussed in this paper. First, it is possible that much of the over-estimation with respect to shorter distances is merely because there is much greater leeway for over-estimation than for under-estimation. Second, the view has been taken that subjects can respond on a ratio scale when called upon to do so, although it may well be that an ordering of distances is all that they characteristically undertake.

Finally, it is pertinent to ask to what extent the concept of cognitive distance can help in our understanding of behavior in space. Establishing the nature of this link should form a vital part of future research. In this context, the present author is currently testing a probability model of consumer spatial behavior, in which real and cognitive distance are inter-changed, in order to determine which one is the better predictor of behavior.

Notes and References

I would like to thank William Clark, Reg Golledge and Gary Moore for their comments on an earlier draft of this paper. The use of the U.C.L.A. Campus Computing Network is acknowledged.

(1) Bratfisch, O., "A further study of the relation between subjective distance and emotional involvement", ACTA PSYCHOLOGICA, 29, pages 244-255, 1969.

(2) Lowrey, R. A., "Distance concepts of urban residents", ENVIRONMENT AND BEHAVIOR, 2, pages 52-73, 1970.

(3) Lee, T., "Perceived distance as a function of direction in the city", ENVIRONMENT AND BEHAVIOR, 2, pages 40-51, 1970.

(4) Corso, J. F., THE EXPERIMENTAL PSYCHOLOGY OF SENSORY BEHAVIOR, New York, Holt, Rinehart and Winston, page 257, 1967.

(5) Stevens, S. S., "The direct estimation of sensory magnitudes - loudness", THE AMERICAN JOURNAL OF PSYCHOLOGY, LXIX, pages 1-25, 1956.

(6) Golledge, R. G., Briggs, R., Demko, D., "The configuration of distances in intra-urban space", PROCEEDINGS OF THE A.A.G., 1, pages 60-65, 1969.

(7) Bratfisch, O., "A further study of the relation between subjective distance and emotional involvement", ACTA PSYCHOLOGICA, 29, pages 244-255, 1969.

(8) Lee, T., "Psychology and living space", TRANSACTIONS OF THE BARTLETT SOCIETY, 3, pages 11-36, 1966.

(9) Stea, D., "The measurement of mental maps : An experimental model for studying conceptual spaces", in Cox, K. R., and Golledge, R. G., BEHAVIORAL PROBLEMS IN GEOGRAPHY : A SYMPOSIUM, Northwestern University Studies in Geography, 17, pages 228-253, 1969.

(10) Lee, T., "Perceived distance as a function of direction in the city", ENVIRONMENT AND BEHAVIOR, 2, pages 40-51, 1970.

(11) Lowrey, R. A., "Distance concepts of urban residents", ENVIRONMENT AND BEHAVIOR, 2, pages 52-73, 1970.

Ann Sloan Devlin

Department of Psychology
University of Michigan
Ann Arbor, Michigan

Abstract

Despite extensive indication that humans characteristically experience fascination
and pleasure in their contacts with nature, novices often display uncertainty, apprehension, and even fear as a function of being in a natural area. The focus of the
research reported here is on the prior knowledge that might enhance the encounter
with the natural setting for people with minimal familiarity with it. This entails
the development of cognitive representations about a specific natural environment
based on substitute experiences. The paper describes some of the problems that must
be solved to achieve this, and some of the tangible accomplishments to date. In particular, four areas of concern are examined: (1) an effective representation of the
area in question; (2) games that involve junior-high school aged children in dealing
with critical aspects of the information; (3) selection of a natural area suitable
for such procedures; and (4) development of dependent variables allowing one to
assess both preference and knowledge of the natural area studied.

Introduction

The study of cognitive processes operating in the environment is not a totally unex-
plored domain, not, that is, if one is addressing himself to the environments of the
city. Lynch's (1) explication of the notions of legibility and imageability in the
cityscape has pointed the way to examining what makes components of that environment
graspable, comprehensible, understandable, and pivotal for orientation.

However, what is known of the cognitive processes operative in the natural environment? Very little, at this point. In many senses, the natural environment is more
in need of examination as it may little longer remain easily open to examination.
What are, then, the important components of the environment, an environment which
man finds preferable to others (2)? Why is the natural environment so compelling
for mankind, so satisfying and restful? While one legislatively tries to put a clamp
on the increasing and diverse forces cutting back the opportunity to experience natural environments, one can at the same time experimentally begin to examine the pivotal cognitive components of the natural environment which render it understandable
and "mappable." This study explores the key components of an experience which makes
the novice in the natural environment more like one who has security in his knowledge of that environment. The experience sought is that which will precipitate the
metamorphosis of the tenderfoot into the more confident and adept cognizer of the
natural environment, sure in his ability to orient himself and trust his internal
representation of that environment.

The paper presented here is an attempt to point out the issues involved with research in the area of cognitive mapping of the natural environment and the directions which have thus far been taken in examining this area of research. The research reported here is a part of a larger program of research in the area of cognitive mapping and information-processing directed by Rachel and Stephen Kaplan. With obvious pertinence to the subject matter of the symposium, the first section of the paper will address itself to the important relationship of cognitive mapping theory to the focus of the study. Subsequent sections will deal in some detail with four major areas of progress in the development of this research program.

Cognitive mapping theory: Relation to knowledge of the natural environment

The beginning steps have been taken in moving toward the question of the key experiential components of the natural environment by examining the effect of prior knowledge on the experience of the natural environment. The particular focus on knowledge was the result of the observation of apprehensive and fearful reactions on the part of children visiting an unfamiliar natural area, a forest or nature center for example, for the first time. It was felt that if prior knowledge could be provided to the children before an outing, as that in a classroom session, the fears would be abated by the knowledge gained in the classroom and much less would be categorized as "unknown" by the young explorers.

The attempt to combat fear by providing information to increase one's knowledge is linked directly to some underlying assumptions about cognitive mapping theory. Orienting oneself and finding one's way in familiar and unfamiliar environments alike are central to human survival functioning. The initial steps of formation and eventual "cohering" of a cognitive map are tied directly to the observer's having had some experience with and hence knowledge of the environment to be mapped. His ability to orient himself depends upon this map formation. The motivation, therefore, for gaining knowledge of the environment is necessarily quite high. In the formation of a cognitive map, the information-processing needs of recognizing and predicting, evaluating and taking action, are also met (3). Thus, acquiring knowledge of the environment which aids the formation of a cognitive map is crucial in providing for the satisfaction of human needs. Human beings become uncomfortable when the necessary knowledge for map formation is not available and adequate functioning in the environment is jeopardized. The presentation of knowledge of the environment is therefore critical in maintaining human well-being.

The actual forms of the information presented in the study, path structure and topographical features, are specific components of the natural environment which are presumably helpful in orientation. Lynch found paths to be the most important in a series of orienting dimensions in his studies of the urban environment. Through use of these two knowledge variables, one can begin to examine the impact of prior familiarization on an eventual actual "knowing" of the environment. In time, this kind of research should be pivotal in indicating what types of knowledge most satisfactorily aid the novice in moving from the shaky stages of unstable and diffuse map formation to the sureness of the adept cognizer of the natural environment.

A study in "knowing" the natural environment

The study involved both a classroom procedure, in which the knowledge of the natural environment was presented in map-game format, and an actual outing to a natural site. The subjects were two groups of seventh grade students who were enrolled in a "small school" within a public junior high school. Forty-one males and 44 females completed all phases of the study. The experimental condition consisted of students who played map-games based on the actual park to be visited while the control group played games based on a different area not-to-be-visited. There were approximately equal numbers of males and females in the experimental and control groups. The hypothesis was that those students who had been prefamiliarized with the games based on the site they eventually visited would demonstrate a greater knowledge of that environment and more confidence in their knowledge than would those students who played games based on a site differing from the one they visited.

Primary research dimensions

A number of areas have received attention in the planning and carrying out of this study and are central enough to be involved in any similar examination of the natural environment: (1) map rendition; (2) games; (3) natural setting itself; (4) dependent variables.

Map rendition- What one is striving for is a map which will make the formation of the cognitive map as straightforward as possible. The rendition given the subjects must be easily comprehensible. When one moves from a standard two-dimensional roadmap variety into the additional dimension of depth, the difficulty of the task increases exponentially. What one wants to convey to the scanner of the map is a miniature, a "view from the hill." More specifically, rendering the map at an oblique angle and rendering the drawing so that the viewer is placed at the summit of the view gives him sight of the entire vista. With this miniature, the viewer is approaching the situation of already possessing a cognitive map of the area, sketchy though it may be. What one is trying to do is provide a basis for the cognitive map which has done much of the gathering and pulling together of the information for the viewer; it is a precognitive map, if you will. Just as the cognitive map itself is a condensation of more spatial information than one can in general experience in any given instance (4), so this miniature, the map rendered at an oblique angle, gives the reader more information than he could ordinarily perceive. Thus the miniature has condensed the information the area contains so that it is easily within the grasp of the viewer. The information is layed out, the obscuring trees and underbrush removed or whatever, so that the observer can view all from the vantage point the oblique view gives him. This kind of a map rendering might be a shorter route to developing an internal representation of the environment. This goal, however, has not yet become a reality.

In the present study, due to a time constraint and project deadline, the final product was far from the stated goal and was recognized as inadequate before the subjects were run. The map proved to have a detrimental effect on the knowledge absorbed by the students. The use of modified contour lines, in a cloud-shape to indicate both elevation and foliage areas simultaneously proved not only to be confusing for the students, but for a number of adults who examined the maps as well. Alternative procedures are currently being explored; clearly this is a critical area for further research.

With respect to the map rendition, one of the most interesting findings that has surfaced through these studies is that a little knowledge can, in fact, be harmful. The human being's perceptual and cognitive processes are highly refined for obviously survival-oriented reasons. A map which appears complete and relatively detailed and yet in reality is much different from the area it depicts is more harmful than an incomplete picture in that it begins the formation of a cognitive map which does not match the reality; when the image in the head and the perception of the reality clash, as they did in this study, confusion results. The map the experimentals played with was obviously misleading with regard to various expectations they had. Many more experimentals than controls indicated that the park entrance differed from their expectations ($X^2=7.15$, df=1, $p<.01$). The experimentals also differed from the controls in their reaction to the number of trees they expected ($X^2=8.89$, df=2, $p<.025$) with the experimentals finding many more trees than they had anticipated. This mismatch of expectation with reality can, possibly, be traced back to the use of the cloud-shaped contour lines to indicate both elevation and foliage; it is quite plausible that subjects did not realize that those lines indicated tree-filled areas.

In addition, the control group, who played a map-game based on an area different from the one they visited and only saw the map of the site actually visited for a few moments before exploring it, showed more confidence in their ability to orient themselves and navigate through what was, to them, an unfamiliar environment, than did the experimentals who should have been quite familiar with the area after two game sessions with the map depicting it. In response to the question, "Was it hard to find your way back to the beginning?" there was a significant difference between the experimentals and controls ($X^2=6.30$, df=1, $p<.025$) with the controls demonstrating more assurance with their many more "no" responses. The same trend was shown in the responses to the question, "Do you think you know the park well enough to be a friend's guide?" with the controls again exhibiting confidence with their "yes" answers ($X^2=5.5$, df=1, $p<.025$). It is also possible that the knowledge that the experimental group did absorb was so mismatched with the reality of the site that it placed a restraint on their willingness to venture beyond the boundaries of the map. Using the "Draw where you went" measure on the structured map as an indication of the area covered from the starting point, the controls demonstrated a greater "adventurousness" trend than did the experimentals (t=2.0, df=83, $p<.05$). The experimentals were much less eager to do any real exploring.

Games- The game development has proceeded at a much faster and smoother pace than the map rendition. The use of games in the classroom rather than a typical lecture or lesson plan format was chosen for a number of reasons. First of all, games seem to be intrinsically compelling to children, more compelling certainly than the normal lesson format. Secondly, games can easily be modified, by an elaboration of the rules, for instance, to introduce new concepts or features of the natural area, and games do not require the constant supervision and instruction of the teacher as does the presentation of a lesson. There are, however, specific concerns with which one must deal in order to have a successful game. The games themselves cannot be so intrinsically glamorous as to detract from the information presented. In an earlier study, a large masonite playing board, covered with a drawing (in pastels) of the natural area and finally covered by a clear acetate playing grid proved to be as enticing as a banana split at the Dairy Queen; the players were so captivated by the professionalism of the game that they suggested it be marketed with Parker Brothers. The grid overlay, though clear acetate, was marked off with black ink in one-inch squares and may have relegated the information in the underlying terrain to a position of secondary importance. Players were eager to move across the board toward certain "surprise squares," indicated with variously colored opaque squares. In their eagerness to pick up and retain the cards available at these squares in a monopolyesque manner, the subjects may have given little attention to the topographical features and path structure. In retrospect, these features of the game were independent of the actual goals of the study and this separation seemed critical in the lack of information absorbed by the subjects in this earlier study.

The game must also not be so competitive that the players become so interested in scoring points, gathering surprise square cards, or whatever, that the information that could be absorbed in scoring those points is lost. Neither can the game be too expensive to reproduce in large numbers, if, as was done in the present study, each pair of students is to receive their own game kit. Thus, an easily lithographed original has proven to be a desirable method in terms of keeping production costs low; the major expense is in the man-hours required to produce the original. The size of the original to be duplicated is also important, and unless reduction before duplication has been considered, the original should be no larger than the maximum size reproducible in the given lithographing machine.

The formats of the games themselves used in this study, the Battleships and 20 Questions games, were successful for a number of reasons. The games conformed to the above-mentioned specifications of reasonable attractiveness, moderate competitiveness, low cost and proper size. Furthermore, the games were modified from familiar and well-liked children's games and were not difficult to teach those uninitiated or to refresh those whose memories were weak. In addition to involving chance and skill, the games involve curiosity and discovery, certainly important motivators.

In the Battleships game, each player was given a map with only half of the total path structure of the area, and the object was to discover where the opponent's path structure was and thus gain a complete path structure map of the area.

In the 20 Questions game, each player had a full map of the area, including a full path structure. Thus, if a player did not complete the path structure in the Battleships game, the information was again made available to him in this second game. In the 20 Questions game, each player had different locations circled on his map as possible hiding places. The object of the game was to discover where one's opponent was "hiding," by selecting questions from a question pile pertaining to the topographical features of the area. Unlike the usual 20 Questions format, the player in this modified form must be able to first read the map in order to select pertinent and logical questions. The 20 Questions format used in the study thus places a significant burden on the players to be able to read the map before they are able to make progress in the game. The information to be transmitted to the subjects is thus inseparable from the actual game-playing. A number of students became so adept at the game that they began selecting their own hiding places and creating their own questions, showing real understanding of the terrain with which they were dealing.

Natural setting- The natural setting is another dimension along which there has been a great deal of movement since the earlier study. In the exploratory study, a park was used which proved to be too architecturally defined, that is, there was little uncertainty in the setting. From any position in the park, the subjects could readily return to the large central open area from which they could easily see their "starting point." Thus, the site demanded too little in the way of orienting skills or use of prior knowledge in finding their way. In the most recent study, a site was found which was a second growth region having been rolling farm land fifty years earlier; the area was thus far denser than a typical mature forest. The land, owned by the city on the outskirts of town, had not been manicured or developed in any way and was used by horseback riders for its bridal paths and by the townspeople for walks of a Sunday afternoon variety. Once past the entrance into the woods, a fence which prohibited motorcycle use, the student was immediately enclosed by a dense woods which possessed a complicated path structure, not easily traversible nor easily "imageable" with a single visit. It took the experimenters a number of visits, in fact, before the path structure formed a coherent image in their heads. The kind of natural environment which offers a reasonable challenge, as this one did, is a desirable area for this kind of research.

The length of the visit is a variable with which there has been little opportunity to experiment. The visits have thus far been limited, through an understandable obligation to the school system, to an hour in length. Motivation to absorb information might be increased if the subject were to eventually spend longer periods of time in the natural environment.

It is desirable to find a site where knowledge is going to make a difference; this requires that the site not be comprehensible at a glance, that it be dense enough to avoid seeing wandering peers on a neighboring path, that it be varied, intricate in places, and that it present the chance that one might not make it back to the beginning, that getting lost is a definite possibility. Perhaps the best way of determining whether a site meets these specifications is having a number of people individually explore the area, rate it on a number of these dimensions, and then compare the ratings.

Dependent variables- Finally, work has been focused on dependent variables. How, after all, is one to assess what has been accomplished if not by the use of the dependent variables. The attack here has been pointed in a number of different directions, as there are a number of levels on which assessment can be made. Immediately after the subjects returned from exploring the woods, they were provided with a clipboard, a pencil and the first in a series of three instruments: an unstructured map, a structured map, and a brief questionnaire. The unstructured map requested that the subject draw in the missing path structure, giving the subject only the main "branch" to the network to which he was to add the various other branches. The structured map, distributed after the first maps were collected, provided the subjects with the complete path structure. The subjects were first asked to draw where they went, in order to gain some idea of the distance and area covered. The directions which followed asked the subjects to fill in or mark the site of various topographical features, as hills, pine groves, a stream, the compass directions, and broad paths. As a method of assessing certain kinds of knowledge of the environment, the use of these structured and unstructured map forms has been quite effective. They approach asking the subject to put his internal representation of the environment on paper. The third instrument, a short questionnaire, assessed the subject's likes and dislikes concerning the trip, how the experience matched his expectations for it, and the confidence he had in his knowledge of the environment. The questions about matching expectancy with reality can be helpful in revising and adjusting the map to better prepare one for what will be experienced in the actual environment.

Conclusion

The studies carried out thus far have been most informative in pointing out that a hypothetically related prior experience, in these studies provided by the map-games, can make a difference in the experience of the actual natural environment. More specifically, it has been seen that knowledge can be harmful if it leads to the formation of a confusing and inadequate cognitive map. There has also been a substantial refinement along each of the four dimensions involved in the research in this area, the map rendition, the games, the selection of the natural setting, and the dependent variables.

The results of this study reinforce the importance of the cognitive map for adequate functioning in the environment. When one's map is inadequate, as was the case for the experimentals in this study, confidence in one's ability to orient and navigate in the environment drops. Further studies should provide a fuller picture of what is involved in rendering an adequate "view from the hill" or miniature. What is required is a procedure which would facilitate the formation of the image in one's head, of one's internal representation of the natural environment.

Notes and References

(1) Lynch, K.   THE IMAGE OF THE CITY. Cambridge, Mass.: MIT. 1960.

(2) Kaplan, S., Kaplan, R., & Wendt, J. S.   Rated preference and complexity for natural and urban visual material. PERCEPTION AND PSYCHOPHYSICS, 1972, 12, 354-356.

(3) Kaplan, S.   Cognitive maps, human needs, and the designed environment. In Preiser, W. F. E. (Ed.) ENVIRONMENTAL DESIGN RESEARCH (EDRA 4). 1973.

(4) Kaplan, S.   Knowing man: Towards a humane environment. ET AL., 1973, in press.

(5) The project reported here is a part of a research program on cognitive mapping in natural environments directed by Rachel and Stephen Kaplan and sponsored by the Forest Service, USDA. I would like to thank Hillorie Applebaum for her assistance throughout the project.

David L. George
2222 Woddingham Drive
Troy, Michigan 48084

Abstract

Current interest in directional orientation has been limited to the question of <u>how</u>
the organism manages to learn its relative position in space. Of less interest has
been the question of how subjective experience of orientation might help or hinder
orientation related behavior. The hypothesis here under investigation is that total
"frame dependence" is an inherent characteristic of spatial perception. Present empirical evidence suggests otherwise, with people typically able to account for non-
rectilinearity by means of mapping. It is suggested that this is in spite of ongoing
total frame dependence. Two methods for discerning frame dependence, map drawing
and pointing, were contrasted. It was hypothesized that significantly more dependence would be revealed by the pointing technique. The hypothesis was confirmed.

Introduction

The readmittance of imagery as a legitimate concern of psychologists has coincided
with the birth of environmental psychology. Nevertheless, the behavioral approach
is still dominant enough to cause much imagery to remain inaccessible because of
the lack of clear-cut accompanying behavioral manifestations. In some spheres of
research the emphasis has been on discovering the extent to which subjective estimates of quantifiable bits of experience differ from the objective situation. The
example that comes most readily to mind is the extensive research on distance perception. The non-veridicality has most likely received attention because of the
ease with which it is revealed through direct verbal accounts. It is important to
keep in mind, though, that only by restricting prior information about the distance
relations can the experimenter be assured that the subject is relying wholly on
"felt" or phenomenal distance in his estimate of objective distance. An inaccurate
"feeling" of distance can obviously persist even after objective relations are
learned. Indeed, one can first learn that two sites are equidistant from a reference site before visiting either, only to report after traveling to each that one
seems to be a different distance than the other.

There has been an unfortunate failure to extend this consideration to distance's
complementary phenomenon, directional orientation. In both the theoretical and empirical works on the subject, emphasis has been on determining how people manage to
maintain a sense of orientation, with the matter of subjective experience of orientation being wholly neglected. Consider this passage from Hart and Moore's (1)
review of spatial orientation studies:
>   "Spatial or geographic orientation as used in this review, refers to the <u>way</u>
>   (emphasis mine) an individual determines his location in the environment."

It is unwisely limiting to define geographic orientation this way. They acknowledge in another passage that external representations can only provide a glimpse at
the external cognitions, but by limiting concern to the way one determines one's

place in space, they restrict interest to how external representations might be aided by, (or might overcome) the organizational peculiarities of internal representations. It is suggested here that frequently an individual is able to find his way about despite, and not because of, his particular orientation, in much the manner that perceived distance can often be a hindrance in attempting to objectively report distance relations.

This study was prompted by the desire to lend some empirical weight to a personal theory of directional orientation. The theory rests on two fundamental postulates, the first of which states that each visual field necessarily assumes a phenomenal orientation with respect to any previously perceived field. Such an orientation involves only the perceived spatial relationship between the coordinate systems of the respective fields, that is, the relation between intra-field relations. This does not necessitate that the "whereabouts", (locus), of one field with respect to another be perceived. This secondary type of orientation does not inhere in the perception but can be discovered given the necessary presence of an axial orientation for each field, as well as some knowledge of the relevant distance relations.

The second postulate concerns the possible ways in which two fields may relate phenomenally. Applying just the first postulate, any pair of fields would assume one of an infinite number of orientation possibilities between them. The second postulate states that each internal coordinate of a visual field is perceptually parallel to one of the two coordinates of any other field, hence limiting to just four the number of possible orientation relations between two fields. It is with this latter postulate that the present study will deal.

"Frame dependence" will be the expression used to designate the tendency to overrely on the structure of the immediate percept when judging an abstract spatial feature. The term has been used extensively in the literature dealing with perception of the vertical. Considerable research has been directed at discovering the relative importance of postural and visual cues. Gibson and Mowrer (2) though the contributions of visual factors in the perception of the upright to be important, but concluded that gravitational (postural) factors are logically prior and hence psychologically more fundamental. Asch and Witkin (3) on the other hand, provided strong evidence that visual cues were more important. In one study, subjects stood directly before a mirror tilted backward so as to effect a 30 degree slant. They were dependent on the scene to the extent of judging a rod moved within the scene to be objectively vertical when it was moved only 3.5 of the 30 degrees required to fully counteract the initial tilt. Their findings supported the famed Gestalt psychologist Koffka (4), who maintained that the visual space created its own framework, with the main lines therein assuming the function of vertical and horizontal.

In recent years, despite the flurry of interest in discovering sources and styles of orientation, almost no attention has been given frame dependence on the horizontal plane (essentially a sub-area of directional orientation). While it would be difficult to speculate on the causes of this neglect, it is doubly ironic. First, those interested in determining the relative contributions of postural and visual factors might have contrasted the degree of dependence exhibited in vertical judgment with the degree displayed in judgment of lines on the horizontal plane, when postural cues are less important. (Except when standing in one grid while observing another rotated grid, there is essentially no "present" postural information for horizontal plane orientation. The absence of a horizontal plane equivalent to gravity, such as a naturally experienced centrifugal force, precludes a postural difference between facing in one direction while standing erect, and facing another way.) Secondly, displacement of the vertical plane is seldom a practical concern, the visual cues rarely being ambiguous. Conversely, the absence of a consistent geographical grid in most locales is common.

It is necessary to reach far back into the literature to find horizontal plane frame dependence mentioned. Binet (5), intrigued by his own experiences of "disorienta-tion" (which the reader can regard as synonomous with inconsistent orientation), re-quested colleagues to relate any instances of experienced directional illusions. In summarizing the reports he stated,
"Generally, the illusion is equivalent to the effect of a rotation of 180 de-grees and that is why most writers compare their impressions to turning or reversal. But we have cited two cases in which the reversion of objects appeared to be only 90 degrees."
This suggests frame dependence, though only indirectly. The phenomenal rotation of the visual field with respect to its normal experienced orientation takes place only through 90 or 180 degrees. Peterson (6) also noted a tendency for directional illu-sions to be either 90 or 180 degrees. He implied that this was culturally caused when he suggested it was due to thinking spatially in terms of the four cardinal directions. Trowbridge (7) had subjects in New York City point to various distant places. As he reported,
"The average error was 30 degrees clockwise. ---accounted for by reason of the prevailing idea that the chief avenues in New York lie approximately north and south. Actually they lie 29 degrees (clockwise) from the meridian."
In this instance, the estimate of the locus of distant sites has been impaired. Frame dependence has caused the longitudinal streets of Manhatten to be perceptually isomorphic with the N-S axis of a map.

Mapping techniques have often been used as a means to discover people's orientation schemes, and subjects have repeatedly demonstrated that they are able to account at least partially for irregular streets in a dominant rectilinear system. Even though an individual may be able to accurately represent a street as lying at a nonright angle to another, it is not wise to conclude that this is how the person is pheno-menally oriented while actually on the particular street.

As an analogy, consider the fact that when viewing a movie, people of western cul-tures typically perceive a three-dimensional representation. Though this is appar-ent to most of us through first-hand experience, we could not have verified the fact by having subjects re-create a movie scene on paper. Moreover, any pragmatic be-havior related to moving about the movie screen would not be hindered by the fact that the individual sees the picture as three-dimensional. Despite all this, it would be absured to exclude from concern the perceived three-dimensionality, of in-terest precisely because it contributes greatly to the ongoing perception. In the instance of orientation, too, what the person draws is not necessarily congruent with what he "sees". Some frame dependence is typically revealed, it is suggested, only because people must often rely on their original perception when other informa-tion is lacking. (The two-dimensionality of the movie screen, on the one hand, is a well known fact, while the angle at which a given pair of streets meet is not so well known.) Though the individual may find his way about an area with no difficulty and may know the an les at which the different streets intersect, it is still meaningful, phenomenally, to speak of inconsistent orientations.

The following experiment was carried out in Los Angeles with the hope of showing that mapping is an invalid means by which to discern cognitive directional maps. The degree of slant accounted for by map-drawing was contrasted with the degree accounted for less directly, by pointing. Subjects pointed to the same location twice, once while on each of two streets forming an acute angle. It was hypothesized that more frame dependence would be revealed by pointing than by mapping.

Method:

Subjects: 34 U.C.L.A. undergraduates participated in the experiment, in partial fulfillment of a psychology course requirement.

Test Area: The experiment was carried out in Westwood Village, just south of the campus. The walk included three streets (see fig. 1). The upper segment of Broxton is parallel with Westwood Blvd., with Le Conte forming right angles with these streets. The lower segment of Broxton forms a 35 degree angle with Westwood Blvd.

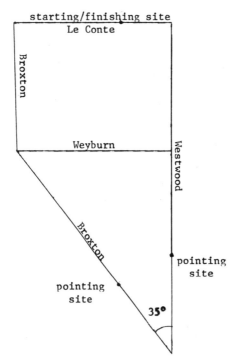

Procedure: I met one subject at a time at a pre-arranged meeting site on Le Conte, instructing the subject to pay careful attention to the surroundings as he took the walk and to keep in mind the course that was followed. The subject was then shown a map of Los Angeles, oriented so that the north on the map aligned correctly with objective north. I first carefully showed where we stood, and then pointed out two districts, downtown Santa Monica and a segment of Ventura Blvd. It was explained that these areas were similar to Westwood Village in retail trade. The subject was advised to keep the two areas in mind, with the explanation that he would be asked to compare Westwood Village with the other areas both during and at the conclusion of the walk. The direction of walk was randomized, with half following a clockwise direction, and half counter-clockwise. The subject was stopped at the first site (fig. 1) and asked to judge which of the two reference areas the immediate surroundings most suggested. It was added that had he never been to one or both of the areas, he should simply use his estimate of what the unknown area was like in making his decision. Immediately following a response, subject was handed a metal rod and was instructed to place it on the pavement so that it pointed directly toward the selected area. The angle of point was noted. The walk then continued until the second pointing site was reached. The same bogus comparison question was asked, but regardless of the similarity choice subject was instructed to point the rod at the same area that he had previously pointed toward. Returning to the starting site, the subject was given a 3 by 5 card, pen, and ruler, and was instructed to sketch a map of the path followed, indicating with an "x" the starting/finishing site and the two pointing sites.

Design: An Identical Subjects Design was used, with each subject both drawing a map and pointing to the same area twice, once from Westwood Blvd., and once from Broxton. Two measures of frame dependence were thus gained for each subject, the perceived angle of Broxton and Westwood indicated directly on the map, and the perceived angle inferred from the two pointings.

Results:

The results supported the hypothesis that more frame dependence would be revealed by pointing than by mapping, with a mean mapping angle of 25.6 degrees and a mean pointing angle of 7.8 degrees (35 degrees indicating perfect estimate, with no frame dependence). A T-test revealed these results to be significant at the .01 level. Some subjects, evidently in the confusion of frame dependence, actually pointed in a manner indicating that they accounted for angularity, but in the wrong direction. Even interpreting these negative scores as positive yields results that prove significant, with the re-interpreted pointing mean of 12.9 and a T-score of 2.82, significant still at the .01 level.

Discussion:

Again consider the different ways in which orientation may be regarded. If we merely wish to determine the extent that one is able to account for the angularity of streets, the map speaks best in his behalf. Given a critical choice situation and a brief period of time in which to make a decision, the evidence suggests that angularity is within most people's cognitive store. However, as stressed already, orientation, when the places in terms of which one is oriented are of no immediate practical concern is also of interest if we wish to discover how the image of one visual field can affect one's cognitive ordering of a new field.

Frequently, I have observed people motion in an altogether incorrect direction while mentioning a particular place. As an extreme example, I have often witnessed people, while in their own house or apartment, consistently point in the same wrong direction when referring to a nearby and constantly visited location. Taking advantage of such situations, I have asked these poorly oriented individuals a short time afterward to point toward the place that they had so recently been unable to. Lo! A moment's thought and a close approximation to the objective direction is indicated by the outstretched finger. The moment's reflection brings about a sudden ability to point correctly. Are we to conclude that this individual's cognitive map represents an isomorphic ordering of the relations between his apartment and the nearby location, as his purposeful pointing behavior would incline us to conclude, or shall we accept the earlier, less conscious, and wholly non-pragmatic pointing? Again, this depends on whether we wish to regard the whole matter of orientation as a practical, way finding concern, or as a perceptual phenonomenon of first interest for the way that it contributes to the ongoing image.

Though attention in this study has been restricted to the cognitive ordering of visual fields with clearly defined internal coordinate systems, the basic principles already put forth can apply to the way one perceives curved paths. The more aesthetically inclined planners and architects have long criticized the preponderance of rigid straight-lined design. The implication has been that the straight line is the work of man torn from nature, striving for mathematical simplicity while divorcing himself from the organic, curve dominated environment. Accepting the observation that curvature dominates the natural scene, an intriguing survival benefit can be seen to derive from (and perhaps actually explain) frame dependence, at the same time vindicating the straight line by explaining its natural origin. By the physical principal of inertia, bodies remain at rest or continue motion in a straight line unless acted upon by some external force. Extending this principle, however crudely, to the locomotive behavior of the early hunting homo sapien (as well as related species), consider the beneficial effect of frame dependence when the need arose to follow a naturally created path. The organism objectively changes his direction of travel when the path curves, but phenomenally he continues in the same direction. Indeed, the very coherence of the path is strengthened by frame dependence. The modern manifestation of the path is the freeway, and interestingly, one rarely hears of an inattentive driver ignoring a gently curving portion of the road and continuing straight ahead. With the benevolent guide of frame dependence, the "straight ahead" corresponds to the changed direction.

In summarizing the practical consequences of frame dependence, it is worthwhile to distinguish three categories of inconsistent orientation: (1) that type having no practical consequences, either because the initial disorientation is offset in the opposite direction or because the disorienting path is the only one connecting the locations; (2) that type of inconsistent orientation involving a wrong notion of the locus of a reference site, despite consistent axial orientation. This can be caused by inconsistent axial orientation at some point on the path linking the fields which, though being offset in the opposite direction, impairs the perceived locus relation. As a result, though consistently orienting the second field's coordinate system with respect to the first field, inaccuracy will likely result when an alternate path is chosen to return to this first field. (3) There is axial disorientation, with the accompanying misperception of locus.

The design implications of all the above are by no means clear. If efficiency in moving about is to be the sole criterion of street design, obviously the grid pattern should prevail. But the vast majority of places are frequented regularly by the same people, most of whom, after perhaps some initial confusion in orienting to a non-rectilinear system, would be able to establish a workable, albeit inconsistent, orientation scheme. This raises the question of whether the maximum ease in getting about the area for passers-through and newcomers should take precedence over the visual benefits likely to be derived from a less regular system. And, of course, this in turn depends on the nature of the place being designed.

References

(1) Hart, Roger A., and Moore, Gary T., "The Development of Spatial Cognition: A Review," PLACE PERCEPTION RESEARCH REPORT, NO. 7, Chicago, 1971

(2) Gibson, J. J., and Mowrer, O. H., "Determinants of the Perceived Vertical and Horizontal," PSYCHOLOGICAL REVIEW, 45, page 300-324, 1938

(3) Asch, S. E., and Witkin, H. A., "Studies in Space Orientation: 1. Perception of the Upright with Displaced Visual Fields." JOURNAL OF EXPERIMENTAL PSYCHO-LOGY, 38, pages 325-337, 1948

(4) Koffka, K., GESTALT PSYCHOLOGY, New York, Harcourt Brace, 1935

(5) Binet, M. Alfred, "Reverse Illusions of Orientation" PSYCHOLOGICAL REVIEW, 1, pages 343-350, 1894

(6) Peterson, Joseph, "Illusions of Direction Orientation," JOURNAL OF PHILOSOPHI-CAL AND SCIENTIFIC METHOD, 13, pages 225-228, 1916

(7) Trowbridge, C. C., "On Fundamental Methods of Orienting and 'Imaginary Maps,'" SCIENCE, 38, pages 886-897, 1913

Georgia Zannaras
Department of Geography
The Ohio State University
Columbus, Ohio 43210

Abstract

This study examines the effects different spatial forms of cities have on the importance attached to environmental features which are to be used as way-finding clues. A sample of college students performed tasks of identifying and assigning importance ratings to a number of environmental features which they expected to use in describing a particular urban travel route to a stranger. The study included three spatial forms and two environmental displays. Analyses of variance for the ratings revealed the varied spatial forms did affect the importance assigned to environmental features.

Introduction

Much research has verified the existing relationship between the environment and the cognitive processes of the individual within urban settings in the fashion that "what is seen is dependent upon what is there to be seen" (2), but many questions remain. Not all urban places have the same spatial structure. Thus, one might ask if a particular structure facilitates or hinders the development of an image (3). Another inquiry may ask whether or not the same environmental features are equally important to observers regardless of the spatial structure of cities. The research reported here examines the second question.

The studies of Lynch (4), Carr and Schissler (5), and Jones (6) have implications for the present work. These studies have mainly focused on small parts of the urban area. They present two important findings. The perception of the urban environment is definitely related to the actual environment. Similar types of features are mentioned in both areal and linear (sequential) images. From this base, we can probe the effect different spatial forms of cities have on the importance attached to environmental features which are to be used later as clues in way-finding.

Environmental Displays

In defining city structure, it becomes clear that the usual laboratory of the geographer --the out-of-doors-- is not adequate for the proposed research. As most geographers are reluctant to substitute abstract indoor environments for reality, a compromise is made. Four environmental displays are used: maps, scale models, slides, and an actual field trip. The latter two displays necessitate using real cities, but this presents no great problem. Three cities whose generalized land use patterns fit the three physical models of urban structure previously defined in the geographic literature are chosen (7). A land use index, M, representing the degree of zonality in the land use plan indicates City I has

214

a zonal distribution of land uses, City II a sectoral distribution, and City III a mixed distribution which is somewhat closer to II than I. The maps and scale models are fashioned according to the genralized plans of the cities and labeled simply City I, City II, and City III. Due to problems of representation and scale, the maps portray only the generalized land uses and traffic features. The scale models include all the features found on the maps as well as a variety of specific features such as churches and a few features unique to each city such as named commercial establishments or government buildings. The present paper reports only the findings of the map and scale model experiments.

Hypotheses and Analyses

The research upon which the present report is based involves three sets of hypotheses. One set concerns the accuracy of an individual's perception of the location of a given "cue" (8) relative to (a) its distance-zone from the city center; (b) its land use classification; and (c) its linear distance from the city center. The hypotheses concern the differences in the means of the accuracy measures for different spatial structures. A second set of hypotheses concern the mean importance assigned by individuals to way-finding cues in different structures. The final set of hypotheses examines the means of both the accuracy and the importance measures when the observations are grouped by personal characteristics of the respondents rather than by city structure. This study deals only with the importance of features under different city structures, and as shaped by personal characteristics.

The effects of spatial structure and selected individual characteristics

The major hypothesis states that city structure significantly explains the variations in the mean importance assigned to the environmental features or cues by a sample of respondents. Furthermore, it is believed the features of land use will be most important in the concentric structure while those of traffic will have greater significance in the sector model.

Although both the environment and the characteristics of the individual enter into the image formation process, it is hypothesized that city structure has a greater discriminatory power than any of the individual characteristics examined. That is, city structure will account for more of the variation in the mean importance measures than will any of the individual characteristics. By using a college sample, it is possible to control for individual differences such as socio-economic class, age, etc. Therefore, the individual characteristics for which testing is performed are those which are thought to have a direct influence in environmental images: (1) length of residence in a large urban place (operationalized by a three-way classification: (a) 0 years, (b) 0-3 years, and (c) more than 3 years); (2) urban experience (defined as the place where the individual spent most of his life up to age 18: (a) rural, (b) small city, or (c) urban/suburban environment); (3) patronized shopping location (specified as (a) downtown or (b) shopping center); and (4) navigational experience (operationalized by the agreement expressed to the statement "I find traveling in an urban area confusing."). Checking on the individual characteristics first requires examining the importance measures to determine which form, if any, best explains the variation. Then it is necessary to examine the importance measures successively in terms of the subgroups of the sample where the grouping is done on the basis of a single characteristic such as patronized shopping location. Although it is hypothesized that city structure will best explain the variation in the importance measures, it is felt that of the personal characteristics considered, the length of residence in a large urban place will be most meaningful in discriminating between cue importance over all features.

Analyses

A number of analyses of variance were performed on the importance ratings given to the environmental features which appeared on the routes selected by a sample of 110 college students (9). The first analysis involved testing the relationship between city structure and importance for each of the environmental features. The other analyses tested the relationship between individual characteristics and the importance assigned to a feature. Interest was in the F values and the ordering of the means for each environmental feature in the city structure analysis.

Results

The maps and scale models were analyzed separately. Some comparisons can be made between the two. The results of the nalyses of variance for the maps are discussed first.

Maps

The F values indicate that cities differ significantly with respect to mean importance for five features: (1) high density residential land use, (2) low density residential land use, (3) institutions, (4) railroad crossings, and (5) streams (F values: 4.166, p .05; 16.891, 25.901, 5.921, 8.367, all p .01). Of the five features, two are land use features upon which the map and model spatial structures are defined. Railroad crossings and streams have an indirect effect on land use patterns. Institutions are often sprinkled throughout the urban scene, although most are not found in the central core of cities. Looking at the ordering of the means (Graph I), it appears the means of Cities I and III are close together and are different from the mean of City II for railroad crossings and streams. Although all the structures had these features, the difference may be the result of the real city upon which structure II was based. City II is an abstracted model of a city which is an exchange point for two railroads in one of the heaviest railroad freight districts in the United States. The stream in City II appeared at the extreme edge of the map and had only a few routes crossing it. In the other cities, streams crossed or paralleled several routes, some of which were located near the central part of the city.

The graph of the means also shows that City III is separate from I and II with respect to the residential land use and institution features. Again, the difference may be the result of the real city (III) of which the map is an abstraction. City III had a greater number of institutions than did I and II. The residential variables are not as easily explained. City III has the smallest mean for low density residential and the largest for high density residential. The difference may simply be a size factor since City III had relatively speaking a greater proportion of its area in high density residential land use than did Cities I and II.

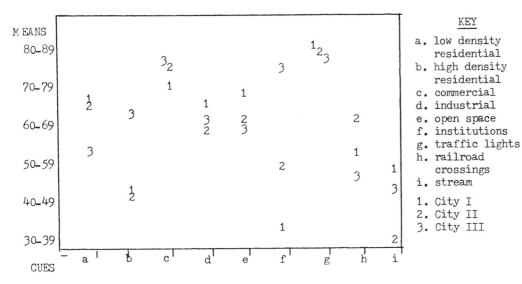

GRAPH I: MAPS—CUE IMPORTANCE MEANS BY CITY STRUCTURE.

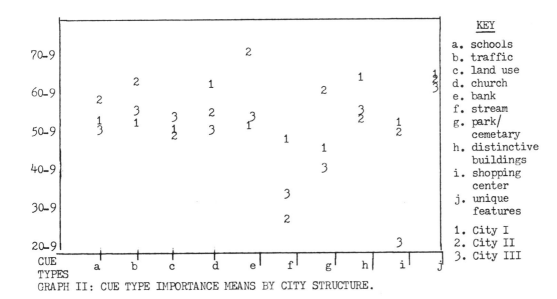

GRAPH II: CUE TYPE IMPORTANCE MEANS BY CITY STRUCTURE.

Also, due to scale problems, the map of City III did not extend to the limits of the real city and therefore, a smaller area of low density residential land use was present along the routes.

The F values also show that the cities do not differ significantly with respect to traffic, open space, and commercial and industrial land use. The graph shows the means of the three structures are quite similar on each of these variables. Calculating an overall mean for each of the nine features indicates the four variables for which the cities did not differ significantly had the highest values. This result promotes the idea that the four features are thought to be dominant in all city structures by the subjects and are therefore rated highly important; whereas, the remaining five are not as dominant in all structures, but are more apt to serve as distinguishing features along routes which taken together are reflective of the structure of the city.

Comparing the discriminatory power of city structure and the selected individual characteristics, we find that a larger proportion of the variables exhibit significant F values when discriminated by each city type than when discriminated by any given individual characteristic. I.e., five of the nine features have significant F values when classified by city type versus from zero to three out of nine for the personal characteristics. Navigational experience was the most important personal characteristic by this criterion, accounting for significant F's on three variables.

Scale Models

The F values of spatial structures for the models indicate the cities discriminate significantly with respect to six types of environmental features: (1) traffic, (2) church, (3) bank, (4) stream, (5) distinctive buildings, and (6) parks/cemetaries (F values: 8.293, 6.357, 10.672, 12.263, 5.532, 7.252, all p .01). They do not discriminate on importance for four types of environmental features: (1) schools, (2) land use, (3) shopping centers, and (4) unique features. The types in the analysis of the models are in some instances a composite of several features. For example, land use is a composite of seven single land use features (high density residential, low density residential, commercial-downtown, commercial-strip, industrial, institutional, and open space) and traffic a composite of four single traffic features (traffic lights, railroad crossings, street direction signs, and freeway evidence). The graph of the means suggests City II is different from Cities I and III on all types except churches and shopping centers. (Graph II) The number of churches along prominent routes in Cities I and II was unusually large. The shopping centers in City III often occurred in the built-up urban area and therefore, were not as dominant visually as those in Cities I and II.

A second part of the major hypothesis is more applicable to the analysis of the models than the maps. It is felt that the land use variable will be most meaningful for the concentric structure while the traffic variable will best explain the differences in the sector structure. Thus, the expected ordering of the means for land use is II, III, and I (going from high to low). The obtained ordering is III, I, and II. The expected ordering of the means for traffic is I, III, and II, while the observed ordering is II, III, and I. Traffic generation may offer a possible explanation for the deviations of the observed and expected ordering of the means.

In concentric structures where land use changes occur along routes, one expects the land uses to have a visual significance. Often each land use generates a different amount and type of traffic. Therefore, it may be that traffic is more salient than land use to the individual driver. In sector structures, land use is the same throughout the sector; thus, one expects traffic to be fairly constant as well. This may cause the attention of the motorist to wander to other features in the environment.

Comparing the discriminatory power of city structure and the selected individual characteristics, we again find that a larger proportion of the variables exhibit significant F values when discriminated by each city. That is, six of the ten types have significant F values when classified by city type versus from zero to five out of ten for the personal characteristics. Patronized shopping location was the most important personal characteristic by this criterion, accounting for significant F values on five variables. The remaining three personal characteristics appeared to be almost equally non-important.

Comparison of Map and Model Findings

Both the maps and models are abstractions of real cities. Neither is an exact replication of the real city on which it is based nor of each other. The map display, due to scale and representation limits, is necessarily more generalized than that of the model display. Thus the results are not directly comparable, but a few comparisons are possible.

Consider the discussion of the previous section that land use has greater importance in concentric structures and traffic in sector structures. In the analysis of the models, the types, land use and traffic are composites of the appropriate individual environmental features. In the map analysis, the features are individually represented. The graph of the means for maps shows an observed ordering of I, II, and III (from high to low) for traffic lights. Combining the features of traffic lights and railroad crossings gives the ordering: II, I, and III. A comparison of the orderings of the means for land use is more difficult since there are six different land uses with six orderings. The predicted ordering of II, III, and I is never observed for any of the land use features. Combining the means for the six and calculating a composite mean for land use on the maps, results in an ordering of III, II, and I. The saliency of traffic in the concentric structure and the attraction of land use in the sector structure is again a plausible explanation.

Graphs I and II indicate the means for the variables become somewhat depressed as the environmental display becomes less abstract. In a free recall situation, observers are more apt to think in terms of specific features such as buildings rather than generalized features such as land use. They record and report environmental features in a like manner. Having to work almost entirely with generalized features on the maps, the respondents appear to have consistently rated the map items higher than the model items.

In the analyses testing the discriminatory power of city structure and selected individual characteristics, similar results occur for both the maps and models. In each case a large proportion of the variables exhibit significant F values when discriminated by city structure. By this criterion, the personal characteristic of length of residence in a large urban place appears equally non-important for the two displays. Urban experience is slightly more important on the maps than on the models. Patronized shopping location is the most important personal characteristic for the models while navigational experience is most important for the maps. At this point, one wonders how much of the difference is due to the abstract qualities of the environmental displays.

Conclusion

The study supports the relationship between the physical environment and the selection of environmental features that has been mentioned by others. It also suggests that variations in the arrangement of land uses in cities do influence the importance attached to environmental features as possible way-finding clues. Among the most interesting aspects of the study, however, are the questions it raises concerning the personal characteristics which are thought to have some influence in the perceptual selection and organization of environmental information. The results suggest more meaningful ways to represent an individual's commerce with the urban environment are necessary. Still other possibilities for understanding the relationship between the individual characteristics and cognitive representations may warrant investigating further Kelly's (10) thoughts on personal constructs.

Notes and References

(1) The author acknowledges the support given by the AAUW during the period in which this research was conducted and an NSF grant which covered the cost of materials. The author also thanks R. C. Jones for his comments.

(2) Carr, S. and Schissler, D., "The City as a Trip: Perceptual Selection and Memory in the View From the Road", ENVIRONMENT AND BEHAVIOR, 1, pp. 7-36, 1969.

(3) Carr, S., "The City of the Mind" in Ewald, W. R., ENVIRONMENT AND MAN, Bloomington, Indiana University Press, 1967.

(4) Lynch, K. THE IMAGE OF THE CITY, Cambridge, MIT Press, 1960.

(5) Carr, S. and Schissler, D., "The City as a Trip: Perceptual Selection and Memory in the View From the Road", ENVIRONMENT AND BEHAVIOR, 1, pp. 7-36, 1969.

(6) Jones, M., "Urban Path-Choosing Behavior: A Study in Environmental Clues", in Mitchell, W. EDRA 3, Los Angeles, 1972.

(7) Thomlinson, R. URBAN STRUCTURE, New York, Random House, 1969.

(8) "Cue " and "feature" are used interchangeably in the paper.

(9) See Golledge, R. and Zannaras, G., "The Perception of Urban Structure" in Eastman, C. and Archea, J. EDRA 2, Pittsburgh, 1970, for details on data.

(10) Kelly, G. A THEORY OF PERSONALITY, New York, Norton, 1963.

BUILDING THE IMAGERY OF SAN FRANCISCO. AN ANALYSIS OF CONTROVERSY OVER
HIGH-RISE DEVELOPMENT, 1970-71.

Alcira Kreimer
Department of Landscape Architecture
College of Environmental Design
University of California
Berkeley, California 94720

Abstract

This study attempts to explore the "image" of San Francisco as it is created by the
newspapers. The main assumption is that the perception and evaluation of the urban
environment is to a great extent shaped by verbal and iconic frames of reference
selected by the media. In this process, newspapers play a central role in influencing not only political decisions on the urban environment, but also public consensus about the possible alternatives for action, their value and their consequences. The specific topic of research is the controversy in local newspapers over
the proposed construction of high-rise buildings in San Francisco during 1970-71.
The analysis focuses on the themes of the articles, the actors involved in the controversy, the strategy of their action, the environmental attributes attached to
San Francisco, and the mythology that the controversy created about the city.

Introduction

Communication about the urban environment is shaped by words as much as by iconic
images. Newspapers contribute largely to creating a representation of San Francisco, its image is much written about and discussed by the press. This will be
the focus of the study: the specific topic of research is the controversy in the
local newspapers over the proposed construction of high-rise buildings in San
Francisco during 1970-71.

The description of the environment by the press reflects, on the one hand, codifi-
cations and representations of the environment that come forth from the collective
image (Boorstin, 1961; Strauss, 1968); on the other hand it modifies or guides the
environmental perceptions of the public. The media select and combine units of
information. They provide the public with some important patterns through which
the public "reads" and perceives the city. In the controversy, the newspaper talks
about different places, buildings and urban qualities that are assembled by the
narration in a relation of contiguity. This is one of the mechanisms they used for
building up the image of the city. The controversy over high-rise development is
important because it deals with one of the processes that shape the city. The
production process is here publicly discussed and, to some extent, the newspaper is
the mediator between the community, which, in this case, exerted pressure to block
the construction, and the decision-making groups (i.e. the Board of Supervisors).
The study explores these central hypotheses:
1. That decisions about physical development are partly formed by verbal imagery
propagated by the media and that this imagery is selective.
2. That different actors involved in the decisions select different images and
axes of meaning to support their positions and systematically avoid talking about

other images and axes of meaning.
3. That certain journalists play key roles as ideological leaders. They will select and give attention to different environmental subjects, perspectives and positions, creating, thus, an imagery of the city. This imagery of the city is again,
only one among many possible others, all of which imply different perspectives on
the city.
4. That the legitimacy of the imagery is class-based.
5. That a mythology is created -- a rhetoric of controversy -- which hides the
biases and underlying interests of the different actors.

The context of the study: In the last seven or eight years there has been a great
deal of discussion in San Francisco about the development of new-high rise buildings.
Newspapers played an active role in it both reflecting attitudes and shaping them.
There has been an evolution in the urban values and in the meaning of the imagery of
San Francisco, in both its iconic and written aspects in the last years: "modern"
and "fast growing" city were positive attributes in the early 60's while "preservation" and "tradition" replaced them in the 70's. In order to understand how the
image of San Francisco is generated by the media, I have analyzed one of the high-
rise controversies, the one concerning the proposed U.S. Steel building. The
building, a Skidmore, Owings and Merrill project, was to be a high-rise 550 feet
high on San Francisco's Waterfront. The Waterfront height limit needed to be
changed in order to allow the U.S. Steel tower. A few months after the proposal
the controversy was raging. The arguments focused not only on the building itself
and the Waterfront, but also on the whole image of San Francisco, its development,
and growth. After one year long of inflamed debate, in February 1971, the Board
of Supervisors voted a 175-foot maximum height limit on the portion of the Waterfront where the 550-foot U.S. Steel building was to rise. The project was therefore killed.

The study: methods

This study on the U.S. Steel controversy is based on 80 articles selected at random
among those carrying information about the proposal and its influence on San Francisco's environment, published by the SAN FRANCISCO CHRONICLE between December 1969
and May 1971. The content analysis focused on the themes of the articles, the
actors involved in the controversy, the strategy of their actions, the environmental attributes attached to San Francisco and the mythology that the controversy
created about the city. The images (photos, drawings, graphics) published in the
articles to accompany the written account were also analyzed, although this analysis
is not included in this report.

The themes of the articles

I have organized the material of the articles into 5 thematic areas. Each thematic
area is an area of meaning created by the common semantic elements of certain words.
The five main thematic areas surrounding the central subject of high-rises and U.S.
Steel are the following: 1) Political environment (the actors); 2) Strategic game
(actions); 3) Economic environment; 4) Physical environment (physical and geographical aspects) and 5) Axiological environment (values). (See components of each
thematic area in graphic 1.)

1. The political environment (actors)

In favor of the building	Opposition to the building	Arbitrating bodies

Port Commission
Chamber of Commerce
International Longshoremen's
  and Warehousemen's Unions
Downtown Association
U.S. Steel Corporation
Construction Industry
San Francisco Planning and
  Urban Renewal (SPUR)
Mayor Alioto
Skidmore, Owings and
  Merrill
San Francisco Art
  Commission
The Editorial Section of
  the San Francisco
  Chronicle
	Citizen's Waterfront
	  Committee
	Alvin Duskin
	Herb Caen (San Francisco
	  Chronicle)
	Charles McCabe (San
	  Francisco Chronicle)
	Northern California
	  Architects
		Board of Supervisors
		City Planning
		  Commission
		Bay Conservation
		  and Development
		  Commission (BCDC)

2. The Strategic Game (actions)

Inputs	Processing	Outputs
Proposal Opposition Picketing Protest Alvin Duskin Advertisement	Study Debate Delay Vote	Approval Blocking

3. Economic Environment

+Consequences of the building	−Consequences of the building
Revenues for the city Employment	Increase of taxes Increase of city services Requirement of new freeways Increase in number of commuters

4. The Physical Environment

Geographic characteristics	Valued elements	Other cities or built environments	
		Good	Bad

Location
Topography:
  Bay
  Hills
  Flatlands
	Views
	Height
	Access to water
	Open Space
	Scale
	Color
	Variety
		Mill Valley
		Big Sur
		Monterrey
			New York
			Chicago
			Waikiki Beach
			Chinese Wall
			Alcatraz

5. Axiological environment (values)

Human	Civic	Urban
Quality of life Emotion Human rights Aesthetics	History Tradition Future	Deterioration Conservation Uglification Beautification Naturalness Imageability Visibility

GRAPHIC I.

The actors in the controversy

The different actors involved in the controversy selected different images and axes of meaning to support their position and systematically avoided talking about other images and axes of meaning.

1. The main groups in favor of the building were the developer (U.S. Steel Corporation), the architects (S.O.M.), the Port Commission, the Unions, the Chamber of Commerce and the Mayor of San Francisco.

2. The main actors who opposed the building were the columnist Herb Caen, the conservationist groups and Alvin Duskin, a dress manufacturer. Herb Caen, whose column in the SAN FRANCISCO CHRONICLE is one of the most successful in the Bay Area press, played one of the key roles in the opposition to the building. He was clearly an ideological persuader who, positively and emphatically, based his arguments on the environmental and life-style values of the city: preservation of San Francisco's small scale, views, tradition. His role was so important because he alone provided the opposition with its most articulate ideology by talking about all the pro and con points broached into the controversy.

3. The arbitrating bodies were the Board of Supervisors, the City Planning Commission and Bay Conservation and Development Commission (BCDC).

The Strategy of Actions

In the graphic (II) I want to expose the skeleton of the chronology, showing the strategy of the actions undertaken by the two opposed groups. In the development of an action, some significant issues or subjects might determine or change the course of action (Bremond, 1963). The logic of the actions follows two patterns: a) each group develops over time a series of arguments: it has to maintain, then, a certain degree of coherence in its arguments, i.e. if the group who favors the building says that taxes will not increase because of it, and that it will have a positive effect on the environment, the "pro" group cannot, later on, support an increase in taxes on the grounds that the positive effects of the building justify the tax hike; b) the development of each group's arguments evolves when it must answer the points introduced by the adversary group. In this case, for instance, the conservationists found a most important ally in Alvin Duskin: he was able to sustain the conservationist position and answer, as well, the economic arguments introduced by the groups in favor of the U.S. Steel. In a sense, his intervention brought about a tie between the opponents in the area of "economic arguments." From there, the controversy shifted back to the purely environmental area. It was decided, ultimately, in terms of environmental considerations.

The Environmental Attributes Used in the Controversy

If we look back upon the controversies about the Bank of America, the Alcoa, the Transamerica or the U.S. Steel building, (all high rise projects built in San Francisco in the past seven years) we see that each one centered around different cultural and urban attributes. Attributes are elements of the language that become "attached" to the topics and thus qualify them within a specific semantic

THE LOGIC OF ACTIONS

AGAINST	IN FAVOR
	PROPOSAL (two proposals for the Waterfront: U.S. Steel and Ford, Dec. 1969)
	STUDY by a Planning Commission to change building rules to allow higher buildings in the Waterfront.
RECOMMENDATION of 84 ft. limit by Planning Director	
	REJECTION OF LIMIT by City Planning Commission
DECLARATION against Manhattanization (Annual Planning Conference of SPUR, Sept. 1970)	
ANNOUNCE by two supervisors of decision to fight U.S. Steel	ADOPTION of 550 ft. height limit by Planning Commission therefore APPROVAL of U.S. Steel
PROPOSAL to Board of Supervisors to vote on 550 ft. height	
	SUPPORT to U.S. Steel from Alioto and Chamber of Commerce
	Opponents of 550 ft. lose in Board of Supervisors to put the issue on the ballot.
ALVIN DUSKIN CAMPAIGN: ("Skyscrapers are economically necessary but only if you own one.")	
HEARING	Labor leaders and Chamber of Commerce ask APPROVAL of U.S. Steel project to Board of Supervisors
	Board DELAYS ACTION on height limit instead of approving 175 ft. limit.
ALVIN DUSKIN CAMPAIGN to submit height limits to a POPULAR VOTE	
San Francisco Supervisors BLOCK U.S. STEEL (February 1971)	
Recommendations to set up regulations to MAINTAIN the VALUES (environmental) "we believe are important."	

GRAPHIC II.

area (Barthes, 1967a). In this case, the topics of the argument are the U.S. Steel and the city of San Francisco. The different attributes work together in providing a framework for the narration; they are the elements of paramount importance in the shaping of a mythology. Each attribute carries, in each case, a positive or a negative "sign." This qualification is cultural and it varies with each urban-architectonic style or ideological frame of reference: thus, in the early 1960's "tall" was marked as positive: "I'm at home where the tall buildings grow...I'll take the vertical city." (H. Caen, SAN FRANCISCO CHRONICLE, July 1960). In 1970, it is negative: "The entire concept of Manhattanization or 'verticality' seems old fashioned." (H. Caen, SAN FRANCISCO CHRONICLE, September, 1970).

The topics are semantically organized by the following attributes: identity as a city, visibility, authenticity, scale, coherence and harmony, and color. I will determine for each attribute the main pairs of opposed meanings, and a checklist of the words related to each opposition pole and utilized by the newspapers to configurate the semantic area of the attribute. The relative importance of the attributes can be seen in Table II.

Table II

Mentions	Attributes
More than 35%	Identity (36%)
Between 25-35%	--
Between 15-25%	Visibility (19%)
	Authenticity (18%)
Between 5-15%	Scale (9%)
	Harmony (6%)
Less than 5%	Color (1%)
Other	

Attributes of Identity

San Francisco appears as "The City" -- the model of the ideal city. The image on which this concept is built assumes that San Francisco is different from another model, that of "problem cities," the archetype of which is New York. Its identity and idealized image derive from its character, color and variety and most especially from its geographic implantation and its connection with the water. About the relationship city/water, Barthes (1970), writes: "There is a relation between the road and the water; and we know quite well that the cities that are the most 'resistant to meaning' and to which, often the inhabitants have trouble adapting are those cities without water, without a river, without a lake, without a stream. These 'waterless' cities present difficulties for living, for reading them." The identity is reinforced in the newspaper controversy because San Francisco is identified with other places which have similar topographic characteristics (hill and sea), and appear as uniquely "good" environments: Mill Valley, Monterrey, Big Sur. The opposite examples are, on the one hand, places with "standardized characteristics" (Waikiki Beach) and, on the other hand, "problem cities" (Manhattan, Chicago).

Pair of opposite identi*y attributes:

Components:	Ideal City	Problem Cities
	San Francisco	Other American Cities
	The City	Manhattan
	Singularity	Chicago
	Uniqueness	Standard Cities
	City in hills	Flat cities
	On the seashore	Inland
	Mill Valley	Waikiki Beach
	Monterrey	
	Big Sur	

Attributes of visibility

A complete openness, allowing a multiplicity of views, is considered optimum for the
city. Visibility is linked to "legibility": the more one can find one's precise
location in relation to the city's surroundings from different spots in the city,
and the greater the possibility of achieving a structured "reading" of the city,
the better. The topic of views appears as an important matter in its own right.
It is so unquestionable a value that it is not even necessary to justify its importance. Both parts in the controversy consider it a valuable topic: the conservationists use it as a flag and as an argument, while the developers do not attack it,
saying, "The proposed skyscraper would have 'minimal effects' on views and the sky-
line." In all the collected material only in one case the argument of the views
was disdained and even openly attacked: "To hell with those people who live on Nob
Hill who worry about having their view destroyed." (Harry Bridges, leader of the
International Longshoremens' and Warehouse Union). Perhaps it is important to point
out that the only opinion in which the topic of the views is set aside comes from
a Union leader. This difference in the perception of San Francisco can be related
to the way of life of different social classes and their prejudices with regard to
the quality of life in San Francisco. A sociological analysis should be done to
test the hypothesis that environmental values correlate with social class orientations. In this light, the high-rise controversy could be approached from the point
of view of an inter-elite fight.

Main Opposition:	Visibility	Blockage
Components:	Openness	Encirclement
	Legibility	Enclosure
	Visual access	Hemmed-in space
	Transparence	Obstruction
		Barrier to views

Attributes of Authenticity

San Francisco is presented in the controversy as "true," "authentic" and, therefore, opposed to "false"; a natural environment as opposed to an "artificial" and
superurbanized one: a city with a strong tradition, history, good taste and spirit
of conservation. The controversy opposes the old buildings to the new ones. For

the opposition groups, "old" has maximum positive meaning. Even when Herb Caen
talks about "new" he is referring to old structures with a new meaning: "some new
buildings in San Francisco add new vistas, open up new spaces, add greatly to the
joy of living in the last best city in the U.S.: Ghirardelli Square, the Cannery,
The Ice House and similar projects of civilized scale are pluses." All three, are
in fact old structures which have been readapted to new uses: the old built structure remains, and the use shifts (i.e. from a Chocolate factory to a Shopping Center). On the other side, the Corporations and the U.S. Steel supporters attach importance to the image of a modern city. Chuck Bassett (from S.O.M.): "If I had my
way, I'd tear it down tomorrow (the Ferry Building)...in fact I'd tear down every
building in town except the City Hall...Forward into the past." The image of San
Francisco as a traditional city, a museum piece, is associated with a definite
group of sophisticated people: the traditional elite, the San Franciscans who le-
gitimated history and tradition by giving value and meaning to old, antique objects.
To this group, "Manhattanization" is anathema. The image proposed by the corporations is supported instead by other social groups: for instance, by the unions for
whom the functionality, bigness and modernity of the objects represent jobs. The
subjectivity of categories such as good taste/bad taste can be seen in the history
of art or of fashion: "Beauty is not a quality inherent in things themselves, it
exists merely in the mind which contemplates them and each mind sees a different
beauty." (Hume, 1970)

Main Opposition:	Naturalness	Artificiality
Components:	Tradition	Computerized thinking
	History	"Plastic" environments
	Heritage	Manhattanized
	Good taste	Dehumanization
	Conservation	Modernity
	Aesthetics	New
	Emotionality	'unrefined' social groups
	Museum piece	
	Humanity	
	Old Style: Victorian, sophisticated elites	

Attributes of scale

Scale is a very important element in the humanized nature of San Francisco, which
according to the terms of the controversy, is "the last possible city in the U.S."
Little things are important to the quality of San Francisco. "The old timers who
knew what San Francisco was all about, built their buildings to scale and made the
city grow beautiful. The giants have passed and now we have rich pygmies with ego
problems" (H. Caen). Associations with fables and plots are continually made:
Gargantua, the giants and the pygmies, David and Goliath. Of course, the giants,
Goliath and the rich-pygmies-with-ego-problems are the Corporations and David, the
San Franciscans. Height is the attribute of scale which was at the center of almost all the discussions. This subjective scale of height is crucial to the image
of San Francisco. What is considered "high" here would probably be considered
normal in New York or Chicago.

Main Opposition:	Civilized scale	Uncontrolled growth
Components:	Human scale	Super-urbanized
		Inhuman
		Massiveness
		Disproportionate height
		Giraffe

Attributes of harmony, coherence

This set of attributes reflects a balanced internal relation in the city and, as well, between the city and the bay. The harmony comes from perfect ecological adjustment between the urban environment and the water. In this category, the concept of enclosure and blocking is "naturalized" by some metaphors like Chinese Wall, Waikiki Beach. The opposition to high-rises uses them to symbolize the rupture in the natural continuity city/bay. Waikiki Beach is nature destroyed as a consequence of massive anonymous tourism, of development and of high-rises.

Main Opposition:	Equilibrium	Imbalance
Components:	Natural profile	Interruption of natural profile
	Positive integration	Waikiki Beach
	Access to the Water	Discon. city/water
	Continuity	Rape of the Bay

Attributes of Color

The controversy presents San Francisco as both colorful and white in opposition to darkness. The color is given by the variety and richness of elements both architectural and human. This dimension "humanizes" the city. The predominant light tonality of the city was broken by the new black buildings (Bank of America, Alcoa). The color, although it is not one of the most important attributes in the case of the U.S. Steel building, was the fundamental attribute in the Bank of America issue. In the U.S. Steel controversy, the color is mentioned as an attribute of the city and of its diversity. "Thanks to the keeper of the flame, the colorful, the individual, the old San Franciscan...Thanks to the little things that give the city its true tone and texture" (H. Caen). "These are 'natural' colors, while the new buildings are felt as 'unnatural.' Bank of America, Crocker, Alcoa and all those other dark buildings thrown up by newcomers with cold New York hearts..."

Main Opposition:	"Natural" colors	"Unnatural" colors
Components:	White, light	Black
	Colorful	Grey (lack of color)
	Diversity of colors	Homogeneity of color
	Warm	Cold

The mythology of the controversy

In this reading of the high-rise controversy, we see concepts used which apparently convey very well defined meanings, such as San Francisco, Manhattan, Mill Valley, San Franciscan, Waikiki Beach. What is the role of these concepts in the building of the controversy? The newspaper narration presents some characteristics which I will call "mythical" and certain concepts which are keys to the mythology. Their function is to attach metaphorically a value to the main subject under the appearance of a fact, as a "concrete reality." (Barthes, 1967b) The context of the high-rise controversy can be reduced to a mythological inventory which states some concepts and relates them to a conceptual system as if they were facts and not values. In the previous analysis I cited certain concepts whose relation to others is taken as mandatory or as a "natural" meaning. Such concepts are the "mythical operators" of a larger mythology that applies to the image of San Francisco. Myths conceal the underlying reasons of the controversy: the location of big corporations in San Francisco, or the goal to convert the city into a financial empire, the "Wall Street" of the West, or the fight between two elites.

The analytical reading of a given myth implies both a search into the structure of the myth and into the context which organizes the mythological universe. For example, in order to grasp the qualities attached to the term "Manhattanization" (dirtiness, crime, etc.) and those that are excluded (modern metropolis, for instance), we have to resort to the mythology existent in public opinion. In the narration these qualities appear as naturally inherent to the concept, as if the only natural meaning of Manhattan really was dirtiness, urban problems, crime. Similarly, the meaning attached to Waikiki Beach changes according to the contextual frame in which it is included. In the U.S. Steel controversy, Waikiki Beach is an example of nature destroyed by man. But "destruction" is conceived only in a "conservationist" oriented mind, because Waikiki Beach is the tourist goal of thousands of lower middle class people. The travel section of the same newspaper is full of advertisements praising the marvels of the "Waikiki Paradise."

The two positions in the myth: The core of the controversy is the confrontation between two opposite views of "what the outsiders want to do to San Francisco so that it stops being what it is and changes its way." Each of the two large adversary groups structures its own mythological narration from a specific perspective: a) those opposed to the U.S. Steel emphasize the mythical argument of "San Francisco" (ideal city, unique); b) those in favor of the U.S. Steel propose the mythology of progress through technological advance and enormous projects. The two antagonistic positions permit us to discover how the image of each adversary is established in the narration: the San Franciscan and the Outsiders; those who wan to protect San Francisco, "different from other cities," and those who think that San Francisco would be better if it accepted the alleged key to American urban progress, high-rise development. This helps to explain the strategy of the leaders of the opposition: they succeeded in combining in their favor a mythology supported by marginal and anti-establishment sectors (intellectuals and artists) with a mythology supported by the traditional local elites. The convergence of anti-establishment and traditional sectors around historical preservation and conservation urban ecology, and the taste for nature, represent different things for each of the sectors in the anti-U.S. Steel coalition. The anti-establishment "intellectual" rejects the increasing power of corporations on the life of the city and its inhabitants. The traditional elites, find in this theme signs and criteria with which to establish social "legitimacy."

Conclusion

I have proposed a reading of one of the issues that has helped to shape -- along with many others -- the image of San Francisco. I have interpreted the material and tried to show the multiplicity of meanings underneath the positions of the various newspaper items. My objective was to show how the explicit and implicit meanings give rise to a mythology of San Francisco. In other words, these meanings shape an ideology which influences both the actual and the future image of the city and therefore affects the plans for the city's development. In the case of the U.S. Steel building, the opposition was strong enough to block the plans for the building. This analysis of the rhetoric of the controversy allows us to understand its value base and, as well, the values and imagery which it helped to build. The systematic knowledge of the media's role concerning questions as important as the urban environment is indispensable if we want to avoid in the words of G. Gerbner: "the selective habits of participation in one's cultural environment (that) limit each of us to risky and often faulty, extrapolation about the cultural experience of heterogeneous communities. Informed policy making and the valid interpretation of social response increasingly require general and comparative indicators of the prevailing climate of the man-made symbolic environment." (Gerbner, 1969)

References

Barthes, R. SYSTEME DE LA MODE, Editions du Seuil, 1967a, pages 119-157.

Barthes, R. MYTHOLOGIES, Ed. du Seuil, 1967b.

Barthes, R. Semiologie et urbanisme, L'ARCHITECTURE D'AUJOURD'HUI, December, 1970, page 13.

Boorstin, D. THE IMAGE. A GUIDE TO PSEUDO-EVENTS IN AMERICA, Harper and Row, New York, 1961.

Bremond, C. Le message narratif, COMMUNICATIONS #4, Editions du Seuil, Paris, 1963, pages 4-32.

Gerbner, G. "Toward 'Cultural Indicators': the Analysis of Mass Mediated Public Message Systems" in G. Gerbner et al. (Ed) THE ANALYSIS OF COMMUNICATION CONTENT, Wiley and Sons, 1969, page 124.

Hume, D. A Treatise of Human Nature, quoted by George Baird in "La Dimension Amoureuse in Architecture," in Jencks, Ch. and Baird, G. (Ed) MEANING IN ARCHITECTURE, Braziller, New York, 1970, page 95.

Strauss, A. THE AMERICAN CITY: A SOURCEBOOK OF URBAN IMAGERY, Chicago, Aldine, 1968.

Gary T. Moore

Department of Psychology
Clark University
Worcester, Massachusetts 01610

Abstract

This paper summarizes part of a theoretical and empirical study of developmental and stylistic variations between and within people in the organization of knowledge of large-scale physical and social environments. Propositions from an interactional-constructivist theory are advanced and hypotheses regarding between-individual developmental differences in the representation of the spatial layout of a city are derived and tested. It was found that: a) sketch maps can be reliably sorted into three levels of representation: undifferentiated egocentric, differentiated and partially coordinated, and abstractly coordinated and hierarchically integrated; b) these levels characterize developmental differences between people and are not significantly related to age, sex, or general intellectual aptitude; c) performance on certain spatial thinking tasks is related to level of representation of the city as a whole; and d) this performance is also related to degree of familiarity with different parts of the city.

Introduction

This study was designed to test parts of a developmental theory of environmental cognition advanced in an earlier paper (2). The general background of the study will be presented and then an empirical study testing one aspect of this conceptualization will be briefly summarized.

The general position is advanced that transactions between people and their environment are mediated by the knowledge or cognitive representations they have of the environment, and that these representations are constructed by each person operating as an active organism dynamically balancing and synthesizing inner organismic factors and external environmental demands. That is, the position is adopted that behavior is not directly affected by the environment and that there is a difference between reacting to and knowing about the environment such that the influence of external environmental variables on behavior is mediated by the way the environment is conceived and structured by the individual. It is also held that far from being passive recipients of external forces moving them to conform to the demands of the external stimulus situation, and far from being driven primarily by biological factors and inherited patterns of response, people are active organisms continually adapting to the world in response to an interaction between both inner organismic factors (including not only genetic and biological factors, but also values, goals, intentions, etc.) and external factors (including social, cultural, and historical factors, as well as immediate human and non-human situational factors). In short, the theory advanced argues that cognitive representations are important mediators of behavior and are constructed through a series of organism-environment transactions. Methodologically, it is assumed that external, symbolic representations (like verbal descriptions, sketch maps, models, psychophysical scales, etc.) reflect these internal, cognitive representations.

Developmental analysis. The present question is whether external representations can be ordered developmentally and, if so, what the nature is of the differences and transformations between levels.

There are at least two fundamental ways of looking at development. In common usage, development is seen as changes over time or in relation to age, and it is assumed that these changes entail progress, i.e., that which occurs later is considered in some way more advanced than that which occured earlier. But there are a number of problems with this time-bound view (3): there are no grounds for assuming that all changes entail progress; the view precludes the developmental comparison of contemporaneous events like the behavior of two individuals or groups; and the view precludes the developmental analysis of cyclically recurring events within the same person. An alternative conception of development focuses on the organization of behavior and dispenses with any necessary association between development and time. Development may therefore be defined formally as qualitative changes, differences, or variations in the organization of behavior such that developmentally more advanced behavior is more differentiated than lower forms of behavior and logically includes and hierarchically integrates lower stages and the behaviors associated with them. This definition is consistent with the particular formulations advanced by Piaget, Werner, and other developmental theorists (4) and leaves as an empirical question whether or not particular developments are associated with age.

There are three contexts in which development may be investigated: we may look for developmental changes in the behavior of an individual, group, organization, society, etc. over extended periods of time; for developmental differences between individuals or groups; and for developmental variations within an individual or group in relation to the demands of particular situations (e.g., stress, anxiety, different intentions, different environments, and so on).

With regard to the understanding of space and the environment, considerable evidence indicates that the ontogenetic development of children's knowledge of space, i.e., spatial cognition, passes through four stages: sensorimotor space without representation, intuitive or preoperational space, concrete operational space, and formal operational space(5). On the basis of extrapolations from general theory and from the findings on spatial cognition, it has been suggested that the ontogenetic development of representations of the large-scale environment passes through three stages: egocentric, fixed, and coordinated reference systems, and that these stages are systematically related to the stages both of general intellectual development and of fundamental spatial cognition (6). Some writers have treated these systems as developmentally ordered, while others have seemed to treat them as different styles of representation, not developmentally ordered (7). Structural analysis of the properties of these systems indicates, however, that they are more easily and parsimoniously interpreted in developmental terms. There is also some suggestion that the microgenetic development of coming to know a new environment passes through the same three stages (8).

A major intent of the present study was to broaden these conceptual categories and to define a general set of developmental levels applicable not only to ontogenetic and microgenetic development changes, but also to developmental differences between individuals and developmental variations within the same individual, and applicable not only to the organization of knowledge of the spatial environment, but also to the organization of knowledge of the everyday social and political environments.

Several different dimensions may be employed for the developmental analysis of behavior. The two most general--degree of complexity of organization and degree of integration--have been mentioned, to which may be added degree of concreteness versus abstractness and degree of egocentricity versus coordination of viewpoints. Together these dimensions may be used to define three essential developmental levels of any representation: a) undifferentiated concrete egocentric, b) differentiated and partially coordinated in fixed subgroups, and c) abstractly coordinated and hierarchically integrated (9). The remainder of this paper reports part of an experiment conducted to test whether representations of the environment may be analyzed in these terms and whether these levels characterize developmental differences between people in the representation of the same city. (Data has also been collected on within-individual variation and on the organization of overall verbal impressions of the city, but due to space limitations this data is not reported here.)

As there is no way to directly observe an internal cognitive representation, the only way to test for certain properties of it is to test logical deductions from it. The most commonly used method has been the analysis of some form of external representation like a sketch map, verbal description, etc. In the present case, a second means was also used. One of the characteristics of development is inclusion, i.e., that each stage of development logically includes and integrates lower stages and the behaviors associated with them. Thus it follows that individuals whose sketch maps are at what is postulated to be a developmentally more advanced level (e.g., abstractly coordinated) would be expected to accomplish certain cognitive operations characteristic not only of their own level but also of the lower level (e.g., partially coordinated), while individuals at the lower level, though accomplishing operations characteristic of that level, would not be expected to accomplish operations of the higher level. The operations chosen were associativity (the association in thought of points in space in different orders such that the same terminal point may be reached by different routes) and reversibility (the reversing in thought of the order of points such that a path can be retraced back from the terminal to the starting point).

Method

The experiment was conducted in two sessions, the first to determine the developmental level of each individual's representation of the spatial layout of a city, and the second to investigate between-individual developmental differences in other cognitive spatial operations. Both sessions were tape recorded.

First session--production of sketch maps. Ss for the first session were 51 teenagers drawn at random from grades 10 through 12 of a Worcester high school. Ages ranged from 15;9 to 19;4 with an average of 17;4. There were 30 girls and 21 boys. All Ss had lived in the city for at least three years.

The first session involved two tasks. First, Ss were asked to draw a sketch map of the city of Worcester including as many different parts of the city as possible. Ss were encouraged to verbalize what they were drawing and how they decided where to put different things. Next, Ss were asked to fill-out a 5-point scale of famiarity with each of 15 different areas of the city.

Intermediate analysis--classification of sketch maps. In order to assign Ss to conditions for the second session, three judges were each given an eight-page set of criteria and were asked to independently sort the sketch maps into three levels of representation: undifferentiated egocentric, differentiated and partially coordinated, and abstractly coordinated and hierarchically integrated, and subsequently to order the maps from lowest to highest degree of organization. (The written criteria were prepared ahead of time and were pretested in a pilot study involving other Ss and judges.)

Second session--tests of other cognitive operations. Ss for the second session were 32 students, 16 drawn at random from each of Levels II and III on the basis of the intermediate analysis. Provision was made to insure that the subject groups were approximately equivalent in terms of two indices of general intellectual aptitude-- verbal and mathematical measures of the SAT and SCAT tests--and three other variables--age, sex, and grade level.

The second session involved four sets of tasks (two of which concerned hypotheses and data not reported in the present paper). Ss were asked to give two sets of alternative directions between pairs of points in the city (i.e., the associativity task) and then a set of directions back to the first point (i.e., the reversibility task), in each case for points in two areas of the city of low personal familiarity and two areas of high familiarity. The areas to which questions pertained were drawn from each S's responses on the scale of familiarity. Finally, as a test-retest reliability on the stability of the initial classification of sketch maps, Ss were asked to draw a final sketch map of the city incorporating a given set of 22 elements.

Results

Ordering of sketch maps. The sketch maps were classified in accordance with the written criteria into three developmental levels. Of the 51 $\underline{S}s$, 3 were classified at Level I, 29 at Level II, and 19 at Level III. Interjudge reliabilities were found to range from .73 to .92 (p<.01). Examples of representations at each of these levels (including two varieties of Level II representations) are shown in Figure 1.

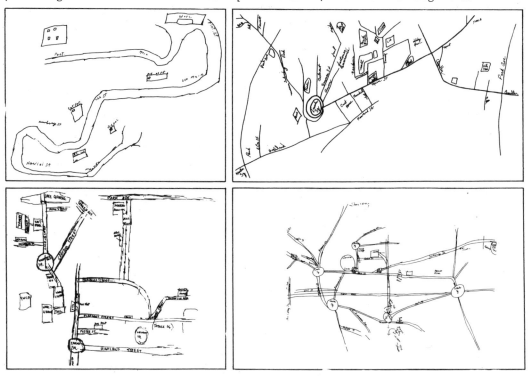

The Level I, undifferentiated egocentric representation on the upper left is a long, serpentine-like route comprised of personally significant street segments bearing little resemblance to the geographical relations between these streets. Of the two examples of Level II, partially coordinated representations, the upper right is of the linear-route variety, i.e., organized around one long street and extentions to it, and the lower left of the point-radial variety, i.e., organized around two different reference points. Finally, on the lower right is a typical example of a Level III, abstractly coordinated representation, characterized by the parts being embedded in an overall geometric organization, in this case comprised of five major traffic circles and the interconnecting routes. Test-retest reliabilities were .91 (p<.001).

Five analyses were conducted to determine if there were any relations between level of sketch map representation and intellectual aptitude, age, sex, or grade. No significant relations were found between level of representation and either of two measures of general intellectual aptitude (SAT: $F=1.64$, $df=1$, 24; $p>.20$; SCAT: $F=2.64$, $df=1$, 29; $p>.10$--intellectual aptitude scores were not available for all $\underline{S}$s; these data are based on Ns of 26 and 31 respectivly) nor between level and age ($F=1.0$, $df=2$, 48; $p>.60$). There was a moderate though non-significant relation with sex, males representing the city at a slightly higher level than females ($X^2=4.1$, $df=2$; $p<.10$), and a significant relation with grade, graduating high school seniors representing the city at a higher level than other high school students ($X^2=6.75$, $df=1$, $p<.01$).

Associativity and reversibility tasks. Four analyses were conducted on the associativity and reversibility data. Interjudge reliabilities on the determination of accuracy of directions ranged from .77 to .91. The results are summarized in Table I.

Table I. Relation between Level of Sketch Map Representation and Success versus Failure on Associativity and Reversibility Tasks for Familiar and Unfamiliar Areas

Associativity Task	Familiar Areas		Unfamiliar Areas	
	Success	Failure	Success	Failure
Level II	6	10	1	15
Level III	14	2	6	10
Reversibility Task				
	Success	Failure	Success	Failure
Level II	12	4	4	12
Level III	16	0	10	6

The results indicate that success on the associativity task of giving directions between points in different parts of the city is positivly related to higher levels of sketch map representation of the city as a whole both for pairs of highly familiar areas (Fisher's exact test: $p<.005$) and for pairs of unfamiliar areas (Fisher's test: $p<.05$). It was also found that degree of success on the associativity task for combined areas (measured on a 5-point scale) was positivly related to level of sketch map representation (Mann-Whitney U: $z=5.01$; $p<.001$).

The results also indicate that success on the reversibility task is positivly related to level of representation for unfamiliar areas (Fisher's test: $p<.05$) but not for familiar areas.

A further analysis was conducted to determine if patterns of success and failure for the same $\underline{S}$ were related to degree of familiarity the different areas. This data is presented in Table II.

Table II. Relation between Level of Sketch Map Representation and Patterns of Success and Failure on Associativity and Reversibility Tasks

	Success on Fam. and Unfam.	Success on Fam., Failure on Unfam.	Success on Unfam., Failure on Fam.	Failure on Both
Associativity Task				
Level II	10	5	0	1
Level III	4	10	2	0
Reversibility Task				
Level II	4	8	0	4
Level III	10	6	0	0

The results indicate that on the associativity task both Level II and Level III Ss did significantly better on familiar areas than on unfamiliar areas (Sign test: N= sum of middle columns =17, x= sum of lesser column =2; $p<.01$) and likewise on the reversibility task (Sign test: N=14, x=0; $p<.01$).

Summary and Discussion

Evidence has been presented, first, that sketch maps of a large-scale spatial environment can be reliably sorted into three developmental levels : undifferentiated egocentric, differentiated and partially coordinated into fixed subgroups, and abstractly coordinated and hierarchically integrated. This finding lends empirical support to the structural analysis that these three levels of sketch maps reflect three essential developmental levels of cognitive representation of the environment. The high reliabilities indicate that people's responses are stable over short periods of time.

Second, it has been seen that developmental differences between individuals in representing the same environment can be characterized in terms of these developmental levels. These developmental differences are not significantly related to age, sex, or general intellectual aptitude, but are related to high school grade level.

Third, the results indicate that for the most part there is a significant positive relation between two measures taken to be reflections of internal cognitive representation: level of sketch map representation of the city as a whole and performance of certain cognitive spatial operations.

Finally, fourth, the results indicate that independently of overall level of representation, individual's accomplish the cognitive tasks relatively more often on subjectivly familiar areas than on unfamiliar areas. These findings are consistent with the interactional-constructivist theory underlying the study.

Notes and References

(1) This paper is based on a thesis entitled DEVELOPMENTAL VARIATIONS BE-
TWEEN AND WITHIN INDIVIDUALS IN THE COGNITIVE REPRESENTATION OF
LARGE-SCALE ENVIRONMENTS being submitted in partial fulfillment of the
M.A. degree at Clark University, 1973. The research has been supported under
a Fellowship Grant from the Canada Council. My thanks especially for super-
vision and assistance from Drs. Leonard Cirillo and Seymour Wapner.

(2) Moore, G. T., Elements of a genetic-structural theory of the development of
environmental cognition, In W. J. Mitchell (Ed.) ENVIRONMENTAL DESIGN:
RESEARCH AND PRACTICE, Vol. 2, Los Angeles: University of California,
1972, pp. 30-9-1 to 30-9-13.

(3) Kaplan, B., Meditations on genesis, HUMAN DEVELOPMENT, 1967, X, 65-87.

(4) Piaget, J., THE PSYCHOLOGY OF INTELLIGENCE, Totawa, N.J.: Littlefield
Adams, 1963; Werner, H., COMPARATIVE PSYCHOLOGY OF MENTAL DEVEL-
OPMENT, New York: International Universities Press, 1948.

(5) Piaget, J. and Inhelder, B., THE CHILD'S CONCEPTION OF SPACE, New York:
Norton, 1967; Piaget, J., Inhelder, B., and Szeminska, A., THE CHILD'S
CONCEPTION OF GEOMETRY, New York: Basic Books, 1960; Laurendeau, M.
and Pinard, A., THE DEVELOPMENT OF THE CONCEPT OF SPACE IN THE
CHILD, New York: International Universities Press, 1970.

(6) Hart, R. A. and Moore, G. T., The development of spatial cognition: a review,
In R. M. Downs and D. Stea (Eds.) COGNITIVE MAPPING: IMAGES OF SPATIAL
ENVIRONMENTS, Chicago: Aldine-Atherton, in press; and Moore, Elements
of a genetic-structural theory, op. cit., cf. diagram on p. 30-9-4 (Ref. 2).

(7) For the developmental interpretation, cf. for example, Shemyakin, F.N.,
Orientation in space, In B. G. Anan'yev (Ed.) PSYCHOLOGICAL SCIENCE IN
THE U.S.S.R., Vol. 1, Washington: Office of Technical Services, 1962, pp.
182-255; for the stylistic interpretation, cf. for example, Appleyard, D.,
Styles and methods of structuring a city, ENVIRONMENT AND BEHAVIOR,
1970, II, 100-117.

(8) Hart and Moore, The development of spatial cognition, op. cit. (Ref. 6).

(9) The logic of this derivation, detailed descriptions of the levels, and the criteria
for their determination, along with other details are presented in Moore,
DEVELOPMENTAL VARIATIONS BETWEEN AND WITHIN INDIVIDUALS,
op. cit. (Ref. 1).

Alfred J. Nigl and Harold D. Fishbein
Department of Psychology
University of Cincinnati

Abstract

This research was designed to elucidate the cognitive aspects of the coordination of perspectives. Two experiments were conducted with 272 children from various preschool and elementary school classes. Children were asked to determine another person's perspective by choosing one of a set of four photographs presented to them. Besides the veridical photograph, photographs representing various types of spatial confusions (errors) were included in each set. The data analysis revealed that the most frequent spatial error made was the one in which the right and left halves of the stimuli were reversed. Back-front confusions were also made frequently by the younger children. Hypotheses were offered concerning the cognitive operations employed in solving the task.

Introduction

In recent years, a substantial amount of research activity has been directed towards uncovering the processes by which children develop an understanding of space. Jean Piaget, one of the most influential theorists in the field of cognitive development, has been primarily responsible for the current emphasis on research in this area. In his theory, a distinction is made between various types of space; topological, projective and Euclidean. Children supposedly master topological spatial relations first and then, sometime later, are able to comprehend projective and Euclidean spatial relations. Piaget and Inhelder (2) devised the "coordination of perspectives" task to study the development of children's understanding of projective space. To be successful on this task, children must integrate various visual perspectives into a total framework or system.

In the typical coordination of perspectives task, a child is seated facing an array of objects, e.g., pasteboard mountains, toys, geometrical shapes, and several photographs or drawings of them. Either the experimenter, himself, or a doll then takes a viewing position of the objects different than that of the child and the child is asked to point to the photograph or drawing which looks like what the experimenter (or doll) can see. The child demonstrates his ability to coordinate perspectives by pointing to the correct photograph or drawing. Under very simple experimental conditions, children as young as three years old have been able to successfully coordinate perspectives, e.g. Fishbein, Lewis and Kieffer, (3) and under more difficult conditions, children twelve years old made 40% errors on this task, e.g. Laurendeau and Pinard, (4).

The theoretical position of this paper is essentially that presented by Fishbein, et. al. (3). The major aspects of the theory are that coordination of perspectives is mediated by both social and cognitive factors, that social and cognitive development involve the successive acquisition of different modes of thinking, and finally, that the different modes are coexisting. From the results of their experiments Fishbein, et. al. were able to formulate three stages of social development. In the first stage, called "egocentric" children operate under the rule "You see what I see." When a child is using this rule he attributes his perception to others and makes egocentric errors, i.e., he points to the picture that shows what he sees. Empirically, more than 50% of the errors made in their experiment by all age groups were egocentric errors. In the second stage, called "non-egocentric", children operate under the rule "If you are not in my place, you do not see what I see." When a child uses this rule, he does not make egocentric errors, but is correct only by chance. In the third stage, called "empathic", children operate under the rule "If I were in your place, I would see what you see." When a child uses this rule he does not invariably perform without error. He still has the problem of figuring out what the other person sees, and this is a function of the difficulty of the task and the child's level of cognitive development.

The present two experiments are concerned with elucidating the developmental aspects of the cognitive factors in coordination of perspectives. These factors refer to the child's understanding of the relationships between objects along the three dimensions of Cartesian space, which we refer to as "left-right", "back-front", and "up-down." The methodology employed in these experiments is unique in that the photographs used were designed to uncover certain of the confusions children have about these relationships. Specifically, in Experiment I, on each trial the children were presented with the following four photographs: a veridical one, one in which the left and right halves were reflected, one in which the back and front halves were reflected, and one in which both left and right, and front and back were reflected. The latter is equivalent to a 180° rotation of the object array. In Experiment II, the objects were presented·on a two-tiered platform, and instead of the 180° photograph, a top-down reflection was used. A child displays a lack of understanding of left-right relationships, for example, when, instead of pointing to the correct photograph, he points to the photograph which depicts the object array with the left and right halves in a reversed or reflected position.

In both experiments age and number of objects (complexity) were varied between different groups of children. Based on related previous research it was hypothesized that older children would make fewer errors than younger ones; that more errors would be made in response to the more complex than to the less complex object arrays, and that the most frequent error would involve a left-right confusion, and the next most frequent, a back-front confusion.

Method

Experiment I was a 4 x 3 x 4 mixed factorial design in which age (four levels) and complexity (3 levels) were between-subject factors, and position of the experimenter (4 levels) was a within-subject factor. Experiment II was a 4 x 2 x 3 mixed factorial design, similar to Experiment I, except that only two levels of complexity were used, and the experimenter took only three viewing positions. In Experiment I the subjects were 144 white working-class and middle class children from the Cincinnati public schools. There were 36 children from each of the following grades:

pre-school, first, third, and fifth. In Experiment II, the subjects were 128 white working-class and middle-class children from the Cincinnati public schools. There were 32 children from each of the following grades: kindergarten, second, fourth, and sixth.

Seven objects were used as a stimuli. They were constructed in a manner such that they looked the same following successive 90° rotations, e.g., a cube, a cylinder, a sphere.

The procedure was very similar in both experiments. The child was seated at a rectangular table on which a certain object display had been placed. A board containing the four types of photographs described above was placed in front of the child. Each photograph was taken from a position on the same horizontal plane of the objects. The experimenter read a standard set of instructions to the child and then sat at a randomly chosen position around the table. He then asked the child to point to the picture that showed exactly what the experimenter saw. After the child made his response, the experimenter gave him corrective feedback, either by acknowledging that his response was correct or by pointing to the correct photograph. The experimenter then changed his position and asked the child again to point to what the experimenter saw. In Experiment I, the experimenter sat, on different trials, next to the child, at the two sides of the table, and across from the child. In Experiment II, he sat next to the child, across from him, and at one side.

In the first experiment each child received thirty-two trials, four for each of eight different stimulus arrays, and in the second experiment each child received thirty trials, three for each of ten different stimulus arrays. There were three object conditions in the first experiment; one group of children was presented with stimulus arrays comprised of three objects, another group was given five objects, and a third group was presented with seven objects in each stimulus array. In all cases the objects were placed along the sides of a rectangular surface, forming the shape of the letter "L". In the second experiment, there were two object conditions; one group was presented with four in each array and the other group was presented with seven objects. The objects in this experiment were randomly placed on the rectangular surface, but with the constraint that from each viewing position of the experimenter at least one object would be interposed in front of one other object.

The primary difference in materials between the two experiments was that in the second experiment a two-tiered platform was used and objects were placed on two levels instead of just one. This change was necessary to provide children with the opportunity to make up-down errors.

Results

In Table 1 are presented the mean number of correct responses in Experiment I as a function of the number of objects, age, and position of the experimenter. The maximum possible score for each cell is eight correct. An analysis of variance performed on these data indicates that overall performance was lowest for the nursery school children who performed at about chance level, intermediate and approximately the same for first and third graders, and highest for the fifth graders (F = 64.9, p < .01.) However, neither the Number of Objects (F = 1.77, p > .05) nor the Sex main effects (F = 2.12, p > .05) were significant. Overall, children gave the fewest correct responses when the experimenter sat across from them, an intermediate number when he sat at the two side positions and the greatest number when he sat next to child, the position which is designated "Front" in the table (F = 100, p < .01). A significant Age by Position of Experimenter interaction was also obtained (F = 8.12, p < .01.) This is largely attributable to two factors: First, for the nursery school children, performance at the front and side positions was very similar, whereas for the other children this was not the case; Second, at the front position, performance substantially increased with increasing age, whereas at the side and across positions this was not the case.

Table 1
Mean Number of Correct Responses For Experiment I

Object Number	Position	Age			
		Nursery	First	Third	Fifth
Three	Left	2.83	3.58	3.17	5.33
	Right	2.50	3.83	3.83	6.00
	Front	2.83	5.58	6.42	7.58
	Across	.83	1.42	2.67	3.83
Five	Left	3.33	3.58	4.41	5.41
	Right	3.66	4.25	4.33	5.58
	Front	2.00	4.67	6.83	7.33
	Across	1.33	1.33	2.83	3.50
Seven	Left	2.75	3.67	3.66	4.25
	Right	2.50	3.92	3.50	5.08
	Front	2.08	5.17	6.75	7.42
	Across	1.17	1.92	1.83	3.00

The types of errors the children made generally conform to what was predicted. For all age groups, for all levels of complexity, and for three of the four positions of the experimenter, i.e., except the right side, the most frequent error involved choosing the left-right reflection and the next most frequent involved choosing the back-front reflection. A binomial test indicated that for all the above conditions the hypothesized pattern, left-right errors > back-front errors > 180° rotations, occurred significantly greater than expected by chance (p < .05 in all cases).

Finally, one other error is of interest. When the experimenter sat across from the child, the 180° photograph actually represented the child's view of the objects. Hence, the child's choice of this photograph could be considered an egocentric error. The first graders made 20% egocentric errors, the nursery school children 16%, the third graders, 12%, and the fifth graders, 6%.

In Table 2 are presented the mean number of correct responses in Experiment II as a function of number of objects, age, and position of the experimenter. The maximum possible score for each cell is ten correct. As can be seen, the results from this experiment were highly similar to those of Experiment I. The analysis of variance indicated that the Age and Position of Experimenter main effects were statistically significant (F = 26.95, p < .01; F = 175.62, p < .01 respectively), whereas the Sex and Complexity main effects were not (F = 3.46, p > .05, F < 1.0, p > .05 respectively). Also, the only significant interaction was the Age by Position of Experimenter (F = 5.27, p < .01), as in Experiment I.

Table 2
Mean Number of Correct Responses For Experiment II

Object Number	Position	Age			
		Kindergarten	Second	Fourth	Sixth
Four	Side	3.06	4.00	4.00	6.00
	Front	5.06	6.81	8.44	8.63
	Across	2.75	3.60	4.19	4.38
Seven	Side	3.25	3.88	3.63	5.93
	Front	4.94	7.19	8.75	9.63
	Across	3.44	2.94	2.93	5.06

Regarding errors, as in Experiment I, the most frequent for all age groups and all positions of the experimenter, was a left-right confusion, and the next most frequent was a back-front confusion. A binomial test indicated that for all the above conditions the hypothesized pattern of left-right errors > back-front errors > up-down errors occurred significantly greater than expected by chance (p < .05 in all cases).

Discussion and Conclusion

Since pre-school children performed, approximately, at chance level and kindergarten children gave better than chance performances, it can be concluded that, for the population of children studied, the cognitive factors required to coordinate perspectives emerge sometime between the ages of five and six. The fact that the fifth and sixth graders in the present experiments made errors on approximately 33% of the trials indicates that full development of these factors requires a very long time span. These findings are consistent with the results of Laurendeau and Pinard (4) and hence have some generality beyond our population.

Of particular interest in this regard are the Age by Position of Experimenter interactions which were significant in both experiments. Recall that at the "Front" position performance uniformly and extensively improved with age, whereas at the "Side" and "Across" positions performance improved much more slowly with age, and on occasion, was essentially the same between adjacent age groups. Further, performance was generally better at the Front position than at the other positions, the exception being that for the nursery school children in Experiment I. This implies that the coordination of perspectives task can be construed as consisting of two subtasks, one corresponding to the Front position, and the second corresponding to the other positions. The subtask at the Front position is a recognition task in which the child is, in effect, asked to match a photograph to his view of the three-dimensional array of objects. In order to perform this task successfully the child must build a schema of the array which includes the spatial relationships between the objects. The data indicate that this ability is apparently lacking in the four year old, rapidly increases and levels off at about ten years of age. In a matching task using two-dimensional single letter-like forms, Gibson, Gibson, Pick and Osser (5) found that by eight years of age children made fewer than 10% errors on both rotations and reversals which is less than, but consistent with, the performance of the second graders in Experiment II.

The subtask at the Side and Across positions encompasses the processes underlying recognition but, additionally, includes a more "conceptual" aspect. In this subtask the child must "figure out" what the other person sees, build up a schema of this perspective, and then match this schema with one of the photographs. Thus, the performance differences between the older and younger children on the coordination of perspectives task may be attributable, in part, to differences in "recognition" capabilities as well as to other cognitive factors. One of the most important of these factors seems to be the ability to rotate a stimulus display mentally, in other words, to imagine how objects would appear if one's orientation were shifted in a specifiable manner. This ability seems to emerge between the ages of ten and twelve.

The error data are consistent with the above argument that recognition is a common feature in both subtasks. In both experiments, at all positions of the experimenter, and for all age groups, the pattern left-right errors > back-front errors > 180° errors (or up-down errors) was the dominant pattern.

The finding of such a small percentage of egocentric errors in Experiment I was unexpected and apparently inconsistent with the results of studies by Laurendeau and Pinard (4) and Fishbein et al (3). In their experiments children were given the opportunity on every trial to make an egocentric error. In Experiment I, only at the Across position was an egocentric error possible. Further, in Experiment I, unlike the previous experiments, left-right and back-front reflections were presented on every trial. These procedural differences may have had the effect of making egocentric errors less compelling than in previous research.

The failure to find a complexity effect in the present experiments was surprising. In the Fishbein et al (3) experiment performance was significantly better when one object was used than when three were used. A possible explanation of these findings is that a threshold effect is operating. In these experiments, a minimum of two objects is needed in order to construct left-right, back-front, and up-down reflections. Any additional objects above two provide redundant information, and hence do not increase complexity regarding these spatial relationships. If this explanation is correct, then one would predict that performance with two objects would be inferior to that with one object, but equivalent to that of the object conditions that were used in the present experiments.

Finally, in previous experiments children were discovered to employ certain social-cognitive rules as they attempted to determine what another person's perspective looked like (3). These co-existing rules could be hierarchically arranged, that is, some rules were more primitive than others and resulted in unsuccessful performance. Although similar social-cognitive rules could not be detected in the performance of children in the present experiments, some hypotheses can be formed to describe how children arrived at the choices they made.

Three types of cognitive operations (extraction, matching and inhibition) seem to be involved in children's attempts to coordinate perspectives. The initial process is one of extracting sufficient information from the environment to build up a schema concerning how the objects are spatially arranged for a particular perspective. After children have an internal representation of this perspective, they must then match it to one of the external representations (photographs) presented to them. In order to carry out both of these operations, children must be able to inhibit their own view of the environment to avoid making an egocentric error.

Errors are made when children have difficulty performing one or more of these cognitive operations. It is conceivable that a particular experimental situation might make one of these processes more difficult for the children than the others. Hence, in the Fishbein, et. al. (3) experiments nursery school children performed well where the matching operation was relatively simple i.e. neither back-front nor left-right reflections were presented, but the inhibition of egocentric responding was relatively difficult. In the present experiments nursery school children performed at about a chance level where the matching operation was very difficult.

Notes and References

(1) This research was supported by Grant No. OEG O 72 1616 from the Office of Education, Department of Health, Education, and Welfare.

(2) Piaget and Inhelder, B., THE CHILD'S CONCEPTION OF SPACE, London Routledge and Kegan Paul, 1956.

(3) Fishbein, H., Lewis, S. and Kieffer, K., Children's understanding of spatial relations, DEVELOPMENTAL PSYCHOLOGY, 7, pages 21-33, 1972.

(4) Laurendeau, M. and Pinard, A., THE DEVELOPMENT OF THE CONCEPT OF SPACE IN THE CHILD, New York, International Universities Press, 1970.

(5) Gibson, E., Gibson, J., Pick, A. and Osser, H., A developmental study of the discrimination of letter-like forms, JOURNAL OF COMPARATIVE AND PHYSIOLOGICAL PSYCHOLOGY, 55, page 897, 1962.

Roger Peters

Department of Psychology
University of Michigan
Ann Arbor, Michigan

Abstract

Behavior of wolves both in the field and in captivity provides evidence that they,
like humans, have cognitive maps. A description of wolf marking behavior, which
creates an external representation of the marker on certain features of the environment, permits some inferences about what features are important to wolves, and hence
likely to occur in their cognitive maps. It is suggested that the marks may serve a
mnemonic function, helping wolves to remember and recognize important places. Comparison of the elements found in drawings of the cognitive maps of men with the ex-
ternalized elements of the cognitive map of the wolf permits the inference that the
structure of the cognitive map is at least in part an adaptation to the problem of
efficient travel in a large area.

Man was a hunter for ninety-nine percent of his evolutionary history. His ability to
conceive large areas is an adaptation to this way of life. It is the purpose of this
paper to show that some of the principles behind this ability can be elucidated by
comparing human conceptions of large areas with those in other hunting species.

Both men and wolves evolved as social hunters of big game. Big game means big areas
to cover, and big areas mean it is easy to get lost. Men and wolves have both had
millions of years to evolve solutions to the problems of getting lost, whether "lost"
means separation from your fellow-hunters, not knowing a quick way back to your
young, or where your prey is headed. The scale of the hunting area is roughly similar in the two species. Although we don't know the areas covered by prehistoric man,
maximum long-distance traveling speed is the same in wolves and men - about 5 mph.
The maximum distance that can be covered in 24 hours is also the same - about 100
miles.

In both wolves and men, a solution to the problems of hunting over large areas seems
to be a representation of the environment, in short, some sort of map. Although the
word "map" is suggestive and possibly useful, we can be sure this "map" is not very
much like an aerial photograph. For one thing, as in even the detailed evaluations
and plans of the landscape architect, there is an enormous amount of simplification.
The simplifications that occur depend on the function which the representation must
perform. For example, a topographic chart simplifies terrain in ways very different
from those of a road map. On the other hand, representations that serve the same
purpose might well contain some similar kinds of simplification. Both men and
wolves have evolved systems for throwing away much of the information in the environment, and for attending to the rest. Thus the "maps" of wolves and men may contain

many of the same kinds of elements or principles of organization because both species evolved the map as a solution to the problems of hunting big game in groups. Some of these problems are (1) how to remember the locations of a large number of key places (rendezvous sites where young are left, feeding grounds of prey, water, food caches), (2) how to get to any of these with a minimum expenditure of time and energy, and (3) how to avoid predators or hostile conspecifics.

A few years ago I helped Drs. R. and S. Kaplan with studies of cognitive maps of natural areas. Although the tasks varied somewhat and the subjects were different in age, background, and experience, the maps they drew showing as much as possible of what they remembered (1) contained the same kinds of elements: landmarks, regions, intersections of paths, and the forest edge. Sometimes these were organized in a linear sequence by their placement along the line representing the path they followed. In other instances, the organization in addition preserved some spatial relationships among the major regions and landmarks. On some occasions, maps were drawn first showing the boundaries of the area, with the other elements then located in relationship to these edges.

The same kinds of elements appeared in all the maps, and these were the same kinds that appeared in the maps of urban areas drawn by the subjects in the Lynch (2) and DeJonge (3) studies. These elements are paths, nodes (i.e., key points), regions, landmarks, and edges. Our results further resembled Lynch's in the predominance of paths as organizing features.

The emergence of the same kinds of cognitive elements in human conceptions of very different kinds of environment raises several questions. To what extent are these "universal" elements adaptations to our hunting past? To what extent must designers regard them as givens? To what extent are they artifacts of the map-drawing procedure? If the same kinds of simplification occur in other species whose way of life resembles that of our ancestors, we have some reason to believe that these kinds of simplification are "universal" in a profound sense. If we find evidence for the same cognitive elements in the wolf we can be sure that these elements are not merely a product of the process of drawing a map or of exposure to maps in our culture.

Finding similarities between the cognitive maps of wolves and men does not imply that wolves are very much like people. In fact, they are quite different in all respects save hunting in groups over large areas. But just as one can learn a lot about streamlining by studying animals as different as porpoises and sharks precisely because they are so different, studying animals as different as wolves and men may shed some light on the adaptive significance of the principles of environmental cognition.

Before turning to evidence about the maps of wolves, it is useful to consider some alternative methods of finding one's way. It is conceivable that an animal might learn all the paths he needs by rote, and find his way around the way a human does when following direction in a strange city ("turn left at the second intersection, go downhill half a mile, turn right," etc.) Or he could always retrace previous routes, using cues from his trail or the trails of his fellow hunters. The first of these alternatives would make great demands on memory. The second place him at the mercy of whether that could obliterate his trail. Neither alternative allows much

flexibility or such "insightful" behavior as short-cutting, which depends on a knowledge of some spatial relations.

Cognitive maps are more useful to animals that have large, but limited ranges than to
animals with small ranges or to nomads. Animals that rarely return to the same
places have neither the experience necessary to learn relations among them, nor the
opportunity to apply their knowledge of these relations. Wolf packs have exclusive
ranges (territories) varying in size from about 40 to about 120 square miles, and
these territories remain stable from year to year (4). Consistent use of the same
territory is a necessary, but not sufficient condition for the utility of a cognitive
map. There are, however, four kinds of spatial behavior that not only indicate that
wolves use cognitive maps but suggest ways in which they would have been useful to
our hunting ancestors.

1. In winter, when not constrained by pups, a pack can in a single day, cover distances that are appreciable in relation to the size of its territory (5-10 miles).
Thus, it is not lack of mobility that confines the movement of a pack. Nor is it
active defense, a pack does not patrol its territory often or regularly, but may remain in a small part of it for days or weeks at a time (5). Wolves, therefore have
an amount of experience which would make it possible for them to form a map.

2. Wolves usually travel along roads and well-used game trails, rather than fight
their way through brush or deep snow. Their territories, therefore, consist of networks of paths, rather than an undifferentiated area. Occasionally, however, they
leave a trail to take a short-cut, sometimes to another trail, sometimes merely to
eliminate a hairpin bend in the trail they are following. It is difficult to imagine
intentional short-cutting in the absence of some kind of cognitive map (6).

3. Another piece of evidence comes from the behavior of traveling packs. Particularly when game is scarce, one or more pack members will split off, and join the rest
at a point several miles and hours away. It is possible that packs re-group by howling, but howling is effective only over relatively short distances. It is therefore
likely that wolves know at least in a general way where the others are headed and
alternate ways of getting there.

4. Rendezvous sites are places where pups are left when they are still too young to
hunt with the pack. Wolves seem to be able to return to their rendezvous site from
any direction, which would imply that they know where it is in a way that does not
depend on any particular route. This suggests a more or less map-like conception of
the area around the rendezvous site.

Understanding the underlined elements of the cognitive maps of wolves and how they depend upon
their way of life requires entering the perceptual world of a species whose sensory
apparatus is very different from ours. Not only are wolves' powers of olfactory
acuity and discrimination orders of magnitude greater than ours, but smells are, as
Hall (7) suggests, a much more vivid and real part of the wolf's world than we can
imagine. For wolves, the reality of an object may lie much more in its smell than
in its visual properties. Canines are often even more interested in each other's
smells than in each other's bodies. When I introduced a female wolf to two captive
males, they spent the first few minutes of their access to each other investigating

the smells left in the other's pen. Only when this exploration was complete did they begin to sniff, look at, and touch each other. Smells are so important to all canines that one would expect them to be a primary medium of perception of the physical and social environment.

As anyone who has worked with them knows, wolves also smell in a reflexive sense. They are sources, as well as receivers, of odor, and continuously alter, as well as investigate, their olfactory environment. A wolf leaves a scent on the ground where he lies. A walking wolf deposits scent with the sweat from his footpads. Wolves' eliminative products have characteristic odors readily detectable even by the attenuated olfactory ability of humans. Moreover, they engage in several behaviors, collectively known as scent-marking, which make their odors more readily detectable. Scent-marking has several characteristics which suggest that it is intimately involved with the wolf's perception and cognitive of his physical environment. According to Kleiman's (8) classic definition, scent-marking is always directed at particular features of the environment. She defines scent-marking as:

> urination, dafecation, or rubbing of certain areas of the body which is
> (1) oriented to specific objects
> (2) elicited by familiar conspicuous landmarks and novel objects or colors, and
> (3) repeated frequently on the same object.

The particular features of the environment that are marked by wolves become vivid olfactory entities, set off from their unanointed surroundings, by complex and fascinating odors. These vivid entities probably perform several functions, but the kinds of features that are marked strongly suggests that one of these functions has the facilitation of the major occupation of the wolf, traveling in search of prey.

Wolves mark their paths every 300 meters, on the average (9). Scent-marks occur at intervals short enough so that their odor plus the odor from sweat glands in the feet makes the path an olfactory as well as a visual unit. Paths traversed by the pack will be distinguished by the pack's odor, even after the footprints and their odor have disappeared.

Scent-marks are not only distributed along paths, but also concentrated at junctions. About a third of the scent-marks found in winter, and most of the scent-marks found during the summer (when wolf-tracks and urine-marks are much more difficult to detect) occur at trail junctions.

Junctions are one example of what Lynch refers to as a node, a key point that can be entered. Rendezvous sites are another kind of node, and they also seem to be marked in a special way. The key paths into and around a rendezvous site, and especially their intersections, seem to be marked with great frequency. This generalization is tentative, based on only three cases, but the extremely high frequency of marking around these three rendezvous nodes is probably not an accident. Wolf pups are almost defenseless and will sometimes approach intruders with curiosity. The high frequency of marking may well serve as a warning to animals that would otherwise enter the rendezvous site and harm or scatter the pups.

In Lynch's taxonomy of spatial elements, nodes which can be entered, are distinguished from landmarks, which are salient features external to the imager. When the image is olfactory, distinctions between internal and external, hence between nodes and land-marks, become somewhat arbitrary. Kills are the events of supreme importance in the lives of wolves, and the place where a kill has occurred is important not only for historical reasons, but because it marks an area where hunting has been good, and may be good again. Kills are salient, surrounded as they are by up to 24 hrs. worth of eliminative products, readily detectable by the human nose at over 100 meters, but exactly where in the process of digestion the node becomes a landmark concerns us no more than it does the unfortunate victim.

Smelly objects like dead animals, scats, especially those of prey species, or particularly pungent vegetable decay also form salient features for wolves. They quickly transform these landmarks by rubbing their shoulders and mane on them. The classic explanation for this highly predictable behavior is that it functions to make an unfamiliar object less threatening by applying body scent to it. Some body scent probably is transferred to the object, but much more scent is transferred from the object to the wolf. In any case, distinctions between the internal and external worlds are again blurred. Of greater significance is the fact that wolves who have rubbed on smelly objects carry representations of these features on their manes, where they are invariably investigated by fellow pack members as part of the greeting ceremony which occurs whenever they meet.

Urine-marks are frequently concentrated on conspicuous objects known as scent-posts, which are often squirted in turn by each member of the pack. Scent-posts probably retain odor long after the odors of distributed urinations have faded. Scent-posts probably perform many functions, but it is likely that one of these is to act as an olfactory landmark, because they are often established at key junctions. Wolves are more likely to remember a place that has been associated with a ceremony, and when any one of them returns to the scent-post, he will be reminded that this was a place visited by the pack. It is quite possible that wolves can tell how old a scent-mark is, and acquire temporal information as well.

Although there is no clear evidence that wolves are capable of conceiving either regions or edges, there is some information which suggests that they might. For one thing, the boundaries of their territories are quite sharply defined. Although there seems to be a narrow border between territories where there is some overlap of the pack positions, (as determined by radio-location), this border is small in relation to the dimensions of the territories (10). This implies that wolves either know their territories well enough to know where the edges are, are attracted by some features of their own territories, and/or repelled by some features (e.g., scent-marks) of neighboring territories. The behavior of lone wolves also is also suggestive. Lone wolves stay out of established territories, and as they travel, they move along territory edges, often sketching the exact shape of the interface between two territories with their route (11).

Wolves do not preferentially mark the edges of their territories, but the density of marking within a territory is high enough so that an intruder moving along a path will quickly encounter the scent of the owners. Territorial regions and edges may therefore be maintained by purely emotional responses (attraction and repulsion) to scent-marks.

Whether or not wolves have internal images (concepts) of the environmental features they mark, they seem to attach importance to the same elements that form a human cognitive map. These elements are probably organized by paths, since the main occupation of the wolf is traveling. Definite edges contribute to imageability, and the clarify of the territorial edge, however it is maintained, may help organize the map of the wolf. The olfactory representation every wolf carries on his mane may serve an organizing function, similar to the 1-dimensional maps carried by bushmen on their spear-throwers (12). Analysis of the chemicals used by wolves in scent-marking shows that they are complex mixtures which could code large amounts of information about the identity, age, and emotional and sexual condition of the marker, and about how old the mark is. In the greeting ceremony, wolves could be exchanging large amounts of information not only about emotional state, but about where each of them has been, and what they encountered.

We can never really enter the mind of the wolf, nor can we know for sure if the features he marks, uses, and avoids correspond to elements of his cognitive map. Short-cutting, multiple directions of approach to familiar areas, and re-formation of the pack indicate that paths and nodes are probably represented mentally, as well as marked externally. Wolves respond to landmarks, regions, and edges, but we do not know how these features are conceived, if they are conceived at all. However, all these elements are essential parts of a description of the spatial and marking behavior of wolves. These elements, particularly paths and their intersections, appear in the movements and scent-marking behavior of all the other social carnivores: lions, hyenas, and hunting dogs (13). Thus their appearance in human cognitive maps is neither coincidence, artifact, nor purely cultural.

Notes and References

(1) Devlin, A. S. Some factors in enhancing knowledge of a natural area. In Preiser, W. F. E. (ed.) ENVIRONMENTAL DESIGN RESEARCH, Vol. 2. (EDRA 4). 1973.

(2) Lynch, K. THE IMAGE OF THE CITY. Cambridge, Mass.: MIT. 1960.

(3) DeJonge, D. Images of urban areas. JOURNAL OF THE AMERICAN INSTITUTE OF PLANNERS, 1963, 29, 266-276.

(4) Mech, L. D. Territoriality in timber wolves. Paper presented at American Institute of Biological Sciences Symposium. August, 1972.

(5) Peters, R. & Mech, L. D. Scent-marking and territory maintainence in timber wolves. Paper presented at American Institute of Biological Sciences Symposium. August, 1972.

(6) Kohler has shown that dogs, which are closely related to wolves, easily solve spatial problems which involve insight, e.g., moving away from a goal object in order to move around an obstacle. In Kohler, W. THE MENTALITY OF APES. New York: Random House, 1924.

(7) Hall, E. T.   THE SILENT LANGUAGE. New York: Anchor. 1969.

(8) Kleiman, D.   Scent-marking in the canidae. SYMP. ZOOL. SOC. LOND. No. 18, 1966, 167-177.

(9) Peters, R. & Mech, L. D.   Scent-marking and territory maintainence in timber wolves. Paper presented at American Institute of Biological Sciences Symposium. August, 1972.

(10) Mech, L. D.   Territoriality in timber wolves. Paper presented at American Institute of Biological Sciences Symposium. August, 1972.

(11) Mech, L. D.   Territoriality in timber wolves. Paper presented at American Institute of Biological Sciences Symposium. August, 1972.

(12) Pfeiffer, J.   THE EMERGENCE OF MAN. New York: Harper & Row. 1972.

(13) Schaller, G.   THE SERENGETI LION. Chicago: U. Chicago Press. 1972.

(14) I am grateful to Dr. L. D. Mech for assistance without which I would have been unable even to begin the study of wolves, and to Dr. S. Kaplan without whose inspiration and encouragement I might never have tried. This research was supported in part by the U. S. Forest Service.

Susan Saegert
Research Supervisor
Environmental Psychology Program
The Graduate School and University Center of the City University of New York
33 West 42nd Street
New York, New York 10036

Abstract

Hypotheses concerning cognitive and behavioral effects of crowding are developed by
looking separately at its two physical components: number of people in a space and
amount of space per person. The first would tend to increase cognitive complexity
and uncertainty in the situation and the difficulty of organizing behavior. The
second would make others in the situation more salient as stimuli and require
greater coordination of behavior. Together these factors would tend to produce
cognitive overload and behavioral constraint. Supporting results from an exploratory study conducted in a mid-Manhattan department store are reported.

Introduction

In 1895, Gustave Le Bon [1] proclaimed that "An individual in a crowd is a grain of
sand amid other grains of sand which the wind stirs up at will." In 1962, Calhoun
[2] said similarly unflattering things about crowds of mice and based his comments
on systematic experimental evidence. A fairly large body of literature has developed on the socially and physiologically pathological effects of crowding in animals
[3,4,5,6,7,8,9,10,11,12,13,14,15,16,17] A somewhat less systematic and coherent set of
findings indicates that crowding may, under some circumstances, have similar consequences for humans [18,19,20,21,22,23].

Generally the effects of human crowding seem neither as consistent nor as dramatic
as those found in research on animals [24,25,26,27,28,29]. Many of the studies of
human crowding are susceptible to methodological criticisms that would be tedious
to pursue here. However, the divergence of the animal and human findings, and the
internal inconsistency of studies of human crowding have implications for our understanding of crowding phenomena. First, the greater cognitive capacity and, therefore, organizational alternatives of humans may make the effects of human crowding
more variable. Secondly, the operational definition of crowding varies from study
to study making comparison difficult. All investigators agree that the physical
situation involved in crowding is one of high density. That definition has at
least two separable components: number of subjects in the group and amount of
space per subject. Some researchers have manipulated density by keeping the total
amount of space constant, but increasing the total number in the group; others have
kept the number constant, while decreasing the size of the room to achieve a high
density situation. The analysis of crowding phenomena in terms of cognitive overload and the need for organization of behavior that is to follow will make clear
the importance of cognitive capacity. The second point, that the effects of group
size may be different from the effects of spatial restriction, receives empirical

support from two studies, one of animals (30) and one of humans (31), in which these two factors were independently manipulated.

Group Size

First, the consequences of increased group size will be examined from the point of view of the subject in a crowded situation. Since we are interested mainly in human crowding we will think of increased group size as involving increased numbers of people. More people provide more sources of stimulation. Potentially each may change his behavior, thus increasing the subject's uncertainty about the state of his environment at any particular time. The relationships possible in the situation increase with the number of people; even in a situation of aggregated strangers, the more people, the more partners in eye contact, accidental touching, negotiation during movements and so on may be encountered by the subject. The larger the number of people in a situation, the more diverse their characteristics are likely to be, again increasing the complexity of the situation.

Therefore, the subject will necessarily be limited in his ability to conceptualize thoroughly and unambiguously the situation because of the complexity of the environment and its potential for change. Also, perhaps the level of stimulation in the situation will heighten the subject's level of arousal. At this point, demands of the task, the subject's expectations, familiarity with the situation, situational norms, the actions of people in the situation and the structure of the physical environment would all be expected to shape the direction of the subject's attention, his feelings and behavior.

The research on effects of group size on organized groups offers some interesting insights into the importance of number. Thomas and Fink (32) review numerous studies of the effects of group size and conclude the following: (a) increased group size tends to decrease members' satisfaction with the group, apparently because size limits communication within the group, (b) tasks are often performed more quickly by small groups, (c) tasks in which speed is not the most important criterion tend to be performed better by larger groups, (d) larger groups tend to break down into cliques and factions. The authors conclude that more people in a group result in more resources being available and more demand being made. As number of members increase, the heterogeneity of demands and resources also will tend to increase. This greater number and heterogeneity will strain the ability of members to organize exchanges of demands and resources optimally. However, these factors also raise the probability that tasks could be performed well and that diverse satisfactions could be obtained. The potential relational complexity of a large group increases the number of alternatives a person has, increases the need for choice and guarantees that some alternatives must be foregone. The formation of small cliques and factions in large groups indicates that people have difficulty with such complex situations. James (33) found that the overwhelming majority of natural groups were dyads.

From this discussion of group size, it seems that increasing density by increasing the number of people in the situation would also increase the cognitive complexity of the situation for the subject. There are more elements in the situation, more possible changes and more decisions to be made in the pursuit of activities. These effects would not necessarily occur if density were increased by decreasing the space available for the same number of people.

Space Per Person

We now can turn our attention to the ways in which being in a small space rather than a large one may affect the subject. Both alternatives for behavior and the attention of the subject are likely to be influenced. First of all, freedom of movement is constricted. Certain activities that could be carried out easily in a larger space become impossible. Secondly, if there is more than one person in the space, the need for coordination of activities increases. Thus, individual activities may suffer while certain group activities that require physical exchanges or communication may be facilitated. Interaction, at least on a minimal level, cannot be avoided. Finally, others as sources of stimulation become more salient because of their proximity.

Research on "personal space" indicates that people choose their distances from others on a culturally defined basis and take into account the particular cultural meaning of the other's characteristics (34,35,36). Further, the type of interaction and interpersonal evaluation expected influence the choice of distance from the others(37,38). At the very least then, a person operating with others in a restricted space might be expected to feel a loss of freedom to use spacing differentially as he might in other situations.

Further, there is evidence that people, at least in some public settings, react to being approached "too" closely by fleeing (39). Of course, the idea of "too close" will be dependent on the particular situation and characteristics of those interacting. Nonetheless, these findings do suggest that people will respond negatively to the close proximity of another person under some circumstances.

One consequence, then, of spatial closeness to others in a restricted area would seem to involve loss of freedom and flexibility. If one wishes to be close in a large room, one can move closer, but if one wishes to avoid someone in a small room, it would not be possible. Most of us have probably experienced the difficulty of ignoring someone who is right by our side even when that person is irrelevant to our plans and thoughts. The experienced subway rider, for example, may learn to read on a crowded subway, but not, I suspect, without learning to increase control of his attention. The situations in which crowding is positive are characterized, I would expect, by general liking and trust for the others present as well as a desire or need to attend to them and interact.

In many naturally occurring crowded situations, a person is faced with both rather large numbers of others and spatial restriction. Thus, the situation in which he must act is cognitively complex and limits his ability to choose a particular action or even, I think, a particular attitudinal strategy. These exigencies do not necessarily mean that the person will experience the situation as unpleasant or stressful, but merely that fewer and fewer activities can be successfully and easily carried out in the situation and that the possibility of frustration becomes higher.

In such situations, the person, as Le Bon remarked, may indeed resemble a grain of sand swept about by the wind. Cognitive control may be quite difficult to attain in a crowded situation. For this reason, simple, regimented and/or spectator activities become more appealing, whereas flexible, individually determined and multi-dimensional behavior would become problematic. In short, activities that require the person to assess the environment, plan, test and then reorganize behavior on the basis of feedback would be difficult.

An Exploratory Study

In an exploratory study carried out in New York, Elizabeth Mackintosh and I focused on the problem of attaining cognitive clarity in a crowded situation. The site we chose was a mid-Manhattan department store that had regular periods of high and low density in November and December. In this setting, number of occupants in a defined space varied. Thus, increased density involved both spatial closeness and increased numbers. We would predict, then, that our subjects would have some difficulty in controlling their attention and would not gain a clear picture of the environment.

We chose a shoe section with identifiable boundaries as our experimental area. Experimental times were chosen to assure high or low density. Paid female subjects were asked to describe twelve shoes in the area; they were given a page for each description with columns of blanks for one or two word phrases. The subjects were informed that they would have twenty-five minutes, or about two minutes per description, in which to complete the task and a clock on the wall was pointed out to them. The experimenter then left and returned when the time was up. The subject showed the experimenter the location of the shoes she had described in the order she had described them and the experimenter noted this down. The two then went to a relatively secluded part of the store where the experimenter asked the subject some background questions. After this, the subject was asked to draw a map of the shoe section in as much detail as she could remember; five minutes were allowed for this task. Then the subject was asked to remember and describe the same shoes she had previously described in the same order. Finally the subject rated the shoes for likeability and gave a subjective estimate of the crowdedness of the shoe section.

The descriptive task can be seen as the focal goal of the subject in the situation. Memory for description is memory for those things the person was attending to most strongly during the experimental period. The map drawing, however, taps the subject's incidental memory of the situation. These two tasks will be discussed in terms of what they imply about the subject's cognitive processes in the high and low density condition.

Subjects in the high density condition tended to remember somewhat less of their shoe descriptions but this tendency was not strong ($t=1.31$, $df=24$, $p \sim 10$). This tendency suggests that while memory for the focal task is somewhat disturbed, this disturbance is not great.

The effects of density on the types of maps drawn were much more striking. The percentage of large objects, such as chairs and display stands remembered, was much higher for low density subjects (t=1.83, df=26, $p < 0.025$). Subjects in the crowded condition misplaced more of the recalled objects than did uncrowded subjects (t=1.97, df=23, $p < 0.05$). Further, the subjects in the high density condition used fewer words to label their maps than did subjects in the low density condition (t= 1.78, df=24, $p < .05$). Overall, the high density subjects seemed to have a less detailed and less correct picture of the area in which they had been working.

One interesting result emerged from the analysis of the total distance subjects walked during the shoe description task. Although there was no difference between the amount of distance covered by subjects in the two conditions, the distance covered was much more variable in the high density condition (t=9.20, df=10/13, $p < .01$). This finding may indicate that whereas subjects in the low density condition used about the same strategies for performing their task, and the environment did not interfere, in high density situations, subjects' strategies diverged or the environment structured their alternatives in divergent ways.

The shoe descriptions were rated for number of positive and negative affective words. Subjects in the high density condition tended to give somewhat more positive descriptions (t=1.59, df=22, p (1-tailed $< .10$), p (2-tailed $< .20$)). This trend did not reach statistical significance; however, it is congruent with other findings indicating females experience more positive affect in crowded conditions.

The account that has been given of the position of the subject in a crowded situation focuses on the immediate relations of the subject to the environment; it does not deal with processes over time. Nor does it lead us to expect that any particular person will behave aggressively or feel anxious or elated in a high density situation. Rather we are concerned with identifying the components of the environment and the relationship between these and the person's task set, expectations and available strategies. The regularities we expect arise from the quality of information presented to the subject, the physical constraints and opportunities for behavior and the limits of the subject as an information processor and decision-maker.

References

(1) Le Bon, G., THE CROWD (1st Edition 1895), New York, Viking, 1960.
(2) Calhoun, J. B., "Population Density and Social Pathology", SCIENTIFIC AMERI-CAN, 206, pages 139-148, 1962.
(3) Chitty, D. H., "Mortality Among Voles at Lake Vyrwy, Montgomershire, in 1936-39", PHILOSOPHICAL TRANSACTIONS OF THE ROYAL SOCIETY OF LONDON, B. 236, pages 505-552, 1952.
(4) Christian, J. J., "Social Subordination, Population Density, and Mammalian Evolution", SCIENCE, 168, pages 84-90, 1970.
(5) Christian, J. J., Flyger, V., Davis, D. E., "Factors in Mass Mortality of a Herd of Sika Deer (Cervus Nippon)", CHESAPEAKE SCIENCE, 1, pages 79-95, 1960.
(6) Davis, D. E., "Physiological Effects of Continued Crowding" in Esser, A. H. (Ed.), BEHAVIOR AND ENVIRONMENT, New York, Plenum Press, 1971.
(7) Green, R. G., Evans, C. A., "Studies on a Population Cycle of Snowshoe Hares on Lake Alexander Area", JOURNAL OF WILDLIFE MANAGEMENT, 4, pages 220-238,

267-278, 347-358, 1940.

(8) Green, R. G., Larson, C. L., "A Description of Shock Disease in the Snowshoe Hare", AMERICAN JOURNAL OF HYGIENE, 28, pages 190-212, 1938.

(9) Keeley, K. "Prenatal Influence on Behavior of Offspring of Crowded Mice", SCIENCE, 135, pages 44-45, 1962.

(10) Morris, D., "Homosexuality in the Ten-Spined Stickleback", BEHAVIOR, 4, page 233, 1952.

(11) Morrison, B. J., Thatcher, K., "Overpopulation Effects on Social Reduction of Emotionality in the Albino Rat", JOURNAL OF COMPARATIVE PHYSIOLOGICAL PSYCHOLOGY, 69, pages 658-662, 1969.

(12) Myers, K., Hale, L. S., Mykytowycz, R., Hughes, R. L., "The Effects of Varying Density and Space on Sociality and Health in Animals", in Esser, A. H. (Ed.), BEHAVIOR AND ENVIRONMENT, New York, Plenum Press, 1971.

(13) Southwick, C. H., "Intergroup Agonistic Behavior", BEHAVIOR, 28, pages 182-209, 1967.

(14) Stott, D. II, "Cultural and Natural Checks on Population Growth", in Montagu, Ashley (Ed.), CULTURE AND THE EVOLUTION OF MAN, New York, Oxford University Press (Galaxy Books), 1962.

(15) Susiyama, Y., "Social Organization of Hanuman Lengurs", in Altmann, S. (Ed.), COMMUNICATION AMONG PRIMATES, Chicago, University of Chicago Press, 1967.

(16) Thiessen, D. D., Rodgers, D. A., "Population Density and Endocrine Function", PSYCHOLOGICAL BULLETIN, 58, pages 441-451, 1961.

(17) Wynne-Edwards, V. C., ANIMAL DISPERSION IN RELATION TO SOCIAL BEHAVIOR, New York, Hafner, 1962.

(18) Griffitt, W., Veitch, R., "Hot and Crowded: Influences of Population Density and Temperature on Interpersonal Affective Behavior", JOURNAL OF PERSONALITY AND SOCIAL PSYCHOLOGY, 17, pages 92-98, 1971.

(19) Hutt, C., Vaizey, M. J., "Differential Effects of Group Density on Social Behavior", NATURE, 209, pages 1371-1372, 1966.

(20) Lantz, H. R., "Population Density and Psychiatric Diagnosis", SOCIOLOGY AND SOCIAL RESEARCH, 37, pages 322-326, 1953.

(21) Loring, W. C., "Housing and Social Problems", SOCIAL PROBLEMS, 3, pages 160-168, 1956.

(22) Plant, J. S., "Some Psychiatric Aspects of Crowded Living Conditions", AMERICAN JOURNAL OF PSYCHIATRY, 9, pages 849-860, 1930.

(23) Schmitt, R. C., "Density, Health and Social Disorganization", JOURNAL OF AMERICAN INSTITUTE OF PLANNERS, 32, pages 38-40, 1966.

(24) Freedman, J. L., Klevansky, S., Ehrlich, P. R., "The Effects of Crowding on Human Task Performance", JOURNAL OF APPLIED SOCIAL PSYCHOLOGY, 1, pages 7-25, 1971.

(25) Freedman, J. L., Levy, A. S., Buchanan, R. W., Price, J., "Crowding and Human Aggressiveness", JOURNAL OF EXPERIMENTAL SOCIAL PSYCHOLOGY, 8, pages 528-548, 1972.

(26) Galle, V. R., Gove, W. R., McPherson, J. M., "Population Density and Pathology: What are the Relations for Man?", SCIENCE, 176, pages 23-30, 1972.

(27) Martin, A. E., "Environment, Housing and Health", URBAN STUDIES, 4, pages 1-21, 1967.

(28) Mitchell, R. E., "Some Social Implications of High Density Housing", AMERICAN SOCIOLOGICAL REVIEW, 36, pages 18-29, 1971.

(29) Winsborough, H., "The Social Consequences of High Population Density", LAW

AND CONTEMPORARY PROBLEMS, 30, pages 120-126, 1965.

(30) Myers, K., Hale, L. S., Mykytowycz, R., Hughes, R. L., "The Effects of Varying Density and Space on Sociality and Health in Animals", in Esser, A. H. (Ed.), BEHAVIOR AND ENVIRONMENT, New York, Plenum Press, 1971.

(31) Smith, S., Haythorne, W. W., "Effects of Compatibility, Crowding, Group Size, and Leadership Seniority on Stress, Anxiety, Hostility and Annoyance in Isolated Groups", JOURNAL OF PERSONALITY AND SOCIAL PSYCHOLOGY, 22, pages 67-79, 1972.

(32) Thomas, E. J., Fink, C. F., "Effects of Group Size", PSYCHOLOGICAL BULLETIN, 60, pages 371-384, 1963.

(33) James, J. A., "A Preliminary Study of the Size Determinants in Small Group Interactions", AMERICAN SOCIOLOGICAL REVIEW, 16, pages 474-477, 1951.

(34) Leibman, M., "Sex and Race Norms and Personal Space", ENVIRONMENT AND BEHAVIOR, 2, pages 208-246, 1970.

(35) Little, K. B., "Cultural Variations in Social Schemas", JOURNAL OF PERSONALITY AND SOCIAL PSYCHOLOGY, 10, pages 1-7, 1968.

(36) Little, K. B., Ulehla, Z. J., Henderson, C., "Value Congruence and Interaction Distances", JOURNAL OF SOCIAL PSYCHOLOGY, 75, pages 249-253, 1968.

(37) Dosey, M. A., Meisels, M., "Personal Space and Self-Protection", JOURNAL OF PERSONALITY AND SOCIAL PSYCHOLOGY, 11, pages 93-97, 1969.

(38) Leipold, W. E., PSYCHOLOGICAL DISTANCE IN A DYADIC INTERVIEW (Ph. D. Thesis), University of North Carolina, 1963.

(39) Felipe, N. J., Sommer, R., "Invasions of Personal Space", SOCIAL PROBLEMS, 14, pages 206-214, 1966.

FOUR   SELECTED INSTRUMENTS AND MEASURES IN ENVIRONMENTAL ANALYSIS: A METHODOLOGICAL CRITIQUE

Chairman: William Michelson, Department of Sociology,
University of Toronto

Authors: William Michelson, "Time-Budgets In Environmental Research: Some Introductory
Considerations"

Dagfinn Aas, "Attempts At Describing Milieu:
The Behavior Setting Survey"

Robert B. Bechtel, "Architectural Space and
Semantic Space: Should The Twain Try to
Meet?"

Gerald Davis and Virginia Ayers, "Photographic
Methods of Research On Behavior In The Human
Milieu: New Developments and Critique"

Robert W. Marans, "A Perspectus On Survey Research For Environmental Planning"

Donald Appleyard and Frances Carp, "The BART
Residential Impact Study: A Longitudinal
Empirical Study of Environmental Impact"

William Michelson
Professor of Sociology
University of Toronto
Toronto, Ontario

Abstract

This paper presents some introductory considerations on time-budgets in
environmental research, including: 1) what is a time-budget, 2) its application
to environment, 3) how one uses it and 4) its major pitfalls. An example of its
use is presented, together with a few relevant bibliographic citations.

1. What is a time-budget?

A time-budget is a record, presented orally or on paper, of what a person has done
during the course of a stated period of time. It usually covers a 24 hour day or
multiples thereof. The record is taken down with precision and detail, identifying
what people have done with explicit reference to exact amounts of time. It is
usually presented chronologically through the day, beginning with the time that a
person gets up in the morning.

The information that is normally gathered in a time-budget consists of the time an
activity began, the time it ended, the nature of the activity per se, the persons
who were present and active in the given activities, and, not least, the exact
location where the activity took place. In practice, a certain minimum duration of
activities to be considered must be decided upon, and this minimum generally ranges
from about ten to fifteen minutes: shorter activities are usually grouped into a
somewhat more general category of activity until such time as they form a minimum
time period.

2. Why use a time-budget?

In environmental analysis, explanation of behavior may come from a number of
individually fruitful and complimentary approaches. If we want to explain behavior
with reference to environment, we could ask, first, if the physical dimensions of a
given physical environment allows minimal opportunity for a behavior to occur. If
the answer is no, then it is highly unlikely that the behavior will occur in that
setting regardless of all other motivations, perceptions, and the like. On the
other hand, even if a given behavior is permitted by the environment, this does not
necessarily mean that it will take place. For this to occur, a set of factors
generally referred to as perception must occur satisfactorily. Nonetheless, opportunity and perception alone do not explain the eventual behavior (even environmental behavior) with reference to socio-cultural factors, which perscribe what
should occur in a given setting. Even then, of course, there is no necessity for
behavior to be explained by environmental factors alone, and a whole host of purely
social and psychological factors may indeed explain the observed behavior.

What I should like to stress from the foregoing is that regardless of the necessity
to consider the valid and fruitful 'soft' approaches to the man-environment interface, it is nonetheless behavior which is occurring within the environment. When
one thinks particularly of environment from the opportunity perspective, it is clear
that the opportunity provided or not is for some form of active behavior. This
being the case, it is necessary to have a standard, reliable, and fruitful method
with which to assess behavior in any given environmental setting (micro or macro).

From a methodological point of view, it is also desirable to have an approach which
deals in detail with qualitative information about everyday human life(not just the
bizarre aberations we find so interesting), but which does so in a quantitative
manner from which critical analysis is possible. Just as it may be desirable to
assess peoples' representations of reality when dealing with questions of perception
and culture, it is unquestionably desirable to have a form of objective measurement
of reality when probing the nature of behavior itself.

What a time budget gives you is a simultaneous record of behavior, spatial usage and
social structure - all viewed simultaneously with respect to any activity or event,
and weighted quantitatively according to the time devoted to it. This measure is
relatively unique in its ability to deal simultaneously with all three of these
considerations in quantitative form.

Furthermore, as a relatively standardized, objective method of measuring aggregate
behavior, use of this method in repeated fashion (i.e. on different occasions with
the same population) enables the measurement of change in human behavior, presumably
in response to a stimulus which one wishes to measure. Comparison through space is
equally applicable; if one wishes to measure the differences in behavior in two
distinct environmental settings at the same time, this is an appropriate measure.

Hence, it is possible to use the time budget as a basis, at one level, for internal
space planning. If one is planning for aggregates, for example, one can document
trends within a group in terms of the usage of internal space, attitude toward
privacy as illustrated by actual use, as well as illustrative information on user
needs as illuminated within the constraint of an existing situation.

On a more macroscopic basis, time-budgets are used for a basis for facility planning,
both from a physical planning and social planning point of view. It is quite
common for stochastic models of daily activity to be built on the basis of time-
budget data, so as to assess the linkage of facilities to one another in common
practice.

On a pre-planning basis time-budgets are used to explore the nature of everyday
activity among large groups in the population. For example, time-budgets have been
used to explore the age at which children become independent of their parents, so
as to serve as a basis for future design; apart from ideology on the subject, a
time-budget can detail exactly for how long and under what circumstances, for example, children are independent of their parents.

Finally, time-budgets can serve environmental research as an aid in project evaluation. If certain activities are expected to appear among the population, as a

consequence of a newly built environment, or if life is supposed to change in a particular direction, the time-budget should provide requisite and detailed information which would support or fail to support the expectations.

3. How do you use a time-budget?

A time-budget can be administered either as part of an interview (i.e. orally) or in questionnaire form. In the latter case, this is known as a time diary. Which method is used is largely a function of the time period which you wish to cover as well as the return that you expect to get. At least one study has shown that when you are concerned only about the activities of the immediately preceding day, it does not matter whether one uses interview or diary approaches. However, if you wish to gather information on more than a single day, the diary is far superior. The usual practice is to leave a diary with a respondent, outline the period for which the diary should be completed by the respondent, then arrange a time for study personnel to pick up the completed time diary; on the last occasion, he looks through the time diary and tries to fill in any apparently missing pieces. The trouble with the time diary, however, is that in spite of their best intentions and promises, many people do not follow through and complete the diary. There is also little chance to question or to discuss their categorization of activities; whoever, picks them up may spot questionable activities, but it is normally only blanks that draw strong attention at that time.

An interview relies on a respondent's memory of the period involved and, therefore, a valid reconstruction is generally possible only for the previous day to day degree of detail. Nonetheless, the co-operation rate is very much higher. The oral time-budget, however, takes a great degree of interviewer time, and frequently interviewers discover that they have at least as much difficulty as their respondent, since quite some strain is involved in ensuring that all levels of detail are completed for as complex a matter as a person's day.

Time-budgets are normally coded and placed on data cards and/or tape for future analysis. Coding a time-budget is generally extremely time consuming and hence, expensive. Furthermore, analysis can be extremely aggravating. Individual researchers have worked up computer programs to facilitate time budget analysis, which they are in the process of making available. Nonetheless, there is as yet no standardization of programs nor any regular arrangement for program distribution. Needless to say, with great amounts of information on large numbers of persons, great amounts of computer time are taken simply by reading the information already on tape, let alone analyzing it.

Information is usually placed on tape in the form of recurring fields, each one of which deals with one episode during the day - that is, an activity, the times involved in it, the people involved and the location. Standard social science analysis programs may be used with time budget data to a greater extent if one episode is placed on one card; the problem with this, however, is that it usually creates an unreasonable number of cards in the data file, which further prolongs the machine reading process. One major difficulty in conducting analysis is that the number of episodes a day will vary greatly by the respondent.

The coding process can be greatly simplified by the use of pre-coded instruments, selected from among a number of possible activity categories. This would be an ideal solution except that, with a general population, prior studies have shown that time budget analysis is relatively fruitless unless a wide variety of categories is utilized (about 100). This is too large a number for an untrained respondent to utilize accurately. Researchers have found it possible to precode with a smaller number of categories in specific contexts where expected behaviors (or at least the only behaviors in which the researchers were primarily interested) were much more limited in number.

4. What are some of its major pitfalls?

While I emphasized above some of the major reasons why people use time-budgets, one should also emphasize many of the difficulties involved, if some of them are not already apparent. It is difficult for interviewers and expensive, to boot. It is relatively accurate and your chances for completion are great if you want to deal with only a short period of time, hoping that with a decent size number of persons studied, the time period chosen would be representative; however, it is difficult to measure longer periods of time. It is difficult and expensive to analyze, regardless of the eventual reward of doing so. For purposes of microanalysis, moreover, it is especially necessary to get absolutely accurate and detailed locational information; this places special demands on the interviewer and the respondent, which are fulfilled only under ideal conditions.

A final pitfall worth mentioning is related to the interpretation of time budget data. It is inherently a measure of what exists now under current conditions, and not what might be under other conditions. It is ideal for use in evaluation. Under other circumstances, however, one must always be aware of the range of constraint above and beyond those constraints which you wish to measure, which may be accounting for the behavior observed. In other words, what you see people doing is not always a measure of what people might want to do in the best of all worlds. How they might change under realistic alternative conditions is something not intrinsic to time-budget data, but which must be used in its interpretation. Under certain circumstances, time expenditure may be utilized fruitfully analogous to the marginal utility of money in Economics, but such interpretation must be undertaken carefully.(1)

5. How about an example?

In a study I have been conducting, I have been interested in assessing the aggregate behavioral implications of residence in high rise apartments as compared to single family homes. In the greater Toronto area (2) we have interviewed a number of families, controlled according to their income and their stage in the life cycle, who have chosen to move to single family homes and to high rise apartments from a variety of previous types of residence. We have interviewed them at several points in time; before they moved (but after their decision to move), two months after and one year and two months after. We hope to go back again at a point four years and two months after the move. At each point in the process we have included time-budgets in oral form to the husband, wife, and one child in the family.

This is not the place to describe the study in detail, but some illustrative example of what we are doing with time-budget is our present intent. We expected, for example, that certain types of behavior are likely to be inhibited by the spatial context of high rise apartments as they are currently constructed. Other aspects of behavior are enhanced and are a major attraction within the high rise complex. On the basis of previous studies and of some popular mythology, for example, we expected that neighboring was something more common in houses than in apartments, while passive activity such as television watching was more common to the high rise (in implicit lieu of alternative active activities save a few specified ones). Furthermore, since sports facilities are characteristic of high rise apartments in this area, we expected more active participation among those moving to high rise apartments. Among men, there is a popular feeling that they do fewer things when living in high rise apartments, such as house repairs and handyman activities. Hence, it is possible to use the time budget longitudinally, to see if people moving from a house to an apartment differ significantly from those making the opposite move with respect to characteristic activities. The table presented is a rather simple one drawn from a considerable larger matrix of time budget data on these people. It presents the amount of time women spent on a selected weekday and on the previous Sunday in visiting, active soports, and television watching, and similar data is presented for the men on active repair and handy craft work in the home, on active sports and on T.V. watching.

The data are arranged in terms of whether people increased, decreased, or remained the same in the time devoted to the particular activity from before their move to the period two months after their specific move.

One can see from this aggregation of data that at least one of our expectations – that people moving from apartments to houses would increase their visiting more than those making the reverse move – is largely unsupported by the data, although more people moving to apartments do decrease their visiting. All the other expectations were supported, although the differences in sports participation are not nearly as dramatic as anticipated by the respondents themselves before their move.

The point of these examples, however, is not to argue overly about a few substantive hypotheses, but rather to illustrate how one might manipulate time budget data in an environmental research context.

Much modern work on time-budgets is still unpublished. However, a few helpful published works are cited as follows:

(a) Chapin, F. Stuart, Jr., "Activity Systems and Urban Structure: A Working Schema". JOURNAL OF THE AMERICAN INSTITUTE OF PLANNERS 34 (January): 11-18, 1968.

(b) Chapin, F. Stuart, Jr., and Henry Hightower, Household Activity Systems - A Pilot Investigation. Chapel Hill, N.C.: Institute for Research in Social Science, 1966.

(c) Cullen, Ian and Vida Godson, Networks of Urban Activities: The Structure of Activity Patterns. London: Joint Unit for Planning Research, University College London and The London School of Economics, 1972.

(d) Hagerstrand, Torsten, "What About People in Regional Science?" Papers and Proceedings of the Regional Science Association 24 (January): 7-24, 1970.

(e) Hemmens, George C., The Structure of Urban Activity Linkages Chapel Hill, N.C.: Centre of Urban and Regional Studies, 1966.

(f) MacMurray, Trevor, "Aspects of Time and the Study of Activity Patterns". TOWN PLANNING REVIEW 42 (April): 195-209, 1971.

(g) Michelson, William and Paul B. Reed, "The Theoretical Status and Operational Usage of Life Style in Environmental Research". Toronto: Centre for Urban and Community Studies, University of Toronto, Research Paper No. 36, 1970.

(h) Patrushev, Vassilii D., "Aggregate Time Balance of a Nation as a Means of Forecasting the Proportions of Human Activity". SOCIETY AND LEISURE 2: 5-19, 1971.

Notes

(1) One way of assisting this type of interpretation is by adding a column to the usual time-budget format which will allow respondents to evaluate the activity, its location and/or the time devoted to it.

(2) Under the sponsorship primarily of the Central Mortgage and Housing Corporation, but with generous assistance in the initial stages as well from the Canada Council.

Table 1 -- <u>Changes in Selected Uses of Time by Type of Residential Mobility</u>

		Type of Mobility					
Activity		Home to Apartment			Apartment to Home		
		Less Time	No Change	More Time	Less Time	No Change	More Time
a. Wife	Visiting (Weekday)	21%	58%	21%	14%	64%	22%
	Visiting (Sunday)	19	51	30	25	41	34
	Active Sports (Weekday)	2	87	12	4	95	2
	Active Sports (Sunday)	5	90	5	6	88	6
	Watching TV (Weekday)	33	25	42	41	29	30
	Watching TV (Sunday)	33	23	44	23	41	36
b. Husband	Active Sports (Weekday)	12	74	13	2	93	5
	Active Sports (Sunday)	16	65	19	5	80	15
	Watching TV (Weekday)	23	35	42	36	31	33
	Watching TV (Sunday)	23	19	58	33	30	37
	House Repairs (Weekday)	26	71	3	5	74	21
	House Repairs (Sunday)	29	58	13	23	53	25

ATTEMPTS AT DESCRIBING MILIEU: THE BEHAVIOR SETTING SURVEY

Dagfinn Aas
Research Associate
Norwegian Building Research Institute
Oslo 3, Norway

The larger context

I will not reopen the debate on the relationship between thinking and language, but just make a note of the fact that it is easy to be led astray by one's own language. We are easily led to believe that phenomena for which we have words and concepts exist in the real world. This problem is of particular interest when researchers in some countries work with concepts that translates badly into another language.

My title includes the "french" word milieu, for which I am told it is difficult to find an American counterpart. In Norway we do have the concept - miljø - and on the top of everything it has become a very popular word - the word is "in".

The good milieu is first of all the healthy, sound and ecologically balanced natural environment, but the word is equally much used in connection with the work-place and the residental neighborhood. There is at present in Norway an almost remarkable interest in these phenomena; both interest and concern and a consequently great demand for research on the same problems.

The standard of living is at present high in Norway. The basics in terms of food, clothing and shelter is provided for at least in an international comparison. We all know of the constantly escalating and expanding need structures as more of the basic needs are satisfied. This growing interest in milieu could then be seen in the same perspective as just "raffinement" of the public interest.

I do not think this is the case. As we through steadily improving technology have improved elements of our material culture to a very great extent we have at the same time produced imbalances in the more inclusive systems of elements. Our wrist watch might be a technological wonder but our possibilities for meaningful relations with people in our own territory might be very slim. The interest in milieu and related problems is coupled with awareness that we more and more have to study larger contexts to acquire the necessary knowledge to improve our total life.

The very practical question which are phrased for the researchers are of this kind: Does it matter how we build the dwellings, the houses and the neigbor-hoods for living and working, or has the human being a capacity for adapting so he can live in drastically different environments? Yes and no. The great differences between the world's habitats testify to the adaptability, but the question raised here will always be phrased in a narrower nontext in terms of states, regions or nations.

"For what does it matter" is the next logical question and "the life and existance of the inhabitants" is the corresponding answer.

It is the problems related to the description and measurement of this last complex phenomena we here will deal with, life and existance constitute our dependent complex of variables. In order to communicate better let us however, first describe the particular research problem involved and describe the possible complex of independent variables.

Design of studies on milieu

All practical studies need to be delineated or cut down to a size that correspond to the resources available - and most studies suffer thereby. The difficulty lies in the way we define certain variables out; they are taken as given and thereby unproblematic.

Most studies in my mind, and particularly studies of milieu, should resemble a double- or multi-layered cake. In studying life and existance in residental neighborhoods, the first layer - the primary study - would typically embrace description of the immediate physical and social structures present. It would be through these that the first set of explanatory factors for a particular distribution of activities would be found. Factors in the larger community or the larger society will however, often be taken as given. Now then, the second-layer study is the one that attacks this larger context and which tries to explain why the particular constellation of people and environmental structures have come into being. Such a study will require a historical approach and a careful **assessment** of the particular economical frameworks at the national level within which the building and financing of housing takes place.

This is really no radical idea as it correspond to previous demands for constantly changing the sets of independent and dependent variables. This strategy however, is of paramount importance in studies of milieu.

The demand for a historical approach need some few comments. The particular period of time that we aim at including in our studies of residental milieu in Norway does not span more that the years since World war II. In this period however, we have seen a tremendous change and develpment going on, in particular with respect to the technology of building. The philosophy and policy of building and housing has likewise undergone great changes in this period. Unless we study this process of change we will not be able to understand the particular situation of the present.

Anyway, any study of these factors will in the end have to be related to what we defined as our main dependent cluster of variables - the life and existance of the people under study.

Operationalizing the concept of milieu

A description of people's life and existance will be the way we can obtain a description of the milieu itself. At the center of attention will be the human

activities with particular care given to the concrete structures within which
these activities take place.

It is particularly on this last point that the traditional sociological approach
is short of being sufficient. With its typical stress on the interpersonal
relationships important aspect of the environment is being left out and taken
as "given" and unproblematic. Associated with this bias is a tendency to rely
first and foremost on information obtained by questioning people; information which
relates the people's experience of their activities and which cannot be taken as
description of the same behaviors.

We have stressed above that milieu refers to the dynamic interaction of humans
and their environments and it goes without saying that both of these main aspects
must be described. That we will need to obtain a description of this phenomena,
preferrably by observational methods, might need more clarification.

What we encounter here is the old conflict between the emic and etic approach in
research as Pike, Harris and others have expressed it. We are actually in most
research obtaining information along both these avenues, although we often
short circuit the process and confuse the issue, for example
by asking our respondent to give descriptions of the concrete phenomena. The
researcher might even be   satisfied with assumptions about the environmental
structures the respondent reacts to. Among natural scientist we often see this
the other way around; the researcher is making assumptions as to the human
reactions relevant for the concrete objects under study.

In studies of milieu we will need data on people's experience; their satisfaction
and wellbeing but in order to formulate a policy of action - and this is of
paramount importance in this context - we will need independent descriptions
and measurements of an etic kind; that is, first of all based on observational
methods. This we turn to now.

At present we have two avenues to follow to obtain this information. The methods
are partly developed but much more work is actually needed before we have fully
useful research tools.

The one is that of "time-budget methods" and the other is the so-called "behavior
setting survey". The former should be known to most, the latter refers to the
ideas developed by Roger Barker in his works on ecological psychology. I will
here assume that the readers are familiar with both techniques and in the
following only comment upon aspects of the methods that are relevant for my
arguments.

The reason why these two appraoches can be listed under the same heading is
that they both produce detailed and "complete" descriptions of activity and
behavior-in-milieu. They are both etic approaches by which we observe and record
the real world without imposing preconceived structures to any large extent.

Both approaches make use of time and duration as major descriptive dimensions;
the isolated elements have a beginning, duration and an end. The activities

recorded are continous in time and both techniques provides criteria by which
time periods can be defined.

The major difference between the methods has to do with the unit of analysis.
Traditional time-budget refer to single individuals while behavior settings
refer to a community. Community in this context is defined first of all with
respect to the time and space dimensions and not with respect to the humans
involved. (In passing L would like to point to the need of developing corresponding
methods using the household as a unit).

As we have stressed the points of similarity between the two techniques one should
expect quite similar results stemming from the use of the two techniques. None
has tried to compare across in this respect and the traditional systems for
coding time-budget information has not been developed with behavior settings in
mind. This is possible and it would provide a solution to the problem of obtaining
the same degree of generality for the timeperiods/behaviors for a person throughout
the day. The day for the individual would then consist of a series of behavior
settings in which he participated, time periods in isolation and timeperiods
in transit.

It is of course only by "summing across" all individuals that we get information
that refer to the milieu as such. In this way the behavior setting survey will
be a much more direct description as the behavior settings consists of "synomorphs"
as Baker calls it, an interactional phenomena where humans and environment is
interlocked in and through behavior or activity.

The behavior setting survey can be designed to yield information of various kinds,
the most general being the number of settings in a particular community and the
size and/or importance of each in terms of persons and hours.

Much critisism has been levelled in Norway against the postwar building of
dwellings and in particular the new sections of the towns that have been built
according to careful plans. The quality of the milieu in these neighborhoods
is said to be low. Simple behavior-setting surveys provide an answer, and as
a matter of fact a basis for such critisism. It is first and foremost in
terms of a very small number of behavior settings that these communities differ
from others. The quality of the houses might be high, but the possibilities for
varied activities are very few.

In his original studies, Barker performed his surveys as total surveys of total
communities. This has been necessary as a first step, but the same approach can
be used in larger communities, parts of same, within organizations or very
limited areas and also for specific periods of time. The movement of the
population will however have to be described independentaly if conclusions are
to be drawn for the participating individuals.

The original set of descriptive dimensions are likewise not a fixed set. They
as other that might be proposed, will all be alternatives that can be exchanged
and definitely improved upon as more experimentation takes place.

Describing the socio-cultural life of a town by the behavior setting approach

In concluding we will here give a short description of an attempt to produce
a description of the socio-cultural life in a middel sized town. The town has
80000 inhabitants and is situated at the southwest coast of Norway. The study
deals with the role of the local government in providing the facilities and
funds necessary for socio-cultural activities. The term "socio-cultural" indicates
that we go beyond the traditional cultural activities.

From the outset it was perfectly clear that no complete survey of such activities
could not be done without extensive participation from many people in the town.
In this way the study is an experiment in extensive participation in the research
process.

A first delineation was performed by making up a list of the sectors to be
studied: Theatre, music, exibitions, museums, film, dance, clubs, debate, lectures,
libraries, religion, out-of-school education and sports. This is all leisure
time activities and the next step consisted of identifying the organizations and
institutions in these sectors that would be potential sponsors or concrete
instigators and leaders of specific events and arrangements. The arrangements
themselves will constitute a sub-set of behavior settings and we aimed at
obtaining help from the central people in each setting.

The list of organizations and institutions ended up having about 750 entries. Some
of these were larger organizations with subgroups responsible for different
arrangements. The number of potential fieldworkers thereby exceded 1000 persons.

We were able to activate about half of these who performed dayly reporting for
four months. The registration of the single event or arrangement was done with
the help of a two-page questionnaire containing information about: location and
physical structures; time, duration and cyclical pattern; participants, number
of different age- and sex groups and performers vs. audience; program and sequence
of activities and lastly, economic aspects.

Our material is not complete, but complete enough so that the research group will
be able to fill in the missing information through interviewing which presently
is under way.

One of the reasons why this operation has been possible is the simple fact that
it is relatively easy to convey the meaning of a behavior setting. There might
be many settings taking place in a particular community, but the consolation lies
in the fact that the number is not infinite. Quite on the contrary and the
activities and artifacts that constitute the settings are readily observable
phenomena. Sofar we have identified about 1500 different behavior settings. We
expect the number to be somewhat higher and we will bring along results from the
analysis for the meeting in Blacksburg in April.

Robert B. Bechtel
Director of Research
Environmental Research & Development Foundation
4948 Cherry Street
Kansas City, Missouri 64110

Abstract

Nine methodological problems are discussed in the use of the semantic differential in environmental research: 1) confounding of denotative and conotative meaning in presentation of the stimulus, 2) ambiguity of reference points in presentation of a complex stimulus, 3) lack of representativeness of semantic scales, 4) lack of representativeness in the population studied, 5) lack of representativeness in architectural environments, 6) lack of representativeness in the media of presentation, 7) confusion of response modes among new and habitual modes of behavior, 8) overemphasis on orthogonality of factors, and 9) ambiguity of derived factors. Solutions based on probabalistic functionalism are recommended.

Introduction

The semantic differential is a widely used instrument in the study of subject responses to architectural stimuli. Craik (1), Hershberger (2), Collins (3), and Seaton and Collins (4) are only a few of the more comprehensive studies done in this field. The original text on the semantic differential (5) has now been augmented by a more sophisticated group of studies reported in Snider and Osgood (6), and recently some very incisive criticisms of semantic differential methodology have come out in the literature (7)(8). Nine problem areas have been uncovered: Problem One. Osgood, Suci, and Tannenbaum (9, p. 290) state: "The semantic differential taps the connotative aspects of meaning more immediately than the highly diversified denotative aspects". Allport (10, p. 19) defines denotative meaning as being that with which we can come in contact. Nouns are denotative. They define objects we can touch, smell, taste, see. Adjectives, on the other hand, are not denotative, they connote objects. Given the same architectural stimulus, a subject responding in denotative fashion would say, "That's a house," while a subject responding in connotative fashion might say, "It's warm, soft, small and cozy." People are usually aware of the differences between houses, churches, and factories, and it might seem easy to pass off the importance of denotative meaning. But when the stimuli become highly ambiguous, the results are often semantic chaos. This happened when non-artists judged abstract art, for example (11, p. 293). And the researcher can never relax in assuming what is clear for the subject. For example, on my own first extensive presentation of stimulus words to subjects for semantic differential measurement (12) there was a denotative confusion which produced a semantic storm. When presented with the stimulus word "China" just enough subjects felt it denoted crockery to conflict with those who felt it denoted a country in Asia, to markedly influence results.
Problem Two. Related to, but not the same as the above problem, is the reference point within the stimulus. When researchers present a stimulus in the design realm they often assume that the subject responds to the whole stimulus rather than some

part of it. This is an assumption which has not been tested and it is again a likely source for semantic confusion. For example, to return to our house stimulus again, it may be quite likely that some subjects react to the amount of window space (or lack if it) while others are intrigued by the slope of the roof, and still others (followers of Wright, perhaps) by the way if fits into the contour of the landscape.

Problem Three. Semantic space, as it has been defined by well over 1,000 studies (13) seems to have three basic dimensions, Evaluation, Power, and Activity (EPA). These dimensions are actually a part of the structure of language itself, and they seem to exist in a fixed ratio to one another. Miron (14, p. 319) states:

"Put in terms of meaning, our language (and most interestingly, other languages as well) exhibits more Evaluative than Potency synonyms and, in turn, more Potency than Activity Synonyms. Accordingly, the variation observed in natural language qualification predicts the Evaluation, Potency, Activity factor order (but see Osgood's (1971) rebuttal). But this naturalistic condition may be grossly distorted if equal numbers of scales are used to represent the "normal" factor prominences, especially when the number of concepts being rated is small."

What Miron is saying is that when concepts in language are being rated by semantic differentials, in order to be truly representative, the scales should emulate the E-P-A ratio found in the language structure by having roughly twice as many Evaluative synonyms as Power, and twice as many Power as Activity.

Problem Four. It was recently pointed out (15) that the use of college sophomores as subjects in social psychological experiments has increased through 1969, despite the fact that many authorities (16)(17) hoped for and predicted a trend toward more representative populations. In the architectural research world the tendency to use the available university population is equally compulsive. However, except for university buildings, the students represent building users even less than they represent adequate social psychologically relevant populations for experiments. Elderly, who constitute a population of 28,000,000 in the United States continue to be vastly underepresented in these studies, and they, along with other persons who may have handicaps or special requirements in environmental adaptation are estimated to total 40,000,000 or 20% of the total population (18). The problem is doubly compounded when the architect wants to be able to tell how people will react to his design without actually building it. The semantic differential seems to be an easy way to get a favorable or non-favorable response. The design is presented sometimes even to random samples of the population as a whole. But never can the true user population be sampled because they have yet to occupy the building. The result is, user populations are never tested and semantic differentials have yet to demonstrate validity for the prediction of user satisfaction.

Problem Five. As Hershberger (19) states, it would be extremely difficult to obtain a representative sample of architectural environments. Yet, if a standardization of semantic space related to architectural environments is ever to be realized, this task must some day be undertaken. Perhaps it need not be so overwhelming if more general architectural principles and architectural styles can be standardized. Collins (20)(21) has made a start in attempting to standardize evaluations of architectural environments but has not dealt with the problem of representativeness. It would seem a fair appraisal of the field to say that most researchers have taken the case study approach and are waiting for a sufficient accumulation of data before attempting any statements representative of all architectural environments.

Problem Six. Seaton and Collins (22) compared the presentation of environments through various media such as models, colored slides, black and white slides and seeing the real building. Yet this study did not cover (nor was it their purpose) other media such as television tape, movie film in color and black and white. Hershberger (23) raises the question of whether any media are really adequate to represent the architectural environment. For although a comparison of the view of a real building with slides and models makes a measurement of the visual contact with the stimulus, actual contact with an architectural environment involves many sensory modalities such as sound, smell, touch, temperature and adaptation to all of these over time (24).

Problem Seven. Barker (25) pointed out that a new situation is one in which the subject is easily influenced and easily led. Thus in any new situation, such as being asked to rate a stimulus on a semantic differential, the subject is oversensitive to cues around him. For this reason Rosenthal (26) and others have discovered that subjects are uncannily sensitive to being influenced by researchers. Likewise, when seeing a building for the first time they are likely to notice aspects that would go unheeded if they went by it every day. The first time a subject enters a building he is experiencing an exploratory mode of behavior. Thereafter, when he regularly uses the building he is experiencing an habitual mode of behavior (27). It is the latter mode that is of more importance in evaluating the architectural environment for it is the habitual use of the building that determines its success or failure. A building cannot be evaluated before it has acquired its habitual patterns of behavior. Yet no semantic differentialshave as yet been linked to habit patterns. The closest link has been to semantic impressions of persons seeing a building for virtually the first time.

Problem Eight. Miron (28) criticizes semantic differential studies for their overemphasis on orthogonality of factors. It may be, of course,that many factors occur in oblique (that is, related or correlated) rather than orthogonal (unrelated) relationships. But this, and the next problem, may be an indication that factor analysis itself needs to be re-examined as the sole technique for analyzing semantic differential data.

Problem Nine. When it comes to meaning, the meaning of a factor is as much a problem as the meaning of a stimulus or a response. For example, in his list of preferred factors, Hershberger (29) places the scale active within the factor Aesthetic. Now, of course, no one questions the high loading of the scale on the factor but there is a question of why the factor should be called aesthetic. When one sees that exciting has an even higher loading than active, it begins to look as though we may have really uncovered the Activity factor of Osgood, Suci and Tannenbaum (30). But no, unique, simple, and specialized are also loading fairly high on the same factor, and perhaps the factor could be called aesthetic to encompass these various meanings. But what is this? Strong which clearly belongs in a Potency factor is also in Aesthetics and loading about the same on both! How then can the Factors be distinguished?

Possible Solutions to the Problems. The astute observer will notice that solving one or more of the problems may result in solving one or more of the others. For example, choosing carefully representative scales may also result in orthogonal and/or more clearly labelled factors. An underlying principle beneath all the solutions is Brunswik's (31) probabalistic functionalism. In order for the semantic differential to tell us something about architectural space it must approximate the probabalistic occurrences of nature in language, architectural environments, media, and behavior. The denotative and ambiguous aspects of the stimulus (Problems one and two) could probably be ameliorated by Honikman's (32) suggestion to ask the subject what particular part of the stimulus he is responding to most (and then what part is next most salient, etc.). In this way it would become clear whether the denotative meanings were similar and whether subjects were responding to different aspects of the stimulus. Problems one and two and others like it tend to cause individual differences on the semantic differential to overwhelm the differences between concepts of objects rated. Heise (33) suggests the way to help overcome this difficulty is to use means of scales across subjects as data for the correlations rather than raw scores of subjects. Miron (34) offers the proposition that when means are not used the factors may be confounded as in Reed's (35) study. Problems three, four, five and six deal with the problem of representativeness. The failure to represent the natural distribution of language as it relates to architectural environments by choosing equal numbers of scales for each dimension can lead to confounded factors. Likewise the selection of subjects, media and environments needs to be as representative as possible. The suggestion to measure the habitual mode of behavior is really an admonition to sample the most representative type of behavior in architectural environments. The last two problems may be solved by trying new methods of cluster analysis. Tryon and Bailey's (36) methods use pivotal variables to define clusters rather than depending on the ingenuity of the researcher to guess underlying dimensions. Further, overlapping variables can be eliminated by preset instructions, producing a much cleaner set of clusters than is obtainable by ordinary factoring. There is a further advantage of being able to classify subjects by their semantic differential scores to determine if any natural grouping scored significantly different from any other group. It can be used as a test of control groups or a determination of significant individual variation. Finally, what is the goal of the use of the semantic differential in architectural research? The ideal would be to produce a semantic index that would tell us the connotative meaning of every conceivable architectural configuration. But even if this were done, would we have anything really useful? The semantic differential is quite similar to many attitudinal measures, and one must bear in mind Wicker's reviews (37)(38) that show there are possibly insurmountable obstacles in predicting human behavior from attitudinal measures. And is that not the true goal of semantic differential research, to predict human behavior for any architectural setting? It is well to bear in mind Altman's (39) remarks at the 1971 APA convention that self report methods are probably not going to be the way to unlock the needed information about behavior in architectural environments and that direct behavioral observation methods need to be developed for this purpose.

References

(1) Craik, K., The Comprehension of the Everyday Physical Environment, JOURNAL OF THE AMERICAN INSTITUTE FOR PLANNERS, Vol. 34, 1968, 29-37.

(2) Hershberger, R., Toward a set of semantic scales to measure the meaning of architectural environments. in Mitchel, W. (ed.) ENVIRONMENTAL DESIGN: RESEARCH AND PRACTICE, Proceedings of the EDRA 3/AR 8 Conference, UCLA, Vol. one., (pages not numbered) 1972.

(3) Collins, J., Scales for evaluating the architectural environment. Paper presented at the annual convention of the American Psychological Association, Washington, September, 1971.

(4)   Seaton, R., and Collins, J., Validity and reliability of simulated buildings. in Mitchel, W. (ed.) ENVIRONMENTAL DESIGN: RESEARCH AND PRACTICE, Proceedings of the EDRA 3/AR 8 Conference, UCLA, Vol. one, 1972, (pages not numbered).

(5)   Osgood, C., Suci, G., and Tannenbaum, P., THE MEASUREMENT OF MEANING, University of Illinois Press, 1957.

(6)   Snider, J., and Osgood, C., SEMANTIC DIFFERENTIAL TECHNIQUE, Aldine, 1969.

(7)   Heise, D., Some methodological issues in semantic differential research, PSYCHOLOGICAL BULLETIN, Vol. 72, 1969, 406-422.

(8)   Miron, M., Universal semantic differential shell game., JOURNAL OF PERSONALITY AND SOCIAL PSYCHOLOGY, Vol. 24, 1972, 313-320.

(9)   Rosenthal, R., EXPERIMENTER EFFECTS IN BEHAVIORAL RESEARCH, Appleton, Century, Crofts, 1966.

(10)   Allport, F., THEORIES OF PERCEPTION AND THE CONCEPT OF STRUCTURE., Wiley and Sons, 1955.

(11)   (Same as reference #5)

(12)   Bechtel, R., A COMPARISON OF MANIFEST ANXIETY, ATTITUDE CHANGE, AND COGNITIVE NEEDS AND STYLES, Susquehanna University honors thesis (unpublished), 1962.

(13)   (Same as reference #7)

(14)   (Same as reference #8)

(15)   Higbee, K., and Wells, M., Some research trends in social psychology during the 1960's. AMERICAN PSYCHOLOGIST, Vol. 27, 1972, 963-966.

(16)   McGuire, W., Some impending reorientations in social psychology: Some thoughts provoked by Kenneth Ring, JOURNAL OF EXPERIMENTAL SOCIAL PSYCHOLOGY, Vol. 3, 1967, 113-123.

(17)   Sears, D., and Abeles, R., Attitudes and Opinions, ANNUAL REVIEW OF PSYCHOLOGY, Vol. 20, 1969, 253-288.

(18)   Vash, D., Discrimination by design: Mobility Barriers. in Mitchel, W. (ed.) ENVIRONMENTAL DESIGN: RESEARCH AND PRACTICE, Proceedings of the EDRA 3/AR 8 Conference, UCLA, Vol. one, 1972.

(19)   (Same as reference #2)

(20)   Collins, J., PERCEPTUAL DIMENSIONS OF ARCHITECTURAL SPACE VALIDATED AGAINST BEHAVIORAL CRITERIA, University of Utah, Ph.D. Thesis, 1969.

(21)   (Same as reference #3)

(22)   (Same as reference #4)

(23)   (Same as reference #2)

(24)   Helson, H., ADAPTATION LEVEL THEORY, Harper and Row, 1964.

(25)   Barker, R., ADJUSTMENT TO PHYSICAL HANDICAP AND ILLNESS: A SURVEY OF THE SOCIAL
       PSYCHOLOGY OF PHYSIQUE AND DISABILITY.   Social Science Research Council, 1953.

(26)   (Same as reference #5)

(27)   (Same as reference #2)

(28)   (Same as reference #8)

(29)   (Same as reference #2)

(30)   (Same as reference #5)

(31)   Brunswik, E., Representative design and probabalistic theory in a functional
       psychology., PSYCHOLOGICAL REVIEW. Vol. 62, 1955, 193-217.

(32)   Honikman, Basil, An Investigation Between Construing Of The Environment And
       Its Physical Form, in Mitchel, W. (ed.) ENVIRONMENTAL DESIGN: RESEARCH AND
       PRACTICE, Proceedings of the EDRA 3/AR 8 Conference, UCLA, Vol. one, 1972,
       (pages not numbered)

(33)   (Same as reference #7)

(34)   (Same as reference #8)

(35)   Reed, T., Connotative meaning of social interaction concepts: An investigation
       of factor structure and the effects of imagined contexts.   JOURNAL OF PERSONA-
       LITY AND SOCIAL PSYCHOLOGY, Vol. 24, 1972, 306-312.

(36)   Tryon, R. and Bailey, D., CLUSTER ANALYSIS, McGraw Hill, 1970.

(37)   Wicker, A., Attitudes vs. actions: The relationship of verbal and overt
       behavioral responses to attitude objects., JOURNAL OF SOCIAL ISSUES,
       Vol. 25, 1969, 41-78.

(38)   Wicker, A., An examination of the "Other Variables" explanation of attitude-
       behavior inconsistency.   JOURNAL OF PERSONALITY AND SOCIAL PSYCHOLOGY.,
       Vol. 19, 1971, 18-30.

(39)   Altman, I., Remarks summarizing a symposium on Consumer Behavior and Environ-
       mental Design at the American Psychological Association Convention, Washington,
       D.C., September 4, 1971.

PHOTOGRAPHIC METHODS OF RESEARCH ON BEHAVIOUR IN THE HUMAN MILIEU: 4.3
NEW DEVELOPMENTS AND CRITIQUE

Gerald Davis   Virginia Ayers
President   Department of Architecture
TEAG - The Environmental Analysis Group   Massachusets Institute of Technology, and
1575 West Georgia Street   Senior Programmer
Vancouver 5, B.C., Canada   TEAG - The Environmental Analysis Group
    and Seattle, Wash.; Burlingame, Calif.

Abstract

This paper outlines general methods, uses, and specific techniques for using
photography in research for environmental design. The relationship of photographic
techniques to other aspects of environmental research is placed in context, and
seven categories of specific use are discussed. One is discussed in detail, with
illustrations. Problems and methods for analysis are reviewed. Examples are given,
and a listing of equipment and supplies. Some of the content, and much in the
symposium presentation, was developed as a special project in the last six months
to evaluate and advance techniques of photographic research for practical use in
day-to-day work.

Introduction

There is relatively little literature on this subject - the typical reference being
a paragraph or two. The occasional useful exception (1) is insightful, but technically out of date and methodologically of limited relevance to the environmental
designer. The following paper, therefore, is a preliminary attempt to suggest a
general methodology, and certain specific techniques based on equipment and experiences during the recent past.

Context and Related Content Knowledge

Photographic methods appear generally useful within a larger context of research,
which also includes other types of data gathering and a variety of analytical
methods. Except where the research objectives were extremely limited, we have not
been successful in using photographic methods as our sole data source, nor do we
know of other studies that contradict this general statement. Our experience has
been that:

1. One should not take research photographs, if possible, without first observing
and, to some extent, understanding not only the general context but also the
specific behaviour that is being photographed. The images to be photographed and
analysed need to be planned, rather than taken "as opportunity arises".

2. Usually more than one iteration is required to complete an analysis. For example:

(a) going to the site and observing within the context of the research hypothesis,
perhaps as participant observer; (b) photographing selected elements of the activity, according to the research plan; (c) analysing the film that has been

obtained; (d) returning to the site to further observe and study aspects of the behaviour which were not clear from the initial round of observation and photographic recording; (e) analysing the new data, and planning additional data gathering by film and possibly by other methods to interpret and answer the questions which have been raised as a result of the above; and (f) recycling as required to complete development of a solid data base responsive to the hypothesis for the research.

3. It is not generally possible to know and understand the physical, social, cultural and functional context before filming without a preliminary investigation. Therefore, before any filming is undertaken, the investigator should define which aspects of background data he needs to know for his particular project, and research methods he has chosen. Some of this data will come, in part, from observation and measurement (as using meters to measure light level or color, or tape measure to record floor plan and other critical dimensions); other data will come from interviews or related survey methods, etc. This research should not, however, modify the behaviour to be photographed. For instance, interviewing people on an escalator tends to affect their normal behaviour on the escalator because they are looking and interacting with a stranger instead of responding to the overall environment.

It is often of great value in planning and analysing the photographic research data to interview professionals and managers, or staff, to understand their perceptions of how their original objectives were or were not achieved, for example, the staff of an airline know why the load factor on a particular flight (airplane arrival or departure) is high or low, or why the particular people on such a flight are rushed or frustrated, or otherwise behaving abnormally.

Useful Contexts for Photographic Methods

We note seven main contexts in which photographic methods of research may have substantial utility, or even advantage, over other methods of research.

1. Space and Activity Inventory. Photographic methods, typically using very wide angle lenses and 35mm slides, can survey and inventory the entire physical context of a setting or environment, and in addition can provide the details that emphasize particular aspects of significance. The principal advantage of this method of inventorying is that the material can be studied in depth, at the convenience of the researcher. However, the work has to be done in a very systematic, structured way, for which special rules must be developed, adapting the general principles to each single instance or project, and it is best done by those who will also do the analysis.

2. Gather Data for Later Counting and Evaluation. Not only do photographic methods often provide greater accuracy than do individuals observing the same scene, but the data can be re-run, and, in effect, the situation can be re-created for checking or for extraction of further information. A single individual with a camera can, in some instances, obtain more information of a useful type than a whole army of people with counters and clipboards, and yet at the same time be unobtrusive.

3. Study a Sequential Experience. Sometimes the photographs can become the main basis for the analysis. This is true when the analyst takes a sequence of photographs as he walks through and experiences the space. Often what he perceives and chooses to photograph, either as general pictures or as details, will be quite different from what someone who sees the spatial sequence only as a set of separate images would photograph.

4. Communicate an Image. Visual recording of experiences and perception also permits effective communication and analysis of the visual components of an "image" of an environment.

5. Participant Observation. Under some circumstances, participant observation may provide realistic and valuable opportunities for photographic methods of research, entirely compatible with the nature of the participant activity. For instance, when one is studying tourist activity and a camera is taken for granted then the use of a camera for a minute or two may gather enough data so that the observer is then free to spend the bulk of his time and interest experiencing and participating in activities as required by the research plan.

6. Activity at Behaviour Settings. We find photographic methods, combining both time-lapse photography and still photography, is an almost indispensable component of a thorough-going analysis.

7. Understanding Normal and Special Behaviour in Specific Functions and Environments. It is often extremely valuable to use photographic images for recording and analysing in depth that behaviour which exists only for a few instants, but which recurs in a variety of contexts. By selecting contexts for comparison so that certain variables are controlled, it is possible to compare accurately many kinds of behavioural details from modest amounts of film. When used with other research methods it is possible to begin to predict what behaviour can be expected in certain situations.

This kind of research was used as an early phase in a study of behaviour on escalators and moving sidewalks. The purpose of this first phase of photographic data gathering was two-fold: (1) to reveal technical and procedural problems, and (2) to collect enough data to formulate an outline of theory from which the remainder of the study could be planned. Data was gathered over eleven days of the holiday season of December 1972/January 1973 at two airports (Seattle/Tacoma and San Francisco) by the authors and Francoise Szigeti.

a) Preliminary Planning. Movies would be taken at 6 frames per second (fps), which is fast enough to show continuity of movement yet slow enough to conserve film and allow longer runs without changing films. Some projectors run at 6fps, so "real-time" can be simulated. Because the timing mechanism of the Braun Nizo can be set only approximately, yet we wanted to time accurately the duration of events, we would photograph in multiples of 30 second modules. At the same time, a second photographer would take colour slides using two Nikon cameras, with a wide angle lens (24mm) to record the context and large scale characteristics of behaviour, and with a long focus lens for detail (105mm). A third member of the team would keep time and records. We listed what should be photographed and at what locations, to ensure we would have the necessary data for comparative analysis. We designed recording forms for written data on general environmental conditions, dimensions, population characteristics, the date and location where movies and slides were taken, with room for a diagram and general notes, etc. (3)

b) Gathering Data. Prior to taking any photographs, we obtained permission from the management and scouted the site, observing behaviour, searching for desirable vantage points, checking light levels, comparing angles of views in the different lenses. This enabled us later to make informed decisions in response to the behaviour we were observing and recording, as it happened. (Details in procedures become very important in the field, all assumptions must be made explicit, and all decisions reached with the understanding of the whole team. This control and coordination is essential.)

The first films were processed and quickly scanned; the recording forms were improved; then one member of the team returned alone to one of the sites to take additional slides, timed movies, and notes covering some additional view points.

c) Identification-coding Films Before Analysis. In this kind of study it is necessary to be able to identify each slide, film module and person shown on film by a unique code. Each roll of film is identified by the photographer, using the month in which the roll is started, whether it is a roll of movie film or slides, and the number of the roll within the month. This is followed either by the slide number within the roll, or the sequence number for movies; e.g., GD 72-12-M2-6 is a movie code. Thereafter, bunches of people can be numbered as they come into view, and individuals can be numbered within bunches; in this case, in the order in which they step on or off the escalator. The coding system should separate the data into small enough pieces that the film can be explored heuristically and quickly coded in just the parts of interest; in addition, small errors in counting people are isolated in small pieces of film. Specific frames can then be identified by the bunches or individuals in them if a frame counter is not available, which allows film to be analysed on an inexpensive editor. The identification coding is added to the original log made when the film was taken.

d) Analysis. There are a number of systematic but heuristic ways of starting to look at films. One method is to take a fairly rich piece of film and brain-dump with it, noting all ideas that occur and trying to be explicit about bits of behaviour that are so common that they are difficult to see. Often it is useful to view a segment of film at many different speeds, forwards and backwards in order to see more each time. Another method is to scan a lot of material with only one hypothesis or point of view in mind. It is difficult to stay with one idea in the face of so much rich material but it is worthwhile; even the inevitable distracting insights tend to be useful. (2) Data from photographs can be converted to format suitable for entry into computers, permitting complex analysis. Punch card analysis with only a sorter, or the simple cross-reference decks for hand-sorting, etc, are also used.

Slide GD-12-5-1 (Context)   Slide GD-12-4-16 (Detail)

Slide GD-12-5-21 (Context)   Slide GD-12-5-23 (Detail)

e) Examples of Photographic Data and Analysis. The four cropped prints of slides shown here illustrate a few of the preliminary findings which are part of the outline of theory of "normal" and "special" behaviour on escalators and moving sidewalks used to plan the study. Approaching groups start ordering themselves sequentially in a zone of 10 feet to 5 feet from the first escalator step (indicated in the photograph by a line of tape on the outside of the escalator). In this same zone, an adult will put down or pick up a child in anticipation of getting on the escalator. There appears to be a second zone, within 5 feet of the first step, in which order has been established by the order in which the zone is entered. Density is frequently quite high in this zone. Within this 5 foot range of the first escalator step are seen most of the minor adjustments frequently exhibited in the behaviour of the approach: grabbing a child's hand; switching an object from the outside hand to the inside hand (when proximity to a companion has defined a hand as "inside"); taking a hand out of a pocket; freeing one hand from a two-handed carrying position.

The Photographic Research Team

We are seeking to create methods whereby the single individual, on projects with low budgets, can be relatively effective in data gathering with cameras. The principal problem, we find, is that when one individual has to use many skills simultaneously the error rate often increases. In our experience, a team of two people seems to be the optimum number, permitting greater control and replicability of photo-recorded data and of other observations.

Specific Methods, Techniques and Technical Comments

1. Context Data. To avoid "photographic quoting" out of context, one should try to get data both as the observer perceives the behaviour or sequence of activities, and as the participant perceives them. The observer may be located some distance from the subjects of the research, and where people do not normally go, such as: a balcony; a mezzanine; through an overlooking window, etc. We then find it is also necessary to record photographically the situation as perceived by the subject.

We usually take a series of wide-angle photographs at regular intervals down a travel path, including at all major turning points, openings in the route, side views, etc. Where signing or other things focus attention, an exposure is taken with a long-focus lens to record the detail that the participant focusses on. On entry to a major space, a left-right pair is usually taken (two exposures from the same position with the left one matching up to the right one at the centre of the observer's field of view). If the lens has a 24mm focal length for a 35mm slide, for instance, then by projecting both slides side-by-side, the horizontal angle of view approaches the full range that one sees.

2. Equipment. We now normally use the following equipment, but emphasize that these choices are relevent to our needs and may not be appropriate for other circumstances: (a) 35mm equipment. Normally two Nikon FTn bodies, one with a 24mm f/2.8 lens and one with a 105mm f/2.5 lens. We also carry at all times a 55mm f/1.2 lens, and closeup and doubler lens, attachments. We use the 55mm f/3.5 Micro-Nikkor lens for closeup details, and occasionally the 200mm f/4.0 Nikkor lens for long details. We also carry a Rollie-35; (b) Super-8 equipment. Camera is Braun Nizo S-560 with zoom lens 7mm-56mm f/1.8. Projector is Kodak MFS-8 Ektographic. Editor, Braun SB1. (c) Film. For consistancy and to reduce human error, all film is high speed Ektachrome by Kodak, ASA 160 in daylight, except where in very low light we use Kodak 4-X reversal film 7277 with ASA 400 daylight. All work is done with "available light"; (d) Light metering equipment. Light level, General Electric type 213. Light temperature, Gossen Sixtacolor.

References and Footnote

(1) Collier, John Jr., VISUAL ANTHROPOLOGY: PHOTOGRAPHY AS A RESEARCH METHOD, Holt, Rinehart and Winston, Inc, 1967.

(2) Ibid., chapter 7, page 70.

(3) Due to shortage of space in this publication, we do not include a copy of our standard form, but we would be happy to provide a sample sheet on request.

Robert W. Marans
Institute for Social Research and
Department of Architecture
The University of Michigan
Ann Arbor, Michigan 48106

Abstract

This paper discusses two important dimensions of survey research vis-a-vis environmental planning - those of geographic scope and survey design. Sprinkled throughout the discussion are examples of past, present and projected research of the Survey Research Center at the University of Michigan. The paper also discusses a number of appropriate purposes for conducting surveys and suggests ways in which the survey can be used in conjunction with other methodological approaches in providing information to the planning and design professions.

Introduction

There is basic agreement that the so-called environmental design professions are in a state of rapid change. Technological advancements with respect to building materials, energy sources and construction techniques, new legislation and changes in individual values and life styles have all contributed to the tumultuous state within which the professions must now work. To further complicate matters, a number of behavioral scientists have taken an active interest in public policy matters including those related to the environment. Many have become intrigued by the potential influence of environmental phenomena on a variety of behaviors and attitudes of people. In order to pursue their interests, economists, sociologists and psychologists have developed research programs and projects aimed in part at determining the role played by environmental phenomena with respect to human performance. In doing so they have brought to bear techniques and tools developed and used by their respective disciplines. Recently, the appropriateness of using these research techniques and tools when addressing the kinds of problems and issues faced by the environmental design professions has been questioned by a number of social scientists. (1, 2, 3, 4) By raising such questions, further debate has been generated among the potential users of the research - namely the architects, environmental planners and others who formulate policies which, directly or indirectly, deal with environmental phenomena.

In order to help clarify the issues centered around the methodological debate, it is important that those who use research findings understand the value of each approach, their basic differences and how they can be used in conjunction with one another. In part, our symposium is intended to contribute to this understanding.

One approach which can be useful in providing information for architects, environmental planners and policy makers is the survey - a technique used widely in social science research and with increasing regularity by people from the design professions (5, 6, 7). By surveys, I mean the systematic collection of data from populations or samples of populations through the use of personal interviews or other data gathering techniques involving direct contact with people.

286

In this paper I would like to discuss two dimensions of survey research - those of geographic scope and survey design. Included in this discussion will be examples of our work in the Urban Environmental Research Program of the Institute for Social Research. I will also discuss some appropriate uses of survey research with respect to the planning and design professions and suggest ways in which the survey can be used in conjunction with other methodological approaches.

Geographic Scope of Surveys

Although surveys can vary greatly in their geographic scope, architects and planners are most familiar with those that focus on small geographic areas such as an individual building, a housing project or a single neighborhood. These surveys are usually designed to learn something about the residents such as who they are, their attitudes toward particular environmental or social attributes and their uses of space within dwellings or in the neighborhood as a whole. Ideally, surveys conducted in single neighborhoods or other special environmental settings should be performed within the context of a more comprehensive field study. The field study, according to Katz (8), enables the social scientist or planner to study a single community or group in terms of its social structure - that is, the interrelations and interactions of the structural parts including behavior and the physical environment. Specifically, it attempts to directly observe and measure the on-going processes that are taking place within the community or group setting. This means that the field study either attempts observations of behaviors such as social interaction or thoroughly investigates the reciprocal perceptions and attitudes of people who play interdependent roles in that setting. This thorough investigation would include carefully planned surveys or interviews with all or a sample of the people involved. The survey, therefore, in order to have its full impact as a device for learning about the residents of a specific geographic area, should be viewed as one of several possible data gathering techniques. The study of married student housing by Festinger, Schachter and Back (9) and the more recent works of Gans (10, 11) best typify the use of surveys in a more comprehensive field investigation.

Unfortunately, field studies of single geographic areas are all too rare. The types of insights obtained from such in-depth studies can not be expected from a survey alone. Nor does a survey represent more than the responses of a single group of people in one geographic area at a single point in time. For instance, it may be useful for the planners in Boston to know how a working class population responded to forced relocation, but it would be unwise if these and other planners were to infer from that the reactions of other segments of the population to a relocation proposal. Small area surveys certainly can provide useful feedback to designers of that area or of a new environment to which these people are expected to move. But such surveys are often costly to initiate, they don't provide the in-depth knowledge that is necessary for developing a theory of the impact of the physical environment on behavior nor are the results always generalizable to other people in other environmental settings.

At the other end of the geographic spectrum are surveys which are national in scope. The most widely known surveys of this type are those conducted by the Harris and Gallup organizations. Less known but perhaps of greater interest and importance to planners and policy makers are the national studies of the Institute's Survey

Research Center at The University of Michigan. For more than 25 years, the Survey Research Center has maintained a national sample of the population of the United States and a well-trained staff of interviewers. Since the sample is representative of the population as a whole, the respondents are distributed throughout the country and include people who vary widely in their socioeconomic and demographic characteristics. They also vary with respect to the types of residential environments in which they live.

Perhaps the best known of the Survey Research Center national studies are the annual Surveys of Consumer Finances. Among the topics covered by these studies is consumer behavior with respect to the housing market. A wealth of information on housing transactions including the distribution of and attitudes toward home ownership have been collected over the years for different age, income and family life-cycle groups.

The potential use of such data for planners and policy makers is great. For instance, one can tell for any age, income or family life-cycle group their attitudes, expectations and behaviors with respect to purchasing or renting a home. Furthermore, this information is available for different regions of the country, providing a basis of comparison for responses from studies of small geographic areas such as communities or neighborhoods.

When such studies attempt to elicit responses to the physical dimensions of housing and the environment and relate these responses to objective measures of environmental conditions, the findings can become useful to architects and urban designers as well as planners. Whereas data are now available which enable us to explain how different segments of the population in different regions respond as consumers to the housing market, the collection and analysis of new environmental data dealing with specific features of dwellings and neighborhoods ranging from the amount of private outdoor space to the frequency of rubbish collection can contribute to the architects and urban designers' understanding of how different population groups respond to environmental conditions.

One major advantage of national surveys emerging from this discussion is the ability of such surveys to differentiate between sub-groups of the population in their responses to different environmental settings. As we noted earlier, such comparisons are rarely possible in samples of single geographic areas where population compositions and components of the physical and social environment do not vary greatly.

When surveys dealing with specific issues or specific populations are conducted, data from national surveys covering the same issues can provide a useful basis for comparison. Does the population being studied differ from the population of the United States as a whole or with comparable sub-groups in other parts of the country? Are environmental conditions in the location under study different than conditions existing elsewhere? If such conditions are similar to conditions elsewhere, to what extent does the local population perceive them differently and why? These and similar questions suggest that national surveys on the relationship of people and the physical environment can provide useful baseline data with which data from specific area surveys can be compared.

Thus far our discussion of the scope of surveys has focused on the two ends of the geographic spectrum. It is obvious that surveys can be designed to cover populations living in areas larger than a housing project and smaller than the nation as a whole. But it is less obvious that surveys can be designed to deal with populations which are distinguished by some common behavior, experience or other characteristic. There have been surveys of college graduates, recent home buyers, people who ride public transit, visit wilderness areas and other equally specialized kinds of people. Samples of these groups are selected because these people have special significance in relation to the objectives of a study. For instance, a proposed study of the past, existing and anticipated living arrangements of the elderly and those approaching retirement will use as its respondents a) those people in the national sample who are over 55 years old, b) people in the national sample between 35 and 55, and c) the living parents of the people in b). In this way we can focus on a pre-retirement group as well as a substantially larger group of people over 55. Part of our analysis will compare the living arrangements of the over 55 group retrospectively with those living arrangements as perceived by their children who fall in the sample. Similarly, a recent survey of people who choose to live in innovative new environments drew its sample from residents of Radburn, Columbia, Reston and two in-town redevelopment areas. (12)

Although most surveys conducted during the past 25 years have been based on samples of large heterogeneous populations, there has been an increase in recent years in the proportion of studies of populations of a more restricted character - either in terms of who they are or where they live. Undoubtedly, such studies of people in special circumstances and environments will continue as we realize that our understanding of these people vis-a-vis the environment is limited.

Types of Survey Designs

Whenever survey data are to be collected, a decision must be made as to the specific design which data-collecting will follow. This decision is based on a variety of factors ranging from the hypotheses to be tested and relationships to be explored to the size of the research budget.

Cross-section surveys are most widely used because they are relatively simple in design and low in cost. This survey method is the best way to determine the characteristics and behaviors of a population or sub-groups of that population at a single point in time. (13) Furthermore, much of the data derived from such surveys are presented in the form of distributions and can be used by planners and designers. For instance, the contention of many planners that neighborhood parks are not being used by the majority of children living around them has been supported in part by distributive information from a recent national recreation study. (14) The study showed that over two-thirds of all children between 2 and 9 years old played in the yards of their homes. An additional 15 percent played in the street or sidewalk area near home while only 5 percent played in a local or neighborhood park. When the distance to the nearest park was considered, the situation improved somewhat but not as much as some park planners would lead us to believe. In those households located within 2 minutes of a local park, one out of four young children played there while slightly less than two-thirds played in their yards or on the street or sidewalk near their homes. The implications of such findings pose a number of important questions for planners and researchers with respect to the future of urban parks and recreational needs of young people.

A survey also can be used to identify relationships between different groups and specific attitudes, expectations or behaviors or in determining the amount of time a group devotes to various activities. However, the establishment of relationships does not reveal whether these relationships are stronger or weaker than they had been at an earlier period. Nor does the allocation of time as determined by a single survey suggest which activities are gaining or losing in importance or popularity. For example, a 1965 national study of outdoor recreation showed that participation in bicycling for people over 12 years old was low relative to other forms of recreation. However, when rates were compared with data from a similar study conducted four years earlier, it was noted that participation in bicycling grew faster than any other activity over the four-year period. This illustration suggests that repeated cross-section surveys at successive points in time offer one approach to getting at changing events, attitudes or behaviors.

As part of our current social indicator work, we are identifying a number of residential environmental conditions and people's assessments of them. We are also measuring satisfaction with housing, neighborhood and community. (15) Repeated measures in subsequent cross-section surveys will enable us to assess changes in these objective environmental conditions and people's responses to them in terms of their expressions of satisfaction and residential mobility. Furthermore, it will be possible to analyze these data in relation to the timing of governmental economic and social policies such as those dealing with housing or income subsidies for low income families. As modelling techniques improve, this information can be used in understanding and predicting how segments of the population will respond in the future to programs and environmental designs for housing.

Although the respondents in these successive surveys will be different, the universe from which the samples are drawn will be identical. Thus, by using probability sampling techniques, we will be able to discern trends from the data over time. Moreover, the systematic use of fixed questions, open-answer techniques and identical procedures for measuring objective environmental conditions is essential if comparisons are to be made from repeated cross-sectional surveys.

Repeated cross-sectional surveys are not the only way of capturing changing experiences and attitudes of a population. Another way is through reinterview panels (longitudinal surveys) in which the experiences and behaviors of a select group or groups are traced in repeated interviews. This approach has been advocated by planners and designers who seek information on how certain environmental configurations alter people's behaviors. But it should be noted that, whether in small area or national studies, high costs relative to sample size is a major problem of panel interviews. There are the costs of following, finding and interviewing people who are no longer clustered geographically as they were when first surveyed. There are also costs associated with paying respondents who are being asked for repeated cooperation and for allowing their names and other identifications to be kept on tap for a period of time. Finally, there are additional costs in dealing with the complex problems of editing, data management and maintaining elaborate record files.

Despite higher costs and budgetary and manpower limitations, there are some obvious advantages to collecting data from the same individuals over, say, a 5-year period. First of all, surveys are often criticized on the grounds that certain types of variables can not be measured retrospectively. In part this criticism is justified with respect to variables which are subject to change over time and which can only be ascertained by objective measurement (or subjective judgements) by someone other than the respondent. For example, it is impossible to determine the condition of the dwelling that the respondent lived in 3 years earlier, unless someone had assessed that dwelling as part of a survey conducted at that time. Similarly, although it is conceptually possible to measure attitudes retrospectively - "How satisfied were you with your neighborhood 3 years ago?" - it is clearly inappropriate to do so if such attitudes are to be used as a basis for explaining subsequent behavior such as moving.

Secondly, longitudinal surveys have the advantage, compared to single retrospective surveys, of reducing errors in response which may be attributable to faulty memory. This is especially true if one is interested in analyzing changes in transportation, recreation or other forms of behavior appropriately determined by the survey method. Other advantages of longitudinal studies are associated with the study of developmental processes that an individual or family goes through over a period of time and with the study of causation. (16)

A proposed Institute for Social Research longitudinal study which aims at capturing the above advantages will investigate people preferences for housing and community in terms of what they pay for and get when purchasing a housing package. Presumably, the results of this study would help elected representatives and planners decide how scarce resources would be allocated. Information also would be useful to architects and urban designers who are interested in how segments of the population respond to various environmental configurations and change.

We propose to do several things as part of the study. First, we would interview people about their past and present environments and the detailed things they like and dislike about them. Then we would return several years later to the same dwellings and talk to the people who live there. If the people have moved, we would follow them to their new dwelling. For each dwelling and neighborhood we would collect data on a number of objective attributes ranging from things potentially manipulable by architects and urban designers to local public services such as the quality of schools and parks and rubbish collection.

The analysis can provide much useful information. For those who have not moved but whose neighborhoods have changed, we can find out how they currently assess their environment before and after the change and, in the second interview, what they think about the changes that have taken place. Those who have moved are even more interesting because they can now describe the new environment they are in, and we can compare those ratings with the concurrent rating made in the old environment. We can also ask movers to describe the neighborhood they used to live in as a check on what they told us earlier, and as part of the explanation as to why they moved. Moreover, in the original dwellings from which the first people moved, we will have new residents whose attitudes can be ascertained and compared to the original residents of the dwellings. In this way we can develop information in both changing and unchanging environments about the responses of different groups to the same situation.

Finally, we will be in a position to identify those environmental attributes and changes in them which influence peoples' decision to move from one neighborhood to another.

Besides sample cross-section survey designs, repeated cross-section surveys and re-interview or longitudinal study designs, there are surveys based on contrasting samples and population experiments, the latter used to measure the effects of change which is consciously introduced. (17, 18) The population experiment has received considerable attention lately with respect to OEO and the housing allowance programs and could be considered an appropriate way of assessing the effects of specific environmental changes.

Some Appropriate Uses of Surveys

Throughout this paper, I have suggested a number of purposes for doing surveys. Basically, these involve describing, explaining, evaluating and predicting some phenomena involving people's responses to the environment. These survey results can be used as input into discussions of policy revolving around some problem or issue. The results, however, can not determine policy directly. But they can keep policy makers aware of the feelings, desires and behavior of diverse groups in the population. I am including architects, urban designers and planners in my definition of policy maker.

Unlike many other methodological approaches, surveys can provide information on "who", "how", and "why". Specifically, this involves questioning people about their social-personal-economic characteristics, their levels of information, their attitudes, opinions, expectations and motives. At another level, questions about individual behavior can be asked. However, these questions tend to be more appropriate to gross forms of behavior such as changing residence, purchasing a new house or other major life events or participating in a particular outdoor recreation activity. At a more finite level of behavior e.g. activities performed around the house, the survey may not be the most appropriate method of obtaining data. While frequency of engagement in an activity is generally a reliable bit of information obtained through interviews, surveys are inappropriate for determining the qualitative aspects of a behavior or its dimensionality. For example, we can use a survey to find out how many times during the past week a person went swimming at the local pool - but it would be difficult to ascertain directly what prompted the individual to swim on each occasion, who he went with and the nature of his entire recreational experience including other activities he may have performed simultaneously. To capture the entire experience would require a battery of questions far exceeding the time limitations of normal interview, that is, assuming an individual can recall and articulate each dimension of the experience.

Of increasing importance to survey work is the collection of objective environmental data to be analyzed in conjunction with attitude and behavioral data. For any respondent in a survey we are able to identify and quantify several dimensions of his physical environment such as the size of his dwelling or yard, the degree to which the latter is enclosed, the amounts and kinds of open space in his neighborhood, the layout of structures and the dwelling unit density at which he lives. Three factors enable us to obtain this information at relatively little cost. First, aerial photographs and large scale maps are available and reveal much information about the physical environment. Second, we can train interviewers to make assessments of certain quantitative and qualitative aspects of the environment. Finally, cluster sampling techniques which can select 3 to 10 respondents living adjacent to each other allow us to identify an environmental characteristic of a neighborhood and assign its value to each respondent. For instance, if the sample of 100 people in a community were scattered, each respondent would have his own set of neighborhood characteristics. By clustering respondents in, say units of four, each cluster would have its own set of characteristics. Therefore, only one-fourth as much information would have to be collected. Admittedly, our ability to identify and measure a great variety of environmental attributes of the respondent's home and larger residential environment is limited at this time. We are now making efforts to improve this capability. As we do so, our understanding of the interrelations and interactions of individuals and their residential environment should increase.

Implicit in our discussion thus far is the fact that surveys, to the extent that they deal with man-environment interactions and interrelations, do so through a study of the final outcome. That is, the processes of these interactions and interrelations are inferred from the statistical analyses of the survey data. With survey research, it is impossible to directly observe, measure and analyze on-going processes. Moreover, it should be evident that, as these processes become more complex, and if a high degree of precision and accuracy is required in the data, the survey technique has severe limitations. Undoubtedly, there are other limitations associated with the use of surveys as the principle means of obtaining data on a wide range of issues and problems associated with the environment. These limitations need to be explored in conjunction with the special problem or issue with which the researcher or environmental planner deals and will not be considered in this paper.

Nevertheless, it is possible to consider the survey as an appropriate technique to be used in conjunction with other methodologies. As we indicated earlier, field studies of small areas requiring an in-depth understanding of the on-going interactions and interrelations among individuals and between them and their environment can use surveys to complement and/or validate information obtained through observation techniques. While the latter approach may provide insights as to how some residents of a small housing development behave, the survey can be used to systematically determine if the behavioral pattern is really characteristic of all residents. Furthermore, it can be used to ascertain attitudes and expectations which then can be assessed in relation to behaviors. If one is interested in determining the influence of past experiences on present forms of observed behavior the survey can provide this information as well as other aspects of the individuals' or groups' background.

At the Survey Research Center, interviews are being used to provide complementary information about the time families spend in child-rearing activities. The basic methodology involves the use of personal diaries complemented with an experimental beeper system. But the data that eventually will be analyzed will be derived from surveys as well as time budgets.

Observational information about attributes in the environment ranging from the use of parks and playgrounds to the amount of litter in the streets can tell the planners something about the behavior of people living in that environment. But they provide little insight as to the human meaning attached to these conditions. What is accepted as good or bad by those who do the observing or use the information to make policy may appear different to different segments of the population whose lives are affected by such policies. In order to obtain a more balanced picture of the conditions which really exist in, say a neighborhood, surveys can be used to complement information derived from observation.

Finally, we mentioned that surveys at the national level can provide a basis for comparison of findings derived from studies of small geographic areas. These small area studies could be based on one or several surveys and/or other methodologies. Furthermore, where observational techniques may generate hypotheses about relationships between individuals and their environments, surveys (at the national level) could be used to test hypotheses with respect to other populations and other environmental settings.

References

(1)   Gump, Paul V., The Behavioral Setting: A Promising Unit for Environmental Designers," LANDSCAPE ARCHITECTURE, January, 1971.

(2)   Bechtel, Robert B., "Social Goals Through Design: A Half Process Made Whole"; paper delivered at the American Institute of Planners Conference, Boston, Massachusetts, October, 1972.

(3)   Proshansky, Harold, "Methodology in Environmental Psychology: Problems and Issues," HUMAN FACTORS, 14(5), 1972.

(4)   Patterson, Arthur H., "Unobtrusive Measures: Their Nature and Utility for Architects" in J. Lang, et al. (eds.) BEHAVIORAL ASPECTS OF ARCHITECTURAL DESIGN, 1973, (forthcoming).

(5)   Committee on Housing Research and Development, "Families in Public Housing: An Evaluation of Three Residential Environments in Rockford, Illinois," Urbana-Champaign: University of Illinois, 1972.

(6)   Sanoff, Henry, "Housing Research and Development," paper presented at a symposium on Housing and Mental Health, School of Architecture, University of Maryland, March, 1972.

(7)   Levin, M.S. and S. Sachs, "Some First Returns on Planned Unit Development," paper presented at the American Institute of Planners Conference, Boston, Massachusetts, October, 1972.

(8)   Katz, Daniel, "Field Studies" in (L. Festinger and D. Katz, eds.) RESEARCH METHODS IN THE BEHAVIORAL SCIENCES. New York: Holt, Reinhart and Winston, 1953.

(9)   Festinger, Leon, S. Schachter and K. Back, SOCIAL PRESSURES IN INFORMAL GROUPS, New York: Harper and Row, 1950.

(10) Gans, Herbert J., THE URBAN VILLAGES, New York: The Free Press, 1962.

(11) Gans, Herbert J., THE LEVITTOWNERS, New York: Random House, 1967.

(12) Lansing, John B., Robert W. Marans and Robert B. Zehner, PLANNED RESIDENTIAL ENVIRONMENTS, Ann Arbor: Institute for Social Research, The University of Michigan, 1970.

(13) Morgan, James N., "How Useful is the Cross-Section Sample Survey?" MONTHLY LABOR REVIEW, February, 1972.

(14) Mandell, Lewis and Robert W. Marans, PARTICIPATION IN OUTDOOR RECREATION: A NATIONAL PERSPECTIVE, Institute for Social Research, The University of Michigan, 1972.

(15) Marans, Robert W. and Willard Rodgers, "Toward an Understanding of Community Satisfaction " in A. Hawley and V. Rock (eds.) SIGNIFICANCE OF COMMUNITY IN THE METROPOLITAN ENVIRONMENT, Washington: National Academy of Science; 1973, (forthcoming).

(16) Parnes, Herbert S., "Longitudinal Surveys: Prospects and Problems," MONTHLY LABOR REVIEW, February, 1972.

(17) Campbell, Angus and George Katona, "The Sample Survey: A Technique for Social Science Research," in (L. Festinger and D. Katz, eds.) RESEARCH METHODS IN THE BEHAVIORAL SCIENCES, New York: Holt, Reinhart and Winston, 1953.

(18) Glennen, Thomas K., "Using Experiments For Social Research and Planning", MONTHLY LABOR REVIEW, February 1972.

Donald Appleyard
Professor of Urban Design
University of California
Berkeley, California

Frances Carp
Research Psychologist
University of California
Berkeley, California

Abstract

This paper describes a multiple survey method of assessing the impact of a large
environmental project on its immediate surroundings. A model of environmental impact is proposed as the basis for collecting data.

The Bay Area Rapid Transit system (BART) has begun operations after over ten years
of planning. This paper will concentrate on the study of external BART impact --
BART's effects upon the residential quality of areas through which it will run.

The BART impact study is focussed on the impact of BART on the residential areas
through which it will run.

1. It is an empirical assessment of impact and human response to this impact.
2. It is geared to the collection of a wide range of measures whose effective-
    ness as indicators of environmental impact will be evaluated in order to
    select the most relevant for subsequent use.
3. It is committed to monitor impacts over a period of time to compare before/
    after conditions and of sufficient length to rule out Hawthorne (1) and
    sleeper effects (2).
4. It will provide immediate information on the impact of BART to aid in the
    planning and management of BART's right-of-way and station areas.
5. It will develop predictive models of impact that may be applied to future
    transit extensions and future transit systems.
6. It will in its later stages compare the environmental impacts of BART with
    those of the routes of freeways, buses, and other urban transportation
    systems, thereby assessing BART impact realistically, in context.

This study focuses on the effects of BART upon the physical, social and functional
environments of impacted populations. It will look at BART's effects on the everyday lives of those who live around the system, on the amenity qualities of their
physical environments, on their social contacts, and on their access to local facilities. Many of these impacts may be termed perceived environmental impacts, since
the residents will be aware of them; others, of which they may be unaware, such as
a slow increase in traffic volumes on local streets may be termed effective environmental impacts. Impacts of BART on the natural environment will be considered if

296

they affect the amenity quality of the physical environment for its residents through, say, unsightly erosion or other deterioration of their perceived residential area.

The external environmental impacts of BART will be both direct and indirect, local and regional. The <u>direct local</u> effects on residential neighborhoods -- effects on such variables as <u>ambient noise</u>, local access patterns, safety, privacy, territoriality, physical character, social networks -- should be relatively easy to measure and clearly attributable to BART. However, the secondary or <u>indirect local</u> effects -- which may be more important in the long run -- will be more difficult to attribute regarding causation. Indirect impacts of BART, say those mediated through traffic patterns around stations, can be assessed with fine-grain traffic information. Similarly, the impacts of land use, population, and zoning changes around BART can be assessed, but their attribution to BART becomes less clear. Has a new office building located near to BART because of BART of because of a regional shopping center?

Sampling Impacts Over Time

The impacts of a project are expected to change over the several phases of its evolution. The phases that appear to be significant in the evolution of the BART system (Figure 1) are:

1. Pre-project history   prior to 1962
2. Site clearance and construction   1962-1971
3. Post-construction and pre-opening   1971-1972
4. Opening of operations   1972-1973
5. Post-opening and impact stabilization   1974-future

Since the study did not commence until after construction was complete (Phase 3), the prior history of impact will be gathered through examination of secondary data and through the interviews, which include questions on the respondents' perceived history of BART's impacts. All pre-BART perishable data -- i.e., that which would be lost once the system started to operate -- was collected during the summer and early fall of 1972. Subsequent waves of data collection are scheduled for the summers of 1973 and 1974.

The "site clearance and construction" phase (Phase 2) may have most impact around stations with large parking lots and in the "cut and cover" type of subway sites such as on Market Street in San Francisco or along Hearst Avenue in North Berkeley. The construction phase of transportation projects often includes the destruction of buildings and relocation of families and users, and the generation of noise, dirt, fumes, and heavy truck traffic. The post-construction, pre-opening phase (Phase 3) may be a hiatus in which relief from construction impacts is mixed with anticipation of the opening.

The "opening" phase (Phase 4) of BART will probably be the time in which people will be most vulnerable and sensitive to impacts. It could be a "honeymoon" period; it could be one of surprise and disappointment. In the first few months of the system's opening BART has frequently been front page news, sometimes favorable, sometimes unfavorable. This will probably be a time when people are most aware of and articulate about environmental impacts such as annoyance from lights or added traffic around the stations. Later they may well have adapted to environmental changes or have screened them out of awareness. It is therefore a most important time to interview people. However, early studies in the General Electric plant at Hawthorne determined that almost any change in management had a favorable effect on production -- withdrawing benefits such as coffee breaks, as well as introducing them, but in many cases the favorable reactions were temporary "Hawthorne effects" (3).

The "impact stabilization" phase (Phase 5) will be difficult to identify as beginning at any particular moment. It may be characterized by a stabilization of attitudes, and by the emergence of various adaptations in behavior, which may include altered ways of using neighborhoods and outdoor spaces, physical changes to homes such as protective walls or outdoor lighting, even to population changeover in certain neighborhoods. The best strategy for identifying arrival at this phase will be comparative analyses of the repeated annual data collections. Comparisons between the 1973 and 1974 data may show such stabilization, or, if impact responses are still in change, a subsequent wave of data collection will identify it. Total stabilization may never arrive. Identification of the regularized period may need relative rather than absolute criteria to separate the period of high awareness and rapid adaptation from that of low awareness and minor behavior change. Patronage may slowly increase (as happened on the Lindenwold Line in Philadelphia) and land uses around the stations may continually change, so that impact responses in some areas may take many years to stabilize. The identification of the stabilization phase will also be complicated by the phased opening of different sections of the BART system over a one year period.

Two control sites have been selected which are several miles from any BART station or track (4). The two control sites were selected by a statistical selection process to be as similar to the more common types of BART site as possible. Data will be gathered on these sites to distinguish whether changes recorded on the BART sites are part of Bay Area trends or attributable to BART.

Systemwide Design

Because of the very large number of variables which must be included in statistical procedures to clarify (1) the impacts of BART as distinct from those of secular events which occurred during the time interval and (2) the ways in which BART impacts are mediated or modified by characteristics of (a) BART itself, and of the (b) physical and (c) social context, large sample data representative of the impacted population are necessary, if generalizable conclusions are to be drawn.

Therefore, as one research strategy, an impact zone was defined as that comprised of residential areas within one mile of BART (5). Of necessity, considering the limited relevant evidence available at this time, the definition of "impact zone" was in large part arbitrary. However, existing evidence and extensive preliminary field observations suggest that the direct environmental effects of BART and many of the secondary environmental effects will be confined to residential areas within one mile of BART.

Moreover, it is anticipated that, insofar as changes reflect BART impact, they will occur in systematic patterns about BART stations and BART lines. Generally, the intensity of BART impacts will depend upon proximity to BART. Effects are anticipated to be greatest upon residential areas immediately contiguous to BART stations and lines; and effects are expected to diminish or decay with distance from the rapid transit facility, most of them dissipating before reaching the outer limit of the impact zone. For each type of BART-impact, a particular "gradient of effect" in relation to BART is hypothesized.

To implement this system-wide research strategy, interview data have been collected from 2541 persons 18 years of age and older who live within one mile of BART, throughout its length (6). Census descriptors of the social context and geographic descriptors of the physical context have been recorded for the residential site of each of these 2541 respondents (7).

The sample size and full coverage of the BART system will allow multivariate analyses to study BART impacts as they vary according to (1) the local configuration of BART, and the local (2) physical and (3) population characteristics. Obviously, the exact size and shape of any BART impact will depend not only upon distance from the facility, but also upon the characteristics of BART in that area; upon the land contour and intervening barriers; upon proximity to other transportation facilities such as freeways, arterials, airports, and railroads; and upon other characteristics of local land use, as well as upon the composition of the local population. It is exactly because of the rich variety of factors which modify the basic relationship between BART impact and distance from BART that a large number of sites, representative of the entire range of possibilities, is requisite to adequate analysis of BART impact.

Selected Site Strategy

The system-wide design has limitations in relation to the study's goals. Even a large sample provides rather thin coverage within a small environmental unit such as a cluster of city blocks which might constitute a neighborhood. In order to understand BART impacts upon the quality of residential areas, it is necessary to make fine-grain studies in a few selected small areas. These detailed, intensive studies are an essential complement to the broad-gauge, representative approach, for full investigation of BART impact upon the residential quality of areas through which it runs.

Consequently, special sites were selected within this interface, some for unique characteristics which will be helpful in understanding BART impact; some because they share many characteristics with other BART sites, and therefore are in some measure representative of a larger number of interface situations. Intensive, detailed observations have been made in these sites of residents behavior, behavior traces, and other environmental variables (8). A supplement of 600 interviews has been conducted with respondents who live within these special sites, to provide more intensive coverage of residents' evaluations of their neighborhoods, which will be used to validate the selection of "environmental indicators."

Twenty-five sites of predominantly residential character immediately around the stations or channels were therefore selected for a supplement of interviews with persons who lived in close proximity to each other and to BART, and for a more detailed physical environmental analysis (9). The most significant variables in the selection of sites have been:

1. station versus channel sites;
2. elevation of the tracks: elevated, grade, subway, tunnel;
3. adjacent transportation channels: freeway, railroads, arterial streets;
4. housing value, density, ethnic character, and income of surrounding residential environment;
5. flat or valley corridors.

Eleven stations and fourteen channel sites have been selected. Each site extends for about one quarter of a mile along the tracks and straddles the tracks for one quarter of a mile on each side.

A Socio-Environmental Impact Model (Figure 1)

The classification systems for environmental impact statements are usually organized by environmental types, e.g., air, water, noise pollution, vegetation, soils, wildlife, visual impacts, while their relative meaning or importance to impacted populations is seldom discussed. The model on which the selected sites study is based considers (A) environmental change and (B) population response.

A. Environmental Change

To assess environmental change, first consider the possible interrelations between two parts of the environment. If we call one the impacting unit, it will have its own ambient conditions, as well as its environmental emissions such as noise, air pollution, overlook points, territorial expansion, or external visual expression. The impacted unit will possess its ambient conditions as well as receiving the impacts from the first unit. The quality and magnitude of the impact will be affected by modifiers such as distance, barriers, reflectors which may increase or dampen the impacts.

In most cases the impacted unit will have its own emissions which will have their impact on the impacter.

In a residential area, hundreds of spatial units are interacting with each other in this form. We shall call these interactions which take place prior to BART's initial construction, general ambient conditions. From this initial set of conditions, the direct and indirect impacts of BART on the locally impacted units constitute the framework for measuring environmental change. Their character will be outlined in the next section.

Meanwhile, besides the impact of environmental change on population response, news media reports, columnists and editorials may affect population responses. If, for instance, the news media report noise intrusions or crime increases in one residential area and attribute them to BART, perceptions and evaluations of all other areas can be affected. For this reason a preliminary media analysis program has

FIGURE 1: A SOCIO-ENVIRONMENTAL IMPACT MODEL

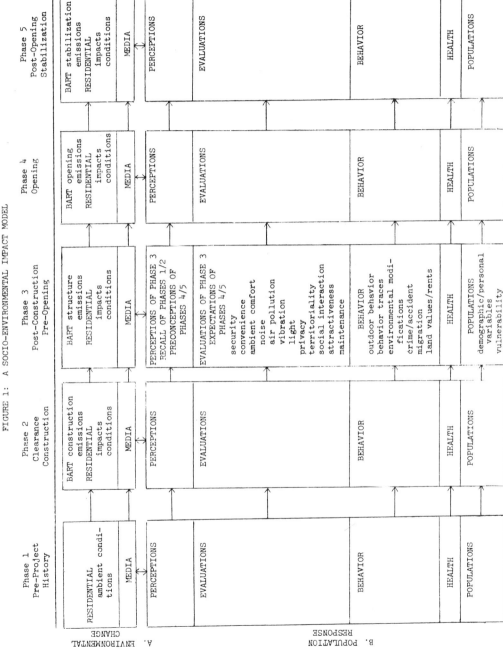

been initiated.

B. Population Response

The effects of these various environmental changes on the residential populations will be assessed through as wide a range of response measures as possible. Changes in perceptions, evaluations, and behavior will be measured. Measurement of changes in physical and mental health were contemplated but temporarily rejected due to their expense. The characteristics of impacted populations will be gathered through interviews.

In the following sections we will illustrate some of the ways we hope to measure environmental and response change by identifying the spatial units of impact and response to be sampled and the measures of impact and response to be related to each other.

The urban environment as used and perceived is an amorphous agglomeration of over-lapping and changing spatial units. It is not a collection of discrete entities, as many neighborhood planning studies would have us believe. The task of identifying spatial units of analysis is therefore a precarious one. Yet certain units are the focus of change and the focus of impact, and for purposes of comparability between sites and between types of impact, units are extremely useful. Since the subject of study is the physical, social, and functional environment, the units of analysis should be based on salient features of each of the three systems. Although physical and behavioral units are not always congruent in the urban pattern (10) (11), nor congruent with perceived spatial elements -- paths, nodes, landmarks, districts, edges (12) -- our strategy will be to focus on units where congruence between the physical, behavioral, and perceived is likely to be high.

Changes may occur in four kinds of impacting units:

1. The BART station and channel areas where existing land uses, transportation facilities, and environments are replaced by BART facilities.
2. Adjacent transportation channels where changes in traffic levels and types related to BART might occur.
3. Adjacent land uses that might change due to BART's presence.
4. Non-BART-related transportation and land use changes occurring in the area such as urban renewal projects, freeway construction, or facilities already in existence prior to BART.

It will be necessary to gather information on the behavioral and environmental conditions of each impacting unit, which will involve collecting detailed traffic and land use information as well as detailed information on BART, the speed and frequency of BART trains, etc. The environmental emissions of the impacting units, including such characteristics as noise and pollution emissions, overlook points, territorial invasion, and visual disruptions should also be assessed.

Within residential areas four types of impacted unit are being considered:

1. Homes: particularly the homes of those being interviewed.

2. Street blocks or some portion thereof: street blocks are clear physical units and are sometimes behavioral units, but they vary in size, which makes comparability difficult and which suggests the need to use standard sized portions of street blocks.
3. Access paths: access across the tracks between neighborhoods and to local facilities may be disrupted by BART; selecting typical access routes from equidistant points (e.g., 100 yards, 200 yards) on either side of the tracks may constitute a comparable measure.
4. Local facilities: the impact of BART on local open space, on commercial facilities, schools, libraries, etc. may affect the everyday quality of the residential environment, and will therefore be considered.

Both ambient conditions in the impacted units and the environmental impacts of BART and other impacting units upon them will be observed.

In addition to assessing change in impacted units, it will be useful for certain measures to sample the impacted zones. These may be identified from the patterns of impact derived from the units, or from measurement at points selected at various distances from the tracks. For instance, measures of noise level or visual intrusion will be taken at varying perpendicular distances from the tracks at different points along the system.

Impacted Populations

The characteristics of the population in each of the selected sites will be analyzed from the interviews and from census data. Their representativeness will be checked against the 2500 random sample interviews. Characteristics such as length of residence, age, occupation of chief wage-earner, education, household composition, marital status, home ownership, household vehicular ownership, household income, and perceived health have been recorded in the interviews.

The intensity of BART's environmental impact on various population groups can be assessed both through environmental measures of change in their residential areas and through the perceived intensity of impact as reported in interviews taken in each area. The vulnerability of different population groups to environmental impact will be assessed through interview questions on such matters as health problems and sensitivity to noise, and through respondents' evaluations of the relative importance of various impacts. Lower-income groups, for instance, may feel more vulnerable to aspects of BART impact which affect employment, income, rent, and neighboring, while affluent groups may feel more vulnerable to BART impacts on comfort, convenience, and aesthetics.

Environmental Concerns

The departing point for assessing environmental impact has been the listing of possible environmental concerns that might be held by various impacted populations with which to evaluate BART's impact. These environmental concerns include:

1. Safety: safety from hazards on the tracks, from construction, from BART cars or the live rail, and from hazards due to traffic or poor sidewalks,

etc. around the stations for pedestrians or automobile drivers; safety from crime in streets or in residences, which may increase or decrease around the stations and rights-of-way.

2. Convenience: auto, pedestrian, and bicycle access to local facilities, particularly transit stops, stores, schools, parks, churches, and the like as well as to friends and neighbors.

3. Ambient comfort:
   a. Noise: noise levels due directly to BART or to indirect effects such as traffic.
   b. Air pollution: fumes, smells, dust, or dirt due to BART or to local traffic.
   c. Vibration: air- or ground-borne vibration due to BART or local traffic.
   d. Microclimate: sun and wind conditions changed by BART structures and parking lots.
   e. Light: day or night lighting levels from BART trains, the shadows from BART structures, the glare from parking lots, or the headlights from local traffic.

4. Privacy: visual intrusion from the BART trains, station platforms, and parking lots; indirect visual intrusion from strangers and through traffic in the area.

5. Territoriality and personal control: degrees of perceived personal control, felt responsibility, and involvement in local streets and neighborhoods and in physical improvements to those neighborhoods.

6. Social interaction: contacts with local friends and relatives, and involvement in community activities which may be affected by severance due to the BART tracks or to BART-related changes in local traffic levels.

7. Attractiveness and maintenance: degree of perceived aesthetic quality, identity, imageability, naturalness, cleanliness, and maintenance of street blocks and neighborhood.

These concerns have been expressed by neighborhood residents in other studies (13), (14), (15), (16). Our task in the BART study will be to see which of these are important to different impacted populations and to assess the valence (positive or negative) and magnitude of BART's impact on such concerns.

Response Measures

We expect to find evidence of response to the above environmental concerns in people's perceptions, behavior, and conscious evaluations of the state of their environment. Response to environmental impact cannot be fully assessed or explained without some understanding of each component of the model. Environmental change may bring about changes in perceptions, in behavior, or in evaluations, and changes in each may be affected by the others. If we only look at attitudinal change -- for instance, in response to noise -- and find relatively little change in a person's verbal attitudes, we may still miss a behavioral change -- such as a move of his bedroom to the other side of the house from the noise source; or we may miss a change in perceptions -- that he can no longer hear certain sounds that he could hear before such as natural sounds -- because ambient noise has risen. Thus, the configuration of his perceived environment is changed, although his attitudes have roughly the same valence as before.

A thorough examination of evaluations, perceptions, and behavior will help explain response to environmental change. For instance, if people feel that a transportation route intrudes on their neighborhood, it will be useful to know what size they perceive their neighborhood to be. There is some evidence that perceived territory differs according to social class (17). Hence, perceived environmental impact may differ by social class under identical environmental conditions. In another case, a person who plans to use BART may feel more friendly towards it in his own neighborhood than if it were useless for him. Differences in attitudes under these conditions would not be understood unless perceptions and expected behavior were known.

Evaluations and perceptions will be obtained from the interviews; various aspects of spatial behavior will be obtained from a variety of sources, including interviews, direct field observation, and secondary data.

Conclusion

The techniques of environmental impact assessment designed for the BART study are aimed at exploring as comprehensive a set of impacts as possible within budget constraints, and, through multivariate analysis, having these environmental measures of impact validated by evaluational, perceptual, and behavioral responses. Validated environmental measures, i.e., those with high weights in the multiple regression analyses, will be confirmed as good indicators of environmental impact; those with low weights will be dropped or considered less important. Some iteration is likely. The validated environmental impact measures from this study can then be applied to other impact situations.

Despite the complexity of the impact measures, the measuring instruments, once developed, should be relatively simple to apply. Interviews take only one hour of time per respondent. The environmental observations are planned to take two people one day each for every 1/4 mile by 1/4 mile residential area, supplemented by another day of office data collection. The behavioral observations took two observers three days for each site where repeated measurements were needed to ensure an adequate sample. Such levels of assessment should not therefore be beyond the capability of most planning operations; and once the measures are validated, it is likely that the numbers of measurements will be reduced.

The fineness of these measures might seem trivial and unnecessary to some people. We would argue that the minutae of the everyday environment is what people often value -- small details and configurations that are quite fragile and can be destroyed easily by large-scale intrusions, but which affect people's sense of well-being in an environment, their sense of privacy, of friendliness, of caring for a piece of territory. If we are concerned with the survival of remote species of wildlife on this planet, we should be as much concerned with the less dramatic but more immediate conditions in the places where people live.

References

(1) Roethlisberger, F. J. and Dickson, W. J., MANAGEMENT AND THE WORKER, Cambridge, Massachusetts, Harvard University Press, 1939.

(2) Krech, David, Crutchfield, Richard S. and Livson, Norman, ELEMENTS OF PSYCHOLOGY, New York, Alfred A. Knopf, 1969.

(3) Roethlisberger, F. J. and Dickson, W. J., MANAGEMENT AND THE WORKER, Cambridge, Massachusetts, Harvard University Press, 1939.

(4) Carp, Frances, Appleyard, Donald, et al, "BART Residential Impact Study: Report on Selection of Control Sites with an Introduction on Control Strategies." In preparation.

(5) Carp, Frances M., Appleyard, Donald, et al, "BART Residential Impact Study Report on Pre-BART Interview Method and Data," BART Impact Studies Interim Report No. 2, Institute of Urban and Regional Development, University of California, Berkeley, October 1972.

(6) Carp, Frances M., Appleyard, Donald, et al, "BART Residential Impact Study Report on Pre-BART Interview Method and Data," BART Impact Studies Interim Report No. 2, Institute of Urban and Regional Development, University of California, Berkeley, October 1972.

(7) Carp, Frances M., Appleyard, Donald, et al, "BART Residential Impact Study: Report on Rationale and Procedures for Collection of Geographic, Census and Secondary Data for the System-wide Strategy." In preparation.

(8) Appleyard, Donald, Carp, Frances M.,et al, "BART Residential Impact Study: Rationale and Procedures for Collection of Behavioral and Environmental Data for the Special Site Strategy." In preparation.

(9) Carp, Frances M., Appleyard, Donald, et al, "BART Residential Impact Study Report on Pre-BART Interview Method and Data," BART Impact Studies Interim Report No. 2, Institute of Urban and Regional Development, University of California, Berkeley, October 1972.

(10) Appleyard, Donald, "Why Buildings Are Known: A Predictive Tool for Architects and Planners" in ENVIRONMENT AND BEHAVIOR, Vol. I, No. 2, December 1969, pages 131-156.

(11) Steinitz, Carl, "Meaning and the Congruence of Urban Form and Activity" in JOURNAL OF THE AMERICAN INSTITUTE OF PLANNERS, Vol. XXXIV, No. 4, July 1968, pages 233-248.

(12) Lynch, Kevin, THE IMAGE OF THE CITY, Cambridge, Mass., M.I.T. Press, 1960.

(13) Appleyard, Donald and Lintell, Mark, "The Environmental Quality of City Streets: The Residents' Viewpoint" in JOURNAL OF THE AMERICAN INSTITUTE OF PLANNERS, Vol. XXXVIII, No. 2, March 1972, pages 84-101.

(14) Michelson, William, MAN AND HIS URBAN ENVIRONMENT: A SOCIOLOGICAL APPROACH, Reading, Mass., Addison-Wesley Publishing Co., 1970.

(15) Wilson, Robert L.,"Livability of the City: Attitudes and Urban Development" in URBAN GROWTH DYNAMICS IN A REGIONAL CLUSTER OF CITIES, Chapin, F. Stuart, Jr., and Weiss, Shirley F., New York, John Wiley and Sons, Inc., 1962, pages 359-399.

(16) Lansing, John B., et al, "Planned Residential Environments," Prepared for the U.S. Department of Transportation, Bureau of Public Roads, Survey Research Center, Institute for Social Research, Ann Arbor, 1970.

(17) Orleans, Peter, "Urban Experimentation and Urban Sociology" in Science, Engineering, and the City. A symposium sponsored jointly by the National Academy of Sciences and the National Academy of Engineering, Washington, D.C., National Academy of Sciences, 1967, pages 103-117.

FIVE   DESIGN LANGUAGES AND METHODS

Chairman: Charles H. Burnette, AIA, Philadelphia, Pa.

Authors: Charles H. Burnette

               Geoffrey Broadbent, "Methodology In The
                   Service of Delight"
               Peter D. Eisenman, "Notes On Conceptual
                   Architecture II A"
               Mario Gandelsonas, "Semiotics As A Tool
                   For Theoretical Development"
               Kenneth J. Hiebert, "The Opposition Of Images
                   As A Means In Developing Sign-Symbols For
                   Visual Communications"
               J. Christopher Jones, "Designing A Response
                   To The Whole Of Life?"
               Richard I. Krauss, "The Design Process: What
                   Data Means"
               Chris McDonald, "Complementary Symbol Systems"
               Thomas P. Moran, "The Cognitive Structure
                   Of Spatial Knowledge"
               Philip Thiel, "On The Discursive Notation
                   of Human Experience And The Physical
                   Environment"

DESIGN LANGUAGES AS DESIGN METHODS

Charles H. Burnette, Dean
School of Architecture
University of Texas at Austin
Austin, Texas 78712

Abstract

An overview of the papers presented in the EDRA4 Symposium on Design Languages and
Methods is offered which notes a switch in reference from methodological models
spawned by industry and war to those of the more humanistic disciplines. The
distinction between design language and design methods is noted as is the need for
their integration to augment natural problem solving thought. The use in design
of dialectic ideas drawn from linguistics is discussed and the implications for
design of computer models of spatial experience based on the simulation of thought
is suggested.

Introduction

The invited papers assembled in this section all address issues related to the
manner and means by which information is organized, expressed and brought to
bear on problems of environmental design. However, the intention behind their
collection is to suggest that there is a significant reorientation now underway
in thinking about the design process, an orientation characterized by a shift
from conceptual and methodological models spawned by the needs of industry and
war to those that are inherently more humanistic and relevant to the broader concerns of environmental design.

The references for earlier models of design method, drawn primarily from the
disciplines of operations research and systems engineering, were heavily biased
by single variable optimization, dollar valued cost-benefit analysis, binary and
heirarchical decision models and other concepts consistent with the narrowly
focussed problems for which they were developed. Having been found wanting, perhaps as much because of the values attached to their success as by their uneasy
fit to problems of environmental design, conceptual modesl from these early sources
are giving way to those from more broadly oriented humanistic disciplines such as
psychology, linguistics, communication and art itself. While they explore concepts drawn from these more humanistic disciplines, environmental designers are
also beginning to come to grips with the actual context of need with which they
are primarily concerned. Indeed, current rethinking of the issues raised by
Design Method may be characterized as a recognition of the problems inherent in
the representation of the content of design on the one hand and the involvement

of the designer and his client with the process of designing on the other.
Both of these issues have risen from the actual needs of designing.

They also underline the distinction between the content of design and its conduct;
between that which is fundamentally a description of the "state" of a situation
and that which describes the way one state is transformed into another; that is,
between Design Languages and Design Methods. Thus Design Languages is understood
as referring to systems for representing and communicating the content of designs,
while Design Methods describe the processes by which this content is handled or
transformed.

The failure to make appropriate use of this distinction between content and method
may have contributed substantially to the recent confusion in design method as well
as to the failure to perceive the utility for designing of theoretical work related to architectural representation and meaning. For example, many people have
taken Christopher Alexander's renunciation of heirarchical organization in "A City
is Not a Tree"(1) to be a refutation of design method rather than what it was, a
recasting of the descriptive representation on which method should operate.
Similarly, his recent preoccupation with behavioral information as content for a
design language available to any user does not deny the need for some process for
the synthesis of these partial descriptions.

New Orientations

It is significant that while some investigators, like Alexander, have refocussed
on questions of Design Language(2), others have focussed on methods and strategies
relatively independent of their content. A case in point is the paper by Christopher Jones, "Is Designing A Response to the Whole of Life?" which makes use of
a strategy of random choice applied to a field of potentially relevant information.
Such a methodological device is as rationally purposeful as any other. Its goals
are simply different and its value in a given context depends on the problem and
the consequences of its use. As a strategy for solving problems, however, random
choice is relatively inefficient(3) as it is dependent for its success on the
number of trials, the content and the scope of the field of choice over which it
operates. While more efficient strategies are finding their way into design as
the algorithms and subroutines of computer based processing of design information,
their integration into a general system for design has floundered largely due to
a failure to find an adequate system of representation; one which augments the
normal functioning of human thought and communication in design. (4) (5)

In general, architects and design researchers are only now beginning to examine
the representational processes and needs as they occur during actual design problem
solving. Richard Krauss, who has carefully studied design activity (6), describes

its exploratory, recursive and constructive nature in his paper, "The Design Process: What Data Means." In his argument for practical, intelligible methods, expressible in the users terms and extendable by him, Krauss seems to suggest a language like organization for design in which both the content and the operation are transformable as well as transferrable within certain norms of communication and usage.

The prospect of achieving an integrated language of design is complicated by the inherent limitations of symbolic notation as Chris McDonald so ably shows in his paper on "Complimentary Symbol Systems." Nevertheless, natural languages such as English offer provocative models in which both content and operations are integrated. The semantic, syntactic and pragmatic aspects of such languages, as well as the data, routines and executive controls of computer processing, are suggestive regarding how this integration might be organized for design.(7)

However, architects and design researchers are only just beginning to explore the implications of such linguistic ideas. For example, the technique of the structural anthropologist (8) and the linguist, in which a corpus of observed communications is subsequently analyzed to produce a systematic description relating significant elements and their use, has apparently not been employed in the study of design method. Yet, as Geoffrey Broadbent points out in his paper, "Methodology in the Service of Delight," there are certain modes, certain general patterns of thought which are recurrent in design. As he indicates, once recognized, these strategies may be used to describe or to constitute a design method. As units of comparative synthesis between one visual image and another, such design strategies are not without similarity to rhetorical and poetic devices in verbal languages. As such, they seem potentially more valuable as guides for the modeling of useful operations in designing than, for example, the listing of elements and their relations in a matrix. This seems so primarily because they stand as dialectic units richer in scope and flexibility, while at the same time more practical in guiding synthesis than the binary relationships of a matrix with its verbal elements, arbitrary relationships and unspecified scope.

The power of a visual dialectic approach as a formal method of design is suggested by Ken Hiebert in his paper,"The Opposition of Images as a Means in Developing Sign Symbols for Visual Communication." This use of a semantically rich qualifying image to transform the background understanding or syntax provided by a context image directly integrates content and method. The forms are the content and their opposition is the method.

In "Notes on Conceptual Architecture IIA," Peter Eisenman extends this discussion of a dialectic use of dual images to the spatial environment, pointing out that the syntactical structure there is not given simply in perception (one knows of

the environment behind and out of sight) (9) and direct perception is thus qualified in the mind by unseen but acquired and perhaps even archetypal organizations.
While this is true, the visible rhythms of the spatial environment, the proportional markings of a surface syntax may be deliberately played against one another
to confound the eye and the mind alike as the recent work of Michael Graves demonstrates.(10)

A greater scope for the consideration of oppositional ideas in design is suggested
by Mario Gandelsonas in his paper on "Semiotics As a Tool for Theoretical
Development." He notes that one of the functions of language is to preserve and
communicate understandings. This provides a stable context against which the
arbitrary play of theory can be meaningful and potentially creative.

While the methodological use of dialectic ideas is of interest in the study of
Design Method, and is suggestive of how visual imagery might serve to organize
units of thought, the question of how such units might be represented and related
remains.

In his paper "On the Discursive Notation of Human Experience and the Physical
Environment," Philip Thiel explores the problem of the symbolic description of
environmental structure experienced over time.

Tom Moran goes on to demonstrate that a coding of environmental experience relative to a path can be given an operational form for computer simulation. He gives
an explicit and dynamic form to the dialectic idea that the appropriate units of
design knowledge are not static facts but rather context dependent actions.How-
ever, the great importance for design method of his paper, "The Cognitive Structure of Spatial Knowledge," is that it demonstrates the possibility of modeling
design as the mental simulation of the experience of space in time. Architects
have long been familiar with the process of visualizing space in order to simulate an experience of it in their own mind in order to assess its design. That
this abstract modeling process might be made explicit and become transferrable
and transformable within some common usage is a revolutionary idea for design
method and language alike, yet one being rapidly developed in computer sciences.
(11) (12)

It is one with the potential to deal with the problems of spatial representation
in a manner compatible with human thought processes in problem solving and design.
(13)

References

(1) Alexander, Christopher, "A City is Not a Tree," ARCHITECTURAL FORUM, April
    and May, 1964.

(2) Alexander, Christopher; Ishkawa, Sara; Silverstein, Murray, A PATTERN LANGUAGE WHICH GENERATES MULTI SERVICE CENTERS, Center for Environmental Structure, 2701 Shasta Road, Berkeley, California, 1968.

(3) Bruner, Jerome; Goodnow, Jacqueline and Austin, George, A STUDY OF THINKING, New York, John Wiley, 1965, p. 85.

(4) Negroponti, Nicholas, THE ARCHITECTURE MACHINE, Cambridge, MIT Press, 1970.

(5) Feigenbaum, Edward and Feldman, Julian, COMPUTERS AND THOUGHT, New York, John Wiley, 1965.

(6) Krauss, Richard, "Improving Design Decisions: Recommendations For a Computer System for Use by the British Government," in William J. Mitchell ENVIRONMENTAL DESIGN: RESEARCH AND PRACTICE 2, University of California at Los Angeles, January 1972.

(7) Burnette, Charles, AN ORGANIZATION FOR COMPUTER AIDED COMMUNICATION IN ARCHITECTURE, #69-21-327, Ann Arbor, University Microfilms, 1969.

(8) Levi Strauss, Claude, STRUCTURAL ANTHROPOLOGY, Garden City, New York, Doubleday, 1967.

(9) Ittleson, William, THE PERCEPTION OF THE LARGE SCALE ENVIRONMENT, New York Academy of Sciences, April 13, 1970.

(10) Carl, Peter, "Towards A Pluralist Architecture, PROGRESSIVE ARCHITECTURE, February 1973, p. 82.

(11) Reitman, Walter, COGNITION AND THOUGHT, New York, John Wiley, 1965.

(12) Feigenbaum, Edward, "Information Processing and Memory," in Donald Norman (ed.) MODELS OF HUMAN MEMORY, New York Academic Press, 1970.

(13) Simon, Herbert, THE SCIENCES OF THE ARTIFICIAL, Cambridge, Massachusetts, MIT Press, 1969.

Geoffrey Broadbent
Head of School of Architecture
Portsmouth Polytechnic
King Henry 1 Street
Portsmouth PO1 2DY

Abstract

This paper discusses the flight from rationality, the social and political reasons which prompted some of the more notable exponents of design method to withdraw from the field. It then discusses the characteristics which all buildings will have in terms of the Hillier, Musgrove, O'Sullivan "four function model", suggesting that even where user-participation extends to eliminating the specialist designer altogether, the creative mechanisms by which 3-dimensional form is generated will remain what they have been throughout history: pragmatic, iconic, analogic, canonic. These provide a basis for analysing the procedures adopted by a highly creative group of building designers: the Taller de Arquitectura of Barcelona, whose working methods enable many people, including non-architects, to participate in the design process.

Introduction

Asked some time ago to write a "state of the art" piece on design methods for Perspecta 15, I was tempted to reply: "There is nothing to say; design method is dead". (1) It certainly seemed so at the time, especially as some of its major exponents had withdrawn from the field, stating fairly potent reasons for doing so.

These were rooted in that drift from rationality which seems to have permeated Western cultural life in the last five years or so. With the vogue for "participation" the belief that any attempt by the "expert" - the artist designer - to foist his views on the long-suffering public should be strenuously resisted, and the means by which he does it suppressed. Design methods, in this view, formed part of that foisting mechanism.

The Nature of Buildings

But whoever actually does the design, however democratic the procedures by which a design is achieved, the finished building actually will display certain characteristics which were outlined by Hillier, Musgrove and O'Sullivan at EDRA 3.(2) These may be summarised as follows:-

Any building whether we like it or not, and whether the designer(s) intend(s) it to or not, will:-
1. Enclose spaces for certain human purposes. The actual division of spaces may facilitate or inhibit specific human activities, it may also provide security.
2. Modify the external climate thus providing conditions in which human beings may be more or less comfortable in visual, thermal and actual terms.
3. Act as a system of signs or symbols into which people may read meanings
4. Modify the values of the materials from which it is built, the land on which it stands and possibly of the adjacent properties.

314

At one level, these are mere truisms, yet they do provide a useful check list against which the designers' ordering of priorities can be assessed, thus forming a basis for the criticism of buildings in design and of completed buildings.

And even if this "four-function model" like most so-called theories of architecture, is merely a polemic, it describes very effectively, the characteristics which some of us think architecture <u>ought</u> to have.

Modes of Designing

It may be, however, that the nearest we shall ever get to a "theory" of architecture will be a theory of design-behaviour which predicts - with probabilities - the ways in which architects, or anyone else who tries to generate 3-dimensional built form will act whilst they are actually trying to design. Certain mechanisms <u>seem</u> to have been used, in this context, by designers throughout history; starting long before there were any professional architects. I have described these elsewhere(3)(4)(5) and can only summarise them here:

<u>Pragmatic design</u> - in which materials are used, by trial-and-error, until a form emerges which seems to serve the designers' purpose. Most forms of building seem to have started in this way. Mongait (6) illustrates an early example; a mammoth hunter's tent excavated at Pushkari near Novgorod-Seversk made from the available building materials: some rather spindly trees, some small stones and after that the bones, tusks and skins of the mammoths; all that was left after the meat had been eaten. The site, as excavated, suggested that the mammoth hunters had built three interlocking tepee-like frames from the available timbers and perhaps from the mammoth tusks. They had then laid mammoth skins over this framework, weighting down the edges with stones and the bones. So the most improbable of materials were used to form a very effective shelter; the available resources were allowed to determine the form. We still tend to use this mode of designing whenever we have to use new materials, as in the case, say, of plastic air houses and suspension structures. It is only very recently, after two decades of pragmatic design, that theoretical bases for the design of such structures are beginning to emerge.

<u>Iconic design</u> - in which the members of a particular culture share a fixed mental image of what the design should be "like". Often encouraged in "primitive" cultures by legend, tradition, work-songs which describe the design process (7) by the mutual adaption which has taken place between ways of life and building form - as with the Eskimo's igloo - and by the conventions of craftsmanship which take a long time to learn but, once learned, are difficult to abandon. We still set up icons - such as Bunshaft's Lever House in New York (1952) which became the fixed mental image for a generation of architects and clients as to what office buildings should be like. User-participation is perhaps the most potent mechanism of all for the repetition of design icons.

<u>Analogical design</u> - the drawing of analogies - usually visual - into the solution of one's design problems. This seems to have started with Imhotep (c.2,800 BC) in designing the Step Pyramid complex at Sakkara; given the problem of building, for the first time, in large blocks of stone, he drew visual analogies with existing brick tomb-forms, timber-framed and reed-mat houses, for the overall building forms, with lotus buds or flowers and snakes heads for the decoration, and so on. Analogy still seems to be the mechanism of "creative" architecture, as with Wright's use of water lily forms in the Johnson Wax factory office (1936), his own hands at prayer in the

Madison, Wisconsin Chapel (1950) not to mention Le Corbusier's crab-shell roof of
Ronchamp. These are direct analogies (8). Much 20th century architecture has drawn
on painting and sculpture as sources of analogies, (Constructivism, Purism, de Stijl);
but analogies can also be drawn with one's own body (personal analogy) and with
abstract, philosophical concepts (as in the present preoccupation with indeterminacy).

Analogical design requires the use of some medium such as a drawing, for translating
the original into its new form. The first Egyptian design drawings date from the same
period as Imhotep's pyramid complex and the drawing itself begins to suggest possibilities to the designer. He sets up grids and/or axes to make sure that his drawing
will fit on to the available surface; these "suggest" regularities - symmetries and
rhythms - which had not appeared previously in architecture. Any design analogue -
a drawing, model, or even a computer program, will "take over" from the designers and
influence the way they design.

Canonic design - the grids and axes of these early design drawings took on a life of
their own; it became clear that the second-rate artists could emulate the work of a
master by abstracting from it the underlying systems of proportion. Once this view
had been formed - that art and design could be underpinned by abstract proportional
systems - it received a massive boost from the Greek geometers (Pythagoras) and
Classical philosophers (Plato, etc.) who believed that the universe itself was constructed of cubes, tetrahedra, icosahedra and dodecahedra and that these in turn were
made up of triangles. The Platonic triangles underlay medieval Gothic design (9).
Whilst much 20th century design has been based on similar precepts; it is the basis
of all modular systems, dimensional co-ordination, prefabricated systems building
and so on. New mathematical techniques and computer aids are likely to boost even
further this interest in the abstract Geometry of Environment (see book of that title(10).

Applications
I have shown elsewhere (11) that these four modes of designing; pragmatic, iconic,
analogic and canonic, seem to underlie all the ways in which architectural form has
been, or can be generated. These may be used singly or in combination and, taking
Alexander's point that the most convincing demonstration of a design methodology is
its actual practice, I should like to demonstrate how - without being at all familiar
with the terms, a highly imaginative form of building designers - the Taller de
Arquitectura of Barcelona - have actually developed a methodology which combines them(12).
Only one of the Taller is fully qualified, with a Spanish Licence to practice. The
others include poets, writers, musicians, a sociologist, an economist and so on.

They seek to avoid the bleak sterility of most current mass housing and this has
involved them in a continuing reassessment, at many levels, of what it means to live
in cities, what it is that makes them attractive, how housing can be planned in such
a way that at any moment people can choose between privacy and participation in the
community. All this has been building up to the massive project for a Ciudad en el
Espacio for Madrid, a project which has yet to be realised, although in working
towards it, the Taller have produced some impressive enough results. These include
the Barrio Gaudi, a low cost, high density neighbourhood (1965 to date) at Gaudi's
birthplace, Reus, near Tarragona; Kafka's Castle an apartment hotel behind Sitges
(1966); and La Manzanera, a holiday village at Calpe near Benidorm (1965 to date).
Other projects include Le Cheval de Monaco, their entry for a competition won by
Archigram in 1969; La Petite Cathedrale for the new town of Cergy-Pontoise near
Paris and Walden 7 for the Taller's own site in Barcelona. The last two are in final
stages of planning and will be started on site during 1973.

The Taller's methodology was developed around the Barrio Gaudi design and certain geometric studies (Canonic design), which I shall describe in some detail as a point of reference. Designing seems to have proceeded in the following stages and whilst these were all achieved manually, thos marked (CG) could have been initiated by computer-aided design techniques, especially if som interactive graphic system had been available. The letters, A, C, I and P in the margin indicate Analogic, Canonic, Iconic and Pragmatic approaches to design respectively, whilst the figures 1) 2) 3) and 4) indicate those of the four architectural functions considered at each stage.

Stage 1   Determine plan- forms for the individual dwellings. A Spanish Government
1) limit of 65 square metres per dwelling reduced this effectively to an exercise in
C   the generation of topological permutations with 1, 2, 3 or more bedrooms, kitchen and bathroom, clustered about a central living space. Two sets of plan-permutations were prepared, one with orthogonal and one with diagonal geometry.(CG)

Stage 2 Take the plan forms thus generated and cluster groups of 3, 6 and finally 12
1) dwellings around access courts, giving one set of orthogonal and one set of
C   diagonal clusters. Eliminate plan forms which cannot be so clustered.(CG)

Stage 3 Check clusters against a range of environmental control parameters; that no
2) dwelling should face directly into another one; that the unobstructed view from
C   any window should be at least 60 metres, etc. Eliminate clusters which fail to meet these parameters.(CG)

Stage 4   Evaluate prefabricated building systems in terms of compatibility with
4) agreed plan forms, costs, availability in Spain, etc. Conclude that none is
P   suitable.

Stage 5   Design a prefabricated system with concrete frame, floor slabs, wall
4) panels, staircase, balcony units, etc. Eliminate on grounds of cost.

Stage 6   Design an in-situ system in which concrete frame is compatible with both
4)1)orthogonal and diagonal plan forms, retaining stairs, balconies, etc. in concrete
A/I/P but with walls in hollow tile and brick.

Stage 7 Given that each cluster of dwellings is known to "work" in terms of planning environmental control and structure, the "form" in which these clusters are put together as an overall housing development will be quite arbitrary. Given also
3) that a particular 'life style' has to be rehoused, examine the physical environment in which that life style was formerly held, in sociological, architectural
A/I and poetic terms. Draw formal analogies with that original, incorporating into th new development at the scale of overall layout, building groups (streets, squares), individual buildings and details (roofs, windows, etc.) thus offering those who are to be moved an identifiable sense of "place" within which the old-life style can be reconstructed.

In the methodology for designing the Barrio Gaudi, therefore, the Taller utilised my four modes of designing; canonic design for the initial geometrical exercises, pragmatic design for the structure and their system of environmental checks, analogic design in generating the overall form, iconic design for certain detail and so on.

I could cite half-a-dozen other projects in which the Taller have used my four modes of designing - individually and in combination. Most of these follow a similar procedure; generate a range of possible plan forms as a topological exercise; cluster

these in various ways and eliminate those which can't be clustered; check the
clusters against certain environmental parameters and eliminate those which fail to
meet them. Determine an overall form with reference to local conditions, using
visual and other analogies. At La Manzanera, a "pop fantasy village" near Calpe,
one group of housing derives by analogy from the local vernacular and another,
Xanadu, from the Penon de Ifach, a Gibraltar-like rock standing out in the bay.
La Petite Cathédrale (for Cergy-Pontoise) looks exactly what the name implies - a
whole suburb with shops, schools, parking and housing draped over the form of a
Gothic Cathedral.

Conclusions

Before the Taller demonstrated otherwise, most of us had supposed that three factors
in particular inhibited the exercise of creativity in architectural design, namely
cost, planning, construction or other statutory constraints and - as Alexander would
have it - the exercise of systematised procedures in the management of design. Yet
the Taller use a highly developed methodology which seems to be the key to their
success in bringing non-architects into the building design process.

Some of their procedures are mathematically-based and these lead to the generation of
solutions in such variety that it hardly matters when some of them have to be eliminated. That, of course, results from the checking against various constraints,
structural, environmental and so on, which form an essential part of the Taller's
systematic method. The crucial point is that instead of starting with the constraints and then complaining that they are hamstrung, the Taller start with possibilities and then eliminate those which prove not to be possible. And finally - but
perhaps most convincing of all - the Taller's buildings are quite remarkably cheap.
So, far from inhibiting creativity, their procedures and methods actually encourage
it. Design method therefore is far from dead. It is alive, well, living in
Barcelona and providing some of the most beautiful, habitable and economical
architecture to be had anywhere.

References

(1) Broadbent, G, "The Present State of Design Method Studies" in PERSPECTA 15
(2) Hillier, W R G, Musgrove, J, & O'Sullivan, P., "Knowledge and Design" in
    Mitchell, W J EDRA 3, Los Angeles, 1972.
(3) Broadbent, G. "The Design Process", in Starling, J., ULM REPORTING BACK
    CONFERENCE, Attingham Park, 1967.
(4) Broadbent, G, "The Deep Structures of Architecture, paper for SYMPOSIUM ON
    ARCHITECTURE, HISTORY AND THEORY OF SIGNS, Barcelona, 1972 (conference proceed-
    ings to be published by Collegio de Arquitectura, Barcelona).
(5) Broadbent, G. DESIGN IN ARCHITECTURE, John Wiley & Sons, London & New York, 1973
(6) Mongait, A, L, ARCHAEOLOGY IN THE USSR (trans M W Thompson 1966), Harmondsworth,
    Penguin, 1955.
(7) Alexander, G, NOTES ON THE SYNTHESIS OF FORM, Harvard. University Press, Cambridge,
    Mass, 1964.
(8) Gordon, W.J.J., SYNECTICES: THE DEVELOPMENT OF CREATIVE CAPACITY, Harper &
    Brothers, New York, 1961.
(9) Frankl, P. "Secrets of the Mediaeval Masons", ART BULLETIN XXVII March 1946
(10)March, L. & Steadman, P. THE GEOMETRY OF ENVIRONMENT, RIBA Publications, London
    1970
(11)Broadbent, G. DESIGN IN ARCHITECTURE, John Wiley, London, New York, 1973
(12)Broadbent, G."The Road to Xanadu" article for ARCHITECTURAL REVIEW (forthcoming).

Peter D. Eisenman
Director
The Institute for Architecture and Urban Studies
8 West 40 Street
New York, New York 10018

Abstract

This paper will discuss the problems of the transposition of linguistic analogies
and models to design methods in architecture. Specifically, it will attempt to
show that language and architecture, which seem to be similar modes of communication, are in fact different in one particular aspect. Because of this difference
the use of linguistics models as anything more than an heuristic device in architectural design becomes suspect. This paper will attempt to isolate that aspect
of architectural space which affects communication and meaning in a way which at
present is not able to be modeled either by traditional architectural methods--
history, aesthetics, function--nor by new theories of meaning. In doing so this
paper takes a position against the application of existing linguistic, semiological and communicational models to architecture. Furthermore, it is proposed that
we must develop our own models more related to the actual "stuff" of architecture.
The following is both a position and an introduction to such development in the
context of syntactic or formal concerns.

This paper is intended for two purposes: First it is a critique of existing approaches to architecture using the idea of language or a design language as a
basis. Second it is an outline of my own position, which has evolved parallel to
this critique. Two almost opposite directions in particular may be seen as antecedent to the ideas in this presentation. They concern a fundamental question in
any architecture of the form-meaning relationship. One, more conservative, was
essentially continuing a tradition of German art history developed at the Warburg
Institute in London. While the people involved were essentially art historians,
their influence on the architecture of the 60's through such people as Rudolph
Wittkower and his pupil, Colin Rowe, in England and America, was no less profound.
Another supposedly more innovative direction was concerned with an attempt to
study on a more methodologically rational basis physical design (initially manifested in industrial design) and architecture. The major thrust of the work of
such people at ULM as Tomas Maldonado, Abraham Moles and Giu Bonsieppe can be
seen to be exemplary of this intention. The difference between the two directions might be summarized as follows: the former group was concerned with types
of meaning--with problems of iconography and symbolism; the latter group was concerned with problems about the nature of meaning--with such problems as the
nature of sign systems in the physical environment and with the lack of an agreed
upon sign convention between the form of the environment and the meaning which
accrues to it.

Partly because of a desire for rationality of method and partly because they were involved in an analogous problem, this latter group turned to disciplines outside of architecture and art history: to linguistics and, more specifically, to semiology. These external models were thought to provide not only a more rigorous and even more scientific frame of reference, but also, they were thought to possess characteristics which were analogous to the form-meaning relationship in architecture.

In the 1960's, most of the European manifestations of the use of linguistics and semiology in an architectural context were based on the work of Ferdinand de Saussure, in particular, and more recently on French structuralism in general. The appearance of a book such as Meaning in Architecture, while significant for its mere existence at that time and for its title, which indicates the particular bias of its contributors, is probably more important in that it was, in a way, a signal to the end of a period which expressed an explicit series of preferences characterized primarily in terms of what is excluded from consideration. Fundamental to these preferences was a concern for meaning as opposed to form.

While this is obviously an oversimplified and schematic introduction, it is useful in that it provides a background to the problem of the form-meaning relationship and to the propositions which will be put forward below. Fundamental to my proposal are the following considerations:

1) The elimination of semantic considerations and the focus on syntactics; that is, the consideration of formal elements or regularities seen as a potential system of marks.

2) The understanding that what is perceived--the particular configurations in the built environment--is only one aspect of a more complex phenomenon, that there exists in any environment an underlying structure which ultimately affects communication.

Traditionally in architecture, considerations of form have played an important role. Previously these considerations were basically concerned with aesthetic problems, with the analysis and the design of specific configurations having proportions, size, scale, contrasts of texture, color and light. Beyond this concern for the physical properties of elements there was equally a concern with relationships--sequence, interval, location, etc.--between elements. These concerns are not aesthetic but more appropriately syntactic in that they are concerned with relationships. However, they are syntactic only in what will be called a surface structural sense. For example, a column or an entry facade in itself may be considered as a formal and thus syntactic element. A description of a particular shape, texture and coloration of a column or a facade would provide us with information concerning the actual physical form, which is only the surface structure. Equally, the relationship of a column to a wall--their location, proximity, direction, etc.--which provides information of a syntactic nature is still information regarding the specific or surface configuration. Thus, it can be said that even when architecture was concerned with formal relationships, i.e., syntax, these were relationships of the elements or objects themselves, i.e., shapes, or the relationships between shapes in a specific environment--dimension, size, scale, etc. This was the limit of syntax. But this did not account for another or underlying level--a more complex phenomenon which can be detected in a specific environment.

3)   This underlying structure can be described in terms of a set of <u>conditions</u> and a set of <u>operations</u> which would link this underlying structure with the particular configuration.

A further difference between my proposition and other work being done in syntax is in the nature of the description of this underlying structure. If we analyze the nature of the formal information potential in any specific context we can see first, that there is information which is <u>iconographic</u> and <u>symbolic</u> and comes primarily from cultural sources which are external to the environment. This information seems to be the product of a cultural interpretation of the formal relationships in the specific context. These exist at a real, actual level, where an individual is aware of them through his senses: perception, hearing, touching, etc. But there is another aspect of information affecting this iconographic interpretation which seems to be derived from another level of relationships. These exist in a more abstract sense; they cannot be seen or heard, but they can be known. In attempting to define the nature of this underlying structure one may consider <u>ways</u> in which formal information may be manifest. The first and most obvious is in a relationship to what may be called a <u>notational order</u>. This order seems to be a description of <u>any</u> formal regularities which may be seen in a specific environment. A notation can be made from the <u>actual geometry</u> of any shape. A second way in which formal information is manifest comes not from the actual geometry or from pure physics alone, but rather from two things: one, from the way in which the individual conceives of <u>space and form</u> and two, from the particular way the underlying structure forms relationships in a specific configuration. For example, the idea of forms existing in a state of shear can be said to be information which derives from comparing two sets of formal relationships, <u>an actual condition</u> in relation to <u>some prior condition</u>. A prior condition is a <u>description</u> of certain formal regularities which when conceived of as juxtaposed to produce a relationship with the actual geometry which cannot be marked yet is implied in the environment.

Again, this information does not derive solely from the pure geometry or pure physical facts in the environment alone but both from our capacity to conceive of these geometries in relation to some prior configuration and from the nature of the actual shapes themselves to suggest this prior configuration. While there are many possible combinations of formal regularities in an underlying structural description and while all architecture may have such an underlying structure, only some of these descriptions possess this capacity to be manifest as a prior condition and thus to produce formal information.

This relationship to a prior condition also may affect our use of a space. For example, because of the difference between the conception of an actual configuration and the conception of its relationship to a prior condition, it is possible to conceive of different ways to approach and enter spaces. These ways seem to

be influenced by our conception of this <u>relationship</u> to a <u>prior condition</u>. And
as was said before, while this other information may be given a notation, it does
not derive from the physical fact alone but rather from the capacity of the relationship between actual facts and prior conditions to <u>generate</u> or imply other
interpretations, and also from our capacity to receive this information. It is
possible to articulate this other aspect of the problem by considering the capacity of the individual--using, perceiving and moving in space--to receive certain
information which is present in that space which is other than notational (that
is, it does not derive either from the specific configuration or from the relationship of the specific configuration to a prior condition); to be able to interpret this, and to turn it into mental constructs. This type of information, while
involving the individual, involves him in his purely conceptual or mental capacity
and has little to do with his culture, aesthetic predilections or taste. Again,
this information is not derived from the actual shape but from the information inherent in the <u>relationship</u> between <u>shapes</u>. This second type of information derives
from what we may call a <u>relational</u> order.

4) The two different types of relationships can be modeled by what I have called
   a dual deep structure.

Syntactic information as defined here is not concerned with the meaning which accrues to elements or actual relationships between elements but rather with the
<u>relationship</u> between <u>relationships</u>. It is not information inherent in the actual
environment, but rather it is information received in our mental construct of the
relationship between the actual environment and a conceptual environment. The
primary factor in this type of information is the activity of the underlying level
of formal relationships, previously not brought to any conscious level of formulation but no less present. These relationships exist in what is called here the
<u>deep structure</u>. The syntactic dimension of architecture can be initially conceiv-
ed of as a dual level structure; it is a model which we are imposing on the existing conception of architecture in an attempt to uncover, define and make operative
further relationships which may be inherent in any specific configuration. These
relationships, it will be argued, pre-exist in any environment and also in our
capacity to conceive of them; and, therefore, these relationships provide information to us whether by design or not, or whether we are even conscious of receiving
this information.

5) But there is a further problem which at present cannot be modeled by a dual
   deep structure. It concerns what I will call the <u>virtual</u> nature of architectural space. While the dialectic potential of actual and virtual exists in
   all physical phenomena, its manifestation in architecture is held to be unique.

There is another level of information which seems to exist in any configuration
which is more difficult to systematize. This touches something in the nature of
architectural space which might be considered archetypal. That is, the capacity
of a certain deployment of form and space to suggest a level of formal information which cannot be understood from a marking of the actual geometry alone but
rather is derived both from the implications which are spatially inherent in the
actual geometry and from the capacity of the individual in space to receive this
information.

But the dual deep structure cannot model the nature of architectural space itself. Let us for a moment take another approach in an attempt to build such a model. Consider for a moment architectural space in relation to painterly space and sculptural space in that all three are activities involving physical integers of some kind. In both painting and sculpture there is an inherent dialectic between the observer and the space, which is not initially present in architecture. Whatever real space there is in painting and sculpture, the observer is usually outside of it; his relationship to that space can be considered virtual rather than actual. Thus, any understanding he has of that space, whether perceptual or mental, will always be in a sense conceptual in that he can never experience the actual space.

Now in architecture all experience of the space is actual, and one cannot have a virtual experience per se. Here is a central problem for architecture: It is all real, and our relationship to it is initially actual. Now if one posits that all physical reality has inherent in it a capacity for an opposite or virtual state, because of the capacity of certain spatial relationships to present a potential continuum from actual to virtual, then somehow we must be able to take this factor into account in any model concerned with the generation of architectural space, again, because this dialectic between actual and virtual may be active even if not designed or consciously interpreted. It is precisely because the individual has the capacity not only to perceive and actually walk through the space but to conceive of that space that he will receive information which he will translate into conceptions. Therefore, if an architecture can make one more aware of the actual space, e.g., its actual height, and an individual might from this awareness have a more precise understanding, e.g., why it's high, of the actual space and the information--beyond high, e.g., as a transition, sequence, definition--potentially available in it, then this awareness might be made possible by the presence of an intentional virtual structure. In other words, since there is always the possibility in architecture of a virtual experience as well as a real experience, they both might be predetermined. However, in architecture as opposed to the other plastic arts this virtual condition must be built into architectural space; it does not exist a priori. While these qualities remain latent in any environment, they must be modeled in both a surface and deep structural description. The exact nature of that difference in the space, what causes this difference, how it relates to a set of formal regularities in a deep structure, and what are the capacities in the environment in certain juxtapositions to produce this difference is in the nature of work to be developed in the future. It is enough here to merely point to this difference.

6) This initial description instead of being considered as a single deep structure is now thought of as a deep dual structure.

From these two deep structures, each with an internal dual structure, it is hoped that one can create a condition of conceptual and perceptual parity through the acknowledgement of this deep structure in the specific environment. The deep structures will be raised to a level of consciousness and therefore contribute more precisely to a potential understanding of the environment. Again the production of this state of parity remains a problem of transformation.

Mario Gandelsonas
Fellow, Co-Director of the Generative Design Program
The Institute for Architecture and Urban Studies
8 West 40 Street
New York, New York 10018

Abstract

In recent years, many theories based on semiotic models have been developed in architecture. But in comparison to similar developments in other fields, these
theories have not led to positive results in architecture except in a few isolated
cases. First, architects have limited knowledge of linguistic and semiotic concepts and transfer them to architecture. Second, and more important for articulating the position to be presented here, when these models are transferred no distinction is made between what we shall call ideological theories and theory in
a more strict sense. It will be my position that the clarification of these points,
especially the second one, must precede any work of general theoretical development
and in particular the development of a semiotic theory of architecture.

Introduction

In the last ten years linguistics and semiotics have played a fundamental role in
the field of the so-called social sciences: anthropology, psycho-analysis, aesthetics and philosophy have been, among others, the disciplines most profoundly
influenced by linguistics. By adopting it as a model there is an acceptance of
linguistics as a "pilot science." In this role linguistics have been used as the
basis for theoretical development in these disciplines.

Architecture has also used linguistic and semiotic models, but with the exception
of a few isolated cases this use has not led to positive results: first, because
architects have limited knowledge of linguistic and semiotic concepts and, consequently, about their transference to architecture. Second, and the more important
for articulating the position to be presented here, when these models are transferred no distinction is made between what we shall call ideological theories and
theory in a more strict sense. It will be my position that the clarification of
this point must precede, in general, any work of theoretical development and in
particular the development of a semiological theory in architecture.

The Confusion between Communication and Signification

Part of the problem we find in recent semiotic developments in architecture stems
from the fact that semiotic concepts, not distinguished from "similar" concepts
belonging to other theoretical fields dealing with communication and meaning--
semiotics, communication theory and traditional semantics--are used and confused
in a random and arbitrary fashion. This can be seen in the existing confusion in
the use of the notions of communication and signification, which produces a situation where there is no clear definition and distinction made between communications

theory and semiotics seen as a theory of signification. If semiotics is to become an important tool for the development of architectural theory it would seem important to clarify the distinction between the notion of communication and the notion of signification, and their particular relevance for architecture.

In the definition of semiotics given by Saussure[1] the notion of communication does not appear, for the precise reason that it is a different distinct phenomenon from signification. The study of the communication phenomenon, analyzing how signs are sent and received, differs from and should not be confused with a study which analyzes "what the signs consist of" or "what laws determine them."[2]

The notion of communication in fact is related to a characteristic universal to any system of signs: all systems of signs are used for communication between individuals. In contrast, the notion of signification depends on the particular internal structure within a given cultural system, such as that given to architecture, cinema or literature. The particular structure of such cultural phenomena stems from their existence as social institutions and not from their use by individuals. In architecture, for example, the particular signification of, say, Japanese buildings is related not to their functional use, which is similar to the use of buildings in other cultures--i.e., shelter, gathering, etc.--but to the internal structure of an architectural system of signs determined by the social and cultural context. In other words, where the notion of communications is related to the function and use of a system, the notion of signification indicates an internal relation within a given system; communication is concerned with the use and effects of signs, while signification is concerned with the nature of signs and the rules governing them.[3] This difference implies, firstly, that even if we understand the factors which are part of the process of communication, we still may not know anything about the nature of signification itself; secondly, that since signification depends on the specific nature of the different systems of signs, it has to be redefined for each different semiotic system according to the way its internal structure works and according to what makes each internal structure different. This, then, is precisely the subject matter of semiotics--to consider the different semiotic systems as devices which produce signification and to determine how this signification is produced.

Theory and Ideology

To clarify our position about the role of semiotics in the development of a theory of architecture I shall present a set of propositions concerning the nature of the relationships between theory and ideology. This is a problem common to any science and for that reason should be redefined in the specific case of architecture before any theoretical work may begin. It is possible to say first, that any scientific theory seen as the production of knowledge is built on the basis of a dialectical relationship with an ideology--that is, on the basis of an ideology and at the same time radically opposing it. It is this dialectical relationship which separates scientific theory from ideology. Second, ideology functions as an obstacle in the production of knowledge.[4]

Ideology can be seen as a certain set of representations and beliefs--religious, moral, political, aesthetic--which refer to nature, to society and to life and activities of men and women in relation to nature and society. Ideology has the

social function of maintaining the structure of society by inducing people to accept in their consciousness the place and role assigned to them by this structure.
Thus, even if ideology gives a knowledge of the world, it is a certain knowledge,
limited and distorted by this function.[5] Ideology in a way alludes to reality,
but it only offers an illusion of this reality. Architectural ideology represents
this same kind of distortion. In this sense it can be seen as the summation of
Western architectural "knowledge" in its entire range, from commonplace intuition
to sophisticated "theories" and histories of architecture. In this context ideology has explicitly claimed to serve the practical needs of society by ordering and
controlling the built environment. Nevertheless, we hold that the underlying function of the ideology is in fact the pragmatic one of serving and preserving both
the structure of society in Western social formations and architectural practice as
part of it. At the same time it works as an obstacle to real knowledge by preventing both the constitution of Theory and its development. Its function is not to
produce knowledge but to actively set itself against such production.

In opposition to this ideology we propose that a theory of architecture is necessarily placed outside ideology. This theory would describe and explain the relationship between society and the built environment of different cultures. Theoretical work in this more restricted sense uses as its raw material no real or
concrete "things" but beliefs, notions and concepts regarding those "things."
These notions can be transformed by means of certain conceptual tools such as abstract models, the result being knowledge of these "things."[6] Architectural
ideology, considered as part of a given society and culture, provides part of the
raw material. It is our belief that semiotics might provide the conceptual tools.

The relationship between theory and ideology might be viewed as a continuous struggle where ideology defends a type of knowledge whose major effect is the preservation of existing social systems and their institutions, rather than the explanation
of reality. There have been many examples in history of this relationship. Ptolemy's theory of the universe, which corroborated biblical texts, was supported by
the Church for centuries against any other models which could explain more accurately the same reality. In opposition Copernicus' theory was the result of a
conceptual mutation of such an ideology. He literally destroyed Ptolemy's notion
of geocentrism, and he separated his theory from this ideology by "projecting the
earth into the skies."[7] In return the condemnation of Copernicus by the Church
was the attempt to suppress a new conception where man was no longer the center of the world, and the Cosmos was no longer ordered around him. The theological ideology, which originally opposed the Copernican conception. finally absorbed
it by re-accommodating the theological structure. In this process of dialectical
relationship between theory and ideology two different stages must be distinguished: the first is that of productive transformation when the ideology is initially
transformed to provide a theoretical basis; the second, that of methodological reproduction when the theory is developed as an entity separated from ideology. In
this sense, Copernicus' studies correspond to the first stage, where the theoretical work consist essentially in the subversion of a given ideology.

In architecture, we have yet to see a "Copernicus" to introduce the first stage of
theoretical explanation. Indeed we have only recently begun to perceive first the
need to analyze the relationships between theory and ideology and second the

potential power of semiotics as a tool for developing theory.

The specific form of the relation between theory and ideology in architecture can be seen through the ambiguities created by the fact that some architectural ideologies have had a more or less systematized appearance, which has been emphasized through the title of "theory." In recent years this ambiguity has been accentuated in several pseudo-theoretical developments, by "using" models from different fields such as mathematics, logic, behaviorism or philosophy. These models are applied introducing a superficial order but maintaining the ideological structure inasmuch as this introduction of theoretical models is determined by an objective which is to solve technical problems rather than by the production of descriptive-explicative theories as an activity in itself.(8)

This introduction of models from other fields, which has been called ideological consumption, creates an illusion of theory but only prevents its development.(9) In this paper we won't discuss this problem. Instead we will discuss the role of semiotics as a tool for the development of theory.

Semiotics as a Tool for Theoretical Development

Semiotics, the theory of the different systems of signs, is considered to be only a first stage towards a future general theory of ideologies. Semiotics was conceived simultaneously but separately by both Peirce and Saussure. Ignoring each other's work, they established the possibility of semiotics as a science of signs. Peirce elaborated a logical structure by classifying the world and thought in different categories of signs, which are defined by their role of representing, taking the place of another thing, evoking it as its substitute. These signs are seen as linked between themselves in endless chains within a unique and global system.(10) Saussure contributed to semiotics by postulating the notion of a plurality of systems of signs or semiotic systems and by adding that natural language has to be considered as one of the various semiotic systems. This thesis implies that signs function in a different way, according to the systems they belong to, that semiotics must establish the differences and similarities between systems of signs and that semiotics must investigate the status of language among the different systems of signs.(11)

From this constitutional period up to now different semiotic models have been developed in different fields; both the positive and negative aspects of these developments have been widely discussed.(12) It has been pointed out that in particular, the fields of literature, painting and architecture demonstrated the negative aspects. And these are precisely the fields where the difference between theory and ideology has not been acknowledged. As a result of this attitude most of these works were considered as mere terminological substitutions that only maintained and sometimes even reinforced existent ideologies.

In my opinion, in the first step of a theoretical development in architecture we must use semiotic concepts as "negative" conceptual tools; that is, semiotic concepts should be used for a critique of architecture as an ideology. As an example of this critical work we will refer to the important semiotic concept of "arbitrariness," which in my approach has the role of beginning the transformation of architectural ideology.(13) We must remember that in Saussure's procedure this concept has a similar role, as a tool to oppose and criticize the ideological conception of language as representation. This thesis of arbitrariness enables Saussure to do away with the representative thesis about the nature of language.

In traditional semantics meaning itself is considered inherent to the word.(14) For Saussure words only take meaning according to their place within language considered as a semiotic system. On the other hand, Saussure is opposed to the thesis of "inherent meaning," where the "meanings" of the components of language mirror their content--that which they represent.(15) Language he sees as a system of signs, structured upon an internal, arbitrary relationship not determined by thought but the result of a social "contract."

Because he understands language as a system not determined by its content, he establishes the conditions for the definition of an autonomous theoretical object of linguistics: the "langue." The importance of arbitrariness in language rests not only with the notion itself but with the introduction of socio-cultural hypotheses in linguistics that replace the "naturalistic" hypothesis.

The concept of arbitrariness has not yet been introduced in semiotic theories of architecture just as the distinction between traditional semantics and semiotics has never been made in architecture. Traditional semantics only makes explicit an implicit conception of meaning which has served as a basis for architectural ideology from classical treatises to the more modern functionalist approaches. In the sense of traditional semantics, objects in the environment have been understood to have inherent meaning. A traditional semantic conception therefore only reinforces and maintains architectural ideology, functioning as an obstacle for the production of knowledge. This conception of "inherent meaning" is incompatible with the semiotic conception where meaning is determined by a system.

An important semiotic conception such as arbitrariness has never been considered because it conflicts with the "inherent meaning" assumption. To establish the notion of arbitrariness in architecture is also difficult because it contradicts ideological notions such as function or expression. To postulate the linkage between object and meaning as arbitrary implies a denial of the supposed natural linkage between function and the form of the object, which in turn exposes its socio-cultural nature. That is, to attribute a certain function to an architecture fact implies an underlying convention.

The fact that these notions of function and inherent meaning work as an obstacle for introducing the notion of arbitrariness explains, first, why there has been no suggestion of its application to the field of architecture and, second, why, instead, a notion such as "motivation" has been introduced.(16) "Motivation" perpetuates the understanding of the built environment as a result of functional demands or as communicating a meaning which is determined by what has "motivated it." This merely reinforces ideological views which emphasize the natural or causal character of architectural form while denying its conventional and socio-cultural nature. The notion of arbitrariness, showing that the form-function "pair" cannot be explained in itself, indicates the necessity to explain it in terms of its relationships with other "pairs" within a system of conventions. In general, we can say that if any sign would be an imitation of what it represents, one would explain it in itself without having a necessary relation with other signs in a system. But as a sign cannot be explained in itself, the role of semiotic theory is to investigate the nature of this system.

Conclusion

Semiotic investigation in architecture is limited by the fact that it does not acknowledge the relationship between theory and ideology, a problem that is prior to any theoretical development. This limitation can be seen in the failure to recognize theoretical problems such as a) the difference between the system underlying Western architecture and systems underlying other architectures, b) the particular conditions and differences between the production and consumption of architectural "messages" and "discourses" in the context of Western culture, c) the specific nature of the creative aspects of Western architecture which cannot be compared to the selection and combination operations on linguistic repertories or the generation of sentences.

In my opinion, any future task of theoretical development "on" architecture must be based on analyzing the specific form of the battle against architectural ideology which is manifested in the specific difficulties faced by semiotics in the field of architecture.

References

(1) De Saussure, Ferdinand (1915) COURSE IN GENERAL LINGUISTICS, McGraw-Hill, New York, 1966.

(2) Ibid.

(3) Valesio, P. "Toward a Study of the Nature of Signs," SEMIOTICA III2, Mouton, The Hague, 1971.

(4) Agrest,D., Gandelsonas,M. "arquitectura/Arquitectura," MATERIA (Cuadernos de Trabajo), Buenos Aires, 1972.

(5) Althusser, L. FOR MARX, First Vintage Books, New York, 1970.

(6) Ibid.

(7) Koyre, A. THE ASTRONOMICAL REVOLUTION, Ithaca, Cornell, 1969.

(8) Agrest, D. EPISTEMOLOGICAL REMARKS ON URBAN PLANNING MODELS (lecture),I.A.U.S. New York, 1972.

(9) Agrest, D., Gandelsonas, M."Semiotics and Architecture: Ideological Consumption or Theoretical Work,"to be published in OPPOSITIONS 1, IAUS, New York,1973.

(10) Peirce, C.S., Buchler,J., ed. PHILOSOPHICAL WRITINGS OF PIERCE, Dover, New York, 1955.

(11) Benveniste, E. "Semiologie de la Langue," SEMIOTICA I 1, Mouton, 1969.

(12) Kristeva, J. "Le Texte Clos," LANGAGES 12, Didier-Larousse, Paris, 1968. Scheffer, J.L. review of Marin, L. "Elements pour une Semiologie Picturale," SEMIOTICA IV 4, Mouton, 1971.

(13) Gandelsonas, M. "Un Enfoque Teorico de la Arquitectura," SUMMA 35, Buenos Aires, 1971.

(14) Lyons, J. INTRODUCTION TO THEORETICAL LINGUISTICS, Cambridge University Press, 1968.

(15) Ducrot, O., Todorov, T., DICTIONNAIRE ENCYCLOPEDIQUE DES SCIENCES DU LANGAGE, Seuil, Paris, 1972.

(16) Agrest, D., Gandelsonas, M. "Semiotics and Architecture," op. cit.

THE OPPOSITION OF IMAGES AS A MEANS IN DEVELOPING SIGN-SYMBOLS FOR VISUAL   5.4
COMMUNICATIONS

Kenneth J. Hiebert
Professor of Graphic Design
Philadelphia College of Art

Abstract

A method of research in the development of visual sign-symbols utilizing opposing
images has been developed at several schools of design, notably the School of Design
(AGS) in Basle, Switzerland (1) the Graphic Design graduate program at Yale University and the Philadelphia College of Art. The goals of this research are to obtain
maximum potential from the visual in those areas where the visual is particularly
effective: the formal symbolization of salient, primary qualities of an idea. By
searching for such essential qualities in a sign-symbol, an abstract form is developed which presents an idea instantly and in an overall way. While an effort is made
to supplant the verbal to the extent possible, the approach tries to delineate those
areas where verbal and visual each perform best.

Introduction

This approach utilizes programmatic means (2) to develop the message content of the
abstract symbols. This involves finding expressions which are polar opposites and
is accomplished by an inductive process of writing and sketching the ideas that must
be conveyed clearly in a communication. A deductive-reductive approach is then
employed to reconcile the specific message requirements. Great stress is placed on
the recognition of good answers, some of which may be inadvertent spin-offs of the
reconciliation process. This places the designer in the role of perceiver. As such
he goes beyond his role as programmer to find additional means to energize the form
by further concentrating or differentiating it.

Highly abstract sign-symbols stand in contrast to illustrations: illustrations
tolerate a greater measure of error in symbolizing and a greater degree of super-
fluity. The complementary relationship between words and pictures is an assumption
in illustration, and the process of receiving messages depends on a deciphering
process rather than visual recognition alone.

In fact, all of the examples shown function as illustrations in the context of this
paper because they are used to make a point described in verbal terms. They serve
to amplify a verbally stated idea and would function very differently if encountered directly. (3)

As has been stated, the basis for these studies is a programmatic thinking process,
usually both verbalized and visualized, which attempts to identify opposite, generic
forces which characterize the subject of a communication. These are converted to
visual equivalents which provide the syntactical structure within which appropriate
oppositional characteristics are made visible. The image which evolves is considered good if a tension (4) between opposing images is apparent and an apparent movement
between them is found in the sense indicated by the following oppositions:

syntax-related	semantic-related
pattern	pattern disruption
convention	invention
generality	uniqueness
structure	detail
latent	apparent
ground	figure
universal	particular

The interaction of two opposing meanings requires that the contrast must be perceived immediately. To achieve this a good sign is required and this is composed of a good pattern and a signal pattern mutation. (5)

The criteria for pattern goodness have been stated by W.R. Garner (6): a. the more visible the redundancy which characterizes the pattern, b. the faster the response, and c. the more accurate the response, the better the pattern. Further, "good patterns have few alternatives" when measured against these criteria. Our research has tended to substantiate this: major alternatives which can be perceived quickly and accurately are few. E.g., rapid scanning of a visual field to discern its organization is reliable when it must discern only a few gradients, preferrably placed in a quasi-geometric progression. The following number sequence can be perceived immediately and consistently well without counting (7): one, two, three, several, many.

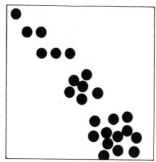

Our experience of the value of simple, tree-like, logical patterns of organization, of which the number progression is an example, is in contrast to our desire to produce images with the information-rich characteristics of the semi-lattice. (8) Since the semi-lattice presents a greater number of subsets, it also presents greater latitude for differentiation. The cross-functioning of syntax image and its qualifying semantic image is more durable and more complex if this occurs in a variety of ways.

This is true even of a simple image: a block letter i lacking a definite field relationship is contrasted with the same letter within a field. The i form placed in a field consists not only in a relationship between its parts, but a relationship between the positive form and the negative space simultaneously. If the size, shape and placement of these elements is guaged to produce a condition of tension, a

rapid flux between the parts and the sets is perceived: an elementary kinetic has
been presented. This condition is important for communication and memorability; it
is also important when forms belonging to the same system are interrelated in
different systems are mixed. Motion within an image tends to facilitate circulation
in and out of it.

Excesses of pattern produce decoration -- or alienation through non-involvement.
Excesses in assertion of the exceptional or disruptive aspects also produce alienation because connections to the known cannot be found.

Pattern excesses are especially a factor in modern technology where the mass production of like units is a commercial necessity and the temptation is strong to let
this necessity be the total rationale for form. (9) In the face of the determining
properties of the image, our tendency is to never accept a purely repetitive pattern,
ipso facto, as a possibility for communication.

This applies not only to physical characteristics of elements, but to redundancy
in the use of symbols where these become progressively trite and impotent through
overuse. Generally overuse seems to come from thinking too much about the original
character of a symbol as remembered and not thinking enough about its new application and how many of the original qualities need to be retained so that the tension
between its pattern, including in this case the repetition through time, and the
new use can result in a vital, new connection.

The following example is from an investigation on the use of an obsolete symbol--
the castle--where the purpose is to achieve a new level of meaning by confrontational
combination with contemporary symbols. A castle form, derived from one of our more
common accesses to it--the chessgame--is used as a consistent syntactical referent.
The fact that the synthesis with the qualifying semantic image in each case points
to a different and surprising interpretation of the castle symbol shows us how empty
our notion of castle is. (The epitome of the emasculation of the castle as symbol
is the appearance of the crown as a tiny embroidered medallion on a sports shirt!)

But symbols are keys to existence. They are the antithesis of harmlessness, emasculation and cuteness. Finding the tension between the symbol as continuity and as

a means to fresh thought is the basic task of visual communication.

There are other contributing, and often inhibiting, factors in the perception of symbols. Style is one of these where one tends to react to the syntax more as an overall look than as a context for the behavior of component figures. Overbearing style tends to generally inhibit communication, but it is very useful for manipulation because it requires less serious perceptual involvement than oppositional images.

In the castle series the definition of constant and changing factors to produce a string of simultaneously coherent and diverse images results perforce in a style. Viewed in isolation and large scale on the screen the style characteristic is less important; in the publication where the same images are a ganged into a language matrix, the overall style becomes more important and the potency of single images diminishes. Contrasted with this are pairs and groups of three where certain juxtapositions produce image reinforcement. The perception of style may be linked with pattern excess.

The problem of defining the relation between tired or conventional symbols and
cliche content to produce a new image is further demonstrated in a sign-symbol design
for the Center for Planning, Design and Construction in Philadelphia. It is possible
to identify three different aspects of the organization:

1. its function as a centralized agency,
2. its activities scope:
   planning, design, construction
3. its member groups.

Any one or combinations of these would be useful for identification. Since the
process of interaction among the organizations belonging to the Center is complex,
a way was sought to symbolize this aspect as well. Thus a combination of all three
aspects was attempted. A hierarchy in terms of scale was established. The letter
C was chosen for its immediate associative value and its essential roundness and
simplicity, useful in representing a focal point or center. But instead of accepting per se a stylistic version of the letter, those factors which distinguish it
from other letters in its subset of round forms--O and G--are exaggerated. The
factor distinguishing it from O is the lack of closure; from G it is the accenting
of the terminals of the broken line: with C the upper terminus is accented; with
G it is the lower terminus.

A bold treatment of the resulting two main parts allows for their further articulation.

The letter form provides an intrinsic program of direction of movement. This
direction is counterclockwise beginning with the upper terminus.

The stage is now set for introducing symbols for planning, design and construction.
The controlling ideas applied to these are:

Planning   point of origin
                                data array
                                collection

Design   link between
                                translation
                                differentiation
                                giving form

Construction   filling in
                                weight
                                conclusion

The rationale for a strictly sequential arrangement of the six member groups is
less important for the following reasons: they do not neatly fit the three activity
categories (planners are architects, architects are planners, all areas require construction specifications and drafting skills, etc.) Secondly, while these are the
founding members of the Center, membership is openended and the new identification
mark should not overdefine individual member identities.

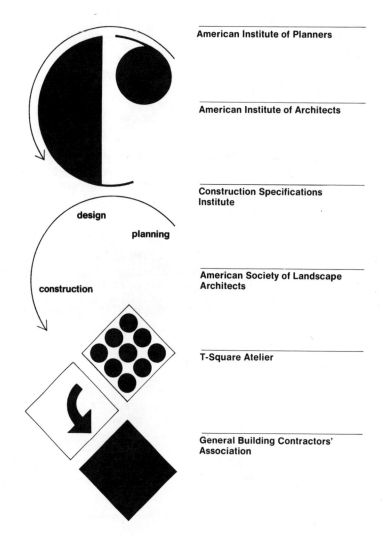

American Institute of Planners

American Institute of Architects

Construction Specifications Institute

American Society of Landscape Architects

T-Square Atelier

General Building Contractors' Association

The following symbolic references seemed a. useful and b. simple enough to be brought into the already complex symbol structure:

 Synonomous with planning symbol already defined.

 The existing symbol for the Philadelphia Chapter is a bold-faced **a**. It is the only symbol of a member group simple enough as a form to be directly usable.

 The number and dimensioning arrow as symbols of precision specifications.

 The tree as a landscape symbol.

 The **T** refers dually to the letter and the tool.

 The filling of a form as with concrete has its source in GBCA's own symbol where a similar idea constitutes a minute detail.

The integration of all the ideas noted resulted in this form which can now be compared with the original program. Partially submerged member group references can be sifted out and compared with their sources.

The retrospective explanation of the process is more orderly than its reality: it is a process of perceptual search. The forms emerge at partially predictable and unpredictable points. Performance is based on recognition.

There is a final comment to make about the complexity of the image: influencing the result was the designer's desire to produce a "complex" symbol form and his belief that the Center was a plausible subject for this treatment. Whether in the long run the degree of complexity tolerated in the result will be seen as a fault or advantage is for the reader to determine.

Finally, an example of the use of a field of elements as a context for achieving differentiated repetition is considered. First, however, a description of the symbol element itself: A symbol was designed for a hypothetical vocational guidance agency. An analysis of the program suggested punctuation marks for question and answer as being an appropriate syntax. The following more universal ideas serve to condition the conventional visual forms for these marks:

Question ?	Answer:
nebulous	focussed
unknown	known
wandering	directed

Correlates for visual syntax include the following:

curvilinear	rectilinear
random	ordered
soft	hard
loose	tight

A field or pattern of identical symbol units seems useful as a syntax to convey the
idea of narrowing a choice. The results, produced by a process of progressive rotation and subtraction (also incidentally aspects of vocational choice), are these
configurations. Randomly generated form elements empirically determined to be
distracting to the desired image were sorted out in a manual process. Note, however,
that some noise is a significant part of the image.

The implications of these experiments for the design of larger environments include the following:

1. That the opposition or contrast of visual properties of images rather than style provides a primary base for the compounding of images where each must preserve its identity.

2. The oppositional character of space as a component rather than background results in radically improved perception. The placement of man-made sign-symbols in any environment, including the natural, requires viewing the environment as a sign image or assemblage of sign images.

3. Tension is more important than balance as an organizing principle because of the clarifying contrast relationship between syntax and semantic images.

4. For many kinds of communication in the street, whether for traffic control or commercial identification, purely visual signs if properly designed could do a faster job of orienting the user than either verbal or combination verbal-visual signs. Most traffic-adjusted information is of necessity terse information. It is in those areas where simple information must be comprehended immediately and dynamically that visual language functions most effectively.

5. Subtler differentiation among visual values, necessary as a human factor and contrasted with simple overall organization, is made more possible when oppositional characteristics are used. Smaller or quieter elements are not overpowered by large or noisy ones if they are recognized as parts of a whole.

6. The real success of the use of opposing images for environmental clarification depends on certain unifying characteristics in the syntax which makes comparison between opposites possible and useful. This implies planning the semiotic aspect of a sign environment, especially the definition of the interrelation between syntax and semantic images. Our current work in urban graphics at Yale is concerned with the planning of urban graphic environments.

NOTES AND REFERENCES

(1) Armin Hofmann's GRAPHIC DESIGN MANUAL, Reinhold, 1965, shows examples of sign-symbol qualities in visual communication based on confrontation of opposites.

(2) Karl Gerstner published DESIGNING PROGRAMMES in 1963, Niggli, and extended the segment related to typographic programs in his KOMPENDIUM FUER ALPHABETEN: SYSTEMATIK DER SCHRIFT, Niggli, 1972, soon to be published in English by MIT Press.

(3) The performance of these signs is impaired by the contradiction between their intended use as direct communicators and their present use as illustrations. However, since the examples vary somewhat in the degree of success with which they function to combine configuration and meaning--which is the intent--only a partial context for evaluating performance is provided. A further diminution of effectiveness occurs in the small-scale.

(4) Tension is the opposite of balance and derives from contrast. Equal relationships tend to be static and not useful for communication.

(5) Every objective visual communication has a precise level at which meaning is measured and where it must be unequivocally successful. We can speak of this as the effective semantic as compared to the limited semantic reached when abstract forms are brought into opposition without objective concurrence on their meaning.

(6) W.R. Garner, "The Goodness of Patters", AMERICAN SCIENTIST, Jan.-Feb., 1970.

(7) Counting is a translational rather than perceptual operation.

(8) Christopher Alexander finds the semilattice as structure to be truer to human interactions than tree structures, "A City Is Not A Tree", DESIGN (London), February, 1966. The need to express rich diversity of visual circuits, however, needs to be coupled with strong points of orientation as shown by Kevin Lynch, THE IMAGE OF THE CITY, MIT, 1960.

(9) This is equally true for typography and architecture.

An imaginary conversation between EDRA, Graham Stevens, Carl Jung, Immanuel Kant and Walt Whitman.

Composed automatically by a chance process at the request of

J. Christopher Jones
The Open University
Bletchley, Bucks, England.

Abstract

When EDRA told me that I was to speak on "Design Languages and Methods" I remembered having once written that

> "methodology should not be a fixed track to a fixed destination
> but a conversation about everything that could be made to happen.
> The language of this conversation must bridge the logical gap
> between past and future but in doing so it should not limit the
> variety of possible futures that are discussed nor should it
> force the choice of a future that is unfree".

This conversation is hardly possible while the language of design theory remains so narrow and machine-like so I have employed a chance process to compose a wider but imaginary conversation between five voices: EDRA, an artist-designer, a psychologist, a philosopher and a poet.

Introduction

The voices in the conversation are as follows:

> EDRA speaks some randomly chosen titles from the Conference Program,
>
> Graham STEVENS (1) tells, <u>in his own design language</u>, how the idea of making inflatable environments came to him in a flash,
>
> Carl JUNG (2) speaks a paragraph he once wrote about method,
>
> Immanuel KANT (3) speaks sentences randomly chosen from his "Critique of Pure Reason",
>
> Walt WHITMAN (4) speaks randomly chosen lines from "Song of Myself".

I chose Kant because there is such a similarity between the language of design theorists and that of his philosophy. (Someone once said Kant's writing is illuminating but difficult: it should be read first for the fourth time.) I chose Whitman because I love his exuberant American vision and because it contains so much of what is missing from our own writings.

The chance process, which decided who should speak next, and which chose statements at random from the texts, is adapted from the way John Cage (5)
composes his lectures.

EDRA   IMPLEMENTATION OF STRATEGIES LEADING TO ENVIRONMENTAL CHANGE.

STEVENS   During 1964-65, I spent a year with other students organising a move-
            ment to change our educational system, culminating in the Stockholm
            Students' Symposium passing a resolution that students should have full
            participation in all aspects of their education: selection, assessment,
            course content, lectures etc; it also passed a resolution that exams
            should be abolished.

EDRA   GAMING AND SIMULATION

STEVENS   With all these negative aspects it seemed necessary to start from the
            beginning - from nature, the body, and peoples' behaviour; investi-
            gations into what was needed and how it could be done.

JUNG   An ancient adept has said: 'If the wrong man uses the right means,
            the right means work in the wrong way.

STEVENS   The relevant aspects of the course being studied were given by
            Professor Page on environmental physics, which also included the
            physics of the body; G. Broadbent on the theory of design, including
            the creative process and kinetic art.

EDRA   DESIGN LANGUAGES AND METHODS

KANT   I shall, therefore, restrict myself to the simple and equitable
            demand that such reasoners will demonstrate, from the nature of the
            human mind as well as from that of the other sources of knowledge,
            how we are to proceed to extend our cognition completely a priori,
            and to carry it to that point where experience abandons us, and no
            means exist of guaranteeing the objective reality of our conceptions.

WHITMAN   I have instant conductors all over me whether I pass or stop,

WHITMAN   At the cider-mill tasting the sweets of the brown mash, sucking the
            juice through a straw,

WHITMAN   And peruse manifold objects, no two alike and everyone good,

KANT   Now, as every principle which imposes upon the exercise of the under-
            standing a priori compliance with the rule of systematic unity, also
            relates, although only in an indirect manner, to an object of experience,
            the principles of pure reason will also possess objective reality and
            validity in relation to experience.

WHITMAN   Divine am I inside and out, and I make holy whatever I touch or am touch'd from,

WHITMAN   Approaching Manhattan up by the long-stretching island,

WHITMAN   There is no stoppage and never can be stoppage,

KANT   It is evident from the remarks that have been made in the preceding sections, that an answer to this question will be far from being difficult or unconvincing.

JUNG   This Chinese saying, unfortunately all too true, stands in sharp contrast to our belief in the 'right' method irrespective of the man who applies it.

STEVENS   These studies, coupled with experiences in painting, meditation, rock music, slum housing (I was deeply dissatisfied with current architecture, its limited concern with small sections of the environment, its rigid unresponsive, immovable demand that people adapt to their environment instead of having it adapt to them) led to the Spacefield project.

KANT   But this representation, I think, is an act of spontaneity; that is to say, it cannot be regarded as belonging to mere sensibility.

JUNG   In reality, in such matters everything depends on the man and little or nothing on the method.

EDRA   IMPLEMENTATION OF STRATEGIES LEADING TO ENVIRONMENTAL CHANGE

WHITMAN   The connoisseur peers along the exhibition-gallery with half-shut eyes bent sideways,

KANT   We cannot even cogitate time, unless, in drawing a straight line (which is to serve as the external figurative representation of time), we fix our attention on the act of the synthesis of the manifold, whereby we determine successively the internal sense, and thus attend also to the succession of this determination.

WHITMAN   This the touch of my lips to yours, this the murmer of yearning,

STEVENS   Spacefield assumed immediate importance in the way in which it brought together and unified all the other, isolated experiments and interests, at the same time answering the dissatisfaction with architecture

JUNG   For the method is merely the path, the direction taken by a man.

WHITMAN   Adorning myself to bestow myself on the first that will take me,

EDRA   DECISION MAKING TOOLS

WHITMAN I will go to the bank by the wood and become undisguised and naked,

KANT   For, granting that certain responsibilities lie upon us, which, as
         based on the ideas of reason, deserve to be respected and submitted
         to, although they are incapable of a real or practical application to
         our nature, or, in other words, would be responsibilities without
         motives, except upon the supposition of a Supreme Being to give effect
         and influence to the practical laws : in such a case we should be
         bound to obey our conceptions, which, although objectively insufficient,
         do, according to the standard of reason, preponderate over and are
         superior to any claims that may be advanced from any other quarter.

KANT   Transcendental freedom is therefore opposed to the natural law of
         cause and effect, and such a conjunction of successive states in
         effective causes is destructive of the possibility of unity in
         experience, and for that reason not to be found in experience -
         is consequently a mere fiction of thought.

JUNG   The way he acts is the true expression of his nature.

KANT   For if they are to have something more than a merely logical signifi-
         cance, and to be something more than a mere analytical expression of
         the form of thought, and to have a relation to things and their
         possibility, reality, or necessity, they must concern possible
         experience and its synthetical unity, in which alone objects of cog-
         nition can be given.

JUNG   If it ceases to be this, then the method is nothing more than an
         affectation, something artificially added, rootless and sapless,
         serving only the illegitimate goal of self-deception.

WHITMAN Give me a little time beyond my cuff'd head, slumbers, dreams, gaping.

JUNG   It becomes a means of fooling oneself and of evading what may perhaps
         be the implacable law of one's being.

STEVENS Its particular form was mainly derived from a piece of tactile sculp-
         ture made in 1965, designed to express the idea of containment -
         fullness, emptiness, filling and emptying, texture, weight, volume
         of content etc.

KANT   For, as in the former case the cognition (conclusio) is given only as
         conditioned, reason can attain to this cognition only under the
         presupposition that all the members of the series on the side of
         the conditions are given (totality in the series of premisses),
         because only under this supposition is the judgment we may be consider-
         ing possible a priori; while on the side of the conditioned or the

inferences, only an incomplete and <u>becoming</u>, and not a presupposed or given series, consequently only a potential progression, is cogitated.

EDRA   QUANTITATIVE TECHNIQUES IN ENVIRONMENTAL ANALYSIS

JUNG   This is far removed from the earth-born quality and sincerity of Chinese thought.

<u>STEVENS</u>   <u>While considering these properties, the nature of toy balloons assumed greater importance.</u>

(EDRA'S instructions were to complete the paper in 5 pages or less, so I decide here to silence the other voices so that Graham Stevens has space for his story. JCJ)

<u>STEVENS</u>   The idea of the balloon as a flexible, tactile skin, completely expressive of containment, simply came in a flash while I was walking down a street.

Balloons were filled with water, soap solution, salt, beads etc., and when air was used, one became much more aware of air as a material, with its own kinetic properties.

The whole exercise was immediately popular with the people around, with its range of sexual and humorous connotations - people squeezed, stretched, rubbed, poured and ejected water and soap solution, swung, dangled, threw, made noises, sucked and passed around the balloons from one to another.

Knowing very little about the technical aspects of air structures and having only seen photographs of warehouse-type structures, the Space Field project had to be worked out using models, discussions, contacting high-frequency welding equipment manufacturers and making up the structure in borrowed factory space over a weekend.

This was done by a process of trial and error for determing fan-size, material thickness, amount of wind-loading, on-site repairs, anchorage, creep; until finally a week later, failure then success showed what kept the structure up or down, and anchored to the ground. Through this experience, the nature and potential of the air structure, beyond that of storage function, became apparent.

REFERENCES

1. Stevens, Graham, Blow-up, ART AND ARTISTS, May 1972.

2. Jung, Carl Gustav, THE SECRET OF THE GOLDEN FLOWER, (Translated by Wilhelm Richard), Routledge & Kegan Paul, London, 1962. p.83.

3. Kant, Immanuel, CRITIQUE OF PURE REASON (translated by J.M.D. Meiklejohn) Dent: London, Dutton: New York, 1934.

4. Whitman, Walt. LEAVES OF GRASS, New American Library of World Literature (Signet Classic), New York, 1954.

5. Cage, John, SILENCE, MIT Press, 1966.

Graham Stevens: "Pneumatic Environment" at the Paris Biennale 1971

Richard I. Krauss, Principal
Andrea Nagode, Nancy Edelman Phillips, Research Associates
Environmental Design Group
14 Arrow Street
Cambridge, Massachusetts 02138

Abstract

Knowing what kinds of conceptual frameworks are applicable in environmental design depends on understanding what designers do. The design process is described as iterative looping between "supply" (forms, technologies, resources) and "demand" (needs, objectives). This design activity is seen as a learning process, with the designer considering alternatives as his understandings grow from his own concerns and those of users. From these views, guidelines for information frameworks emerge. They should be open-ended rather than "complete"; allow the designer to consider any relationship he is interested in; grow with the designer's understanding rather than structure his problems. Two systems that begin to meet these criteria are IMAGE, a computer system based on graphic manipulation of "use-volumes", and PAK, a planning technique aimed at enabling the users of an environment to exercise some control over its design, development, and use.

In order to discuss what are significant frameworks for conceptualizing designer operations, it would be helpful to begin by describing what designers do. For it is the character of the designer's role that determines what sorts of concepts he needs to handle, in what ways information ought to be classified, and what the responsibilities are in dealing with it.

Basically the designer's function is to suggest ways of altering the environment so as to support and enhance human activities. He invents, for what he perceives as needed, possible environmental systems that can aid in fulfilling these needs. To responsibly carry out his work he must have two concerns: a continual attentiveness to human needs and an understanding of the workings and potentials of the environment.

In the abstract what environmental designers do can be described as the "solving" of supply/demand problems, with needs, as the designer understands them, forming the "demand", and the form/space configurations he can offer to meet them forming the available "supply". The designer's responsibility, however, goes beyond sheer problem-solving and matching-up of supply with demand to the projecting of new kinds of demand and new ways of meeting it. Through his concern for ways in which the environment can affect and serve people, the designer can perceive needs his clients are not necessarily sensitive to themselves, and he can help them become conscious of and able to articulate them. Through his ability to learn about clients' needs and to learn from his experience in manipulating space and form, the designer can develop physical possibilities for serving the needs he and his clients discern when the environment can aid in meeting them.

348

The designer attempts to relate various elements -- the needs of users, the characteristics for physical form that these imply, issues of technology and construction, and the resources and constraints afforded by available sites and funds -- balancing them in trial ways and changing them so as to produce progressively better resolutions of the design problem they pose. The process can be represented schematically (Diagram 1) as a repeated looping from demand issues to supply issues and back: the designer proceeds from his conception of a set of needs to the invention of a form to fulfill it, then checks his proposed form against need and comes to a new understanding of need based on issues the new form has brought to light, then makes a still newer form to meet the revised conception of need, and so on until he is satisfied -- or has run out of time.

In order for this iterative process to take place responsibly and insightfully, the designer's concern has to extend over a wide range of issues. Diagram 2 suggests the array of elements and their logical connections with each other. On the demand axis there are conceptions of how the as-yet unbuilt environment will have to perform, and, working backward, there are the various levels of considerations that generate these criteria: projections of what people will do in the built facility and notions of the broader objectives that the user activities will express or serve. On the supply side there are physical form possibilities, traced forward through the projected determinants of what is available and allowable; through the cost and technological implications of development, construction, use, maintenance, and resources.

The designer's attention not only moves back and forth from one axis to the other, it should also be able to move along each axis in order to enrich his understanding of it. That is, he must not only know what sort of performance criteria are desired but also be able to understand why: a necessity that means the designer must be given access to the sources of these criteria -- the people who have defined them and (if these are not the same) the people for whose use the facility is intended. For without this access his understanding of demand elements will be both superficial and rigid, a set of fixed constraints rather than an ingredient of a learning process. Similarly -- with regard to the supply axis -- if he is aware of the construction implications of a form alternative but not its projected maintenance implications, his design decisions may be based on inadequate and misleading predictions of relative costs.

While the foregoing diagram attempts to show a meaningful way of grouping the elements involved in the environmental design process, our sense is that human beings do not normally learn, understand, or invent in ways as linear and orderly as this image suggests. Because the ranges of supply and demand alternatives are infinite the architect must continually select among them. His paths are not based on generalized methodological principles or on logic but follow from his own personal values, modified by and responsible to the values of the people he serves. Thus the designer's own central concerns are critical in influencing the direction he takes: they are the main impetus to the way in which he structures an understanding of a problem, formulates questions about it, and focuses the search for solutions.

Diagram 3 is an attempt to make visualizeable this notion about the design process. It represents the architect's complex patterns of acess to and connection among the elements arrayed in Diagram 2, and suggests how his grasp of a given problem grows as he understands an increasing number of elements -- both in terms of each other and in relation to his core of concerns, which is shown as the center of a set of radiating lines which grow as he inquires and understands new elements and their relationships.

Though concerns and elements are complexly interwoven in the highly individuated design processes we are describing, it is possible to distinguish two sorts of operations that designers commonly perform as they try to broaden and enrich their problem/solution understandings.

First, surveying alternatives in any given range of elements, devising variations on them or creating new ones. (This operation is represented by lateral arrows in Diagram 4.) "Surveying Alternatives" can include such activities as the investigation of a range of possible structural systems or claddings for a given facility; it can also take the form of attempts to examine the range of applicable objectives in order to locate or discover those that might aid in judging the significance of a possible space/form configuration.

Second, tracing the meaning of an element in one range in relation to those in other ranges, especially in relation to the designer's central concerns. (This is represented on Diagram 4 by radial arrows.) "Tracing meaning" refers to the searching out of chains of implications and consequences, from demand to supply or supply to demand. It includes attempts, for example, to evaluate a form alternative in terms of the contribution it makes toward facilitating some desired set of user activities, or in terms of the construction costs it is expected to entail. From another starting point, it includes attempts to understand the significance of some set of user/designer objectives for various space-allocation schemes.

In light of the two images of the design process put forward here -- iterative looping between considerations of demand and supply, and the forming of complex webs of understanding among elements viewed, ultimately, in terms of intuitive, felt concerns -- a possible design scenario can be outlined as follows. Ranging over a field of alternative forms ("surveying"), the designer makes a preliminary choice and uses it provisionally as a straw man to focus questions on. He studies it in depth ("tracing meaning") to identify or at least sense its relationships with other elements and with the concerns he currently gives most weight to. Finding it wanting, he rejects it in favor of a new straw man (perhaps responding to a revised conception of demand) whose implications he explores until it, too, has to be rejected. The pacing of these operations seems to involve first a deliberative, focused concentration on each successive form, followed by a more fluid time of reexamination, reaction, imagination, and invention while the new straw man takes shape. With each exploration the architect learns, increases his understanding of the links between elements in the environmental design/development process, and strengthens his convictions about their meaning in the light of his concerns. By these means, he approaches a clearer perception of what those concerns really are and the degree of their relevance to the situation at hand.

For as we have indicated before, the architect's core of concerns is not something inviolate; it is essential that it change as he learns. It varies somewhat with each new design situation, and in the course of any given project it is influenced and altered by new understandings which come both from the architect's form explorations and from his interactions with other participants in the design process. In particular the architect must be attentive to the concerns, feelings, objectives, and predispositions of the people whose lives will be affected by his work. Inevitably his own values and past experiences will shape how he inquires of and what he succeeds in understanding about potential users of the environments. But he should maintain as much openness as possible to interaction with and communication from users, so that his core of concerns can be enriched, qualified, and when necessary, altered in response to what he learns from and about these people.

In light of these views of the designer's activity, we can propose several guidelines about the kinds of conceptual frameworks that will be of most relevance to him. In particular we will attempt to describe what an information system should be like if it were to be congenial to these notions of design.

First, it is important that any set of concepts be tentatively considered -- they should stimulate modifications, extensions, encourage additions in any direction that the designer's evolving understanding directs -- rather than being closed or aspiring to "completeness." For example, we should not attempt to construct "universal" information systems, because universal systems are complete by definition and do not allow for the introduction of ingredients whose relevance was originally unforeseen.

Moreover, insofar as a taxonomy pretends to be universal, it precludes the existence, or at least the utilization, of alternative taxonomies. The structure of an information system or conceptual framework inevitably depends on the purposes for which it was designed. Most schemes for the categorization of architectural data are organized around some particular aspect of the development process. Indeed, they are generally only good for such restricted aims. The Construction Specification Institute's catalogues, for instance, are designed to facilitate the job of putting a project out for bids; accordingly, they are structured to reflect building practice and the sequence of construction activity. Sweet's catalogue is categorized for the convenience of buyers and sellers, as a means of giving access to manufactured products. The SfB system, though aiming at universality and more comprehensive than the foregoing ones, is nevertheless useful mostly for organizing the more technical aspects of architecture. Operations control systems, aimed at understanding and controlling the functioning of complex systems, are organized such that each element is viewed in terms of its contribution to the whole. Thus each of these information systems makes accessible a particular segment of the range of elements involved in the design/development process; none is applicable to the entire spectrum of considerations.

And this is as it should be. No single information system can aim at serving all conceivable purposes. No system can anticipate all the possible perspectives and lines of questioning a designer might generate in the course of exploring a problem. Those that attempt such comprehensiveness do the designer an ultimate disservice, for they close off possible lines of inquiry and force him to shape his understandings to the requirements of the information system rather than according to the evolving configuration of the design problem as he sees it.

A second requirement for information systems is that they cover a wide range of issues, for example the whole set implied in dealing with the supply and demand elements mentioned above. In particular they must make accessible the desires and viewpoints of potential users, since this frequently bypassed data is fundamental to any intelligent evaluation of demand elements and to the responsible linking of these with supply. Thus performance-specification systems, for example, are dysfunctional insofar as they codify static criteria for generic "building types" -- schools, low-income dwelling units, government offices -- for this serves to deflect attention away from the needs of real people in specific situations and forces the designer to adopt preordained, inflexible demand criteria.

Third, information systems should also allow the architect to consider at will any possible connection and inter-relationship among elements -- and, in so doing, should enhance his ability to focus on the design as a whole rather than as an aggregation of parts. Here too performance-specification systems serve inadequately, since typically they undertake to set standards of functioning for each separate building component -- floors, ceilings, illuminations, etc. -- and fail to provide ways of dealing with the performance of the whole building as a system for the support of human activity.

Fourth, information systems must be such that they engage the designer's creative intelligence actively rather than appearing to solve his problems for him; they must ensure that the learning process remains his rather than being guided by the dimensions and capabilities of the system. This caveat applies especially to computer systems, for the computer's powers and agility can be seductive and can serve to shield designers from the consciousness and effort involved in following through on their own evolving personal concerns and the implications these have for structuring the design problem. Thus the computer system has to be amenable to full control by the designer, either directly or through an expert liaison. The designer has to be in a position to select and shape the kinds of operations the system performs. If not, he will be at a loss to use the computer for his own purposes as an instrument in helping him pursue the questions generated by his felt concerns and by his continual efforts at intermingling needs and form.

We have been involved with the conceptual development of two frameworks for design information which, we hope, begin to meet these aims.

The first is the initial development (with Tim Johnson) of a computer system called IMAGE which is now operating at MIT. It is based on the notion that an architectural problem has two sides, that someone has needs, and that they can be met by providing a suitable environment. Hence, the basic unit that the system manipulates has two aspects and is called "use-volume." The designer invents these units (living-room, locker-room) and then applies, with weighting, any set of constraints to each (e.g., their proportions, their qualities such as privacy, circulation, visual access) or to a number of them (e.g., their proximities, distances, sequences, exclusivities). The system then applies these constraints to a graphic display of the use-volumes and makes them move with respect to each other to descrease the errors in the constraints formulae in the displayed solution. The designer can modify the forms or the constraints interactively as he learns from the solutions displayed. Our hope is that the vocabulary of use-volumes and constraints is open-ended enough to allow the designer to invent and modify forms in whatever ways his growing understanding of the problem suggests. The major constraint then, is the user's ability to understand and translate his problem into either the constraint language or form.

The second information system is a planning technique called PAK (Planning Aid Kit), based on one developed (with Michael Brill) under the sponsorship of the National Institute of Mental Health. The aim of the system is to make the elements of a design problem (see Diagram 2) be understood by the users of an environment so that they can exercise some control over its design, development, and use. The process is a series of meetings which correspond very roughly to the steps in Diagram 2. The net effect of such meetings is that the participants begin to gain a notion of how their environment can be designed to meet their needs, and (if the administration of it is left in their hands) of how to continually modify it, or their aims for it, when they see a need to do so.

The general criteria developed above for information systems deal less with substantive issues than with what the vehicles for such systems are -- the technology (e.g., computers, performance specification techniques) used and the ways of administrating them. It is these which must permit an open-ended understanding of how the environment is developed and used and must improve such understandings in both architect and users.

These latter prescriptions have at base ethical aims that each person, whether designer or user, have an appropriate role in the on-going development of the environment; that he have sufficient understanding about it to be able to reflect on its relation to him in the deepest sense and then to be able usefully to act. To the extent that a conceptual framework hinders or restricts the open-ended pursuit of such reflections or actions it is harmful. In order to be of real value, then, the intellectual abstractions that information systems represent, and the ways in which they can be manipulated and applied, should be both extendable and intelligible in significant ways by the people who are its users.

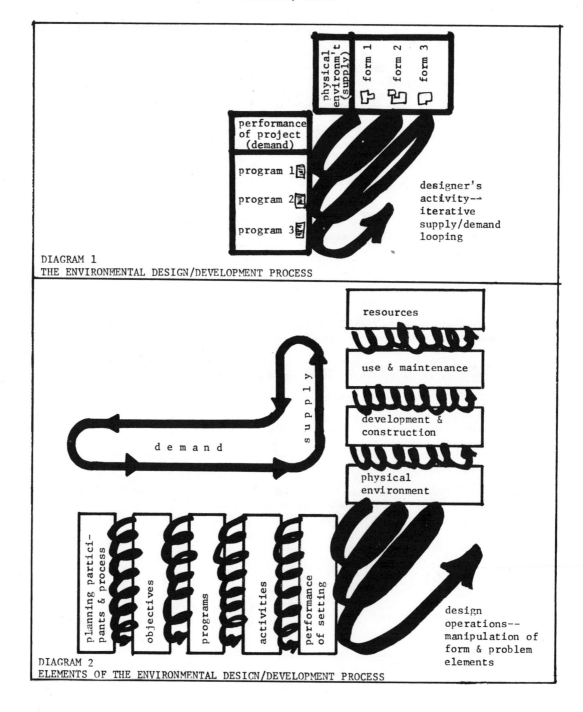

DIAGRAM 1
THE ENVIRONMENTAL DESIGN/DEVELOPMENT PROCESS

DIAGRAM 2
ELEMENTS OF THE ENVIRONMENTAL DESIGN/DEVELOPMENT PROCESS

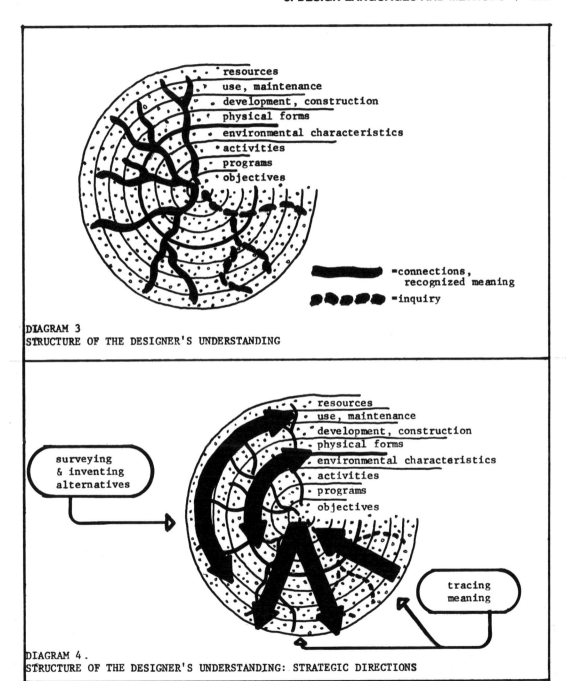

DIAGRAM 3
STRUCTURE OF THE DESIGNER'S UNDERSTANDING

DIAGRAM 4.
STRUCTURE OF THE DESIGNER'S UNDERSTANDING: STRATEGIC DIRECTIONS

Chris McDonald
Research Officer
Department of Geography
University of Leeds
Leeds LS2 9JT, England

Abstract

This paper is concerned with the written languages of policy making and design.
It advances certain principles for the specification of symbol systems to best
represent one's problem area and decision procedures. In the context of relatively rich problem areas, and relatively formal decision procedures, any given
symbol system evidently has a limited capacity to convey information. Due to this
capacity constraint, the overall representational task is often split between several symbol systems. Some of the advantages and disadvantages of such complementary
systems are examined, using languages developed for metropolitan planning as a case
in point.

Introduction to the Representational Issues

Written or printed languages, due to their explicit, preservable and reproducible
nature, have long been recognised as playing a key role in mankind's decision making capabilities. The author's investigations of that role have been guided by
two related questions. Most broadly, what types of symbol system ought policy
makers to be using, if the potential contribution of written languages to policy
making is to be fully exploited? And more particularly, how rich (as distinct
from parsimonious) and how formal (i.e. well-defined, disciplined and standardized), should the languages of policy making be?

These questions are important since there appears to be a necessary trade-off here
between richness and formality. The outstanding example, perhaps, is in the contrast between natural and mathematical languages: natural languages being much the
richer; and mathematical languages, much the more formal (1,2,3). Although there
are many languages with some intermediate mix of richness and formality -- e.g.
legal dialects of natural language, engineering and architectural drawing, computer
programming languages -- there seem to be basic constraints in symbolic form and
symbol using processes, preventing the evolution of individual systems which are
both highly rich and highly formal. It is thus usual to resort to specialist
languages, offering distinct perspectives upon the total problem, at different
junctures of a policy making process.

Clearer criteria for splitting the overall representational task in this fashion
would help provide a sound basis both for the selection between existing symbol
systems; and for the specification of new systems which promote more suitable
mixes of formality and richness. The present paper addresses this need, but with
the more limited aim of clarifying how many distinct symbol systems are required
to handle any given decision phenomenon. Our arguments will be illustrated by
reference to one pair of artificial languages -- the "planning situation chart"

and the "planning process diagram" -- which is under development as a design and decision aid for metropolitan land use and transportation planning.

Briefly, this particular representational system was conceived in order to overcome the weaknesses of more conventional models of the planning process: such as the macro-level "generation-elaboration-evaluation" paradigm (4). A need was felt to portray planning as a _dialogue_ between _participant groups_ over _time_: a _cyclic learning process_, in which both _political and technical statements_, about _specific properties of alternatives_, gradually contribute to consensus on some _composite_ course of action. While not necessarily inconsistent with conventional paradigms, it was believed that a more convincing (and eventually more practical) representation would require such attributes of planning to be denoted as formally and explicitly as possible. And the "situation chart" and "process diagram" were specified to fill that need. So that the questions for us, in this case, are: "Why have _two_ separate symbol systems? Why not just _one_? Why not _more_?

The summary nature of this paper must be stressed. The reader is referred elsewhere for a thorough treatment of the broad issue of "appropriate" representation, and for a detailed definition and discussion of this particular experimental language system (5).

Explicit Nature of a Symbol System

Our attraction to the _written component_ of language derives from its ability to augment certain capabilities of the individual human mind and individual human experience. Writing enables man to circumvent his limited channel capacity; to supplement his memory size and span; to carefully relate past and present observations; and to readily expose them to the critique of a wider community. It is the "_explicating_" power of writing, in the formulation and communication of data and ideas, which encourages much of the discipline of science and technology.

Writing consists of material deposits -- such as ink on paper -- which take on a conventional form, to yield _symbols_. These in turn take on positional conventions, to form _symbol systems_. And when a symbol system also has a processor or _user_ -- for which or whom it has an interpretive significance -- then let us say one has a _language_. Finally, to the extent that distinct languages interlock, and are readily used in conjunction, a _language system_ may be said to operate.

In order to talk about complementary symbol systems, we need some agreement as to what delineates a single symbol system. Where does one end, and another one begin? For our purposes, this distinction is best made initially on syntactic grounds. The _extent_ of a symbol system consists of that set of expressions, consistent with the positional conventions of the system, each member of which, when written explicitly in its entirety, can be reasonably scanned and comprehended as a whole. In short, while expressions which cannot _individually be comprehended as a unity_ may be associated with some language system; these expressions must be decomposed into more manageable sub-expressions before we recognize them as belonging to an explicit symbol system. By the same token, a single language system may be associated with several symbol systems.

This is illustrated by our experimental languages. On their most theoretical
level, we have introduced (6) a set of "sentential matrix" expressions, such as:

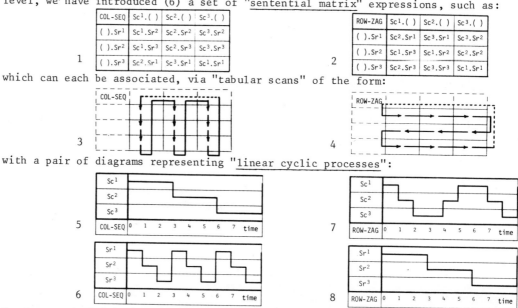

which can each be associated, via "tabular scans" of the form:

with a pair of diagrams representing "linear cyclic processes":

Now by our definitions, although these expressions may all be considered part of
the same language system, they belong to three different symbol systems. Within
each group (e.g. Figures 3 plus 4) one has expressions sharing common syntactic
conventions, which can readily be interpreted alone. But between groups (e.g.
Figures 1 plus 5), the only way to find a common syntax is by considering the two
expressions to be one: and this composite expression could not be conveniently
and convincingly comprehended as a whole.

The extent of a symbol system for human processing is thus determined by limitations in the size and complexity of a single written expression, which man can
visually and mentally manage as an integrated whole. Clearly, this will partly be
a function of his mode of use. The same symbolism, even in the same syntactic
context, may be interpreted quickly and connotatively one minute, and in a deliberate and rigorous manner the next -- by the very same person. Nonetheless, this
criterion for extent keeps a symbol system faithful to its role of "explicating"
information: a discipline which other components of a language system need not
fully satisfy. The significance of such pragmatic considerations has been noted
previously elsewhere (7,8).

Matching Symbol and Phenomenon

So far we have been speaking of the syntax of symbol systems, independent of their
semantic possibilities, or the meanings with which they may be associated. Let us
now refer to one planning interpretation of the "sentential matrix" of Figure 1,
and the corresponding "linear cyclic processes" of Figures 5 and 6:

COL-SEQ	genertn	elabrtn	evalutn
indstry	gen.hsg	elb.hsg	evl.hsg
housing	gen.shp	elb.shp	evl.shp
shoppng	elb.ind	evl.ind	gen.ind

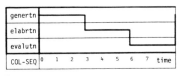

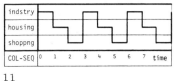

9   10   11

Figure 9 is a way of specifying that the generation of plans for industry (i.e. column labelled 'generation', row labelled 'industry') should be followed by the generation of plans for housing (i.e. entry in cell at intersection of that row and column). This is to be followed (back to row and column labels) by the generation of plans for shopping, and so forth. Figure 10 then plots the sequence in which generative, elaborative and evaluative capabilities are invoked; while Figure 11 is an equivalent plot of the sequence in which plans for industry, housing and shopping are processed. The author has shown how many different patterns for proceeding may be formalized in a similar manner.

What of the match of symbol and phenomenon in this example? Evidently one employs various components of symbolic form (words, straight-lines, directions, areal sub-spaces, etc.) to denote various elements of the microcosm of concern (types of plan, types of planning capability, passage of time, etc). Using these symbols together with positional conventions (allocation of words to cells, registration of lines at points in time, etc) ensures that the complete expressions analogue meaningful relations or behaviours of the basic elements (sequencing rules in Figure 9, procedural patterns in Figures 10 and 11). The correspondence rules involved may range from extremely direct "iconic" matches (e.g. the similarity in shape between ancient pictograms and physical objects), through to devices of "abstraction" (9) and "substitution" (10). And there are less obvious levels of organization. For instance, even though one may be using very abstract symbols as a basic building block, it is often advantageous to resort to relatively strong and direct correspondences in constructing more complicated expressions (11).

Let us indicate how critical these rules of correspondence are. In the "linear cyclic process" language of Figure 11, the various planning tasks (such as "generation of plans for industry") were denoted by horizontal lines or links. Each line is the same, and the nature of each task cannot therefore be completely and explicitly identified: it is simply beyond the capacity of this symbolic form to do so. However, the expression does succeed in conveying very vividly the pattern in which industrial, housing and shopping capabilities are needed over time: indeed, in laying out this pattern for rigorous examination. By contrast, the "sentential matrix" language of Figure 9 clearly specifies the complete composition of successive tasks; but fails dismally in portraying the sequence in which the various planning capabilities must be invoked. In this case, the planner's tasks are denoted not by lines, but by a character-based symbolism in which the individual characters are meaningless.

This latter use corresponds to the main use of characters in natural (but not mathematical) languages: and is central to the capability of natural languages to accommodate great richness. Such abstract characters, though not as bold or connotative as more diagrammatic symbolisms -- indeed, because they are not as bold or connotative -- have a strange representational power. For, strung together in different combinations they enable numerous syntactically distinct symbolic chains to be devised, and to be readily associated with unique meanings. Yet they achieve this richness on the basis of a handful of letters which are, in natural language, meaningless themselves. Without such abstraction at the character level, there could never have been such a limited number of simple symbols. And without such a limited number of simple symbols, there could never have been that degree of symbol sharing and ease of reproduction, which have so enhanced man's communicative powers.

Requisite Variety and Multiple Systems

In contrast to the syntactic definition of "extent", the range of applicability of a symbol system will be defined in terms of semantic properties of its microcosm of concern. That is to say, the range of a symbol system consists of that set of phenomena which are better analogued or represented by its expressions, than by expressions from any other symbol system. (Note that what is included in this range will again be dependent upon the purpose, perspectives and rigor of the language user.) Each symbol system thus presumably has a limited range of applicability. And many expressions within the extent of a symbol system may have no corresponding significance within its range: they may not represent anything particularly well.

By way of illustration, let us consider a variation upon the "procedural patterns" phenomenon of Figure 11, which could still be within range of the linear cyclic process syntax -- i.e. would be better analogued by its expressions, than by those of any other symbol system. Suppose we now identify the horizontal bands with participant groups, and the horizontal links with procedures, pursued within those groups over particular periods of time (Figure 12). (If one considers groups of industrial, housing and shopping planners this emerges as a modest reinterpretation of the language.) Suppose also that we now utilize a redundant component of the

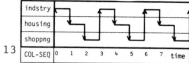

symbol system -- the vertical line or link -- to represent statements passing between the participant groups at particular points in time (Figure 13). Then the complete expression becomes a plausible representation for a chain of planning dialogue. Indeed, it can be argued that it is an extremely good representation: that this perspective upon planning is well within the range of our syntax.

In fact, quite complex patterns of dialogue may be conveniently portrayed and analyzed (Figure 14), and it is this version of the symbol system which constittutes the author's "planning process diagram" (12). Two strengths of the representation are readily apparent. The first is its explicit "time" dimension: the diagram disciplines one to record when a statement was, is, could or should be made. The second is the explicit "participant" dimension: the diagram disciplines one to ask by whom the statement

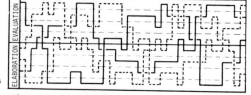

is issued, and to whom it is directed.   However, one serious weakness of the diagram is also evident.   Only when one is able to refer as explicitly and systematically to the content of the statements -- to indicate which are commands to do what, for example -- will we have a convincing model of the planning process.   This part of the task, however, lies outside the range of our symbol system.   The present syntax has insufficient capacity to convey the additional information;   while further embellishment would result in unmanageable expressions.

But this is just one instance of a very common dilemma, having to do with the requisite variety (13) of the match between symbol and phenomenon.   Many problem situations and decision procedures are so complex as to be outside the range of any feasible symbol system: i.e. no single system extends to include syntactic expressions, which can be reasonably comprehended in their entirety, rich enough to analogue every essential semantic distinction.   These worries are bad enough when one includes pragmatic dimensions, such as "reasonably manageable and familiar" in one's definition of "reasonable" comprehension.   They are drastically heightened as soon as one also wishes to embrace such desiderata as "reasonably formal and systematic" -- for this desiderata is only satisfied by relatively abstract, well-defined and parsimonious systems.

So, given some complex area of interest which one desires to represent, various types of solution emerge.   If the whole area is to be served by a single symbol system, there are two extremes: one can use a very rich system, sacrificing much in formality;   or one can use a very formal system, sacrificing much in richness. The former tends to lead to error and confusion, the latter to oversimplification. But one could also have a solution in which the representational task is divided up among a number of distinct symbol systems, each of them providing some trade-off between richness and formality appropriate to its particular sub-area or sub-perspective.   On the face of it, since each distinct symbol system would now represent only a proportion of the total area of interest, there could be a far better match (in terms of both richness and formality) between symbol and phenomenon, within each system.   What one apparently stands to lose, however, is the same degree of consistency between these separate symbol systems as would be encouraged were they all components of one single, integrated, explicit system.   There may be an intolerable sacrifice in immediacy of associations, and in feeling for the whole. Those, in outline, are the advantages and disadvantages of multiple symbol systems.

A Chart to Complement the Process Diagram

We therefore introduced a second symbol system, in our case example, to better explicate the structure and substance of the statements of a planning dialogue.   This complementary language portrays a planning situation at a point in time.   It utilizes a form of sentential matrix

	empirical DOES-HAVE	projected WOULD-HAVE	hypothetcl COULD-HAVE	preference SHOULD-HVE	political WILL-HAVE
CHAR-X_1	PERF-X_{11}	PERF-X_{12}	PERF-X_{13}	PERF-X_{14}	PERF-X_{15}
CHAR-X_2	PERF-X_{21}	PERF-X_{22}	PERF-X_{23}	PERF-X_{24}	PERF-X_{25}
CHAR-X_3	PERF-X_{31}	PERF-X_{32}	PERF-X_{33}	PERF-X_{34}	PERF-X_{35}
CHAR-X_4	PERF-X_{41}	PERF-X_{42}	PERF-X_{43}	PERF-X_{44}	PERF-X_{45}
CHAR-X_5	PERF-X_{51}	PERF-X_{52}	PERF-X_{53}	PERF-X_{54}	PERF-X_{55}

15

(Figure 15) in which various classes of statement used in planning -- expressed in terms of verbal prototypes -- are assembled into associative list structures. The first row of Figure 15, for example, specifies that:

CHARACTERISTIC-X_1 DOES-HAVE PERFORMANCE-X_{11}, WOULD-HAVE PERFORMANCE-X_{12}, ETC. The corresponding columns, embracing all five characteristics, then represent data-bank (empirical statements), trend-state (projected statements), alternative (hypothetical statements), criterion set (preference statements), and plan (political statements), respectively. And the entire expression is a very simple, abstract version of the author's "planning situation chart" (14).

These definitions may be extended to include other classes of statements, and more sophisticated statement structures. But the key notion is that the logical patterns in such a table of statements have implications for action. Indeed, "problems" represented in the tabular planning situation, may be "resolved" by the modification and addition of statements, to obtain a new pattern. This is illustrated by the simple situation of conflicting interests in Figure 16; tackled, in the case of Figure 17, by presenting proposals suggesting give-and-take on some scores (CHARACTERISTICS 1,2,3,7,8,9) and mutual-compromise on others (CHARACTERISTICS 4,5,6).

	projected WOULD-BE			group p SHOULD-BE	group q SHOULD-BE
CHAR-X_1	MED			HI	LOW
CHAR-X_2	MED			HI	LOW
CHAR-X_3	MED			HI	LOW
CHAR-X_4	MED			HI	LOW
CHAR-X_5	MED			HI	LOW
CHAR-X_6	MED			HI	LOW
CHAR-X_7	MED			HI	LOW
CHAR-X_8	MED			HI	LOW
CHAR-X_9	MED			HI	LOW

16

	projected WOULD-BE	alternty a COULD-BE	alternty b COULD-BE	group p SHOULD-BE	group q SHOULD-BE
CHAR-X_1	MED	HI	LOW	HI	LOW
CHAR-X_2	MED	HI	LOW	HI	LOW
CHAR-X_3	MED	HI	LOW	HI	LOW
CHAR-X_4	MED	MED	MED	HI	LOW
CHAR-X_5	MED	MED	MED	HI	LOW
CHAR-X_6	MED	MED	MED	HI	LOW
CHAR-X_7	MED	LOW	HI	HI	LOW
CHAR-X_8	MED	LOW	HI	HI	LOW
CHAR-X_9	MED	LOW	HI	HI	LOW

17

But these statements in the planning situation chart surely bear some relation to the statements in the planning process diagram? Can one not then imagine a planning situation for which administrative, legal, logical and heuristic rules for proceeding, are also incorporated in the chart? And could not these rules be applied repeatedly to data, trends, alternatives, criteria and policies, to guide the generation of an "output" stream of statements -- which might in turn be plotted as a chain of dialogue in the planning process diagram? Moreover, as this dialogue is generated, could not the state of the chart also be updated by the modification and addition of statements: i.e. does not the planning situation itself evolve alongside? In this way one begins to achieve a framework for the formal representation of planning as a continuing dialogue about the value and composition of a set of performance statements.

Enhanced Capacity of Separate Systems

So we have broken the representational task down, analoguing distinct perspectives by separate symbol systems. But our justification till now has been rather negative: given the degree of formality we wished to encourage, it simply did not seem feasible to handle the essential features within a single explicit system. However, there are much more positive reasons for resorting to multiple languages.

For if one relaxes the requirement that all aspects of the microcosm of concern be represented at once, in a single unified system, then one has a <u>greater freedom of choice, among available symbolic forms</u>, in constructing one's analogue.

That is to say, one can reuse and reinterpret some symbolisms from one's basic stock, in various specialist syntactic systems, without much fear of ambiguity or contradiction.   And one can switch others for fresh symbolic elements, more suited to the perspective at hand.   Taken to its limit, this positive assertion would be that separate languages are <u>essential</u> to capture separate classes of phenomena. Each, in our case, takes advantage of the natural expressiveness of a particular type of linear symbolism (links and characters), deployed in a particular type of diagrammatic format.

With separate languages, both extent and range may be increased.   <u>The same symbols can take on new meanings</u> (consider the contrasting interpretations of areal sub-spaces in chart and diagram): each language providing a distinct context.   And the <u>same meanings can be given different symbols</u> (consider the contrasting denotations for the "statement" unit): each language providing a distinct perspective. Such mechanisms are permissible -- indeed necessary -- within a sophisticated <u>language</u> system.   But they are dangerous within a single, explicit <u>symbol</u> system, if ease and reliability in writing, scanning, manipulation and interpretation are to be preserved.

Contrasting Attributes of Chart and Diagram

Thus each of our two languages is able to handle its specialist perspective much better than were it combined into a single symbol system.   The <u>sentential matrix syntax</u> has a tremendous potential for dealing formally with categorical entities, with interactive relationships, with completeness and consistency checks, with aggregative structures, and with the systematic scanning and manipulation of lists and arrays.   On such grounds it is an ideal representation for a complex of issues at a point in time.   Similarly, the <u>linear cyclic process syntax</u> has a fine connotative attraction for the analoguing of a time-related sequence of activities and events, and the patterns in which associated messages are distributed between a number of established reference groups.   On such grounds it is an ideal representation for the procedural aspects of continuing planning.

There is a further balance in the way these languages complement each other.   <u>The process diagram is less general than the situation chart</u>: it has a less rich syntax, and it invokes far more definite and specific assumptions about the phenomena it depicts.   The entities, properties and relationships portrayed in the process diagram are a <u>subset</u> of those represented, albeit less vividly, in the corresponding sequence of situation charts.   The process diagram provides, in effect, a <u>more specialist and more parsimonious representation of a certain sub-situation from an evolving chart</u>.   Indeed, it is only one of several more-specialist-and-parsimonious languages which could be usefully related to the situation chart.   Accompanying the relative boldness of the diagram, of course, are all the advantages (e.g. of relative rigor), and all the disadvantages (e.g. of relative oversimplification), which were alluded to earlier.

These contrasts in subject matter are accompanied by contrasts in the <u>functions</u> of each language, vis-a-vis the other, in the total system. It is the planning situation chart which is able to present the decision making situation, to the language user, in <u>a form most faithful, immediate and relevant to his decision perspective</u>, at any point in time; and this results in an emphasis upon the chart as the principal working tool in the two-language relationship. The chart, in effect, poses the practical question "Where does one go from here?" In modification and manipulation of statements on the chart, one is able to explore and examine various strategies. And in interpreting the output -- one aspect of which might be a planning process plot -- one is led to revise and evaluate those strategies. <u>The two languages are thus ultimately used in close conjunction.</u>

Finally, what of the <u>interface</u> between distinct, but complementary, symbol systems? Need the switch from one to another be as ad hoc as it tends to be between mathematical and natural languages? Clearly not, since we have already seen more <u>formal links</u> forged between the sample systems in this paper. At the weaker extreme, the situation chart and process diagram are positively interlocked by virtue of their <u>common definitions</u> (e.g. the "statement" unit), and their <u>complementary definitions</u> (e.g., "point-in-time" versus "over-time"). At the stronger extreme, we have offered an abstract version of the symbol systems -- recall Figures 1 to 8 -- in which there is a quite <u>mechanical mapping</u> from certain aspects of the chart into certain aspects of the diagram. Nonetheless, the difficulty of achieving a careful and consistent mapping between <u>richer</u> symbol systems, should be a persuasive factor in limiting the proliferation of specialist languages.

Conclusion

Various writers have stressed the importance of obtaining different perspectives, via different modes of representation, in the processes of policy making and design (15,16). This paper has attempted to suggest several principles which should govern the number of specialist written languages employed in any complex problem area. Multiple symbol systems are needed because of the capacity limitations of an individual symbolic expression. But the advantage of being able to reuse and reinterpret a limited stock of symbolic forms, has to be offset by the absence of explicit connections between the separate symbol systems.

References

(1) Gorn, S., "The Computer and Information Sciences and the Community of Disciplines", BEHAVIORAL SCIENCE, Vol. 12, No.6, 1967; page 445.

(2) Keenan, E.L., "A Logical Base for a Transformational Grammar of English", TRANSFORMATION AND DISCOURSE ANALYSIS PAPERS, No.82, University of Pennsylvania, Philadelphia, 1970; page 3.

(3) Winograd, T. UNDERSTANDING NATURAL LANGUAGE, Academic Press, New York, 1972.

(4) Boyce, D.E., Day, N.D., McDonald, C., METROPOLITAN PLAN MAKING, Regional Science Research Institute, Philadelphia, 1970.

(5) McDonald, C., THE ROLE OF FORMAL SYMBOLIC REPRESENTATION IN COMPLEX POLICY MAKING PROCESSES, Ref. 72-1416, University Microfilms, Ann Arbor, 1972.

(6) McDonald, C. and Boyce, D.E., "Concatenation, Tabular Scans and Cyclic Processes", paper prepared for presentation at ACM-SIGPLAN Symposium on Two-Dimensional Man-Machine Communication, Los Alamos, New Mexico, 1972.

(7) Cherry, C., ON HUMAN COMMUNICATION, 2nd Edition, The M.I.T. Press, Cambridge, 1966; page 79.

(8) Russell, B., "Introduction to Principia Mathematica", in Egner, R.E., and Dennon, L.E. (eds.), THE BASIC WRITINGS OF BERTRAND RUSSELL, Simon and Schuster (Clarion Books), New York, 1961; page 162.

(9) Foerster, H.V., "From Stimulus to Symbol -- The Economy of Biological Computation" in Buckley, W. (ed.), MODERN SYSTEMS RESEARCH FOR THE BEHAVIORAL SCIENTIST, Aldine, Chicago, 1968; page 179.

(10) Chao, Y.R., LANGUAGE AND SYMBOLIC SYSTEMS, Cambridge University Press, New York, 1968; page 200.

(11) Chao, Y.R., LANGUAGE AND SYMBOLIC SYSTEMS, Cambridge University Press, New York, 1968; page 199.

(12) McDonald, C. and Boyce, D.E., "Prototypical Forms of Dialogue for Metropolitan Planning", paper presented at 40th National Conference of the Operations Research Society of America, Anaheim, California, 1971.

(13) Ashby, W.R. "Variety, Constraint, and the Law of Requisite Variety", in Buckley, W. (ed.) MODERN SYSTEMS RESEARCH FOR THE BEHAVIORAL SCIENTIST, Aldine, Chicago, 1968.

(14) McDonald, C. and Boyce, D.E., "Tabular Form as a Language for the Planner", paper presented at 54th Annual Conference of the American Institute of Planners, San Francisco, California, 1971.

(15) Eastman, C.M. "On the Analysis of Intuitive Design Processes", in Moore, G.T. (ed.), EMERGING METHODS IN ENVIRONMENTAL DESIGN AND PLANNING, The M.I.T. press, Cambridge, 1970; page 30.

(16) Simon, H.A., "The Theory of Problem Solving", in PROCEEDINGS IFIP CONGRESS 71, Invited Papers Volume, North Holland, Amsterdam, 1971; page 265.

Thomas P. Moran
Department of Computer Science
Carnegie-Mellon University
Pittsburgh, Pennsylvania 15213

Abstract

Human visual imagery is being investigated by careful analyses of spatial visualization tasks. Some protocol-gathering experiments were run on a simple task of learning a path in space. Using a psychologically-structured computer system, the protocol behavior was simulated in detail, showing that the cognitive structure of spatial knowledge can be explained by symbolic structures and processes (as can other
human problem-solving processes). This kind of research is important to several
aspects of design theory and research.

Introduction

Let me begin by apologizing for pretending to be a design researcher. For the past
year or two I have been working on my doctoral thesis in computer science--which is
really a piece of research in cognitive psychology--but which I believe can be
viewed (through rose-colored glasses?) as a piece of basic research in design
theory. Let me present a very brief, non-technical picture of my current project
and you may judge its relevance for yourself.

Visual Imagery

The substance of my thesis deals with the nature of human visual imagery. Imagery
is the subjective experience of being able to "see" something in the "mind's eye"
without having that something in front of your eyes. E.g., assuming that you are
not there at this moment, imagine your bedroom; can you look around the room? Most
people claim to understand what imagery is, though some claim it to be more vivid
than others. (1)

Visual imagery is a very useful mental skill. Picturing something to oneself is a
good way to remember it. Much recent work in experimental psychology has confirmed
that using imagery increases the amount and accuracy of material that can be memo-
rized. (It is the basis of a mnemonic technique known to the ancient Greeks for
memorizing long speeches.) People use imagery in their everyday reasoning and
problem-solving (e.g., giving someone directions to your house). Many problems have
been developed to isolate the ability to visualize. (2) E.g., rotate the letter "Z"
by 90 degrees; what do you have? which way did you rotate it? does it matter?
Finally, note that imagery is also used in the design process. The designer must
imagine the product before it is built. Of course, he may use aids like drawings,
but even the process of making a drawing requires a mental image.

An image is a mental construction from memory (unlike perception which can draw on
the input from the visual system). Ignore the subjective experience of imagery.
The question I am interested in is what precisely does one know--what information

366

does one have--when one has an image? Is imaging characteristically different (e.g., a continuous analog process (3)) from other kinds of knowing? (This is a key issue.) What is the structure of an image? What operations can be performed on an image? What are the limits of imagery, i.e., what can be imagined and what can't?

My hypothesis is that imagery is an abstract symbolic process, not unlike other symbolic processes, except that it deals with spatial information. This is a parsimonious hypothesis since we know that symbolic processes are the basis for most human thinking. (4) The issue is whether or not symbolic structures and processes can represent and account for imaging behavior. The problem is that imaging behavior is covert; the imager does not exhibit much measurable activity which gives clues to the nature of his imagery. However, one of the properties of imagery (5) is that it is hindered by overt visual activity (e.g., looking around the room), but that it is relatively unaffected by overt verbal activity (e.g., talking). This suggests that we can have someone talk about his imaging while doing it.

The Path Task

To get a hold of some imagery behavior, I performed some exploratory experiments with a very simple spatial task. A blindfolded subject was asked to imagine a blank, two-dimensional plane in front of him and to locate himself at some point in the plane. The experimenter then verbally gave him a series of directions (North, South, East, West). For each direction the subject imagined a line of unit length being drawn in that direction on the plane from his current location. The subject then tried to understand (visualize) the path thus far drawn by organizing it in some way. He then described the path and repeated the direction sequence of the path to the experimenter. The subject was allowed as much time as he wanted at each move, and he was free to determine his own cognitive organization of the path.

The experiments were tape-recorded and transcribed. These verbal protocols are the data from which the subject's imaging process must be inferred. The following are the direction sequences for two of the experiments:

       Problem 1: N E S E S E S E N E S S E E N E N W W N

       Problem 3: N E N E N W N E E E S W S E S S W S W N W S W N

(To encourage you to try the task out on yourself, I have not included drawings of the paths in this paper. You will find it helpful for the following discussion to make the path drawings.) The last section of this paper presents a short segment of the subject's protocol from Problem 1.

A Basic Model of the Human Processor

To understand both the processing requirements of these path problems and the subject's behavior in them, I have built a model of the subject in these tasks. The model is a computer program which simulates the subject's memory and mental processing. The program is embedded in a special kind of programming system which is a basic model of the human information processor. What distinguishes this kind of system and program from earlier computer simulations is the clear way in which psychological assumptions are embodied in the system and the detailed way in which the program works with these assumptions.

In brief, the programming system contains a short-term memory (STM) and a long-term memory (LTM). The STM is an ordered list of symbolic expressions which represent the system's immediately accessible knowledge. The expressions can be arbitrarily complex, but STM may contain only a few (about 10-20) of them. STM is constantly changing. New expressions are pushed into the front of STM, forcing out old expressions at the back, thus keeping the length of STM constant. STM functions as the central focus and stimulus of all the system's processing.

The LTM is a (potentially) unlimited collection of symbolic rules of behavior. These rules are of the form   condition --> action. A condition is a set of patterns to be matched against the expressions in STM. An action is a set of simple symbolic transformations (e.g., inserting and deleting symbols in an expression, creating a new expression, etc.) on the expressions in STM. These rules are the only form of permanent knowledge allowed to the system. The operating principle of the system is: if the condition of any rule in LTM matches any of the current expressions in STM, then execute the action of the rule, which changes the state of STM, thus causing another rule to apply; and so on, in serial fashion. The system has a mechanism for unambiguously selecting applicable rules. Hence, once we declare some rules to the system and "push the button", it performs according to those rules. In other words, the rules are the program. (6)

The Model of the Subject

Given the basic system, a set of rules (a program) was designed to represent the subject's ability to perform in the path problems. The system goes through the following cycle on each input move: [1] Listen for the new move direction. [2] Create a new expression describing a line in the move direction. [3] Recognize other new figures by combining the new line with other parts of the path. [4] Integrate the newly recognized figures into the current overall path description. [5] Verbally describe the newly incorporated elements of the path. [6] Review the entire path description and repeat the sequence of moves in the path.

While working on a path problem, the system creates several different kinds of expressions in STM. Many are descriptions of figures such as lines, corners, boxes, step patterns, S-shapes, etc. E.g., the expression
> (L12 LINE VERT SOUTH P1 NORTH P2 MOVE NORTH)

represents a northward moving line, labelled internally as L12, from point P1 to point P2. Note that the symbol LINE is not the word "line" (although they are related). A symbol is an abstract entity; its semantics (meaning) is only defined by the rules that use it. E.g., a simple rule (in English) using LINE is:

> Given a new LINE, and another LINE orthogonal to
> and sharing an end point with the first LINE
> --> create a new CORNER expression with
>   the shared end point as the corner point.

If the expression   (NEW L23 LINE HORIZ WEST P2 EAST P3 MOVE EAST) were in STM along with the previous expression, then the above rule would produce in STM an expression like   (NEW C123 CORNER P2 WEST L12 NORTH L23 ...) .

But there are other types of expressions in STM. Some hold verbal input/output information (7); some represent goals; some are markers and place-keepers. Thus many expressions are devoted to spelling out what the system is trying to do at any moment and how it is doing in its attempts. I call these "control" expressions. They are especially important because they give a purposeful structure to the (potentially chaotic) sequence of rule executions.

It should be pointed out that it is only this kind of task analysis--taking into account the whole range of processes necessary to perform the task--that brings out the importance of control knowledge and how it interacts with the figural knowledge to produce the observed behavior. The system could be viewed as being either goal-directed or data-directed, depending on whether the rules that are currently executing are conditioned on control expressions or on "data" expressions; but in fact it is hard to separate these out since both are happening together.

The Internal Representation of Paths

Consider how the system internally represents the incoming information. It does not just make a list of directions--the simplest strategy allowing the reconstruction of the path--but rather it interprets the directions spatially by grouping elements into visual patterns and relating these patterns. E.g., from the protocol sample we see that both the subject and the program encode the beginning of Problem 1 as an upside-down box (ss 146-147) followed by a pattern of steps (ss 149-155) followed by an S-figure on its side (ss 160). The structure of this encoding is basically a hierarchy of spatial configurations and elements, as can be seen in the tree diagram following the protocol sample.

The reason for this more complex strategy is the limited size of STM. Much of the system's processing must be devoted to managing STM. Expressions can be encoded by embedding them in other (higher-level) expressions (8) (e.g., the rule example in the previous section). This preserves an indirect access to the embedded (lower-level) expressions, even if the latter should be pushed out of STM. On the other hand, (higher-level) expressions can be decoded ("opened up") by explicitly writing their embedded expressions in STM. These operations of encoding and decoding expressions may be viewed as climbing up and down the hierarchy tree.

Aside from the hierarchic relations, the most pervasive encoded relation is "next-in-time"; this is primarily due, of course, to the sequential nature of the task. All figure expressions are marked so that the time sequence of their parts can be recovered. In fact, the rules use this sequence information more than the spatial information.

One of the interesting features of the system's behavior is that it often predicts what directions will come next. E.g., when a step pattern is recognized, it expects the pattern to be continued. If an expectation is thwarted, the system sometimes has to reorganize its representation; but the system remembers this event (e.g., see ss 154-157 in the protocol sample), and it becomes a permanent part of its knowledge of the path.

Another important feature of the internal representation is its abstractness--symbol structures are neither verbal nor visual. They are not visual because only a very small part of the information that would be immediately available with a visually presented drawing of the path is explicitly represented. That they are not verbal is indicated by the amount of processing necessary to generate verbal descriptions from them.

The function of the description rules is to convert the internal symbolic descriptions into a grammatical string of words (or more accurately, into symbols close to words; e.g., L12 cannot be communicated externally, but LINE can). This process also entails the selection of the appropriate information to verbalize and the use of the problem context in constructing the output. The system does not produce real English, but only English-like symbol sequences, as can be seen in the right column of the protocol sample. Although the program is a bit more verbose than the subject, notice that its output is quite consistent with the subject's verbalizations.

The internal representation of the path is also used for spatial processes (imaging?), such as spatially relating the current location in the path to previous parts of the path. Another process is the elaboration of the bilateral symmetry relations in Problem 3. These processes use the sequential and hierarchic relations in the internal descriptions, as well as the spatial relations. We see, therefore, that imaging behavior depends on more than just spatial information.

The most important feature of this representation is that it is a mixed bag. Temporal, spatial, and part-whole relations are intermixed with records of special events of the encoding process. Visual images cannot be isolated as separate structures. The subject does not exhibit (in the protocol) any kind of knowledge that cannot be explained by this kind of symbolic encoding and the rules to act on it.

But to be honest, I must admit that the current program misses some subtleties of the subject's behavior. In Problem 1 the subject often complains that the path "keeps dragging out" to the east; and by the end of Problem 3 he knows that he is near the beginning of the path, but not exactly where. However, it appears that these can be explained by expanding the internal representation to include some higher-level spatial relations between the sub-configurations of the path descriptions, allowing the system to rely less on its sequential relations. In any case, all the subject's knowledge of the path seems to comfortably fit a symbolic representation.

Relevance to Design

What does all this have to do with the topics of this conference? Let me just hint at a few areas of contact.

[1] The path task could be considered (though it was not intended this way) as a very abstract model of one aspect of environmental imagery. The path is learned by sequentially travelling over it, just as a city is learned. The account just presented accords well with the findings of Lynch (9), Appleyard (10), and others: the path is understood mostly in terms of local relations; knowledge of the whole is

rather fuzzy; the time sequence of features and events plays a central role; etc. What this suggests to me is the possibility of extending this kind of detailed analysis of the human processor to the more complex domain of city imagery. This would enable us to get a hold of some precise specifications of what knowledge of a city is and how it is learned.

[2] An understanding of imagery is necessary to an understanding of the psychology of the design process. My analysis of the nature of imagery fits well into the larger (symbolic) context of the design process, which involves both form and function. The structural description of images is central to a theory of cognitive representation which is vital to a theory of representation in design. (11)

[3] This research relates to the problem of interfacing between the designer and the computer. As an exercise, we could consider an extension of my program to the task of conversing (in language and drawings) with people on the topic of spatial configurations. To do this well, the computer must have a compatible "cognitive map" of the spatial world, which is what this research is working rowards. This view is supported by the recent research on language understanding systems (12) which is finding that a deep understanding (a semantic base) of this kind is essential to language communication.

[4] Finally, the programming techniques of this research have a lesson to offer about the form of design knowledge. The idea of the condition-action rule says that the units of knowledge are not static facts, but rather context-dependent actions. In other words, knowledge can be defined only in the contexts in which it is used. (13) This notion is compatible with the "pattern language" (14) approach to design knowledge. The issue here is the nature of a more-or-less formal framework for specifying design knowledge so that it can be communicated between designers and so that it can be assimilated by the computer. Using such a framework, I have suggested elsewhere (15) how the computer might be used as a design advisor.

These suggestions are rather superficial. Regretfully, I do not have the time nor space to pursue them further here. But each of these areas is ripe for study; and they show that the detailed psychological study of cognitive structures has an important place in design research.

Sample Protocol Segment

This segment is taken from the end of move 15 of Problem 1. The subject is reviewing the whole path. The numbers at the left are speech segment (ss) numbers.

ss	subject's protocol	program output
144	Uh, I can review what I have,	(REVIEW)
145	Just so I don't forget it.	
146	Uh, you began with a box,	(BOX
	(pause)	
147	uh, going upside-down,	OPEN SOUTH)
	(pause)	

148	uh, up, over, and down.	(MOVE NORTH EAST SOUTH)
		(THREE STEPS)
149	And then you did a step,	(STEP TWO)
		(MOVE EAST SOUTH)
150	a step,	(STEP THREE)
	(pause)	
151	a step means over, uh, to the east,	(MOVE EAST
152	and then down,	SOUTH)
153	[Uh huh.]	
	(pause)	
154	Uh, then you did, uh,	
	(pause)	
155	you began to go on the fourth step	(BEGIN STEP FOUR)
156	across and/	(MOVE EAST)
157	but you came up.	(EXPECT FAIL INSTEAD MOVE NORTH)
		(S-FIG)
	(pause)	(BOX OPEN NORTH)
		(BOX OPEN SOUTH)
158	At which point you went over	(MOVE EAST
159	and down, and	SOUTH)
	(pause)	
160	made that S-shape.	
		(LINE LENGTH TWO)
161	And then you dropped down,	(MOVE SOUTH)
		(TWO BY TWO BOX OPEN NORTH)
		(LINE LENGTH TWO)
162	went over two,	(MOVE EAST EAST)
163	and up one,	(LINE NORTH)
164	and that's where we are right now.	

The diagram at the right shows some of the program's cognitive structure of the first 15 moves of the path in Problem 1. The program's internal representation is actually much more complex, but this diagram covers these aspects reviewed by the program above. Hierarchic relations are indicated horizontally and sequential relations vertically.

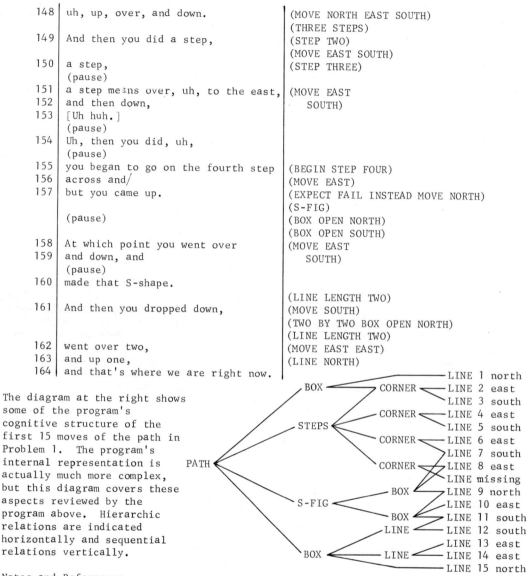

Notes and References

I would like to acknowledge the help and encouragement of my thesis advisor, Dr. Allen Newell. This research is supported by the Advanced Projects Research Agency of the Office of the Secretary of Defense, contract F44620-70-C0107, and is monitored by the Air Force Office of Scientific Research.

(1) For a general discussion of imagery, see Ulric Neisser, COGNITIVE PSYCHOLOGY, Appleton-Century-Crofts, 1967, Chapter 6.

(2) A typical visualization problem on intelligence tests is one involving the painting, cutting, and counting of imagined cubes. An extensive analysis of this task was done by George Baylor, "A treatise on the mind's eye", Ph.D. Thesis, Carnegie-Mellon University, 1971. His research is the logical predecessor to my own.

(3) The hypothesis of the analog nature of imagery is being pursued by Roger Shepard in a series of experiments on mental rotation. See, e.g., R. N. Shepard and J. Metzler, "Mental rotation of three-dimensional objects", SCIENCE, vol. 171, pp. 701-703, 1971.

(4) E.g., Allen Newell & Herbert Simon, HUMAN PROBLEM SOLVING, Prentice-Hall, 1972.

(5) See Lee R. Brooks, "Spatial and verbal components of the act of recall", CANADIAN JOURNAL OF PSYCHOLOGY, vol. 22, pp. 349-368, 1968.

(6) These kinds of rules are usually called "productions" and this kind of system a "production system". The case for a production system as a model of the human information processor is made by Newell & Simon in Chapter 14 of HUMAN PROBLEM SOLVING, Prentice-Hall, 1972.

(7) The system has primitive LISTEN and SPEAK operators for simulating verbal input/output. These operators work by reading and writing in STM.

(8) This is sometimes called "chunking". See, e.g., the classic paper by George Miller, "The magical number seven ...", PSYCHOLOGICAL REVIEW, vol. 63, pp. 81-97, 1956.

(9) Kevin Lynch, THE IMAGE OF THE CITY, MIT Press, 1960.

(10) See, e.g., Donald Appleyard, "Notes on urban perception and knowledge", Proceedings of EDRA 2, 1970.

(11) Concerning the importance of representation, see Herbert A. Simon, THE SCIENCES OF THE ARTIFICIAL, MIT Press, 1969.

(12) See Terry Winograd, UNDERSTANDING NATURAL LANGUAGE, Academic Press, 1972.

(13) See Winograd (above) for an advocacy of the procedural definition of knowledge.

(14) Several reports on the pattern language by Christopher Alexander and his associates are available from the Center for Environmental Structure, Berkeley, California.

(15) Thomas Moran, "(Artificial, intelligent) architecture: computers in design", ARCHITECTURAL RECORD, March 1971.

Philip Thiel
Professor of Architecture
College of Architecture and Urban Planning
University of Washington
Seattle, Washington 98195

Abstract

Discursive notational tools are needed for the time-based abstract simulation of proposed environmental-contingent experiences, and of the experienciable environments
hypothesized as necessary to facilitate or evoke them. In association with the
identification of User-Participant characteristics and situational roles such tools
will forestall the most serious designer errors. An Experience-notation is necessarily based on information elictable from User-Participant responses to subsequent
iconic simulation, and may be scored in terms of Actions, Feelings, and Thoughts.
An Environment-notation is keyed to a path-contingent sequence of Scenes, and may be
scored in terms of Space, Place, and Occasion.

Introduction

Given the technological imperative of man's ecological and social condition, as
environmental designers and social scientists we have no option other than the continued development of the tools by means of which we attempt to understand and guide
our transactions with the physical and social environments.   In the emerging
circumstances of our finite resources, increasingly diversified patterns of mobility,
and of socio-environmental egalitarianism our traditional professional normative
stereotypes no longer serve, and we are faced with the necessity of developing a
whole new order of tools for (A) the operational specification of our proposed environmental-contingent experiences; for (B) the description of the experienciable environments which will presumably facilitate, support, or evoke these intentions; for
(C) the simulation of these hypothetical environments; and for (D) the elicitation
of the situational responses thereto of the putative User-Participants of these
environments.

This formulation of our design task, when combined with the associated cybernetic
operation of the management of the built environment, may be given the comprehensive
name of the Envirotectural Process.   It is essentially concerned with the matter
of environmentally-contingent human experience, and assumes that the individually-
evocative and socially-facilitative affect of this experience is the ultimate purpose for any intentional intervention in the environment (as well as the ultimate
consequence of any other intervention, inadvertent or otherwise). By making this
purpose explicit all our other sub-purposes, activities, and tools may be seen in a
proper ends-means perspective.

Environmental experience, or the perception of the physical environment, is based on
the extraction of information latent in the sensory stimulation available at our
body/environment interface, which in a general sense is the outer surface of our

skin. This stimulation exists in the ambient fields of matter and energy in which we live, and whose patterning on a point-by-point basis is specific to and therefore specifies that environment. Perception then is the active, individualistic process of the probabalistic determination of the invarients in this environment-specific patterning, and is obtained in the process of our movement in and through these fields. This dynamic time-based nature of our denotative and connotative reading of our environment has fundamental implications as to the type of simulation appropriate to the Envirotectural Process.

Simulation, defined as the manifestation of an essence of a situation before or aside from the fact of its reality, is a basic element of the Envirotectural Process. It is as old as man, and from prehistoric cave-walls to the contemporary cathode-ray tube has served as man's de facto crystal ball by providing a means for making decisions in the face of alternate courses of action. Simulation, as a part of the technological instrumentation of man is a parabiological sociocultural means for adapting to the environment, and a key factor in determining and qualifying man's relations with his environment. Thus our consciousness of the environment, and the nature of our intentional interventions therein are limited to what we can communicate to ourselves and each other with our existing means of simulation.

Langer (1) differentiates between the discursive and the presentational modes of communication; which in the former involve a successive order of data, as in the case of writing, music, dance, and the cinema; and in the latter, a simultaneous order, as in the case of maps, plans, photographs, paintings, and models. Our professional means of communication have always been of the latter type, and have scarcely changed since the time of the Renaissance. One of our major blind spots and operational incapacities has been due to the lack of discursive means of environmental simulation, and only recently have attempts been made to fill this gap with computer-aided simulations of environmental sequences, and cinematographic and closed-circuit representations of virtual movement in environmental scale-models. But it should be noted that these means for discursive simulation are limited to iconic forms in the visual mode, suitable to the later iterations of the Envirotectural Process; and that they require expensive instrumentation. A prior operational necessity are means for the inexpensive, convenient, and rapid discursive description of hypothetical experienciable (or actually experienced) environments in analytic and synthetic abstraction, in multisensory modes, so as to facilitate evocation of the designer's initial imaginative formulations and their external communication to others. Some precedents for such discursive notations exist in the fields of music, dance choreography, television, and cinematographic design, and a few embryonic environmental notations have been developed and published in recent years.

Another of our operational incapacities has been due to the lack of a similar discursive means for the specification of the generic, archtypical, intended experiences we propose for a given group of user-participants (UP), in a given situational time-place-occasion (TPO) context. Our capabilities in this area are presently exemplified only by the very occasional (and post facto) casual verbalizations of a few designer's intentions. Without a prior explicit formulation of the ultimate purposes of our environmental interventions, for use as a performance specification, we have in fact no criteria for the evaluation of our operations.

General Specifications

The conceptual bases of these notations should be comprehensible to beginning design students, and once learned, the notation itself should become "invisible" through familiarity in use. The graphic indications should involve nothing more than the freehand use of any common writing instrument, and no special graphic skill or equipment should be required. The notations should use time as the basic reference: either virtual, phenomenological, subjective time; or on-line, "real", objective time. They should be suitable for either prescriptive or descriptive use; as a means of specifying proposed Experiences (EXs) or Environments (ENs), or of recording actual EXs or ENs, and in either event and case should be capable of specification to any desired degree of exactness from a rough "guesstimate" to a precise measurement. The conceptual or operational independence of components of EX and EN should also be represented in the notation, so that various types of analysis or different degrees of design will be possible.

Experience Notation

For practical purposes the content of EX-notation should be based on measurable UP responses in the simulation laboratory or real-world field, and limited to inferences from multiple independent measures. Thus we are constrained to the use of direct observation of overt body behavior, and indirect observation of covert somatic processes through instrumentation, and to UP verbalizations of introspected consciousness. This material is notated here as the EX in the three parallel streams of Actions, Feelings, and Thoughts.

Actions include the voluntary and involuntary muscular body activity, on a macrofocus level, and are divided into three sub-categories: Whole Body Actions, involving passive, transitory, and active configurations of the body as whole; Interpersonal Actions, involving attentive, vocal, gestural, and contact behavior with other human beings and living creatures; and Manipulative Actions, involving interactions with inanimate objects. This information is coded in pre-defined vocabularies and notated separately in terms of its successive occurance and duration with reference to a parallel vertical time-line. An additional analytical channel records the summated power level.

Feelings are taken here to mean the affects of the emotions, as inferred from overt and covert muscular and glandular body changes, as associated with the responses of the autonomic nervous system. The notation of the flux of emotion over time is made by coded indications of kind and intensity in terms of Plutchik's model, (2) and with event and duration similarly related to the above same time-line. A separate analytical channel of the intensity envelope is included, to denote the (undirectional) level of arousal.

The Thought channel concerns the stream of consciousness, as available from introspection and empathic observation. A general index to the content of thought is the 10 X 10 matrix of biologically basic "Primary Message Systems" described by Hall; (3) coded in association with the indication of their occurance and duration in time on three channels representing the Designative, Appraisive, and Prescriptive modes of signification. An additional analytical channel characterizes the locus of thought; in either perceptual environmental awareness, or in conceptual inward attention.

User-Participant Characterization

Any such EX-score achieves significance only in conjunction with an identification of the characteristics of the one or more UP groups involved, and of the TPO context of their involvement. In requiring this in Phase A of the Envirotectural Process, and by the use of UP analogues in Phase D, the designer transcends his own limitations in anticipating the signification of his proposed environment to the actual UPs, and thus eliminates the source of his most fatuous errors.

UPs are differentiated in terms of their situational TPO roles, and the physiological, demographic, historic, and motivational correlates of their Transducers, Coders, and Attenders: which are the perceptual filters mediating between the public physical environment and the private phenomenological environment.

Transducers are the receptive units of our perceptual systems whose potential capabilities in transferring information from one system to another are genetically determined, experientially developed, and prosthetically supplemented. Coders incorporate the sets of conditioned and learned responses; or the collection of habits, attitudes, preferences, images, skills, and languages developed or acquired through evolutionary selection and the informal experience and the formal training of enculturation. Attenders operate in real time to monitor the afferent streams of signals from exterior and interior sources of stimulation in terms of a hierarchy of long and short-term need-states, and the accessibility of categories of role-determined situational sets.

The TPO context has been dealt with at length by Barker (4) as the "behavior setting", and consists of one or more conventionalized patterns of behavior in association with a correlated pattern of space and furnishings. Barker's six "zones of penetration" into behavior settings provide a general categorization of situational role, and an EX-score must be written not only in terms of a specific UP-group characterization, but also for one or more TPO roles such as these.

Environment Notation

The physical world may be described as an aggregation of locally differentiated Spaces, each determined by a perceived invariance in sensory pattern in a given sensory mode. Thus we have visual, olfactory, auditory, thermal, and tactile Space. Scene may be defined as the combination of all the multi-modal Spaces coexisting at a given point, at a given moment. This physical environment is experienciable only in the course of our movement through it, from Scene to Scene, and the EN we encounter then is a consequence of the path we follow through the general environment, and of our position, body-orientation, and rate of movement thereon. The notation of path is accordingly the index to the EN-score. The path-movement we are concerned with is that of the UP's body as a whole, as it changes position in space over time, relative to a given initial position. The notation for this involves time and distance (subsuming rate of motion), and the characteristics of turns left and right, and of ascents and descents.

For convenience in dealing with the manifold complexity of the EN, we may adopt a theatrical model, and consider Scene to be composed of visual Space, established by Surfaces, Screens, and Objects. This empty stage-set achieves a degree of individuation as a Place through its qualification by Props, Finishes, and multi-sensory Effects; and a sense of Occasion by the presence of Men, Women, and Children as actors. Space, Place, and Occasion thus represent the major components of the EN-score, each of which is in turn composed of an open-ended variable number of sub-channels concerned with discrete categories of information, all coordinated with reference to the path-movement notation.

Space exists in varying degrees of explicitness, depending on the number, position, and type of establishing elements; and in terms of variable numbers of simultaneously occupied In-Spaces. Out-Spaces occur in View-relationships. Changes in the attributes of these conditions and of the type of connections between In-Spaces are notated at the time-distance they occur, in terms of either an $180°$ "fish-eye" hemispherical projection (HP) or a more abstract notation; depending on both the form-quality of the Space and its degree of explicitness. Supplementary numbers indicate Space dimensions and eccentricity with respect to UP position.

Props are the generally three-dimensional thing-like objects, large or small, temporary or permanent, stationary or movable, animate or inanimate; Finishes are the generally two-dimensional color and texture attributes of all the environmental surfaces (including the sky and ground, Space-establishing elements, and Props); and Effects are the luminous, sonic, olfactory, thermal, tactile, and kinetic fields and events. Higher order attributes of these furnishings, such as Prop-density, frequency distributions of hue, value, and chroma, and of pattern sizes (scale), luminous key, chiaroscuro, temperature effect, etc., are variously notated in occurance and duration.

The attributes of Occasion are Composition, including number, age, sex, and socio-economic class; Occupation, including activity, nature, role, and manner; the UP-Relationships, including personal, transactional, and spatial. These may be alpha-numerically coded, in conjunction with positional relationships as indicated in the HP, and similarly specified in temporal occurance and duration.

Prospects

The notations outlined above have been taught to a variety of design students in Japan, Scandinavia, and America while still under development. Approximately 120 hours of studio and field work are required to develop an elementary competence in their use. The open-ended nature of their format invites collaborative development and supplementation, and hopefully many others will participate in this work.

References

(1) Langer, S. K. PHILOSOPHY IN A NEW KEY, New York, Mentor, 1951.

(2) Plutchik, R. THE EMOTIONS, New York, Random House, 1968.

(3) Hall, E. T. THE SILENT LANGUAGE, New York, Doubleday, 1959.

(4) Barker, R. G. ECOLOGICAL PSYCHOLOGY, Stanford, Stanford Univ. Press, 1968.

SIX   COMPUTER AIDED DESIGN

Chairman: Michael Kennedy, Department of Architecture,
University of Kentucky

Authors: Michael Kennedy, "For The Environment: Major
Thrusts In Computing Activity"
Nicholas Negroponte, "Futures In Computing
Activities"
William J. Mitchell, "Vitruvius Computatus"
Charles M. Eastman, "The Challenge of Design"
Charles F. Davis, "Do We Need the Computer?"
Peter W. House, "From Technique To Analysis"

Michael Kennedy
Department of Architecture
University of Kentucky

Abstract

The days of ad hoc computer programs to aid environmental designers are, or at least
should be, coming to an end. How do we integrate the knowledge and expertise we
have gained? What are the advantages and dangers of developing larger systems?
Where do we put our energies and resources in the future to assure both that computers will be used as a design tool and that their use will result in a truly better
environment?

Introduction

What I have to say will take only a very few moments and a very few words. The
question has been asked: in what direction should we put our energies to make the
computer a careful tool in environmental design? Should we concentrate on simulation, on solution enumeration, on artificial intelligence, on systems analysis,
on number crunching, on graphics, or perhaps on some total system which will allow
us to drop a quarter in a slot at one end and get a cube foot of well designed space
out at the other.

We have, thus far, built a monument to ad hocery and we are no closer to any
cohesive whole that all of us together would claim-on any level or scale from
product design to national planning.

It has been said that using a computer forces a person to define his problem. This
statement assumes that you have a goal already in mind.

I submit that we, together, have neither a goal nor a well defined problem. For
this reason, if for no other, we have no overall theory on the use of information
handling equipment for improving our environment through good design and the
implementation.

We have an advantage -- larger selection -- or disadvantage -- those of us who
traffic in computers at some point we must say what the inputs are and what their
forms are; and we must say what outputs we want. We have all done this individually.
Now, I believe, we must do it in a concerted effort.

I propose that we enumerate and describe those qualifiable or symbolically represent-
able elements and components which affect our lives and futures from the energy used
by a building to the importance of relaxing in a private space; from the concentration
of sulfur dioxide in city air to the probability of getting a particular proposal
through a crooked planning communication.

I am not proposing that we develop a data base for the environment; rather a definition of the form of such a data base.

Once we have done this, several things could happen. We could partition our results into two sets: those items to be dealt with by machine and those dealt with by man. We might have a limit for tying, with modification, many of our ad hoc efforts together. And we just might begin to see congruence between types of information which could lead us to the development of a comprehensive system for using a computer in environmental design.

Nicholas Negroponte
Architecture
MIT
Boston, Massachusetts

In 1967 and 1968 we saw a burst of enthusiasm for computer aided design, for the most part stimulated by the emergence of computer graphics. At the time only a few architects could program; of that group only a handful understood the workings of a computer. Since then, architectural education has yielded a large population of designers trained in information processing, capable of initiating or overseeing computer projects more substantive than those that replace the humdrum activities of office practice and more realistic than those that emulate mankind. At the same time, since then, we have seen a radical drop in costs associated with computation (in some areas, a drop of tenfold and more).

Conspicuously, this drop in cost and rise in expertise has been matched with a decline in enthusiasms and a heightening of skepticisms. In short, we can confidently say that computers have so far had only a very marginal impact on the design profession; their major contribution has been to public relations and, perhaps, engineering.

I postulate that this decline results from two phenomena and one paradox, and that the future of computer aided design can only be seen as a change in or confrontation with these, as opposed to a technological jump some might envision.

1) Computers are intellectual engines that allow us to simulate human behavior. As such, in developing computer programs we are forced to scrutinize our methods and ask such questions as: "How do people design?" and "How does architecture evolve?". ..I suggest that we don't have the vaguest idea of "how..." and consequently are stymied at every turn, except in endeavors to write the most banal programs. In other words, until we recognize that computers are not only machines for mimicking what is understood, but are also vehicles for exploring what is not understood, we shall continue to make only small pokes at our knowledge of architecture. As with psychology, for example, I believe architecture will develop sound theories through and only through computation and the new way it has provided us to view the world.

2) A schism exists between what we can do and what we want to do with computers. This is not a simple split that exists with most scientific pursuits, it is a complicated dicotomy of interests that has led to a professional ambivalence. On the one hand what we can do is so simple and petty that involvement from the design professions is minimal; automation takes place in those areas of least theoretical challenge. On the other hand, an area of study like machine intelligence forces researchers to examine such basic cognitive studies that the practitioner (of architecture) finds disinterest because the topics are too distant from his current activities. In short there is a major gap between immediacy and substance which results primarily from the fact that (it appears) understanding and emulating design (the verb) cannot be achieved in babysteps. It is difficult to find problems and projects that can be tackled with modesty and, at the same time, have a future in ultimate goals.

3) Finally a paradox. There exists a discrepancy in roles. Four years ago in a
similar brief statement I would have claimed that the future of computers in
architecture was the complete replication of human endeavors and the substitution
of the human design by a machine far more intelligent. While this is probably the
eventuality to expect someday, it is worth reviewing the position in the context of
"Who does the designing?" If you take the position (as I do) that the meaning we
ascribe to things far supercedes their physical embodiment, then the role of
designing should surely reside with those most attached to the metaphorical being
of that chunk of the built environment. This works well for housing and not so well
for airports and hospitals. In any event, this implies a partitioning of "competence"
and "talent" in a scheme of what I have called "design amplifiers", where competence
of design is resident in a machine and the talent (of ascription, for the most part)
is with the person(s) to which the environment is meaningful. The paradox results
from the need to provide a smooth, congenial, suggestive, inviting, friendly, understanding interface that can draw inferences and recognize intentions. The intelligence of such an interface may contradict the partitioning and put back a middleman.
A possible, but undesirable result is a population of surrogate architects.

William J. Mitchell
Head, Architecture/Urban Design Program
School of Architecture and Urban Planning
University of California
Los Angeles, California

Abstract

There now exists an extensive body of theoretical and technical literature concerning
computer-aided architectural design. Its principal (indeed almost exclusive) focus
is the question of how computer-based techniques can facilitate the process of design.
This paper is concerned with the different and ultimately much more interesting
question of what the development of computer-aided design might imply for architectural
form. It argues that the notions of architectural form which implicitly underlie much
of the emergent theory of computer-aided design may be most usefully viewed as a direct
continuation of the classical academic tradition of elementary composition. This
tradition embodies an Aristotelian conception of form, and its evolution may be
traced from antiquity.

The Academic Classical Conception of Architectural Form: Elementary Composition

The evolution of the classical tradition in architecture is a long and subtle story,
and it is certainly not my intention to attempt to fully summarize it here. But to
prepare the ground for the argument which follows, it is useful to recall some of
the important stages and concepts.

In his well-known discussions of the forms of animals Aristotle developed a general
systematic framework for comparative analysis of the forms of things:

> If we were going to speak of the different species of animals, we should
> first of all determine the organs that are indispensable to every animal,
> as, for example, some organs of sense and instruments of receiving and
> digesting food, such as the mouth and stomach, besides organs of locomotion.
> Assuming now that there are only so many kinds of organs, but that there
> are differences in them...I mean different kinds of mouths, and stomachs,
> and perceptive and locomotive organs...the possible combinations of these
> differences will necessarily furnish many varieties of animals. (For
> animals cannot be the same which have different kinds of mouths or ears.)
> And when all the combinations are exhausted there will be as many sorts
> of animals as there are combinations of the necessary organs.(1)

In other words, forms were conceptualized combinatorially. They were seen as compositions constructed from limited sets of fundamental, elementary components. The
development and formalization of a similar concept of elementary composition in
architecture may be traced from Vitruvius' discussion of the orders through Renaissance
theorists such as Alberti and Serlio to its first fully systematic expression in the
pages of J.N.L. Durand's famous Precis (1802). Durand defined sets of elementary
components (columns, arches, walls, etc.), then explicitly demonstrated how wide

ranges of alternative forms might be systematically built up by combining them in
different ways. The approach was transmitted into the twentieth century largely by
Julien Guadet's massive Elements et Theories de l'Architecture (Paris, 1902). Guadet
like Durand was Professor at the Ecole des Beaux Arts, a position of immense influence. He was, as Reyner Banham has pointed out, the master of Auguste Perret and
Tony Garnier, and his book "formed the mental climate in which perhaps half the
architects of the twentieth century grew up." Banham has summarized the conception
of built form upon which the Elements is based as follows:

> The approach is particulate; small structural and functional members
> (elements of architecture) are assembled to make functional volumes,
> and these (elements of composition) are assembled to make whole buildings.
> To do this is to compose in the literal and derivational sense of the
> word, to put together. (2).

Conceptions of Form in Computer-Aided Design Systems

I suggest that the conceptions of built form which underlie most current approaches
to computer-aided design are very much in the direct tradition of Durand and Guadet.
This begins to be clear when we examine the role of representation techniques in
design, and the particular techniques by which representations of buildings are
stored in computer memory.

An architect normally generates a design for a building by operating upon some
convenient representation or partial representation of that proposed building until
the state of the representation consists of two-dimensional projections of edge-
lines of three-dimensional forms, drawn in pencil on paper, and the operations
performed upon it are making and erasing projected edge lines.

A computer-aided design system replaces this pencil and paper representation of the
design with a systematic symbolic description (consisting of numbers and words)
stored internally in the computer's memory, and the operations performed upon it are
manipulations of symbols in accordance with the laws of logic and arithmetic.
Unlike in a normal traditional design situation, the nature and sequence of these
operations may not always be directly determined by the human designer, but may be
wholly or partially under the control of some stored computer program. In other
words, the design process may be wholly or partially automated.

A symbolic description of this type is known as a data structure. To develop a
useful data structure for computer-aided architectural design it seems necessary to
conceive of architectural forms as divisible into sets of discrete and uniquely
identifiable elements and to develop some consistent systematic notation for identifying and describing those elements and the important relations between them.

Now there is a very close conceptual relationship between data structures of this
type and the classical academic treatises on design discussed earlier. In each
case, the Aristotelian method of systematic analysis and descriptions of form is
followed. A limited set of essential elements, for example the elements of the
orders, the "elements of architecture" and "elements of composition" of Guadet, and
the primitives of the data structure, are first defined. Each of these elements is

allowed a certain range of variation of type and dimension, and by assembling combinations of variations on the elements widely varied architectural forms are generated. In this sense computer-aided design as it is currently approached may be seen as a direct extension of the academic classical tradition of elementary composition and particular computer-aided design systems as embodying particular theories of architectural form in much the same way as the treatises of Serlio, Durand, and Guadet.

Is this continuity of the academic classical tradition of elementary composition in a rather unexpected way merely a historical curiosity of little practical consequence? I suggest not. It indicates that computer systems cannot be regarded as formally neutral tools in the design process. On the contrary, their use can be expected to demand acquiescence to particular formal disciplines. This implies several things. Firstly it becomes clear that the design and development of satisfactory computer-aided design systems is not simply a technical task to be left to systems analysts, engineers, and programmers. It demands a high level of architec-tural skill and capacity for rigorous analysis of built form. Secondly, as architects begin increasingly to work with such systems they will need to devote as much attention to understanding the vocabulary and syntax of form implied by the data structures of those systems as the classical architects of old devoted to study of the orders. Finally, if increasingly sophisticated systems become capable of automatically performing increasingly comprehensive design tasks, we can expect the designs which emerge from them to be characterized by particular stylistic traits. If computer systems become architects they may be academic classicists, heirs to Durand and Guadet.

NOTES

(1) POLITICS, 1290, trans. Jowett

(2) Reyner Banham, THEORY AND DESIGN IN THE FIRST MACHINE AGE, Second Edition, Praeger, 1967.

Charles M. Eastman

Associate Professor
Institute of Physical Planning
Carnegie-Mellon University
Pittsburgh, Pennsylvania 15213

While there are many ways to define design, the following provides particular insights into its process and purposes. Here, design is defined as the synthesis of physical elements so as to maximize the positive value of difference of the whole over the sum of its parts. From this perspective, everyone designs, in choosing clothes to wear or arranging furniture in a home. It is only the scale and complexity of certain design tasks that justify professions being devoted to it. Along with language and music, design is a fundamental synthetic skill that challenges and sometimes exhibits man's highest intellectual resources. For these reasons, intensive efforts to understand design processes are justified, so as to better understand ourselves, our history and to better determine our future.

The computer is probably the most important tool available for studying design. While designers usually talk as if they are synthesizing form, most design involves the synthesis of <u>information about form</u>. The computer, as an information processing mechanism, has already allowed the processes of design to be broadened beyond those fitting human capabilities. The languages of computing also provide an important means for describing design activities. Any process of design that has been unambiguously described and which relies on unambiguous subprocesses can be simulated on a computer. Thus it provides an excellent medium for testing hypotheses regarding different aspects of a theory of design. The gain in understanding resulting from simulation of design and other human synthetic skills may be one of the computer's most important contributions.

The aspects of a theory of design are generally agreed upon to include:

(a) A set of representations capable of depicting a problem at different levels of detail;
(b) A method for identifying and agreeing upon objectives;
(c) Methods for evaluating alternatives in terms of (often complex) goals;
(d) Procedures that generate alternatives, preferably in response to prior evaluations;
(e) a control process that sequences decision making among the different representations and maintains the bookkeeping for each of them.

An important qualification is that (d) the generation of alternatives, involves the definition of both the parameters that describe the alternatives as well as the values assigned to them. Form generation is more than choosing the optimal values for a pre-defined set of variables. Many of these aspects have received study and important results have been gained. Earlier EDRA proceedings and issues of the DMG-DRS Journal provide some of the reports describing them. No work has progressed very far in integrating these elements of the design process. Yet it is in their larger organization that most interesting phenomena occur. All theories of design are in their infancy.

In this short space, I wish to focus on one issue arising from the aggregation of these subprocesses. Parallel to the decomposition of problems into sub-problems (with possibly different representations) is the decomposition of goals into sub-goals. The information required to achieve this decomposition is both detailed and varied. Consider the hierarchy of goals in the design of a suitcase. The goal of durability leads to such subgoals as those regarding the abrasion, tear, and impact resistence of materials, structural properties of the shell and impact and shear considerations for all protruding parts. Some of these subgoals will have a greater impact on durability than others. Furthermore, this is only one level of the hierarchy and each subgoal will have further subgoals for its realization. The value of the solution thus can be greatly affected by the choice made of subgoals. We know that human capabilities in identifying subgoals vary greatly. To date, their treatment has been largely inductive. Some attempts have been made to enumerate the subgoals in particular design areas, as in the texts on site planning and the work by Kira and Alexander. In many problem areas, though, enumeration of all possible subgoals is impractical. As there are just too many different conditions to consider.

In many areas, goals and subgoals are context dependent. In the luggage problem, for example, quite different subgoals are derived from structural requirements and the need to keep clothing in place for soft-sided and hard-sided designs. General methods for organizing subgoals that respond to these issues may be possible. By specifying the contextual conditions under which they apply, a set of conditions could define the subgoal's appropriate application in (possibly many) different problem domains. That is, a formalism could be developed that could identify these subgoals relevant to a particular context. Such a computer system, to be an important contribution, would have to go beyond a simple cataloging and indexing of goal structures. Given the use of a suitcase, empirical studies could derive which of its attributes most affect durability. That is, sensitivity analysis could also be applied to determine the relative importance of different subgoals. The opportunities for contributions to the understanding and advancement of design in the area of goal structuring have yet to be explored in detail. (Marvin Manheim's thesis provides one example of this sort of sensitivity analysis for a single class of subgoals.)

Goal structuring is only one question of theoretical and practical importance in a theory of design. The role of prototypes, design languages, methods for gaining input form a breadth of users and methods of long range analysis are other important areas for study.

While design is a universal capability of man, only a few professions have been concerned with its development and study. As designers, it seems that we should assign high priority to the analysis of design. Rather than deemphasizing form synthesis and embarking on studies of social science, political science or engineering, we would do well to make design knowledge and theories about it our province.

Charles F. Davis
Skidmore, Owings & Merrill
New York, New York

Introduction

For ten years architects and environmental designers have been aware of the general
potentials of computers. Yet today there is little significant usage within the
design professions or the design schools. I think we should wonder why. There are
at least two basic reasons. We have solved the wrong problems or we have solved the
unimportant ones.

We make these mistakes because we ask the wrong questions. Most often it is "How
can I use the computer?" or "What can I do that is really nifty with the computer?"

Conferences like this one serve to perpetuate this kind of question by encouraging
people to say "Oh, look what I did with the computer! What did you do with it."
Though it is all my own doing, and I accept the responsibility, I resent being here
today participating in a discussion on how we should use the computer or how it
will be used in the future.

This experimental approach to computers may have been necessary ten years ago and
may be useful as a teaching aid today. But by now we should have reached maturity.
There are signs of emerging maturity in the schools. Now instead of teaching drafting
techniques, we teach computer programming. In 10 more years we will have reached
puberty and the computer programming course will have disappeared. At that point
we will understand that the computer is only a tool which is to be used when it is
needed. You don't use a sledge hammer to tighten a bolt.

Let us now begin thinking of the computer as a programmatic tool which is a part
of everyday life. Let us ask now how we as architects and designers can improve
the quality of the built environment. If the computer offers us a solution to some
felt need then we shall certainly use it.

Do we need the computer to design or layout spaces? I thought that is what we did
best or at least what we enjoyed most. In other disciplines people are not so mis-
guided as to let a machine do all the fun work while they do all the drudge work.

Do we need a computer to check us and verify that we have not made mistakes? We do
make mistakes, some of which the computer could catch. We may let our consulting
engineers put their ducts and beams in the same physical space. There is no question
that the computer could be useful here. However, it is probably not the most
reasonable allocation of resources and energy. We could accomplish a great deal
more and for less effort by restructuring the design and decision making processes
in the firms. We should be able to eliminate 99% of the mistakes we make now and
all of the important ones. All that computer applications in this area have to
offer is that they will not cause change. We can continue to do things in our old
sloppy ways.

Do we need a computer to manage information? Architects spend at least 3/4,
and more probably 90%, of their time managing or searching through mismanaged
information. A small percentage of their time and effort is spent in design, decision
making and drafting. This area of application lacks some of the built-in natural
glamour of the first two but there is no doubt that it can revolutionize architecture
and related design professions. Today, information is power. Look what has happened
to the banking industry in the past 10 to 15 years. Once bankers were freed by the
computer of the record keeping tasks they were able to discover what the money business was about. Today, banking has been revolutionized and is one of the fastest
growing industries.

I am not saying that architecture will or should go the way of banking. Only that
once architects and once those of us who get our kicks working with computers
and those in similar fields have more immediate access to the information they need
and in a form appropriate to their needs whether it comes from a computer or a book
or microfilm or word of mouth they will then have the time and energy to discover
what the built environment is about.

Dr. Peter W. House
Environmental Protection Agency, Washington, D.C.

The computer industry, both in its hardware and software phases, is probably one of
the best available examples of the sociologist's concept of "cultural lag", far sur-
passing the earlier example of the industrial revolution and the steam engine. If
one examines the concept of the computer, and begins to look at it through the eyes
of its various protagonists, a multi-faceted and almost humorous mosaic begins to
emerge.

The "computer-nik", largely interested in hardware, has been one of the dominant
forces in the computer field over the last couple of decades. His interest is in
machines which have larger capacity, faster incore speed, and smaller size. Added
to this are a large number of peripherals, ranging from the nearly obsolescent
paper tapes to cards; from remote terminals to magnetic tapes at the terminal; and
from tape drives to disks. The range of highly specialized gadgets available for
the computer today is staggering. It extends from graphics and terminals, to
computers with all types of interpretative capacities, designed to enormously
simplify the jobs of specific sectors of the user industry.

In addition, there exists an even more varied software industry. The range of
this group encompasses competitive compilers which do one or more of the tasks
sgemented to the computer with greater speed or higher efficiency; and the almost
uncountable number of generalized and specialized software packages built for
specific applications or hawked to specified segments of the community.

Also, there are the information specialists, and the modelers, who have begun to,
among other things, interpret the world in terms understandable to the computer.
They have begun to structure the thinking of many of the theoreticians and policy
makers in such a way as to facilitate that task, and to facilitate the use of
computers directly.

Finally, there are the users themselves. Policy and decision makers, in both the
public and the private sectors, must make sense out of the model-computer output
to guide their actions day to day. Inasmuch as there is generally a high correlation between the age of the decision maker and his policy-making power, it is
accurate to say that the most powerful policy sector is usually almost completely
unfamiliar with the analytical techniques of the computer itself.

Taking just these four sectors and analyzing them, both individually and in relation
to each other, results in a highly interesting anomaly. Not only do the four sectors
not communicate with each other, but there are great differences, both in need and in
sophistication, within each of the sectors. Additionally, it would appear that each
of the sectors acts independently of the others; often resulting in great expenditures
of time, effort and funds by one sector producing no measurable payoff to the others.

We are told that such "carryings-on" are characteristic of what must be changed.
What is unclear is the reaction of the policy maker, who is already faced with a
world where change is rapid and problems come at a staccato pace. The lag is exceedingly costly.

WORKSHOPS

SEVEN ACTION RESEARCH IN
MAN–ENVIRONMENT RELATIONS

Chairman: Edward H. Steinfeld, School of Architecture and Gerontology Center,
Syracuse University, Syracuse, New York 13210

Participants:

James Filipczak, Institute for Behavioral Research, Silver Spring, Md.
Stephen Kerpen and David Marshall, People's Housing Inc., Topanga, Cal.
Omar K. Moore, Dept. of Sociology, Univ. of Pittsburgh, Pittsburgh, Pa.
Leon A. Pastalan, Dept. of Architecture and Institute of Gerontology, Univ. of
   Michigan, Ann Arbor, Mich.
James Chaffers, Dept. of Architecture, Southern Univ., Baton Rouge, La.
Donald Conway, American Institute of Architects, Washington, D.C.
Stephen Margulis, National Bureau of Standards, Washington, D.C.
Justin Gray, Justin Gray Associates, Cambridge, Mass.
Louis Sauer, Louis Sauer Associates, Philadelphia, Pa.

Abstract

This workshop explores ways in which research projects can be settings for environmental design, management and policy making endeavors at the same time that they generate new knowledge. Four research projects are presented that have such potential. The projects vary considerably in subject matter and background of the investigators. This helps to identify the many ways in which the above goal may be reached, identify common problems and provide a setting for all participants and the audience to gain insights from one another.

Introduction

Research focusing on existing man-environment systems often fails to provide meaningful information for planning, design, and policy decisions. It often takes several years before pioneering work is recognized and findings and their decision making implications are accepted as new paradigms. Furthermore, by the time research results are obtained and widely disseminated, the nature of the problem it sought to solve often has changed drastically. Finally, the urgency of the social and environmental problems with which decision makers are faced leaves virtually no time to investigate existing systems for answers to problems. The call is clearly for action rather than research. However, action without understanding or imperfect understanding often makes things worse rather than better.

If man-environment research is to be more effective in helping to solve problems, approaches must be developed that can overcome excessive time lags and respond to rapid change and urgent needs for answers. One kind of research that can meet this challenge is "action research" where new environments or environmental management systems for everyday use are planned and implemented as "experiments" with the underlying assumption that they will be analyzed by real time feedback and modified until near-optimal conditions are achieved. This concept includes feedback that can be applied on an extended time frame. That is, where a building program or designer's future work becomes the setting for modification, not just the setting which has been studied.

As action research proceeds, informal and formal information networks disseminate the latest findings from the experimental environments. These settings become "demonstrations" for decision-makers to observe and the research staff becomes a source of well informed and well-trained consultants who can aid others, not only by passing on scientific knowledge, but also by disseminating equally valuable information for solving implementation problems. The process of action research provides an environment in which the distinction between research, planning, design, implementation, and use is overcome--researchers themselves become decision makers. This ameliorates the problems of more conventional research discussed above, although it does raise certain other problems, such as insuring objectivity of findings and developing client centered interests in research personnel.

This workshop seeks to explore the implementation of action research by presenting four different projects which can be placed under this rubric. The four presentations were prepared in writing by panelists for the benefit of discussants who reviewed only the initial drafts of the papers and submitted written comments as well. These items appear below. The broad range covered by the four projects illustrates the potential of action research approaches. What all share in common is a commitment to improving some part of the physical world while learning more about how that world affects people's lives.

It is hoped that this workshop, by examples and discussion, will encourage more researchers to provide a direct service to people as they gather information about them and more designers to assess the impact of their work on people's lives as they design for them. Finally, it is hoped that those already engaged in action research may learn something from others working in different contexts.

In addition to those who have submitted papers for publication, there will be four other participants. Donald Conway, Director of Research, American Institute of Architecture, will be a discussant, and Louis Sauer, Architect and Justin Gray, Planner, will be commentators on the verbal discussion that occurs.

Panelists's Paper: A Reflection on Privacy and Programming in Prison
By James Filipczak

CASE II (Contingencies Applicable to Special Education) was a project conducted six years ago by the Institute for Behavioral Research at the former National Training School for Boys in Washington, D.C., a federal training school for 14-21 year old juveniles serving states east of the Mississippi River and the District of Columbia. Approximately one-half of the commitments were from the District; one-half of the inmates were white; one-half were charged with interstate transportation of stolen vehicles; most were social and educational dropouts. This situation fostered recurrent intercultural and racial friction.

CASE II was an early attempt at the application of behavior management (or modification, if you prefer) to a penal environment. It intended to develop procedures that could establish and maintain educational behaviors for such juveniles within a controlled and supportive setting. It was organized as a residential school-within-a-prison, having 24-hour per day control over the program of its students. CASE II was planned to provide all perquisites for student life, including housing, dining, education, social programs, community interactions, and (in this case) supervise the parole process. Limited interaction with the institution was maintained, for religious services and vocational training. Clearly, the environment proposed for CASE II would play as functional a role in the overall program as the learning procedures, materials, and consequences.

CASE II students and staff (including training staff of the NTS) worked for approximately two months on the design of the social and living programs and of the environment itself. The largest step toward the final environmental plan included the separation of various staff and student requirements onto the four floors. The ground floor (previously used as a recreation and leisure area) was converted into the sleeping quarters and "quiet area" for the students. During the Planning phase, both the students and the staff were compelled to note strongly the need for student privacy in this area. It was felt that this privacy should function to serve the intra-personal needs of confined teenagers with only minimal consideration for custodial supervision. Second, the students should have the opportunity to disregard such private facilities or make personally-directed changes in the originally conceived environment. Two types of private space were planned and installed: 1) private student sleeping quarters; and 2) private showers. Limitations in funds precluded installing other apparently desirable private accomodations such as enclosures around toilets. This ground floor area was termed the "Home Floor" by the students and also contained small-group meeting areas for the students, a counseling and office space for the NTS correctional officer, automatic clothes laundering machines, and so forth. Most of their time spent on home floor construction was devoted to the private rooms. Each of these rooms enclosed a 6' by 8' rectangle of floor space, divided by semi-permanent celotex and 2 x 2 wood framing. Each contained a bed (salvaged from surplus NTS stocks) and mattress, a chair, a private lamp, and a combination desk/clothing storage unit. The NTS administration would not permit closing these rooms off with doors, but entry ways were staggered along two corridors to insure no direct interior observation from the officer's desk. The officer could, however, observe movement between rooms. Clearly, these rooms were neither palatial nor wholly pleasing to a designer's eye. Initially, the student's reactions were "Wow, we did it." and "Boy, that sure looks neat." (fitting in verbal approximations of actual vocabulary for this audience.) Students expressed distinct relief when they were permitted to move into this home floor from their former cottage dormitories. The later development in and redefinition of this original planning and construction took place over an 18-month project period and provided striking examples of student preferences and behavioral or attitudinal changes.

However, the home floor was but one element of a high integrated approximation of the outside world. CASE II was conducted as a token economy where students earned points (analagous to money) for demonstrating criterion-reference performance on a range of educational, social, and vocationally oriented learning programs. The principal means of sustenance in this economy was through work done on educational materials (reading, English language, math, social studies, and science) on the third and fourth floor of the cottage. The environment devised for CASE II's Educational program included two classrooms (one used as a library and small group study area), an audio-visual projection room, an area for staff and student interaction while checking progress on individualized and self-paced learning materials, a large space accommodating private study offices for each student, and a testing room. This space was air-conditioned and provided with the most necessary amenities for study—learning materials, light, sound control, teachers to help it along, and distinct motives (both increased educational competence and the point earnings). Students were generally most attentive to the tasks at hand and educational data show distinct changes in performance related to both variations in types of point payment and availability of additional outside educational and vocational opportunities. At times, however, even the hardest working of them took some time off. Even though the students were able to choose the type of study situation in which they could work, over 95% of the individual study time was spent in the private study office. Students seldom took advantage of the group area as a study tool, but preferred it as a quiet area for taking earned time off from study.

The main, or first, floor of the cottage served a variety of student and staff-related functions. Principal staff offices, data management, and counseling space was made available. However, student activities took up the bulk of the first floor's space. Rather than utilize the NTS operated student dining hall, CASE II provided its own cafeteria service. This permitted both the staff and students to define food preferences, to eat in a mutually supportive and socially directed atmosphere. Students were able to select preferred foods and the staff management was able to shape and direct such choices (to enhance cultural interchange and understanding) by varying prices and creative advertising. Students paid for their meals through the point economy, using earnings from educational, social, and pre-vocational programs. Most leisure time on the first floor was spent by the students in the CASE II lounge. Here, the students were able to shoot pool, drink a coke, and eat snacks, smoke, dance to the strident rhythm of the jukebox (records selected by the student government, of course) work on model-building projects, shoot the breeze with their friends, play ping-pong, read, study, snooze, or use selected gaming devices, e.g., pin ball machine. A separate room, off the main lounge, provided space for television viewing (even beyond the normal lounge-closing time, if you had the points to spend). Each diversion, of course, cost points (again, all prices set cooperatively between the staff and student government). Adjacent to the lounge, CASE II provided a "store" where students could purchase with their point earnings both necessities and luxuries (such as civilian clothing and gifts for family and friends) that previously were available on a "forced-choice" basis in the NTS commissary (only Wings cigarettes available, for instance). The store's services and materials also provided a distinct stimulus to the activities and operations of the home floor.

Rooms that had originally appeared bare, spartan, and foreboding were transformed into individual masterpieces of interior design ingenuity. Playboy centerfolds, new clocks, radios, television sets, framed photographs of family and friends, drawings, calendars, pillows, and bedspreads vied with bright paint and wall hangings to create an atmosphere of ownership and pride. Considerable time, effort, and points were expended in this decorating process. Banking data from the project indicate that the students' leisure time activity preferences changed coincidentally with the increasing sale of items for use in private rooms. Fewer hours and points were expended in active leisure activities in the lounge, and students devoted both time and points to home floor diversions. For most CASE II students, this was their first private space. Their comments to other students often indicated possessiveness of this space--"Get out of my room; this is my room. I paid 800 points for this room, and you have to ask me if you want to come in." Interestingly, a stronger opposite effect was found. A number of students decorated their rooms similarly, and named the "street" that abutted their rooms "the Ville." Eventually, two of these students removed the partition between their rooms and created a "suite" suited to their friendship and tastes. Such space manipulation proliferated and the students were found to wear "civilian" clothing almost consistently. On entering the cottage, visitors commented on the apparent similarity to a "regular" school.

Eventually, CASE II home floor contained three double-occupancy suites, one four-man pad, and a range of redesigned, decorated, and highly personalized private rooms. Students invited friends into their rooms to watch television, to do homework jointly, to help write letters to parents and girlfriends, to play cards, or simply to b.s. It should be noted that students were not required to rent these private rooms. Each student could choose to save all of the points he was earning in his learning programs to spend (as cash) after his parole. In theory, a student could choose to never partake in any CASE II rental or leisure spending program. If he so chose, he would be provided a regimen similar to that of a regular NTS inmate. He would eat a more bland meal served on a metal tray. He would sleep on a dormitory-style bunk and store his belongings in a regulation locker. He would also wear NTS-issued khaki clothing and draw an "issue" of ten cigarettes per day. He would also be permitted participation in all learning and recreational programs that did not require specific point entrance fees. Over the term of CASE II, seven students spent a total of sixteen weeks in this status--which was termed "relief". Only two students voluntarily chose to spend one week each on relief status--and then for only one week each. During this test of the system, each of these two students repeatedly commented to their friends that there was "no way" they'd ever try that again. The rest of those students on relief simply did not have sufficient points to avail themselves of room and meal option.

CASE II counselors discussed the conditions of relief status with each of these students. The most frequent comments concerned the "difference" between relief and the "real world" programs available in CASE II. Students were also concerned that the relief area provided them with no respite from interaction with other students and that their sleeping accommodations subjected them to the scrutiny of every passing student and staff member. Many said (and followed through) that they would like to spend every night for a week in their rooms, entertaining no visitors and just goofing off. In a major debriefing of 16 students, the majority indicated that there were three "best-like" features of CASE II: 1) the food; 2) the private rooms; and 3) the academic learning program.

The private rooms and other CASE II amenities obviously functioned in ways other than to satisfy the students' homemaking needs. As a part of the overall contingency system of the project, they were integral (to what extent, one will never know) to the backup for point earnings on academic learning activities. It should be noted here that the academic achievement of CASE II students always exceeded (and often more than doubled) that of "normal" students in a traditional school program. Further, there were gains noted in measures indicating more general types of intellectual and interpersonal functioning--these paralleling the social behavior development noted in the students' home floor and other leisure area activities. For example, the average student Intelligence Quotient increased from entry to the project to its close a total of over 16 I.Q. points, well beyond high levels of statistical significance. There were few doubts that the improvements found in student achievement and performance during CASE II were spurious.

However, these gains were achieved at a cost of $1.75 per student per day more than the existing NTS penal program. The question here, of course, is whether the foremost objective is reduction of costs or effectiveness of programs and change of student behavior.

One objective of the CASE II project was to train staff of the NTS to carry through proven procedures to their everyday operational activities. A large-scale program of training was incorporated into CASE II for such purposes and the NTS eventually assumed a range of procedures similar to those of CASE II (particularly in the academic program). These steps were undertaken to insure that the NTS would have a more viable program as it relocated in new facilities (called the Robert F. Kennedy Youth Center) in Morgantown, West Virginia. Unfortunately, as is the case in other programs, many of the staff trained by CASE II chose not to relocate at the new facility. Many of these staff members were black and found the atmosphere of West Virginia potentially not conducive to their family situation. Moreover, no funds were available either through the original sponsoring agency or through the Bureau of Prisons to insure interaction of CASE II staff with staff of the new training school facility. Similar discontinuity between proven research activities and subsequent practice can arise in even the most closely monitored and viable federally sponsored programs. Although the environmental planning of the new facility incorporated certain features of CASE II in an attempt to foster the degree and kind of privacy that had been the hallmark of CASE II, subtle differences were noted. For example, private sleeping quarters were constructed as permanent facilities in the institutions, either as tiled cubicles in the intake cottages or as cell-like (and nondecorable) rooms for "high-status" living quarters for more advanced inmates. The differences may well have been more subtle, but could well be as functionally dissimilar to CASE II as those occurring due to loss of trained staff. Students, of course, had no hand in their planning.

In conclusion, it must be noted that the total set of results from CASE II is mixed. Students were found to learn academic skills far beyond national norms, engage in new and appropriate social behaviors with their peers, interact more viably with their families, help shape and maintain a working model of the "real world" in a penal setting, and express highly valued pleasure through the entire process. Yet, the principles and practices of CASE II have not been widely applied in penal settings since the cessation of CASE II activities.

Reasons for this lack of application (or, further investigation) include abhorrence of behaviorally-based intervention strategies, lack of familiarity with environmental design procedures for program establishment and conduct, ineffectiveness of dissemination strategies and programs, and simple unwillingness to change. Yet, it has been found here that the fusion of design and behavioral principles can be effective in the operation of a program of penal intervention for juveniles. Such procedures have been extended recently to provide useful alternatives in the circumvention of the penal system entirely--the conduct of preventive and community-based treatment facilities. Here may well lie the future for viable social and environmental change procedures

Panelist's Paper: Health and User Needs in Low Income Housing (1)
by Stephen Kerpen and David Marshall

We feel that where human needs, including preferences, are not being met in low income housing, there is a resulting health impairment, both psychologically and physiologically. It is these human needs, their relationship to both the physical housing requirements and the people in the housing process making decisions that influence the satisfaction of these requirements, that are the subject of this paper.

Although no administration has yet committed itself to providing an adequate supply of low income housing, there has been considerably more housing built in the last few years than in previous years. Albeit not really low income housing. In most cases however, where this housing has been built, it has not been designed to meet the health needs of the people nor has it involved the people in the design process. This is especially true in publicly financed housing. This situation, coupled with restrictive budgets and a lack of adequate architectural programs, results in designs that do not reflect the life styles or the living patterns of the community. Further, it seems to indicate that those responsible for making decisions about the housing are not aware of the relationship between housing and the health of the residents.

This study came about as a result of an original survey made in New Haven by the office of Louis Sauer Associates. (2) They were the architects for two FHA Section 236 cooperative housing projects, Canterbury Gardens and Harmony House, developed by the New Haven Redevelopment Agency. Originally, one of the projects was designed based on criteria established by the various institutional clients, i.e., the New Haven Redevelopment Agency and the Federal Housing Administration, and the architect felt that these criteria did not accomodate the existing life styles of the potential users. The New Haven Redevelopment Agency granted a request by the architect to survey a limited number of potential residents in order to establish key architectural relationships and to test the initial design for its effectiveness in providing what the potential user says he needs and wants. A sample of only six families was used due to the lack of time and inability to identify eligible families. The families were selected, on the basis of family size and make-up (i.e., number of children, sex of the children, heads of household, etc.), from the New Haven Redevelopment Agency's relocation workload. As it happened, none of these six families moved into the housing project.

The results of the survey were used to change the unit plans and to support other design decisions which reflected residents' preferences of land use. We used this project as an example to find out the utility of a user need study in providing for the health needs of residents of low income housing. To analyze this we sought to answer three questions. First, because the sample used in the original survey was small and because the families sampled did not move into the development, we wanted to know whether one could generalize the values of six families and project these values to the actual project residents. Secondly, we wanted to know if the design of the housing, based on the initial New Haven Survey, met selected health criteria of the user. And thirdly, we wanted to know what kinds of decisions, made by professionals in the housing process, affected the health needs of the users.

User Preferences

To answer the first question we wrote a user preference interview. (3) This interview checks the major conclusions drawn from the original New Haven Survey regarding use, size and location preferences in addition to the relationships of spaces within the units, adjacent to the buildings and elsewhere on the site. The interview results show that most of the families were in agreement with the conclusions of the original six families. There were a few exceptions, but these differences may be attributed to the dissimilar housing experiences of the people.

Only one of the original six families had a television in their bedroom in comparison to over 80% of the families in the recent interviews. Because of this, the majority of families now use the bedroom for watching TV as well as for sleeping rather than sleeping only as indicated in the original survey. Most of the original families lived in apartments and they state that they did not feel a front porch was necessary. In the recent interviews, everyone had a covered entry at grade level and the majority wanted a front porch even if they had to give up space elsewhere. Only half of those in the original survey expressed a need for privacy fencing around their yard but all those interviewed in the new housing wanted the yards fenced for privacy. Originally everyone said they would use a private yard. Now, with everyone having access to a yard, only 80% use them. The original survey showed three of the six families wanted a separate den-type area for viewing TV and four of the six wanted a basement. Those living in the new housing were more satisfied and their needs for additional space were quite different.

Health Needs

Secondly, to determine if the design of the housing met the selected health criteria of the user, we researched, analyzed and finally established specific physiological and psychological health criteria for housing. We found many inferences to the existence of psychological health criteria and felt that the difficulty in scientific measurement was no reason to negate them. We therefore took both of these health criteria and grouped them into human needs categories that we selected after a review of the literature of various psychologists, psychiatrists, and cultural anthropologists. We then linked the health criteria to physical requirements of housing. For example, one of our health criteria states that children have to develop friendships and learn rules of social behavior. The physical requirement that satisfies this is to provide specific play areas for children.

We then determined the physical housing requirements in the original New Haven Survey and linked them with one or more health criteria. To determine if those physical housing requirements, i.e. the design of the project, met the health criteria we designed an open ended interview. The majority of those interviewed confirmed that their housing was providing most of the requirements for a healthy and safe environment.

Units: The majority of the families were satisfied with the size and location of the kitchen-dining area. There was an interesting variation, however, in one type of unit which serves as an example of people often reacting to what they are familiar with. In Canterbury Gardens, where some units had a visual separation between the kitchen and dining areas, 63% of the families said they wanted the separation. At Harmony House there was no separation and only 25% said they wanted it. The rear yard, located off the kitchen-dining area, was generally satisfactory to everyone. However, twice as many people in Canterbury Gardens were satisfied with it because a gate in the fence (available in half of the units interviewed) allowed a second means of access to the house. Most families were also satisfied with the size and location of the livingroom except those having smaller living rooms--55% of those people were dissatisfied with its size. Although circulation caused furniture problems in both types of living rooms, it was not used as a reason for dissatisfaction.

More than 57% of those interviewed complained of noises between adjacent living areas, particularly in the stairwell. The units were separated by a masonry wall on one side but a double wood stud wall on the other side caused a disturbing noise transmission. Over 90% of the families were satisfied with the number of bedrooms and their location, but only 70% thought they were large enough. This was probably due to the number of larger families with older children in the Harmony House community. Some families, whose master bedroom faced the street, were dissatisfied with this room location. There was general satisfaction with the bathrooms except that those units without a half-bath on the first floor wanted one. Although only one accident was reported, 29% of the families did complain of wall hung lavatories being loosened by children leaning or hanging on the fixtures. (It was felt to be a potential source of serious accidents.) All but one of the families felt strongly about their need for a laundry area within their unit and all felt the one they had was large enough. Seventy-seven percent were satisfied with its location (in a separate room adjacent to the kitchen). Eighty-eight percent had some laundry equipment (50% had a washer only and 38% had a washer/dryer).

Buildings: The greater majority of the families were satisfied with the entry areas to their units and felt it gave them an identity and sense of community. Fifty-nine percent of the families used the area for contact with their neighbors and, although, almost all the families felt it was too small for a children's play area, 14% indicated it was used as a gathering point for older children and friends. Nineteen percent wanted the front porch area fenced to better define it as a private and more secure area. Ninety-one percent of the families said the rear yard was quiet and private. They most often used it as cook-out area (defined as relaxing family meals and large gatherings of friends or relatives). Sixty-six percent said young children did not use the rear yard and only 17% used it as a play area for pre-school children. (The high number of working parents may account for this low percentage.) Fifty-two percent of the families were satisfied with the extra outdoor storage provided. The large number of those dissatisfied was because the storage was located in the front rather than at the rear.

Site: More than 90% of the families were satisfied with the location of the children's play area. Fifty-two percent felt the area was too small. One-third of the families reported that their younger children used the area. There was also some dissatisfaction with the lack of equipment for older children and these families thought some of the community's problems of vandalism and child harassment might be due to this. Others felt that providing this equipment might draw outsiders and cause additional problems. The majority of families park their cars in assigned stalls but many park in unused stalls so as to park close to their units. The lighting in the parking area, community open space, and walkways, is considered adequate. Over 90% felt safe walking from their car to their home.

Reflecting the large percentage of private ownership of laundry equipment, only 31% of the families used the community laundry facilities. Almost one-quarter of the people using the facilities were displeased with the number of machines and maintenance. The facilities were located away from major activity areas and showed signs of vandalism and maintenance neglect. The community trash collection facilities are large dumpster containers located in the parking areas. Ninety-one percent of the families were satisfied with the location and 83% with the size. At Canterbury Gardens, the dumpster is located where parked cars sometimes block access to the area resulting in problems for the collection companies.

Professional Roles: Thirdly, we wanted to know what kinds of decisions, made by professionals in the housing process, affected the health needs of the users. Although we identified over one hundred types of professionals involved in the housing process, it was beyond the scope of this study to investigate more than two of these professionals: the architect and the owner/developer. An interview was developed following the same organization of the health-housing survey in which we asked a series of open-ended questions.

The owner/developer decisions regarding health criteria showed a primary concern with the safety of the people. This concern was reflected in decisions regarding their requirements for kitchen and laundry equipment, construction details and design requirements for site planning. They were almost as concerned with psychological security and had specific design requirements regarding people controlling their housing environment. Other requirements were based on concern for disease prevention, privacy and user identity.

In designing the communities, the architect responded to health criteria which concern the owner/developer, but he also made decisions which indicated his concern for other health criteria. The architect's primary concern was based on the people and their need for identity. Most of the architectural decisions involved providing the residents with a sense of individuality, defining the area under their territorial control and responding to the specific requirements dictated by the life styles of the people. This concern for identity was not limited to the individual units but extended to the need for community identity. The architect shares the owner/developer's concern for the safety and privacy of the residents, making special efforts to control vehicular circulation on the site as well as provide proper separation between various activities in the units.

Both the owner/developer and the architect made additional decisions which related to people's needs for control of natural amenities, aesthetics, rest and relaxation, and recreation.

Conclusions

First, families now living in the development were in agreement with the conclusions of the original six families indicating that the original families could project their values for future residents. Secondly, the design of the housing did generally meet selected health criteria of the user. Thirdly, the owner/developer was mostly concerned with decisions regarding the safety of the people. The architect was also concerned with safety, and in addition, was concerned with the residents' need for identity. A general, and probably most important, conclusion that can be made from this study is that if low income residents are involved in the planning and design process, the resulting housing will reflect their needs and life styles. Therefore, the user need study technique is appropriate in providing for the health needs of residents of low income housing.

Future

We have explained one level of a framework to answer questions posed by the objectives of this study--the identification of the physical requirement of housing. We have explained links between physical housing requirements and health criteria. We used, as an example, the provision of children's play areas to enable the formation of friendships and to learn the rules of social behavior. There is a need to go further than this level. A second level delves deeper into this requirement. Although the links make clear what must be provided, they do not investigate the kinds of activities that might be included. For example, in the play area for children there might be field sports, quiet games, loitering areas, etc. A third level of development might involve identifying the size and location of each physical housing requirement. Successful examples of these requirements from throughout the country, could be shown with photographs and sketches. A fourth level is a system of accountability. Each professional in the housing process could be linked to the physical housing requirement that is affected by the decisions he makes. If these four levels of development were realized, the resulting framwork could be used to assure the quality of future housing developments. People involved in the housing process could use it as a guide to insure proper design. Moreover, the consumer would be able to use it as a system of accountability because he would have available to him a listing of the individuals and agencies in the housing process who make the decisions affecting all aspects of housing.

Footnotes

(1) Based on report for Department of Health, Education, and Welfare, Public
     Health Service, Contract No. HSM 99-72-89, an evaluation of the utility of
     "User Needs Assessment Techniques" in providing for the health needs of
     low income housing.

(2) The original survey has been published in the EDRA Conference Papers, 1972,
     and in the May, 1972, edition of Progressive Architecture.

(3) All interviews made in this study were conducted with 21 of the 28 residents
     living in the 3 and 4 bedroom 2-3 story townhouse units.

Panelists's Paper: A Dynamic Assessment Paradigm for Environmental Design Research(1)
by Omar K. Moore, Ph.D.

The present paper perhaps best can be thought of as an extension of some basic
procedures which are commonly used in architecture. The procedures in which I
allude are those which are placed under the rubric of "rendering", i.e., that
set of techniques for making a possible structure, or an ensemble of structures,
realistically vivid for a client. These procedures range from the "parti" of a
design study to an elaborate multi-faceted presentation rendering. It is my
thought that if I share with you the elements of what I term a "Dynamic Assessment
Paradigm," and if you would think of this paradigm as an advanced form of
"rendering," we would be in a better position to learn from each other. An outline
of the Paradigm is given below.

   Dynamic Assessment Paradigm

A. Productive Stimulus Material
B. Penecontemporaneous Context
C. Opinionnaire I (individual opinions solicited)
D. First Group Discussion with Vote (issue drawn from Opinionnaire I)
E. Long-Term Historical Context
F. Opinionnaire II (individual opinions solicited)
G. Second Group Discussion with Vote (issue drawn from Opinionnaire II)
H. Dynamic Projective Test
I. Third Group Discussion (Topic: subjective meaning of projective test)
J. A Reflexive Retrospective View of the Problem

I devised this paradigm as one part of my research project's work in evaluation
and assessment. A student of mine, Susan J. Smerd, used the Paradigm in a study of
how inner-city ghetto residents might react to advanced educational technology
were it to be made widely available to them. The best way to appreciate the
Paradigm is to read her case study (2) and a continuation of it done jointly by
another student of mine, Francine E. Jefferson, and me. (3)

The rationale which underlies the Dynamic Assessment Paradigm is the set of design principles which I formulated as the heuristics for creating "clarifying environments." It goes beyond the scope of this paper to present these principles here; they are explained in fair detail in "Some Principles for the Design of Clarifying Educational Environments". (4)

The Paradigm itself is a sequential outline for the way in which "clients" or "subjects" are to spend approximately six hours. The object of having people go through the Paradigm is to help them formulate a clearer conception of what they really want. For example, if an architect were trying to find out whether a client would approve of, and be satisfied with, a novel hypothetical building, the analysis of his probable responses becomes a bewildering array of contrary-to-fact conditionals. The point of using the Paradigm is to make a possible future real for the client. For a short period of time, we need to make tommorrow . . .[his] permanent address (5), to borrow a phrase from e.e. cummings, and the way to do that, borrowing again from cummings, is to . . .move away still further: into now. (6)

Let us turn to the outline of the Paradigm. There are several things which we should note about it. It has ten parts. These parts are so ordered that a number of experiential dimensions are varied systematically. As people go through the various phases of the Paradigm, we are looking for attitudinal constancies which may emerge as invarient elements. Specifically, what are the experiential dimensions which are being varied in the Paradigm? Using Smerd's study as an example, she did the following things:

A. Productive Stimulus Material. The stimulus material consisted of two identical prototypes of advanced educational technology. However, she varied the socio-physical context of the prototypes. One was placed in the context of the elite "white establishment" and the other was placed in the context of an inner-city ghetto. The differences in the responses to the same thing gives one a sense of how important "context" is for the client. (Smerd's subjects were high school students from a Pittsburgh Inner-city school. They constituted a reasonably representative sample of the girls in this high school. There were 24 subjects; she carefully matched them to form 12 pairs. All were Black. Members of each pair were assigned, randomly, to either the White Context condition or the Black Context condition.)

B. Penecontemporaneous Context and E. Long-Term Historical Context. These two parts of the Paradigm form a contrasting pair as far as time is concerned. We want to know both how a client sizes things up if his attention is directed toward short term immediate concerns and long-range interests. Following each of these two parts of the Paradigm, there is an opinionnaire to be filled out and a group discussion. The analysis of the opinionnaires and the discussions can give us a sense of what is time invariant and what is not.

C. Opinionnaire I (individual opinions solicited) and D. First Group Discussion With Vote (issue drawn from Opinionnaire I). There are several things which should be pointed out about these two parts of the Paradigm. In Part C we are getting at opinions expressed privately. In Part D the outcome is the consequence of a group process. This motif of contrasting opinions given in private, as opposed to being given in public, is built into the Paradigm. Phases F and G of the Paradigm similarly provide for private versus public responding. Also, Phase I involves group activity, whereas J is a matter of individual interviews. The reason the Paradigm involves an alternation between responding privately as an individual and responding in an open-group setting is that we want to get some notion about how malleable our client's opinions are. Also, we want to know about whether there is a discrepency between opinions expressed in individual as opposed to group settings. In Smerd's study, there was a large measure of consistancy between private and group opinion, but it might have been otherwise, and we would have been in a position to know it. It should go without saying that the content of the opinionnaire and the topic chosen for group discussion would depend upon the nature of the problem to which the Paradigm is addressed. However, there is one point which should be made plain. It is part of the rationale of the Paradigm to make predictions about how the opinionnaire will be answered and about how the vote will come out at the end of the discussion. Failure to predict accurately is to be taken as a warning signal that one has got hold of the problem by the wrong end.

H. <u>Dynamic Projective Test</u>. Up to this point in the Paradigm, the client has been faced with situations which are structured in meaningful ways. The point of using a projective test here is to get some sense of his latent symbolic meanings. In terms of varying contexts, we are contrasting structured versus nonstructured contexts.

J. <u>A Reflexive Retrospective View of the Problem</u>. This final phase of the Paradigm calls for the client to sum up his emerging position. This final step is an interview conducted along the lines of Lazersfeld's Reason Analysis. (7) In the Jefferson-Moore study, the interviews were conducted via Picturephone--advantage was taken of Picturephone's optionally reflexive properties.

Even the thumbnail sketch of the Dynamic Assessment Paradigm given here probably is sufficient to suggest to the reader that this approach is extremely complex. It calls for a suitably designed physical system to go with it. I have designed such a system; it is called the Responsive Evaluation and Testing System (RETS). A sketch of the system is presented below. It is this facility, plus the rationale of the Dynamic Assessment Paradigm which, I am suggesting here, may be thought of with profit as an extension of the concept of rendering as this notion is used in the field of architecture.

Footnotes

(1) My remarks here constitute a precis of a paper entitled "A Dynamic Assessment Paradigm for Architecture." This paper and an associated case study, which make a unit, can be obtained from a nonprofit organization at cost plus handling charges. Inquiries should be directed to the Responsive Environments Foundation, Inc., 146 Oakhurst Road, Fox Chapel, Pennsylvania 51215.

(2) Smerd, Susan J., Advanced Educational Technology and the Attitudes of Inner-City High School Students, in QUALITY CONTROL AND SELF-ESTEEM: PART 2A, AN EVALUATION OF THE PITTSBURGH CLARIFYING ENVIRONMENTS PROJECT IN THE HILL DIS-TRICT, Pittsburgh: The Responsive Environments Foundation, Inc. December, 1972 14-90.

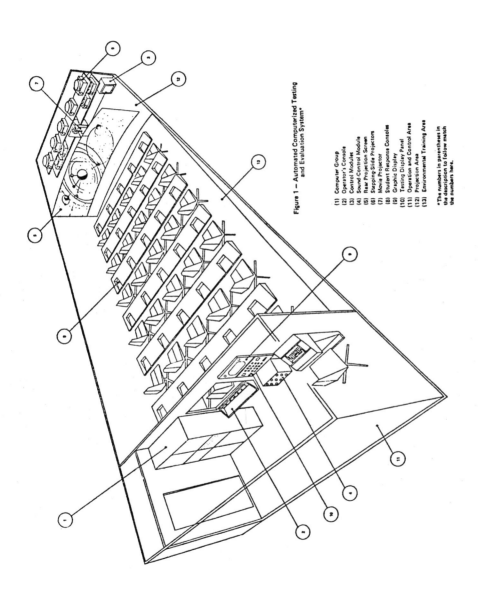

Figure 1 – Automated Computerized Testing and Evaluation System*

(1) Computer Group
(2) Operator's Console
(3) Control Module
(4) Sound-Control Module
(5) Rear Projection Screen
(6) Stepping-Slide Projectors
(7) Movie Projector
(8) Student Response Consoles
(9) Graphic Display
(10) Testing Display Panel
(11) Operation and Control Area
(12) Projection Area
(13) Environmental Training Area

*The numbers in parentheses in the description to follow match the numbers here.

(3) Jefferson, Francine E. and Omar K. Moore, Picturephone as an Instrument for Conducting Interviews, in THE PERSONALIZATION PRINCIPLE AND REFLEXIVE DEVICES: PART 2B, AN EVALUATION OF THE PITTSBURGH CLARIFYING ENVIRONMENTS PROJECTS IN THE HILL DISTRICT. Pittsburgh: The Responsive Environments Foundation, Inc. January, 1973.

(4) Moore, Omar K. and A.R. Anderson, Some Principles for the Design of Clarifying Educational Environments, HANDBOOK OF SOCIALIZATION THEORY AND RESEARCH, ed. David Goslin. Chicago: Rand-McNally Company, 1969, 571-613.

(5) cummings, e.e., All Ignorance Toboggans Into Know, POEMS 1923-1954. New York: Harcourt, Brace and World, Inc., 1944.

(6) Ibid.

(7) Lazersfeld, Paul F., QUALITITIVE ANALYSES. Boston: Allyn and Bacon, Inc., Chapter 8, 183-202.

Panelist's Paper: Involuntary Environmental Relocation: Death and Survival (1)
by Leon A. Pastalan, Ph.D.

The negative effects of relocation of elderly patients in terms of high incidence of death and serious illness have been suggested in several studies. At the same time, Blenkner (2), Goldfarb (3), Lawton (4), and others have presented evidence that the consequences of relocation are not entirely consistent from one subsample to the next, suggesting that relocation results in high mortality and morbidity rates for some older patients and lower mortality and morbidity rates for others. In addition, Novick in Montreal has reported significantly lower death rates following relocation when a program of pre-move preparation was instituted and patients had wide choices to make in selection and design of the new facility. Apparently, then, the consequences of relocation depend on the particular conditions involved. In reviewing the literature on relocation through 1967, Blenkner noted the urgent need for further investigation in this area, with quite literally many lives at stake. It was with this imperative in mind that we began our study of environmental relocation.

Design

There were two experimental and one control settings that constituted a vital part of our research design. The two experimental settings gave us a chance to study two kinds of relocation. One experimental setting was a county medical care facility which was closing its doors (Washtenaw Co. Medical Care Facility, Ann Arbor, Michigan). The other experimental facility was a county medical care facility also but it was only moving from an old frame building to a new building located on the same property (Lapeer County Medical Care Facility, Lapeer, Michigan). Thus, we could contrast changes in staff, in program, in patients, and the physical environment, all of which were involved in the first setting with a change in the physical environment only in the second situation. The control facility was a county medical care facility which remained stable and unchanged (Sandusky County Home, Fremont, Ohio). All three facilities were essentially county nursing homes. The average age of the population was in their mid-70's, their median length of hospitalization was three years and the majority were afflicted with multiple physical and mental impairments.

The major hypothesis to be tested is that the fate of the patient following relocation measured by morbidity and mortality is not determined by chance, but is a complex function of six classes of independent variables: the characteristics of the patient himself, the attitudes of the staff members who serve him prior to relocation, changes in characteristics of the physical environment, changes in relationships patients have with their physical environment, changes in services the patient receives, and the extent of formal preparation of the patient for relocation. Since our concern at this conference is largely on the environment, I shall focus on that part of our study that has mainly to do with the environment-behavior interface.

Change in Physical Structure

It is important to study objective changes in the physical environment accompanying relocation, since these may significantly affect the behavioral responses of the patient. For instance, De Long has noted that the distance of functional spaces such as recreational areas from patient rooms plays a large role in the amount and frequency of use. The same is true of the accessibility of settings within a facility. Thus, structural variables, such as the presence or absence of ramps and elevators which facilitate movement within a building, must be taken into account.

De Long (5), Lawton (6), and Lecompte (7), have all presented evidence to indicate that friction-laden encounters occur among patients and between patients and staff when functional values assigned to spaces are unclear or ill-defined. Therefore, boundaries and other cues that serve to define the functional uses of various spaces must be noted too. These physical characteristics are being documented for the experimental and control facilities. It is expected that the greater the differences which impede patient movement and independence between pre-move and post-move settings, the higher the mortality and morbidity rates. Conversely, the greater the differences which facilitate patient movement and independence, the lower the mortality and morbidity rates.

Home Range

A second important area of study is home range, defined as the total number of behavior settings penetrated by a patient during a typical day. Behavior settings are physically distinct areas where on-going patterns of behavior independent of specific individuals have been established. Through initial observation and questioning of staff and patients, we have been able to establish a list of behavior settings for each facility studied. Typically included are such things as dining room, lounge or dayroom, workshops, etc. To examine characteristic activity patterns within the home range, patients are being interviewed before relocation and during each of the four follow-up periods. They are asked what they do during a typical day, and are questioned about their use of each behavior setting identified for that facility. These measures will enable us to assess the changes which occur in patterns of activity for each patient. It is assumed that if a patient does not adapt readily to the new environment, this will be reflected in a reduction in his home range, i.e., he will routinely penetrate fewer behavior settings. It is expected that a patient who suffers a severe reduction in his home range will die sooner than the patient who does not experience such a reduction.

Spatial Autonomy

The relationship that exists between a patient and his physical environment is viewed here essentially as one of control or autonomy. It is assumed that patients occupy a fixed place within the environment whose physical aspects they cannot basically change. Inhabiting a given portion of this space, they may identify with it regardless of who in a strictly legal sense owns it. Over time the patient may come to regard this portion of space as his. He symbolizes this relationship by the arrangement of environmental props (such as furniture) and self markers (personal artifacts such a family pictures, etc.) and by the attitudes he adopts toward others regarding how they use his space.

We have designed a number of questions to ascertain how much control a patient has over the various types of functional spaces found in his home range. We ask patients to tell us about those rooms or spaces they think of as their own, and about their favorite places. Interviewers probe for specific things about these spaces that make them special to the patient, and note use of environmental props and self markers. Patients are also asked about restrictions on their freedom of movement and problems encountered in maintaining their autonomy, in an attempt to identify the degree to which staff control the spaces within the hospital and keep the patients' spatial autonomy to a minimum.

Privacy

Privacy is also recognized as a highly valued amenity for all humans. Privacy may be defined as the right of the individual to decide what information about himself should be communicated to others and under what conditions. In a previous paper, I identified four basic states of privacy: solitude, autonomy, anonymity, and reserve. (8) Westin (9) notes that privacy plays a significant role in helping an individual to fulfill his need for personal autonomy, emotional release, self-evaluation and limited and protected communication. Privacy for limited and protected communication has two general aspects. First, it provides the individual with opportunities he needs for sharing confidences and intimacies with those he trusts—spouse, family members, personal friends, and close associates at the hospital. Second, privacy through limited communication serves to set necessary boundaries of mental distance in interpersonal situations ranging from the most intimate to the most formal and public. We have modified the Privacy Preference Scale developed by Nancy Marshall (10) on a community sample for use in an institutional setting. The questionnaire is scored for preferences for the four states of privacy previously mentioned. We have developed a number of questions aimed at an assessment of the manner in which the individual copes with problems of protecting his privacy. This makes it possible to trace changes in a patient's preference for privacy over time, and compare it to the actual levels of privacy attained pre and post move.

Results

The results of our study are in the process of being analyzed, thus what data will be reported here are based on selective and preliminary analysis.

It was initially felt that higher mortality would be found in the Washtenaw County patient population because the disruption was far more severe than for the Lapeer Country patients. For instance, the Washtenaw patients suffered a rupture in the patient-staff support network since the staff did not move to the new location. The familiarity of the physical setting was also drastically altered as the patients went from an old three story structure of a turn of the century design to a modern glass and brick, single story "H" shaped layout. Finally the patient to patient support network was altered because it was not always possible to keep roommates together. Then, too, this patient population had to adjust to and integrate with a patient population already residing at the new location. The Lapeer population on the other hand, moved from an old wood frame structure to a modern two story facility. Essentially the remainder of their vital support networks remained intact. The results show however that after a 12 month post relocation period, the mortality rates for Washtenaw and Lapeer were 43% and 37% respectively. Only a 6% difference between the two facilities.

Mortality Rate - Pre and Post Relocation

	4-6 Mo.Pre	1-3 Mo.Pre	1-3 Mo.Post	4-6 Mo.Post	6-8 Mo.Post	9-12 Mo.Post	Total Deceased
WCMCF/WL	3 (5%)	6 (10%)	8 (13%)	4 (7%)	3 (5%)	2 (3%)	26 (43%)
LCMCF	0 (0%)	4 (11%)	2 (5%)	2 (5%)	5 (13%)	1 (3%)	14 (37%)

Predictors of Mortality

Preliminary analysis indicates that the best predictor of mortality is health status and cognitive functioning. Those patients who had the highest mortality were the sickest in physical terms and suffered more severe cognitive impairments. Conversely, those patients who were most intact survived best. Home range as an environmental variable shows early promise of being a strong predictor of mortality. Those patients who had 10 or more behavior setting penetrations during a given day all survived. Those who had 7 or fewer penetrations were highly vulnerable.

Mortality Related To Number Of Home Range Areas
(Lapeer County Medical Care Facility)

No. of Areas	1	2	3	4	5	6	7	8	9	10	10 or more
Alive	2	2	2	1	0	3	2	2	1	1	5
Dead	3	0	0	1	1	2	2	0	1	0	0

	6 or Less	7 or More
Alive	10 (32%)	11 (35%)
Dead	7 (23%)	3 (10%)

The other environmental variables such as spatial autonomy, privacy preferences, environmental coping style do not seem, at this juncture of analysis to be strong predictors of mortality. There is some optimism, however, that they may be effective predictors of change in a patient's status, i.e. predicting whether a patient will improve or deteriorate as a result of the move.

The Washtenaw patients had the benefit of a preparation program which was focused on environmental familiarization. The patients were divided into two matched groups, one group received a direct familiarization experience which was made up of 5 separate visits to the new facility with appropriate problem solving tasks and spatial orientation sessions. The other group received one visit to the new facility with follow-up sessions viewing slide presentations, tape recordings of familiar sounds, staff visits from the new facility, and group review sessions. The multi-visit preparation program proved to have a dramatic impact on mortality. The mortality rate in the single visit group was 52% (13 out of a total N=24) as opposed to the multi-visit group at 27% (7 out of 24). The groups showed no significant difference at time of baseline data collection in age, sex, physician and registered nurse vulnerability ratings of those likely to die; occupational therapist ratings of ADL, dependency and physical limitations; mental status questionnaire responses; behavior observation level of activity or number of behavior settings encountered. These mortality rates seem to support the benefits of multiple exposures to new surroundings as an aid to environmental orientation. It raises questions however, as to what might be the optimal number of visits or most beneficial environmental factors to which one should be exposed. (11)

Footnotes

(1) The research described in this paper is supported by an NIMH grant No. 5-R01-MH 20746-02, co-principle investigators are Norman C. Bourestom and Leon A. Pastalan.

(2) Blenkner, M. "Environmental Changes and the Aging Individual", GERONTOLOGIST 7, (1967), 101-105.

(3) Goldfarb, A.I., Fisher, M. and Gerba I. "Predictors of Mortality in the Institutionalized Aged," DISEASES OF THE NERVOUS SYSTEM. 27 (1966), 21-29.

(4) Lawton, M.P. and Yaffe, S. "Mortality, Morbidity and Voluntary Change of Residence by Older People," JOURNAL OF THE AMERICAN GERIATRICS SOCIETY, 18 (1970), 823-831.

(5) DeLong, A. "The Micro-Spatial Structure of the Older Person: Some Implications of Planning the Social and Spatial Environment" in Pastalan, L.A. and Carson, D.H. (eds.) SPATIAL BEHAVIOR OF OLDER PEOPLE, Ann Arbor, The University of Michigan, 1970.

(6) Lawton, M.P. "Ecology and Aging" in Pastalan and Carson, Op. Cit.

(7) LeCompte, W.F. and Willens, E.P. "Ecological Analysis of a Hospital Location Dependencies in the Behavior of Staff and Patients" in PROCEEDINGS OF THE

ENVIRONMENTAL DESIGN AND RESEARCH ASSOCIATION MEETINGS, Pittsburgh, Pa., 1970.

(8)   Pastalan, L.A. "Privacy as an Expression of Human Territoriality" in Pastalan and Carson, Op.Cit.

(9)   Westin, A.F., Privacy and Freedom, New York, Athensum, 1967.

(10) Marshall, N. "Environmental Components of Orientations Toward Privacy" in PROCEEDINGS OF THE ENVIRONMENTAL DESIGN AND RESEARCH ASSOCIATION MEETINGS. Pittsburgh, Pa. 1970.

(11) Space does not permit a detailed explanation of study results. For a more extensive description, please write to the author c/o Institute of Gerontology or Department of Architecture, the University of Michigan.

Discussion Paper
by James Chaffers, D. Arch.

(Ed. Comment: The papers reviewed here are initial drafts of the proceeding panelists' papers which were subsequently revised.)

Given that "research" is often used as an excuse for inaction, the continuing emergence of "ACTION research" as a respected and respectable problem-solving methodology within scientific circles is encouraging. Unfortuantely, it may also be a powerful catalytic agent for some very reactionary theatrics both outside and within this same circle. For while the potential for positive change and innovative problem solving inherent in the action research concept would appear as reasonably obvious, strong resistance to the broad (many would no doubt say, "radical") implications posed by its required depth of commitment and the ultimate intent of its central thrust should be perceived no less so. In time, such resistance, manifested primarily as a series of sophisticated intellecutal hurdles, will most assuredly be asserted at every opportunity by those who feel threatened--probably in a manner that stresses at least temporal immediacy.

The strained theatrics of this resistance will take a little longer to surface; but once visible, will attain ever higher levels of reactionary hysterics (pegged to the assumed and actual effectiveness of action-orientated research) as rising numbers of researchers and research supporters who profit from a maintenance of the status quo seek to legitimize prevailing perceptions of order and normalcy. In the main, such legitimization will be sought by fashioning rationales and counter-points that hopefully work either to neutralize the CHANGE-orientated, status quo-challenging concept of action research or that succeed (somehow) in having the guts of its plainly clear intentions portrayed and internalized as a basis for further INaction.

Notwithstanding my rather pessimistic conjecture (not intended as cynical rhetoric), I am hopeful that critical masses of researchers will continue taking note and cues from the likes of such idea projections as have been developed and actualized by our panelists--and push on.

In this vein, a key issue in research paradigms--certainly not unknown to most of us assembled here--is the relationship of the researcher to his client or subject. In reviewing the efforts of Kerpen and Marshall, Pastalan, Moore, and Filipczak, one can sense and appreciate (above all else, I think) a conscious effort on their parts not to subjugate the values/reference frames/knowledge structures, etc., of their respective clients to those of their own. This is a critical, extremely sensitive aspect of any social research effort--cited often in contemporary journals--yet the predominance of professional values, inferences and knowledge in tension (if not open conflict) with the values and indigenous wisdoms of increasing numbers of clients (being "helped") mark it as an apparently frequently violated principle; a methodological weakness that could prove disasterous in action-orientated research, considering its collaborative and applied nature. Certainly it will require a major transformation among most students of Architecture, trained as they are, from and within a very narrow value-base that is exclusive of most others.

Looking at other dimensions, I am convinced that the budding concept of action research--and its explicit aim of optimizing designed environments through a kind of early error identification and correction system--is sure to be a tremendous aid in motivating design and planning students and professionals to be more critical of their own strengths and weaknesses, and far more conscious of the real/actual impact of their future work on human affairs. Further, staying or being required to stay in touch with the use(s) of environments they have designed should go far toward defining and emphasizing their (our) extended "accountability" to ultimate users--a very serious (though largely neglected) phase of design evaluation that goes far beyond the classic, but now rudimentary, concerns of sanitation and safety. The efforts of Pastalan and Kerpen and Marshall clearly speak to both these points, but perhaps their importance and relevance is best underscored when one views the colossal failures of this country's so-called "public housing/urban renewal" developmental efforts of recent vintage.

In attempting to integrate the concept of action research (in community settings) into ongoing educational programs for designers and planners, there are four goals that I view as paramount:

Ways to find and develop new opportunities for broadened and continuing involvement by ultimate users in the total process of environmental development--to help us better define, classify and accomplish prioral needs within an expanded reference frame.

A structured means for testing educational achievement outside the classroom/school context.

A means for heightening communications and expanding communal efforts among ourselves as professional designers while broadening our working base of information.

The development of more effective/comprehensive means for implementing the valid outcomes of our research efforts.

Having said the above, my closing statement relates to an uneasiness about what I sense as the current prevailing perception of the action research concept. In my view, it would appear, by its very nature, to be an idea that is far more in rhythm with an advocacy/participation/developmental-type paradigm than one that is merely prescriptive--perhaps more than we are prepared to admit or accept. Meaning, essentially, that if in our definitional praise of the action research concept we simply stress such gains as a reduction of the (presently, intolerable) time lag gap between presentation and application of valid research findings and/or the strength of this concept as a viable mechanism for responding more quickly to changing environmental conditions, without looking at the required changes in the nature and outlook of the researcher engaged in such research, we may yet fall far short of comprehending and applying the full force of its enormous potential.

Discussion Paper
by Stephen T. Margulis, Ph.D.

(Ed. Comment: The papers reviewed here are initial drafts of the proceeding panelist's papers which were subsequently revised.)

According to Dr. Edward Steinfeld, the workshop organizer, this workshop should explore ways of obtaining reliable information for design and policy decisions, at the time when they are needed, in order to help solve urgent environmental and social problems. As a recommended vehicle toward this end Dr. Steinfeld suggests we treat socio-physical environments in everyday use as "experiments" which would be analyzed by real time feedback and modified until near-optimal conditions are achieved. Bouterline in his discussion of "environmental management" (1) identified the characteristics of this approach:

[First,] unlike the designer, who must make decisions about components without knowing the nature of the whole system or its exact functions, the environmental manager knows most of the components . . ., how they work together, the specific users and their specific activities . . .

[Second, management decisions] are reversible, affect the immediate environment of a specific population of users within a short time of taking action, and are made within the context of preexisting, ongoing social-physical systems.

From this perspective the papers by Pastalan, Filipczak, and Moore fit these characteristics.

Pastalan discovered two county medical care facilities which planned to relocate patients in new facilities. Relocation is painful for the healthy (2); it can be lethal for the elderly. The study, a natural experiment in a field setting, included two facilities varying in extensiveness of relocation-related changes plus a third (non-changing, stable) control facility.

The major prediction, that extensiveness of change would affect mortality, was not supported. However, several predictors of mortality have initial support: reduced home range and cognitive and physical impairment. But it is unclear whether, as Pastalan argues, reduced home range is a determinant of nonadaptation and a prelude to death or whether it is a consequence of severe cognitive and physiological impairments which, in turn, are determinants of nonadaptation and death. Subsequent analyses should settle questions like this and provide back-up for a program to mitigate relocation-related death and illness. Hopefully future natural experiments on relocation will assess program effectiveness rather than what happens in the absence of preparation for relocation.

Filipczak and his associates created a physical, social, and educational environment within an established penal institution using a token economy system. The project, called CASE II, was a success but it did not survive intact the physical relocation of the training facility. The teachers, unlike Pastalan's elderly patients, could and did refuse the transfer. Notwithstanding relocation, why didn't a successful program obtain strong institutional support? Filipczak offers a number of reasons. Not among them is the congruence if any between the investigators' and the administrators' criterion for success. If recidivism was the administrator's criterior for judging penal rehabilitation success and if, for whatever reason, this was not part of CASE II, then the results may have been unpersuasive because they did not address the policy or perspective of the key user of the results.

Moore presents a Dynamic Assessment Paradigm. The paradigm attempts to create conditions for obtaining meaningful judgements from people about what was initially for them, hypothetical or unfamiliar. Its use demands careful preparation by the investigator. Participants have spent six nearly-continuous hours working through the first nine steps of the paradigm, and apparently with sustained interest. This is a plus. Moore recommends the paradigm in conjunction with RETS for environmental designers who want to test ideas in advance. (RETS has extensive audio-visual, display, and feedback capacity. Thus the participant can "visit" and react to hypothetical or unfamiliar settings.) The recommendation has appeal. But one may ask if a flexible, adaptable, perhaps costly, and relatively untested system is worth the investment, compared with alternative approaches.

Kerpen and Marshall's aim is to develop residential design requirements which reflect psychological, social and physical health needs, broadly conceived. Toward this end, as I understand them, they recommend the following steps: 1. develop health requirements, 2. get personal preferences of future (eligible) occupants, 3. based on preferences, develop physical/design requirements to meet health requirements, 4. construct and occupy the housing, 5. study the occupants to determine whether the design requirements meet the health requirements. This approach involves serious analytic problems. Fortunately, they can be solved by fiat! Nevertheless the basic problem remains. It is: how do you get from A to **B**, where A and B, respectively, may be a construct and a method, an observation and a requirement, a psychological construct and a spatial construct, a requirement and a criterion, and the like. For example, the attitude concept is central to understanding user preferences, yet to appreciate the construct-method gap one need only peruse articles on this problem. (3) The problems of relating behavioral and spatial constructs is as difficult. (4)

In all, these papers are consistent with the goals of this workshop. They attempt to get reliable information on urgent social and environmental problems. However, it is too early to estimate their influence. Overall, the papers have reinforced three personal beliefs. First, applied research must be supplemented by basic.

research. We need to sharpen our tools and concepts and must determine boundary conditions for our generalizations. Second, we must maximize the persuasiveness of our results: we must get the right person the right information in the right form at the right time. Third, the importance of environmental management has been under-rated and that is a serious mistake. It is a powerful source of behavioral control that lends itself to exciting studies.

Footnotes

(1) Bouterline, S. The Concept of Environmental Management. In H.M. Proshansky, W.H. Ittelson, & L.G. Rivlin (Eds.), ENVIRONMENTAL PSYCHOLOGY: MAN AND HIS PHYSICAL SETTING, New York: Holt, Rinehart & Winston, 1970. Pp. 496-500.

(2) Fried, M., Grieving for a Lost Home in R. Gutman (Ed.), PEOPLE AND BUILDINGS, New York: Basic Books, 1972. Pp. 229-248.

(3) Scott, W.A. Attitude Measurement. In G. Lindzey and E. Aronson (Eds.), HANDBOOK OF SOCIAL PSYCHOLOGY (Rev. ed.) Vol. II: Research Methods. Reading, Massachusetts: Addison-Wesley, 1968. Pp. 204-273.

(4) Buttimer, A. Social Space and the Planning of Residential Areas. ENVIRONMENT AND BEHAVIOR, 1972, 4, 279-318.

EIGHT   IMPLEMENTATION OF STRATEGIES
LEADING TO ENVIRONMENTAL CHANGE

Chairman: Henry Sanoff, Community Development Group, School of Design, North
            Carolina State University, Raleigh, North Carolina

Participants:

Terry Alford, Dept. of City and Reg. Planning, Univ. of N. C., Chapel Hill, N. C.
Gary Coates, Dept. of Design and Environ. Analysis, Cornell University, Ithaca, N.Y.
Larry Goldblatt, Dept. of City Planning, MIT, Cambridge, Massachusetts

Introduction

The intention of this workshop is to stress the relatedness of research to implementation, particularly since it is appropriate to explore new and more effective
methods for designers to intervene as agents of environmental change. This workshop will re-examine the concept of interdisciplinary activity to include participation from representatives of component parts of problems; conceptualization, fact
finding, analysis, design, planning, evaluation, and training. To this end, the
presentations will describe the link between research activity and implementation of
findings or environmental change.

This re-definition of "interdisciplinary" will require the involvement of new participants in the problem solving process that here-to-fore have been excluded. The
approach seeks action and relies on a wide array of expertise from problem component areas. While the content areas are not related, the primary purpose of the
workshop is to examine strategies, methods, and linkages for environmental change.

Architecture, Prisons and People
Larry Goldblatt
Massachusetts Institute of Technology
Cambridge, Massachusetts

A project was undertaken in a youth detention center to see how certain aspects of
the inmates living environment influence stressful behavior. Through studies of
friendship networks (socio-grams) and territoriality, an attempt was made to understand the nature of the inmates perception of crowding and, subsequently, strategies for altering those perceptions. Through a participatory planning effort,
environmental changes were made more consistent with the inmates image of a "workable" environment. Additional modifications of their living environment included
an "activity" room for quiet and private use, as well as changes in the color
scheme of their living environment.

420

Rural Housing Rehabilitation

Terry W. Alford
Department of City and Regional Planning
University of North Carolina - Chapel Hill, North Carolina

The primary focus of the project is on the identification and implementation of strategies, for the improvement of substandard housing conditions in rural areas. Initial studies of rural housing markets revealed that new construction, except in rare cases of public housing, was totally inaccessible for the rural poor. Attempts to reach low-income groups through technological breakthroughs have also met with great difficulty in rural areas. Initial research conclusions suggested that any attempt to improve the quality of housing in rural areas must recognize the problems expected in rural communities: lack of technical expertise, management skills and organizational ability, dominance of existing housing stock, low levels of capital investment, underdeveloped financial institutions, and high costs of new construction. As a means of accommodating each of these problem areas, research efforts were directed toward two broad-based objectives:

(1) The development of a "new rehabilitation technology" for rural housing, based on:
  (a) the physical condition of the existing substandard housing stock, and
  (b) the socio-economic characteristics of rural households occupying substandard dwelling.
(2) The development of information systems and organizational structures for utilizing the "new rehabilitation technology" based on three sub-objectives:
  (a) to encourage participation by private enterprise in housing rehabilitation through technical assistance in marketing, management, and production techniques for home repair,
  (b) to establish non-profit housing rehabilitation corporations as an integral part of multi-county planning and development agencies, and
  (c) to initiate community based non-profit corporations for purposes of home repair.

An analysis of data was made from an extensive survey of 394 households, representing open country and towns of less than 2,500 population, in the 41-county area of Coastal Plains North Carolina. Data describing the physical character of each household's dwelling were used to derive a system of 16 categories of rural house types accounting for 84 percent of all house types represented in the sample. Additional data on household expenditures and general economic status are being used to derive criteria for financial eligibility for housing rehabilitation. For those families occupying typical houses who are financially eligible, standardized rehabilitation schemes are being provided. Demonstration projects, in each of the aforementioned sub-objectives to establish rehabilitation organizations, have also been initiated and are now in various stages of development.

The development of a community-based non-profit rehabilitation corporation has been the most successful strategy and is currently operating as both construction firm and lending institution. The development of this consumer controlled corporation in the rural black community of Princeville, North Carolina is a way in which research programs directed toward problems of regional development may be integrated with local processes of community organization and awareness.

Environmental Design and Action Research: A Case Study of a Partial Success

Gary Coates
Dept. of Design and Environmental Analysis
Cornell University
Ithaca, New York

The major problem facing the environmental design professions is one of integrating the activities of design, implementation, and evaluation (research) in a manner that contributes to the resolution of an immediate problematic situation while advancing our understanding of the processes and consequences of environmental and social change. It is argued that an action research model, adapted from the social sciences, provides a reasonable framework for the introduction and observation of planned change.

Assuming that evaluation of failure as well as success contributes to the advancement of science (and design) this case study provides a vehicle for elaboration and discussion of a model of action research for environmental design. To do this, an outline is given of the problem as initially given, the chosen strategy of research and design, the process of design implementation, and the results of not following up this successful (the design was built) beginning with an ongoing program of research and training.

Since this project involved college students and a local community in the design and construction of an outdoor learning environment for children in a Head Start program, the prospects for a successful action research program in a university setting are evaluated. It is concluded that radical changes in the existing academic and political structure are necessary before any further success can be expected.

Finally, it is argued that commitment to an action research approach to environmental design necessarily raises issues of power and social responsibility. Rather than a "value free" outsider, the designer and researcher should be a committed but critical participant in a long-term effort to achieve community process and outcome goals. This supportive role suggests considerable flexibility in research methodology, with more emphasis placed on such techniques as participant observation and informal interviewing. More importantly, specific methods for feeding back information to user groups must be developed and evaluated, and mechanisms for ongoing environmental and/or social change must be built into the role relationships among the participants. This model implies joint collaboration between the action research group and the user community within a mutually acceptable ethical framework.

It is hoped that workshop discussion can focus on these and related issues as they relate to the case study presented as well as other concrete examples of real world problems.

An Alternative Strategy for Planning an Alternative School

Henry Sanoff   and   George Barbour
Community Development Group   Sandhills Mental Health Center
School of Design   Pinehurst, North Carolina
North Carolina State University
Raleigh, North Carolina

The process began when the Wallace O'Neal Day School in Pinehurst, North Carolina, chose a participatory planning approach to develop their building program through the creation of a parent-child teacher coalition.

The process for reaching this objective is frequently referred to as a "charrette", from the French term which in architecture implies a period of brief but intensive planning. In its present adaptation, a charrette is an activity that brings community members and experts together for a limited time period to study specific community problems. The essential ingredients are:
1. A problem to be solved
2. Community members willing to participate
3. Experts in both substantive and process areas
4. A commitment to implement the plans and recommendations of the charrette

The first of the charrette sessions began with the children who were asked to respond to educational goals through various modes of expression. Through collaborative poetry, rating scales, archetypical drawings, and role playing games, the children characterized their aspirations, perceptions, and ideals for their educational environment.

The adult members of the school community--parents, teachers, board members--also were involved in similar activities in addition to a "learning objectives" game. This game consists of four steps sequentially related and played by groups of four or more individuals. The steps include selection of educational objectives, learning methods for implementing objectives, relationships between participants and the nature of the physical enclosure, and finally, physical settings representative of the physical environment. The game encourages confrontation, trade-offs, and establishes linkages between educational objectives and alternative environments.

The final and most intensive sessions involved the assessment of the statements generated from the formal tasks into a consensual set of objectives for the Wallace O'Neal School. Four of the most important tasks were: (1) developing a sense of responsibility, (2) producing an atmosphere of trust, (3) developing motivation for learning, and (3) developing a realistic self-image.

Following the generation of goal statements, appropriate learning methods were associated with "activities" as well as the student-teacher relationship.

Each activity was analyzed, utilizing data recording sheets which ultimately became a building program for the architect, selected by the school's building committee.

Chairman: Peter W. House, Director, Environmental Studies Division, Environmental Protection Agency, Washington, D.C. 20460

Participants:

Steven C. Carter, International City Management Association, Wash., D.C.
Joel Gordon, Dept. of Natural Resources, Commonwealth of Puerto Rico, San Juan, P.R.
Larry Taylor, Integrated Regional Environmental Management (IREM) Project, San
   Diego County, California

Abstract

In the three years since the National Environmental Policy Act has been in existence, the Federal, state and local governments have moved vigorously in the direction of cleaning up the environment. Now that these agencies have experienced some short-range success in various areas by focusing on the more obvious and more easily remedied environmental problems, the more pervasive problems become more paramount.

This panel shall focus on two of these problems, both of which are in the area of environmental management. The first is a realization that the long-run environmental problem is not going to be simply cleaning up our air and our streams, but is, rather, going to be in prevention mode and, in a lower key, will include an increasingly demanding search for institutional change. Second is the ever more obvious fact that, although the Federal Government can give direction in terms of standards, the real solutions are at the regional and local levels.

It is the purpose of this panel to gather together representatives of state, regional and local government who are actually attempting to manage the environment so that they can report on their problems and solutions. The work of these people and the results of studies done in these areas will be used for input to a major EPA-sponsored conference scheduled for May and concerned with the full range of environmental management, from research to implementation.

TEN ENVIRONMENTAL ASSESMENT METHODOLOGY

Chairman: Edward R. Ostrander, Department of Design & Environmental Analysis,
Cornell Univ., Ithaca, New York 14850

Participants:

Tarja Cronberg, National Bureau of Standards, Washington, D. C.
Robert Helmreich, Department of Psychology, Univ. of Texas, Austin, Texas
Robert Hershberger, Architecture, Arizona State Univ., Tempe, Arizona
Charles C. Lozar, DERL, Champaigh, Illinois
Sam Sloan, People Space Arch. Co., Spokane, Washington
Lorraine Snyder, Department of Design & Environmental Analysis, Cornell Univ.,
    Ithaca, New York

Abstract

Broadly conceived, questions of environmental assessment methodology pertain to a
sequential process that incorporates problem definition, creation of research
strategies, selection and development of data gathering instruments or techniques,
data collection and analysis, translation of the information into forms relevant
to design decision making, and the subsequent evaluation of the design solution
against criteria. The workshop contributors will each deal in depth with specific
elements in the assessment process that they have concentrated on professionally,
and the group will seek to clarify the strengths and weaknesses in the entire
process by drawing on the focal concerns of each contributor.

Introduction

> Conferences, symposia, and vast bibliographies keep exhorting toward
> "interdisciplinary collaboration", but the specifics of how to col-
> laborate have been elusive.   Perin 1970

The concept environmental assessment methodology no doubt means many things to
many people. Personal interests and special training may direct one investigator
to concern himself with explicit details of questionnaire construction or fixed
response intruments. Others choose to involve themselves with the pragmatics of
the assessment process and value questions such as which users shall be heard when
feedback is sought. The hypothesis generating merits of observational techniques
that are relatively unobtrusive intrigue some investigators, while instruments
that require the user's conscious effort and demand careful discriminations appeal
to still other researchers. Continuing work on all of these fronts is essential
if meaningful assessment of the built environment is to be understood and the
process of assessment made more accurate, dependable, and relevant.

However, as Perin (1) suggests in her quotation, we have difficulty collaborating or even patiently sharing ideas. The practicing architect who works under the pressure of deadlines and his client's urgings finds it easy to get impatient with the academic researcher who develops methods in what appears to be a time frame that has no relationship to real-world schedules. The conscientious methodologist working on the improvement of a technique that does not yet even have standardized instructions or who is developing a paper-and-pencil instrument for which there has never been reliability and validity studies becomes distressed at what he considers to be the "quick and dirty" research philosophy of the man in the field.

If we can stand back and dispassionately survey the state of environmental assessment methodology and its application we can probably agree that there is more than a grain of truth in the concerns each party is expressing.

There are those who feel that sound expertise in a given area creates a narrowness of focus that can outweigh the strengths of the in-depth mastery. A possible solution is to broaden the specialist's frame of reference and competence - so he can take into account more dimensions of the problem than he could heretofore. This may be the generalist-specialist argument in a new wrapper with the idea being to become a bit more general. In some settings it may take the form of the two-culture argument that C. P. Snow emphasized in his writings several years ago. The scientist thinks and operates in one fashion, while the artist or humanist operates in quite a different fashion. Participants in this workshop include people whose interests are focused on various phases of the environmental assessment process. Each one is quite knowledgeable in his particular domain. Each one is also reasonably sensitive to the professional norms and constraints under which his colleagues work as they deal with other aspects of the assessment process. Our objective is to expand our understanding of the way the constraints and norms shape options and even dictate solutions. We are looking for realistic trade-offs that are not made at the expense of compromises in the quality of decisions.

Workshop Strategy

Suggestions from this group on ways to improve the quality of environmental assessment should range widely because the participants have concentrated on different phases of the environmental assessment process. Each participant has developed a brief paper directed to an issue of particular concern or offering an example of research that is aimed at improving the assessment process. The papers have been circulated so each participant will briefly describe the issues which he will address in this workshop.

Following that declaration of issues we will break up into several assessment problem groups. The key participants will lead the discussions. The give and take in some groups may include quite specific questions about techniques or statistical matters. In others the discussion may be on a much less concrete level dealing with philosophic questions and ethical concerns. The entire group will come together following the problem group discussions to summarize the conclusions they have reached.

Issues

The range of participants' concerns are shown in the brief summaries of the issue papers described below.

Cronberg, T. and Saeterdal, A. "From Surveys to Performance Tests"

There is a gap between the methods used to study man/environment interactions and methods for evaluation of the performance of a physical element. In the former case the environment is usually the static component and user variables such as behavior, perception and attitudes are measured. In the latter case the user is standardized to load, size, etc., and the physical solutions are varied. A procedure of data collection, incorporating both types of methods is described. In a step-wise procedure the information provided in one step is integrated with the information needed in the next step in order to establish a correlation between the built environment in use and the performance tests of the physical elements.

By starting the procedure with general studies not directed toward specific physical elements an attempt is made to take into consideration all factors relevant for the performance of a physical element. By gradually directing the study towards certain situations of use critical for the performance of the physical element and by analyzing these situations the factors influencing the performance may be standardized at certain levels, varied and controlled in experimental conditions. The four-step procedure includes: 1) identifying the problems, 2) identification of user groups, activities, and physical elements relevant to the problem, 3) analysis of the critical user/activity/physical element interaction, 4) verification of the performance requirement.

It is important that these two principally different activities - collecting and analyzing data and decision making - are clearly separated.

Secondly, it is important that the two processes are coordinated to eliminate the intuitive short cuts, leading to the neglecting of important information or to preservation of existing solutions.

Ostrander, E. "The Environmental Analyst's Tool Kit: Options and Cautions"

After the assessment research strategy has been developed and thought has been given to the kind of information desired, a decision must be made on the most appropriate methods to use in gathering data. Available approaches include unobtrusive methods such as the hodometer and participant observation that require little or no cooperation from those functioning in the environmental setting. Various forms of systematic observation may be obvious to the users being studied but may require little in the way of their active cooperation. Traditional social science data gathering techniques such as the interview or open-ended questionnaire make a somewhat greater demand in the form of participant cooperation. Another set of instruments including rating scales, the semantic differential and the Q-Sort may require considerable cognitive work on the part of the user. Which instrument should be chosen or what combination of techniques should be included in a battery are questions that will be discussed.

Criteria to consider include the nature of the information needed, degree of rapport with users, time available to collect and process the data, cost, reliability and validity of the technique.

Snyder, L. "The Primary Level of Space Inquiry: Systematic Observation"

There are definite advantages to be gained by using observational approaches when dealing with environmental assessments, especially when working in an unfamiliar setting or with a group of users that have certain unique characteristics. Often the observations can be made without disrupting the ongoing patterns of behavior so the researcher gains an overview of the situation. In addition, a sensitive observer accumulates information from which to generate design hypotheses and hypotheses regarding user behavior. Observation can provide a range of information about the spaces, the users, specifics of behavior, functionality, design and spatial arrangement. A case study drawn from the observation approach used on the Cornell Gerontology Project is used to illustrate the adaptation of the observational approach to an institutional setting and the aged residents. Graphic techniques for communicating the findings of systematic observation are described. Recommendations are made concerning observational procedures, data recording forms, and modes of presenting findings.

Helmreich, R. "Systematic Observation and Longitudinal Studies: Some Considerations"

It is one thing to carry out systematic observations in traditional settings over short periods of time, but when the environment is an under-sea habitat placed on the ocean floor for a seven-month period new problems of data gathering and analyzing are introduced. The under-sea habitat study is the case in point for discussing these issues. One of the programs was an intensive study of the aquanauts' psychological reactions to confinement and isolation. Project requirements included the data being objectively coded observations, not subjective impressions of feelings or performance. The researcher was also required to gain his data through unobtrusive measures that would not interfere with on-going behavior. The research approach involved continuous monitoring of all compartments of the habitat by closed-circuit television and open microphones with continuous coding of behavior into predetermined categories on machine readable punch cards. The experience gained in the work on exotic environments is used as a basis for considering the merits and weaknesses of longitudinal studies by means of systematic observation.

Cass, R. and Hershberger, R. "Semantic Scales to Measure the Meaning of Designed Environments: Hershberger-Cass Marker Set"

One of the shortcomings in most of the instruments available for use in environmental assessment is the absence of a standard version of that instrument. Each investigator selects his own items or components, thus creating a custom-built instrument. These instruments have such limited use that it is difficult to draw conclusions based on the findings. The development of standardized instruments is an important task. The Hershberger-Cass Marker Set of semantic differential scales offers items that have been developed empirically.

Nine orthogonal dimensions of meaning and one superordinate evaluative dimension have been identified in this study. The primary set of scales representing these dimensions in the Hershberger-Cass Marker Set should now be considered the absolute minimum essential for comprehensive coverage of the range of semantic meanings attributable to the designed environment. The alternative set of scales proposed in the Base Set can be used in whole or in part in place of the ten primary scales for subject matter or respondent groups where their use would be more appropriate. The factors in the set are: general evaluative, utility evaluative, aesthetic evaluative, activity, space, potency, tidiness, organization, temperature, and lighting.

Lozar, C. "Location-Specific Behavioral Episodes Using Time Lapse Film and the Semantic Differential"

The problem of the analysis of attitudes and behaviors in environment in most previous research is the lack of identification of distinct environment-behavior units to which the results can be related. An empirical study of location-specific behavior settings was conducted using the semantic differential and time lapse photography in a military dining hall. The first part of the study dealt with a comparative evaluation of attitudes toward a visual sequence in an old and a new dining hall using the semantic differential as a measurement technique. Viewing positions in the dining hall were selected and slide simulations were used to get reactions. Significant differences were found favoring the one setting over the other. As a second part of the study time lapse photography was used to carry out an overt behavioral analysis in the dining hall. Objectives were to describe overt behavioral patterns, queing situations conflict and accident areas, and table preference patterns in the food acquisition and eating areas. Results showed preferences for areas for seating, conflict, situations in food acquisition and queing behavior. Problems in the use of the semantic differential and time lapse photography are enumerated and solutions suggested.

Sloan, S. "In Practice Problems of Research Oriented Production"

When the architect in practice uses a research oriented approach to design decision making his perspective is not the same as that of the academic researcher. The "measurement of an environment" implies that we could assign a positive or negative value to space... which is most likely impossible. At least, I believe it is fair to say that it is impossible if the value is to be placed on a scale responsible to human needs.

A more realistic assumption may be to posit that we can measure existing values of an environment as to their effects upon specific individuals engaged in the production of particular and definitive tasks. From this information it may be possible to predict the probability of the environment to either support or deny the success of a person or persons to accomplish a defined task.

The dimension necessary to breach the gap between subjectivity and objectivity in designing and evaluating environments is infinite. If subjectivity is to give way to a more objective approach to design, then the establishment of a baseline from which to relate is the first and most essential step.

It appears safe to assume that (at least) the greater number of human beings on earth live their lives in pursuit of happiness. If we define happiness as "the absence of frustration", then we may relate environments to people on the basis of whether or not a spatial setting produces frustration in the minds of its occupants. This position is developed and supporting evidence cited.

References

(1)   Perin, C. WITH MAN IN MIND, Cambridge, 1970.

ELEVEN   GAMING AND SIMULATION

Chairman: Ervin J. Bell, College of Environmental Design,
              University of Colorado, Boulder, Colorado 80302

Panelists:

Sidney Cohn, Dept. of City & Reg. Planning, U. of N.C., Chapel Hill
Alan Feldt, Environ. Simulation Labs., Univ. of Michigan, Ann Arbor
Daria B. Fisk, Dept. of Architecture, U. of Texas, Austin
John Hershey, Environmental Specialist, Blue Bell, Pa.
Margrit Kennedy, GSPIA, U. of Pittsburgh, Pittsburgh
Michael Kennedy, Dept. of Arch., U. of Kentucky, Lexington
Phillip Patterson, Environ. Protection Agency, Washington, D. C.
Bob Proctor and Bruce Dains, Coll. of Environ. Design, Univ. of Oklahoma
Raymond G. Studer and Richard H. Hobson, Div. of Man-Environment
   Relations, Penn State U.
Louis H. Summers and Edward H. Seeley, Engineering, Penn State U.

Content

Workshop/Urban Gaming: An accessing tool or key to environmental
                        decision making.
Purpose: To introduce gaming as a tool for the upgrading of the
urban environment. After short descriptive presentations of
variously scaled urban games, the panel will discuss the various
dimensions of urban games and their role in the improvement of
the environment.

The purpose of urban gaming may fall into one or more of the following:
   a) Identifying or exposing problem areas
   b) Identifying or exposing the decision making process
   c) Generation and development of innovative means to resolve
      problem areas (or to improve the environment)
   d) To be a means for a dynamic experiential learning process for
      people to make decisions on the form of their own environment.

Thus, urban games might be used in community and individual non-expert
decision making, education and research.

One attempt at dimensioning the urban gaming tool is illustrated in the following diagram (Figure 1.).

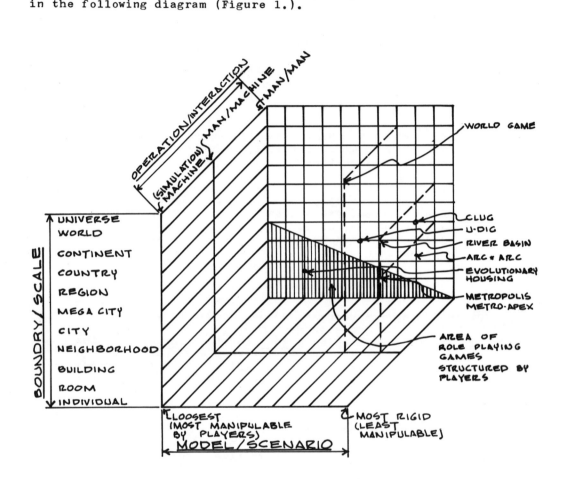

URBAN GAMING DIMENSION CUBE

Figure 1.

In summary: We will look at dimensioning or describing urban gaming as a tool for people to meaningfully <u>access</u> the decision making process in upgrading the environment.

A LETTER TO THE WORKSHOP CHAIRMAN

Daria B. Fisk

School of Architecture
University of Texas
Austin, Texas 78712

Could we begin by trying to recap what individuals have mentioned and
been up to, but in a way which cross-relates things and more or less
categorizes them, beginning to provide a general framework for looking
at the whole topic of gaming and design (or planning, it doesn't
matter what you call it.) It seems to me we could use some of the
things which you've already distinguished as relevant - like loose
vs. tight analogies, flexibility and manipulability of the game and
in turn, of the model. I think it would be useful to look at some of
these things in terms of the context and purpose in which and for which
different games were designed and built. What were some of the
original motivations behind them? A need for more effective decision
making? A need to explain, or understand, a complex and dynamic system?
A need to bridge the gap between the theoretician and the practioner?
Or what? Was the context a real and pressing need, demanding a
workable outcome (as we might say of war games) or was it a more
relaxed and removed academic context, associated with no necessary
action and consequences in the larger world? Do we find a direct
relation between the nature of the original context, and associated
purpose, and the eventual usefulness of these games? This might
raise questions like whether or not the game maker has a personal
interest in keeping the inner working of his model itself somewhat
obscure. Are people reactors in the system, or are they actors in it?
Is the model on which the game is based basically mechanistic or not
and might there not be a direct correlation between the mechanistic
nature of the model and the degree of freedom which it allows, or
even, introduces? Note, for example, the frequent impossibility of
introducing new variables into games, despite the frequency of doing
so in so-called "real life". Can the game, or model behind it, accept
a change in the rules - can the player propose a "whole new ball game"?

In some sense it's like asking if games are capable of handling really
substantive issues, and modes of operating, or if they are more like
exercises. After a very short time of playing CLUG, for example,
there inevitably comes the request to incorporate values which are
not solely economic, but there is no apparent way to do it. So it
exaggerates that part of the system which it is interested in, and
with which it can clearly and quantitatively deal. We might suggest
that gaming which approaches qualitative concerns has more parallels
with some experiments in group therapy in psychology than with many of

the things we have been talking of in this workshop. Some examples
which begin to work in the design world seem to be some of the things
Lawrence Halprin has been trying, and, at a totally different end of
the spectrum, the sort of thing Jan Wamplar has been doing in Boston,
or Troy West in Pittsburgh - where the games are real life, with the
players gaming (in a sense) things which are vital to their own lives.

When this is applied to the question of verifiability, which people
seem to be somewhat concerned about at the moment, what becomes so
obvious is that the context and purpose of a game are at the crux of
the matter. If the game and gaming process is actually simply one
step in the decision-making process, and is seen as having very direct
implications for action (or to put it more strongly, intentions toward
action), then it is verified by the effectiveness of the action that
ensues. I would submit that when you have difficulty verifying a game,
it is largely because the game is merely an exercise - playing it
doesn't make a difference to the players, or anyone else, in real terms.
There are no real world consequences associated with the thing.

I realize this is hardly an outline for discussion or, even more
important, for participation. These are some of the things which I
think it could be very profitable to deal with, though - especially
as they again point toward one of the basic dilemmas which has
plagued this conference for a number of years - which is just the
problem of theory and practice finding a common and workable ground.

Perhaps in terms of an outline, or whatever, we could, for one, ask
people to comment on what they see as the potentials of gaming as a
useful tool. What hopes do they hold, what paths do they see as
fruitful? Are there any glimmers which they can point to for encouragement? Jack Hershey's work seems to offer one terrifically
encouraging example, at least as I see it. I very much agree with
what you mentioned as the possibility of games as a means of entry
into the decision-making process. As a democratic tool, games hold
fantastic potential - but, at the same time, that potential is not, I
don't think, inherent in games. One could just as easily devise games
to overwhelm people with their own insignificance in the face of huge
and complex systems. One could just as easily distribute games so
exclusively as to make decisions easier and more influential for
handfuls of people, rather than for the general public. Take a look
at the games we are likely to discuss here today. How many of them
have been available except to a small, exclusive group of players -
were any of these even conceived as everyday, layman's tools?
Certainly in terms of cost most of them haven't been. Witness, too,
the recent proliferation of newsletters, gaming groups, etc.,
reinforcing the in-grown and exclusive nature of the whole enterprise
with a sort of false security, allowing people to sit back and assume
that their games are actually doing something.

Perhaps we could make a pact to refuse to hold any more gatherings or to produce any more publications on gaming, until we are ready to do so to a much more general audience, on Applied Gaming - or call it what you will. Games as tools toward self-organizing systems. If we could actually get people at this workshop working together on a plan of action to really try to make some of these games, or combinations of them operational,in real world terms, then we would begin to be really doing something. With the people who will be collected for the conference, we should find a very rich ground for problem identification. Imagine the challenge and excitement of trying to apply gaming to some of these, simultaneously in different places and so forth, with each person's effort the richer for knowledge of the other people's progress, failures, false starts and so forth.

At any rate, I do think we should make every effort to avoid having this workshop turn into another discussion for its own sake - but really use it to provide a firm impetus and purposeful direction for some of the potentials which are still only dimly on the horizon.

U-DIG GAME

Ervin J. Bell

Associate Professor
College of Environmental Design
University of Colorado, Boulder

Urban Development Investment Game (U-DIG) was developed as a response
to the need for a gaming tool for the understanding of urban dynamics
and for research into urban innovation to improve the quality of
urban life.

Three to eight teams of one to four players play in multiple sessions
of three to four hours each. A board illustrating a neighborhood
plan is used. When an opportunity to purchase occurs to a team,
computer developed investment tables are consulted for aid in the
decision to buy. Buying, selling, building and bidding all may take
place in the course of play. Year end pay-offs are made after
income tax in a simple bookkeeping procedure. Interest rates and
occupancy rates fluctuate. Mortgages are available at the current
interest rate. Thus the economic rules are closely patterned after
the real world. After an initial period of play, the players become
familiar with the dynamics of real estate economics and the basis
for decisions that determine the urban form.

In a second version, a news item is distributed that announces the
elimination of property lines. Property owners own a proportional
share of a block. They can now build dwelling units on top of units
owned by others in a common structure that crosses streets within the
same density limitations as the first version. Rules are set that
establish ground coverage and the relationship on each level above
ground. This is one version in which an experiment with a change in
one factor in urban form determination is varied to result in a new
form, the "quality -of-life" merits of which can be debated. Other
rules may easily be changed to study the effects, thus the research
possibilities exist.

The value of U-DIG lies in its worth as a tool for understanding
existing urban situations (Version One) and as a research device
to help develop a better quality of urban life (an example is Version
Two). In Version Two, the game sessions indicate some of the problems
of planning, phasing and blending a growing mega-structure with an
existing urban fabric.

Raymond G. Studer   Richard H. Hobson
Professor and Director   Graduate Assistant
Division of Man-Environment Relations   Division of Man-Environment Relations
College of Human Development   College of Human Development
The Pennsylvania State University   The Pennsylvania State University
University Park, Pennsylvania 16802   University Park, Pennsylvania 16802

Abstract

An operant discrimination learning model is adopted to explicate and pretest urban movement systems via simulation. A multimodal simulation experiment is identified to refine the model. The initial stage of this study, a computer simulation using SIMSCRIPT 11.5, is described in terms of program structure, input and findings.

Introduction

Environment-behavior incongruence related to urban movement contributes significantly to the pathology of urban existence. An aborted engagement, the needless waste of time and energy and a host of unconsummated behavioral objectives--such frustrations are a product of muddled environmental structures and spatial codes. These add tremendously to the stress of urban life, just as a monotonous, naive physical order can add to the boredom of urban life. Being lost or confused in a complex urban setting produces human dislocations ranging from a mild form of stress to outright catastrophe for the participant. How do humans come to successfully negotiate complex movement systems--find their way, develop appropriate, uniform responses to an array of environmental elements in spite of highly variable ontogenies? People no doubt develop appropriate responses to environmental codes and structures as they do to linguistic codes and structures (1) and these are probably every bit as subtle and orderly.

Behavioral Development in Urban Environments

Competence in negotiating a complex urban environment can be seen to involve several possible strategies. For example: 1) a person may internalize an overall map of the area he inhabits and thus locate himself with reference to this internalized spatial network, 2) he may internalize key landmarks and relationships among them as a means of making spatial decisions, or 3) the environment in question may be organized around a system of codes the conceptualization of which allows the inhabitant to "read" even unfamiliar aspects successfully. Perhaps there are other modes of viewing this phenomenon and perhaps a person negotiates environments utilizing all of the above. Our investigation focuses upon the patterns of acquiring and maintaining new behaviors through interaction with environments organized to facilitate their acquisition. The participant's internal organization of environmental information, i.e. environmental cognitions (2), lies outside the concerns of this study, which rather examines changes in behavior in the presence of this information.

Because the physical design problem assumes the need to facilitate new forms of behavior, the fundamental issue is how stimuli can be ordered to accomplish this. The techniques of operant conditioning have been demonstrated as highly effective in addressing such problems both in laboratory (3) and in applied settings (4). The methods for bringing operant behavior under the control of elements of the environment involve an analysis of the spatial/temporal relations between behavior and its consequences. These affect the probabilities of the behavior's recurrence. Specific behavioral topographies are affected when appropriate contingencies of reinforcement are temporally and spatially ordered.

Aspects of new environments can come to accommodate new behaviors through discrimination learning. Operant research indicates that appropriate responses to certain stimuli emerge as these are differentially reinforced in their presence. An important aspect of simulating the probable effects of new environments on behavior is a description of the manner in which an environment can be spatially and temporally arranged to contribute to behavioral acquisitions via stimulus control (5). This is the strategy adopted in this simulation experiment.

Simulation and Urban Movement Systems Design

The behavior-contingent environmental design and management strategy explicated by Studer (6,7) argues for the necessity of modeling and simulating of proposed environment-behavior ensembles. The designer's task is to produce an environment-behavior ensemble predicted to support the behavioral objectives of the participants with the highest probability. Our understanding of man-environment relations is insufficient at this time to even begin to deal with such design problems analytically. On the other hand, the implementation of untested and unrefined models, i.e. direct experimentation, is both inordinately expensive and involves significant social, biological and psychological risks. Lacking appropriate algorithms, congruence of environment-behavior ensembles can only be pretested via some form of simulation. A behavior-contingent approach requires that the proposed environment be pretested in terms of the behavior system it will produce.

The following represents the first of a multistage study to refine and validate a simulation model which facilitates more reliable predictions regarding environments for human movement behaviors. The approach is to move from an abstract to a real situation through several iterative stages as a means of enriching and validating the model, i.e.: 1) computer simulation (described below), 2) infrahuman simulation, 3) human simulation, and 4) a human field experiment. These four experiments dealing with comparable variables should result in a simulation with high fidelity and richness. Beyond the resulting availability of this applied tool, noteworthy research linking computer, infrahuman and human laboratory and field experiments will have been documented.

Computer Simulation of a Simple Discrimination Learning Process

Movement environments inevitably present the participant with a number of options. The following analysis assumes that, the behavioral objectives of the system have been identified, that a general network has been developed and a desirable, i.e. normative, route through the system has been defined and requires validation.

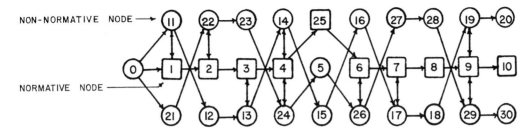

NON-NORMATIVE NODE →

NORMATIVE NODE →

We are given a situation in which individuals are moving from point to point through a space, e.g., a building or a city. "Points" are not geometric points, but areas, e.g., a given block or corridor. We will refer to these as nodes. People can occupy a node, or move from node to node with certain probabilities. At normative nodes, (with which certain stimulus arrays are associated), individuals are reinforced; and this reinforcement increases the probability of appropriate choices in the future. Since the events modeled are most easily visualized as discrete rather than continuous, a discrete language has been selected for this program, i.e., SIMSCRIPT 11.5 (8). Since no sharp distinction can be made between the program and the model in SIMSCRIPT, the latter can best be explicated through a discussion of the program.

Nodes are conceptualized as permanent entities. Paths and persons are viewed as temporary entities. Nodes can be terminating nodes or normative nodes or neither, and there is exactly one node which is both. Associated with every node is a BUNCH of people--those currently at that node. Associated with every path are two nodes-- the origin off the path and its destination. Associated with every person is a probability--his P.PROB which reflects the extent to which he has "learned the system". Events occur in the model when a person enters the system, when he makes decisions regarding the next node, and when he leaves the system. Other events include various reports and the end of the simulation.

Input to the program includes the number of nodes in the system, and their names. Also read into the program is the number of normative nodes and their names, as well as the number of terminating nodes and their names. For every node, the number of other nodes to which it is possible to go from the original is read in as well as the probability of an unlearned person taking that route. Other input data include: the average decision time at a node, average individual interarrival time, the time required to recycle from a termination point to the starting point, the total number of people moving through the system during the simulation, and the time between reports.

As a person enters the system he arrives at the starting node, whose name is 0. At this time he is faced with a decision. There may be any number of possible exit nodes, and associated with each node is a route. There is only one requirement for the probabilities associated with these routes: they must sum to one. We can introduce the additional requirement that they be equal, but this requirement is not built into the program. Rather, the probability associated with each route is read in (to depict particular environmental characteristics or ontogenies of the participants). The time required to make the decision to move to the next node is established Monte Carlo style based on an exponential distribution whose mean has been read in. If the individual selects a normative node, his P.PROB is increased by 0.1. For a given node, each of the exit nodes of that node determines a path--the path whose origin is the person's present node and whose destination is the exit node. Then, PROB (PATH) is altered by the new probability associated with normative path, i.e.: [1-PROB (PATH)] [P.PROB (PERSON)] + PROB (PATH). Output is an account of the way individuals respond and learn in the system through time. We have run the simulation with various sets of input data. Results are available.

References

(1) Pike, K., LANGUAGE IN RELATION TO A UNIFIED THEORY OF A STRUCTURE OF BEHAVIOR, The Hague, Mouton and Co., 1967.

(2) Stea, D. and R. Downs (Eds.), "Cognitive Representations of Man's Spatial Environment", ENVIRONMENT AND BEHAVIOR, Vol. 2, No. 1, June, 1970.

(3) Honig, W. (Ed.), OPERANT BEHAVIOR: AREAS OF RESEARCH AND APPLICATION, New York, Appleton-Century-Crofts, 1966.

(4) Ulrich, R., T. Stachnik, and J. Mabry, CONTROL OF HUMAN BEHAVIOR, Glenview, Scott Foresman, (2 vols.), 1966, 1970.

(5) Terrance, H. S., "Stimulus Control" in Honig, W. (Ed.), OPERANT BEHAVIOR: AREAS OF RESEARCH AND APPLICATION, New York, Appleton-Century-Crofts, 1966, pages 271-344.

(6) Studer, R. G., "The Dynamics of Behavior-Contingent Physical Systems" in Proshansky, H., et al (Eds.), ENVIRONMENTAL PSYCHOLOGY: MAN AND HIS PHYSICAL SETTING, New York, Holt, Rinehart and Winston, 1970, pages 56-76.

(7) Studer, R. G., "Human Systems Design and the Management of Change", GENERAL SYSTEMS, XVI, 1971, pages 131-143.

(8) CASI, SIMSCRIPT 11.5 USER'S MANUAL, Consolidated Analysis Centers, Inc., 12011 San Vicente Boulevard, Los Angeles, California, 1971.

Margrit I. Kennedy
Department of Urban Affairs
Graduate School of Public and International Affairs
University of Pittsburgh
Pittsburgh, Pa. 15213

Our success in getting urban decision-makers to participate in urban simulation-games has been limited in the past. Among many possible reasons one seems to me particularly critical: that decision-makers have little understanding that games provide risk free experimentation, yet also relevance to real life situations.[1]

To a student, playing the urban decision-maker is a game with learning utility. To an urban decision-maker, playing the urban decision-maker is as much as working overtime, and without understanding the experimental latitude, has little perceived utility. There are, however, examples[2] that demonstrate gaming as having perceived utility by decision-makers, of which the following is one:

Urban Design Associates, Pittsburgh, was asked to design a multi-usage community center for a new town in New York, and decided to involve the users in a series of (person-only) games. Users in this case were not only local people but also agencies, institutions and the private sector from state, metropolital and local levels. Everyone was asked to identify himself by his/her first name only, and with this opportunity to leave their everyday professional roles unidentified they could simply be people together addressing common (and each other's) problems without simulating or assuming particular roles. The series consisted of seven rounds, each building on the outcome of the previous one. Over the seven rounds participants gained deep insights and made special inputs into common and special needs, and identified the programs, problems, and solutions for their center. The architects are now transforming the programs into three-dimensional design in continuing dialogue with the participants.[2]

It is hoped that the benefits of this approach will last beyond the implementation stages of the design; and that this mixture of game-charette-brainstorming-and-community-sensitivity-training will initiate on-going revitalization of the agencies and institutions involved through participation of the users in the decision-making process.

NOTES

(1) A more explicit theoretical framework for the use of urban simulation-games can be found in: Margrit I. Kennedy, "Education and Urban Planning as Congruent Events," in Steven J. Kidder and Alice W. Nafziger, PROCEEDINGS OF THE NATIONAL GAMING COUNCIL'S ELEVENTH ANNUAL SYMPOSIUM, Baltimore, 1972.

(2) A description of the game will appear in: David Lewis, "A Community Determines What Its Center Is," in Declan Kennedy and Margrit I. Kennedy, THE INNER CITY, Paul Elek Publications, London, 1973.

Sidney Cohn
Department of City and Regional Planning
University of North Carolina
Chapel Hill, North Carolina

Housing Crisis is a systemic game designed to assist in training personnel in non-profit housing agencies but with relevance for low-income housing in general. The game simulates the development of low and moderate income housing in moderate size cities. Its major objectives are to teach sponsors to develop long-range programs in contrast to individual projects, i.e. to plan, and to be aware of the social and political factors which impinge on the success of such programs. Secondary objectives include reinforcement in training in the financial, programmatic and technical aspect of low-income residential development.

The game instructions describe the existing socio-political situation in the community as well as community perceptions of low-and moderate income housing. The game is played on a board simulating a hypothetical city by three teams of two or more persons, each round of play simulating one month of development time. The general structure of the city is described as well as the land uses and demographic conditions. Potential sites of varying characteristics can be brought into the market by the players, in part stochastically, each site being described as to number and type of units, costs of land and development, construction time, etc. As sites are acquired by the players, construction kits are provided simulating their development. Variable interest rates as well as exogenous factors outside the control of developers but which can influence development are introduced stochastically at each round of play.

Each team initiates the game with $60,000 in capital and competes to develop the greatest number of houses. $500 profit is accrued for each dwelling unit successfully completed. Success, or winning, though involving some chance, is highly dependent upon knowledge and skill. It requires that the players continually increase their capital through a sound long-range program including the efficient management of finances, the proper analysis of site conditions, the proper interpretation of social and political conditions, and to a minor degree, knowledge of housing and housing programs. A computerized version of the game has also been developed.

Robert Proctor and Bruce Dains

School of Architecture, College of Environmental Design
The University of Oklahoma
Norman, Oklahoma 73069

Abstract

Arc*Arc is a basic design decision game combining human behavior with seven elements:
1) evaluation of topography, 2) competitive bidding, 3) design diagnosis, 4) cost
analysis, 5) team interaction, 6) project evaluation, and 7) reality of economics.

Play consists of two basic and sequential games. The primer is a tactical land
development game which contributes working capital for use in the second
simulation. The second game simulates bidding for land; design, construction, and
evaluation of a specific project; and each team's economic reward. The projects
of the second game increase in complexity as new design considerations develop.
Simplified project evaluation may be done by the game director, or a more
comprehensive evaluation by computer, which is recommended for more complex
projects. Projects are evaluated with respect to:

    I.   Form   IV. Construction time
   II. Function   V. Suggested selling price
       A. Climate and solar exposure   VI. Net profit
       B. Percent circulation
  III. Economy
       A. Land cost
       B. Materials cost
       C. Labor cost

Form is evaluated by team discussion and has no economic bearing.

Introduction

Arc*Arc is a simulation developed as a project for an operational gaming studio at
the University of Oklahoma in 1971. The objective was to produce a learning aid
for basic architectural design students. A two-part game resulted.

Primer Game

The first or primer game has the purpose of acquainting the players with each
other and with the physical characteristics of the board while simulating perception
of scale, spacial relationships, and planning.

The object of the primer game is for each team (two to four players) to obtain
maximum cash return for placement of "houses" on the playing board. The economic
reward is a function of the relative position and level upon which the "house" is
placed. The moneys earned in the primer game become the working capital for the
second game.

The primer game takes approximately two hours to explain and play.

Second Game

The second game simulates bidding for land; design, construction, and evaluation of a specific project; and each team's economic reward. The designs are constructed from playing pieces provided in the game. Projects increase in complexity at the discretion of the game operator.

The object of the second game is for each team to obtain maximum cash return for the sale of their architectural projects and consideration of aesthetics. The economic reward is based upon evaluation with respect to:

    I. Function
        A. Climate and solar control
        B. Percent circulation
    II. Economy
        A. Land cost
        B. Materials cost
        C. Labor cost
    III. Construction time

From the evaluation, a "suggested selling price" is given and "net profit" is figured. The "form" of the project is evaluated by team discussion and has no economic value.

The second game takes approximately three hours to explain and construct one project.

Playing Board

The playing board used for both games consists of 676 3/4" blocks varying in height from 3/4" to 2-3/4" which are contained by a wooden frame. The blocks are positioned to simulate the desired topography. The scale of the board changes from one block equals 35' to one block equals 4' in the second game.

Dr. Luis H. Summers and Edward H. Seely
Associate Professor of Architectural Engineering
101 Engineering "A" Building
The Pennsylvania State University
University Park, Pennsylvania 16802

Abstract

Operational Games that combine physical models with human players are explored as useful and efficient tools for the exploration and teaching of architectural processes. Their potential and limitations are discussed. A second part of this paper mentions some salient architectural games in use today. The educational advantages inherent in designing operational gaming simulations are then discussed. The last section describes one procedure for game design used with success by the authors. Six sequential steps commonly used in game design are outlined.

Introduction

The field of architecture has traditionally used a modeling approach to problem solving, design studio projects. Whether the design studio follows the Beaux Arts "sequential design concept", the Bauhaus "originality" concept, or a combination of both, there is always a considerable amount of role playing involved. The "CRIT" plays the roles of enlightened master, client, city planner, etc., while the student plays "Howard Roarke", or as close as he can get to this role. Both the crit and the student are subsequently tested by a board of enlightened experts, "The jurors". The traditional studio system, whether Beaux Arts, Bauhaus, or whatever, works when the master knows all that the students need to know, and when the studio is part of the real world. Today's complex architectural processes cannot be taught by the traditional studio system. The many roles involved in the architectural process have become increasingly more difficult to represent by one actor, the "crit". Traditional studio teaching tends to become neither theory nor practice, but a self fulfilling exercise with its own rules.

In recent years a number of operations research tools have been applied to architectural studio problem solving. The tools, although highly useful for information ordering purposes, fail to model and describe complex interactions, expectations and goals of various participants affected by the building process. In order to introduce complex architectural problems into the studio, a tool is needed that will permit the representation of quantifiable variables such as economics and circulation, and non-quatifiable variables such as politics and emotion.

Since the early 1950's social scientists have been using techniques that combine mathematical models and human behavior, techniques called "operational gaming". In operational gaming, mathematical models and players are combined in a game simulation to examine physical and social consequences of human decisions.

At this stage in its development operational gaming is not being widely used in the architectural decision process; however it has met with great success in the classroom. Some of the reasons why operational gaming is so successful as a teaching tool are: a greater and more complete knowledge of a process is gained by making a gaming simulation involving participants than by describing the interaction in a typical scholarly description of its parts, gaming simulations promote a high degree of involvement; the emotive aspect of learning is not neglected, the consequences of one's moves and decisions are immediately observed, games are self-judging; they avoid authority reactions in the participants, gaming simulations emphasize behavior rather than verbal intentions.

A gaming simulation lends itself to rapid evolution and refinement, a highly desirable trait which contrasts with the more rigid structures of traditional models and teaching methods. When variables or relationships are encountered that can't be readily quantified, heuristics are made that describe them. Comparison of the simulation with the real life situation is then used to modify the rules and the game is played again. This cyclical process of modification and simulation gives operational gaming great flexibility and the ability to deal with variables and relationships that are difficult to quantify.

Some Salient Architectural Games

Since the many operational games available to urban analysis and designers have been extensively reported elsewhere, this paper will exclude a description of urban games.

Table 1, lists some of the better known architectural simulations in use today. While the fields of, user needs in housing, construction estimation, project management, building programming, office practice and introductory design have been gamed, simulations that will model the quality of the built environment are needed. Among the simulations described in Table 1, of particular importance are: LOW BIDDER, THE TRUAX HOUSING SIMULATION, AND THE HOUSE DESIGN GAME. LOW BIDDER, a simple computer-aided simulation of the construction bidding process, has historic importance, since it was one of the first games, along with CLUG, to be introduced into architectural curriculae. The Truax Housing Simulation, is important since it is a very elaborate model that allows the users to make decisions affecting the design of their habitat. This simulation is also concerned with implementation of the findings, therefore it has programmed conflict resolution sessions which facilitate conversation between home dwellers and public administrators. The House Design Game, is important because it introduces models that test the performance of the user-designed house through time. Models for pre-experiencing and evaluating the designed space, prior to building, seem to be desirable inclusion for future simulations.

A comprehensive approach to modeling helps the educator to evaluate, judge, correct, and coordinate his specialized knowledge. In a similar manner, students designing or modifying a game must collect data, conduct research, and examine theory to validate their proposed model. This experience can increase the designer's awareness of model elements and focus on valuable ideas such as validation, constraints, calibration, and sensitivity. Game design encourages communication among participants because the setting is generally informal and a discussion focus such as a playing board is usually available. To make clear what is referred to as the design process, one sample outline for the design of a game is given next: outline the situation or area of interest, define the model of the real system, choose the important roles and their game representation, determine the simulation feedback, outline the space and time dimensions of the game, define the rules and constraints for the game, calibrate and play-test the game.

Table I, Some Salient Architectural Games

LOW BIDDER, W. R. Park, Simulates Conditions for Contract Bidding, Shawnee Mission, Kansas, 1964.
PLANNING AN EDUCATIONAL SYSTEM, C. C. Abt, Cost and Benefit of Alternative Plans, Cambridge, Mass., 1965.
THE GAME, N. Mitchell, Gather Housing Information from User, Cambridge, Mass., 1966.
THREE COLUMN PRE-DETERMINED AVERAGE GAME, H. Sanoff, People's Preferred Housing Arrangement Within Fixed Budget, N. Carolina State University, 1968.
SPATIAL PREFERENCE GAME BOARD, H. Sanoff, Elicits Responses Concerning Preferred Spatial Arrangements, N. Carolina State University, 1968.
ARCHITECTURAL CONTROL PROCESS, S. Cohn, Planning Controls Used in the Regulation of Development, University of North Carolina, 1968.
SITE PLANNING GAME, R. White, Discover Needs of Inhabitants of Housing Project, Yale University, Connecticut, 1969.
UNIT DESIGN GAME, R. White, Discovers Individual Family's Housing Needs, Yale University, Connecticut, 1969.
BEATING THE SYSTEMS GAME, C. R. S., Hospital Programming, Houston, Texas, 1969.
THE MONEY PROBLEM, D. Solomon, Interrelation of Physical and Economic Factors in Design, Berkeley, California, 1969.
DESIGN ROLE PLAYING, J. Fitzgibbon, Exercise Public Interaction Skills of Designer, Washington University, Missouri, 1969.
TOOLS FOR CHANGE, Sim Van der Ryn, Heuristics of Problem Solving, Berkeley, California, 1969.
BEG, J. Ridyard, Problems of Estimating Bidding and Costing, South Australian Institute of Technology, 1970.
CONSTRUCTO, D. W. Halpin, A Computerized Construction Game, University of Illinois, 1970.
TEAM APPROACH TO CONCEIVING AND INITIATING BUILDING PROJECTS, AIA, Teach Language of Finance to Architects, Washington, D. C., 1970.
SIMU-SCHOOL, D. Burr, A Tool for Planning the School of Tomorrow, AIA, Washington, D. C., 1970.
ARC-ARC, B. Proctor and B. Dains, A Basic Design Game, University of Oklahoma, 1971.
THE HOUSE DESIGN GAME, L. H. Summers, The User Designed House, The Pennsylvania State University, 1971.
PROFESSIONAL PRACTICE GAME, J. Bancroft, Two Year Plan for Establishing a Professional Office, Oklahoma State University, 1971.
TRUAX, I. S. A., Solicit Housing Preferences of Low Income Residents, Dane County, Wisconsin, 1971.
HOMEGROWN, D. Fisk, A Housing Alternatives Game, University of Texas, Austin, 1971.
GOAL 26, G. D. Ding, A Game for Housing Education, Virginia Polytechnic Institute, Blacksburg, Virginia, 1971.
INHABS, C. W. Green, A Housing Growth Game, Gloucestershire College of Art and Design, England, 1972.
THE PLANNING GAME, L. A. Daly, Hospital Design Game, Washington, D. C., 1972.

Table I, Some Salient Architectural Games, Continued

EDUCATIONAL FACILITIES GAME, M. Pyatok, Programming and Schematic Design Phase, The Pennsylvania State University, 1972.
SPECIAL EDUCATIONAL FACILITIES GAME, M. Pyatok, School Design for Handicapped Children, The Pennsylvania State University, 1973.
EXERCISE QUINTAIN, J. Laing, Management of a Building Firm, London, England.
OPERATION TAURUS, P. C. Webb, Management of A Building Firm, Hendon Tech., England.
SCHOOL PLANNING GAME, D. W. Meals, Physical and Programmatic Requirements for School Design, Cambridge, Massachusets.
PLAY IBIS, T. Mann, A Design Game Based on the Argumentative Model of Design, Berkeley, California, 1972.
U-DIG, I. Bell, A Neighborhood Development Game, University of Colorado, Boulder. Colorado.

Notes

(1) Due to space limitations the bibliography, which can be obtained from Dr. Summers, is not included in this paper.

(2) A more detailed Table with descriptions may be obtained from Dr. Summers.

TWELVE   BUILDING SYSTEMS

12.0

Chairman:
Gunter Schmitz, School of Architecture & Environmental Design, SUNY, Buffalo, NY 14214

Participants:
Robert Blake, Facilities Engineering and Construction Agency, HEW, Washington, DC
Eric Dluhosch, Architecture Research Coordination, University of California, Berkeley
Kim Judge, National Association of Building Manufacturers, Washington, DC
Walter Kroner, School of Architecture, Rensselaer Polytechnic Institute, Troy, NY
Dr. Edward O. Pfrang, Office of Housing Technology, NBS, Washington, DC
Earl S. Swensson, Architects, Nashville, Tennessee
Jack Warner, Warner Consultants, Washington, DC

Abstract

The workshop attempts to explore the potentials and limitations of building systems. Building systems offer a historic chance for a retarded industry, if they are used as part of systemic approaches. The multiple elements in the general process of building delivery are interlinked and behave as a complex system, affected by outside independent variables. Building systems as technical solutions have to be integrated into the structure of this system. Combined with managerial skills of systems building and backed by user needs analyses they can become effective tools in providing built environments responsive to social needs - offering initial flexibility and built-in adaptibility for future functional changes. To prepare the introduction and growth of building systems on an industrial scale in a competitive economy, several critical areas need attention: comprehensive and reliable data bases, interdisciplinary cooperation, future oriented research, incentives to accelerate innovation processes, market research and development, public information, and education.

Building Systems - Chances for a Retarded Industry

The building industry is notorious for failing to adapt to the needs of our century. Its means of providing for our built environment continue to be strangely out of date. Its production methods are antiquated, distribution is devious, and assembly disorganized. A network of building and zoning ordinances - often contradictory, and almost always obsolete - has to be negotiated, as do all the legal processes involving transfer of land titles, financing, etc. As a result of this archaic system of production, building prices are high, quality generally low, and output inadequate. (1)

Not only could building adopt modern means of production and organization, it also

449

could adapt much better to the social conditions of our day and the needs of tomorrow. The emerging building industry, if to be successful, has to link its objectives to social goals. It has e.g. to become sensitive to the housing crisis existing in the wealthiest society the world has seen. In particular, ways have to be
found that broaden its focus from the lucrative field of middle-income single family
residences to new scales of operations involving the design and construction of
whole communities, communities which will include large population segments now
living in substandard housing and often chaotic environments. This new context will
require a shift from an individual building oriented technology to a system oriented
technology, where sets of components with rules for interaction are developed first,
and then produced continuously, long before they are applied in unique combinations
for unique solutions in unique situations.

Building systems can indeed match user needs as many application examples from the
field of education facilities suggest. The various consortia based school building
systems in Britain - CLASP, SEAC, SCOLA, etc. - are outstanding examples. They were
developed with active participation of educators since their inception, are strongly
user oriented and provide excellent facilities at controlled cost. School building
systems on the American continent like SCSD, SEF, RAS, etc., or the Marburg University Building System in Germany, show similar characteristics. Their importance,
however, goes beyond their initial matching of careful defined functional performance
requirements. Functional needs within buildings, activity patterns, circulation,
etc. do not remain constant and cannot be preplanned over the lifetime of a structure. The built-in adaptibility to future functional change, expansion, etc. makes
these system-built facilities superior to conventional solutions where structures
after having outlived their suitability are still used, but differently and with
sacrifices to efficiency. By devising architectural forms that are open to use
change, able to accomodate unknown functions in the future, designers can contribute to social development in a time noted for rapid change. Functional building
types in the classical sense may decrease in importance, giving way to buildings
with interchangeable functions that may introduce a new type of architecture, a
building system-built environment that, because of its usefulness, will have a good
chance to outlast our present generation.

The current disorganized state of the building industry, the scale of the urban
housing crisis facing the nation and the necessity of a continuous adaption of the
product to changing user requirements all call for a strong systems orientation of
the building process.

Building Systems can be described as a set of rules which apply to the relationships
between kits of parts (building components), developed or selected to function as a
whole. It has become clear, however, that building systems as technical solutions
alone cannot be expected to succeed in a competitive economy. Historic experience
shows that "hardware" systems of building cannot resolve the socio-political problems connected with building. The building process has to be recognized as a
complex network of interacting forces. Materials, products, production, management,
labor, legislation, codes, real estate, financing, marketing, transportation, etc.
are interdependent variables behaving as a system. A reasonable understanding of
the complexity of this system should be a prerequisite for any organization considering to compete on the market place. A recent study identifies the structure

of an important portion of the current U.S. building community: the growing industrialized housing industry (2). It provides potential building systems sponsors not
only with the basic information for a market entry by identifying the linked elements
of the industrialized housing industry in a network diagram, but also selects the
most critical strategic points within the industry's structure that inhibit growth,
and suggests ways how they could be resolved.

It is obvious that in order to become competitive, building systems should be developed in a coordinated Systems Approach, which can be described as a "strategy of
problem definition and solution which emphasizes the interaction between problem
elements and between the immediate problem and its larger context, and which specifically avoids traditional methods of independent or ad hoc treatment of the various
elements"(3). The application of the systems approach to construction - Systems
Building - results in "the organization of programming, planning, design, financing,
manufacturing, construction, and evaluation of buildings under single, or highly
coordinated, management into an efficient total process"(4). Systems building as a
management tool, can be very effective in relating structures to User Needs, "those
conditions which the user of a building considers necessary or desirable as environment and support for his activities, without particular references to how such
conditions are to be physically produced"(5). User needs are transformed in Performance Specifications, "a set of specifications which prescribes a building system,
subsystem, or component for bidding purposes not by its physical materials, shapes,
dimensions, or other physical properties, but by the desired results; in other words,
not by what it is, but by what it does"(6). By stating objectives in performance
terms rather than in terms of particular technologies, alternatives can be compared
in regard to their cost/effectiveness, which will take into account the continous
maintenance and operating costs and costs for changing space layouts, which are
essential for the lifetime economy of any facility.

Systems building, augmented by building systems may even see the return of the user
as force in shaping his environment. Several models of active user involvement in
an emerging housing industry have been suggested with the aim of adapting the building economically to the user rather than the user to the building (7,8). It is this
notion (building systems combined with the managerial skills of systems building and
a decided user needs orientation) that will let building systems contribute substantially to the shaping of a humane world.

Partially industrialized forms of building production concentrating on components
with high technological content (electrical, mechanical, hydraulical) can exploit
the benefits of mass production to the fullest. Subsystems that are compatible
with conventional building techniques in particular have a good chance to succeed
as they imply lower risk and may threaten the vested interests of the traditional
operators in the building process to a much lesser degree than "total" building
system packages. Recent developments seem to prepare the entry of components of
that nature in international markets already(9). In the light of the fact that new
buildings constitute the smaller part of our whole built environment and that much
of the aged building stock is in dire need of rehabilitive modernisation, the market for these components could possibly be broadened substantially.

The future holds great promise but there is a long way to go. Public or private large scale private commitment to capital intensive building processes has yet to happen, but will become inevitable if the gigantic construction needs of the years ahead should be overcome. Mankind seems to have reached a doubling rate of 11 years for its urban population already (10), and the estimated housing need (alone) for the next 30 years is over 1 billion dwelling units (11), more than the total number mankind has built in its entire existence. The scale of necessary operations is unprecedented and requires the development of building systems for mass production on a scientific basis. Limited insights, concepts, preparation time, markets, and resources so far generated limited solutions with limited public acceptance. Some of the failures were and are spectacular and should serve an educational purpose. We would, however, miss a major opportunity in history by not exploiting to the fullest the potential capabilities of science and technology to advance the processes for realizing major improvements in building's delivery time, performance characteristics and cost control.

To this end several critical areas need attention:
· Comprehensive automated data bases for the building industry - depositories of information with automatic selection and updating of information - can provide the planner with a wealth of manipulable information as to facts and their interrelationships. Easy accessible, these data banks will cause multiple technical and managerial developments.
· The building code system is currently undergoing major overhauls regarding scope, content, uniformity, computerization and enforcing processes (12). Deliberate efforts can be made to prevent codes from acting as a brake on development by basing them on performance concepts and by stipulating periodical revisions.
· Professional societies, trade organizations, labor unions, manufacturer organizations, and the like, now largely fragmented and organized around distinct technologies, should open and provide frequent problem oriented forums for crossdisciplinary interaction. The active participation of multiprofessional groups in formulating and implementing medium and long range national building goals would be only logical.
· The systematic use of technological forecasting techniques could assist not only in the articulation of national objectives but also in the definition of technological research requirements in areas where existing research programs are inadequate. However, as the general business horizon rarely extends much farther than the aim of maximizing profits - and as the private economic sector is likely to dominate the development of building systems in the foreseeable future - needs of people and society have to be given sufficient attention in the allocation of r&d funds. Contextual maps with subject matter organized in modules could serve as a basis for cross-support of interrelated projects.
· While most segments of American business and industry respond rapidly to any advances in science and technology and invest much of their manpower and resources in planned experimentation and development, the building industry is notorious for being much less innovative. Judged by standards of the industrial community, building's allocation of funds for research is far underdeveloped. However, even in a situation of scarce financial resources, innovation can be accomplished focusing on technology transfer, the diffusion of existing technology; new ways of applying products   and processes, developed in other areas, to particular problems in building (13). The method is by far less costly and time consuming than original research and development (14,15). A recent government announced

program seems to prepare federal efforts to mount a national program of innovation incentive mechanisms to overcome existing barriers in the civilian sector (16). The building systems industry would be well advised to participate.

· As far as innovative marketing and process management is concerned, industrialized building as a capital intensive activity can learn much from other major industries, which pioneered e.g. with product individualization, or which reduced required investment by being only concerned with design, assembly and marketing, while subcontracting out the actual manufacture of components. Scientific marketing techniques for building systems have to be developed based on a thorough understanding of historical inertia, recognition of acceptance cycles, correct assessment of economic requirements, trend extrapolation, demand aggregation, etc. Matching of industrial objectives with social goals, and continuous economic monitoring with cost/benefit and cost/effectiveness analyses, will essentially guide building systems into a future of mass production and mass markets.

· International or corporate competition may well accelerate the growth of building systems, as may social disequilibria, the ecology movement, or plain challenge. Probabilistic assessments of alternative futures will certainly stimulate and somehow guide the technological development (17). The public, however, is presently ill informed on   alternative futures or not at all. Not a single TV station or newspaper has a technology "daily". Building systems as a study object for design professions is only beginning, to some extent, to intrigue this country's academic community, leaving leaders in the field with only a scant basis of competent personnel for years to come.

To set general building goals without relating them to specific implementation plans helps little. Major political commitments that would ensure such conditions for long-term production in building that it would be easier to plan ahead are nonexistent. In the face of such uncertainty the task of improving the productivity of the building process in this country is formidable. Any systemic and industrial approach for building has to be scientifically prepared. A successful planning of a future of building with systems will largely depend on more effective cooperation between government agencies, industries, labor, finance institutions, business, mass media, user groups, educational institutions and research centers. Management technologies, which play a crucial role in accelerating the pace of progress, are available, distribution, transportation and communication systems exist or can be improved, techniques can be learned, and attitudes can be developed. It is not too late and it may well be an historic chance.

References:

(1) Bender, Richard, SELECTED TECHNOLOGICAL ASPECTS OF THE AMERICAN BUILDING INDUSTRY - THE INDUSTRIALIZATION OF BUILDING, prepared for the National Commission on Urban Problems, New York, 1968.
(2) The Buffalo Organization for Social and Technological Innovation, A MODEL FOR AN INDUSTRILAZED HOUSING INDUSTRY IN THE UNITED STATES, Buffalo, NY, BOSTI, 1972.
(3) Boice, John R., A HISTORY AND EVALUATION OF SCSD- THE SCHOOL CONSTRUCTION SYSTEMS DEVELOPMENT PROJECT 1961-1967, Menlo Park, California, Building Systems Information Clearinghouse/Educational Facilities Laboratories, Inc., no year.
(4) Building Systems Information Clearinghouse, BUILDING SYSTEMS PLANNING MANUAL, Special Report No.3, Menlo Park, California, BSIC/EFL, 1971.

(5) Ibid.
(6) Ibid.
(7) Bender, Richard (1).
(8) Terner, I.D. and Turner, John, F.C., INDUSTRIALIZED HOUSING, Ideas and Method Exchange publication No. 66, HUD, Washington DC, 1972.
(9) TECHNICAL REPORT, Vol. 17, Misawa Homes, Institute of Research & Devel., Tokyo.
(10) Toffler, Alvin, FUTURE SHOCK, New York, 1970.
(11) United Nations, WORLD HOUSING CONDITIONS AND ESTIMATED HOUSING REQUIREMENTS, New York, UN Dept. of Economic and Social Affairs, 1965.
(12) THE IMPLICATION OF A COMPUTER-BASED CODE SYSTEM, School of Architecture & Environmental Design, SUNY at Buffalo, for the National Science Foundation, 1971-1973.
(13) Clapperton, R. Ian, "Developing a Technology Transfer System", BUILD INTERNA-TIONAL, Vol. 5, No. 6, Nov/Dec 1972, p.333-339.
(14) MacFadyen, David J., "Technology Transfer and Improved Housing Production", INDUSTRIALIZATION FORUM, Vol. 3, No. 5, June 1972.
(15) Foster, R.N., "Technology Transfer and Information", INDUSTRIALIZATION FORUM, Vol. 3, No. 5, June 1972.
(16) National Science Foundation, EXPERIMENTAL R&D INCENTIVES PROGRAM, PRELIMINARY PROGRAM ANNOUNCEMENT, Washington DC, NSF, 22 Sept 1972.
(17) Jantsch, Erich, TECHNOLOGICAL FORECASTING IN PERSPECTIVE, Paris, OECD Organization for Economic Cooperation and Development, 1967.

THE BUILDING BLOCK SYSTEM: A RESEARCH AND DESIGN STUDY FOR MODULAR RELOCATABLE   12.1
FACILITIES

Walter M. Kroner
Assistant Professor & Associate Director
Center for Architectural Research
School of Architecture
Rensselaer Polytechnic Institute
Troy, New York, 12181

Abstract

In July 1971 the USAF Civil Engineering Center (CE Center) contracted with
Rensselaer Polytechnic Institute, for its Center for Architectural Research, to
undertake a Research and Design Study for developing a Building System for Modular
Relocatable Facilities. The Building Block Research and Design Study, its official
name, is designed to provide research and design guidance for a system of modular
relocatable facilities which can accommodate a variety of uses, which can be
utilized in a variety of circumstances, which can be recovered and relocated, and
which can provide the necessary cost, time and quality performance.

The Need

As part of its total mission, the CE Center is concerned with providing habitable
facilities which are both rapid-response and variable-term in nature. In addition
to their instant-response facility program (Bare Base Mobility), and their conventional construction program (which takes years to place a facility) there is a need
for a program which provides facilities within 6 months or less, facilities which
can be shipped anywhere around the globe, facilities which can remain in place for
unspecified lengths of time, but can be moved, relocated, and reconfigured several
times over the buildings life-time. Facility types include dispensaries, offices,
dining halls, schools, bachelor quarters, laboratories and are used for military
requirements as well as emergencies and disasters (floods, hurricans, etc.) for
both military and the civilian sectors.

Over the past 7 years the CE Center has provided these types of facilities and
gained considerable experience pertaining to modular relocatable facilities. In
addition many problems remained unsolved especially in the areas of environmental
quality, manufacturing, shipping, storage, erection and general facility use. As
a result the CE Center requested a research and design study which would result in
a building system representing a "quantum jump" for both modular relocatable
facilities and building system developments. The following general design criteria
was established: (1) facilities had to be deliverable within 6 months or less;
(2) the building system had to be of a quality equal to permanent type of construction; (3) one building system had to work for at least nine different facility
types (theaters, libraries, dining halls, officers mess, laboratories, offices,
bachelor living quarters, schools, and dispensaries); (4) the building system had
to be capable of being shipped by land, sea and sometimes air, and erected anywhere around the globe between the arctic and antarctic circle; (5) it had to be
erected using semi-skilled labor; (6) it had to use off-the-shelf technology;

(7) components and subsystems had to be manufactured in the U.S. to minimize the "gold flow"; (8) it had to be of reasonable cost; (9) it had to be procured using the existing delivery/logistic system of the Armed Services procurement.

The Building Block System

While space does not permit a detailed description of the methodology used in developing the Building Block System, the study team developed a basic design concept which allows for a "free" open space (which can be configured and reconfigured in many ways) within a structural frame, and with services distributed from above and below the "free" space. The mechanical and electrical services are connected to utility mains at the periphery of the facility which in turn connect to a separate energy-producing module at the exterior of the facility.

For the design of the system itself we selected the erector-set approach. This approach is one where the Building Block System is a kit of parts which can be put together in erector set fashion, according to a set of rules, allowing for a variety of configurations, facility types, and under a variety of conditions. It is possible to add, delete, and move parts around, disassemble the parts; pack them, ship them to new locations and (perhaps adding or subtracting parts) re-erect them as required. It is critical to point out that the size of the ELEMENTS (the parts) had to be segmented to fit into a 8'x8'x40' shipping container.

We recognized that the "quantum jump" of building system development had to come about thru maximizing the physical integration of subsystems. We had to go beyond the level of integration of lighting/ceiling, atmosphere, and interior partitions as achieved in the SCSD project.

The study team designed a series of building hardware elements, which are used to provide the necessary facilities. An element is a relatively large piece of hardware which, more often than not, integrates parts of a number of functional subsystems which serve as the basis for determining building performance. For example one of the elements, the horizontal sandwich, integrates components of the following subsystems: structure, lighting/ceiling, electric/electronic, atmosphere, plumbing, and finishes. The elements are based on a 5'x5' planning module, and a 20'x30' and 30'x30' structural module. A total of 64 elements have been developed and are aggregated into four element groups: (1) the Structural Element Group, (2) the Enclosure Element Group, (3) the Energy Element Group, and (4) the Equipment Element Group.

The elements are designed with existing components and/or subsystems which are delivered to a central manufacturing point, are assembled, packaged, and shipped to the site and erected without further subsystem integration. Erection is limited to connecting elements to each other according to an assembly guideline. Elements can be installed in various configurations, positions, and slope conditions.

Basically the Building Block System is a steel frame type structure, limited to two stories, and utilizing pier type foundations. A maximum building width of 120' and an unlimited building length establish the overall configuration. The first floor of each facility is always located four feet above finished grade or the highest elevation point.

The Structural Element Group: This group contains 22 elements. There are two types of steel columns (4' and 12' in length), three types of primary trusses (10', 20' and 30'), five types of horizontal sandwiches, five types of horizontal mains (peripheral utility lines) and two vertical mains (vertical utility connections). In addition there are a few smaller elements which complete the structural requirements. The quantum jump of this system is in the horizontal sandwiches. Sandwiches are elements 5' wide, 2' high and all of them are 30' in length. The sandwiches integrate components, of the structural, lighting/ceiling, atmosphere, electric/ electronic, plumbing and finishes subsystems. Thru a hinged panel located at the top of a sandwich, each sandwich covers a floor area of 300S.F. Each sandwich is independently controlled and spans between the primary trusses. Sandwiches are connected end to end and are serviced by the horizontal main which is secured to the structural frame and functions as a main utility spine, located at the periphery of the building. Each 10' section of the horizontal main can serve two sandwiches end to end and by locating a horizontal main at both sides of the building a maximum building width of 120' is possible. The upper surface of the sandwiches functions as a subfloor ready to receive a removable floor finish, or a roof surface taped with a removable joint cover. The vertical mains connect to the horizontal mains and thus provide linkage to the energy modules which house all of the mechanical equipments, also located outside of any facility.

The Enclosure Elements: 13 elements are included in the enclosure elements. Essentially these elements enclose the facility and make it operational. Twelve different wall panels facilitate different appearances, fenestrations, and forms of access. Enclosure panels are located between the columns, and are integrated with the 5'x5' planning module. Wall joints can be reinforced to accommodate wind velocities of 180 mph. In addition a standard fascia panel is provided to enclose exposed trusses, and horizontal mains. As stated previously the roof enclosure is part of the horizontal sandwich which basically is a fiberglass skin, and the joints are covered with a Hypalon tape. This tape can be cut in relocation and retaped in subsequent erections.

The Energy Element Group: Five different energy elements are provided. The energy elements are 8'x8'x20' containers designed to serve various sandwich combinations. They are modularized to facilitate various atmospheric options as well as various utility load conditions.

The Equipment Element Group: This group contains all the elements necessary to configure the interior volume of the various facility types. It includes partitions, various bathroom types and wet spaces, kitchens and storage modules, plumbing electric and atmospheric columnettes, and stair elements. Each element in this group can be moved within the "free" space. Stairs are located at the periphery of the building and can be open or enclosed.

Summary: The Building Block System with its 64 elements, and assembly rules, not only represents a quantum jump for the Modular Facilities Program of the Air Force but for the general Building System Developments as well. It is a quantum jump because subsystems integration were increased and site erection reduced.

THE DEVELOPMENT OF AN OUTPATIENT PHARMACEUTICAL DISPENSARY UNIT BASED ON TASK-   12.2
ORIENTED AND HUMAN-ENGINEERING DESIGN APPROACHES

Earl S. Swensson, A.I.A.
President
Earl Swensson Architects
2104 Sunset Place
Nashville, Tennessee 37212

Abstract

The author was retained by the Research Institute of Pharmaceutical Sciences,
School of Pharmacy, University of Mississippi, Oxford, Mississippi, to participate
in a project to design a model outpatient pharmacy for a 200-bed non-teaching
general hospital, under a grant from General Equipment Manufacturing Company of
Crystal Springs, Mississippi. The planning process discussed in this paper introduces the author's concept of planning based on his "human-engineering" and "task-
oriented" techniques. He outlines the total design process of data collection,
problem analysis, design development, model investigation, prototype planning and
the final production of an innovative design for an outpatient pharmacy unit.

Problem Definition

The Research Institute personnel and the architect were convinced that new pharmaceutical facilities should be planned to enable people to perform their tasks with
comfort and efficiency in which a breakthrough in basic attitudes was mandatory.
The pharmacy facility planners emphasized the elimination of function obsolescence
of design, equipment, and fixtures. The architectural design team then began intensive orientation to the planning parameters already established by the Institute
which included a review of filmed facilities in the United States and of national
surveys of hospital pharmacy facilities. As a member of the planning team, the
author also began an investigation of the drug dispensing system and the emerging
role of the pharmacist as specialist, counselor, and administrator. Continued
problem definition specified functional task centers in a hospital pharmacy facility which would be required for maximum performance. The environmental task centers, the planning team concluded, must enable the pharmacy personnel to accomplish
assigned tasks, provide for adequate storage to control all work, and provide
communications to coordinate all activities.

Concept Development

In his approach to the design solution, the author advanced the basic parameter
that man must be the scale for all planning and that design must be related to human behavior. In developing the design for the pharmacist's task, he utilized
"human-engineering" principles and "task-oriented" standards to enable the pharmacist to assume his proper and best role. Continuing with the functional program
completed by the Research Institute, the architectural design team evolved the
experimental "task-oriented module concept" for a model outpatient dispensary.
Instead of creating new equipment for the unit, they combined a group of total
environments including counters, equipment, walls, seating, and lights with each

458

fixture characterized by its own configuration. The outpatient center thus developed as a self-contained module with interrelated space use that included counters, acoustical panels, rotary drug files, communications, adjustable shelves, client identification board, sink with work space, etc.

Model Development

The initial module design was recycled by the pharmaceutical researchers and architects who spent numerous hours evaluating the task center as a self-contained unit. As the team explored the potential of the module unit, better space utilization was developed for pharmacists and patients accompanied by better drug distribution and control of prescriptions. A second outpatient dispensing module design was completed with further improvements such as a two-station pharmacist module, and innovative six-foot diameter drug storage area equal to 48 linear feet of conventional pharmaceutical storage space. After agreeing to accept the design concept, the production of a full-scale mock-up to test the effectiveness of the outpatient dispensing module design began. Following completion of the factory mock-up, team members from the Research Institute, the architectural firm and selected pharmacists refined and evaluated the module. The final prototype was circular in form and was transferred to the Research Institute for terminal refinement with final evaluation and testing by pharmacists and pharmacy students among others.

Production modules have been patented under the trademark "SystaModule" with a pharmacy dispensing function. The area of the module is approximately 100 square feet, although the marketing information stresses the adaptability of the module or modules into interchangeable units with several space combinations. Unit "A" is described as a service and consultation window with a work counter, narcotics control cabinet, communications system and adjustable gravity-fed and flat shelving. Unit "B" is a shelf unit with gravity-fed adjustable shelving and having dimensions of a 96 1/2 inch width and an 84 inch height. Unit "C" is a utility unit with a 3.3 cubic foot refrigerator, stainless steel lavatory sink, adjustable flat shelving, and electrical and water conduits. The height of the unit is also 84 inches. Unit "D" is a reserve storage area with adjustable flat shelving finished in natural woodgrain vinyl with two sets of double doors. The unit has the same outside dimensions and is interchangeable as Units "A" and "B". Other significant features of the module unit include patient privacy areas, built-in utility systems as described in the four units, stain-resistant, washable vinyl exteriors, a packaged power unit with AC outlets, lighting, heating, and ventilation, and ceiling structure of an acoustical, egg-crate design. The sales prospects also offer as optional equipment sit-stand perch chairs, patient seating, cashier cubicle, etc. The highly versatile module system can be installed in new or existing space without requiring structural changes.

Project Summary

In conclusion, the author believes that the above program and effective results has established his concept of task-oriented and human-engineering in spatial planning as a valid technique.

Swensson, E., "An Innovative Design in Hospital Pharmacy Facilities", AMERICAN JOURNAL OF HOSPITAL PHARMACY, 28, pages 422-446, (June) 1971.

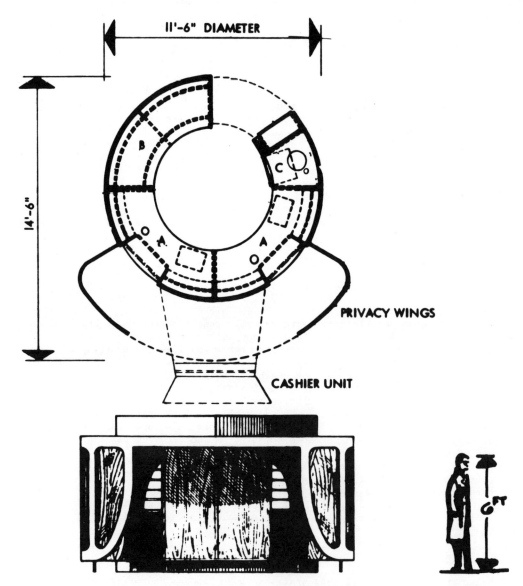

PRIVACY WINGS

CASHIER UNIT

PHARMACEUTICAL DISPENSING MODULE
SCALE: 1/4" = 1'-0"

Jack R. Warner
President, Warner Consultants
75-A G Street S.W.
Washington, D.C. 20024

INTRODUCTION

The following scenario was developed from information gathered from 30 building industry experts and generalists. These persons, serving on a Delphi Panel as part
of a larger study for a building industry trade association, evaluated the probability of 43 events, mostly related to construction, happening by 1980. The events
from this previous study deemed significant form this paper. Additional information is available on request from the author.

THE BUILDING INDUSTRY, 1980

Traditional contractors and subcontractors are facing increasing difficulty in marketing their services, due to the fact that well over half of the buildings procured are through systems building, the management technique that took hold in the
seventies. More importantly, legislation to prohibit traditional, cost increasing
labor practices has been stopped since systems building continues to gain ground
and the quality of workmanship associated with it has forced traditional builders
to improve their product also.

Adoption of federal building codes on the state level has also given systems building a boost by encouraging the manufacturers of building systems to get a "seal of
approval" that allows nationwide distribution. Modular core units, preassembled
wet walls, integrated electrical systems, CATV, low-voltage and pneumatic controls
are just a few of the products that have been developed in conjunction with building systems.

Owner/user building associations, perhaps a spin-off of the consumerism movement,
are now asking contractors to use systems building methods for their jobs. As
organizations, they have become a powerful economic and political force.

Initial union reluctance on a local level to systems building has practically
ceased as their work jurisdiction has changed; field *vs.* factory is no longer a
battle line. The blurring of this line has been aided, in part, by the establishment of junior college and private educational firm apprenticeship programs.

Computer assisted management, design and cost estimating mathods are widespread.
Owner/user associations rely on the cost estimating techniques and many times give
labor-only contracts. Pre-award liaison between design firms and contractors, as
well as others, is encouraged to reduce costs.

Consumers have been demanding longer warranties and higher quality standards to
the point where some contractors have become original equipment manufacturers'
(OEM) representatives for building subsystems.

Of special note is the ingenious application of solid state devices to many applications formerly requiring high power. This has allowed better utilization of
energy and a chance to lessen the energy crisis. The rise of solid state devices
and favorable rulings on cable television has opened this medium as a nationwide
market. Home installed CATV centers have computer, copier, bill paying and other
home management and entertainment devices built in. Many forward looking corporations are installing home "work consoles" for employees to reduce unneeded central-
ization (costing the corporation more money in office space than for the home consoles!) and as their contribution towards keeping unneeded automobile pollution
down.

An increased reliance on government solutions to intra-industry problems has been
the "court" to which other industry segments have brought complaints about too much
vertical and horizontal integration of contractors and subcontractors. Some fear
this merger trend will in the end put building back into the position of the 1970's
when rising costs brought on systems building as a panacea. Now some fear the tail
will wag the dog and are lobbying for yet another solution to the rising costs of
building.

EVENTS WITH PROBABLE OCCURRENCE BY 1980 OR 1985 AS PERCEIVED BY THE DELPHI PANEL

Vertical integration of firms

Non-construction firms buy construction firms

Innovative contracting methods
replace traditional

C/M becomes the major method of
building

Computer assisted methods reduce sub-
bids to labor only

OEM strengthen through life cycle
servicing

Adoption of national urban and rural
growth policy

Adoption of federal building codes
and standards

Special investment tax credit given
to the industry

Increased government spending in
construction and rehabilitation

Performance codes with "seals of approval" will be common

Owner/user associations emerge

Life cycle costing promotes life maintenance by the manufacturer

Warranty and quality standards demanded
by consumers

Continuing shortage of energy

Factory produced assemblies replace on-
site assemblies

Sophisticated solid state controls require skilled technicians

Decreased interest in overtime eases
acceptance of building subsystems

Legislation prohibits traditional
practices where new methods emerge

Bidding competition intensifies with
pre-award liaisons

THIRTEEN   FUTURE ORIENTED TECHNOLOGIES   13.0

Chairman: Wolf Hilbertz, School of Architecture, University of Texas, Austin,
           Texas 78712

Participants:

Edward Allen, Department of Architecture, M.I.T., Cambridge Massachusetts
Robert E. Lucas, School of Architecture, University of Texas at Austin
Joseph Mathis, Symbiotic Processes Laboratory, Austin, Texas
Renato Severino, Urban Technology International, Inc., Westport, Connecticut
Friedrich St. Florian, Center for Advanced Visual Studies, M.I.T., Cambridge,
        Massachusetts
Michael Webb, Rhode Island School of Design, Providence, Rhode Island
Joseph Weber, Academy of Fine Arts, Hamburg, Germany

Abstract

It is the intent of the workshop to discuss future environmental technological
developments and assess their validity according to certain postulated goals.
Five distinctly different papers form the basis for discussion. If a common de-
nominator can be found at all, it is the sometimes strongly expressed discontent
with existing conditions. The cardinal demand expressed is the need to transform
a selfishly man-centered technology into a set of comprehensive systems which can
achieve dynamic symbiotic fit.

Introduction:

Shifting parameters in environmental design philosophy have led to place increased
emphasis on formerly unknown or neglected factors and influences. The consideration of the following areas increasingly influences decisions affecting the natural
and built environments:
1. Ecosystems and strategies for their implementation;
2. Energy conservation and use of resources; and,
3. The socio-political context.

Only recently, interest has begun to center around the emerging field of organism-
environment interaction. Sechenov (1) views the environment in which animals live
as a factor in determining their organization. Therefore, it follows that in the
course of organic evolution an increase in the complexity of the organism and an
increase in the complexity of the environment acting on it are mutually dependent
factors. Life can be seen as a dynamic state of harmony between vital demands and
environmental conditions. The greater the demands, which are resulting from the
higher level of organization, the greater the call made on the environment for the

463

satisfaction of these demands.

Walter (2) contends that by adapting the environment to our models rather than ourselves to the environment, we oppose organic evolution, i.e., that evolutionary
mechanisms no longer apply to ourselves but to our habitat. These two selected
views promote understanding the conceptual development of organism-environment systems in which all parts evolve into ever-higher organizational pattern (3).

Workshop contributions are posed against this background, which inevitably represents somewhat of a personal bias.

Discussion:

Edward Allen, in his paper "The Responsive Dwelling," emphasizes the need for greater participation of the user in the design and erection of his own structure in the
effort to give to the individual maximum control over his own life. In part, this
should alleviate some of the indignities resulting from the "abdication of personal
perogative leading to the faceless little boxes of suburbia." The inclusion of the
user in the design and construction process not only provides "more house for less
money," he says, but also, according to studies made, the individual experiences
   "pride of accomplishment, extending one's self-confidence, obtaining
   a better-constructed house through closer personal control of the
   construction process, acquiring the skills necessary to repair and
   modify one's own dwelling on a continuing basis, and obtaining a
   house with personalized design features which are otherwise unavail-
   able."

Dr. Allen cites in his own work an attempt first to break out of the "tyranny of
the rectilinear module," and later a more ambitious effort to provide easier
and cheaper (and more flexible) construction methods through automation. At present, though, he feels that it is more important to incorporate the individual into
the process now to achieve more autonomous design and construction quickly, rather
than wait for the technological extensions necessary to provide automated and flexible techniques to the user. In order to achieve this end, Dr. Allen points out
three major problem areas: more complete and understandable information on the
design and construction process must be made available to the potential user-build-
er; "easier building technologies requiring less skill, fewer tools, less muscle,
and less time, must be developed" (e.g., plastic versus cast-iron plumbing); and
better administrative and financial organizations must be established to provide
the owner-builder with easier access to money, permits, information, professional
help where needed, and sufficient time to undertake the task. In short, Dr. Allen
advocates the development of technologies to provide a responsive building --
responsive in the sense that the user creates his own space to fit his own needs.
Recognizing the potential future breakthroughs in building technology, he emphasizes that
   "... the key is an enlightened technology, one which recognizes as its
   goal the placement of the individual human being at the center of things."

Some architects, including myself, are working toward a greater development of
building technology through the means of automation, partly to increase the

"responsiveness" of such a system and partly to decrease the tremendous investment of financial and human energy in the present building processes. I must admit that I abhor the useless expenditure of human energy, whether by the construction industry as it exists now or by the user as implied by Dr. Allen's system. However, I must also confess that I see in his guidelines the intermediate means by which we   might   gain greater responsibility and responsiveness to needs so necessary in today's architecture immediately, rather than wait for the technological advancements necessary to facilitate full social and environmental "responsiveness." I am forced to respond, though, to Dr. Allen's closing thought that the individual be placed at the center of things. Obviously, the individual should retain pre-eminence when we talk about man alone, but when we consider man and his environment, I believe that we cannot afford any longer to relegate the status of the environment to second place as a matter of course (4). Here the central problem of freedom and necessity arises (5). So, in the long range, man ultimately becomes a reflection of his environment, and we cannot sacrifice or detriment the present environment in order to provide the individual with short-range benefits.

Wolf Hilbertz and Joseph Mathis present a concept of "Form-Space Manipulation with Computer-Controlled Light Configurations, Interference Patterns, and Photopolymerizable Materials." Light configurations and other energy fields can describe objects three-dimensionally. All energy which can be propagated in a coherent wave form can be used to construct interference patterns: sound, microwaves, infrared and ultraviolet light, x-rays, etc. With on-line computing capabilities, any conceivable shape can be described and changed in real-time.

Photopolymerization of vinyl monomers and other materials has already been demonstrated (6). When an aerosol consisting of a dye-catalyst-monomer mixture or gaseous monomers is introduced into an interference pattern or other energy field, the monomer can be catalyzed selectively, producing an object which maps the contours of the energy pattern.

Material reclamation is facilitated by solvents and molecular chain deterioration by application of certain wavelengths of light.

Coherent radiowave interference patterns can serve as guidance systems for self-propelled material distribution and reclamation hardware, which would construct or reclaim an object conforming to the shape of the pattern.

Application of interference and other energy pattern material manipulation systems would range from the molecular level up to cityscapes, from one-shot techniques to continuous form-space manipulation.

The described system is capable of responding directly to user needs and the syn-ecological setting, thereby becoming a fully integrated factor of socio-political and biological processes.

This proposal seems to be far from implementation. It belongs in a category aptly named by Bloch "goal-directing utopias" (konkrete Utopie) because it has the potential to induce change in environmental and societal structure (7).

In "Architecture and Education," Mr. Lucas sharply attacks educational institutions and the pervading low level of environmental consciousness. The architect today regards himself as a spacial specialist; the success of his work depends on his ego, experience, taste, and luck. In general, architecture is not presently solving larger environmental problems and, in fact, is contributing to those problems. The orientation and outlook of the architect must be changed and the techniques of architecture must be developed further if we are to solve the spacial needs of individuals, the social problems of housing and other structures, and the larger environmental issues of which architecture is a part.

The architect can no longer be a specialist; he must be re-educated to take the role of planner in the general relationship of man-building-environment. This re-education becomes most important in order to provide the research goals and framework in which specialists can work; existing research, atomistic and specialized, can only lead to further scientific disintegration and mis-application to environmental issues. The architect's approach must be broadened in three major areas. First, he must be able to more fully recognize the needs of the individual through research in the social sciences. Second, he must fully recognize the interdependence of man and nature and begin to recognize the needs of the environment. And, finally, he must develop building systems with sufficient flexibility to keep pace with the changing relationship of man and the environment.

If the architect's goal can be redefined as the provision of the best possible "fit" between the three environments of man, architecture, and nature, the building itself becomes the interface between man and nature and as such acts as a stimulus to both. Thus, the architect is not a designer of buildings, but a planner and co-ordinator in the effort to achieve a harmonious and mutually beneficial fit between all levels of the environment.

Renato Severino, in "Future Housing Systems in Architecture," contends that the democratic society necessitates the industrialization of the production of all goods, and in this he believes that we should incorporate the housing industry. Recognizing the need for lower-cost structures with more flexibility for future change, he believes that present so-called "industrial" building processes are unsuccessful because they have used traditional materials and have been financed, built, and sold with traditional methods. As such, the characteristics of low-cost housing are retained: "cheap material, low standard of finish, poor design, questionable public acceptance, poor support by private financing institutions, and above all, an unsound economic justification."

The answer to this problem, according to Dr. Severino, is to totally industrialize the industry, creating a "consumer market" for housing; that is, to re-direct architecture to a total "product" orientation. In such a system, he says, you might order a house from a catalog or department store, including certain options, in the same way we order automobiles from Detroit. He advocates total modularity in such a system as the best way to achieve flexibility. In addition to achieving uniform construction times and controlled costs, this "new" system provides other features as well. In his words:
  "The major feature of a new housing system will be the possibility of covering
   a wide spectrum of the market with a limited number of modules and components,

offering options at several levels to the public for approximately the same amount of money as follows:

1) Choice of size of each room.
2) Choice of type, number and location of bathrooms and utility rooms.
3) Choice of internal layout.
4) Choice of general shape of the house, either two or three modules wide, with one or two exposures.
5) Possibility of growth of the house, by the adding of new modules at a future date.
6) Possibility of buying as part of the house all the furniture and fittings or buying only some, or none."

Dr. Severino obviously feels great concern for the failures of architecture today, but in my opinion is naive to the extent that his system creates more problems than it solves. The reliance on First Industrial Revolution mass-production techniques to solve flexibility and low-cost problems will in effect reduce the individuality of the user and decrease the variety available for his choice; thus he limits the participation of the user and at the same time eliminates all possibility of unique design solution in response to the site, much less to the environment. Thus, in his effort to increase flexibility through modularity and industrialization, he not only enforces social mediocrity but also destroys the two prime motivations for flexibility -- the individual and the environment.

Jos Weber, writing about "Interaction Between Technology of the Built Environment and the Socio-Political Scope, states that optimum technological solutions for most complex problems can be found, but are not used. When and where advanced technological means are employed, only few in the society profit from it.

World progress is essentially not supported by technological evolution, but by strong social and political ideas.

Mr. Weber poses the question whether technological evolution can benefit mankind at all if socio-political evolution has not developed simultaneously and refers to a user-participation model and the realization of a housing project in Hamburg. Here he illustrates the concern that all users of the built environment participate at first in their strictly personal surroundings and, as a result of this experience, later in the whole environment. Mr. Weber concludes:

"Science enables man to comprehend logic in nature in an objective way and to apply the results, but it is man's social and political morality that gives relative value to this knowledge. Therefore science and morality must develop simultaneously if we really want to make progress available to all mankind."

Summary:

I have attempted to briefly and objectively summarize the contributions of all participants, and have provided my own comments and criticisms in light of certain postulates which seem essential. It seems that the progress of architecture should somehow be linked with the progress of life, and in this we can define progress as the ever-increasing ordered complexity of organization and variety available, and the concurrent development of the ability to cope with increasing variety.

In order to accomplish this, technology needs regulative functions derived from the socio-political context; that is, scientific advancement must be more closely linked with the goals of human and environmental life. Unchecked technologies degenerate into technocracies, preventing further social and organic evolution. All technologies must be examined closely for their potential to enhance life-system developments.

In conclusion, attention should be called to an apparent paradox, and a warning for the future must be made. Man, in order to achieve self-realization, has had to structure his environment in a purposeful manner and thus has assumed an increasingly dominant role over the environment. And yet such an anthropocentric attitude is quickly leading to the deterioration of the natural environment, which in turn detriments man's capacity for self-realization and self-fulfillment. The paradox can only be resolved when we come to realize that man and the environment are integrally linked together--that a change in one automatically causes a change in the other which causes a change in the other ad infinitum. Thus, the anthropocentric attitudes of today may benefit man tomorrow, but may cause his destruction next year. We must learn to treat the environment as an equal partner with equally important problems and needs, in order to promote the meaningful existence of man in the future.

References

(1) Sechenov, I. M., ELEMENTS OF THOUGHT, Moscow, pages 414-415, 1947.

(2) Walter, W. G., OBSERVATIONS ON MAN, HIS FRAME, HIS DUTY AND HIS EXPECTATIONS, Cambridge (G. B.), Cambridge University Press, pages 37-38, 1969.

(3) Hilbertz, W. H., "Strategies for Evolutionary Environments," in Allen, C., RESPONSIVE HOUSEBUILDING TECHNOLOGIES, M.I.T., 1972.

(4) Lucas, R. E., "Evolution of Future Environments," in Allen, C., RESPONSIVE HOUSEBUILDING TECHNOLOGIES, M.I.T., 1972.

(5) Maldonado, T., UMWELT UND REVOLTE, Hamburg, Rowohlt, pages 15-16, 1972.

(6) Oster, G. W., and Yang Nan-Loh, "Photopolymerization of Vinyl Monomers," CHEMICAL REVIEWS, Vol. 68, No. 2, 1968.

(7) Bloch, E., UBER KARL MARX, Frankfurt/M. Suhrkamp, page 172, 1971.

FOURTEEN   THE SERVICE INSTITUTION– CLINIC CONCEPT OF THE SCHOOL OF ARCHITECTURE   14.0

Chairman: Professor John W. Wade, Dean, School of Architecture, University of
       Wisconsin-Milwaukee, Milwaukee, Wisconsin, 53201

Participants:

Charles Burchard, Architecture, Virginia Polytechnic Inst., Blacksburg, VA
David Crane, Architecture, Rice University, Houston, TX
Ibrahim Jamal, Building Systems, State Univ. of N.Y.-Buffalo, Buffalo, NY
Sandy Greenfield, Boston Arch. Center, Boston, MA
Ralph Iredale, Architecture and Planning, Univ. of Cal., Los Angeles, CA
Charles Burnette, Center for Design Planning and Construction, Philadelphia, PA
Frederick Moyer, National Clearing House for Criminal Justice, Univ. of Ill,
     Champaign, IL

Abstract

There have now been several proposals from widely different sources for comprehensive service institutions that would provide support for the design practitioner. Many different schools of architecture and several A.I.A. chapter offices provide different forms and degrees of service. Many of these institutions have advocacy operations, research centers and "clinical" modes of instruction. Most of them have the capability of developing into a full services
institution. There would then be a major advantage in linking such a group together as regional service centers to serve the design professions.

In an article that appeared in the Architectural Education Section of the January
1972 issue of the A.I.A. JOURNAL, I described a service institution for the design
professions. I had in mind a parallel with the institutionalized services that
are provided for the medical profession by a major teaching hospital and I included in my description of the service institution such elements as: a consulting
staff, an information center, research groups, equipment and facilities, a service
staff, and an intern program. I described the need for such an institution by
noticing the differences that presently exist between the demands of complex professional practice, the capability for such practice that exists in the medium-
sized or small office, and the information and competence that could be made available through our educational institutions.

In both the A.I.A. JOURNAL article and in a slightly shortened version that appeared in the February 1972 issue of the JOURNAL OF ENGINEERING EDUCATION, I review
the range of problems in professional practice that such an institution could
help to reduce: the inappropriate subdivision of the design fields, non-pertinent

education processes, inadequate licensing procedures, failures in design feedback and communication and inefficiencies in design processes.

This article was, of course, not a unique expression of the ideas contained in it. A.I.A., for example, had already begun to organize the offerings of several automated services to its members. In 1969 there had been a proposal for a national-scope United Engineering Information Service, which is still under study. More recently, in the June 7, 1972 issue of the ARCHITECT'S JOURNAL, Phillip Groves proposed that the R.I.B.A. form a practice association with its members in order to provide those members with a broad range of supporting services. Similar arguments for need have appeared in these several proposals.

The Philadelphia chapter of the A.I.A. has organized a Center for Planning, Design and Construction. Chuck Burnette, the executive director for the center, reports a broad support base from an interdisciplinary group of eight professional and industry associations and a broad group of services including: product display and product and reference information services, computer access and automated services, conference and presentation facilities, and a continuing education program. Through the efforts of Stuart Rose of A.I.A. Headquarters Staff, several other state chapter offices have begun a modest offering of automated services.

In addition to these efforts, there are a number of institutions associated with our schools that are already in operation or that are being planned that incorporate one or more of the ideas that appeared in that original article. Ibrahim Jamal has reported that the School of Architecture at the State University of New York at Buffalo has in addition to the Buffalo Organization for Social and Technological Innovation, two other contract research institutions that offer practical experience for graduate students and services to the public and the design professions. Ralph Iredale is president of an incorporated design practice, called the Urban Innovations Group, associated with the School of Architecture and Urban planning at UCLA that offers services to both practitioners and the public. Dave Crane has organized a similar institution at Rice. Henry Sanoff at N.C. State heads a Community Development Group.

In addition to these institutionalized efforts, there are schools that have operations along the lines of the more conventional research or study centers. These are usually centered around specific topical areas. Robert Dyck at V.P.I. heads a center for Urban and Regional Studies and a center for the Study of New Communities. Fred Moyer at the University of Illinois is director of a National Clearinghouse for Criminal Justice Planning and Architecture. At the University of Hawaii, the research center is combined with a Community Design Center and undertakes tropical research.

There are, of course, so many schools that have Community Design Centers that it would be difficult to mention any one center without having to mention all of the more than seventy that exist. The University of Kentucky reports what appears to be a regional version of the C.D.C. idea in its Appalachian Mountain Program and its Mountain Institute.

Finally, there are several schools that run in-studio operations that are real-client and real-service oriented. Don Grant reports from Cal Poly that their Fifth-Year Systematic Design Methods Option spends the entire academic year in such a service. Don Brown reports from the Boston Architectural Center that their Metro Boston Studio is organized as a directed resource of the city government's Boston Redevelopment Authority.

Our own program at the University of Wisconsin-Milwaukee has begun development along several of the lines. Robert Beckley manages two Community Design Centers and offers an advocacy option within our program. David Hoeh manages a funded program that provides a broad range of planning and design service for the city of Columbus, Indiana and for community organizations in that city. David Sawicki is in charge of a service contract with the state planning agency. We have a proposal presently under consideration by HUD for the pilot study of a services operation to both the public and practitioners and we are beginning a continuing education program. We will hope to collaborate closely with the Wisconsin A.I.A. chapter in both of these areas. Dan Carson is in charge of research development for the School and Amos Rapoport is organizing a man-environment studies program. We have the policy of encouraging in-house service by our instructional studios and we have provided service to a broad range of community organization clients.

The listing of schools and organizations above has obviously not been able to do justice to everyone and I must apologize at this point to those whose efforts have been unintentionally slighted.

Having reviewed, however briefly, the range of service and the variety of organizations which can be thought of as "clinical" operations, it might be well at this point to question accomplishments and to consider possible directions for the future. Several questions have been raised concerning the Community Design Centers and advocacy activities. It is difficult to respond to the comments of Richard Hatch from several years back or of Robert Goodman from quite recently who ask what on-the-ground accomplishments advocate architects and planners can point to. Robert Beckley, commenting on the work in Milwaukee, makes the only reasonable response that I have heard; "We have only been effective when we have helped the community provide itself with a power base." All of us who have worked with Community Design Centers know the difficulty in coordinating volunteer work and scheduling an accord between instructional time demands and real job time demands. What have been the actual accomplishments of the C.D.C. movement? I believe that we should try to find out.

In considering possible directions for the future, I believe that we must examine carefully what needs exist within the design professions. I would like to do so, briefly, before returning to argue for the kind of comprehensive institution described at the beginning of this paper.

Needs within the design professions exist at two levels. Where the design professions are already serving a market they have need for the range of practice aids and services that I have described earlier: information, automated services, contract research, basic research, etc. Where the professions are not serving a market adequately, they need ways in which they can begin to do so.

Among the markets that have not been well served are the housing market, the vernacular building market, the urban design market, the poor client and the "other culture" client. Each of these market areas have not been well served for different reasons. What are these reasons? How can they be served? What are the experiences that the different schools and institutions have had in such service? How can we learn from each other?

It would appear to be possible for each institution that I have described to grow into a full service institution. Such an institution could become an important support for the design profession in its region. It could help to develop, in a coordinated way, services to both those markets which are served and which are not presently served. Each institution, in order to be effective, will need to establish a close relationship with the organized practitioners in its region in order to resolve problems of conflict and possible competition. The practitioners must be a resource to the school and its institution, as the institution is a resource to the practitioner.

It would also appear to be possible to link a number of these comprehensive institutions into a network of regional centers. By doing so any one institution could have its deficiencies supplied by resources in other institutions. The several institutions by being in communication could avoid unnecessary duplication of effort. Together they could develop a common data bank.

It seems likely that such a cooperative linking of resources and information could secure funding support from the profession and from major funding agencies where a single institution struggling alone for such support might fail. It is possible that this EDRA IV Workshop on Clinical Operations can be the initial meeting that will begin to form such a network.

FIFTEEN   OPEN BEHAVIORAL PLANNING

15.0

Chairman: Sam A. Sloan, President, People Space Architecture Company, West 907
         Bridge Avenue, Spokane, Washington 99201

Participants:

Dennis Green, Office of Construction Management, General Services Administration,
         Washington, D. C.
Walter Kleeman, Jr., Consultant, Union Graduate School, Yellow Springs, Ohio

Abstract

This workshop will discuss the behavioral design and space development of a 300-
400 person office for the new Northwest Region of the Federal Aviation Administration in Seattle, Washington; an interdisciplinary team from the fields of architecture, behavioral design, environmental design, social psychology and interior
design research has directed the research-design process for People Space Architecture Company under contract to the General Services Administration. The project
tests the hypothesis that working office people can participate in the design of
their own working environments with confidence and direction; their individual
physical, social and territorial requirements, determined by adroit questioning
and observation, can be translated into design issues/requirements with the aid of
a computer and can then be woven into the total design process.

Introduction

In order to develop a design solution to the contemporary needs of the office worker, the wants of each individual working in a given office environment must be
thoroughly investigated and satisfied as thoroughly as possible within the normal
limits of budgetary and space constraints - the usual communications survey is
not enough.

So that these needs could be accurately assessed, the design team determined that
investigation of 74 Design Issues/Requirements recognized through a cursory examination by the team would provide the necessary data, not only for the meaningful
development and arrangement of working spaces, but also for each individual's selection of artifacts/tools as an integral part of his/her participation in the design of his/her own work station

Before proceeding to the specific investigation of the 74 Design Issues/Require-
ments it was necessary to establish a baseline evaluation of the FAA'S previous
facilities to pre-identify workers' environmental concerns and also to provide the
design team a basis for comparison of workers' reactions to the implementation of
the design of the new offices. After implementation this same analysis of environmental quality will be made of the new facilities to ascertain the effects of carefully devised individual research and user-participation in design upon the actual
quality of the built environment. The initial questionnaire and its results follow:

SYNTHESIS SHEET:

 MAJORITY RESPONSE
SECONDARY RESPONSE

This is your opportunity to help us do a better job of planning facilities.
Please give us your best opinion of the following list of items in this room
by making an appropriate check (✓) on the rating lines. And if you rate something on the poor side, try to tell us what you think the problem is.

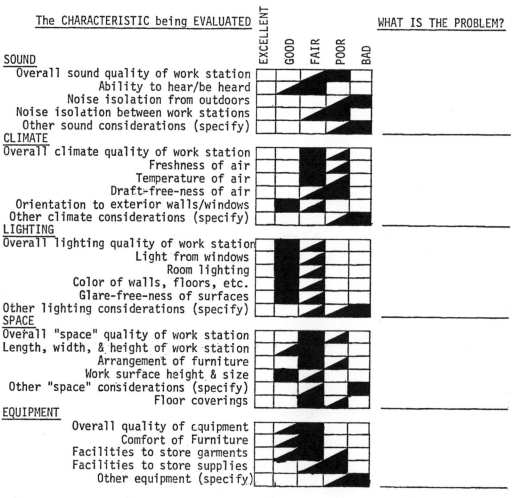

COMMENTS: Perhaps we have missed something in the above list that you'd like to
comment on. Please do so below or on the back of this questionnaire.
We want to know in what ways this building "turns you on" - or off!

From the results of this questionnaire, completed by 185 people it is possible to make certain gross assessments of the existing FAA offices:

THE PRESENT FACILITIES
....have poor to bad acoustical quality
....have fair to poor air temperature and comfort quality
....have good to fair lighting quality and content
....have fair space and furnishings orientation and availability
....have fair to poor equipment and furnishings

After the completion and tabulation of this questionnaire, an interview procedure was instituted including a further questionnaire much more detailed and individualized than the one evaluating the existing facilties. Space does not permit the reproduction of the 7-page questionnaire and interview sheet used, but one salient effort in this process was to provide enough information on each individual so that ACUTE needs could be identified and then checked through cross analysis on a computer. These ACUTE needs are flags which warn the designer to reference the other issues within the category where an acute requirement is indicated. Thus, when Mary Jones reveals an acute need for privacy, the designer can check her answers to questions concerning various types of privacy needs - audio, visual, security or smoking. In this way the answers from the questionnaire and interview become design tools to enable the designer to satisfy individual human needs.

In addition to the privacy criteria above, the 74 Design Issues/Requirements analyzed included:

Personal - proxemic needs on a high-social to anti-social scale; color preferences, bright, medium or none; territorial needs; motility characteristics; hierarchial orientation; agressive-non-agressive traits; need for living plants; extent of disablement, if any; acuteness of sight and hearing; sensitivity to temperature change noise, and visual distraction; adequacy of artifacts/tools such as desks, files, chairs, tables, wall mounted items, machines and storage cabinets.

Maintenance - volume of waste and dirt; extent of interior and exterior traffic

Reuse preference for specific artifacts/tools

Requirements for group work space and group social space

Comfort ratings for seating and work surfaces

Simultaneously with the above part of the study, the widest possible range of artifacts/tools has been developed within space and budget limitations. In this selection process heavy emphasis has been placed on the ergonomic characteris   of the artifacts/tools offered so that as the workers change, the artifacts/tools can be adjusted to successive users and provide for their comfort as well.

An unused section of a hangar near the new facilities is providing a space where each individual designs his/her own work station, with a member of the design team.

Each piece of furniture offered for selection is available so that, when necessary a work station can be arranged in its actual pattern for verification of its workability. The floor is carpeted and a ceiling comparable to the new building is installed in the hangar to simulate the final built space. Typical furniture combinations are developed for executive, supervisory, secretarial and technician tasks at each work station.

If successful, each work station will reflect the personality requirements of the of the individual occupying the station.

Simultaneously, group space is being developed with a proper compromise between individual and group requirements.

The major design issues of group orientation are territory and traffic. They must be assimilated carefully. Personable people must fence for their less sociable workmates and persons requiring privacy should be placed so that they will not be easily invaded.

In the design of group space, and in the design of individual work stations, we are attempting to actualize the basic needs of each worker.

Chairman: Robin C. Moore, Dept. of Landscape Arch., Coll. of Environ. Design,
            Univ. of Calif., Berkeley, California 94720

Participants:

Rob Beasley, Jeff Hayward, Leanne Rivlin, Marilyn Rothenberg, Maxine Wolf,
    Environmental Psychology Program, City University of New York, New York
Sidney Brower, City Planning, Baltimore, Maryland
Nanine Clay, Photographer/Writer, Louisville, Kentucky
Stephen Cohen, Department of Psychiatry, University of Vermont, Burlington, Vermont
Roger Hart, School of Geography, Clark University, Worcester, Massachusetts
Randolph Hester, School of Design, North Carolina State Univ., Raleigh, N. Carolina
Polly Hill, Polly Hill Associates, Ottawa, Canada
Florence Ladd, Department of City Planning, Harvard University, Cambridge, Mass.
Alan Leitman, Community Education, Cambridge, Massachusetts
Robin C. Moore, Department of Landscape Architecture, Univ. of Calif., Berkeley,
    California
Jose Muntanola, Department of Architecture, Univ. of Calif., Berkeley, California
Cornelia Oberlander, Landscape Architect, Ottawa, Canada
Anne-Marie Pollowy, Faculte de l'Amenagement, Montreal, Canada
Lee Shaw, Dan Williams, College of Architecture & Fine Arts, University of Florida,
    Gainesville, Florida
Susan and Michael Southworth, Designers/Planners, Boston, Massachusetts
Chuck Zerner, Department of Architecture, Oregon State, Eugene, Oregon

Abstract

The workshop will be a market place of information and ideas for those seeking to
create through research, design and action, a viable city-wide habitat for children
(and all other living things). It will focus on the public and semi-public space of
the city as an actual and potential play and learning place. Based on what we
already know, we will discuss where research resources should be invested; research
methods; the influence of human and physical factors; design methods; politics of
the child-environment; environmental education; and ways of making designers,
managers, legislators and officials more aware of child-hood needs. An evening
movie/slide program and other events will form an integral part of the workshop.

Orientations, Assumptions, and Definitions

Some children, and mothers, have been inadequately considered as users of the public
outdoors because cities are designed and managed by male adults. Children spend
much of their everyday life in inappropriate surroundings. Often traffic dangers
cut them off from the diversity of the city. Our cities must be opened and made
accessible to children under their own volition, for them to use and learn from

informally. Environmental education is an institutional means of involving kids and
adults together in a joint process of using the real-live environment as a learning
vehicle. Through this process meaning and understanding can be greatly extended
with the adults acting as interpreters, information providers, "door-openers", etc.,
for the kids.

Our specialized and fragmented society has a tendency to treat children as objects,
play as something that only happens in "playgrounds", and learning as something that
happens only in schools. The play and learning process that children engage in
every waking moment is a continuous process in space and time involving all aspects
of the social and physical environment. A play and learning place can be any part
of the environment where children are, e.g., a street corner, transit stop, playground, dime store, etc. The total play and learning space of a city is the sum of
all the places actually used and the pathway networks connecting them. Many play
and learning places often cannot be freely used, e.g., waterfronts, rooftops, industrial land, private open space of all kinds and many public places which are simply
cut-off by traffic dangers.

The amount and distribution of play and learning space varies greatly between cities
and different sectors of the same city. The intensity and type of use is also
variable depending on the physical and social qualities of the place and on the
cultural, economic, personality, sex, age, etc., characteristics of the users. Each
of these factors is important in the delineation of user-groups and they are all
important issues for exploration. Clearly kids are looking for a broad and
fluctuating spectrum of environments to satisfy their needs. Therefore, the child-
environment should be conceived as a diverse and subtly variegated territory in
space and time, allowing kids to interact and learn from each other and adults,
while also allowing for privacy, security and individual action, etc.

A Hierarchy of Systems and Four Levels of Professional Interest

1.   The Macro-Outdoor encompasses all the play and learning environments in a city,
that fall within the area of planning and urban design. Policy making here,
relates to the disposition of space and money and includes, for example, open-
space development, waterfront conservation, bike and pedestrian networks, distribution of playgrounds and schools, standards for housing site layout, etc. Research
needs at this scale are great because we know little about how cities function as a
habitat for the young. We need to know where kids spend their time, how they get
there, what they feel about their favorite places, what their problems are, what
they would like to see changed, etc. We have little idea where public money should
be invested to benefit the young most. Because it is difficult for many people to
understand child issues at the scale of the city, research will be inhibited until
the question has a greater political airing.

2.   The Intermediate-Outdoor covers a variety of multi-use areas, such as parks and
public open spaces, communal space in housing developments, shopping centers, downtown areas, etc. Although community participation is occasionally part of the
planning and design process, it is not common to find the needs of children discussed, even though -- particularly in residential areas -- it is the child who may
be most affected. Feed-back is especially relevant here but generally not available.

Perhaps it should be a requirement of any contract involving public money that feed-back statements, focussed on human response, be prepared when construction is complete. Some tested methods are available for this kind of work.

3. The Micro-Outdoor (and indoor in cold climates) includes specific places where often, by design, children are the predominant users. This includes playgrounds and the myriad of undesignated "kid-places" scattered throughout the city, e.g., street corners, alleys, vacant lots, parking lots, entrance lobbys, transit stops, etc. In these situations interaction between children and their "here-and-now-environment" can be closely observed. Several methods have been tried and more work has been done at this level than any other. Information for designers is available, but scattered! Specific activities such as climbing, sliding, social interaction, water play, etc., have design requirements which can be graphically expressed. They could then be provided for in many different contexts, such as shopping centers, urban plazas, mass transit stations, etc.

4. The Micro-Indoor/Outdoor includes the child's home and immediate surroundings. The indoor/outdoor interface, shop fronts, private yards, driveways, etc., should be highlighted for special attention. This interface is "abrupt" functionally, administratively, and professionally. School yards are the classic example of the indoor/outdoor dichotomy. There is an obvious need for new kinds of indoor/outdoor, transitional, robust, roofed-over-and-heated spaces -- especially in cold climates.

Consciousness and Action

Can the quality of the child's urban life-space be improved? A key question is how to train and educate those who are directly involved in managing the child-environment. Many seem out of touch with their own childhood. How can their consciousness be raised? Value systems need to be examined and new kinds of training developed for environmental teachers, environmental managers, and play leaders who can be unobtrusive. New design and management models which can integrate research and action to make the environment far more responsive to the changing needs of children in particular, need to be explored. The workshop will be whatever you make it!

SEVENTEEN   PLANNING ENVIRONMENTS
FOR THE AGED

Chairman: Thomas O. Byerts, Gerontological Society, One Dupont Circle, N.W.,
           Washington, D. C. 20036

Participants:

Sandra C. Howell, Florence Heller Grad. School, Brandeis Univ., Waltham, Mass.
M. Powell Lawton, Philadelphia Geriatric Center, Philadelphia, Pa.
Steven Demos, Boston Housing Authority, Boston, Mass.

Abstract

This presentation will expand on the Design Evaluation Workshop Technique,
conducted twice recently by the members of this panel. These programs featured
indepth exploration of the design decision making process through the review
of architectural drawings and models of elderly housing. Presentations delivered
by architect/developers were reacted to by social science consultants and
participants from all aspects of the private and public sectors.

This evaluation process is an important vehicle for both direct consultation to
designers and developers and also as a tool for researchers and policy makers
to obtain feedback from "real" operational situations.

This process and principles of good design for the elderly will be discussed.

Introduction

Two multidisciplinary Design Evaluation Workshops on elderly housing programs
have recently been conducted to:
1. expand the interchange between behavioral science consultants
   and design/development teams leading to application of research findings,
2. improve the specific building programs being designed for the elderly,
3. identify the problems and barriers to the production of satisfactory
   environments,
4. generate recommendations regarding housing policy, research design and
   planning,
5. explore the potential for organizing a series of ongoing programs using
   this kind of model.

The first workshop held in June, 1972, conducted by Dr. Sandra Howell, was
sponsored by Brandeis University and NIMH Community Services Division. This
2 day program included 37 participants representing all elements of the housing

spectrum -- builder/developers, designers, researchers, government agencies, social service specialists, advocates and tenants. It featured the detailed presentation of drawings and models of housing for the elderly by several architect/developer teams and reaction by 3 selected consultants (sociologist, psychologist and architect) and participants from the public and private sectors.

The second program was a half-day session held during the December 1972 Gerontological Society sponsored conference Designing Environments for the Elderly in San Juan. Two simultaneous workshops were conducted with 30 conference participants each. A panel of three consultant experts led each session discussion and analysis of the design work that was presented. This program as well as the Brandeis session was tape recorded for further analysis.

Why Elderly Housing

In both programs, discussions were limited to elderly housing building types. While housing for older adults contains specific content areas (research and practice) generic to aging, there is, however, a large body of issues that are generalizable to the entire housing and building scene. Design for this age group rarely excludes use by other ages while the converse is not true.

Housing for older adults ranges in degrees of independence depending on health, financial and physical capacities. It can generally be considered a "semi-closed" system for research. Much of the leading man/environment research has been performed in "pure" institutional settings. The findings of this work are often difficult to relate to open settings.

The tendency for elderly to be more dependent on their proximate environment than other age groups makes the elderly both ideal subjects for study as well as a population group sensitive to and in great need of innovative alternatives. Works edited by Byerts (1), Kaplan (2), Lawton (3) and Pastalan (4) address the main issues of research and practice in this field.

The aged represent a significant and growing population. Daily, 4,000 new "old" people reach 65 years of age - and 3,000 over 65 die. In 1969, according to the 1971 White House Conference on Aging Workbook on Housing (5):

> there were about 19-1/2 million persons aged 65 and over living outside institutions in the United States. Of these, 61 percent were living in metropolitan areas, most of them within the central city itself where the poorest urban housing is concentrated. Among the 39 percent living outside the metropolitan areas, just over 5 percent live on farms. The other 34 percent (6-1/2 million) live in rural but nonfarm localities. And although less visible, there is a higher proportion of poor housing in the rural than in the urban areas.
> Changes Which Affect Housing Needs - The changes associated with age encompass health status and energy, mobility, opportunity for companionship, and the financial ability to occupy or maintain adequate housing.
> So deep is the need to preserve their old life patterns, in spite of these

changes that many older people struggle, often too long, to maintain their old living arrangements. Is this the perversity of human nature or does it reflect the failure of society to provide the spectrum of housing opportunities that would make it possible for older people to better satisfy their needs at any given time?

Sample Workshop Interaction

The technique of design presentation becomes a strong catalyst with the use of 2 or 3 dimensional artifacts exhibited for discussion. The following dialogue was transcribed from the Brandeis Workshop conducted by Howell (6). It is illustrative of the interchange that is generated:

Architect: This site is surrounded by non-residential structures, the streets are heavy volume carriers, the redevelopment authority had setback requirements; 60 feet here and 40 feet there -- we began to think of an inward focused development -- a mini-neighborhood because there was very little to relate to.

Social Scientist: While you are mentioning this inward turning would you be able to say what kind of features determine the inward orientation of your project? Are there structural features consistent with or help to determine inward focus?

Architect: First of all we made a value judgment to say that we wanted to shape the buildings on the site to make the spaces focus inward. Other things we do then tend to reinforce that decision -- materials to use, alternative configurations of buildings. I could have made buildings go the whole way around the outside with big spaces in the middle. I could have made a whole series of little cul-de-sacs. What we did decide was 1) to develop a very regularized building system because we are pressed for cost -- a tough cost per square foot to meet -- an FHA certified cost at that time for this program, 2) because of the triangular shape of the site, instead of running the building this way (points to area on site map) it began to spatially do something different from the usual gridiron, 3) we began to think in terms of what kinds of spaces we wanted to create.

Social Scientist: Am I correct in assuming that in some instances you put the front entrances facing the interior social spaces and in other cases you put back patios -- was this a conscious effort?

Architect: Some, but we didn't think it through or have any hard data. It happened as much by accident as anything else. Security reasons were an after-thought.

Social Scientist: The front entrance isn't necessarily the most frequently used space -- it's a place people are only a couple times a day -- while the patio...

Implications

The content analysis of the issues and details discussed at these workshops can lead to the isolation of a series of points that need investigation, refinement and recommendation. Such new information can be fed back into housing policy development, operational guidelines, educational and continuing educational networks. If each building were considered a hypothesis designed to 1) meet short and long term needs of the users and 2) be a vehicle for the evaluation of better environments, more rapid and substantive progress can be achieved to benefit design of housing for the elderly and the population in general.

References

(1) Byerts, T. (ed), "Preliminary Publication", of HOUSING AND ENVIRONMENT FOR THE ELDERLY, Gerontological Society, 1972.

(2) Kaplan, J. (ed), "The Home for Aged/Nursing Home: Past, Present and Future", THE GERONTOLOGIST, 10, No. 4, pages 261-305, 1970.

(3) Lawton, M. P. (ed), "Housing", THE GERONTOLOGIST, 12, No. 2, Part II (Monograph on International Research and Education in Social Gerontology), pages 3-16, 1972.

(4) Pastalan, L. and Carson, D. H. (eds), SPATIAL BEHAVIOR OF OLDER PEOPLE, Institute of Gerontology, University of Michigan, 1970.

(5) _____, WORK BOOK ON HOUSING, White House Conference on Aging, Washington, D. C., 1971.

(6) Howell, S., DESIGN EVALUATION WORKSHOP: HOUSING FOR THE ELDERLY, Brandeis University, 1972.

Chairman: Michael Kennedy, School of Architecture, University of Kentucky, Lexington

Participants:

Kurt Brandle, Dr.-Ing., Architect, Dept. of Architecture, Univ. of Utah, Salt Lake City
Jeffrey M. Hamer, School of Architecture and Urban Planning, Univ. of California, Los A.
William J. Kovacs, Systems Analyst, Skidmore, Owings and Merrill, New York
Donald R. Fullenwider, Assistant Professor, School of Architecture, Univ. of Maryland
Charles E. Reeder, Director, Research and Development, Morganelli-Heumann & Associates
Edward F. Smith, M.S., Architect, Dept. of Architecture, Univ. of Utah, Salt Lake City
D. Kernohan, G.D. Rankin, G.D. Wallace and R.J. Walters, ABACUS Studies, University
   of Strathclyde, Glasgow

Introduction

This workshop points out, so have several in the past, that there is no general
underlying computer use or automated information handling for environmental designers.
And in the accelerating world in which we live, a lot of time has gone by since
the first ideas which occurred to anyone in this area have been implemented.

We have worked for several years on various ad hoc applications and, in my view, are
not really much closer to any truly overall ability to do or even effectively aid
the design process. I am aware that this is a pessimistic view and I cannot support
it very well but if one examines the papers in this session, and the papers in sessions
of previous, he will find, time after time, small areas of application carved out of
that amorphous entity we call design. And design itself generally excludes questions
such as "What should we be building", and "How should we construct what we have
designed".

Now for the good news. The current papers, though primarily worthwhile variations
on past themes, may indicate a turn towards realism in three important ways.

First, there is an understanding that what is being dealt with by the computer is
information--not aesthetics, not structure, not philosophy--but information.

Next, there seems to be a more definite attempt to get people plugged into the
process in developing solutions to design problems and in evolving, iteratively,
programs to do so. (The sign over the man says "THINK"; over the computer it says
"COMPUTE".)

And lastly, it may be that now some of the messier, not so much fun, but more practical problems are being attacked. The results of this might be programs and sets
of programs which are actually used more than just once to provide the basis for
giving a paper at a conference.

SIMULATING THE EVOLUTION OF URBAN SPATIAL ORGANIZATION

Jeffrey M. Hamer
School of Architecture and Urban Planning
University of California, Los Angeles

Abstract

This work investigates the evolution of urban spatial organization via the exploration of the behavior of very simple form-generation systems. These systems are investigated in order to gain some general understanding of characteristic behavior of forms which grow and transform themselves as a consequence of the operation of deviation-amplifying mutual causal processes. The conceptual framework is akin to that of cellular automata. The method is to simulate the growth of patterns on the computer and identify growth-controlling rules by application of which certain patterns result.

How does a simple settlement evolve into a complex, extensive and subtly structured urban fabric? One approach to beginning to understand this processes is to utilize the concept of deviation-amplifying feedback systems. Maruyama has summarised its relevance as follows:

> Ecological patterns can also be generated by mutual interaction. Let us postulate a large plain which is entirely homogeneous as to its potentiality for agriculture, and that one ambitious farmer opens a farm at a particular spot on it. This provides the initial kick for the process, after which several farmers follow his example and further farms are established around his own. One of the farmers opens a tool shop, and this tool shop becomes a meeting-place of farmers. Than a food stand is established next to the tool shop. Gradually a village grows, which facilitates the marketing of the agricultural products, and so more farms flourish around the village. Industry then develops in the village, and the village grows into a city.

> On what part of the entire plain the city starts growing depends only where the initial accidental kick occurs. The first farmer could equally well have chosen any spot on the homogeneous plain, but once he chooses, a city grows from that spot, and the plain becomes inhomogeneous. If a historian should try to find a geographical 'cause' which made this spot a city rather than some spots he will fail to find it in the initial homogeneity of the plain (at least in this idealized example). Nor can the first farmer be credited with the establishment of the city. The secret of the growth is in the deviation-amplifying mutual causal process itself. (1)

To make practical use of this concept it becomes useful to simulate the development of urban spatial patterns--that is, find some way of representing form and its transformations--and then closely study the behavior of these models. One can attempt to create a complex model whose behavior hopefully will closely approximate a real world phenomenon (the classic example of this approach being the Lowry model). The disadvantage of this sort of procedure is that the behavior of the model is likely to be so complex as to defy any broad grasp of the nature of the relationships between growth rules and the form which evolves. It is very difficult to generalize from the specific cases. (2)

An alternative approach, one which compliments the insights gained from such complex mimetic models, is to explore the behavior of very simple form-generation systems. These systems are investigated in order to gain some general understanding of characteristic behaviors of forms which grow and transform themselves as a consequence of the operation of deviation-amplifying mutual causal processes. This is the approach followed in this study.

The systems chosen for study consisted of two-dimensional arrays of cells, in which each cell may possess one of two states--passive ( ) or active (✱). A 9x9 sample configuration is shown in Figure 1. Neighboring active cells are linked by lines to produce a graphic display of neighbor relationships (Fig. 2). Cells may change state from passive to active or conversely. Whether or not a cell changes state at a given point in time is determined by the current state of its eight neighbors at that time. Thus, transformation rules for cells may be specified by tables as in Figure 3.

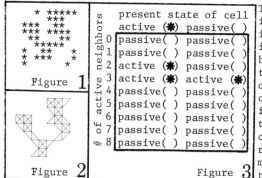

Figure 1

Figure 2

# of active neighbors	present state of cell	
	active (✱)	passive ( )
0	passive ( )	passive ( )
1	passive ( )	passive ( )
2	active (✱)	passive ( )
3	active (✱)	active (✱)
4	passive ( )	passive ( )
5	passive ( )	passive ( )
6	passive ( )	passive ( )
7	passive ( )	passive ( )
8	passive ( )	passive ( )

Figure 3

This specifies the cell's next state, given its present state and the present state of its neighbors. Given the rule system specified by Figure 3 for example, a cell will become active only if it is passive with three active neighbors or active with two or three active neighbors. In all other cases, cells become or remain passive. It is clear that there are 2^{18} possible such tables. Transformations may be made one cell at a time in some type of systematic or random sequence, or transformations may be made of all cells simultaneously. (Incidentally, if we assume that all cells will be transformed simultaneously, the table shown above specifies the rules for John Conway's well known solitaire game, LIFE). (3) Beginning with some initial pattern of active and passive cells, then, a series of forms may be generated by recursive transformation as shown in Figures 4 through 7.

An interactive FORTRAN program, producing output on a storage tube display, was written in order to explore such processes of form development. Investigations so far have focused on the conditions for achievement of stability of form. Some typical system behaviors are illustrated in Figure 8. In general, the form development processes observed have tended to strikingly confirm Simon's observation that the number of stable sub-assemblies present in a system at a given time dramatically influences the time taken to reach stability:

> The effect of the existence of stable intermediate forms exercises a powerful effect on the evolution of complex forms that may be likened to the dramatic effect of catalysts on reaction rates...complex systems will evolve from simple systems much more rapidly if there are stable intermediate forms than if there are not. The resulting complex forms in the former case will be hierarchic. (4)

It is not difficult to see that the existence of stable primitives exerts a 'holding' action on progressively larger areas of space, and so influences not only the

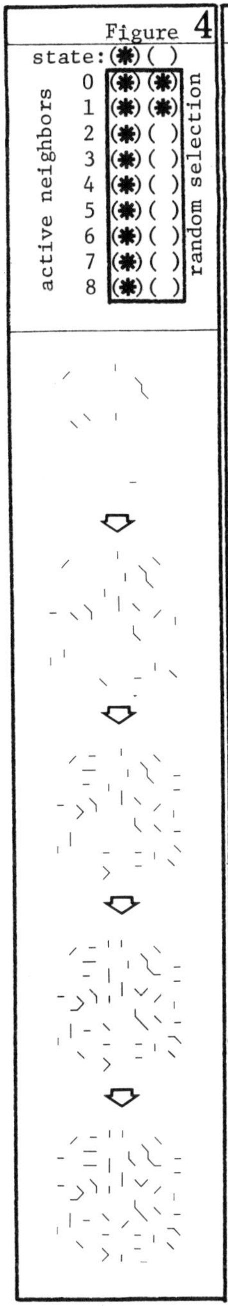

Figure 4

state: (✳) ( )

active neighbors			random selection
0	(✳)	(✳)	
1	(✳)	(✳)	
2	(✳)	( )	
3	(✳)	( )	
4	(✳)	( )	
5	(✳)	( )	
6	(✳)	( )	
7	(✳)	( )	
8	(✳)	( )	

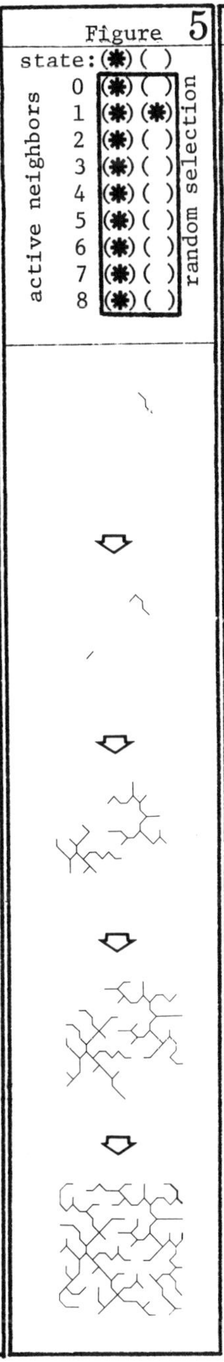

Figure 5

state: (✳) ( )

active neighbors			random selection
0	(✳)	(✳)	
1	(✳)	(✳)	
2	(✳)	( )	
3	(✳)	( )	
4	(✳)	( )	
5	(✳)	( )	
6	(✳)	( )	
7	(✳)	( )	
8	(✳)	( )	

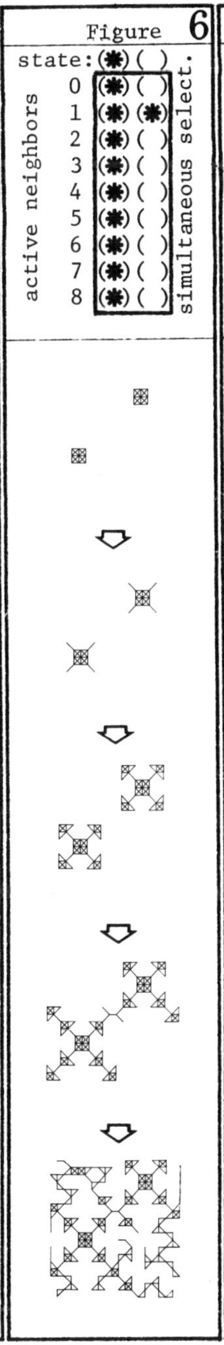

Figure 6

state: (✳) ( )

active neighbors			simultaneous select.
0	(✳)	( )	
1	(✳)	(✳)	
2	(✳)	( )	
3	(✳)	( )	
4	(✳)	( )	
5	(✳)	( )	
6	(✳)	( )	
7	(✳)	( )	
8	(✳)	( )	

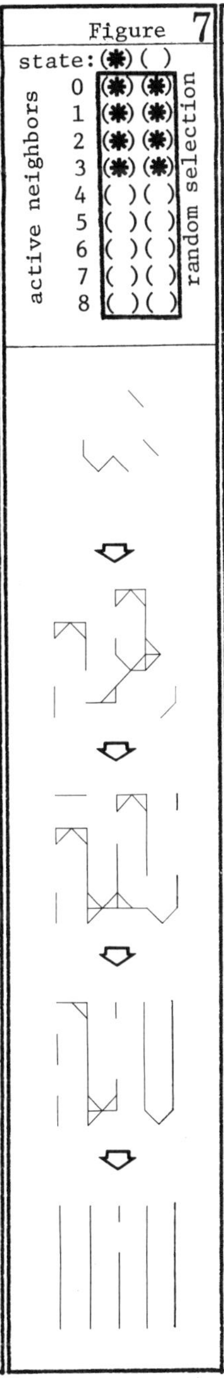

Figure 7

state: (✳) (✳)

active neighbors			random selection
0	(✳)	(✳)	
1	(✳)	(✳)	
2	(✳)	( )	
3	(✳)	( )	
4	( )	( )	
5	( )	( )	
6	( )	( )	
7	( )	( )	
8	( )	( )	

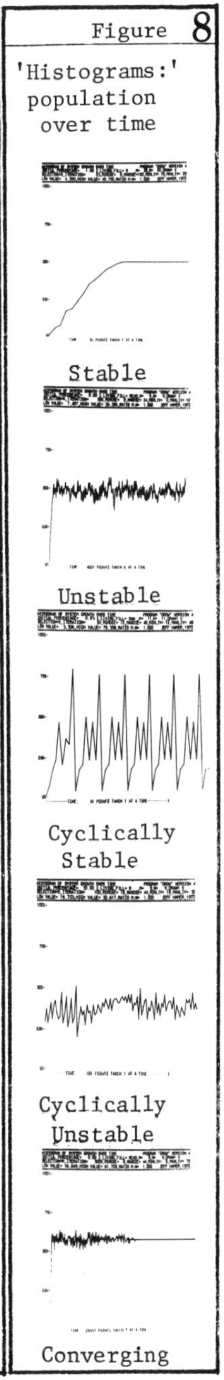

Figure 8

'Histograms:'
population
over time

Stable

Unstable

Cyclically
Stable

Cyclically
Unstable

Converging

order (or lack of it) within a system, but accelerates the rate at which a system will approach a pattern possessing overall stability.

Many other fascinating questions may be investigated. Appearance of symmetrical and cyclical patterns are also often observed, for example. What conditions are necessary for such behavior? The results of these studies may be usefully related to some exciting current work in theoretical biology and cellular automata.(5) While it is premature to make any direct application to urban design and planning, some implications are beginning to become clear. We have demonstrated that very complex, intuitively surprising and unpredictable, pattern growth and transformation processes and spatial organizations may result from the application of very simple rules. This suggests first that producing useful simulations of the development of complex urban spatial structure from simple beginnings may not be such an impossibly formidable task as it might first appear. Secondly, it suggests an attractive alternative to both the master plan and incrementalist approaches to evolving and controlling the urban spatial pattern. By basing 'urban software' (i.e. land use regulations, etc.) on sophisticated theoretical analyses of mutual causality, it may be possible to state very complex, comprehensive and adaptable development strategies in relatively simple and concise sets of rules. Just as the design for a complex organism is encoded and transmitted in a few molecules, so the design for a new town might be encoded in a few pages of symbols. (6)

References

(1) Magoroh Maruyama, "The Second Cybernetics: Deviation-Amplifying Mutual Causal Processes," in Walter Buckley (ed.), MODERN SYSTEMS RESEARCH FOR THE BEHAVIORAL SCIENTIST, Aldine Publishing Co., Chicago, 1968.

(2) Jurg Lang, "Development of an Accessibility-Growth Model," Research Report, School of Architecture and Urban Planning, UCLA, January, 1972.

(3) Martin Gardner, "The Fantastic Combinations of John Conway's New Solitaire Game, 'Life'," SCIENTIFIC AMERICAN, October, 1970.

(4) Herbert A. Simon, "The Architecture of Complexity," PROCEEDINGS OF THE AMERICAN PHILOSOPHICAL SOCIETY, Vol. 106, No. 6, December, 1962.

(5) Maxwell Braverman, Robert Schrandt, "Colony Development of a Polymorphic Hydroid as a Problem in Pattern Formulation," GENERAL SYSTEMS, Vol. XII (1967).
Arthur W. Burks (ed.), ESSAYS ON CELLULAR AUTOMATA, University of Illinois Press, 1970.
Martin, Gardner, "On Cellular Automata, Self-Reproduction, the Garden of Eden, and the Game 'Life'," SCIENTIFIC AMERICAN, February, 1971.
Richard Gordon, "On Stochastic Growth and Form" PROCEEDINGS OF THE NATIONAL ACADEMY OF SCIENCES, 56, November, 1966.
Stanislaw Ulam, "On Some Mathematical Problems Connected with Patterns of Growth Figures," PROCEEDINGS OF SYMPOSIA IN APPLIED MATHEMATICS, American Mathematical Society, 1962.
Peter Cowan, "The Growth of Systems," ARCHITECTURAL DESIGN, Vol. LXI, February 1971.

(6) William J. Mitchell, "Simple Form Generation Procedures," Royal Institute of British Architects/British Computer Society International Conference on Computers in Architecture, University of York, September, 1972.

William J. Kovacs
Systems Analyst
Skidmore, Owings and Merrill
New York

Abstract

The purpose of the proposed system is to aid the planner of physical facilities in exploring solutions and determining feasibility for large scale projects. Emphasis is placed on the structure of the design information as opposed to the nature of specific analysis techniques used within the system. Provision is made for a phased development of project information. Planners progress through these phases in cycles of generating trial solutions, evaluating and selecting "best" solutions. The goals of the system are basically twofold: 1. To establish a flexible planning aid which can respond to the variety of information processing requirements of determining initial feasibility. 2. To provide an information structure which can also prove useful in the later, more detailed, stages of design.

Introduction

Often, in the course of subdividing and quantifying the planning process, some aspects of the overall information structures required for planning are overlooked. This is unfortunate because, to a great extent, Planners and Architects have a need for a comprehensive information system which can span the various chronological stages of the planning sequence and allow for varing levels of detail as a particular project progresses. The time honored success of the working drawing is a testimony to the need for just such a tool. The main service that it provides is one of storing a variety of information for use throughout a project. F.P.I.S. is a computerized tool designed to respond to some of these information processing and storage requirements. It is assumed that the planner already has in mind a general set of initial programmatic goals. With F.P.I.S., these goals can be translated into physical and financial configurations.

System Structure/Software

F.P.I.S. is composed of two software components unified in a single, time-shared environment. RAMIS (Rapid Access Management Information System) is used to define files and retrieve information. Fortran routines are used where more complicated or specialized processing is required.

Data storage is accomplished within the system in basically two modes. Library Files store large amounts of information about a variety of building types, land parcels and cost data. Project/Solution Files provide indexed storage locations for trial solutions generated for a specific project.

Processing within F.P.I.S. can be described in terms of three phases. Each phase represents a stage in the development of the project definition.

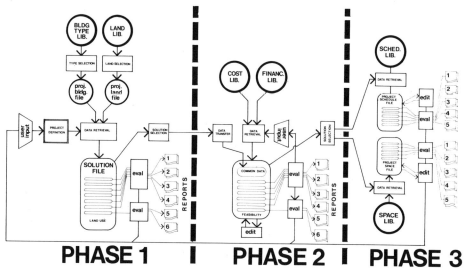

Fig. 1

1. Land Use and Building Type Definition
2. Financial and Physical Feasibility
3. Implementation--Financial Scheduling/ Space Allocation

Assumptions made in one phase are passed on to the next phase where they can be explored in greater detail and with respect to more specific criteria. Each phase includes separate mechanisms for generating solutions, exploring alternatives, and examining results produced at that level.

Phase 1. Land Use and Building Type Definition

The programming of any facility larger than a single structure and involving more than one parcel of land often begins with an explorative study of alternative land uses and building types. Phase 1 is designed to facilitate that process. At the user's disposal is a file containing data about standard building types as well as a file containing information about available or proposed parcels of land. By selecting from these library files building types and land parcels which he feels are appropriate for the particular project, he can begin to examine alternative combinations. Specifically this is done by assigning numbers of building types to a portion of a parcel or combination of parcels. Thus, in effect, a series of land planning units are defined. A set of these units defines a trial solution. As these initial, explorative problem definitions are generated they can be stored in a solution file for comparison. Thus the solution file in Phase 1 is a RAMIS file that contains a set of labeled problem definitions, each constituting a complete initial land use concept. At this point, two kinds of evaluations are possible.

The entire file can be scanned for solutions that exhibit certain characteristics of interest to the planner. For example, the planner might ask to have all solutions ranked by the amount of land required or to have displayed all solutions which contain a certain number of a particular building type.

Detailed reports can be produced from individual solutions in order to make more complete and specific judgements. Of course, the basic function of Phase 1 is to generate a single solution which is sufficiently promising to develop to higher levels of detail. When this solution is chosen, the data which constitutes it is passed to Phase 2 of H.P.I.S.. It is important to note that all other solutions generated in the process of choosing this "best" solution remain in storage and can be chosen as "best" solutions at some later time.

Phase 2. Financial and Physical Feasibility

If Phase 1 can be described as a process of generating an initial land use "image" of the project, Phase 2 becomes a detailed feasibility study of that project image. Costs that were dealt with in gross terms in Phase 1 are decomposed and examined in detail. In this phase the planner deals with physical form and its cost implications. Because many different physical schemes may satisfy the statistical requirements of Phase 1, the planner must now incorporate more information into his decision process. His approaches to problems such as site circulation, topography, building form and orientation become important. As the planner generates responses to these new constraints evaluation reports help him to weigh their impact on the total scheme. Detailed information about building costs and financing can be retrieved from library files or can be directly input by the planner. As the project is examined in more detail, spatially as well as financially, assumtions which seemed feasible at Phase 1 may prove to be untenable. Again a file of solutions is developed, each solution sharing in common assumptions made in Phase 1 but differing in detail. At this point the planner may decide that his initial assumptions made earlier were unproductive and return to choose another solution or he may select a satisfactory Phase 2 solution and continue to the next phase. His decision to do so is based on reports and evaluations such as cash flow, detailed spatial reports, and cost itemizations.

Phase 3 Implementation- Financial Scheduling/Space Allocation

Spatial implementation is explored by generating a list of required spaces based on Phase 1 and 2 assumptions. The listing of spaces can be revised and edited to produce a final spatial configuration. Each space can be assigned relational attributes with respect to other spaces. This is done by describing a kind of relation such as proximity, view or access and assigning a weight to that relation. Reports can be generated for a particular space (or all spaces) listing the strength and nature of relations to all other spaces. Thus, in addition to examining numbers and types of spaces the planner can begin to evaluate emerging relational patterns.

Financial implementation consists of a schedule of financial events describing the operation of the project. Events can be weighed with respect to the time value of money and staging schemes can be explored. In the same way that building types were decomposed into their component spaces, financial amounts can be translated into a series of amounts expended or received over time. As in Phase 2, assumptions which prove to be unresolvable may send the planner back to Phase 2 or even Phase 1 for redefinition. It is important to remember that, having followed particular assumptions to their logical conclusions, the planner is better equipped to tackle this redefinition of the project.

THE EFFECTS OF IMPLEMENTATION ON THE STRUCTURE OF A COMPUTER-AIDED-DESIGN SYSTEM

Donald R. Fullenwider
Assistant Professor
School of Architecture
University of Maryland

Charles E. Reeder
Director, Research and Development
Morganelli-Heumann and Associates
Los Angeles, California

Abstract

This paper describes an automated office interior planning system now in production at Morganelli-Heumann and Associates. This is a package of programs designed to co-ordinate and manipulate design data and produce basic conceptual schemes. It is used as a working example of two issues we wish to discuss here; the impact of the mini-computer for interactive graphic ability and the effects of iteration on the production of computer programs. This second issue, a process versus product orientation to the design of architectural tools, we consider of primary importance.

Introduction

In the past few years of computer-aided-design research, there has been a trend toward developing a systems approach. "Systems", being the outstanding buzz word of the last decade, in our case, is used to mean a process consisting of a series of computer programs manipulating a common data base, and the associated user techniques. The particular system that we are developing is oriented to assist space planners in designing large corporate interiors. This system was approached with the idea of evolving a process that would be useful daily in the design situation. We were not trying to produce a P.R. gimmick or an elaborate pro-duct which claimed everything and did little. In order to implement any new techniques, their relationship to existing design techniques must be understood by the designers who will use them, particularly when the new techniques encompass a more comprehensive model of the design process.

There appears to be major categories of problems in the implementation of a computer-augmented-design process. The first cluster of issues is, obviously enough, to develop the actual network of programs and information modifications. That is, to model the process of the designer and computer in synergistic combination. The second set of considerations

Fig. 1

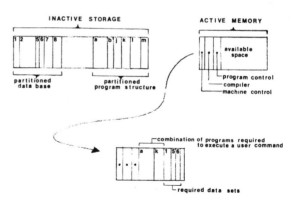

Schematic Manipulation of Program Into Mini-Computer Active Memory

is to make it possible for designers to use, react to, and modify the system; thereby, increasing the sophistication of that interaction. Many researchers have approached this task by partitioning it in just this way. They attend to the first set of problems with little regard for their relationship to the second. This produces a computer system in which the intended users see little relation to the non-computer augmented process with which they presently operate "effectively". In designing this system we considered the process orientation of our undertaking. Our task was to design a system which responded to the user's psychology and operated with the designer at the current level of his design process model. Only in this way can user feedback be established. This feedback is essential to increasing the complexity level of the user-machine interaction and generating more encompassing design process models.

```
*****************************************************************************
*****************************************************************************
*****************************************************************************
DETAILS OF SQUARE FOOTAGE FOR SECTION        13100 SHIPPING SERVICES     W V MOORE
*****************************************************************************
*****************************************************************************
*****************************************************************************

EMPLOYEE WORK SPACES:
=====================
                 A   M-MANAGER SHIP SERV       W V MOORE        4420
                 E   M-SECRETARY               B C JOHNS        4409
                 C   M-ASSISTANT (COMPUTER)    M REEDER         4412
                 C   M-ASSISTANT               TBA JUNE 73      4412
                 B   S-MANAGER SEA TRANSP      J SMITH          4416
                 E   S-SECRETARY               A V VALLERIO     4409
                 D   S-FIELD REP               TBA JUNE 73      4414
                 D   S-FLEET CAPT              C.M. CARSONI     4415
                 B   A-MANAGER AIR TRANSP      M MARTINO        4416
                 E   A-SECRETARY               M DAVISTEIN      4410
                 C   A-FIELD REP               S STEVENS        4413
                 C   A-CORP PIOBETT            P JOHNSONNE      4413
                 D   A-ASSISTANT               TBA JUNE 75      4414
              ==========================================================

              1   A   OFFICES @  270 SQ. FT. =    270
              2   B   OFFICES @  200 SQ. FT. =    400
              3   C   OFFICES @  120 SQ. FT. =    360
              1   D   OFFICES @   65 SQ. FT. =     65
              3   E   OFFICES @   45 SQ. FT. =    135
                       PRESENT TOTAL SQ. FT. =   1230 X 2.00 =    2460

              1   C   OFFICES @  120 SQ. FT. =    120
              1   D   OFFICES @   65 SQ. FT. =     65
                         FOR 73 TOTAL SQ. FT. =   185 X 2.00 =     370
                       TOTAL SQ. FT. TO DATE =   1415 X 2.00 =    2830

              1   D   OFFICES @   65 SQ. FT. =     65
                         FOR 75 TOTAL SQ. FT. =    65 X 2.00 =     130
                       TOTAL SQ. FT. TO DATE =   1480 X 2.00 =    2960


FILING REQUIREMENTS:
====================
      1 TYPE OF FILING                          SECURITY REQ.    # DRAWERS
                                                                 NOW  73  75
        ==============================          =============    ===========
           LETTER FILE DRAWERS                  STANDARD LOCK     10  12  15
           MAP 30" X 40"                        STANDARD LOCK      5   6   7
           COMPUTER CARDS 3" X 7"               STANDARD LOCK     10  15  20
      3 REMARKS:
           COMPUTER CARD FILE NEEDS TO BE IN ROOM WITH THE
            COMPUTER TERMINAL.
                                                       FILING SQ. FT. =


STORAGE REQUIREMENTS:
=====================
      1 DESCRIPTION                                  FEET  DEPTH  OPEN/CAB
        ======================================       ====  =====  ========
           NAVIGATION MANUALS                          6     12     OPEN
           OFFICE SUPPLIES                            12     12     CAB
           20 COATS                                                 CAB

                                                     STORAGE SQ. FT. =
```

FIG. 2

The System

The first attempts at production systems were risky undertakings by avante-garde firms who sank large amounts of capital into software production, and the high-level hardware necessary to support it. (1) Most of this early software was highly machine dependent and was marketed in packages of software and hardware combined.

Since they require a relatively large machine to store and execute the programs, the systems are available only to huge firms; those who can afford the great capital outlay and also can cost-justify the devices in other areas as accounting and management. The mini-computer industry recently has generated many new machines. These machines fall into a low-price range but also have fairly small (8-32K) memories. (2) Certainly, the memories can be expanded to virtually the size of the big machines but that would be defeating the purpose.

The situation we were left with was to develop some way to load a large sophisticated software package with correspondingly large memory requirements into an inexpensive hardward configuartion with its attribute of little active memory. The approach eventually developed was on two levels: to compact the software with more efficient algorithms and to structure the total system so that only part of the package was required for operation at any time.

The Structure of the Package

The package is composed of tiny steps (programs) which produced distinct usable information modifications and passed control onto the next step. The control direction is not linear but can be modified by designer intervention. At the beginning of the job, an information base of relevant data is compiled. The base is modified by the designer and the programs, and becomes an ever-refined source through the design process. The structure is set up so that when the designer decides on the next phase of the process to be implemented, the series of steps which constitute that phase are executed. Each step grabs exactly the information it needs from the large, disc-stored data base and jumps into memory. After doing its thing, it dumps out its modified information back into storage and signals the next step until the phase is complete. (See Figure 1).

Stacking Plan

As with other projects, we approached the task of automating the office planning process with many pre-conceived notions. In this case, we planned to adapt a previously written space allocation program SP-2 (3) to lay out the spaces, which seemed very reasonable. After a detailed analysis of their design process, we developed an initial system of three computer programs.

FIG. 3

The first, "DATMAN" processes questionnaires; the second, "POLES" proposes stacking plans and the third, "SP-20" generates alternative layout schemes for individual floors. "DATMAN" operates in a series of five steps taking information from different questionnaires. The questionnaires are filled out by upper level management, department level management, and the designers assigned to research the existing constraints. The questionnaires are implemented in stages, the earlier, more general sections being used to structure the form of later sections. From these different sources, "DATMAN" builds up a compartmentalized data base which is internally cross-checked. The areas of data are interaction requirements, furniture and equipment requirements, estimated square footages, predetermined area locations, and bureaucratic structure. The information is partitioned into discreet parts and later programs use only parts they need. The designers can have reports produced from this data base which will show the most recent update of information. The reports can break down the information in many subsets, such as all of the filing requirements for the Accounting Division by Departments. (See Figure 2)

After several discussion loops on the information by designers and clients, the information is ready to be handed to "POLES" to produce a stacking plan. A stacking plan for a corporate office is a list of departments and divisions by floor assignment. There are essentially two forces influencing the assignment of departments on floors. First, there is the status factor associated with the upper floors. This tends to pull those elements with the most prestige to the top of the building.

There is another force operating in the opposite direction. Those departments which interact highly with elements outside the building, such as shipping and receiving, function most efficiently on the bottom floors. The remaining areas are assigned usually to the middle floors according to their interactions. These adjacency relationships are important because there is no prestige element to influence the placement of these areas. (See Figure 3) Based on reactions to its output, POLES will continue to modify the plan until a scheme acceptable to the designers and clients is reached.

Taking some information generated by POLES AND DATMAN, SP-20 lays out each floor. An iteration similar to that in POLES occurs until an acceptable scheme is produced. The input required by SP-20 consists of the perimeter of the floor, a list of areas and their required square footages, and interaction relationships between areas. It is possible to indicate special areas on the floor as high priority areas (example, the area in front of a window with a special view or a prestigious corner). The departments and square footages comes from "POLES", the interaction matrix from "DATMAN". The floor layout is generated by the use of a modified implicit enumeration procedure. (4)

The data base is capable of supporting a series of additional programs which takes the design to working drawings and to the scheduling of furniture and equipment purchases. The significance of this work is not in which the programs produce in the way of products (although designers in our firm may disagree), but in the technique. The approach is viable and, as a process, creates sophisticated tools for the designer without exorbitant expense.

References

(1) Steward, Clifford D. and Lee, Kaiman COMPROSPACE: INTERATIVE COMPUTER GRAPHICS IN THE REAL WORLD, EDRA 3/AR8, University of California, Los Angeles, 1972.
(2) Reeder, Charles E. THE SELECTION OF AN INEXPENSIVE, EFFECTIVE MACHINE CONFIGURATION FOR INTERACTIVE DESIGN, AR-9, Chicago, 1972.
(3) Fullenwider, Donald R. SP-1 -- A COMPUTERIZED MODEL FOR STORE PLANNING, EDRA 3/AR8, University of California, Los Angeles, 1972.
(4) Liggett, Robin S. FLOOR PLAN LAYOUT BY IMPLICIT ENUMERATION, EDRA 3/AR8, University of California, Los Angeles, 1972.

D. Kernohan, G.D. Rankin, G.D. Wallace and R.J. Walters,
ABACUS Studies,
University of Strathclyde,
Department of Architecture and Building Science,
131 Rottenrow,
GLASGOW, G4 ONG.

ABSTRACT

The PHASE appraisal package consists of a suite of computer programs.   Each
program is based around a suitable method of representation and is linked to a set
of calculation routines.   The aim of the package is to produce information over a
range of design criteria including the efficiency of circulation and service distribution systems, environmental performance, capital and running cost.   It is
envisaged that the package will be used at the strategic stages in hospital planning
and not in the detailed design of individual departments.   The package is equally
effective whether used in the context of a live design project or for research
purposes.

Nature of Hospital Design Problem

A major sector of many national building programmes is the design and construction
of hospital buildings.   In recent years hospitals have become increasingly large
and complex and consequently more expensive.   An overall aim of the hospital design
is therefore to produce buildings which satisfy a range of design criteria and which
do not exceed predetermined cost limits.

PHASE (Package for Hospital Architecture Simulation and Evaluation) makes a
significant contribution to the realisation of this aim by providing a more informed
base for decision-making during the early stages of hospital design and by tracing
the consequences of design decisions through a range of cost/performance measures.

Hospital design operates at two levels - the design of the total hospital complex
and the design of individual hospital departments.   It is apparent that at the
level of whole hospital design the most important and influential decisions are
made with relation to building form, growth potential, principles of circulation,
supply and disposal and services distribution.   Formal appraisal therefore has its
maximum impact at this level of design and so PHASE is concerned with whole
hospital design and not with the detail design of individual departments.

Form of the package

The appraisal package relies on the designer to make an initial design statement,
about which information is produced so that subsequent design decisions can be made
in an informed manner.   Information concerning the geometry of the built form, site
characteristics, constructional requirements and activity patterns is specified
and is processed through a series of algorithms.   These computations cover a range
of cost/performance measures.   The package is composed of four discrete modules -
data interface, building program, network program, visual simulation program.

1. Data Interface - Program data are structured hierarchically and stored in four
files. The standard data file contains information, environmental conditions, cost
and interdepartmental relationships. Where relevant these data are stored for

each of 40 individual departments (e.g. X-ray, OPD, Pharmacy, etc).

All information which remains constant throughout a hospital design project is stored in the project file. This includes information relating to the contours and orientation of the site, the building life and interest rates.

The scheme file contains the three dimensional description of a proposed design. The geometry is specified by the x, y and z co-ordinates of a reference point, the length, breadth and height, and the angle of orientation for each element of the scheme.

The function of the solution file is to store the cost/performance characteristics of previous schemes.

The inspection and upgrading of all data can be carried out by the interface · routine. During these operations the program initiates a dialogue with the designer.

2. Building Program - The program produces information on spatial performance, functional performance, environmental performance and costs, at synoptic and detailed levels of output. The synoptic output (see Fig 1) consists of descriptions of the scheme followed by a series of indices of plot ratio, site utilisation, compactness, planning, capital and energy costs. The four additional columns of output are the values from the solution file for previous schemes. These are produced to allow comparative evaluation of the current scheme.

Fig. 1.

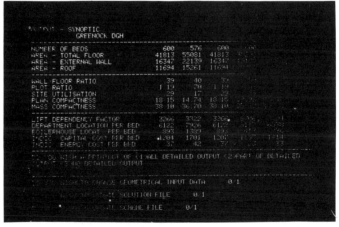

At the conclusion of the synoptic output the opportunity is given to obtain a more detailed output. Under the heading of departmental location the pairs of departments which have significantly contributed to this performance index are identified. High divergence values indicate that the departments have been sited too far apart, low values indicate that the departments have been located closer than is necessary. Capital costs are output for fourteen elements along with running costs for heating, lighting, ventilation and air conditioning. The detailed output concludes with the net heat gains and losses for any specified department.

3. Network Program - The network program is so called because it represents

building circulation and services distribution system as a network.

Measures of activity performance include total travel times for each category of staff, location of lifts and stairs, segregation of non-compatible traffic and optimum sizing of lift installations to avoid congestion.

The services network program seeks to evaluate the layout of the distribution system, location of plant areas, alternative fuel policies and heat transfer media.

Due to the quantity and specific nature of the data required for the network program it is necessary to develop a general data model. Such a program allows the efficient generation of specific data from general information describing the hospital under study such as hospital size, function, operational policies and so on.

4. Visual Simulation Program - This program produces perspective view of any design scheme from any of a number of predetermined viewpoints. The 'hidden lines' are either removed completely or shown dotted. A typical output is shown in Fig. 2.

Fig. 2.

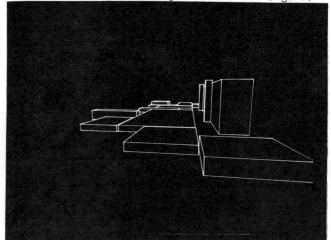

Use of the Package

There are two main uses to which PHASE 1 may be put. The first is in the context of a live design project. Alternative design hypothesis, together with all modifications which are effected on them, are explicitly appraised and evaluated by comparison with indices from previous schemes stored in the solution file. The speed with which modifications can be effected ensures that a vast area of the feasible 'solution space' can be searched for that solution which represents the optimum compromise between conflicting requirements. Moreover, the implications of future change - in type of occupancy, size, functional interdependence etc. can be examined at the outset of a hospital design project.

The second use is as a research tool to investigate the relationships between any pair of building design variables. A program package like PHASE 1 which can simulate, in a controlled way, a large number of alternative solutions in a short space of time, offers a unique chance to study the causal relationships which govern building performance.

THE APPLICATION OF COMPUTER TECHNIQUES FOR THE SIZING AND THE SELECTION OF BUILDING COMPONENTS

Kurt Brandle, Dr.-Ing., Architect
Associate Professor

Edward F. Smith, M.S., Architect
Assistant Research Professor

Department of Architecture, University of Utah, Salt Lake City

1 Introduction

The economic success of building systems development depends very much on the repetitive use of components thus enabling mass production. Extensive modular coordination is necessary for the unification of component sizes. From the unlimited number of possible sizes, the most favorable must be selected with regard to mathematical and material advantage and controlled by functional and aesthetic criteria.

The application of interactive computing based on combinatorial analysis methods facilitates the selection of such component series especially when optimization is part of the programming code. Computer graphics are very helpful not only in visualizing possible component combinations but also in demonstrating their advantages and disadvantages in differing building assembly conditions.

In the following, after remarks on basic modular coordination principles and on component systems, computer programs now in operation will be explained and prototypical applications will be documented.

2 Modular Coordination

Modular coordination has been used in this country up to the present time mainly as a tool for referencing drawings (modular grids). In a few instances it has served for coordinating building systems, such as for schools and offices. By pre-determining the dimensions of the spaces in buildings in modular increments and by dividing the structures accordingly, modular coordination becomes part of the design process. The greater the use of this development in the building industry on a common modular basis, the more feasible will be the interchangeability of building subsystems and components.

Certain parts of buildings lend themselves to modular coordination in different ways than others, depending on the tasks which they have to perform. Load bearing wall components, for example, may have different modular requirements than demountable partitions. Production processes, material thicknesses, limits on shipping weights, jointing configurations, etc., influence component sizes. Many investigations have been related to this subject, especially in Europe (1).

The building as a whole rarely can be divided into a single complete system of coordinated components. It is therefore necessary to break projects down into component systems, the interfaces of which fulfill requirements different from those which connect components of a particular subsystem. In providing such, the modular sizing of components and consequently jointing is much simplified as fewer criteria must be observed.

In developing the component sizes for such subsystems it must be determined whether one, two or three dimensional coordination must be achieved; that is, divisibility in the length, the height and the depth of Assembly Dimensions (2) of particular parts. Cabinetry, for example, located between two walls will have much simpler requirements than a curtain wall system to be used for varying building configurations, including inside and outside corners, and which may need to be compatible with an interior partition system.

3 Combinations of Components

Unifying spaces by adjusting dimensions in increments and adjusting components to modular grids are two procedures for limiting the infinite variety of possible dimensions for building components. A third procedure is the application of combinatorial analysis methods for determining the best set of component dimensions, called Combinatorial Dimensions (3).

After investigating a given building system with regard to assembly dimensions which must be made up of sets of components, combinatorial dimensions for such sets are determined. This is, mathematically speaking, an optimization process. The results are much dependent on the dimensional differences between the assembly dimensions under investigation as well as on the number and size of the members of the set. Many other criteria such as functional requirements, e.g., minimum door sizes, may limit the choice of combinatorial dimensions. Investigations so far have shown that choosing sets of two or three components with the maximum size of the largest one related to the maximum production or transport measurements is most practical.

The smaller the difference between the individual component sizes, the easier it is to achieve assembly dimension series with small increments. This is important for space allocation programs with many rooms of relatively small differences in size which need to be accommodated.

4 Computer Applications

The mathematical relationship in the use of combinations is independent of the dimensional unit which is chosen as a basis. Therefore, additivity may be represented by numerical values only. Dunestone (4) developed charts which allow, using 2 or 3 modular components, the selection of combinations for assembly dimensions with 3 to 29 modular increments beyond a smallest critical dimension.

Brandle investigated advantages of more than 3 components per combinatorial set and determined the best actual component dimensions used for horizontal and vertical assembly dimensions. A computer program called COMB is able to deliver numerically all possible combinations for an unlimited number of assembly dimensions and an unlimited number of component dimensions. The program presently does some optimization, selecting only 5 combinations with the smallest numbers of components, that is, using the largest possible component sizes.

Computer graphics programs are in use which have the full capability to represent modular components on a Cathode Ray Tube (CRT) terminal. Two-dimensional views are usually adequate to show elevations of modular assemblies.

The figures show the numerical output from COMB for a partition wall and the CRT-display of component combinations. The assembly dimensions are 250 and 260, the component dimensions are 18, 24, 34 and 48 inches. The dimension of 34 inches was chosen in this example to accommodate 30-inch doors with 4 inches required for jambs. It may be used also for achieving odd assembly dimensions, that is, for dimensions which are not modular, e.g., for partitions between columns with modular column spacings but varying thicknesses in 2-inch increments. By optimization in the program the largest possible component dimensions are chosen. The display was generated by an existing graphics program from the COMB data. The link between the COMB program and the graphics program has not been completed.

The next task to be undertaken will be to expand the COMB program to handle modular coordination in three dimensions. This will allow for the examination of interfacing and compatibility between the several space enclosing systems currently used in buildings (5). The use and intersection of partition systems with curtain wall systems, ceiling systems and floor systems will be areas of concern. Three-dimensional computer graphics capability will be required to display the results from the expanded COMB program.

Another interesting application of modular coordination that is under study is the optimal cutting of panel building materials in order to achieve the least waste. An initial attempt at solving this problem involved a computer program to specify the cutting pattern for sheets of 4 ft. by 8 ft. plywood or particle board. The cut pieces were to be used in a system of modular cabinetry proposed for the mill. A separate computer program produced a listing of the cut sizes and quantities of pieces required to complete a given set of cabinets.

COMB
ASSEMBLY DIMENSIONS?
☐:
        250 260
COMPONENT DIMENSIONS?
☐:
        18 24 34 48
OPTIMAL COMBINATIONS FOR 250
COMPONENT DIMENSIONS AND REQUIRED NUMBER

48	34	24	18
4	1	1	0
3	1	3	0
3	1	0	4
2	1	5	0
2	4	0	1

OPTIMAL COMBINATIONS FOR 260
COMPONENT DIMENSIONS AND REQUIRED NUMBER

48	34	24	18
4	2	0	0
3	2	2	0
2	2	4	0
1	2	6	0
1	2	0	8

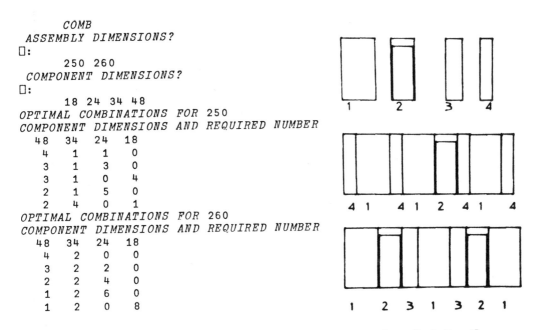

(1) See e.g. Co-ordinating Dimensions for Building Components, Kurt Brandle, BUILDING INTERNATIONAL, Rotterdam, January/February 1971 (includes extensive bibliography).
(2) Assembly Dimensions are partial dimensions of total building measurements. They may be multiples of planning grid increments, e.g., axis-to-axis of walls, or "in-between" dimensions between faces of walls.
(3) Combinatorial Dimensions are component measurements which are selected because of their favorable additive properties in component combinations.
(4) P.H. Dunestone, Combinations of Numbers in Building, London, THE ESTATES GAZETTE, LTD., 1965.
(5) A National Science Foundation grant to Kurt Brandle is being used for exploring such relationships especially towards the open systems approach in design.

Chairman: Richard M. Hessler, Department of Sociology and Section of Health Care
Studies, University of Missouri-Columbia, Columbia, Missouri 65201

Co-authors: Peter Kong-ming New, Department of Behavioral Sciences, University of
Toronto Medical Center, Toronto, Canada

Ramon Hache Jaurigue, Director, Richie Community School, Tucson, Ariz.

Participants:

Manuel Alvarez, Tucson, Arizona
Ramon Jaurigue, Tucson, Arizona
Mike Lugo, Tucson Design Center, Tucson, Arizona
Peter Kong-ming New, University of Toronto Medical Center, Toronto, Canada
Felipe Olivas, Tucson, Arizona
Leo Williams, Portland City Planning Commission, Portland, Oregon

Abstract

The paper applies theory on the relationship between socio-cultural organization and
the design process to citizen participation in the design of low-cost housing.
Types of participation are presented and evaluated relative to introducing social
and cultural factors into the design of low-cost housing. The vehicle for this
application is a workshop where Yaqui Indian and Chicano residents of Barrio Pascua,
Tucson, Arizona, meet with architects and critique specific designs for their
community housing needs. The impact of consumer participation on the profession of
architecture is discussed.

Architecture and Social Change: Low-Cost Housing and Consumer Participation(1)

The relationship between man's social and physical well-being and his material existence is influenced dramatically by architectural design. Numerous substantive
articles and books of great merit have documented the reasonableness and desirability of linking the design process with human qualities of social and cultural
environments and habitats (2, 3, 4). Regarding housing, this work stresses the
importance of defining the human habitat as an unified and extended field for
action, thereby removing the design process from purely technical and scientific
considerations per se and more toward social and cultural factors which have
serious implications for physical form. In reading this literature, one comes
away with the impression that a significant gap exists between words and deeds.
This is especially true in the housing area where much has been written urging

architects and other planners to weigh and include the "invisible" social and cultural factors that have major implications for physical form. Nevertheless, the
development of a methodology for translating the words into deeds has lagged far
behind as evidenced by the dearth of housing designs which reflect the consumers'
cultural contributions.

Mere techniques of low-cost housing design cannot serve in lieu of a truly innovative approach which moves beyond performance standards and concepts of efficiency.
In order to systematically and effectively allow culture and life styles to determine the physical forms of design, the consumer must participate in the design process. In as much as design is a decision-making endeavor, participation in effect
would center on some degree of consumer involvement in the decision-making process.
Quite obviously, the probability of successfully incorporating consumer preferences
and cultural patterns into low-cost housing designs increase dramatically with a
greater degree of consumer participation in the design process.

The traditional antithesis to consumer participation in design is the elitist model
which occurs when individuals plan for others. Perhaps unexampled vividness is the
case of Los Angeles where one architect alone since 1931 has affected the destiny
of more than a thousand square miles of land and in the process has shaped the lives
of countless thousands (5).

One popular approach to consumer participation has emerged under the rubric "performance approach" (6). This model stresses the relationships between the structure,
a house for example, and the performance expected from the structure vis a vis the
satisfaction of human needs. The architect identifies consumer population characteristics and needs within the context of the dwelling and its environment through
systematic field research and performance attributes are translated into building
requirements of a practical nature. A variation of this model establishes the consumer needs through a review of the literature on concepts of territoriality,
proxemics, crowding, privacy, and other social and cultural aspects of human
behavior (7, 8). This approach, while representing an improvement over the elitist
model, is at best only an approximation of consumer participation. In as much as
consumer needs are included in the design process consumers are represented, but
only as passive recipients of structures which are planned for them and not with
them. As a result, the model could be described as quasi-participation.

If we focus on the core issue of consumer participation, namely participation in
the decisions relating to the design process, alternative approaches are evident.
One could cast consumers in the role of advisors to experts but this model has
proved extremely frustrating to consumers who find their advice ignored as often as
taken seriously by the experts. Where this model has been applied within the
institution of health care, much conflict and creative waste has resulted, primarily from the lack of effective consumer participation in decision-making and
absence of an egalitarian relationship between consumer and provider (9, 10, 11).

Another approach, one which we will spend the rest of this paper discussing, is the
consumer-architect commune model. Because many of the details of this model have
been published elsewhere (12), we will not spend time describing its structure and
functions. Instead we should like to apply some of the key principles of the

commune concept to the design of low-cost housing with minority consumers, specifically Yaqui Indians and Chicanos in Barrio Pascua, Tucson, Arizona.

The most important principle of the commune approach is to establish a genuine exchange of power between architect and consumer. This can be accomplished in several ways (13) but basically must involve both parties in a full sharing of the power to influence all decisions in the design process, beginning with the definition of the housing problems and ending with the disposition of finished structures. The exchange principle includes both taking and receiving (14), since both consumer and architect have the power to give facets of enormous value to the design process. The architect has the theoretical and technical knowledge necessary to produce a structure of practical and aesthetic integrity. The consumer, in the case of Pascua residents, are the only experts capable of accurately articulating the requirements introduced into the process of designing human habitation.

Another principle closely associated with the exchange of power is the establishment of mutual expectations regarding roles and knowledge bases. It is encumbent upon both parties to see the world through the eyes of the other which in effect is a fancy way of saying that one must appreciate and understand the style of thought, language and concepts of the other. Professional training often incapacitates one by producing a less flexible and more dogmatic mind while many times a minority perspective automatically turns to the defensive posture in response to genuine, albeit bumbling, approaches from outsiders. For example, an architect working with a Pascua resident on low-cost housing may seek data which he has been trained to believe is essential for the design process. Toward this end, he may strive to gain entry into Yaqui or Chicano homes for the purpose of establishing living patterns, use of rooms, size of rooms, etc. This activity may cause great concern on the part of the resident who values privacy and anonymity highly. Unless the architect truly understands the resident's perspective, he will pursue the request for entry doggedly to the detriment of all concerned. On the other hand, data on proxemics, interaction, and other cultural dimensions are important informing principles and must be considered, but only in a way defined by the Yaqui or Chicano resident. It is highly likely for example, that the resident will not understand why the architect needs to know where a ramada should go or where one works on the cars; since, from his perspective, one puts a ramada where the sun shines and works on a car wherever there is room to do it in comfort, even in the kitchen if it is too cold outside.

Working within the community boundaries of time and style of action is a critically important third principle of the commune approach. Proxemics can be applied to an analysis of the interaction between architect and resident in as much as careful attention to the manner in which community residents negotiate with outsiders and deal with time will enhance the probability of creating a climate which facilitates full consumer participation. To cite Pascua as an example, there is an old saying among Chicanos and Yaquis that refers to Anglo time and Mexican time as very different phenomena. According to this saying, Anglos adhere to rigorous time schedules and in fact measure time by a clock. Mexicans in Pascua measure time relative to social and environmental processes which do not correlate well with the clock. One can see the potential for development of mutual antagonisms, given conflict between these two orientations.

In proposing a commune approach to consumer participation in design, we have barely touched the surface values of an enormously complicated and exciting process capable of producing low-cost housing which truly reflects the cultural needs, practical and aesthetic, of the consumer. Yet, a complex series of issues remains to be resolved, issues which are plaguing other sectors of our society such as health care, education and transportation. For example, how much can human needs realistically be considered in the design of low-cost housing within budgetary constraints? For example, Pascua residents are desirous of low-cost housing which can be individually tailored to family preferences rather than having two or three general plans to choose from. Is it possible to produce the social engineering necessary to meet this request, thereby maximizing congruence between habitat and culture, and at the same time keep the housing low-cost? Furthermore, is it possible for persons from different socio-economic, ethnic, or racial backgrounds to listen and understand the others' perspectives well enough to act in a manner consonant with desires articulated?

Finally, and perhaps of major concern to architecture, consumer participation affects the aesthetic and artistic tradition which has been the central domain of architecture historically. The architect is an artist in as much as a given media is shaped to personal artistic and aesthetic values. The commune approach expands this to include the consumer as a determiner and shaper of the media. By involving those for whom a structure takes on human meaning in decisions of aesthetic and artistic import, one changes one of the primary domains of architecture and thereby the profession itself. Thus, it becomes less a question of how and more a question of willingness to undergo profound change in the nature of one's work and in the relationship to the consumers of our efforts.

Notes and References

(1) Paper resulting from a workshop, "Low-cost Housing for Yaqui Indians and Chicanos," EDRA IV, Blacksburg, Virginia, April 15-18, 1973. The authors wish to thank Manuel Alvarez, Felipe Olivas and Mike Lugo from Tucson for making the workshop possible. Also, we wish to thank Wolfgang Preiser, School of Architecture, Virginia Polytech Institute for his help throughout. Finally, Robert Lehr gave us valuable suggestions and Orah Mockbee edited and typed the paper with consumate skill.

(2) Chermayeff, Sergius and Alexander, Christopher, COMMUNITY AND PRIVACY: TOWARD A NEW ARCHITECTURE OF HUMANISM, Garden City, New York, Doubleday, 1965.

(3) Hall, Edward T., THE HIDDEN DIMENSION, New York, Doubleday & Co., Inc., 1966.

(4) Rapoport, Amos, HOUSE FORM AND CULTURE, Englewood Cliffs, New Jersey, Prentice-Hall, Inc., 1969.

(5) Diehl, Digby, "William Pereira", LOS ANGELES TIMES WEST MAGAZINE, pages 20-23, August 20, 1972.

(6) Wright, James R., "Performance Criteria in Building", SCIENTIFIC AMERICAN, 224 (3), 1971.

(7) Mather, William G., TERRITORIALITY, PROXEMICS, AND HOUSING, Washington, D.C., U. S. National Bureau of Standards Report No. 10401, 1971.

(8) Mather, William G., PERFORMANCE REQUIREMENTS FOR HOSPITAL INTERMEDIATE CARE NURSING UNITS AND PATIENT BEDROOMS, Washington, D. C., U. S. National Bureau of Standards Report, 1971.

(9) Hessler, Richard M., and New, Peter Kong-ming, "Research as a Process of Exchange", THE AMERICAN SOCIOLOGIST, 7, pages 13-15, February, 1972.

(10) New, Peter Kong-ming; Bellin, Seymour; Bagwell, Phyllis; Hessler, Richard; and Schoepf, Brooke, "Entry into Problems", Paper read at Annual Meeting of Midwest Sociological Society, St. Louis, Missouri, April, 1970.

(11) New, Peter Kong-ming and Hessler, Richard, "Consumer Control and Public Accountability", ANTHROPOLOGICAL QUARTERLY, forthcoming, 1973.

(12) Hessler, Richard M. and New, Peter Kong-ming, "Research as a Process of Exchange", THE AMERICAN SOCIOLOGIST, 7, pages 13-15, February, 1972.

(13) Hessler, Richard M. and New, Peter Kong-ming, "Research as a Process of Exchange", THE AMERICAN SOCIOLOGIST, 7, pages 13-15, February, 1972.

(14) Blau, Peter, EXCHANGE AND POWER IN SOCIAL LIFE, New York, John Wiley and Sons, Inc., 1964.

TWENTY   SUBJECTIVE RESPONSES TO ACOUSTIC ENVIRONMENTS

Chairman: Ifan Payne, School of Architecture, M.S.U., Bozeman, Montana 59715

Participants:

T. D. Northwood, National Research Council of Canada, Ottawa, Canada
Ron J. Hawkes, School of Environmental Studies, University College, London
Bill G. Watters, Bolt Beranek and Newman Inc., Cambridge, Mass.

Abstract

This workshop deal with studies of the ways in which people respond in acoustic environments. There will be a discussion of past and current work on subjective responses to noise in general. More detailed discussion will be concerned with speech privacy in offices and hotels, and the acoustic environments of school and concert halls.

Introduction

It is interesting to note that whilst there is in our society an already large and growing interest in the effect of noise upon humans, this area has been largely ignored by workers in the field of man-environment studies. The current general concern with "pollution" has tended to increase the scope of the word's meaning, so that the concept of noise pollution has been created. This refers to the increased intrusion of man-made noise, occurring at its greatest in man-made environments. Yet this aspect of man-environment relations has been largely ignored by those who profess to be concerned with man-environment relations.(1) The reasons for the apparent lack of concern with sensory responses other than visual(2) are histori- cal(3), even though Southworth(4) has pointed out the possible greater importance of auditory environmental stimuli over visual stimuli. As witness of the current state of affairs, a glance at the current standard text on environmental psycho- logy(5) shows that out of 65 chapters there are only two brief references to noise.

As recently as 1971 it was possible for an article entitled Environmental Program- ming for Offices Based on Behavioral Considerations(6) to contain the sentence that "The environmental attributes are those elements which give the activity site its overall character and mood and include such elements as lighting, colour, use of materials, texture and style", without once mentioning the words 'noise' or 'acous- tics'. Yet Peter Manning had already stated that "noise is perhaps the major envi- ronmental problem of offices in city centers".(7) All this lack of concern despite the fact that Michelson in his book, Man and His Urban Environment(8) was able to state catagorically that "high noise levels are related to the incidence of ten- sion".

Some of the problems currently being encountered owing to past lack of interest in the field of subjective noise assessment are well illustrated in the recent introduction of a noise bill by one county council.(9) The proposed bill would have limited all external noise on a piece of property to 55dB as measured on the property line. Now this would be eminantly desirable state of affairs, except for one thing. Not all sound is noise, nor are all loud sounds thought to be noisy by the hearers. Would the county council have banned the birds from singing, or the cows from lowing? Both of which may be loud, but not "noisy". Why, for example is the chopping of wood less "noisy", (even in a situation where it is louder) than the use of a chain saw? These problems of course parallel others in other aspects of the man-environment relationship. What the county council, and all legislative bodies, need is a graph that enable them to set reasonable, logical noise levels, and this, ultimately is what studies of community noise is all about so that our society may, eventually live in an optimum acoustic environment. (See Figure 1)

Where subjective responses to interior acoustic noises are concerned, Yamaguchi(10) stated the research requirements for one specialized environment:

> "1.   To clarify the relationship between acoustical measurements and subjective characteristics of the music hall.
> 2.   To quantify the auditory difference among seats in a music hall.

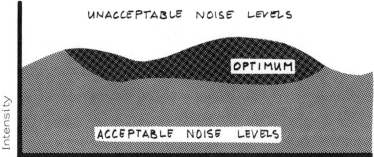

UNACCEPTABLE NOISE LEVELS

OPTIMUM

ACCEPTABLE NOISE LEVELS

Intensity

Physical correlates of subjective responses to noise

FIGURE 1

> 3.   To quantify the auditory differences among various halls."

If this is required for one hearing environment and if noise is indeed linked to tension ailments then how much more important is the study of subjective responses to classrooms, lecture halls and offices. Again, we should ideally end up with a graph somewhat like Figure 2.

The importance of acoustics for man-environment studies is clear. As T. C.Northwood has pointed out there had in the past been "an amassing of information on the physical aspects of architectural acoustics. It is predicted...that the next decade or so will see an equivalent advance on the subjective side of acoustics. Then the physical data, which we are now so adept at measuring, will become relevant to the real life problems of architectural acoustics."(11)

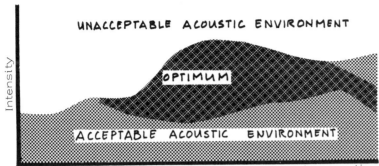

Physical correlates to subjective responses to acoustic environments

FIGURE 2

Notes & References

(1) See Walters, David, in Canter (Ed.) ARCHITECTURAL PSYCHOLOGY, RIBA, 1970, for
      an exception.
(2) See Griffiths, Ian D. Thermal comfort, a behavioral approach, ibid and Payne,
      Ifan, New Methods and Research in Qualitative Evaluation of Architectural
      Acoustics, EDRA 3, Vol. 2, University of California, 1972 as two of the few
      exceptions.
(3) There seem to be two prime reasons for the direction which the field of environ-
      mental psychology took. Firstly, in the initial years, the strong influence of
      psychologist who entered the field and brought with them their "experimental"
      background (often insisting that architects should not meddle with things they
      knew nothing about, i.e., study of the built environment). Secondly, the
      importance of existing methodologies (it is interesting to note the frequency
      with which the name Oswood crops up in the bibliographies, and more recently,
      Barker) and their continued application along a narrow (simple?) path of
      development.
(4) Southworth, M. The Sonic Environment of Cities. ENVIRONMENT AND BEHAVIOR,
      Vol. 1, No. 1, June 1969.
(5) Proshansky, Harold M. et. al. (Ed.) ENVIRONMENTAL PSYCHOLOGY, Holt, Rinehart
      and Winston, 1970.
(6) Moleski, Walter. ENVIRONMENTAL PROGRAMMING FOR OFFICES BASED ON BEHAVIORAL
      CONSIDERATIONS, in ARCHITECTURE FOR HUMAN BEHAVIOR, Philadelphia Chapter of
      A.I.A., 1971.
(7) Manning, Peter, Office Design: A STUDY OF ENVIRONMENT. Pilkington Research
      Unit, University of Liverpool, 1965.
(8) Michelson, William, MAN AND HIS URBAN ENVIRONMENT, A SOCIOLOGICAL APPROACH,
      Addison-Wesley, 1970.
(9) Howard County, Maryland.
(10) Yamaguchi, Kiminori. Multivariate analysis of subjective and physical measures
      of hall acoustics. JASA., Vol. 52, No. 5, November 1972.
(11) Northwood, T. C., Measurements in Room Acoustics - Recent Progress. 82nd meet-
      ing of the Acoustical Society of America; JASA., Vol. 15, No. 1, January 1972.

TWENTY ONE   RELATIONAL AND ANALYTICAL INTELLIGENCE IN DESIGNERS AND RESEARCHERS

21.0

Chairman: Robert B. Bechtel, Environ. Research Foundation, Kansas City

Participants:

Rosalie Cohen, Dept. of Sociology, Temple Univ., Phila.
Sheila Campbell, Dept. of Architecture, U. of Edinburgh, Scotland

Abstract

Commication failures had often occurred in designer-researcher collaborations. It was hypothesized that they may be due to the conflict of Analytic and Relational conceptual styles among them. Exploratory data were collected from conference participants, 97:200 of whom returned mailed tests of conceptual style. Among them there were no clear Analytic or Relational styles at all. Designers and researchers alike demonstrated the use of the Concrete conceptual style. Differences appeared, however, in the field articulation scores of teachers and social and behavioral scientists, and designers. This suggests that perceptual distance is greater among the academic group. A preference for independence and a low value on team effort characterize Concrete style carriers. Thus, communication gaps may be due to the collaboration of independents.

Introduction

The Workshop, ANALYTIC AND RELATIONAL CONCEPTUAL STYLES AMONG DESIGNERS AND RE-SEARCHERS arose because Robert Bechtel had observed that the collaboration of designers and researchers in design projects was often marked by failures of communication. He reasoned that this communication gap may be due to a conflict in the differing conceptual styles which each of these professional groups brought to their common project. Since Analytic and Relational styles had been empirically related to certain classic communication failures in other groups, it was hypothesized that designer-researcher problems might be similarly explained.

A small study was, therefore, planned to obtain some basic information about the conceptual styles of environmental designers and researchers. In February, an instrument was mailed to the more than 200 registrants at the EDRA 4 conference. This instrument consisted of the Cohen adaptation of the Sigel Test of Cognitive Style and the Cohen adaptation of the Witkin Test of Field Articulation. To these were added requests for three definitions for language sampling and half a dozen pieces of personal information. Unfortunately, occupational discrimination was not entirely possible, as the questionnaires were made up without including a full set of occupational possibilities. As a result, our original intent...that of comparing the conceptual styles of designers and researchers...was not possible. Nevertheless, the dominant conceptual styles reflected in the returns on these instruments were of sufficient interest to justify reporting.

Conceptual styles are rule-sets for the selection and organization of sense data for memory storage or for transfer to new situations. They are important because they control in their carriers the possible and permissable relationships among objects, among people and between people and objects, thereby providing individuals with the conceptual means for ordering their environments. These styles also determine for their carriers the perceptual distance between them and their fields. Since the rule-sets which are used by individuals have been observed to change under certain conditions, they are not genetically determined. They appear to have developed proverbally as rules of social organization in the families and other social groups of their users, and to be responsive to changes in the structure of these social relationships.

Four conceptual styles have been identified which are reliable, over time in individuals, and among individuals as they relate to social organization. The four styles are called, Analytic, Flexible, Concrete and Relational. Each of the styles is made up of two cognitive skills, Mode of Abstraction (formal or descriptive), and Field Articulation (field dependent or field independent). The Analytic and Concrete styles are viewed as object-oriented styles because they stress the salience of object-object relationships. The Flexible and Relational styles are, conversely, subject-oriented styles as they place salience on person-person relationships. Such styles are responsible, in part, for the development of certain related behavior characteristics in their users which are sometimes viewed as personality characteristics; they are differentially associated with the development of different kinds of talents and abilities in their carriers; and they are associated as well with individual self-selection into different occupations.

The purpose of a small exploratory study of designers and researchers in environmental design was to attempt to assess what kinds of conceptual styles are used by environmental design professionals and to suggest what they may mean for the profession.

Findings

Of the more than 200 tests mailed out to participants in the EDRA 4 conference, 97 were returned in time for scoring and presentation. Since the occupation question had been unconstructed, 24 of these respondents could not answer this question; and 39 answered so ambiguously that they offered insufficient information for analysis. As nearly as could be determined, there were 29 designers, 11 researchers, 8 psychologists, 9 architects, 5 sociologists, 10 teachers and 1 consultant, some of whom were students. Despite this handicap, analysis of the data was unusually fruitful, because there were no sharp distinctions among the response patterns presented whatsoever, and no evidence, therefore, that the hypothesized distinctions could be supported. In brief, there were no clear Analytic or Relational response patterns in this sample at all; and the language styles used by the respondents in their definitions did not suggest that the expected variation in the sample could be induced by adding other instrumentation to the existing battery.

The dominant response style used by the respondents was clearly and homogeneously Concrete, as measured by the tests of conceptual style and the language samples provided. Among them, only eighteen could be scored barely Analytic, and this in combination with the Concrete style. Of the 10 women in the sample, only two exhibited the characteristic Flexible, or female style: and, of these two, only one used the language style associated with its cognitive counterpart. In the language samples, the definitions of creativity, imagination and intelligence, the Standard English of little elaboration associated with the Concrete style appeared: and when answers were lengthy, they consisted of lists of related responses in perfect Standard English construction with little or no elaboration. Little attention was given to a content analysis of these definitions, although suggestions for further research were clear. The notion of genetic determination (a characteristic of the Concrete explanatory system) appeared voluntarily in 24 of the 97 responses, and, in 67 of them, the manipulation of concepts in relationship to one another in mental space (its common spatial notion) appeared.

Social origins of the respondents were similarly those associated with the development of the Concrete style. Of 96 answering this question, 59 came from small towns or rural areas and 37 from large urban centers. Of the 37 who grew up in large cities, parental occupations were: 8 engineers, 7 businessmen, 7 skilled craftsmen, 5 clerks, government workers or bank workers, 2 salesmen, 2 architects, 2 attorney or physician (presumably in private practice) and 1 each, career serviceman, police officer, cab driver and writer. Despite the breakdown of the occupations listed above, all of these occupations in the families of the designers and researchers are those associated with the Concrete style, suggesting that it may have been stimulated and reinforced in family process.

One observation in the analysis of the data deserves comment. That is, despite the apparent homogeneity in the dominant conceptual styles of designers and researchers, one major difference appeared in their responses. Those who had identified themselves as teachers or professors, along with 5 of 8 psychologists and 3 of 5 sociologists, as a group, had higher field articulation scores than those actively engaged in applied settings. One psychologist found and clearly marked all of the embedded figures presented, a score so rare in the experience of the author that it is noteworthy. Field articulation scores are measures of perceptual distance from one's field, and a measure of preferred social distance. Individuals who demonstrate such scores would be expected to exhibit greater objectivity, greater rigor in their work than those with lower field articulation scores, and a lesser tolerance for working interdependently with other members of a team. The unique characteristic of the Concrete style is that it is one which is used by people who prefer to develop their skills and to do work alone...i.e. independently. The only conclusion possible from these data is that designers and researchers are both independent workers with a strong sense of individuality and craft pride whose social skills and work habits do not lend themselves well to collaborative team efforts.

The small exploratory research attempted as a medium for the EDRA 4 workshop posed more questions than it answered. It cannot be viewed as controlled research for reasons which are mentioned above; however, it did suggest that, by en large, the communication failures which appear among design professionals are not explanable by Analytic-Relational conflicts. The entire group appeared, in the context of thousands of such responses, to be more homogeneous in conceptual style than many occupational groups. However, such observations as the distinction between teacher or discipline carrier and designer in their field articulation scores seems to warrant further research.

Two kinds of implications for use of this information did arise from these findings. They are related to selection criteria for higher education in design related fields, and to the designs which, themselves emerge from this group. Since design professionals who are already working in the field, regardless of the kind of contribution they make to it, appear predominantly to use the Concrete style, such tools as conceptual style measures may provide more effective selection mechanisms than those presently provided, at least in combination with other measures of ability. Secondly, and more importantly, since conceptual styles appear to arise from rules of social organization, and since spatial arrangements affect, to some degree, those social arrangements which are possible within them, the impact of design on the conceptual styles of individuals who use their products may be an important variable in social change.

References

(1) Cohen, Rosalie, PRIMARY GROUP STRUCTURE, CONCEPTUAL STYLES AND SCHOOL ACHIEVE-MENT, Monograph of the Center for Psychosocial Studies, Pittsburgh, Learning Research and Development Center, 1967

(2) Cohen, Rosalie, Fraenkel, G., and Brewer, J., "Implications for Culture Conflict From a Semantic Feature Analysis of the Lexicon of the Hard Core Poor," Hague, LINGUISTICS, No. 44, Winter, 1968

(3) Cohen, Rosalie, "Conceptual Styles, Culture Conflict and Non-Verbal Tests of Intelligence," AMER. ANTHROPOLOGIST, Vol. 71, No. 5, 1969

(4) Cohen, Rosalie, "The Effect of Conceptual Styles on Measures of Learning Ability," in Brace, C.L., Gamble, G., and Bond, J., RACE AND INTELLIGENCE, Amer. Anthropologist Special Issue, 1971

(5) Cohen, Rosalie, "School Reorganization and Learning," in Kimball, S., and Burnett, J., CULTURE AND LEARNING, N.Y., Shenkman, 1972

SUMMARY OF EDRA 4

John P. Eberhard
Dean
School of Architecture and Environmental Design
State University of New York at Buffalo
2917 Main Street
Buffalo, New York 14214

> Our revels now are ended. These our actors,
> As I foretold you, were all spirits and
> Are melted into air, into thin air:
> And, like the baseless fabric of this vision,
> The cloud-capp'd towers, the gorgeous palaces,
> The solemn temples, the great globe itself.
> Yea, all which it inherit shall dissolve;
> And, like this insubstantial pageant faded,
> Leave not a rack behind. We are such stuff
> As dreams are made on, and our little life
> Is rounded with a sleep. (1)

Now just before we put this process of interaction, this frantic file cabinet of
more than 200 papers; this chance to rub up against five hundred other humans who
share at least a portion of our own interests and concerns; just before we put
all of this insubstantial pageant to sleep again for another year allow me to
sum up for us all. To assume a posture of capability for summary of what John
Zeisel has computed must represent almost $500,000 worth of human effort, expenses
and consumption is to assume a posture of some arrogance. My only qualifications
are that I have done something like this several times before. My only apology
is that I could not possibly mention everybody or even read the titles of what
was presented in the twenty three minutes allotted to me. My only possibility
is to convey to you an existential impression of what we have been, and done and
thought about these past few days. By the time the sun comes round again my words
will have vanished into thin air and with them any sense of what I said. (For
those of you who read these words later, I can only suggest that you pass on to
more pleasant things for what I say now will mean even less to you than to those
who were here.)

First I'd like to give you some impressions of our "environment":

One wonders from such far off places as London, San Francisco or Buffalo if Blacks -
burg, Virginia is possible to approach by public transportation. Even as we
deplaned in Roanoke it wasn't clear that those greenbreasted mountains now turning
to purple in the fading twilight were not one of those illusions that would
fade on before us as we approached them in a rented automobile.

With Bob Ward at the wheel and Florence Ladd in the back seat we approached this
citadel of southern gentlemen trained in the art of the military to find its
grey stone halls, sprinkled with new buildings -some to its new heroes the

fightin' Goblers and others one supposes to respond to the new sense of grace
endowed on its campus by the presence of females.

First impressions being the powerful source of future cognition that they are,
how wise it was for Wolf Preiser to arrange that bash with booze in the Armory.
What a stimulus it was to most of us oldtimers at EDRA Conferences to see those
fresh young faces--both male and female--in such great numbers. New grist for
the mills of our mind to grind upon. All through that warm evening liquid with
alcohol and the making of new friendships the acoustical environment was so
heavy with human signals that even with substantial amplification whatever Wolf
was trying to announce got lost on the first synapse of our nervous systems.

Monday morning dawned bright with hope in the warm Virginia sunshine. We could
no longer catch a glimpse of those Blue Ridge Mountains we had seen from the
airport; our man-made environment had surrounded us now but no matter because
while they elude us now they can't be far away and tomorrow we can reach out...
or perhaps as V.P.I. Vice President McKeefery (2) suggested in his opening remarks
the fish would be the last to discover the ocean. An interesting psychological
response to environmental conditioning occurred during Vice President McKeefery's
prerecorded address shown to us on closed circuit television. The audience
cheered or booed at inappropriate times in direct response to their value judgments
of his value judgments. With no direct feedback loop between them and him polite
convention could be dropped.

One was conscious as the day wore on of how many conferences within conferences
the Social Environment encouraged and spawned. If you were bored with the endless
 reading of papers in the acoustical environment, you could retreat to a visual
environment and read them for yourself from the first giant volume of selected
papers; or you could assemble with a small group in a hallway somewhere to talk
about how dense the other participants were; or you could go to Synfoam Two
and extract from its parallel proceedings some knowhow about making synthetic
environments; or you could usually find some bright and energetic people in
the Childhood City room. (3) It even occurred to a few venturesome souls that
they might wander across the campus to find the architecture school and its
great, busy spaces depopulated by the conference or by the excused classes
anyway.

As usual each session, be it a symposium, a workshop, or the delivery of papers,
was not a quiet collection of attentive listeners. People came and went as
the spirit moved them or the speaker didn't. I observed sessions that began
with fifty people grow to 150 and diminished again to eighty. Time lapsed photography would reveal more agitation than a kindergarten playground.

That evening there was a special environmental experience put on by the Haus-
Rucker Corporation. A giant air-filled mattress, was the site of squirming,
awkward but happy, playful bodies bouncing up and down while their sensory
receptors were inundated with sounds and sights--enough to set children screaming--
really groovy was what I heard. I wasn't there because I was in the smoked
filled parlors of EDRA politics having a secret ceremony to select the next
three tribal chiefs.

Tuesday found the morning heavy with rain and moisture that seemed not to dampen the spirit of the 280 students and 280 pros who once again assembled in such places as "Squires Small Ballroom" or "CEC Auditorium" to hear about environments for the American Indian, for wolves, for children, for the elderly (or even elderly females,) etc.; to participate in acoustical environments, visual environments, man-made environments, within natural environments that exist within political environments that are a part of the social environment.

When Heinz Von Foerster (4) was introduced by Hans Esser who was introduced by Wolf Preiser (the germanic trilogy) on Tuesday evening it was with a sense of relief that we could laugh at his statement that we had finally discovered that all of our lives we have lived in the "environment".

Now allow me to give you some impressions of "environmental design research".

Oswald Spengler in the second volume of THE DECLINE OF THE WEST (5) talks about the concept of a cultural pseudomorph. He points to the common fact in geology that a rock may retain its structure after certain elements have been leached out of it and been replaced by an entirely different kind of material. Since the apparent structure of the old rock remains, the new product is termed a pseudomorph. Spengler suggests that a similar metamorphosis is possible in culture: new forces, activities, institutions, instead of crystallizing independently into their own appropriate forms, may creep into the structure of an existing civilization. Something like this, I would suggest, has happened with environmental design research--in all probability with the so called social sciences as disciplines. The paradigms, the structure, the concepts of the physical sciences were there fully developed by the time the social sciences began to blossom, so that instead of developing a new form, the study of man's awareness of himself, the study of man's interaction with man and the studies of man's interaction with the artifacts he creates borrowed the cloak of the physical sciences and became a pseudomorph.

Herbert Simon in his great series of lectures on "the Sciences of the Artificial" (6) makes the distinction between intellectual activity devised to shed new light on those phenomena found in nature and those phenomena associated with man created-or artificial-things. He emphasizes that engineering, medicine, business, architecture, and painting are concerned" not with the necessary but with the contingent--not with how things ARE but with how they might be---in short, with design."

When we devote our minds and our energies into research to illuminate how things might be instead of how things are we face some problems not faced by the physical sciences. Design involves value judgments and value judgments involves man's views of themselves, their fellow man and their common environments. The information gleaned from the sensory processes so eloquently described by Hein Von Foerster last night is massaged within the mind. A lot of the research here is concerned with that internal process of massaging sensory inputs into value systems, judgments about fit, or about beauty or about how things ought to be. To impose a model of rationality upon this activity is to be suspect since we all know that we only rarely make decisions based entirely (or sometimes even in part) on rationality. In the absence of rationality it is difficult to place numbers on the measurement of human decisions (other than probability) and hence the concern expressed by many that we seem to lack a basis of theory in our EDRA research.

Amos Rapoport (7) suggested that it is important to consider why man-environment studies should require theory at this point. Charles Kahn (8) raised the caution that we examine our bias that suggests that all problems may be studied through research methods and techniques with a high probability of success. And Ray Studer (9) suggests in his own inevitable language that "we do not appear to have sufficient technical understanding of the interdependencies amongst most manenvironment systems to understand and isolate dysfunctional aspects, or to predict the direct and indirect effects on contingent systems."

Well what do we do if we are not to dispair as Geoffrey Broadbent says he did a short time ago when he felt that design method research was dead? I like the prescription that Herbert Simon (10) suggests for us:

> The artificial world is centered precisely on this interface between the inner and outer environments; it is concerned with attaining goals by adapting the former to the latter. The proper study of those who are concerned with the artificial is the way in which that adaptation of means to environments is brought about and central to that is the process of design itself.

I would be the last to say that your research interests should be abandoned no matter how esoteric or inessential they may seem to me, because my own notion of what is valuable has changed and will change again. But I also would not be happy with any intolerance on your part about someone else not really being a "researcher". I thought yesterday as I watched Robin Moore describe how he had modified playgrounds for children what a sensitive research machine he was. He didn't use any formal techniques to make his measurements; he didn't measure his problems in quantitative terms; he didn't write down or model in a computer his situation and his alternatives; he just reacted to what he observed happening around him and made little changes in the environment that seemed to please the children with whom he was interacting. It's this interaction with imagination and sensitivity to design opportunities that seems to me so crucial. There are questions of scale--from playgrounds to cities, so that when we intervene at even larger scales we need more sensitive instruments for collecting data, more effective methods than solo action, more advanced technologies than a few hard tools, and as effective social action as is possible. The model is more complex as the problems get larger, but the model is Robin Moore.

And finally a word about the Environmental Design Research Association. This is our fourth meeting--only our fourth. Some people are worried that we convey mass confusion, others that they didn't discover in our midst some "practical" secrets to unlock the doors of their own lack of understanding, but by and large I think it worked. Students got exposed to more good things and more bad things in three days than they would likely get in three months in their normal classrooms.

Lots of us learned about at least one new area of research that interested us.
Experts' egos got reinforced. New alliances emerged. Sometimes we were entertained
sometimes we were bored, but always we were interacting with ideas.

We should be no more or no less discouraged than F. Scott Fitzgerald (11) was
when he reflects at the end of "THE GREAT GATSBY" that:

> Most of the big shore places were closed now and there were hardly
> any lights except the shadowy, moving glow of a ferryboat across the
> Sound. And as the moon rose higher the inessential houses began
> to melt away until gradually I became aware of the old island here
> that flowered once for Dutch sailors eyes--a fresh green breast of the
> new world. Its vanished trees, the trees that had made way for
> Gatsby's house, had once pondered in whispers to the last and greatest
> of all human dreams; for a transitory enchanted moment man must have
> held his breath in the presence of this continent, compelled into an
> aesthetic contemplation he neither understood nor desired, face to
> face for the last time in history with something commensurate to his
> capacity for wonder....

Gatsby believed in the green light, the orgastic future that year by year
recedes before us. It eluded us then, but that's no matter--tomorrow we will
run faster, stretch out our arms farther...And one fine morning--

So we beat on, boats against the current, borne back craselessly into the past.

Bibliography and Notes

(1)   Shakespeare, William, THE TEMPEST IV,i, page 148. Bill was an early observer
      of human interaction who prepared some interesting case histroies to illustrate
      his studies.

(2)   McKeefery, Vice President, WELCOMING REMARKS TO EDRA IV, about 15 minutes into
      presentation. A prerecorded, but unprinted manuscript.

(3)   Childhood City was a conference within the conference organized by Robin Moore
      around those persons particularly oriented to children and their environments.

(4)   Von Foerster, Heinz. A well presented and highly dramatic exploration of the
      relationship between perception and the nervous system. His paper is to be
      published in these proceedings.

(5)   I really borrowed this quote from Mumford's book on TECHNIQUES AND
      CIVILIZATION, so I can't very well tell you where to find it in Spengler.
      You would probably never look anyway.

(6)   Simon, H.A. SCIENCES OF THE ARTIFICIAL, Cambridge, MIT Press, 1969. An
      important piece of thinking. A must on your reading list.

(7)   Rapoport, A. AN APPROACH TO THE CONSTRUCTION OF MAN-ENVIRONMENT THEORY,
      EDRA IV Proceedings, 1973.

(8)   Kahn, C.H. DILEMMAS OF RESEARCH IN OPEN-ENDED PROBLEMS, EDRA IV Proceedings,
      1973.

(9)   Studer, R.G. MAN-ENVIRONMENT RELATIONS: DISCOVERY OR DESIGN, EDRA IV
      Proceedings, 1973.

      (you don't really need page numbers for the last three citations)

(10) This is from the SCIENCES OF THE ARTIFICIAL again, but I'm not going to give
      you the comfort of an "ibid" and page numbers.

(11) Fitzgerald, F.S. THE GREAT GATSBY, New York, Charles Scribner's Son 1925,
      P. 217-218. You probably won't be able to find a copy of this edition since
      I got it out of the original and rare book collection at V.P.I. You get the
      message anyway--I hope.

Note: As is obvious from the above I'm not a great believer in citations. It
      tends to be one of those posturing moves made by social scientists within
      the pseudomorph. In physics and chemistry et. al. it makes some sense,
      I question its value in most EDRA papers other than to make the author appear
      to be well versed in "the literature".

APPENDIX

BEHAVIOR RELATED LITERATURE AND READING EXPERIENCE OF DESIGN STUDENTS

C. Craig Frazier and Neven Travis
Sponsored by Association for the Study of Man-Environment Relations,
A.H. Esser, M.D.; The College of Architecture V.P.I.-S.U., Dr. Wolfgang
F.E. Preiser; and the Environmental Design Research Association

Abstract

In a two phase study, a survey was made of the familiarity of design students with the literature related to design. This was compared to their faculties' emphasized (suggested/required) material. The study's first phase concerned the collation of all behavior-related literature mentioned in 25 reports of 73 solicited ACSA Schools of Architecture, and the frequency of each item was suggested/required. The second phase involved the students themselves and their familiarity with (1) the 30 titles most frequently emphasized by design school faculties, and (2) 4^3 items considered important, yet scarcely emphasized, relating the behavioral sciences to design.

Phase 1 Procedure

On September 25, 1972, to each of the 73 accredited U.S. Collegiate Schools of Architecture, a letter from Dr. Alan Y. Taniguchi, then President, A.C.S.A., was sent recommending participation and explaining the study intentions, together with a letter asking that a "collection of any and all required reading lists for design classes for all instructional levels from (each school's) faculty" be sent for collation. The solicited reading lists arrived throughout October and November and three stages of processing were carried out on 23 sets of returned lists.

(1) Every item submitted was classed as either behavior-related or not behavior-related. "Not behavior-related" material was clearly more associated with architecture, design methods, structure, ecology, systems or information theory, planning, urbanization, creativity, graphic communications, history, construction, etc., than with behavior sciences. There were over 1000 different references submitted, half of which were classed as behavior-related.

(2) Each item classed as behavior-related was recorded on a 3X5 card. This master bibliography includes some 500 individual references. On the back of each reference card the number of times the item appeared in the reading lists of the reporting schools was recorded.

(3) A list of the 30 most frequently mentioned items was compiled for the second phase survey. The list included all references mentioned by at least six of the responding schools, i.e., 25%. The titles and approximate percentages, indicating the frequency emphasized is noted on the table of second phase results. E.T. Hall, C. Alexander/S. Chermayeff et al., R. Sommer, K. Lynch and I. McHarg are the authors currently most frequently emphasized by design school faculties. Also, the diversity of reading lists is clearly indicated in that only 10 authors occur on 50% or more of all reading lists: the great majority of the 500 items in the master bibliography occurred only once or twice.

40	Holland.	WHO DESIGNS AMERICA		6	4	24
75	Jacobs.	THE DEATH AND LIFE OF GREAT AMERICAN CITIES		19	15	28
40	Lynch.	SITE PLANNING		24	24	20
80	Lynch.	IMAGE OF THE CITY		26	24	23
80	McHarg.	DESIGN WITH NATURE		28	29	27
27	Michelson.	MAN AND HIS URBAN ENVIRONMENT		4	5	17
23	Moholy-Nagy.	MATRIX OF MAN		5	11	32
40	Norberg-Schultz.	EXISTENCE, SPACE, AND ARCHITECTURE		11	7	16
40	Norberg-Schultz.	INTENTIONS IN ARCHITECTURE		11	8	16
50	Perin.	WITH MAN IN MIND		6	3	9
57	Proshansky.	ENVIRONMENTAL PSYCHOLOGY		7	5	10
40	Rapoport.	HOUSE FORM AND CULTURE		13	10	11
40	Rasmussen.	EXPERIENCING ARCHITECTURE		32	15	19
27	Rudofsky.	ARCHITECTURE WITHOUT ARCHITECTS		13	29	31
29	Rudofsky.	STREETS FOR PEOPLE		7	21	23
23	Sommer.	DESIGN AWARENESS		4	7	18
80	Sommer.	PERSONAL SPACE		19	16	19
22	Thoreau.	WALDEN		18	29	24
29	Venturi.	COMPLEXITY AND CONTRADICTION IN ARCHITECTURE		17	11	21

"titles of significant value, but not frequently found in ACSA reading lists"

Ardrey. THE TERRITORIAL IMPERATIVE	6	8	17
Barker. ECOLOGICAL PSYCHOLOGY	–	2	6
Calder. THE MIND OF MAN	1	3	15
Commoner. THE CLOSING CIRCLE	1	2	8
Craik. ENVIRONMENTAL PSYCHOLOGY	1	2	5
Dubos. SO HUMAN AN ANIMAL	4	2	11
Esser. BEHAVIOR AND ENVIRONMENT	–	3	8
Ewald. ENVIRONMENT FOR MAN	3	4	8
Festinger. SOCIAL PRESSURE IN INFORMAL GROUPS	1	2	5
Goffman. BEHAVIOR IN PUBLIC PLACES	1	3	6
Lorenz. ON AGGRESSION	3	4	13
Maslow. MOTIVATION AND PERSONALITY	1	3	11
Morris. THE HUMAN ZOO	6	9	31
Neutra. SURVIVAL THROUGH DESIGN	5	7	21
Odum. ENVIRONMENT, POWER AND SOCIETY	2	1	2
Toffler. FUTURE SHOCK	30	19	33

"journals, bibliographies, proceedings"

CPL EXCHANGE BIBLIOGRAPHY	2	3	3
DMG JOURNAL	1	4	6
ENVIRONMENT AND BEHAVIOR	1	6	13
JOURNAL OF APPLIED BEHAVIORAL ANALYSIS	–	2	5
JOURNAL OF ARCHITECTURAL RESEARCH AND TEACHING	–	4	6
LANDSCAPE	–	19	18
MAN-ENVIRONMENT SYSTEMS	1	5	7
NEWSLETTER ON HUMAN ECOLOGY	–	2	8
Archea & Eastman. EDRA TWO 1970	1	6	13
Canter. ARCHITECTURAL PSYCHOLOGY 1970	–	3	8
Mitchell. EDRA THREE 1972	1	5	8
Preiser. EDRA FOUR 1973	–	2	10
Sanoff & Cohen. EDRA ONE 1970	1	4	15

Phase II Procedure

By February 1973, a questionnaire had been generated from the phase one results, which would give an indication of the actual familiarity of design students with both the frequently emphasized material and "other readings considered essential for the understanding of the behavior-design interface." (As stated in the introductory letter from Dr. Robert Harris, President, A.C.S.A.) 4500 copies were distributed to 94 schools of architecture, accredited and un-accredited in the U.S. and Canada.

850 surveys were returned from 48 schools including five in Canada. Preliminary tabulation and analysis indicated:

(1) Familiarity with the required/suggested readings was far greater than with the category of "titles of significant value, but not frequently found in ACSA school reading lists." 13 of the 30 items emphasized by the faculties of the ACSA schools were familiar ('owned,' 'read,' 'heard of') to 50% or more of the design students responding, while only one book, Toffler's FUTURE SHOCK, in the second category was as familiar.

(2) The students of the Canadian design schools had a greater overall familiarity with the literature than the U.S. students. Only 15% of the U.S. students' responses were in the categories 'own' or 'have read', while 24% of the Canadian students' responses fell into those two categories.

(3) The similarity among students' reading habits suggest a predictable range of reading backgrounds in the up-coming generation of architects. A majority own or have read: Giedion's SPACE, TIME AND ARCHITECTURE, Lynch's THE IMAGE OF THE CITY, Toffler's FUTURE SHOCK, and McHarg's DESIGN WITH NATURE, while Rasmussen's EXPERIENCING ARCHITECTURE is owned by more design students than any other book listed (32%).

(4) Design students are not familiar with the journals, bibliographies and proceedings of the man-environment field. The most familiar, Landscape is ready by 19% of the students, and Environment and Behavior by 6%. The proceedings of EDRA I and EDRA II were equally owned, read or heard of by 20% of the design students.

(5) The most frequently mentioned of the 73 items are:

% listed on ACSA reading lists	item listed	approximate % own	read	heard of
	"most frequently stressed by ACSA faculties"			
40	Alexander, etal. HOUSES GENERATED BY PATTERNS	3	14	23
60	Alexander. NOTES ON THE SYNTHESIS OF FORM	9	20	25
40	Alexander, etal. A PATTERN LANGUAGE WHICH GENERATES MULTI-SERVICE CENTERS	2	20	25
27	Boulding. THE IMAGE	4	6	11
80	Chermayeff & Alexander. COMMUNITY AND PRIVACY	28	21	20
38	Cullen. TOWNSCAPE	7	21	21
35	Gans. THE URBAN VILLAGERS	4	8	19
40	Giedion. SPACE, TIME, AND ARCHITECTURE	27	39	23
48	Goodman. COMMUNITAS	12	8	18
26	Hall. THE SILENT LANGUAGE	12	14	22
100	Hall. THE HIDDEN DIMENSION	28	20	24

AUTHOR INDEX

SUBJECT INDEX

Errata for Environmental Design Research, **Vol. 1**
Ed. W. F. E. Preiser

1. Page 21   A critical portion of the first sentence has been omitted. The sentence should read:
"Wilkie found that at the poles of upper and lower class, people tend to be conservative for different reasons, in the upper because they are oriented to peer group expectation, and in the lower to community tradition through lack of confidence in their ability to cope with the environment."

2. Page 73   The missing factor on the bottom of the page should be: "POTENCY."

3. Page 422 The last two lines should read:

   CRAFT 5 x 5 Matrix 58058   .39
          6 x 6 Matrix 58103   1.31

4. Page 507 The actual participants for the Workshop (20.0) on "Subjective Responses to Acoustic Environments" were:

   Dr. T. D. Northwood, National Research Council of Canada
   Dr. Hugo Blasdel, University of California, Berkely
   Dr. Robert Cunitz, National Bureau of Standards.